CliffsNotes®

AP®

U.S. History

CRAM PLAN™

by Melissa Young, Ph.D. Candidate

Contributor: *Joy Mondragon-Gilmore, Ph.D.*

Houghton Mifflin Harcourt
Boston • New York

D1591844

About the Author

Melissa Young holds an M.A. in both history and English, and is currently a Ph.D. candidate at the University of Alabama in Tuscaloosa, where she specializes in modern American history.

Acknowledgments

This book would not be possible without the education provided me by the outstanding professors of the University of Alabama History Department and the hard work of my contributing author/editor Joy Gilmore and all of the editorial staff at CliffsNotes.

Dedication

I would like to dedicate this book to my husband, Martin, whose support and encouragement has been and continues to be invaluable to all of my work.

Editorial

Executive Editor: Greg Tubach
Senior Editor: Christina Stambaugh
Copy Editor: Lynn Northrup
Production Editor: Jennifer Freilach
Technical Editor: Michael H. Kim
Proofreader: Susan Moritz

CliffsNotes® AP® U.S. History Cram Plan™

Library of Congress Control Number: 2018941138
ISBN: 978-0-544-91504-6 (pbk)

Printed in the United States of America
DOC 10 9 8 7 6 5 4 3 2 1

For information about permission to reproduce selections from this book, write to trade.permissions@hmhco.com or to Permissions, Houghton Mifflin Harcourt Publishing Company, 3 Park Avenue, 19th Floor, New York, New York 10016.

www.hmhco.com

Table of Contents

Preface

Congratulations! You've made the decision to take charge of the AP U.S. History course. This book can help you plan your course of study and prepare for the exam. You can use it as a quick reference guide, an in-depth resource, a source for practice, or a refresher on one or more topics in U.S. history. This guide contains a series of reviews that can supplement your textbook and your teacher's lectures. Consider it an organized summary of a massive amount of U.S. history information that will allow you to organize and make sense of essential information necessary to be successful on the AP U.S. History (APUSH) exam.

CliffsNotes AP U.S. History Cram Plan is an easy-to-follow study guide that provides the maximum benefit in a reasonable amount of time. Although it is not meant to substitute for a formal high school AP history class, it provides you with important learning tools to refresh your understanding of the topics outlined in the AP course curriculum framework and key concepts. The skills and concepts defined in this book will not only help you pass the APUSH exam, but will also provide you with exam-oriented approaches and practice material to help you evaluate your strengths and areas of improvement. If you follow the lessons and strategies in this book and study regularly, you will deepen your understanding of U.S. history, which will strengthen your performance on the exam.

Navigating This Book

CliffsNotes AP U.S. History Cram Plan is organized as follows:

- **Introduction to the AP U.S. History Exam** — A general description of the APUSH exam, exam format, scoring, question types, chronological periods, reasoning skills, themes, frequently asked questions, and general strategies.
- **Chapter 1: Two-Month Cram Plan** — A study calendar that provides a detailed suggested plan of action for preparing for the APUSH exam 2 months before your exam.
- **Chapter 2: One-Month Cram Plan** — A study calendar that provides a detailed suggested plan of action for preparing for the APUSH exam 1 month before your exam.
- **Chapter 3: Diagnostic Test** — A shortened version of the APUSH practice exam in Chapter 13, the Diagnostic Test introduces you to the APUSH question types, evaluates your areas of strength and weakness to help you focus your study, and provides you with a baseline starting point.
- **Chapter 4: Period One** — Early Settlement of the Americas (1491 to 1607)
- **Chapter 5: Period Two** — The Colonial Period (1607 to 1754)
- **Chapter 6: Period Three** — Revolutionary America (1754 to 1800)
- **Chapter 7: Period Four** — Early America (1800 to 1848)
- **Chapter 8: Period Five** — The Civil War and Reconstruction (1844 to 1877)
- **Chapter 9: Period Six** — The Gilded Age (1865 to 1898)
- **Chapter 10: Period Seven** — The Rise to Global Power (1890 to 1945)
- **Chapter 11: Period Eight** — The Post-War Era and the Cold War (1945 to 1980)
- **Chapter 12: Period Nine** — The Globalization Era (1980 to the Present)
- **Chapter 13: Full-Length Practice Exam** — Includes answers and in-depth explanations for multiple-choice questions, and sample responses and scoring guidelines for the short-answer, document-based, and long-essay questions.

How to Use This Book

You're in charge here. You get to decide how to use this book. You can decide to read it from cover to cover or just refer to it when you need specific information. Most people find it useful to start by learning *general* reasoning skills, themes, and historical periods to develop a broad understanding of U.S. history before memorizing *specific* facts, concepts, and evidence.

Here are some of the recommended ways to use this book.

- Create a customized study "action plan." Be time-wise because your study plan depends on the total amount of time until the exam date. Preview the cram plan calendars in chapters 1 and 2 to organize your study time.

- Read (and then reread) the Introduction to become familiar with the exam format, time periods, history disciplinary practices and reasoning skills, themes, question types, and test-taking strategies.

- Take the diagnostic test (Chapter 3) to assess your strengths and weaknesses.

- Get a glimpse of what you'll gain from a chapter by reading through the key concepts referenced at the beginning of each chapter.

- Follow the recommended sequence of time periods (chapters 4–12). Within each chapter, take detailed notes on the pages of this book to highlight important facts and topics related to the APUSH key concepts.

- Pay attention to the intermingled callout features in chapters 4–12 that focus on what you need to study to pass the APUSH exam.

  - **Key Facts** — Lists the significant facts of a topic for a quick study reference.

  - **Did you know?** — Covers interesting information about people, places, and events on topics to aid in your overall understanding of a point in history.

  - **Heads Up: What You Need to Know** — Summarizes details about specific content that may be on the actual APUSH exam.

  - **Test Tip** — Offers quick strategies and tips for approaching exam questions.

  - **Historiography** — Offers different scholarly viewpoints so that you can "think like a historian" to reconstruct, debate, or critically think about topics that shape our history over time. For example, the reasoning skills associated with causes and consequences, comparisons and contrasts, and similarities and differences of historical events.

- Use the "Chapter Review Practice Questions" to gauge your grasp of questions on the APUSH exam and strengthen your critical reasoning skills. Although it is tempting to look ahead at the answer explanations, try to simulate testing conditions by answering the questions and writing your document-based question (DBQ) responses before reviewing the explanations. Initially, it may be difficult, but this strategy will reinforce your learning, particularly for writing DBQ responses.

- Test your knowledge more completely in the full-length practice exam in Chapter 13.

If you have moments of self-doubt, keep reminding yourself that even though the material is challenging, it is manageable. Take a deep breath, and know that you can do this by using the content, tips, and practice questions offered in this study guide.

Finally, the lessons and strategies you are learning in this book will help you throughout your high school and college learning experiences. If you make the commitment to follow the lessons and practice regularly, you will not only statistically increase your odds for passing the APUSH exam, but you will also learn skills that can help you manage future college coursework!

Introduction to the AP U.S. History Exam

Teachers and students alike will find *CliffsNotes AP U.S. History Cram Plan* to be a valuable course supplement. This compact book is packed with information about what to expect on the exam, how to approach the questions, how to plan your study time, and how to study the nine major time periods. To enhance your learning, a diagnostic test and a full-length practice exam provide practice questions with complete answer explanations.

As you begin your preparation, know that while the APUSH exam is challenging, it is manageable. You do not need to memorize specific dates, battles, and events. Rather, you will be asked to look at the big picture by looking for important changes, continuities, comparisons, and contrasts within each time period. For example, the APUSH exam might ask how certain events or people influenced the American Revolution or the Civil War. *CliffsNotes AP U.S. History Cram Plan* takes the guesswork out of how to approach questions. So take a deep breath, and know you can do this.

Exam Format

Multiple-choice questions are combined with free-response questions (short-answer questions, document-based question, long-essay question) for a combined scaled score of 1–5.

Note: Format and scoring are subject to change. Visit the College Board website for updates: http://apcentral.collegeboard.com.

Section	Question Type	Time	Number of Questions	Percent of Total Grade
Section I: **Part A**	Multiple-Choice Questions	55 minutes	55 questions	40%
Section I: **Part B**	Short-Answer Questions	40 minutes	3 questions (Note: Answer the first two questions and then choose one question from the next two choices.)	20%
Section II: **Part A**	Document-Based Question	60 minutes (includes a 15-minute reading period)	1 question	25%
Section II: **Part B**	Long-Essay Question	40 minutes (Note: The DBQ and LEQ appear in the same section. Use the 15-minute mandatory reading period to read and plan BOTH essays.)	1 question (Note: Choose one question from three choices.)	15%
TOTALS:		**3 hours, 15 minutes**	**55 multiple choice** **5 essays**	**100%**

Scoring

Scores on your APUSH exam will be based on the number of questions you answer correctly for two separate sections.

> Section I: Multiple-choice and short-answer questions are 60% of your overall score.
>
> Section II: Document-based and long-essay questions are 40% of your overall score.

Based on the combination of the two sections, the scores are converted into a grading scale of 1 to 5. A score of 5 is the best possible score. Most colleges consider a score of 3 or better a passing score. If you receive a passing score, the APUSH exam can be applied as a college course equivalent—two-semester units will apply toward your college bachelor's degree as a U.S. history course.

As a reference, in 2017, more than 50% of the students who took the APUSH exam scored a 3 or higher.

AP Score	Score Translation
5	Extremely well qualified
4	Well qualified
3	Qualified
2	Possibly qualified
1	No recommendation

The APUSH exam is graded on a curve, particularly the multiple-choice questions. Oftentimes, students panic when they get back their first practice exam. "A 65% on the multiple choice? I'm failing!" In reality, a 65% on the multiple-choice questions can be good enough for a 4 or even a 5 on the entire exam, depending on your score on the other sections. Note: For multiple-choice questions, no points are deducted for incorrect answers. If you don't know the answer, take an educated guess because there is no penalty for guessing.

Question Types

The APUSH question types are multiple-choice, short-answer, document-based, and long-essay. Questions measure your knowledge of the main concepts within the context of the nine historical periods. As you approach each of the four question types, consider the following points to receive your best possible score.

- What are the main points within the context of a particular time period?
- What is the broader historical context (what happened before, during, and after)?
- What are the relevant significant themes?
- What supporting evidence will strengthen your analysis?
- What are the reasoning skills?

Multiple-Choice Questions

Multiple-choice questions require that you read and analyze a passage or graphic image and draw reasonable conclusions based on your knowledge of U.S. history and your interpretation of the document. Documents are primary or secondary sources (text or graphic image) that college history students might use in their research. Each question draws from the APUSH key concept outlines and your knowledge of U.S. history.

Key points about multiple-choice questions:

- Multiple-choice questions comprise 40% of your overall score.
- The exam contains 55 multiple-choice questions.
- The questions are grouped into sets. Each set contains one source-based prompt (text or graphic image) and two to five questions.
- Questions ask you to analyze, interpret, or find evidence from a primary or secondary source (historical text, government document, quotation, graph, chart, map, political cartoon, art, or image).
- Select one answer from among four choices in each question.
- No points are deducted for incorrect answers; therefore, there is no penalty for guessing.

Short-Answer Questions (SAQs)

The SAQs are similar to multiple-choice questions, but consist of short written responses. Short-answer questions give students an opportunity to demonstrate what they know by describing examples of historical evidence in a concise response that answers the question. If you answer all parts of the question and apply reasoning skills, the SAQs are a great section to increase your score.

One question is taken from a secondary source (text or graphic image), one question is taken from a primary source, and one question has no source.

Question	Type of Source	Task	Historical Period
SAQ 1	Secondary source	Analyze a historian's argument.	Periods 3–8
SAQ 2	Primary source	Analyze the original historical source and then respond by using the reasoning skills of comparison or continuity and change over time.	Periods 3–8
Choose only ONE of the following (not both).			
SAQ 3	No source	Respond to the question by using the reasoning skills of comparison or continuity and change over time.	Periods 1–5
SAQ 4			Periods 6–9

Key points about short-answer questions:

- Short-answer questions comprise 20% of your overall score.
- The exam contains four short-answer questions, but you are only required to answer three short-answer questions. You must answer the first two short-answer questions and then choose one from the last two questions. Select the period you know more about. It's your choice!
- No thesis statement is required in your written response.
- Write a short analysis that responds to a question with a secondary source, a primary source, or no source. If the question contains a primary or secondary source, you must identify, describe, explain, or provide evidence from the document found in a graph, text, map, or image source.
- Use at least one reasoning skill in your written response (comparison or continuity and change over time).
- Each short-answer question contains three tasks. You must respond to all three tasks to receive full credit.

Document-Based Question (DBQ)

DBQs require that you write an essay with *specific* historical evidence in support of your argument. You will need to analyze (not summarize) the documents, explain the broader historical context, follow a line of reasoning, and provide supporting historical examples to develop your argument.

Key points about the document-based question:

- The document-based question comprises 25% of your overall score.
- The exam contains one document-based question from Periods 3–8 (1754–1980).
- The document-based question contains six or seven documents of historical sources in text (speeches, reports, laws, letters, quotations, declarations), graphs, charts, maps, artifacts, political cartoons, art, or images.
- Write an essay response to identify, describe, explain, or provide evidence from three to six documents.
- Write a response that considers the relationship among the topic question, your thesis argument, and the documents.
- Each point is earned independently. For example, you can earn a point for a historically defensible thesis, but fail to earn a point for not providing an example beyond the documents.
- Essays are considered first drafts and may contain some errors.
- Write a response that addresses all points in the scoring criteria as described by the College Board (see the chart below).

Scoring Rubric for the Document-Based Question		
Task	**Scoring Criteria**	**Possible Points**
Thesis and Claim	Presents a historically defensible thesis that establishes a line of reasoning (**1 point**). (Note: The thesis must make a claim that responds to *all* parts of the question and must *not* just restate the question. The thesis must consist of *at least* one sentence, either in the introduction or the conclusion.)	1 point
Contextualization	Describes the broader historical context of events, developments, or processes that occurred before, during, or after the time frame of the question (**1 point**). (Note: Must be more than a phrase or reference.)	1 point
Evidence	**Evidence from the Documents** Uses the content from at least *six* documents to support the argument in response to the prompt (**2 points**). OR Uses the content of at least *three* documents to address the topic prompt (**1 point**). (Note: Examples must *describe*, rather than simply quote, the content of the documents.) **Evidence Beyond the Documents** Uses at least one additional piece of specific historical evidence beyond those found in the documents that is relevant to the argument (**1 point**). (Note: Evidence must be different from the evidence used in contextualization.)	3 points

Task	Scoring Criteria	Possible Points
Analysis and Reasoning	Uses at least *three* documents to explain why each document's point of view, purpose, historical situation, and/or audience is relevant to the argument (**1 point**). (Note: References must explain *how* or *why*, rather than simply identifying.)	2 points
	Shows a complex understanding of historical development that focuses on the question while using evidence to corroborate, qualify, or modify the argument (**1 point**). (Examples: Explain the nuances of an issue by analyzing multiple variables; explain what is similar and different; explain the cause and effect; explain multiple causes; explain both continuity and change; explain connections across periods of time; corroborate multiple perspectives across themes; qualify or modify the argument by considering alternative views or evidence.)	
Total Possible Points		**7 points**
Note: Each point is earned independently by task. You must respond to **all** tasks to receive full credit.		

Long-Essay Question (LEQ)

The final part of the exam is one long-essay question. Just like the DBQ, the long-essay question requires that you write an essay with *specific* historical evidence in support of your argument. LEQs focus on reasoning skills and often require a great deal of contextualization about broad trends and significant issues in U.S. history—the big picture. You will need to consider not only the overall trends, but also historiographical arguments, long-term developments, and overall characterizations.

Key points about the long-essay question:

- The long-essay question comprises 15% of your overall score.
- Long-essay questions are drawn from broad topics on the key concept outlines.
- The exam contains three long-essay questions from different time periods, but you will choose only one question to write your essay response (periods 1–3, periods 4–6, or periods 7–9). Focus on the time period that is most familiar.
- Each point is earned independently. For example, you can earn a point for a strong thesis, but fail to earn a point for not applying historical reasoning to explain specific evidence.
- Write a response that addresses all points in the scoring criteria as described by the College Board (see the chart below).

Scoring Rubric for the Long-Essay Question		
Task	**Scoring Criteria**	**Possible Points**
Thesis and Claim	Presents a historically defensible thesis that establishes a line of reasoning (**1 point**). (Note: The thesis must make a claim that responds to *all* parts of the question and must *not* just restate the question. The thesis must consist of *at least* one sentence, either in the introduction or the conclusion.)	1 point

Continued

Task	Scoring Criteria	Possible Points
Contextualization	Describes the broader historical context of events, developments, or processes that occurred before, during, or after the time frame of the question **(1 point)**. (Note: Must be more than a phrase or reference.)	1 point
Evidence	Supports the argument in response to the prompt using specific and relevant examples of evidence **(2 points)**. OR Provides specific examples of evidence relevant to the topic of the question **(1 point)**. (Note: To earn 2 points, the evidence must *support* your argument.)	2 points
Analysis and Reasoning	Shows a complex understanding of the historical development that addresses the question and uses evidence to corroborate, qualify, or modify the argument **(2 points)**. (Examples: Explain the nuances of an issue by analyzing multiple variables; explain what is similar and different; explain the cause and effect; explain multiple causes; explain both continuity and change; explain connections across periods of time; corroborate multiple perspectives across themes; qualify or modify the argument by considering alternative views or evidence.) OR Uses historical reasoning (comparison, causation, or continuity and change over time) to frame and develop the argument while focusing on the question **(1 point)**. (Note: Must be more than a phrase or reference.)	2 points
Total Possible Points		**6 points**
Note: Each point is earned independently by task. You must respond to **all** tasks to receive full credit.		

Historical Time Periods

The APUSH exam covers significant events, individuals, developments, and processes in nine periods of U.S. history from 1491 to the present. Because history is not always divided into distinct dates, you will notice that some time periods overlap, but these time periods are very manageable once you understand the big picture.

As you review the time periods in the table that follows, keep in mind that certain time periods receive more emphasis than others. Your review and study for the exam should reflect those percentages. Note: The document-based question (DBQ) and two of the short-answer questions focus on periods 3–8.

Overview of Historical Periods			
Era	Dates	Percent of Exam	Topics
Period 1: **Early Settlement of the Americas**	1491–1607	5%	■ Early contact between Europeans, Native Americans, and Africans ■ European exploration ■ The Columbian Exchange ■ Conflicting cultures and worldviews
Period 2: **Colonial Period**	1607–1754	10%	■ European colonization ■ Interactions between colonists, Europeans, and Native Americans ■ Colonial economic, political, and social developments (slave trade, mercantilism, salutary neglect) ■ The Great Awakening
Period 3: **Revolutionary Period**	1754–1800	12%	■ The Seven Years' (French and Indian) War ■ The Enlightenment ■ Colonial resentment leading to the American Revolution ■ The American Revolution ■ The Articles of Confederation and the Constitution
Period 4: **Era of Good Feelings**	1800–1848	10%	■ The early republic ■ The War of 1812 and the end of the First Party System ■ The development of political parties and Jacksonian Democracy ■ Voluntary organizations, abolitionism, and women's rights ■ Industrial Revolution: transportation, communication, and market advancement ■ Westward expansion ■ Growing sectionalism
Period 5: **Antebellum Era**	1844–1877	13%	■ Western expansion and Manifest Destiny ■ The Mexican-American War ■ Increased immigration and migration ■ Continued sectional tensions over slavery and events leading to the Civil War and the end of the Second Party System ■ The Civil War and Reconstruction
Period 6: **Gilded Age**	1865–1898	13%	■ Economic development and the Second Industrial Revolution ■ The Populist Movement ■ Racial tensions and segregation ■ Migration and urbanization ■ The women's movement ■ Labor unions
Period 7: **Progressive Era**	1890–1945	17%	■ U.S. imperialism ■ The Spanish-American War ■ World War I ■ The Roaring Twenties ■ The Great Depression and the New Deal ■ World War II

Continued

Era	Dates	Percent of Exam	Topics
Period 8: **Cold War Era**	1945–1980	15%	■ The Atomic Age and the post-war boom of the 1950s ■ The Cold War ■ Civil Rights Movement ■ LBJ's Great Society and its rejection by Nixon's "silent majority" ■ The rise of the New Right and the New Left
Period 9: **Digital Age**	1980–present	5%	■ End of the Cold War Era ■ Reagan Era ■ The digital revolution ■ War on terror ■ Globalization and the environment

Disciplinary Practices and Reasoning Skills

To be successful on the exam, you must make sure that you are clear on the AP history disciplinary practices and reasoning skills identified by the College Board.

Disciplinary Practices

Disciplinary practices provide strategies to help you analyze sources and development arguments for your free-response questions.

Disciplinary Practice 1: Analyzing historical evidence. Analyze and explain the significance of historical evidence from primary sources and secondary sources. Ask yourself, "What is the point of view, historical situation, purpose, and/or audience of the source?" and "Is the source credible, or does it have limitations?"

Disciplinary Practice 2: Argument development. To develop your free-response argument, you should: (a) defend your thesis/claim based on historical facts, (b) support your thesis using specific (and relevant) evidence, (c) use one of the reasoning skills listed below to make a connection to the evidence, and (d) consider alternative evidence to corroborate, qualify, or modify your argument.

Primary and Secondary Sources

Before you can decode a document, it's important to be familiar with the differences between primary and secondary document sources. A *primary source* is an original passage, speech, or image that was composed, spoken, or illustrated during a specific time period. Primary sources give you an "inside view" of the particular event by someone who directly witnessed or experienced the historical event. For example, primary sources include government documents, artifacts, letters, diaries, correspondence, books, speeches, and art. A *secondary source* is a "secondhand" account told by a third party who interpreted or wrote about the primary source. For example, secondary sources are often published by historians in historiographies to make a historical claim or argument.

Reasoning Skills

The APUSH test-makers want students to offer *support* and *reasons* for historical facts that connect to the questions.

The four reasoning skills identified by the College Board are bundled into four categories in the table that follows, along with critical thinking questions.

AP U.S. History Reasoning Skills		
Skill	**Description**	**Critical Thinking Questions**
Contextualization	It's important to understand the context of a document to be able to make an interpretation. Context not only refers to a document source, but more importantly to the time period surrounding or inspiring the creation of the document (author, purpose, point of view, and audience). People who lived long ago had different ideas and values, lived in a different *context*, and saw the world in a very different way from the world today. In order to understand history, we must think about the context in which people lived. For APUSH documents, it's all about understanding *historical context* and the author's intended purpose for writing the document in the time frame that it was written.	■ Can I describe what was happening in the U.S. (and the world) when a particular event occurred? ■ Can I connect a particular historical event to broader trends and developments (social, religious, political, economic)? ■ How did the interactions among people with different political views, time periods, and geographic regions shape how the author of a document was influenced?
Comparison	Comparison involves comparing and contrasting perspectives between historical developments so that you can draw conclusions about your findings. To compare and contrast: (1) list the core similarities and differences of an issue, (2) group the similarities and differences, (3) give *reasons* for the compare/contrast issues.	■ What are the similarities and differences of core issues (events or developments) between periods, regions, states, or presidential administrations? (Can these be grouped by themes?) ■ Can I reasonably explain why one state or region was affected by an issue differently than another state or region?
Causation	Causation uses the skill of cause and effect. It involves providing *reasons* for the causes of complex issues that resulted in unexpected developments (called turning points in history). A good way to simplify this causation is to think about the logical sequence: (a) what happened *before* the event, (b) what happened *during* the event, and (c) what happened *after* the event—or cause, event, effect.	■ Can I identify several reasons that prompted an event or development? (And the short-term and long-term consequences?) ■ Can I prioritize the causes and consequences? ■ Can I build an argument by providing a clear and specific chain of events leading up to the event?

Continued

Skill	Description	Critical Thinking Questions
Continuity and Change	Think of continuity and change over time as another level of causation. Continuity and change over time involves recognizing "patterns" in a society that tend to stay the same over time or change over time. These patterns are consistent across the larger big picture of history. For example, you may be asked to identify what is the same and what is different in women's roles in the U.S. during a specific time period, and then compare these findings to women's roles in the U.S. 100 years later.	■ Can I identify what stayed the same and what is different in a region, time period, political party, or racial/ethnic group? ■ Can I identify similar patterns or differences in other time periods? ■ Can I identify the main reasons (causes) that led to decision-making changes in these groups?

Themes

The APUSH exam will expect you to understand common themes from different time periods. Most colleges and universities expect students to master these themes and to understand why particular developments occurred. These themes will guide your studying and help you group documents for your DBQ essay response.

The good news is that the College Board has identified the seven themes (see the table that follows). These themes will help you connect to why certain social, political, religious, geographic, ideological, technological, and economic developments transpired, or why they were repeated in history. Success on the APUSH exam will depend on the connections you make between the content and the deeper understandings of thematic developments relevant to U.S. history.

Theme	Subject	Description	Example
American and National Identity	Citizenship and Ideology	American values, national identity, and definitions of freedom and citizenship have changed over time. This has influenced U.S. foreign and domestic policies, interpretations of the Constitution, and debates over rights, liberties, and the inclusion or exclusion of various racial or gender groups.	How did interpretations of the Constitution affect national identity?
Politics and Power	Politics and Government	Political parties, loyalties, and institutions have developed over time and can be connected to popular movements and reform organizations that have sought to influence change. Various beliefs about the federal government and its role have affected political debate and policy.	How did political affiliations influence motivations for the American Civil War?
Work, Exchange, and Technology	Labor, Economics, and Technology	Technology, global or domestic markets, communication, and the government are the primary factors behind the growth of systems of trade and economic exchange. Labor systems in different regions of the U.S. have had a profound effect on workers, trade patterns, and enterprise.	How did trade and commerce impact the late 19th-century labor systems?

Theme	Subject	Description	Example
Culture and Society	Culture, Religion, and Philosophy	Cultural beliefs have developed in the U.S. over its history. Many social mores and belief systems were transferred from Europe and other immigrant countries, but others were motivated by the way people responded to new environments. Ideas about science, art, gender, race, class, and ethnicity have emerged, changed, and influenced domestic policy and society.	How did the conservative Christian Right change or influence the 20th-century political and social systems?
Migration and Settlement	Physical and Social Environments	People who have moved to and within the U.S. have had to transform themselves by adapting to new social and physical environments. Migration and immigration have occurred in many different periods and have affected particular regions in the U.S.	Why did Americans shift their attention to imperialist expansion in the 19th century?
Geography and the Environment	Regional Geography and Natural and Human-made Environments	Natural and human-made environments have led to social, cultural, and political developments. Geographic factors have expanded and contracted communities, led to competition for resources, and sparked debates about conservation and preservation that have inspired domestic policies.	What was the global significance of the Columbian Exchange?
America in the World	World Political, Social, and Economic Interaction	America not only affected interactions between nations in its Colonial Era, but it has also continued to influence world affairs. Cultural interaction, cooperation, and competition with other countries has prompted specific diplomatic and military actions.	How did the U.S. impact the global political and social climate after World War II?

Frequently Asked Questions about the APUSH Exam

Q: Who administers the AP U.S. History exam?

A: The College Board prepares and scores the APUSH exam. For further information regarding test administration, contact *Advanced Placement Program (AP)*, P.O. Box 6671, Princeton, NJ, 08541-6671, (888) 225-5427 or (212) 632-1780, e-mail: apstudents@info.collegeboard.org, http://apcentral. collegeboard.com.

Q: Are there prerequisites to taking the APUSH exam?

A: No. However, you should be able to read college-level textbooks and write grammatically correct and complete sentences.

Q: How do I register for the APUSH exam?

A: The exam is given in May. If your school offers the APUSH course, contact your AP teacher or coordinator to register. If your school does not offer the APUSH course, visit http://apcentral. collegeboard.com for more information.

Q: Can I take the APUSH exam more than once?

A: Yes, but you may not retake the exam within the same year. If you take the exam again, both scores will be reported unless you cancel one score.

Q: What do I bring to the exam?

A: Bring several no. 2 pencils with erasers for the multiple-choice questions, and bring several pens with black or dark-blue ink for the free-response questions. Bring your 6-digit school code. Bring a watch that does not have Internet access, does not beep, and does not have an alarm. If you do not attend the school where you are taking the exam, bring identification (school-issued photo ID or government-issued ID).

Q: What items am I not allowed to bring to the exam?

A: You cannot bring electronic equipment (cell phone, smartphone, listening devices, cameras, or any other electronic devices). You cannot bring books, scratch paper, highlighters, notes, food, or drinks. Note: You can take notes in the margins of your exam booklet.

Q: Can I cancel, withhold, or change my report recipient score?

A: Yes, you can request to cancel your scores at any time before the deadline. Contact AP Services for deadlines and policies.

Q: How long does it take to receive my score?

A: Once you sign up for a College Board account at www.collegeboard.org/register, you can receive your scores online sometime in July. You will get an e-mail reminding you how to access your scores. You must enter your AP number (the 8-digit number on the labels inside your AP Student Pack) or your student identifier to access your scores.

Q: Should I guess on the APUSH exam?

A: Yes. Your score is based on the number of questions you answer correctly, so there is no penalty for wrong answers. If possible, use the elimination strategy (see pp. 14–15) for multiple-choice questions to increase your chances of guessing the correct answer. Don't leave any questions unanswered.

Test-Taking Strategies

To be successful on the APUSH exam, you must spend time learning about the exam and how best to approach it, study to increase your knowledge, and practice answering simulated questions. This section begins with *general* test-taking strategies and then gives you *specific* information, approaches, and strategies to tackle the questions.

General Test-Taking Strategies

Consider the following general strategies.

- Stick to the College Board key concepts.
- Think and reason historically.
- Know the historical time periods.
- Know the significant themes.
- Know the causes, outcomes, and consequences.

Stick to the College Board Key Concepts

Take the guesswork out of what to expect on the exam and follow the guidelines for the College Board key concepts. The key concepts are the well from which *all* questions are drawn. The APUSH course content can seem overwhelming at first, with so many dates, events, people, movements, wars, conflicts, and social, cultural, or geographical changes—it is a lot to follow! Take a deep breath and understand that the College Board has provided key concepts in the *AP U.S. History Course and Exam Description* that can help you focus on what is testable. They are accessible online.

Think and Reason Historically

Historians study evidence from historical texts in order to interpret and draw conclusions about history. Students who are successful on the APUSH exam use some of the same skills that historians use. These skills are called higher-order thinking skills. Higher-order thinking skills challenge you to think about and draw conclusions as you approach each question. Refer to pp. 9–10 for comprehensive descriptions and examples of AP history reasoning skills.

You can make these reasoning skills more manageable by organizing them into four important overarching categories that historians use:

1. Historians look to see how the broader historical context of a particular time period uniquely impacted the ideas, actions, and social positions in a society (*contextualization*).
2. Historians look for common similarities and differences from other time periods (*comparison*).
3. Historians look for the causes and effects by asking *why* things happened when they did (*causation*).
4. Historians look for common themes (patterns) that link historical events across different periods of U.S. history to see what changed or stayed the same (*change and continuity over time*).

Know the Historical Time Periods

Students who are successful on the exam can identify what preceded and what followed particular events. Use the College Board time frames as bookends. While history occurs on a continuum of cause and effect, it can also be viewed in smaller chunks, which are set apart from others through turning points (events that clearly distinguish the beginning and end of an era). Review the "Overview of Historical Periods" table on pp. 7–8 and pay attention to the way U.S. history is divided in the chapters, but also focus on significant people, like U.S. presidents, political leaders, cultural leaders, reform workers, and activists. Who did what and why? What were their political views? Were these individuals representative of others or were they separated from the majority? Who would have opposed these individuals and why? How can these people be linked to various historical events?

Know the Significant Themes

Pay attention to relevant themes, patterns, and broad trends in U.S. history and think about how these themes overlap or change over time. This is often challenging for students, but if you can remember that the APUSH exam is about seeing the big picture, you should be able to identify the most important themes across different time periods and regions. As a reminder, the themes are described on pp. 10–11.

Know the Causes, Outcomes, and Consequences

Although particular people and events are certainly a large part of U.S. history, the College Board will expect you to emphasize their causes, outcomes, and consequences. Don't just memorize the details; instead, pay careful attention to how they relate to each other and broader regional, national, or global contexts. If you use the road map the College Board has provided and familiarize yourself with the format for exam questions, you can erase many of your worries.

Specific Test-Taking Strategies

It's important to consider the types of questions you are being asked and the specific strategies to tackle these questions. If you start to use these strategies before you even take the exam, you are way ahead of the curve.

Multiple-Choice Questions

Instructions for multiple-choice questions will appear in your exam booklet. Here are specific strategies to help you work through the multiple-choice questions quickly, accurately, and efficiently.

- Budget your time wisely.
- Use the elimination strategy.
- Mark the answer sheet correctly.
- Read each question and document carefully.
- Watch for "attractive distractors."
- Be on alert for EXCEPT and NOT questions.
- Make an educated guess if necessary.
- Practice, practice, practice.

Budget Your Time Wisely

You have 55 minutes to answer 55 multiple-choice questions. You might calculate that you have about 1 minute per question, but this does not include the time it takes to read a passage or analyze an image. Some questions may take more time, while others may take less time. Students who spend too much time dwelling on a single question don't get the score they deserve because they leave insufficient time to answer other questions they could get right. With sufficient practice, you will almost automatically know when a question is taking too much time and when to take an educated guess and move on to the next question. There is no penalty for guessing, so make sure you answer every question.

Use the Elimination Strategy

Take advantage of being allowed to mark in your exam booklet. Eliminate one or more answer choices to narrow down your choices to statistically improve your odds of selecting the correct answer. Practice this strategy as you take the diagnostic test and the full-length practice exam in this study guide.

Keep this marking system very simple and mark your answers in your exam booklet (no need to erase the markings in your booklet because you are allowed to write in your exam booklet). Use a question mark (?) to signify an answer choice as a possible answer, use a diagonal line (/) to cross out an answer choice that is incorrect, and leave the choice blank if you are uncertain. Notice that in the example below, you've just narrowed your chances of answering correctly to 50%.

? A.

B̸.

C.

D̸.

Mark the Answer Sheet Correctly

Make sure that your marked responses on the bubble answer sheet match your intended response. When answering questions quickly, it is common to select the wrong answer choice by mistake. Students who skip questions might make the mistake of continuing to mark their answers in sequence and forget to leave a blank space for the unanswered questions. To avoid this mistake, mark your answers (and any other notes) in the exam booklet before you fill in the answer sheet. If necessary, you will be able to double-check your answers.

Read Each Question and Document Carefully

Don't work so quickly that you make careless errors. Read actively and take notes as you read each document and multiple-choice question (see pp. 19–20 for more information about analyzing a document). Do not make a hasty assumption that you know the correct answer without reading the whole question, the document, and all of the choices to find the *best* answer.

Watch for "Attractive Distractors"

Watch out for answer choices that look good but are not the *best* answer choice (called *attractive distractors*). Attractive distractors are usually the most commonly selected incorrect answers and are often true statements, but not the best choice. Be aware that facts and concepts presented in answer choices may often contain subtle variations that make it difficult for test-takers to narrow down correct answers. Here are some examples of attractive distractor answer choices that should be eliminated:

- Answer choices that answer only *part* of the question and do not directly answer the entire question
- Answer choices that are not related to the correct time period
- Answer choices that are not using the correct AP history reasoning skill
- Answer choices that are not related to both the document and the question

Be on Alert for EXCEPT and NOT Questions

Another common mistake is misreading a question that includes the words *except* or *not*. A negative question reverses the meaning of the question and asks for the opposite to be true. Negative questions can initially be confusing and challenge your thinking. It is helpful to write down brief notes to avoid misreading a question (and therefore answering it incorrectly). To help answer a negative question, treat the answer choices as true or false statements, searching for the answer choice that is false.

Make an Educated Guess If Necessary

Remember, there is no penalty for guessing. If you get stuck on a question, reread it. The answer may become apparent when you take a second look. If not, take an educated guess by eliminating some of the answer choices to increase your odds of choosing the right answer. You have nothing to lose, and quite possibly, something to gain. If you have time, you can always go back to rethink a marked question and change the answer.

If you do not have time to finish the test, save 1 minute of your exam time to mark the answers for all of your remaining unanswered questions. There is no penalty for guessing, so pick your favorite letter—A, B, C, or D—and fill in all of the blank answer choices with this letter.

Practice, Practice, Practice

The College Board recommends consistent practice to attain a high score. This is why we have included practice questions throughout this study guide: Chapter 3 (diagnostic test), chapters 4–12 (review chapters), and Chapter 13 (full-length practice exam). These practice questions include answers and thorough explanations. Be sure to practice in the exam format as often as possible. To benefit from further practice, you can purchase previously administered AP U.S. History exams at https://store.collegeboard.org. Just keep in mind that some exams prior to 2016 may not reflect the most recent format of AP U.S. History, but they are still valuable practice.

Free-Response Questions

Unlike an old-school history test that is just about memorizing facts, dates, and names, for free-response questions, students must do what historians do—interpret historical evidence while reasoning historically. When given historical documents, data, or images, you must be able to write a clear argument, provide supporting evidence, show historical knowledge, and demonstrate strong writing conventions.

This section will give you strategies for the three types of free-response questions:

- Short-answer questions (3 questions, 20% of your score)
- Document-based question (1 question, 25% of your score)
- Long-essay question (1 question, 15% of your score)

Essay Writing

To write effective free-response essays, stay focused on the AP essay scoring rubrics, follow the essay writing strategies in the table that follows, and practice writing essays.

Checklist for Answering Free-Response Questions			
Strategy	**Short-Answer Questions (SAQs)**	**Document-Based Question (DBQ)**	**Long-Essay Question (LEQ)**
1. Stay focused on the question and answer *all* parts of the question.	✓	✓	✓
2. Prewrite to organize your essay in a logical sequence of events.	✓	✓	✓
3. Link AP history reasoning skills.	✓	✓	✓
4. Link the broader historical context (key time periods and principal themes).	✓	✓	✓
5. Link documents to your essay to (a) cite evidence/examples, (b) provide the document's point of view, and (c) corroborate, qualify, or modify your argument.	✓	✓	
6. Write a strong thesis statement.		✓	✓
7. Write an essay with a clear line of reasoning using the standard essay writing format: introduction (with a strong thesis statement), body (with examples and evidence), and conclusion.		✓	✓

Note: Sample essays are available at the end of review chapters 6–11 and on the College Board website found on the AP U.S. History Course homepage.

Stay Focused on the Question

One of the most important strategies is that your essay must stay focused on the question and address *all parts* of the question prompt. To help you stay focused, underline or circle key words in the question prompt before you start writing. For example, if the question reads, "Explain the political and social consequences of 20th-century capitalism," you must respond to *both* parts of the question—political and social consequences. Too often students lose points because they don't respond to all parts of the question.

Note: The APUSH exam asks you to choose between three questions in the long-essay section and two questions in the short-answer section. This is an opportunity for you to focus on a time period that is most familiar. For the LEQ, choose one of the three long-essay questions from different time periods (periods 1–3, periods 4–6, or periods 7–9). For the SAQ, you are expected to answer the first two questions from periods 3–8, and then choose to answer either question 3 or question 4, which addresses two different time periods (periods 1–5 or periods 6–9).

Prewrite to Organize Your Essay

Think before you write by brainstorming, planning, and prewriting to organize your thoughts. The technique of brainstorming means that you should write down all ideas and examples that come to mind. After you brainstorm, organize those ideas in a logical sequence of events. These ideas should emphasize important points, offer historical evidence, and provide the historical context related to the question prompt. (Note: For the DBQ and LEQ, the exam allows 15 minutes to read documents, take notes, and plan both essays.)

If you're stuck and can't think of ideas, read the question a few times and think about one of the AP history reasoning skills. For example, consider the causes and consequences of the historical turning points, or the common similarities and differences in themes during one time period and another time period. Remember that free-response questions are generally designed so that you can receive at least partial credit if you have some knowledge of the subject. Partial responses will get partial credit. Even a response that receives 1 point will be added to your total points. One point may not seem like much, but earning 1 point is better than zero.

Link AP History Reasoning Skills

AP history reasoning skills are at the heart of all APUSH questions: contextualization, comparison, causation, and continuity or change over time. Every essay must include at least one of the four targeted AP history reasoning skills described on pp. 9–10.

Link the Broader Historical Context

Remember to keep your eye on the big picture. Identify and connect the question topic to the broader historical context of different time periods and principal themes. What preceded and what followed the events and developments? Study the historical time periods on pp. 7–8 to help you focus on the big picture of chronological events.

Link Documents to Your Essay

One of the main objectives of the APUSH exam is testing your ability to work with documents in multiple-choice questions, short-answer questions, and document-based questions. This means that you will have to quickly read over a document source or interpret a graphic image, and then organize your answer based on some pretty in-depth critical reasoning.

On free-response document-based questions, you will be required to read short passages, interpret images, or make sense of a graph, chart, table, or map to link documents to your essay so that you can attain your highest possible score by (a) creating groups of common themes in your essay, (b) relating the documents to a historical period, (c) citing evidence that matches the context of the documents to your essay topic, (d) referencing the author's point of view or purpose in your essay, (e) citing at least one additional piece of outside historical evidence, and (f) drawing conclusions about the meaning of the documents to support the argument.

This may seem like a pretty difficult task because these types of questions may challenge your thinking processes. However, these questions may also provide you with an opportunity to excel on the exam because all of the documents are related to the question prompt. According to the College Board, "there are no irrelevant or deliberately misleading documents." The real issue is how to decode all of the documents so that you can connect them to the questions. The good news is that the documents are giving you the information that you need to answer the questions.

How do you accomplish this? What we strongly suggest is that you stop looking at the exam as a test, and start looking at the exam as a puzzle. Your job is to decode the puzzle. The test-makers have given you most of the pieces of the puzzle, and it is your job to figure out how to complete the puzzle by filling in the missing pieces.

Analyzing Documents: A Five-Step Process

As you analyze the documents, ask yourself, "Can I show how these documents are related to my thesis, and can I provide reasons, examples, and proof from the specific facts in these documents?"

The following five-step process will help you analyze the documents.

1. **Decode the documents.** First, preview the documents, circling or underlining key points. This will help you match information from the documents to your question. As you look through the documents, think about how each document might fit with your tentative thesis. Write notes from the documents in the margins of your test booklet, but remember that you don't have a lot of time to take comprehensive notes. Try to keep notes to one or two words and abbreviate when possible.

   As you decode the documents, you will not need to read every detail, statistic, date, or leader in the document. Read quickly to gather context, audience, and other pertinent facts.

   Remember to look for the *context* of the document. Historians find the context by asking *when* and by *whom* the document was written, found in the bibliographic source. If you know the U.S. history time periods, you should have a general sense of events that took place when the document was written, and you should be able to make an educated guess of the major events, ideas, themes, and issues that surrounded the time when the document was written. It also helps to determine what came before and what came after this period (continuity and change over time).

   Find the context by asking some of the following questions (remember to take notes as you answer these questions):

   - Are there headings showing the title, author, and date of the document?
   - Who is the author of the document (male/female, nationality, title, social status)?
   - What is the document's main purpose or point of view, and can I paraphrase the main point in my own words?
   - Can I determine one piece of evidence from the document that supports (corroborates or qualifies) my argument or one that weakens (modifies) my argument?

   Use the information from the context to try to determine the author's intended audience. Who is the author addressing and who benefitted from the document? And why is the author addressing this particular audience during this particular time period?

   After you have completed this process to interpret each document, quickly scan the rest of the document to see if you missed anything, but remember you are just trying to get an overall idea or gist of the passage. Reading, scanning, and taking abbreviated notes should take you less than a minute per document. This step is critical to help you set up your essay response.

2. **Read the documents.** Use speed reading, an important tool when test-taking. In order to avoid reading every word, you must have the mindset that you will not need to know every detail, statistic, date, or leader in the document. Rather, look for the overall gist of the document so that you can draw general conclusions. In some cases, the implications of the document may be more important than the actual details in the document.

3. **Group the documents into thematic categories.** It is likely that you will not be familiar with the author or his or her work, but after decoding the context, this information should help you make an educated guess to determine a relationship between the document and your thesis statement. Ask yourself two questions: "What is the main point of the document?" and "How does the document relate to the question prompt?" This information will help you group the documents into general or specific thematic groups.

   AP Readers want to see that your essay has specific groupings that logically support your thesis. For example, a generalized grouping might be "The social roles during the 18th century." A specific grouping on this topic might be "Documents 1, 3, and 5 characterize women's roles during 18th-century industrialization and the impact on the labor industry."

   Note: If you don't have time to read through the entire document, remember that many authors insert the main idea in the first and last sentences of their writing. Start with the first and last sentences to get a gist of what the author is trying to convey.

4. **Cite evidence from at least three to six of the documents (and at least one piece of evidence not found in the documents).** To receive the highest score possible, you need to be able to explain the fundamental issues related to the question with supporting evidence from at least six documents to support your main thesis and at least one additional piece of historical evidence beyond those found in the documents. When given historical documents, data, or images, you must be able to provide evidence and historical knowledge while constructing a clear argument to support your claims. (Note: Use quotation marks around direct quotes when citing information from the documents.)

   Note: Remember to add the document number when referencing evidence in your essay. For example, "Document 3 vividly describes the brutal methods that were used by the Spanish in their conquest and rule of the New World."

5. **Cite the point of view or purpose from three of the documents.** After you've decoded the documents as described in step 1, it's time to read the documents to gather more information and discuss the point of view from at least three DBQ documents. A surprising number of students neglect this step and lose points on their DBQ essays because they do not successfully address the point of view from three documents. It is not enough to cite the title of a document; you must explain the author's perspective (what influenced or inspired the author to create the document). Think about why the author produced the document during the specific period of time. What is the meaning of the document from the author's perspective? For example, "Document 3 demonstrates the author's point of view in the political cartoon 'Dividing the National Map, 1860.' The context of this image depicts America's strong political divisions during the 1860 presidential election."

Write a Strong Thesis Statement

The introduction of your response should include a convincing thesis statement that tells the AP Reader the main points of your argument within a historical context of U.S. history, the question prompt, and the documents. The thesis statement must be historically defensible. A strong opening paragraph tells the Reader what to expect in the body of your essay and lets the Reader know that you are (1) addressing the central issues of the question prompt, (2) addressing all parts of the question, (3) using multiple pieces of historical evidence or examples, (4) following a line of logical reasoning, and (5) including pertinent themes, periods, and AP history reasoning skill(s) such as context, comparison of similarities and differences, causes and effects, or the changes (or no changes) over time periods.

Do not just restate the question in the thesis statement. AP Readers are looking for your own original thinking. After you read the question prompt, what thoughts jump out at you? Can you provide concrete facts to support your ideas? Write down these ideas as you brainstorm to prewrite a tentative thesis. Underline or circle what you will need to locate in the document(s) and use this information to formulate your thesis statement. Remember, the brainstorming stage is tentative; you can always adjust the thesis statement once you have gathered all of the information from the documents.

Use the Standard Essay Writing Format

Write a clear and legible essay using the standard essay writing format:

- Introduction with a strong thesis statement that focuses on the question prompt
- Body with examples and evidence that are historically defensible
- Conclusion

Paragraph one: The introduction of your essay should focus on a line of reasoning: (a) present a strong main thesis within a historical context, (b) list supporting point #1, (c) list supporting point #2, (d) list supporting point #3, etc.

Paragraphs two, three, and four: Divide the body of your essay into separate supporting points. The body must develop historical evidence by showing *proof, examples*, *evidence*, *analysis*, or *interpretations* of the points in your introduction. This includes evidence that corroborates, qualifies, or modifies your thesis. Think about the thematic big picture of major developments and events to support your argument, and think about the key turning points that caused a shift in developments. Remember that a strong argument not only provides supporting evidence, but also addresses alternative explanations. It is sometimes helpful to use "who, what, where, why, and when" to support your points. And remember to show a connection between each paragraph and your thesis statement.

Paragraph two – Develop point #1.

Paragraph three – Develop point #2.

Paragraph four – Develop point #3.

Note: Continue this process if you have more than three supporting points.

Paragraph five: A lengthy conclusion is not necessary, but your conclusion should expand on important points from your thesis. The Reader will focus on the introduction and the conclusion. Therefore, if you fail to clearly state your points at the beginning of the essay, you have a second chance to provide substance from your thesis at the end.

The following strategic plan of attack summarizes the strategies for all three free-response question types.

A Strategic Plan of Attack

Read the question TWICE and note the directions, prompts, and document sources.

↓

PREWRITE. Gather information from the question, sources, or documents by marking and taking notes about key points. Organize your ideas by prewriting an outline (or list) to prioritize important points and evidence from sources and documents.

↓

WRITING SHORT–ANSWER RESPONSES

No thesis statement.

Answer all three points in each question to receive full credit.

Answer three questions—the first two questions and then choose ONE of the last two questions (the period you know more about).

Keep your answers brief and address historical evidence from the primary or secondary sources (if included).

Use interpretation to historically explain the *content knowledge* related to the question.

Use reasoning skills to address similarities and differences, causes and effects, or changes and continuities over time.

WRITING A DOCUMENT–BASED RESPONSE

Develop a thesis statement that is a historically defensible claim, establishes a line of reasoning, and responds to *all* parts of the question.

Describe the broader historical context of events, developments, and processes. (What happened before, during, or after the time frame of the question?)

Provide supporting evidence that corroborates, qualifies, or modifies your argument.

For the highest possible score, support your argument by identifying, interpreting, and citing specific examples from SIX documents.

Provide at least ONE relevant piece of outside historical evidence not mentioned in the documents.

Provide examples of the author's point of view, historical situation, purpose, or audience from at least THREE documents.

Show the complex relationship among the question prompt, thesis statement, and documents by using historical reasoning (comparison, causation, or continuity and change over time).

WRITING A LONG–ESSAY RESPONSE

Choose ONE of the three question options (the period you know more about).

Develop a thesis argument that is a historically defensible claim and establishes a line of reasoning.

Describe the broader historical context of events, developments, and processes. (What happened before, during, or after the time frame of the question?)

For the highest possible score, use complex understanding of historical development to support your argument with specific facts and examples that corroborate, qualify, or modify your argument.

For the highest possible score, use historical reasoning (comparison, causation, or continuity and change over time).

↓

PROOFREAD AND EDIT. Leave yourself a few minutes to correct errors and make minor revisions.

Chapter 1

Two-Month Cram Plan

The calendar below details a two-month action plan for the APUSH exam. The first step is to determine how much time you have to prepare and then pick the plan that fits your schedule: two-month plan or one-month plan (see pp. 27–29 for a one-month plan). Ask yourself, "How many hours a week can I realistically devote to preparing for the exam?" Be specific. For example, you may be able to study on Tuesdays, Thursdays, and Fridays from 4 to 6 p.m., or you may only have time on Saturdays and Sundays from 8 to 11 a.m. It doesn't matter what plan you pick; what matters is that you stick to the schedule to get your best possible results.

Note: If you are using Internet sources for your additional reading, use at least two trustworthy sources to compare information.

Two-Month Cram Plan	

8 weeks before the exam	**Study Time:** 5 hours
	❑ Chapter 3: Take the diagnostic test and review the multiple-choice answer explanations.
	❑ Compare your multiple-choice responses with topics covered in chapters 4–12.
	❑ Compare your essay responses to the free-response essay-scoring rubrics and to the sample responses provided.
	❑ Browse the APUSH official website: https://apstudent.collegeboard.org/apcourse/ap-united-states-history.
	❑ Read the Introduction.
	    ❑ Study the APUSH exam format (p. 1).
	    ❑ Take notes as you study and memorize the APUSH history disciplinary practices and reasoning skills (pp. 8–10).
	    ❑ Take notes as you study and memorize the APUSH historical time periods (pp. 7–8).
	    ❑ Take notes as you study and memorize the APUSH themes (pp. 10–11).
	    ❑ Take notes as you study the test-taking strategies (pp. 12–22).

7 weeks before the exam	**Study Time:** 3 hours at least three times a week (or as often as your schedule permits) ❑ Chapter 4: Read and take notes on Period One, "Early Settlement of the Americas (1491 to 1607)." ❑ Use additional resources to read more about general and specific topics discussed in Chapter 4. ❑ Reread "AP U.S. History Key Concepts" (pp. 59–60), "Important Events, Terms, and Concepts" (pp. 62–63), and "Study Questions" (pp. 60–61) for Period One. ❑ Answer the chapter review multiple-choice practice questions and compare your answers to the explanations provided. If you miss a question, be sure to note the logic behind the correct answer. ❑ Chapter 5: Read and take notes on Period Two, "The Colonial Period (1607 to 1754)." ❑ Use additional resources to read more about general and specific topics discussed in Chapter 5. ❑ Reread "AP U.S. History Key Concepts" (p. 78), "Important Events, Terms, and Concepts" (p. 80), and "Study Questions" (pp. 78–79) for Period Two. ❑ Answer the chapter review multiple-choice practice questions and compare your answers to the explanations provided. If you miss a question, be sure to note the logic behind the correct answer.

Continued

6 weeks before the exam	**Study Time:** 3 hours at least three times a week (or as often as your schedule permits) ❏ Chapter 6: Read and take notes on Period Three, "Revolutionary America (1754 to 1800)." ❏ Use additional resources to read more about general and specific topics discussed in Chapter 6. ❏ Reread "AP U.S. History Key Concepts" (pp. 103–104), "Important Events, Terms, and Concepts" (pp. 106–107), and "Study Questions" (pp. 104–106) for Period Three. ❏ Answer the chapter review multiple-choice practice questions and compare your answers to the explanations provided. If you miss a question, be sure to note the logic behind the correct answer. ❏ Answer the chapter review document-based question. Compare your response to the scoring guidelines and sample response. ❏ Chapter 7: Read and take notes on Period Four, "Early America (1800 to 1848)." ❏ Use additional resources to read more about general and specific topics discussed in Chapter 7. ❏ Reread "AP U.S. History Key Concepts" (pp. 137–138), "Important Events, Terms, and Concepts" (pp. 140–141), and "Study Questions" (pp. 138–140) for Period Four. ❏ Answer the chapter review multiple-choice practice questions and compare your answers to the explanations provided. If you miss a question, be sure to note the logic behind the correct answer. ❏ Answer the chapter review document-based question. Compare your response to the scoring guidelines and sample response.
5 weeks before the exam	**Study Time:** 3 hours at least three times a week (or as often as your schedule permits) ❏ Chapter 8: Read and take notes on Period Five, "The Civil War and Reconstruction (1844 to 1877)." ❏ Use additional resources to read more about general and specific topics discussed in Chapter 8. ❏ Reread "AP U.S. History Key Concepts" (pp. 173–174), "Important Events, Terms, and Concepts" (p. 177), and "Study Questions" (pp. 174–176) for Period Five. ❏ Answer the chapter review multiple-choice practice questions and compare your answers to the explanations provided. If you miss a question, be sure to note the logic behind the correct answer. ❏ Answer the chapter review document-based question. Compare your response to the scoring guidelines and sample response. ❏ Chapter 9: Read and take notes on Period Six, "The Gilded Age (1865 to 1898)." ❏ Use additional resources to read more about general and specific topics discussed in Chapter 9. ❏ Reread "AP U.S. History Key Concepts" (p. 216), "Important Events, Terms, and Concepts" (pp. 219–220), and "Study Questions" (pp. 216–219) for Period Six. ❏ Answer the chapter review multiple-choice practice questions and compare your answers to the explanations provided. If you miss a question, be sure to note the logic behind the correct answer. ❏ Answer the chapter review document-based question. Compare your response to the scoring guidelines and sample response.

4 weeks before the exam	**Study Time:** 3 hours at least three times a week (or as often as your schedule permits)
	❏ Chapter 10: Read and take notes on Period Seven, "The Rise to Global Power (1890 to 1945)."
	❏ Use additional resources to read more about general and specific topics discussed in Chapter 10.
	❏ Reread "AP U.S. History Key Concepts" (pp. 249–250), "Important Events, Terms, and Concepts" (pp. 254–255), and "Study Questions" (pp. 250–254) for Period Seven.
	❏ Answer the chapter review multiple-choice practice questions and compare your answers to the explanations provided. If you miss a question, be sure to note the logic behind the correct answer.
	❏ Answer the chapter review document-based question. Compare your response to the scoring guidelines and sample response.
	❏ Chapter 11: Read and take notes on Period Eight, "The Post-War Era and the Cold War (1945 to 1980)."
	❏ Use additional resources to read more about general and specific topics discussed in Chapter 11.
	❏ Reread "AP U.S. History Key Concepts" (p. 312), "Important Events, Terms, and Concepts" (pp. 316–317), and "Study Questions" (pp. 312–315) for Period Eight.
	❏ Answer the chapter review multiple-choice practice questions and compare your answers to the explanations provided. If you miss a question, be sure to note the logic behind the correct answer.
	❏ Answer the chapter review document-based question. Compare your response to the scoring guidelines and sample response.
3 weeks before the exam	**Study Time:** 3 hours at least two times a week (or as often as your schedule permits)
	❏ Chapter 12: Read and take notes on Period Nine, "The Globalization Era (1980 to the Present)."
	❏ Use additional resources to read more about general and specific topics discussed in Chapter 12.
	❏ Reread "AP U.S. History Key Concepts" (pp. 353–354), "Important Events, Terms, and Concepts" (pp. 356–357), and "Study Questions" (pp. 354–357) for Period Nine.
	❏ Answer the chapter review multiple-choice practice questions and compare your answers to the explanations provided. If you miss a question, be sure to note the logic behind the correct answer.
2 weeks before the exam	**Study Time:** 5 hours
	❏ Chapter 13: Take the full-length practice exam and review your answers and the explanations and sample responses.
	❏ Based on your performance, identify topics and their corresponding chapters that require further review.
	❏ Use additional resources to read more about general and specific topics discussed in the practice exam.
	Study Time: 2–3 hours
	❏ Based on your review, target general and specific topics.
	❏ Reread the "Test-Taking Strategies" in the Introduction (pp. 12–22).
	❏ Practice writing responses to two short-answer questions and one document-based question (or one long-essay question) using the scoring guidelines on pp. 4–6 to score your essay. Note: Previous free-response question topics can be found online at https://apstudent.collegeboard.org/apcourse/ap-united-states-history/exam-practice.
7 days before the exam	**Study Time:** 3 hours
	❏ Review APUSH Key Concepts for Period One (pp. 59–60) and Period Two (p. 78).
	❏ Study and target specific topics as needed.

Continued

6 days before the exam	**Study Time:** 3 hours ❑ Review APUSH Key Concepts for Period Three (pp. 103–104) and Period Four (pp. 137–138). ❑ Study and target specific topics as needed.
5 days before the exam	**Study Time:** 3 hours ❑ Review APUSH Key Concepts for Period Five (pp. 173–174) and Period Six (p. 216). ❑ Study and target specific topics as needed.
4 days before the exam	**Study Time:** 1–2 hours ❑ Review APUSH Key Concepts for Period Seven (pp. 249–250). ❑ Study and target specific topics as needed.
3 days before the exam	**Study Time:** 1–2 hours ❑ Review APUSH Key Concepts for Period Eight (p. 312). ❑ Study and target specific topics as needed.
2 days before the exam	**Study Time:** 1–2 hours ❑ Review APUSH Key Concepts for Period Nine (pp. 353–354). ❑ Study and target specific topics as needed. ❑ Reread any material you feel is necessary.
1 day before the exam	❑ Relax. You have covered all of the material necessary to score well on the exam. ❑ Get plenty of sleep the night before the exam.
Morning of the exam	❑ Eat a balanced, nutritious breakfast with protein. ❑ Keep your usual habits. Don't try something new today. ❑ Bring your photo ID, ticket for admission, watch (that does not have Internet and does not beep), your 6-digit school code, several sharpened no. 2 pencils with erasers, and a few pens with black or dark-blue ink. Note: Cell phones, scratch paper, books, smartwatches, and food/drinks are not allowed at the testing center.

Chapter 2

One-Month Cram Plan

The calendar below details a one-month action plan for the APUSH exam. The first step is to determine how much time you have to prepare and then pick the plan that fits your schedule: two-month plan or one-month (see pp. 23–26 for a two-month plan). Ask yourself, "How many hours a week can I realistically devote to preparing for the exam?" Be specific. For example, you may be able to study on Tuesdays, Thursdays, and Fridays from 4 to 6 p.m., or you may only have time on Saturdays and Sundays from 8 to 11 a.m. It doesn't matter what plan you pick; what matters is that you stick to the schedule to get your best possible results.

Note: If you are using Internet sources for your additional reading, use at least two trustworthy sources to compare information.

One-Month Cram Plan	

4 weeks before the exam	**Study Time:** 5 hours
	 ❑ Chapter 3: Take the diagnostic test and review the multiple-choice answer explanations.
	 ❑ Compare your multiple-choice responses with topics covered in chapters 4–12.
	 ❑ Compare your essay responses to the free-response essay-scoring rubrics and to the sample responses provided.
	 ❑ Browse the APUSH official website: https://apstudent.collegeboard.org/apcourse/ap-united-states-history.
	 ❑ Read the Introduction.
	   ❑ Study the APUSH exam format (p. 1).
	   ❑ Take notes as you study and memorize the APUSH history disciplinary practices and reasoning skills (pp. 8–10).
	   ❑ Take notes as you study and memorize the APUSH historical time periods (pp. 7–8).
	   ❑ Take notes as you study and memorize the APUSH themes (pp. 10–11).
	   ❑ Take notes as you study the test-taking strategies (pp. 12–22).
	
	 Study Time: 3 hours at least three times a week (or as often as your schedule permits)
	 ❑ Chapter 4: Read and take notes on Period One, "Early Settlement of the Americas (1491 to 1607)."
	 ❑ Answer the chapter review multiple-choice practice questions. If you answer a question incorrectly, make sure you understand the logic behind the correct answer.
	 ❑ Chapter 5: Read and take notes on Period Two, "The Colonial Period (1607 to 1754)."
	 ❑ Answer the chapter review multiple-choice practice questions. If you answer a question incorrectly, make sure you understand the logic behind the correct answer.
	 ❑ Chapter 6: Read and take notes on Period Three, "Revolutionary America (1754 to 1800)."
	 ❑ Answer the chapter review multiple-choice practice questions. If you answer a question incorrectly, make sure you understand the logic behind the correct answer.
	 ❑ Answer the chapter review document-based question. Compare your response to the scoring guidelines and sample response.

Continued

3 weeks before the exam	**Study Time:** 3 hours at least three times a week (or as often as your schedule permits) ❏ Chapter 7: Read and take notes on Period Four, "Early America (1800 to 1848)." ❏ Answer the chapter review multiple-choice practice questions after you have read the entire chapter. If you answer a question incorrectly, make sure you understand the logic behind the correct answer. ❏ Answer the chapter review document-based question. Compare your response to the scoring guidelines and sample response. ❏ Chapter 8: Read and take notes on Period Five, "The Civil War and Reconstruction (1844 to 1877)." ❏ Answer the chapter review multiple-choice practice questions. If you answer a question incorrectly, make sure you understand the logic behind the correct answer. ❏ Answer the chapter review document-based question. Compare your response to the scoring guidelines and sample response. ❏ Chapter 9: Read and take notes on Period Six, "The Gilded Age (1865 to 1898)." ❏ Answer the chapter review multiple-choice practice questions. If you answer a question incorrectly, make sure you understand the logic behind the correct answer. ❏ Answer the chapter review document-based question. Compare your response to the scoring guidelines and sample response.
2 weeks before the exam	**Study Time:** 3 hours at least three times a week (or as often as your schedule permits) ❏ Chapter 10: Read and take notes on Period Seven, "The Rise to Global Power (1890 to 1945)." ❏ Answer the chapter review multiple-choice practice questions. If you answer a question incorrectly, make sure you understand the logic behind the correct answer. ❏ Answer the chapter review document-based question. Compare your response to the scoring guidelines and sample response. ❏ Chapter 11: Read and take notes on Period Eight, "The Post-War Era and the Cold War (1945 to 1980)." ❏ Answer the chapter review multiple-choice practice questions. If you answer a question incorrectly, make sure you understand the logic behind the correct answer. ❏ Answer the chapter review document-based question. Compare your response to the scoring guidelines and sample response. ❏ Chapter 12: Read and take notes on Period Nine, "The Globalization Era (1980 to the Present)." ❏ Answer the chapter review multiple-choice practice questions. If you answer a question incorrectly, make sure you understand the logic behind the correct answer.
7 days before the exam	**Study Time:** 5 hours ❏ Chapter 13: Take the full-length practice exam and review your answers and the explanations and sample responses. ❏ Based on your performance, identify topics and their corresponding chapters that require further review. ❏ Use additional sources to read more about general and specific topics discussed in the practice exam. **Study Time:** 2–3 hours ❏ Based on your review, target general and specific topics. ❏ Reread "Test-Taking Strategies" in the Introduction (pp. 12–22). ❏ Practice writing a response to one document-based question or one long-essay question using the scoring guidelines on pp. 4–6 to score your essay. Note: Previous free-response question topics can be found online at https://apstudent.collegeboard.org/apcourse/ap-united-states-history/exam-practice.
6 days before the exam	**Study Time:** 3 hours ❏ Review APUSH Key Concepts for Period One (pp. 59–60) and Period Two (p. 78). ❏ Study and target specific topics as needed.

5 days before the exam	**Study Time:** 3 hours ❏ Review APUSH Key Concepts for Period Three (pp. 103–104) and Period Four (pp. 137–138). ❏ Study and target specific topics as needed.
4 days before the exam	**Study Time:** 3 hours ❏ Review APUSH Key Concepts for Period Five (pp. 173–174) and Period Six (p. 216). ❏ Study and target specific topics as needed.
3 days before the exam	**Study Time:** 3 hours ❏ Review APUSH Key Concepts for Period Seven (pp. 249–250) and Period Eight (p. 312). ❏ Study and target specific topics as needed.
2 days before the exam	**Study Time:** 1–2 hours ❏ Review APUSH Key Concepts for Period Nine (pp. 353–354). ❏ Study and target specific topics as needed. ❏ Reread any material you feel is necessary.
1 day before the exam	❏ Relax. You have covered all of the material necessary to score well on the exam. ❏ Get plenty of sleep the night before the exam.
Morning of the exam	❏ Eat a balanced, nutritious breakfast with protein. ❏ Keep your usual habits. Don't try something new today. ❏ Bring your photo ID, ticket for admission, watch (that does not have Internet and does not beep), your 6-digit school code, several sharpened no. 2 pencils with erasers, and a few pens with black or dark-blue ink. Note: Cell phones, scratch paper, books, smartwatches, and food/drinks are not allowed at the testing center.

Chapter 3

Diagnostic Test

This chapter contains a diagnostic exam that will give you valuable insight into the types of questions that may appear on the APUSH exam. It is for assessment purposes only to help you to gauge your understanding of APUSH questions. As you take the practice exam, try to simulate testing conditions. The time limits for each of the following sections are estimates based on the amounts that are designated by the College Board for the actual test.

Section	Diagnostic Test	Actual Exam
Section I: Part A—Multiple-Choice Questions	25 questions, 25 minutes	55 questions, 55 minutes
Section I: Part B—Short-Answer Questions	2 questions, 25 minutes	3 questions, 40 minutes
Section II: Part A—Document-Based Question	1 question, 60 minutes	1 question, 60 minutes
Section II: Part B—Long-Essay Question	n/a	1 question, 40 minutes

Answer Sheet for Multiple-Choice Questions

```
 1  Ⓐ Ⓑ Ⓒ Ⓓ
 2  Ⓐ Ⓑ Ⓒ Ⓓ
 3  Ⓐ Ⓑ Ⓒ Ⓓ
 4  Ⓐ Ⓑ Ⓒ Ⓓ
 5  Ⓐ Ⓑ Ⓒ Ⓓ

 6  Ⓐ Ⓑ Ⓒ Ⓓ
 7  Ⓐ Ⓑ Ⓒ Ⓓ
 8  Ⓐ Ⓑ Ⓒ Ⓓ
 9  Ⓐ Ⓑ Ⓒ Ⓓ
10  Ⓐ Ⓑ Ⓒ Ⓓ

11  Ⓐ Ⓑ Ⓒ Ⓓ
12  Ⓐ Ⓑ Ⓒ Ⓓ
13  Ⓐ Ⓑ Ⓒ Ⓓ
14  Ⓐ Ⓑ Ⓒ Ⓓ
15  Ⓐ Ⓑ Ⓒ Ⓓ

16  Ⓐ Ⓑ Ⓒ Ⓓ
17  Ⓐ Ⓑ Ⓒ Ⓓ
18  Ⓐ Ⓑ Ⓒ Ⓓ
19  Ⓐ Ⓑ Ⓒ Ⓓ
20  Ⓐ Ⓑ Ⓒ Ⓓ

21  Ⓐ Ⓑ Ⓒ Ⓓ
22  Ⓐ Ⓑ Ⓒ Ⓓ
23  Ⓐ Ⓑ Ⓒ Ⓓ
24  Ⓐ Ⓑ Ⓒ Ⓓ
25  Ⓐ Ⓑ Ⓒ Ⓓ
```

Section I

Part A—Multiple-Choice Questions

Multiple-choice questions are grouped into sets. Each set contains one source-based prompt (document or image) and two to five questions.

25 questions

25 minutes

Questions 1–3 refer to the following excerpt.

> It is the general concession of all men that the invitation of witchcraft is the thing that has now introduced the Devil into the midst of us. The children of New England have secretly done many things that have been pleasing to the Devil. They say that in some towns it has been a usual thing for people to cure hurts with spells, or to use detestable conjurations with sieves, keys, peas, and nails, to learn the things for which they have an impious curiosity. 'Tis in the Devil's name that such things are done.

> —Source: Cotton Mather, *The Wonders of the Invisible World,* 1693.

1. The excerpt was written in response to

   A. The Puritans' dedication to a City on a Hill, which would provide an example of a righteous government

   B. The Puritans' justification for the torture and execution of several people in Salem

   C. The Puritans' persecution of Catholics and other religious dissenters in Massachusetts

   D. The Puritans' prejudice against Native Americans and slaves, whom they considered to be pagans

2. Based on your knowledge of U.S. history, how were the circumstances of the original Puritan migration ironic to this passage?

   A. Puritans were investors in a joint-stock company and wished to make money.

   B. Puritans were often persecuted in England, their mother country.

   C. Puritans wanted to ensure that they could educate their women and children.

   D. Puritans felt their children were threatened by the secular world and would lose faith in God.

3. Which of the following best describes a different religiously motivated historical development in the British colonies?

   A. Tensions between Old Lights and New Lights during the Great Awakening

   B. Divisions between northern and southern religious denominations in the Antebellum period

   C. Antebellum attempts to free slaves against the wishes of their masters in the evangelical church

   D. The abuse of indentured servants by tobacco growers in Virginia

Questions 4–6 refer to the following political cartoon.

THE DOWNFALL OF MOTHER BANK.

Source: Henry Robinson, "The Downfall of Mother Bank" – *Harper's Weekly,* 1833. Lithograph portrays the "Order to Remove the Public Money" from the Second Bank of the United States.

4. Robinson's political cartoon is a direct reaction to which of the following?

   A. South Carolina's threat to nullify the Tariff of Abominations

   B. Andrew Jackson's fight against Nicholas Biddle and supporters of the Second Bank of the United States

   C. The Cherokees' attempt to receive remuneration resulting from the Indian Removal Act

   D. The crisis associated with the Force Act

5. Based on your knowledge of U.S. history, which of the following best describes a historical development that allowed Jackson to win the election of 1828?

   A. The Market Revolution

   B. Cherokee disputes over the Indian Removal Act

   C. Universal white male suffrage

   D. The annexation of Texas

6. Which of the following was NOT a characteristic of Jacksonian Democrats in the Second Party System?

    A.   Jeffersonian traditions, such as a small federal government

    B.   Usually southerners or states' rights advocates

    C.   Supported the principles of "common men"

    D.   The promotion of economic nationalism

Questions 7–9 refer to the following painting.

Source: John Trumbull, painting of a Revolutionary event (painted in 1819).

7. The conditions shown in Trumbull's painting depict which of the following historical events in 1776?

    A.   France's entry into the war

    B.   The signing of the Declaration of Independence

    C.   Washington's Farewell Address

    D.   The formal separation of church and state

8. Based on your knowledge of U.S. history, which of the following is a true statement about the Second Continental Congress?

   A. It declared war upon the English Parliament and King George III.
   B. Georgia did not bother to attend.
   C. The Battles of Lexington and Concord took place directly after the delegates began to meet.
   D. Some of the delegates' loyalties were torn, so they appealed to the king for the ability to negotiate.

9. Which of the following best describes the colonists' motivations for rebellion?

   A. Colonists were upset about the boycotts of British imports and exports.
   B. Colonists were inspired by enlightened writers, including Locke, Rousseau, and Paine.
   C. Colonists were angry about the French and Indian War.
   D. Colonists were forced to feed and house the British royal troops.

Questions 10–12 refer to the following excerpt.

The magnitude of the American victory led those who had been concerned about American honor to rejoice. But to those who were committed to *Cuba libre,* the war had a bitter end. At the close of the Cuban campaign, it appeared that one of the casualties of war was the prospect of Cuban independence. Although American troops had collaborated with the Cuban insurgents early in the war, by the time the United States negotiated the surrender of Santiago de Cuba in July, relations with the Cuban revolutionaries had deteriorated to such a degree that U.S. troops kept Cuban soldiers from entering the city… Rather than liberating Cuba in the summer of 1898, the United States occupied it until 1902.

—Source: Kristin Hoganson, *Fighting for American Manhood,* 1998. An excerpt about the provocation of the Spanish-American War through the lens of gender-specific political roles.

10. The ideas reflected in Hoganson's excerpt reflect which of the following?

    A. The persecution of Cubans by American soldiers
    B. The political influences resulting in debates concerning peace negotiations
    C. The criticism of the general public concerning the brutality of the war
    D. The complex motivations for fighting the war, which led to its mixed results

11. Which of the following represents the continuation of imperialistic foreign policies suggested by the excerpt?

    A. The war in the Philippines, which resulted in a U.S. provisional government
    B. William McKinley's attack on *yellow journalists,* like William Hearst
    C. Teddy Roosevelt's Rough Riders overtaking San Juan Hill
    D. The establishment of an independent government in Hawaii

12. Based on your knowledge of U.S. history, which of the following best represents the long-term consequences of the Spanish-American War?

    A. The Teller Amendment
    B. McKinley's re-election in 1900
    C. The Open Door Policy
    D. The Platt Amendment

Questions 13–15 refer to the following excerpt.

I want to say that we are not here advocating violence… The only weapon that we have in our hands this evening is the weapon of protest…

If we were incarcerated behind the iron curtains of a Communistic nation we couldn't do this… My friends, don't let anybody make us feel that we are to be compared in our actions with the Ku Klux Klan or with the White Citizens Council. There will be no crosses burned at any bus stops in Montgomery. There will be no white persons pulled out of their homes and taken out on some distant road and lynched for not cooperating. There will be nobody amid, among us who will stand up and defy the Constitution of this nation…

If we are wrong, the Supreme Court of this nation is wrong. If we are wrong, the Constitution of the United States is wrong… And we are determined here in Montgomery to work and fight until justice runs down like water, and righteousness like a mighty stream.

—Source: Martin Luther King Jr., "Montgomery Bus Boycott Speech," December 5, 1955.

13. Which of the following represents the main purpose of King's speech?

    A. King wanted to note tensions within the black community during the Civil Rights Movement.
    B. King wanted to inspire African Americans to unify and protest oppression nonviolently.
    C. King wanted to motivate African Americans to use their political voting power to fight for civil equality.
    D. King wanted to shift the opinions of ministers and others in the white community.

14. Which of the following is NOT a strategy used by African Americans to promote social and civil equality during the Civil Rights Movement?

    A. The promotion of black nationalism and armed self-defense
    B. Legal battles instigated by the NAACP
    C. Appeals for patience within the black community to allow legislation to take its proper effect
    D. The formation of interracial organizations that participated in voting drives and freedom rides

15. Which of the following best describes an example of the ideas expressed in King's excerpt?

    A. Booker T. Washington's accommodation strategies in the early 19th century
    B. W. E. B. DuBois' avocation of a "Talented Tenth" that could lead the black community into equality
    C. Elite black women's organizations during the Progressive Era that sought to better their communities and reputations
    D. Philip Randolph's intention to organize a march on Washington to protest discriminatory employment practices during World War II

Questions 16–18 refer to the following political cartoon.

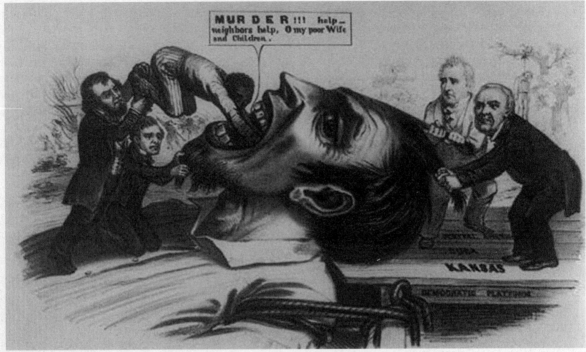

Source: John Magee, "Forcing Slavery Down the Throat of a Freesoiler," 1856.

16. This 19th-century image illustrates which of the following?

    A. Transcendentalist propaganda associated with freedom and liberty
    B. Conflicts between pro-slavery and anti-slavery factions in the Antebellum era
    C. Issues related to the Spanish-American War
    D. The persecution of white activists for African American civil rights

17. Which of the following legislative acts is depicted in Magee's political cartoon?

    A. The Missouri Compromise
    B. The Force Act
    C. The Kansas-Nebraska Act
    D. The Dred Scott Case

18. Based on your knowledge of U.S. history, which of the following presidents was considered a free soiler?

    A. Andrew Jackson
    B. Andrew Johnson
    C. Abraham Lincoln
    D. David Wilmot

Questions 19–21 refer to the following excerpt.

The object of your mission is to explore the Missouri river…or any other river [that] may offer the most direct & practicable water communication across this continent for the purposes of commerce….

Your observations are to be taken with great pains & accuracy…with the aid of the usual tables, to fix the latitude and longitude of the places at which they were taken and are to be rendered to the war office for the purpose of having the calculations made concurrently by proper persons within the US…

The commerce which may be carried on with the people inhabiting the line you will pursue renders a knowledge of those people important. You will therefore endeavor to make yourself acquainted…with the names of the nations & their numbers…it will be useful to acquire what knowledge you can of the state of morality, religion, & information among them, as it may better enable those who may endeavor to civilize & instruct them, to adapt their measures to the existing notions & practices of those on whom they are to operate.

—Source: President Thomas Jefferson, "Instructions for Meriwether Lewis."
Letter written June 20, 1803.

19. Jefferson's letter references which of the following historical events?

   A.   The Embargo Acts
   B.   *Marbury v. Madison*
   C.   Expansion of presidential power
   D.   The Louisiana Purchase

20. Based on your knowledge of U.S. history, which of the following best describes a global motivation for Jefferson's acquisition from France?

   A.   The French and Indian War
   B.   An uprising of African slaves in Haiti
   C.   Economic declines in Spain
   D.   American debates about the interpretation of the U.S. Constitution

21. Which of the following best describes one of the primary reasons that Jefferson sent instructions to Lewis?

   A.   The desire for American expansion and security
   B.   A respect for Native American culture and religion
   C.   Improved relations with the French
   D.   The yearning for additional immigrants, who would be drawn to open land

Questions 22–23 refer to the following excerpt.

...in the West today, we see a free world that has achieved a level of prosperity and well-being unprecedented in all human history. In the Communist world, we see failure, technological backwardness, declining standards of health, even want of the most basic kind—too little food... We hear much from Moscow about a new policy of reform and openness... Are these the beginnings of profound changes in the Soviet state? Or are they token gestures, intended to raise false hopes in the West, or to strengthen the Soviet system without changing it?

There is one sign the Soviets can make that would be unmistakable, that would advance dramatically the cause of freedom and peace. General Secretary Gorbachev, if you seek peace, if you seek prosperity for the Soviet Union and Eastern Europe, if you seek liberalization: Come here to this gate! Mr. Gorbachev, open this gate! Mr. Gorbachev, tear down this wall!

> —Source: President Ronald Reagan, "Speech about the U.S. and
> Soviet Relations in Front of the Berlin Wall," June 12, 1987.

22. Which of the following does the excerpt of Reagan's 1987 speech best reflect?

    A. Reagan's continuing mistrust of the Soviet Union due to Cold War tensions between the U.S. and the Soviet Union
    B. Reagan's ability to appease Gorbachev when international diplomacy was necessary
    C. Reagan's growing respect for the transformative changes taking place in the Soviet Union
    D. Reagan's commitment to positive global rhetoric and freedom

23. Which of the following best describes what tearing down the Berlin Wall represented for Americans?

    A. Political clout for Reagan generated during a period of his unpopularity
    B. A national triumph for the U.S. associated with the economic destruction of the Soviet Union
    C. The symbolic removal of the "Iron Curtain" that Churchill identified in 1946
    D. Soviet military defeat during a time of crisis

Questions 24–25 refer to the following map.

Source: "Tennessee Valley Authority," created 1933–1945. A map of the general planning of the river transport development.

24. Based on your knowledge of U.S. history, the map is best seen as evidence for which of the following?

    A.   Various projects associated with the New Deal
    B.   All of the waterways and rivers of the South
    C.   States that were to receive new forms of hydroelectric power
    D.   A cultural project intended to inform the public of new technology

25. Which of the following was NOT a criticism of the TVA and other New Deal programs?

    A.   The deals gave the federal government and the president too much power.
    B.   The deals nationalized industries that should have remained private.
    C.   The deals were unconstitutional.
    D.   The deals promoted various definitions of freedom and democracy that favored the wealthy.

IF YOU FINISH BEFORE TIME IS CALLED, CHECK YOUR WORK ON THIS
SECTION ONLY. DO NOT WORK ON ANY OTHER SECTION IN THE TEST.

Part B—Short-Answer Questions

2 questions

25 minutes

Reading Time: 5 minutes (brainstorm your thoughts and organize your responses)

Writing Time: 20 minutes

Directions: Write your responses on lined paper. The short-answer questions will *not* require that you develop and support a thesis statement. Use complete sentences—bullet points or an outline is unacceptable. Answer **all** parts of the question to receive full credit.

> NOTE: The following short-answer questions are for instructional purposes only and may not reflect the format of the actual exam. On the actual exam, there are four short-answer questions, but you are only required to answer three questions. Answer the first two questions, and choose to answer either the third or fourth question. Questions 1 and 2 are based on sources with texts, images, graphs, or maps from periods 3–8. Question 3 (periods 1–5) and Question 4 (periods 6–9) have no sources.

Question 1. Use the image below and your knowledge of U.S. history to answer all parts of the question that follows.

Source: James Albert Wales, "The 'Strong' Government 1869–1877." A woman from "the Solid South" carrying Ulysses S. Grant in a carpet bag.

1. Using the image, answer (a), (b), and (c).

   (a) Briefly describe ONE perspective about Reconstruction supported by the image.

   (b) Briefly describe ONE specific historical event or development that led to the changes in domestic policy during Reconstruction.

   (c) Briefly explain ONE opposition to the perception of Reconstruction between 1869 and 1877 depicted in the image.

Question 2. Based on your knowledge of U.S. history, answer (a), (b), and (c).

2. **(a)** Briefly describe ONE specific historical similarity between U.S. immigration in the period 1820–1864 and in the period 1865–1898.

   (b) Briefly describe ONE specific historical difference between U.S. immigration in the period 1820–1864 and in the period 1865–1898.

   (c) Briefly explain ONE specific historical effect of U.S. immigration in either the period 1820–1864 or in the period 1865–1898.

IF YOU FINISH BEFORE TIME IS CALLED, CHECK YOUR WORK ON THIS SECTION ONLY. DO NOT WORK ON ANY OTHER SECTION IN THE TEST.

Section II

Part A—Document-Based Question

1 question
60 minutes

Reading Time: 15 minutes (brainstorm your thoughts and organize your response)
Writing Time: 45 minutes

Directions: The document-based question is based on the seven accompanying documents. The documents are for instructional purposes only. Some of the documents have been edited for the purpose of this practice exercise. Write your response on lined paper and include the following:

- **Thesis.** Present a thesis that supports a historically defensible claim, establishes a line of reasoning, and responds to all parts of the question. The thesis must consist of one or more sentences located in one place—either the introduction or the conclusion.

- **Contextualization.** Situate the argument by explaining the broader historical events, developments, or processes that occurred before, during, or after the time frame of the question.

- **Evidence from the documents.** Support your argument by using the content of six of the documents to develop and support a cohesive argument that responds to the question.

- **Evidence beyond the documents.** Support your argument by explaining at least one additional piece of specific historical evidence not found in the documents. (Note: The example must be different from the evidence used to earn the point for contextualization.)

- **Analysis.** Use at least three documents that are relevant to the question to explain the documents' point of view, purpose, historical situation, and/or audience.

- **Historical reasoning.** Use historical reasoning to show complex relationships among the documents, the topic question, and the thesis argument. Use evidence to corroborate, qualify, or modify the argument.

Based on the documents that follow, answer the question below.

Question 1: Evaluate the extent to which differing views of democracy influenced U.S. domestic and foreign policies from 1940 to 1945.

Document 1

> **Source: Franklin Delano Roosevelt, "Fireside Chat (154)." Evening radio address by President Roosevelt on the necessity of European support. December 29, 1940.**
>
> The Nazi masters of Germany have made it clear that they intend not only to dominate all life and thought in their own country, but also to enslave the whole of Europe, and then to use the resources of Europe to dominate the rest of the world…the Axis proclaims that there can be no ultimate peace between their philosophy—their philosophy of government—and our philosophy of government.
>
> …it is the purpose of the nation to build now with all possible speed every machine, every arsenal, every factory that we need to manufacture our defense material… We must be the great arsenal of democracy. We have furnished the British great material support and we will furnish far more in the future. There will be no "bottlenecks" in our determination to aid Great Britain. No dictator, no combination of dictators, will weaken that determination by threats of how they will construe that determination.
>
> ….We have every good reason for hope—hope for peace, yes, and hope for the defense of our civilization and for the building of a better civilization in the future.

Document 2

> **Source: Charles Lindbergh, "America First Speech," September 11, 1941. Anti-war speech delivered in Des Moines, Iowa, on behalf of the America First Committee, criticizing those groups leading America to war.**
>
> …only one thing holds this country from war today. That is the rising opposition of the American people. Our system of democracy and representative government is on test today as it has never been before. We are on the verge of a war in which the only victor would be chaos and prostration.
>
> We are on the verge of a war for which we are still unprepared, and for which no one has offered a feasible plan for victory—a war which cannot be won without sending our soldiers across the ocean to force a landing on a hostile coast against armies stronger than our own.
>
> We are on the verge of war, but it is not yet too late to stay out. It is not too late to show that no amount of money, or propaganda, or patronage can force a free and independent people into war against its will. It is not yet too late to retrieve and to maintain the independent American destiny that our forefathers established in this new world.

Document 3

> **Source: Sidney Diamond, "A Soldier's Reasons for Enlisting," 1942. Letter from Sidney to his longtime sweetheart, explaining his reasons for joining the war.**
>
> Our mutual friend Thomas Paine has aptly said "My country is the world and my religion is to do good!"... It is true as Goethe suggests that in peace time every one concerns himself with sweeping his own doorstep and minding his own business and things will go well, but at present, the world (which we recognize as our country) fights hopelessly in a maelstrom as it is gradually and seemingly inevitably sucked into chaos. When a man drowns, one scarcely thinks of the future. One hardly sits down to coldly calculate the credits one loses in college, one does not dream of future happiness—
>
> There is no desire to wait and see!!—"Love of country is more powerful than reason itself!" (Ovid)... our country is the entire world and mankind our countrymen!!!
>
> ...Patriotism knows no time, no land, no sea—it is not geographical! It is not scheduled!

Document 4

> **Source: James G. Thompson, "Democracy: Double Victory at Home-Abroad," April 11, 1942. Editorial letter from an African American man to the editor of the *Pittsburgh Courier*. Thompson believed that he should not fight for a nation that discriminated against him.**
>
> Being an American of dark complexion and some 26 years, these questions flash through my mind: "Should I sacrifice my life to live half American?"... "Is the kind of America I know worth defending?" "Will America be a true and pure democracy after this war?" "Will colored Americans suffer still the indignities that have been heaped upon them in the past?"
>
> The "V for Victory" sign is being displayed prominently in all so-called democratic countries which are fighting for victory over aggression, slavery and tyranny. If this V sign means that to those now engaged in this great conflict then let colored Americans adopt the double VV for a double victory. The first V for victory over our enemies from without, the second V for victory over our enemies within. For surely those who perpetrate these ugly prejudices here are seeking to destroy our democratic form of government just as surely as the Axis forces.

Document 5

> **Source: Western Defense Command and Fourth Army Wartime Civil Control Administration. Instructions to "all persons of Japanese ancestry" in San Francisco, California, May 3, 1942.**
>
> Pursuant to the provisions of Civilian Exclusion Order No. 33, this Headquarters, dated May 3, 1942, all persons of Japanese ancestry, both alien and non-alien, will be evacuated from the above area by 12 o'clock noon, P. W. T., Saturday, May 9, 1942...
>
> The Following Instructions Must Be Observed:
>
> ...Evacuees must carry with them on departure for the Assembly Center, the following property:
>
> **(a)** Bedding and linens (no mattress) for each member of the family;
>
> **(b)** Toilet articles for each member of the family;
>
> **(c)** Extra clothing for each member of the family;
>
> **(d)** Sufficient knives, forks, spoons, plates, bowls and cups for each member of the family;
>
> **(e)** Essential personal effects for each member of the family...
>
> No pets of any kind will be permitted... Each family, and individual living alone, will be furnished transportation to the Assembly Center or will be authorized to travel by private automobile in a supervised group...
>
> Go to the Civil Control Station...to receive further instructions.

Document 6

Source: Roger Smith, from the Office of War Information, "New York Girl Scouts," June 1943. Photo of Girl Scouts participating in the opening of the Four Freedoms war bond show. Courtesy of the Library of Congress.

Document 7

Source: Franklin Delano Roosevelt, "Speech at the Foreign Policy Association in New York," October 21, 1944.

Peace, like war, can succeed only where there is a will to enforce it, and where there is available power to enforce it.

The Council of the United Nations must have the power to act quickly and decisively to keep the peace by force, if necessary. A policeman would not be a very effective policeman if, when he saw a felon break into a house, he had to go to the Town Hall and call a town meeting to issue a warrant before the felon could be arrested...

If we do not catch the international felon when we have our hands on him, if we let him get away with his loot because the Town Council has not passed an ordinance authorizing his arrest, then we are not doing our share to prevent another world war. I think, and I have had some experience, that the people of this Nation want their Government to work, they want their Government to act, and not merely to talk, whenever and wherever there is a threat to world peace.

IF YOU FINISH BEFORE TIME IS CALLED, CHECK YOUR WORK ON THIS SECTION ONLY. DO NOT WORK ON ANY OTHER SECTION IN THE TEST.

Answer Key for Multiple-Choice Questions

1. B	6. D	11. A	16. B	21. A
2. B	7. B	12. D	17. C	22. A
3. A	8. D	13. B	18. C	23. C
4. B	9. B	14. C	19. D	24. C
5. C	10. D	15. D	20. B	25. D

Answer Explanations

Section I

Part A—Multiple-Choice Questions

1. **B.** Based on the references to "New England" and "the Devil," and the date 1693, Mather is referencing the witch trials that occurred from 1692 to 1693, choice B. Mather does not reference the City on a Hill concept of governance (choice A), nor the prejudices against the Catholics (choice C) and Native Americans and slaves (choice D).

2. **B.** The best answer to this question is associated with the persecution of the Puritans, who wanted to "purify" (separate) themselves from the Church of England. Although the level of their oppression depended on who was in power, Puritans were often oppressed by various monarchs and royal officials, choice B. While some formed joint-stock companies (choice A), Puritans were not usually associated with pursuing monetary gain. Puritans did educate women and children (choice C) and attempted to reject the secular world (choice D), but these are not reasons why the Puritans decided to leave Europe.

3. **A.** The only possible answer is choice A, which references religious conflicts during the Great Awakening (1730s to 1740s). Be sure to read the question carefully for clues that hint at the correct answer choice. This question specifies the colonial era; therefore, choices B and C, which detail the Antebellum period, can be automatically eliminated. Since tensions between indentured servants and their employers would have been socially, culturally, or economically motivated, rather than religiously charged, choice D is incorrect.

4. **B.** The title of the image should give you a clue about the conflict being depicted. The political cartoon reflects Jackson's battle with the Second Bank of the United States, choice B. The Democratic political cartoon portrays Jackson's decision to remove federal deposits, which he then placed in politically supportive state banks. The left side of the image shows the destruction of the bank's financial temple, and the bank president (the devil) and politicians running for cover. While the Nullification Crisis (choices A and D) and the Indian Removal Act (choice C) both happened during Andrew Jackson's presidency, none of these are the topic of the cartoon.

5. **C.** Remember, the word *suffrage* is the right to vote. Since Jackson promoted himself as a representative of the "common man," he was well liked by new male (white) voters, who were able to vote for the first time because many states had recently eliminated property requirements, choice C. Both the Indian Removal Act (choice B) and the annexation of Texas (choice D) occurred after 1828,

so these answer choices can be quickly eliminated. While the Market Revolution (choice A) may have contributed to economic changes that instigated the federally funded American System (which Jackson rejected), it is not generally linked to his rise to power in 1828.

6. **D.** Democrats promoted the idea that they were the party of the "common man" (choice C) and resented interference of the federal government in domestic affairs, which meant they rejected, not promoted, economic nationalism, choice D. Jacksonian Democrats were usually supportive of small government (choice A) and states' rights (choice B).

7. **B.** Trumbull's painting quite famously depicts the signing of the Declaration of Independence, choice B, but if you didn't recognize it, remember to look for clues in the painting. The question points to a specific event, "historical event of 1776." Since nothing indicates a representative of France (French colors or a French military officer or statesman), the painting does not reflect France's entry into the war (choice A). The painting describes a "Revolutionary" event, which eliminates both Washington's Farewell Address (choice C) and the formal separation of church and state (choice D). Neither of these events occurred during the American Revolution. Notice that there is a large group of men pictured, indicating that it is probably a governing body of some type—in this case, the Second Continental Congress.

8. **D.** The Olive Branch Petition was the final attempt to avoid war. It was composed and submitted to Britain's king by the Second Continental Congress, choice D. The Second Continental Congress did not have the authority of a national government; therefore, the answer is not choice A (it declared war upon the English Parliament and King George III). The Second Continental Congress met to manage the war effort (fighting began more than a year before independence was declared) and to move toward a more formal split with Britain if negotiations were rejected. Georgia didn't attend the First Continental Congress, but they did attend the Second, making choice B incorrect. The Battles of Lexington and Concord (choice C) were essentially the reason that the delegates were meeting (the battles happened *before* the Second Continental Congress convened).

9. **B.** Colonists were inspired by enlightened writers, choice B. The boycotts (choice A) were designed to put pressure on Britain to guarantee the colonists' rights as British subjects, not to cause a larger rebellion. The French and Indian War itself (choice C) was not an inspiration for rebellion either. The British policies as a *result* of that conflict angered the colonists, but they still did not spark demands for a split with the mother country. While the existence of the British troops and the Quartering Act of 1765 (choice D) contributed to the colonists' ire, it did not create an ideology that inspired them throughout the revolution. Although you may have been tempted to select choice D, remember that the question emphasizes motivation. Texts that argued for natural rights, liberty, republicanism, and equality motivated the colonists to revolt and inspired the writing of the Declaration of Independence.

10. **D.** The excerpt requires interpretation based on your knowledge of U.S. history to determine the author's argument. The excerpt notes that some Americans were motivated to enter the war because they desired to fight for Cuban independence, while others were more concerned about their own honor; thus, the motivations were complex, which led to mixed results, choice D. The excerpt discusses the results of the war, but does not note specific persecutions (choice A), political debates (choice B), or public criticisms of brutality (choice C).

11. **A.** The war in the Philippines was more extensive than the Spanish-American War and resulted not only in a treaty that gave the U.S. imperial control, but also a provisional government, choice A. McKinley's struggle with yellow journalists (choice B) and the Rough Riders' battle (choice C) occurred *before* the war, so they cannot be considered continuations. Hawaii was annexed as part of the U.S.; it was not made an independent nation (choice D)—this occurred in 1898, the same year as the Spanish-American War.

12. **D.** The Platt Amendment of 1901, choice D, best describes the long-term consequences of the Spanish-American War. It established policies that banned Cuba from making treaties with nations other than the U.S., created U.S. naval bases in Cuba, and allowed the American military to intervene in Cuban affairs. The amendment gave the U.S. a great deal of power over Cuba and was viewed as a betrayal by resistance fighters. The Teller Amendment of 1898 (choice A) was passed *before* the Spanish-American War in response to the conflict in Cuba. Although McKinley's re-election (choice B) was made possible by the victory in Cuba, other factors were involved in his success. The Open Door Policy (choice C) related to trade and spheres of influence in China.

13. **B.** King is motivating African Americans to unify and protest nonviolently by reminding them in his speech about their own struggles and experiences of victims of violence, choice B. King is also referencing groups that use violence to oppress black Americans in order to demonstrate the justice and legitimacy of their cause. King neither mentions tensions within the black community (choice A), nor political voting rights (choice C). While King could have shifted the opinions of ministers or those in the white community through his speech (choice D), his message is directed specifically to the task at hand, the bus boycott in Montgomery, Alabama.

14. **C.** Appeals for patience within the black community to allow legislation to take its proper effect, choice C, was not a strategy used by African Americans. In fact, most black activists—including Martin Luther King Jr. and more militant leaders like Malcolm X and Stokely Carmichael—rejected pleas for patience, stating that the African American community had been oppressed long enough. Note you are asked which answer choice is NOT an African American strategy. This type of question can be confusing. Select the "false" statement to determine the correct answer choice. The legal battles had been conducted by the NAACP since the early 20th century, choice B. Interracial organizations like the COFO (Council of Federated Organizations) and SNCC (Student Nonviolent Coordinating Committee) were established early in the movement, choice D, and black pride (black nationalism) and armed self-defense were advocated later, choice A.

15. **D.** Randolph's suggestion about a march on Washington is the only form of a nonviolent protest mentioned in the answer choices, choice D. Accommodation strategies (choice A) are the opposite of what King is suggesting here. Both DuBois and the black women's organizations, choices B and C, promoted visions of elitism and had reputations of wanting to build stronger links with white leaders and politicians in order to achieve racial equality. King and Randolph were instead encouraging the full participation of the black community in grassroots organizations and protests.

16. **B.** The title and date, as well as the notation of Kansas and free soilers, suggest that the image is related to conflicts that would have occurred between pro- and anti-slavery supporters in the Antebellum era (1815–1861), choice B. Transcendentalists, like Henry David Thoreau, did not support expansion because they viewed it as an attempt to gain more slave states, choice A. Additionally, Thoreau's writings are not related to propaganda. Tensions were generated from the land received in the Mexican-American War, not the Spanish-American War (choice C). Free soilers were not considered activists for black rights (choice D). Rather, free soilers didn't want to see slavery spread into new territories.

17. **C.** The image is related to the terms of popular sovereignty in the Kansas-Nebraska Act, choice C, which allowed the people of a new state to vote on its status (slave-state or free-state). This could have forced people who did not believe in the expansion of slavery to live in a region that allowed slavery. The Missouri Compromise (choice A) occurred much earlier (1819) and was an attempt by Congress to alleviate, not reinforce or induce, conflicts associated with slavery. The Force Act (choice B) was linked to the nullification crisis and the Dred Scott Case (choice D) was related to African American legal rights, neither of which are referenced here.

18. **C.** This question requires a historical knowledge of President Abraham Lincoln. While not initially an abolitionist, Lincoln campaigned as a free soiler, choice C, and initially assured the South that he would not interfere with slavery in regions where slavery already existed. Andrew Jackson (choice A) became president before the Free Soil Party was established, and Andrew Johnson (choice B) was president after Lincoln, when there was no longer a need for free soil advocates. David Wilmot (choice D) was a congressman, not a president.

19. **D.** Read the question carefully. Jefferson may have expanded his presidential power by purchasing the Louisiana Territory (choice C), but that does not qualify as a historical event, which can only be indicated by the purchase itself, choice D. The Embargo Acts (choice A) and *Marbury v. Madison* (choice B) are associated with other events in Jefferson's presidency; they had nothing to do with Meriwether Lewis and William Clark, who were charged with exploring the newly bought territory in 1803.

20. **B.** Napoleon was horrified and financially drained by the Haitian Revolution, and sought to divorce himself from New World territories like Louisiana that might have caused him problems later; this allowed the U.S. to purchase the territory from France, choice B. Even though the Louisiana Territory had passed to the Spanish after the French and Indian War, it was back in French hands by the time of Jefferson's offer (choice A). Economic declines in Spain (choice C) were unrelated to the purchase; Jefferson bought the territory from France, not Spain. Constitutionality (choice D) was an issue for Jefferson, who went against his own beliefs about presidential authority to make the purchase, but it was not a motivation for his actions.

21. **A.** Jefferson clearly emphasized exploration and indicated that Lewis' measurements would be presented to the war office, which suggested that he was motivated by both expansion and security, choice A. Jefferson did not express respect for the established Native American religion (choice B); he indicated that various information should be gathered to convert the Indians. While the purchase may have improved relations with France (choice C) and provided a draw for immigrants (choice D), neither was the reason for his instructions to Lewis.

22. **A.** Before you can answer the question, it is important to identify the tone of the excerpt as well as the historical context of Reagan's speech. The speech was before the Berlin Wall came down and Reagan's attitude was slightly antagonistic and skeptical, not respectful, of changes within the Soviet Union (choice C). Reagan's words are not intended to appease his rival (choice B), but to challenge Gorbachev. Although Reagan may have communicated his dedication to freedom and peace (choice D), he rarely framed his addresses toward the Soviets in positive rhetoric; he often identified the nation as an "evil empire." All of this indicates that Reagan still mistrusted the Soviet Union due to Cold War tensions which continued between the U.S. and Gorbachev's nation, which is why choice A is the correct answer.

23. **C.** The Berlin Wall was symbolic of the Cold War division between democratic and communist nations, choice C. Reagan's speech did not suggest bartering for political support (choice A); his approval rating ranged from 40 percent to 60 percent. Although economic advantages are hinted at in the speech, they are not associated with the meaning of the destruction of the wall (choice B).The speech did not involve military intervention (choice D).

24. **C.** The question requires students to know a little bit of background information about the TVA (Tennessee Valley Authority), which was intended to bring hydroelectric power to new areas in the South, choice C. Only one New Deal project, the TVA, is depicted in the map (choice A). The map does not include all the southern states, so choice B can also be eliminated. While it may have unintentionally informed the public of new technology (choice D), the TVA was not a cultural project.

25. **D.** This is a NOT question, so you are looking for the statement that is false. Instead of favoring the wealthy, choice D, most New Deal programs favored many of the disadvantaged, which could not be denied. President Franklin D. Roosevelt's critics suggested that New Deal programs were unconstitutional and dictatorial (which are suggested by choices A and C). Critics also complained when it appeared the government was competing with private industry (choice B).

Part B—Short-Answer Questions

Question 1

Reasoning skills: *Comparison* and *continuity and change over time.*

This question asks you to interpret an image that is associated with an artist's interpretation of Reconstruction. You will need to closely examine and then analyze the actions of the figures in the political cartoon. Be sure to think of the image in the context of what you already know about opposing perspectives of the Reconstruction time period. The questions require that you note a domestic policy related to Reconstruction and provide an opposing perspective from the image depicted.

To receive full credit, you must address all three parts. The sample responses for parts (a), (b), and (c) in the table below are for instructional purposes only. On the actual exam, you must write ONE complete short-answer essay.

Part	Task	Explanation	Sample Response
(a)	Briefly describe ONE perspective about Reconstruction supported by the image.	Part (a) can be answered by considering the southern or "Lost Cause" perspective of Reconstruction.	The image references southern interpretations of the consequences of the Reconstruction Act (1867), which split the South into five military districts. The districts broke down racial hierarchies that had been advantageous to wealthy and common whites. Southerners viewed the post-war federal government as oppressive and felt it allowed for corruption at the hands of carpetbaggers and the Grant administration, which was heavily criticized for its scandals.
(b)	Briefly describe ONE specific historical event or development that led to the changes in domestic policy during Reconstruction.	Part (b) can be answered by focusing on the specific legislation that transformed domestic policy during Reconstruction.	There were several key legislative developments that led to changes in domestic policies, including the 13th, 14th, and 15th Amendments. The Civil Rights Acts of 1866 and 1875 (all directed toward African American freedom, voting rights, or social equality) also led to policy changes. Supreme Court cases like the Slaughterhouse Cases or *U.S. v. Cruikshank* that later "nullified" progressive legislation.
(c)	Briefly explain ONE way in which the perception of Reconstruction between 1869 and 1877 depicted in the image was countered.	Part (c) can be answered by considering the Radical Republican or revisionist perception of Reconstruction.	The opposing side of this issue was the perception of Radical Republicans, who rejected the lenient tenor of Johnson's Presidential Reconstruction, encouraged biracial cooperation, and passed legislation that sought to ensure African American civil and social rights. While many northern Republicans were either corrupt or simply hoped to improve their African American voting base in the South, others (like Thaddeus Stevens) believed in equality and hoped the nation could be restructured through free labor ideology and northern investment in southern industry.

Question 2

Reasoning skill: *Comparison* and *continuity and change over time.*

This question asks you to analyze the differences in immigration in the context of two particular time periods. You are being asked to compare and contrast the changes *before* 1865 and *after* 1865, which will require you to have some knowledge of both early immigration and the effect of industrialism and migration on national expansion.

To receive full credit, you must address all three parts. The sample responses for parts (a), (b), and (c) in the table below are for instructional purposes only. On the actual exam, you must write ONE complete short-answer essay.

Part	Task	Explanation	Sample Response
(a)	Briefly describe ONE specific historical similarity between U.S. immigration in the period 1820–1864 and in the period 1865–1898.	Part (a) can be answered by analyzing one specific part of U.S. immigration from both periods that overlaps. The effect of industrialism is relevant as well, given the time periods in the prompt.	Both the Market Revolution (1815–1840) and the Second Industrial Revolution (1870–1910) sparked the need for cheap industrial labor, which was supplied by immigrants in both periods. As a result, skilled work declined and workers were mistreated in both eras because immigrant laborers were often considered easily replaced. Therefore, laborers often worked long hours for low wages and lived in poverty.
(b)	Briefly describe ONE specific historical difference between U.S. immigration in the period 1820–1864 and in the period 1865–1898.	Part (b) can be answered by providing one specific difference about immigration in the specified periods.	Although immigrants were often key figures in U.S. expansion in both periods, native-born Americans migrated on a large scale into North American territories owned by natives or other nations. In the 1840s, individuals in search of land and economic opportunities moved by invitation into what we now know as Texas, which was then a Mexican territory. Disrespectful of Mexican law and culture, Americans eventually overtook the region, establishing their own state, which was annexed by the U.S. government in 1845 and led to the Mexican-American War in 1848.
(c)	Briefly explain ONE specific historical effect of U.S. immigration in either the period 1820–1864 or in the period 1865–1898.	Part (c) can be answered by providing a specific effect of the immigration from either period.	The immigrants of the first period were generally from Western Europe, which meant they were of Irish, British, and German descent. These immigrants had been in the country for generations when Jewish and Italian immigrants began pouring into the country between 1890 and 1920. As a result of their acculturation, many resented the newcomers, which caused tensions in the social makeup of urban centers and generated new definitions of national inclusion and "whiteness" in particular regions.

Section II

Part A—Document-Based Question

DBQ Scoring Guide

To achieve the maximum score of 7, your response must address the scoring criteria components in the table that follows.

Scoring Criteria for a Good Essay	
Question 1: Evaluate the extent to which differing views of democracy influenced U.S. domestic and foreign policies from 1940 to 1945.	
Scoring Criteria	**Examples**
A. THESIS/CLAIM	
(1 point) Presents a historically defensible thesis that establishes a line of reasoning. (Note: The thesis must make a claim that responds to *all* parts of the question and must *not* just restate the question. The thesis must consist of *at least* one sentence, either in the introduction or the conclusion.)	The essay provides coherency throughout the argument and compares and contrasts different views of democracy that influenced domestic and foreign policy from 1940 to 1945. This period centers on World War II. The essay provides a logical line of reasoning in each body paragraph and uses historical facts, trends, and details to support the thesis and contextualize the material.
B. CONTEXTUALIZATION	
(1 point) Explains the broader historical context of events, developments, or processes that occurred before, during, or after the time frame of the question. (Note: Must be more than a phrase or reference.)	A good response provides historical context in the body paragraphs. This essay discusses isolationism, Roosevelt's democratic rhetoric, the cessation of neutrality, and opposing points of view to place the documents in historical context.
C. EVIDENCE	
Evidence from the Documents **(2 points)** Uses at least *six* documents to support the argument in response to the prompt. OR **(1 point)** Uses the content of at least *three* documents to address the topic prompt. (Note: Examples must describe, rather than simply quote, the content of the documents.) **Evidence Beyond the Documents** **(1 point)** Uses at least one additional piece of specific historical evidence beyond those found in the documents relevant to the argument. (Note: Evidence must be different from the evidence used in contextualization.)	To receive the highest possible points, the response must address at least six documents that relate back to the thesis and question. Document 1 provides evidence from President Roosevelt's "chats" that appeal to Americans to defend democracy and the American future. Document 3 expresses a soldier's response to Roosevelt's call to action by taking up arms and enlisting in the Army for the "love of country." President Roosevelt's speech in Document 7 confirms the freedoms that are lost when threats to world peace exist in the world. Document 2 demonstrates the opposite point of view from Charles Lindbergh, who rejected war efforts and supported isolationism. In addition, the essay points to racial prejudices that existed during this time period. While all Americans were encouraged to support the war efforts, Documents 4 and 5 illustrate how American equality and democratic values were not extended to African American and Japanese citizens. The essay provides outside evidence beyond the document when it discusses the relevance of minority perspectives and global concerns—looking to the future by mentioning the United Nations and the Cold War. It also hints at expanding definitions of democracy and inclusion that would be formed in the 1950s and 1960s.

Continued

Scoring Criteria	Examples
D. ANALYSIS AND REASONING	
(1 point) Uses at least *three* documents to explain how each document's point of view, purpose, historical situation, and/or audience is relevant to the argument. (Note: References must explain how or why, rather than simply identifying.)	The response analyzes at least four of the documents using point of view, purpose, historical context, or audience. The essay notes the relevance of each speaker while comparing and contrasting different points of view, shaping the evidence to convey a clear argument.
(1 point) Uses historical reasoning and development that focuses on the question while using evidence to corroborate, qualify, or modify the argument. (Examples: Explain what is similar and different; explain the cause and effect; explain multiple causes; explain connections within and across periods of time; corroborate multiple perspectives across themes; or consider alternative views.)	The essay provides a coherent and well-organized argument and uses the historical reasoning of continuity (i.e., whether policies stayed the same or changed over time). The sample essay argues that domestic and foreign policies were shaped by various definitions of democracy and freedom.

Sample Response

By the time the U.S. entered World War II in 1941, it was already deeply involved in European affairs. Intervention was both rejected and promoted by various politicians and grassroots groups, which continued to use conflicting definitions of democracy to influence mobilization, recruitment, and domestic policy. During the war, the fight was characterized in terms of global freedom to legitimize the Allied cause and increase support for the postwar ratification in October 1945 of the United Nations, an organization that required direct involvement in other countries' affairs. Although interwar policies of neutrality became obsolete as Americans began to accept their status as world leaders, many still recognized the need for improvements at home. This instigated additional tensions that shaped their futures.

During the Great Depression, financial hardship caused most Americans to call for isolationism in order to focus on their own needs. In the 1930s, U.S. policymakers, including President Roosevelt, fought hard to keep America away from developing European conflicts. From 1935 to 1937, Congress passed a series of Neutrality Acts—just as it had before World War I—designed to ban loans or the sale of armaments to belligerents. Yet as early as 1939, Roosevelt became sympathetic to Winston Churchill's appeal to allow Britain and France to buy weapons on a "cash-and-carry" basis, just as they had been doing with non-lethal goods since 1937. Even before the Japanese attack on Pearl Harbor in December 1941, Roosevelt began to fear Hitler's gains in the war, seeing them as spreading fascism, a political ideology that opposed democratic forms of government, and convinced Congress to pass the Lend-Lease Act. Roosevelt spoke to the American people directly in a series of "Fireside Chats" (Document 1) indicating the need for increased mobilization and production in order to defend "our civilization." Sentiments like this later encouraged young men to enlist in the fight, for they—like Sidney Diamond (Document 3)—believed that Hitler had thrown the world "into chaos" and that their patriotism should expand to all nations that held similar governments.

This view was not uncontested. Before the war, grassroots groups like the America First Committee formed to indicate their displeasure with Roosevelt's pursuit of direct involvement in the European war. Charles Lindbergh, speaking on behalf of those still dedicated to isolation (Document 2), used terms promoting democracy and representative government to state that Americans should not be forced to go to war by politicians or special interest groups if they didn't want to. Other people, like African Americans, decided not to reject the war, but to change the meaning of the democratic rhetoric being used to endorse it. They saw their demonstrations of support as a way to continue their fight for civil and social rights, embarking on a "Double V" campaign that would make the tenets of the war more meaningful (Document 4).

Still others were persecuted, sacrificing their liberty at the demand of a government that claimed it was supporting Roosevelt's Four Freedoms, which included the freedom of speech and worship as well as freedom from want and fear (Document 7). While Girl Scouts (Document 6), military units, and both black and white citizens were being encouraged to support the war in the name of democracy, the president's Executive Order 9066 and Civilian Exclusion Order No. 33 forced Japanese Americans (Document 5) to leave their homes for internment camps, violating their status as U.S. citizens. When they attempted to speak out or pursue legal recourse, many were accused of treason or denied their civil rights by the Supreme Court, which—like the continuation of oppression pointed out by African Americans like James Thompson (Document 4)—seemed to question whether the country was practicing what it preached.

When the war ended, the United States embraced a leading role in global affairs, completely rejecting isolationism through its support of the United Nations and becoming the sort of global policeman Roosevelt envisioned. This was also seen as a way to protect democratic forms of government in the future, a way to ensure peace through the active institutions U.S. citizens had come to expect. The level of necessary intervention may have been questioned throughout the Cold War and is even the subject of current debates, but the language of democracy and varying views of freedom continue to influence foreign policymakers. Domestically, the ideals of democracy and freedom have motivated American civil rights activists, feminists, and other groups in the 1950s and 1960s, who have added to the complexity of freedom and influenced the way democracy is defined today.

Chapter 4

Period One: Early Settlement of the Americas (1491 to 1607)

Period One explores the merging of the European Old World and the American New World.

- Early Migration
- Early Native American Societies
- European Exploration (c. 1492 to c. 1600)
- The Rise of the Spanish Empire in the Americas
- The Columbian Exchange
- Compare and Contrast Europeans and Native Americans

Overview of AP U.S. History Period One

Chapter 4 begins by reviewing the motivations and patterns behind early European exploration of indigenous tribal settlements. The focus is on the development of subsistence patterns, social makeup, and attitudes of native societies and Europeans. As Native Americans, Europeans, and Africans came together, the world expanded and a system of trade developed that had devastating effects on the native culture.

Use the chart below to guide you through what is covered on the exam. The curriculum contained in this chart is an abridged version of the concept outlines with topic examples. Visit https://apstudent.collegeboard.org/apcourse/ap-united-states-history/ for the complete updated APUSH course curriculum descriptions and key concepts.

AP U.S. History Key Concepts (1491 to 1607)	
Key Concept	**Content**
KEY CONCEPT 1.1: NATIVE EXPANSION AND ADAPTATION **As native populations migrated and settled across the vast expanse of North America over time, they developed distinct and increasingly complex societies by adapting to and transforming their diverse environments.**	Different native societies adapted to and transformed their environments through innovations in agriculture, resource use, and social structure. Maize cultivation spread from present-day Mexico into the American Southwest. People in the Great Basin and Great Plains developed transient lifestyles. In the Northeast, the Mississippi River Valley, and the Atlantic seaboard, societies developed agricultural and hunter-gathering economies. Permanent villages were established. Hunter-gatherers in the Northeast and what would become California supported themselves with hunting and gathering. Some societies were supported by resources from the ocean.

Continued

Key Concept	Content
KEY CONCEPT 1.2: EUROPEAN EXPLORATION IN THE AMERICAS **Contact among Europeans, Native Americans, and Africans as a result of the Columbian Exchange created significant social, cultural, and political changes on both sides of the Atlantic Ocean.**	European expansion into the Western Hemisphere generated intense social, religious, political, and economic competition and changes within European societies. The Columbian Exchange brought new crops to Europe from the Americas, stimulating European population growth and new sources of mineral wealth, which facilitated the European shift from feudalism to capitalism. The Columbian Exchange and development of the Spanish Empire in the Western Hemisphere resulted in extensive demographic, economic, environmental, and social changes. Spanish exploration furthered widespread epidemics that devastated native populations. The *encomienda* system used Native American labor to support plantation-based agriculture and extract precious metals. The Spanish also imported enslaved Africans to labor in plantations and mines. Livestock transported from Europe had devastating effects on the North American landscape. In their interactions, Europeans and Native Americans asserted divergent worldviews regarding issues such as religion, gender roles, family, land use, and power. As European encroachments on Native Americans' lands and demands on their labor increased, native peoples sought to defend and maintain their political sovereignty, economic prosperity, religious beliefs, and concepts of gender relations through diplomatic negotiations and armed resistance.

Significant Themes

Now that we've discussed the curriculum, let's discuss the significant themes related to this period. The theme-related study questions that follow will help you make mental connections to the context of the "big picture" of this time period. Keep in mind that these questions often overlap and apply to other themes of social, political, religious, geographic, ideological, technological, and economic developments.

Glance through the study questions before you start the review section. Take notes, highlight questions, and write down page number references to reinforce your learning. Refer to this list as often as necessary until you feel comfortable with your knowledge of the material.

Study Questions Related to Significant Themes for Period One

Theme 2: Politics and Power

1. What are the historical developments that influenced European exploration? (Hint: European exploration brought new resources and new sources of wealth, economic and military competition, and the desire to spread religion.)

2. What types of power relations developed in North America during this period? (Hint: Consider the imperialistic relationship of early European explorers and Native Americans.)

3. What was the encomienda system and how did it impact cultural relations? (Hint: Think about *how* and *why* Spanish imperialistic conquerors employed the encomienda system to gain free labor from Native Americans.)

4. What was the Columbian Exchange? How did it impact Europeans? How did it impact Native Americans and Africans? (Hint: The Columbian Exchange was the result of European exploration in the Americas. The exchange stimulated European economic wealth. However, Native Americans and Africans suffered from the exchange, as European diseases spread throughout the New World and European imperialistic motives oppressed Native Americans and Africans.)

Theme 4: Culture and Society

1. How did cultural differences impact the relationships between Native Americans and early explorers? (Hint: Divergent beliefs about religion, gender, land occupation, and ownership led to misunderstandings and conflicts. The Spanish developed a caste system to justify the lower status of Native Americans.)

2. What was the difference between various native cultures in North America? (Hint: Natives were farmers and hunters of various tribes with different languages who often formed alliances of common interests as they adapted to environmental influences.)

Theme 5: Migration and Settlement

1. How did the first Americans arrive in North America? (Hint: Although other explorers set their sights on the Americas, the explorations of the Spaniards brought European settlers to North America.)

2. How did Spanish exploration affect cultural exchange as well as the spread of maize culture in what would become the American Southwest? (Hint: Mesoamerican civilizations were built around the production of maize (corn) as it spread from what is known today as Mexico through the Southwest and across much of North America.)

Theme 6: Geography and the Environment

1. What was the effect of the environment on Native American settlements, societies, and economies? (Hint: The environment influenced certain migratory patterns and regional settlements due to environmental adaptation. Natives and settlers were dependent on climate, water, and agriculture for survival to seek shelter from the effects of nature—heat, snow, rain, etc.—and for trade among other tribal societies.)

Important Events, Terms, and Concepts

The list below shows important events, terms, and concepts that you should be familiar with on the APUSH exam. These and other important terms are printed in boldface throughout the chapter. Because the APUSH exam requires you to pay attention to the historical context and connections rather than details, don't bother memorizing the terms now. Simply place a check mark next to each as you study. You can return to this list to review as often as necessary. After you finish the review section, you can reinforce what you have learned by working through the practice questions at the end of this chapter. Answers and explanations provide further clarification into perspectives of U.S. history.

Event/Term/Concept	Year/Brief Description	Study Page
Beringia	A land bridge in the Bering Strait exposed by drops in sea levels 15,000 to 25,000 years ago. The land bridge enabled Asian tribes to migrate to North America through what we now know as Alaska.	p. 63
Maize culture	Mesoamericans (Mexicans) domesticated maize (corn), and it was embedded into their social and political structures, ceremonial practices, and languages. It was passed down from generation to generation. The maize culture migrated to the American Southwest well before 2000 B.C.E. and influenced American Pueblo tribes. Maize was also exchanged with Europeans in the Columbian Exchange.	pp. 66, 73
Anasazi	The "ancient ones" were considered ancestors of the Pueblo people (200–1300 C.E.). Noted for the cultivation of maize and building a network of communities high on the Colorado Plateau, their best-known urban centers were constructed at Chaco Canyon and Mesa Verde. These multi-story sandstone cliff dwellings housed thousands of people. The descendant Pueblo peoples such as the Hopi and Zuni carried on the Anasazi's mastery of basketry, pottery, and architectural design.	p. 65
Pueblo	The name applied to southwestern Native American people who share a tradition of agriculture, particularly cultivation of corn, trade, and the construction of multi-storied apartments made of stone and/or adobe (1100–1300 C.E.). When the Spanish first encountered the indigenous people of this region, they called their villages built around a central plaza "pueblos" (or towns) and later applied the term to all groups sharing this element of culture. Puebloan people suffered three successive waves of Spanish invasions (soldiers, missionaries, settlers) that often led to violent confrontation including the first known European-Indian war between Spanish conquistadors led by Francisco Coronado and several Pueblo tribes.	p. 65
Iroquois League of Peace	**1142.** A peace alliance in the Great Lakes region of Iroquois-speaking nations that discouraged war between five major native tribes.	p. 66
Aztecs	Mesoamerican people whose capital, Tenochtitlan, was located in present-day Mexico City (1300–1521 C.E.). The Aztecs provided the premier example of a highly developed and complex indigenous civilization in the New World. The Spanish invasion in 1519 established a pattern of conquest that would prove devastating to indigenous people throughout the Americas. Ravaged by smallpox introduced to the population by Spanish invaders and the military defeat led by Hernán Cortés in 1521, only a remnant population of the Aztecs survived.	p. 69
Old World and New World	Old World refers to the Eastern Hemisphere continents of Europe, Asia, and Africa. New World refers to the Western Hemisphere continents of North America and South America, discovered by Christopher Columbus after 1492.	p. 68
Conquistadors	The warriors/explorers from Spain and Portugal. The conquistadors accompanied voyages of discovery to Africa, Asia, and the Americas. The Spanish conquistadors were instrumental to the conquest of indigenous people and laying claim to a Spanish empire in the New World (e.g., Hernán Cortés, Francisco Pizarro, Hernando de Soto).	p. 69
Encomienda system	**1512–1720.** A feudal-style trade-off system imposed in the New World which defined the relationship between prominent Spaniards (*encomenderos*) and indigenous people. Conquistadors, who were the first to conquer regions, were granted land together with its inhabitants. It was an exploitative practice. Indigenous people were required to pay "tribute" to the Spaniards through labor or extracting natural resources like gold or silver.	p. 70

Event/Term/Concept	Year/Brief Description	Study Page
Columbian Exchange	**Late 15th and 16th centuries.** The trans-Atlantic transfer and exchange of livestock, goods, agriculture, and diseases across the Atlantic Ocean that resulted from contact between Native Americans, Europeans, and Africans. The exchange was prompted by the arrival of Columbus in the New World and the subsequent settlement of Europeans throughout the Western Hemisphere.	pp. 71–72

Chapter Review

The United States had a diverse history of indigenous peoples and exploration long before it officially gained sovereignty. The information discussed in this chapter covers several overlapping categories of the initial migration and settlement in North America. Important topics include European exploration into the Americas during early-modern history, the impact of the Columbian Exchange, and the impact of interactions among Europeans, Native Americans, and Africans.

Early Migration

The first people to migrate to North America came from Northeast Asia using a land bridge over the Bering Strait known as **Beringia** (also known as the Bering Land Bridge). The land bridge (which was a former seafloor) was exposed due to changes in climate from glacier activity and drops in sea levels. Through environmental research, scientists have estimated that dry land appeared and people starting migrating from what we know as Siberia, Russia, to Alaska and Canada approximately 15,000 to 25,000 years ago.

Beringia Migratory Patterns

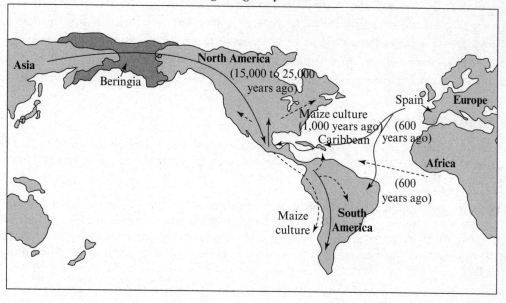

HISTORIOGRAPHY. *Even though American Indians resemble people from Mongolia, China, and Siberia, some scientists debate the traditional migration narrative which holds that people migrated from Northeast Asia. Some archaeologists theorize that part of the region remained flooded and boats were used to cross a small section of Beringia to travel to other parts of North America. Still others place the date either more recently (11,000–13,000 years ago) or suggest that Beringia opened up too late to support the land bridge theory.*

Early Native American Societies

On the APUSH exam it is helpful to think of cultures as being sedentary, semi-sedentary, or nomadic. Early Native Americans adopted *sedentary* societies (groups of people who settled down to live in one territory). Sedentary societies developed in regions that were supported by an environment so abundant in food resources that the people thrived with crop cultivation. *Semi-sedentary* cultures were those who lived for extended periods in one area, perhaps moving seasonally and sustaining themselves through trade, hunting, fishing, and foraging. *Nomadic* people were those who are highly mobile, sustaining themselves principally by foraging and/or hunting.

As natives settled, early forms of social, political, and cultural norms emerged that were based on environmental, climatic, and geographic influences. Early Native Americans formed *tribes* (communities), *kinship* groups (blood families), and social hierarchies to share responsibilities, adapt to the environment, search for water sources, and hunt or gather food sources. Most tribes were based on a *patriarchal* (male-dominated) society centered on the leadership of fathers and other male figures. Early forms of farming were important for human survival. Planting agricultural crops was a much more efficient way to produce food, rather than performing the time-consuming process of gathering berries, roots, and nuts.

TEST TIP: On the APUSH exam, think about the continuity and changes over time of settlements based on nature and the environment. Early inhabitants migrated from Asia to search for land in the Americas to help them survive and thrive. The environment may not seem relevant to this early history time period when Native American societies were just beginning to organize, but it's important to remember that the migrations of these early humans were influenced by environmental factors. As time progressed, humans have continued to be swayed by these same environmental influences, but through industrial advances, humans have also impacted the environment.

Native American Regions

The geographic locations of the first successful American settlements are difficult to determine, but two known regions where early Native American tribes were known to thrive are the Southwest and the Mississippi River Valley.

As tribes expanded, many different languages, cultures, settlement patterns, economies, alliances, and governments developed among almost 200 different tribes (today there are approximately 560 federally recognized Native American tribal groups). While it is true that as Native Americans organized and began trading systems, some were inclined to see other tribes as a threat to their survival, and conflicts arose among the tribes.

Heads Up: What You Need to Know

For the APUSH exam, don't worry about knowing every tribe and tribal sub-group in North America. There are literally hundreds of these groups, and there is simply no utility in knowing them all. Remember, only 5 percent of your score is based on questions from Period One, and there will NOT be DBQ or LEQ essay questions for Period One.

However, you should have a solid understanding of general regional classifications and a few representative tribes from each of these regional groupings that you can use as examples when prompted to provide evidence. The focus of some questions on the exam will address environmental adaptations that set each regional grouping of tribes apart from one another. For example, if a question on the exam highlights the cultivation of *maize* (corn), you should know that domestication and cultivation of maize appears most prominently among southwestern and southeastern Native American groups, particularly in the "four corners" region of Colorado, Utah, Nevada, and New Mexico and in the Mississippi Valley. While the cultivation of corn extended sporadically northward among northeastern tribes, any type of systematic approach to agriculture is not central to the culture of peoples on the Great Plains, in the northwestern coastal region, or the northwest plateau, none of whom, for a variety of environmental factors, cultivated crops to sustain themselves.

The table below describes the regional sections of the future United States.

Native American Regions			
Region	**Mobility**	**Notable Tribes**	**Characteristics**
Southwest	Sedentary	Apache, Hopi, Navajo, Pueblo, and Zuni	The tribes in the southwest region were descendants of the **Anasazi** (the "Ancient People"). The region was arid with two great river systems (Colorado and Rio Grande). Many of these indigenous tribes established beautiful rock cliff dwellings that served as homes in their *pueblos* (villages made of adobe). Others were *nomads* (mobile or semi-mobile) like the Apaches. The native economies were based on agriculture (including corn, squash, and beans), hunting, and gathering. A pan-southwestern trading network developed through the years and exchanged turquoise, feathers, pottery, and excess crops. Modern-day states in the Southwest include New Mexico, Arizona, Colorado, and Utah.
Southeast (Mississippi River Valley)	Sedentary	Chickasaw, Choctaw, Cherokee	The tribes in the Mississippi River Valley were descendants of the Cahokia and were often hierarchical. Some built houses, temples, and burial structures on large earthen mounds, and also developed a writing system. Other southeastern tribes were generally agricultural and had access to an abundance of fertile land and natural resources that easily provided them with food, clothing, and shelter. Cherokees, Choctaws, and Chickasaws have uncertain origins, but some historians believe they developed from lesser-known tribes around the 17th century. Modern-day states include the upper states of Minnesota, Illinois, Wisconsin, and Iowa and the lower states of Missouri, Kentucky, Tennessee, Arkansas, Mississippi, and Louisiana.

Continued

Region	Mobility	Notable Tribes	Characteristics
Great Plains/ Great Basin	Nomadic and semi-sedentary	Shoshone (Numa), Paiute, Sioux, Cheyenne	Tribes on the western plains were migratory due to the climate in which they lived. Later tribes focused on basket weaving instead of producing pottery like the sedentary tribes of the **maize culture.** Because of the region's lack of natural resources due to drought and seasonal weather extremes, they found sustenance through foraging and the hunting of bison and elk, which was made easier after the Spanish brought horses into the New World. Tribes on the eastern plains were semi-sedentary because there were more rivers and precipitation. Modern-day Great Plains states include Montana, North Dakota, South Dakota, Wyoming, Nebraska, Kansas, Colorado, Oklahoma, Texas, and New Mexico; the Great Basin states include Nevada, California, Oregon, Idaho, and Utah.
Pacific Northwest	Sedentary	Chinook, Salish, Tlingit, Haida	The Pacific Northwest was full of animals from land and sea. Chinook-speaking natives supplemented their hunting and gathering with fishing for salmon. Most tribes were located near the ocean. They built large canoes and totem poles carved from giant redwoods. They had hierarchical societies with top tiers of shamans, warriors, and traders who isolated themselves from common natives. Living communally in long houses, they incorporated slavery and head binding into their lifestyles. Modern-day states include Oregon, Alaska, and Washington, and Northern California.
Northeast (East Coast)	Sedentary	Powhatan, Wampanoag, Algonquian, Iroquois, Chippewa, Ottawa, Mohawk	Many of these tribes developed a seasonal lifestyle based on the weather. In the summer months, they lived in portable dwellings (*wigwams*), which made it easier to seek out game and forage. In the winter months, they resided in more permanent communal dwellings (*longhouses*) like their Pacific counterparts. Some supplemented their hunting and gathering with corn and squash crops, but many lived in areas too cold for agricultural growth. Iroquois-speaking peoples formed a confederation of nations (the **Iroquois League of Peace**) that encouraged peace among matrilineal tribes like the Mohawk, the Seneca, and the Oneida. Modern-day states include Virginia, North Carolina, and New York.

Did you know? Do you know where the term *Indian* originated? One version of the story is that Columbus called the natives *Indians* because he purportedly believed that he discovered the trade route to the Indies. What he really discovered were a group of indigenous civilizations spread out between North America and Mesoamerica. The term *Native American* was popularized in the 1970s as an alternative to *Indian* because it more accurately describes indigenous people who were born in the Americas. While indigenous people prefer to be referred to by their specific nation or tribe name, *Native American* is the official legal term used in the United States.

European Exploration (c. 1492 to c. 1600)

The Vikings were the first explorers to the New World (they settled for a short time in Newfoundland around 1000 C.E.), but the Spanish were the first Europeans to settle and colonize the Americas. When the Spaniards arrived, nothing in European philosophies, religious texts, or experiences had foretold of these entirely new civilizations that had existed for centuries long before European contact. The indigenous civilizations that Europeans encountered were completely different from their worldview. Some natives, like those who lived in the Northeast, lived in a farming confederation that included trade zones throughout the Mississippi River Valley. Others were *nomadic* (traveled from place to place). Some lived in the Southwest and created whole cities out of rock. Still others in Mesoamerica (today's Mexico, Central America, and South America), such as the Aztecs, Mayans, and Incas, created cities and kingdoms that dwarfed the European cities of the time.

Heads Up: What You Need to Know

For the APUSH exam, you should know the reasons that motivated Europeans to explore the New World. Some of these reasons include political and religious power, the desire to find new resources for trade and economic power, the need for a new trade route, and an interest in learning about the outside world and undiscovered lands. Through technological and scientific advances in ships and their design of sails, Europeans were able to make the long journey to the Americas.

Key Facts That Led to European Exploration

Before we cover the voyages of Christopher Columbus, let's discuss some of the key developments in the 15th and 16th centuries that motivated European exploration.

The impact of the Reformation. The *Reformation* was a European movement from c. 1515 to c. 1650 that was aimed at a new way of thinking about religion—Protestantism. Protestantism challenged the powerful Roman Catholic Church and changed the face of 16th-century Europe. Through the efforts of Martin Luther, who challenged the Church's abuses, particularly the selling of indulgences for sins, the Catholic Church was divided. This division caused political and religious conflicts in Europe, especially after a Counter-Reformation was established to generate support for the Catholic Church. Exploration was often stimulated by religious motives and the desire to freely practice or spread either Protestantism or Catholicism. After settling, new religious orders like the Jesuits brought faith to the Americas, while others sought out new converts amongst the Native Americans to replace the lost Catholic populations of Northern Europe.

The pursuit of power. When the Catholic Church became less powerful in Western Europe, many powerful rulers were able to consolidate city-states and local principalities that were once controlled by noble families or feudal lords. As political power centralized and feudalism declined, nation-states developed under monarchs who had a desire to fund voyages to the New World for political and religious world power, trade, and land expansion.

The impact of the Renaissance. Mathematical, astrological, and scientific advances during the 16th-century *Renaissance* (a time of rebirth in Europe) motivated many people to look at the world in new ways. Scientist Nicolaus Copernicus was the first to establish the *heliocentric theory* (sun-centered universe) c. 1514 and inspired Galileo Galilei to provide further proof that the sun, not the earth, was the center of the universe. As a result, Galileo stood trial for heresy against the Catholic Church, c. 1633. Though few scholars actually believed in a flat earth during this period, the concept of the *geocentric theory* (Earth-centered universe) was used as a battleground for larger issues associated with the Reformation and exploration.

The search for a new trade route. The European desire for new trade routes led to the explosion of kingdoms looking for leverage. Keep in mind that around 1492, Muslim powers encircled almost all of Christian Europe. Faced with hostile Muslim powers, Europeans had two main choices of trade routes: Europeans could travel south, around the Cape of Good Hope at the bottom tip of Africa, or they could try to forge a path west, directly to China and India. It was in search of this westward route around the globe that Portuguese and Spanish explorers got their start.

The Rise of the Spanish Empire in the Americas

Portugal and Spain set out to find a new trade route to China and India for land and resources. Since both were Catholic nations, the competition among explorers threatened to split apart the Catholic Church, but Pope Alexander VI negotiated an agreement, the **Treaty of Tordesillas** (c. 1494), between Portugal and Spain. All areas discovered east of Europe would go to Portugal, and all areas discovered west of Europe would go to Spain. The one exception was Brazil, which had already been settled by the Portuguese.

Portugal's Explorations

The first nation to explore was Portugal because it was located north of the Mediterranean, right along the Atlantic Ocean, and its biggest neighbor was Spain, which had just consolidated its two biggest kingdoms under Spain's Queen Isabella of Castile and King Ferdinand of Aragon. Most importantly, Portugal had a chance to increase its trade without having to worry about either of its European or Muslim competitors, but it needed to have a new trade route to do this.

The king of Portugal's son, Prince Henry the Navigator, found a way. Prince Henry started a school to train maritime explorers. Portuguese mariners like Bartolomeu Diaz, Vasco da Gama, and Pedro Álvares Cabral were some of the first Portuguese Europeans to explore the world. They mapped the coasts of Africa and Brazil and traveled as far as Japan and India. Their experiences led to maritime advances in shipbuilding, navigation, and cartography that made expeditions easier. The Portuguese also discovered the **Atlantic Trade Route** so that Europeans no longer had to travel through land occupied by the Ottoman Empire.

Spain's Explorations

In the 15th century, Spain seemed an unlikely country to become the dominant power in Europe. Its culture was considered pitiful, its military was respectable but hardly legendary, and its customs were considered backward and superstitious. And yet, because of its efforts to explore in the Americas, Spain had dramatically risen to become the dominant power in the world, a place it would hold for nearly a century.

Spain in America

Spain began its process of discovery, conquests, and colonization in the islands of the Caribbean, from Hispaniola to Cuba, Puerto Rico, and smaller islands. Some islands that were later conquered by the British or Dutch, such as Jamaica and Trinidad, were first settled by Spaniards.

"In 1492, Columbus sailed the Ocean Blue." Students have used this rhyme for decades to remember the year in which the Italian explorer, Christopher Columbus, set out on his momentous voyage across the Atlantic Ocean. Christopher Columbus was commissioned by Spain to explore the West and as a result, not only did he discover the West Indies, but he also set his sights on America. Columbus' voyages led to the permanent settlement of the **New World** (America) by people from the **Old World** (Europe).

Before we discuss the colonization of America and trade exchanges to and from Europe, let's cover some of Spain's other conquests: Mesoamerica (Aztec civilization) and South America (Inca civilization).

Spain in Mesoamerica and South America

It's important to understand that Spanish explorations didn't stop when Columbus discovered America. During the early 16th century, Hernán Cortés of Spain decided to make an expedition to the continent of North America. In 1519, Cortés and about 500 men landed in present-day Veracruz, Mexico, and marched into the heart of the **Aztec Empire** (now called Mexico City). Cortés was able to negotiate with the Aztec emperor, Montezuma, who initially tried to appease Cortés. Fearing an uprising, the Spaniards held Montezuma hostage and eventually killed him and demolished the Aztec Empire. With the leader of the empire destroyed and huge numbers of Aztecs dying from smallpox and other diseases, it was all too easy for the Spaniards to acquire land and enforce a new empire.

Did you know? The Aztecs did not always live in Mesoamerica (today's Mexico). The **Olmecs** (1600–200 B.C.E.) and the **Toltecs** (900–1186 C.E.) were the first two empires. They established a centralized authority and created a center of trade networks. South of these large empires were the **Mayans** (c. 300–900 C.E.), who were a confederation of smaller kingdoms known for trade. The classical empires of the Olmecs, Toltecs, and Mayans disappeared from 900–1524 C.E., possibly due to climate changes. The Aztecs migrated to Mesoamerica after these civilizations.

After Cortés' conquest, Francisco Pizarro made an expedition to South America. After many years of failed attempts, Pizarro made his way into the heart of the **Inca Empire** in the Andes mountain region in 1532. He encountered Atahualpa, the Inca emperor. Atahualpa had over 100,000 men; Pizarro had fewer than 200. The Spaniards used cunning wit, gunpowder, and their horses to crush an exponentially larger Inca army. Another empire had been conquered, seemingly overnight, by an intrepid band of Spanish **conquistadors.**

Heads Up: What You Need to Know

For the APUSH exam, you should be familiar with the Spanish term *maize* (corn). Maize played a significant role in the lives of indigenous Mesoamericans long before the Spanish arrived. Scholars believe Aztec and Mayan tribes domesticated maize as an agricultural crop between 5,000 to 6,000 years ago. It was an essential part of life, considered sacred, and was used to celebrate the growing seasons, harvests, and religious festivals. This ensured cultivation rituals would be passed down from generation to generation.

The **maize culture** from Mesoamerica moved north to the American Southwest through the natural migration of farmers. The maize culture influenced the development of several American Pueblo tribes. Because corn was easy to transport and preserve, it also became one of the crops shipped to Europe through the Columbian Exchange.

The Impact of Spanish Colonization

European monarchs were more likely to fund expeditions in an effort to achieve greater wealth, especially after the Spanish found an abundance of gold and silver in Mesoamerica and South America (Peru) in the early 16th century.

When Spanish *conquistadors* (conquering soldiers) settled in Mesoamerica and other regions of South and Central America in the 16th century, several thriving indigenous civilizations already existed, including the Aztecs (in what is now Mexico), the Incas (in what is now Peru), and the Andeans (in what is now Bolivia, Peru, Ecuador, and Argentina). The Spaniards set out not only to militarily conquer these natives, but also to extract natural resources and labor for economic gain.

The Spanish Encomienda System

In 1512, the Spanish monarchy under King Charles V began granting conquistadors and colonizers (often known as *encomenderos*) large grants of feudal *encomiendas* (land and labor grants). Under the Spanish papal bull of 1493, known as the *Inter Cetera* (Doctrine of Discovery), and *Leyes de Burgos* (set of Spaniard laws), the encomenderos were responsible for the religious education and care of the natives who worked on the estate. The doctrine and laws authorized subjugation and conversion of any people "discovered" in new lands on behalf of the Spanish Crown and the Christian faith.

When the Spanish Empire granted conquistadors a plot of land, natives were required to work on the land in exchange for protection against other tribes. This system of feudalism was supposed to appoint a protective lord to guard and Christianize the natives on the land. The system was disguised as a benefit to protect the natives, but it was primarily used to enslave the natives and use them for labor.

Since many indigenous societies were subject to hierarchies that culminated in a single leader like the Aztecs' Montezuma, natives adapted quickly to the new system. But because the colonists used this system to establish a ruthless form of slavery, it was heavily criticized by religious leaders like **Bartolomé de las Casas,** a Dominican missionary and first-appointed "Protector of the Indians." De las Casas considered the system inhumane and wrote extensively about the acts of violence committed on the natives.

In 1542, a set of new laws was issued, *Leyes Nuevas,* replacing the *Leyes de Burgos* as a result of ongoing pressure for reform of the **encomienda system.** The laws continued to allow encomenderos to demand tribute from indigenous people, but prohibited slavery. Labor was to be compensated in wages and encomienda charters expired upon the death of the encomendero, ending the hereditary passing of an encomienda from an encomendero to his heirs. The Leyes Nuevas met resistance in Spanish America, particularly in Peru where Gonzalo Pizarro, half-brother of Inca conqueror Francisco Pizarro, led a revolt of encomenderos against the Spanish Viceroy. Despite resistance, the Leyes Nuevas led to the freedom from bondage for many natives in 1720.

Heads Up: What You Need to Know

Although only 5 percent of the APUSH exam contains questions from this period of U.S. history, you should be able to identify and explain the causes and consequences of the Columbian Exchange. The debates surrounding Bartolomé de las Casas' criticism of the treatment of Native Americans may also appear in multiple-choice questions.

The Columbian Exchange

The **Columbian Exchange** was described in Alfred Crosby's book, *The Columbian Exchange,* as a system of trade, transference, and migrations that resulted from European colonization in the Americas. The exchange fundamentally transformed both the New World and Old World as it brought together global cultures. For example, the introduction of new food crops to Europe, particularly the potato, transformed European diets and contributed to a population boom. Crops such as sugar, tobacco, rice, and cotton from Europe via Asia were subsequently introduced to the Caribbean, Brazil, and North America, which led to the development of extensive plantation slave societies in the New World. Most importantly, from the perspective of the native population in the Americas, diseases from Europe and Africa also brought biological diseases to indigenous populations of the Americas that caused devastation and death. This inhibited the natives' ability to defend themselves against conquest.

The Columbian Exchange

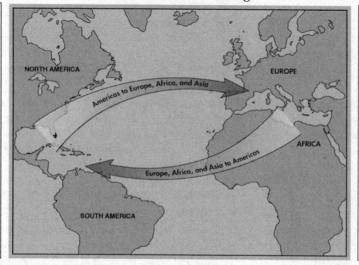

From the Americas to Europe, Africa, and Asia:

- Beans
- Cocoa
- Corn
- Pineapples
- Peanuts
- Peppers
- Potatoes
- Pumpkins
- Squash
- Sweet potatoes
- Tobacco
- Tomatoes
- Turkeys
- Vanilla
- Gold and silver

From Europe, Africa, and Asia to the Americas:

- Bananas
- Citrus fruits
- Coffee beans
- Disease (smallpox, influenza, typhus, measles, malaria, diphtheria, pertussis)
- Grains (barley, oats, rice, wheat)
- Grapes
- Honeybees
- Livestock (cows, horses, pigs, sheep)
- Olives
- Onions
- Peaches
- Pears
- Sugarcane
- Turnips

Key Facts about the Columbian Exchange

	Description	Impact
Exchanges between Europe and the Americas	A variety of agricultural products, plants, and livestock was exchanged between Europeans and the native cultures, including tomatoes, bananas, potatoes, turkeys, sheep, horses, and cattle.	New fruits and vegetables were introduced to the European market. Eventually, many served as production staples for future colonists, which increased the need for African slave labor. Potatoes (a South American product that was inexpensive and easy to grow) became a primary food source of the European working class. The introduction of horses to the New World by Europeans helped Native Americans to hunt, travel, and battle. Other European livestock—especially pigs, cattle, and sheep—had devastating ecological effects on the landscape and limited many natives' ability to grow sustainable crops.

Continued

	Description	Impact
Gold and silver from the Americas transferred to Europe	Natural resources like gold and silver were discovered throughout Mesoamerica in the 16th century. Native labor was used to extract the ore and enrich the Spanish economy.	The Mesoamerica discoveries of gold and silver had a significant impact on the growth of the European economy. Spain became the richest and most powerful nation in the world. However, Spain was unable to manage its wealth and overstretched its finances. Spain had several wars, inflation, high import taxes, and internal rebellions, which negatively affected its common citizens and caused the decline of Spain as a world power.
Racial mixing	As Spanish colonists took Native American women and African women as wives and concubines, they created diverse societies with complex caste systems.	Racial mixing was more common and accepted in Mesoamerica than in North America, which was later settled by British colonists. Still, a complicated caste system existed with many hierarchical tiers related to an individual's level of racial composition. European blood was considered the most accepted, Native American blood was in the middle, and African slave blood was the least accepted. An **encomienda system** was used during the Spanish colonization of the Americas. Towns and lands of conquered natives were granted to people based on a class system. It was a hierarchy system that determined who would inherit property, conduct business, or serve in important social or political positions.
European imperialistic motives	As Europeans were exposed to Native American and African cultures, they began to debate the nature of their differences and how various people should be viewed and treated.	Natural resources were important for supporting the wealth of European economies. In search of a rationalization for oppressing colonial societies, Europeans began to use religion and race to justify their own supremacy and instill exploitative governments and economies. Many Europeans believed that since "darker peoples" were "barbaric" and "pagan," they could be mistreated or forced to labor in mines or on plantations. This attitude was debated by missionaries and scholars who suggested that these actions were only a greedy effort to maintain wealth and power.
Cultural adaptation and resistance	Some Africans and Native Americans violently resisted Spanish invasion and enslavement, while others adapted to the demands of their oppressors by adopting Christian or European social mores. Still others retained aspects of their cultural identities by holding onto various traditions and religious beliefs.	Africans who were enslaved by Spanish conquistadors served in military conflicts as they accompanied their masters while exploring. Some Africans even rose up through the ranks to become encomenderos. Some indigenous tribes, especially those who resided in remote or interior regions of the colonies, were often difficult to control and fought to retain their independence. Others migrated to unoccupied areas of the Americas. In the 17th century, most Native Americans were subjugated through military efforts, missionary expeditions, bureaucratic expansion, and European settlers' desire for land on the frontier.
Annihilation of indigenous populations	Exposure to European diseases like cholera, measles, influenza, and smallpox annihilated many Native American tribes in the New World.	Native Americans had no immunity to European diseases. A demographic catastrophe occurred that wiped out approximately 90 percent of the Native American population. Many scholars actually attribute the ease of Spanish conquest to this factor.

Compare and Contrast Europeans and Native Americans

European and Native American worldviews share several similarities, but the two groups had cultural differences that often made communication and negotiation difficult.

Europeans	Native Americans
Political and social similarities. Both Europeans and Native Americans formed patriarchal (male-dominated) societies. Both lived in communities, held specific religious beliefs, and developed leaders and governing bodies that advised the rest of their populations.	
Labor. Europeans divided specific work by gender. Women's roles were clearly defined as domestic responsibilities. Europeans did not believe that women should farm the land. This frequently caused Europeans (who assigned heavy lifting and harsh agricultural production to men) to claim that Native Americans "mistreated" their women.	**Labor.** Although both groups divided work by gender, farming and working the land were often *egalitarian* (equal). Women were left to farming and domestic responsibilities, while men hunted, defended the tribe, or engaged in war.
Religion. Europeans were *monotheistic* (believed in one god); they worshipped God as the single authority over all humans. Initially, Europeans held that Native Americans were superior to pagan Africans, who were considered barbarians, instead of "noble savages" who simply needed to be introduced to Christianity. By the 16th century, however, many colonists rejected these beliefs for premises of white supremacy that justified oppressive practices. Europeans in the Old World were horrified by tales of native cannibalism and violence, suggesting that these "uncivilized" peoples should be controlled.	**Religion.** Native Americans were *polytheistic* (believing in many gods) and promoted a balance between man and nature. Native Americans did not judge or criticize the European religious beliefs.
Landownership. Europeans considered land as property to be owned for one's personal enrichment or sustenance.	**Landownership.** Native Americans considered nature sacred and believed that the gods graciously allowed human beings to use the land, plants, and animals. Native Americans did not understand the concept of property ownership because they believed their relationship with the land was supposed to be reciprocal and respectful. This caused misunderstandings in territorial negotiations and treaties related to the sale or use of land.

Chapter Review Practice Questions

Practice questions are for instructional purposes only and may not reflect the format of the actual exam. On the actual exam, questions will be grouped into sets. Each set contains one source-based prompt (document or image) and two to five questions.

Multiple-Choice Questions

Questions 1–3 refer to the following image.

BURNING A PERUVIAN TO MAKE HIM TELL WHERE THE GOLD IS.

Source: John William Orr, "Burning a Peruvian to Make Him Tell Where the Gold Is," 1858. Spanish soldiers under the command of Francisco Pizarro torturing someone from the Inca Empire in 1520–1548.

1. The circumstances in the image depict which of the following?

 A. The encomienda system
 B. The violence associated with Spanish conquest
 C. Successful native resistance to Spanish conquest
 D. The wealth and property obtained through Spanish conquest

2. Which of the following historical developments best describes a motivation for European exploration?

 A. The Spanish Inquisition
 B. The French Revolution
 C. The *Reconquista*
 D. The Reformation

3. Based on your knowledge of U.S. history, which of the following does NOT describe the way Native Americans responded to Spanish colonial rule?

   A. Native Americans used violence to resist the Spaniards in an attempt to retain their political and physical sovereignty.
   B. Native Americans adapted to the demands of the Spaniards.
   C. Native Americans preserved important tribal bloodlines since Spanish men would only choose European women as wives or concubines.
   D. Native American tribes migrated to remote regions with rugged terrain that the Spanish found difficult to access and control.

Questions 4–6 refer to the following excerpt.

   The impact of the smallpox pandemic on the Aztec and Incan Empires is easy for the twentieth-century reader to underestimate. We have so long been hypnotized by the daring of the conquistador that we have overlooked the importance of his biological allies. Because of the achievements of modern medical science we find it hard to accept the statements from the conquest period that the pandemic killed one-third to one-half the populations struck by it. Torbido Motolinia claimed…"They died in heaps, like bedbugs."

   —Source: Alfred Crosby, historian, *The Columbian Exchange,* 1972.

4. Which of the following does Crosby's excerpt best reflect?

   A. The transfer of biological agents as a result of the contact between Europeans, Africans, and Native Americans
   B. The inadequacy of ancient Aztec and Inca healing practices
   C. The 20th-century reader's defense of disease as a primary cause of Native American death
   D. The limited amount of death that occurred as a result of smallpox

5. Which of the following best expresses Crosby's interpretation of first contact?

   A. Crosby is praising the deeds of Spanish conquistadors.
   B. Crosby is commenting on the impact of disease on conquest.
   C. Crosby is discussing the importance of Motolinia's statement.
   D. Crosby is comparing Native Americans to bedbugs.

6. Based on your knowledge of U.S. history, which of the following best describes a significant result of the Columbian Exchange?

   A. Debates regarding the nature of race increased.
   B. A demand for African and Native American slave labor fell as food choices rose.
   C. The exchange of goods and livestock caused a decline in the European market.
   D. An influx of gold and silver into the European economy caused prices and taxes to drop in Spain.

Answers and Explanations

Multiple-Choice Questions

1. **B.** Even though the engraving is dated in the 19th century, what is depicted is the reputed violence of Spanish conquistadors in the New World, choice B. The subjugation of natives through the encomienda system (choice A) is not referenced, and only gold is mentioned, not the wealth and property obtained by the Spanish (choice D). Although native resistance is depicted (choice C), it is not interpreted as successful, for the indigenous man is clearly suffering and might even be killed during his torture, while the Spanish continue to control the situation.

2. **D.** The "Protestant" Reformation (c. 1515 to c. 1650), choice D, is the best answer because it decentralized Europe and contributed to the demise of feudalism, creating competition among nation-states and monarchs who ordered and funded exploration. The Spanish Inquisition (1478–1834), choice A, was part of the Counter-Revolution (which could be considered to play a role in the inspiration for exploration). The French Revolution (1789–1799), choice B, and the Spanish and Portuguese *Reconquista* (c. 711–c. 1492), choice C, are European events, but they are chronologically unrelated to the period of exploration.

3. **C.** This is a NOT question, so you are looking for the statement that is false. Spaniards often took African or Native American women as wives or concubines, which caused an elaborate caste system to develop throughout Spanish America, making choice C the correct answer. Many tribes resisted (choice A) or migrated (choice D). To prevent future violence, some tribes adapted to the demands of their conquerors (choice B); this was easier for those who had hierarchical societies and were accustomed to paying tribute or working for a particular leader or group.

4. **A.** The excerpt reflects a transfer of disease through biological agents that Native Americans were unable to fight, choice A. The inadequacy of ancient healing practices (choice B) is neither mentioned nor relevant, and Crosby clearly discusses both the massive amount of death, not limited amount (choice D), and the 20th-century reader's difficulty in perceiving this sort of death because of modern medical science, not their belief that it was the primary cause of death (choice C).

5. **B.** It is important to read the question thoroughly in order to determine precisely what it is asking. Here, the question specifically asks about the author's interpretation of first contact. While Crosby does discuss the importance of the primary source (which compares Native American deaths, and thus the natives themselves, to bedbugs), the excerpt's main objective is to note the impact of smallpox and state that 20th-century readers often become too caught up in the deeds of the conquistadors to recognize it. The quote neither praises Motolinia nor any Spanish conqueror, but is analyzing a factor of conquest instead, choice B.

6. **A.** Specific New World crops like tobacco and sugar became staples of colonial production, which increased the need for slave labor (not decreased, choice B) and sparked debates about race and the treatment of Native Americans and Africans, making choice A correct. Labor was also needed to mine and extract gold and silver for colonial export to Europe, which caused an increase in European market prices and import taxes, not a decline (choice D), when gold and silver flowed into the European economy. Choice C, the exchange of goods, actually sparked a rise in the market, not a decline.

Chapter 5

Period Two: The Colonial Period (1607 to 1754)

Period Two explores important events and developments from early American colonization of the Spaniards, English, Dutch, and French.

- Early North American Settlements
  - Spain's Settlements (c. 1492)
  - Britain's Settlements (c. 1607 to 1754)
- British Colonies
- British Colonial Geographic Regions
- British Colonial Economics
- British Colonial Societies
- British Colonial Slavery
- British Colonial Culture
- British Colonial Government

Overview of AP U.S. History Period Two

Chapter 5 covers the motivations and patterns behind European colonization in North America. While it describes settlement patterns related to the Spanish, Dutch, and French, the main focus is on the British colonies, which would soon form the United States. The historical developments discussed in this chapter explain the similarities and differences among various colonies' economies, societies, and government that are relevant to the APUSH exam.

Use the chart below to guide you through what is covered on the exam. The curriculum contained in this chart is an abridged version of the concept outlines with topic examples. Visit https://apstudent. collegeboard.org/apcourse/ap-united-states-history/ for the complete updated APUSH course curriculum descriptions and key concepts.

AP U.S. History Key Concepts (1607 to 1754)	
Key Concept	**Content**
KEY CONCEPT 2.1: COLONIZATION AND MIGRATION PATTERNS **Europeans developed a variety of colonization and migration patterns, influenced by different imperial goals, cultures, and the varied North American environments where they settled. They competed with each other and Native Americans for resources.**	Spanish, French, Dutch, and British colonizers had different economic and imperial goals involving land and labor that shaped the social and political development of their colonies as well as their relationships with native populations. Spanish efforts to extract wealth from the land led them to develop institutions based on subjugating native populations, converting them to Christianity, and incorporating them, along with enslaved and free Africans, into Spanish colonial society. In the 17th century, early British colonies developed along the Atlantic coast, with regional differences that reflected various environmental, economic, cultural, and demographic factors. Competition over resources between European rivals and Native Americans encouraged industry and trade, and led to conflict in the Americas.
KEY CONCEPT 2.2: EXCHANGES WITH GREAT BRITAIN **The British colonies participated in political, social, cultural, and economic exchanges with Great Britain that encouraged both stronger bonds with Britain and resistance to Britain's control.**	Transatlantic commercial, religious, philosophical, and political exchanges led residents of the British colonies to evolve in their political and cultural attitudes as they became increasingly tied to Britain and one another. Like other European empires in the Americas that participated in the Atlantic slave trade, the British colonies developed a system of slavery that reflected the specific economic, demographic, and geographic characteristics of those colonies.

Significant Themes

Now that we've discussed the curriculum, let's discuss the significant themes related to this period. The theme-related study questions that follow will help you make mental connections to the context of the "big picture" of this time period. Keep in mind that these questions often overlap and apply to other themes of social, political, religious, geographic, ideological, technological, and economic developments.

Glance through the study questions before you start the review section. Take notes, highlight questions, and write down page number references to reinforce your learning. Refer to this list until you feel comfortable with your knowledge of the material.

Study Questions Related to Significant Themes for Period Two

Theme 1: American and National Identity

1. How did colonial governments operate? How were they alike? How were they different? (Hint: Colonies were operated and/or governed through a) joint-stock companies, b) proprietorships, or c) the royal monarchy. The colonies were settled by the British—note that New Amsterdam (New York) was first settled by the Dutch—but they had distinctly different geography, governance, religions, and economies and are sometimes categorized as southern colonies, New England colonies, and middle colonies.)

2. How can colonial attitudes be linked to definitions of freedom in the Revolutionary Period? (Hint: You may need to read both chapters 5 and 6 to answer this question completely. The ideas of freedom and independence from the Mother Country—Britain—began in colonial settlements and were apparent in events like Bacon's Rebellion, the Great Awakening, and the Dominion of New England. These events showed that growing colonial resentments against Britain were beginning to take shape.)

Theme 2: Politics and Power

1. What was Bacon's Rebellion and why was it important? (Hint: Bacon's Rebellion was a brief colonial civil war that took place due to a conflict among Native Americans, a class war against the Virginian elites, and unfair government leadership. It is historically important because it was the first colonial rebellion; the result was that it strengthened the hierarchy in colonial society and regulated slavery as a race-specific labor system that replaced indentured servitude.)

2. What kinds of conflicts existed between various colonies and the British government? (Hint: Conflicts associated with governance, class, and trade.)

3. What was the reaction to slaves revolting? (Hint: The Stono Rebellion.)

Theme 4: Culture and Society

1. How did the Great Awakening and the rise of the tobacco merchants influence attitudes that would lead to the American Revolution? (Hint: Think about the New Light movement during the Great Awakening and the concepts of egalitarianism and separation of church and state. Consider the tobacco industry, the growth of elite tobacco plantation owners in Virginia, unfair tobacco crop practices instituted by the southern stratified class system, and the growing frustration of the yeomen farmers against the gentry.)

Theme 5: Migration and Settlement

1. Why did the Spaniards settle in North America? (Hint: Spanish colonies conquered regions in today's New Mexico, California, Arizona, Texas, and Florida—as well as Mexico and Central America. The Spaniards wanted to expand world dominance, gain wealth, and spread religion.)

2. What were the causes of colonial migration to North America, especially the region that would become the present-day United States? (Hint: European migration to the New World was inspired by new opportunities for monetary gain, territorial expansion, and land ownership.)

3. How were the colonies different from one another? (Hint: Think about their economies, geographies, trade, response to the natives, religious and family institutions, governments, etc.)

Theme 6: Geography and the Environment

1. What were the effects of triangular trade? (Hint: The mercantile trade among three Atlantic port regions helped to rectify trade imbalances and gain wealth for Europeans, but the consequences had far-reaching effects on human lives—the introduction of slavery.)

Important Events, Terms, and Concepts

The list below shows important events, terms, and concepts that you should be familiar with on the APUSH exam. These and other important terms are printed in boldface throughout the chapter. Because the APUSH exam requires you to pay attention to the historical context and connections rather than details, don't bother memorizing the terms now. Simply place a check mark next to each as you study. You can return to this list to review as often as necessary. After you finish the review section, you can reinforce what you have learned by working through the practice questions at the end of this chapter. Answers and explanations provide further clarification into perspectives of U.S. history.

Event/Term/Concept	Year/Brief Description	Study Page
Roanoke Island	**1585.** The first attempt at British colonization failed. The settlers left behind in Roanoke were never seen or heard from again.	pp. 83–84
Virginia Company	**1606–1624.** A joint-stock company (also known as the London Company) that established the first British colonial settlement at Jamestown in Virginia. It generated its money from tobacco exports.	p. 85
Indentured servitude	A form of labor in which immigrants from Europe worked for a period of time (generally 4–7 years) in exchange for passage to the British colonies.	p. 86
House of Burgesses	**Est. 1619.** The Virginia colonial assembly, the first form of representative government in North America.	p. 87
Pilgrims and Puritans	Religious sects that established colonies in Massachusetts. The Pilgrims believed in separation from the Church of England, and the Puritans wanted to purify the Church of England.	p. 88
Quakers	Known as the *Society of Friends,* a tolerant religious group that settled in what is now Pennsylvania.	p. 91
Salutary neglect	Britain's failure to strictly regulate or send strong bureaucrats to govern its colonies.	pp. 97–98
Navigation Acts	**1651–1663.** A series of legislative acts that tied colonial trade to Britain through restrictions associated with shipping, imports, and exports.	p. 92
Bacon's Rebellion	**1676.** A brief civil war in Virginia that resulted in the burning of Jamestown. It ushered in the change from indentured servitude to African slavery as a primary source of labor in the South.	p. 87
Salem Witch Trials	**1692.** A series of public trials created by mass hysteria in Puritan Massachusetts over accusations of witchcraft. It resulted in the persecution of more than 200 people and the death of at least 20 people.	p. 90
Stono Rebellion	**1739.** An armed slave revolt occurring in South Carolina.	pp. 95–96
Triangular trade	A system of colonial trade based on mercantilism that was designed to enrich mother countries. It exchanged goods, agriculture, and slaves across the Atlantic Ocean.	pp. 92–93

Chapter Review

The information discussed in this chapter covers several overlapping categories of European colonization including the regional, cultural, governmental, and religious differences in the settlement patterns of the British colonies. The behaviors and tensions associated with Native Americans, indentured servants, and African slaves are also covered, as well as colonial trade and economic developments.

TEST TIP: When considering any period of American history on the APUSH exam, remember to think like a historian. History never occurs in a vacuum; look for connections that are relevant during each period. For example, during the colonial era, there were various motivations for European colonization and vast differences between colonial regions. The British were not the only ones to settle in North America—many different types of people came in contact with each other for the very first time. This caused new attitudes, conflicts, and behaviors to arise in different regions over the centuries—mainly because of the culture that the colonists (Spanish, Dutch, French, and British) brought with them and their interaction with each other, Native Americans, and African slaves.

Early North American Settlements

As introduced in Chapter 4, Europeans were driven to resettle in the Americas in the 1500s and early 1600s. Settlers came from different ethnic, social, and religious groups.

By 1607, the English created the first permanent settlement in Jamestown, but other Europeans also made their claim to North America. The Spanish in New Spain, the French in Canada, and the Dutch in New Netherland were not about to let the English take over the great economic potential of the continent. With the founding of Jamestown and the rapid expansion and growth of Britain's colonies on the east coast of North America, a global competition for markets and imperial power was set in motion.

By 1754, competition among European powers had driven the Dutch out and kept Spain in a state of status quo. As you will see later in this chapter, Europeans made their mark on political, economic, and social developments in North America, but the fight for control of the continent came down to a contest between Britain and France.

Heads Up: What You Need to Know

On the APUSH exam, you should be familiar with the reasons that Europeans were motivated to make the long journey across the Atlantic to America.

- Economic competitiveness, which motivated nations to seek economic wealth through business ventures and mercantilism.
- Europe's poor economic conditions including a decline in wages. Many landowners were converting farming fields into livestock pastures, and workers lost their jobs. America offered new job and economic opportunities.
- Europe's overpopulated cities.
- Europe's growing religious intolerances. Catholics and Protestants continually battled for control in the New World, just as they did in Europe.

HISTORIOGRAPHY. *The historical perspectives of the early American settlements are often based on* Eurocentrism *(the worldview centered on European historical perspectives and European culture). For example, the term "New World" was developed by Europeans' Eurocentric point of view, but North America wasn't new; it had been inhabited by indigenous people for thousands of years. On the APUSH exam, you might want to use the concept of Eurocentrism in your essay responses to relate the overall context of beliefs and values during this time period compared to other cultures such as the indigenous people.*

Spain's Settlements (c. 1492)

Following Portugal's lead, Spain began exploring the world as early as the 15th century, searching for a westward path to trade with India for spices and silks. Spain's historical importance was that it commissioned Christopher Columbus to explore the Western Hemisphere, which led to large European settlements in the New World. Spain's discovery of lands filled with gold and silver (like Mexico and Peru) inspired others to search for lands they could colonize.

Key Facts about Spain's Settlements

Spain wanted to spread religion to the New World. Missionary zeal was inspired by the Reformation, a religious movement sparked in Europe by Martin Luther, whose protests against the Catholic Church became the basis for Protestantism. The Counter-Reformation arose to defend Catholic practices and Spain, a Catholic country, was at the forefront of the fight for "souls." By 1535, the Spanish claimed much of the future southwestern and central United States. There was no gold in these territories, but missionaries and Jesuit priests felt it was important to convert the native populations to Catholicism by establishing missions and living among various tribes. In addition, Spanish *conversos* (Jews who adopted Christianity) often fled to the New World to escape religious intolerance in Europe.

Spain established forts. To defend their land, the Spanish built forts (*presidios*) in their settlements.

Spanish Southwest (New Mexico, California, Arizona, Texas). The Spanish settled in South America, Central America, and Mexico and established missions to claim their territories including the Southwest (now the United States: New Mexico, California, Arizona, and Texas). Unfortunately, natives were often enslaved by the Spaniards, just like in the British colonies.

Pueblo Revolt (also known as Popé's Rebellion) of 1680. The Pueblo Revolt was an uprising of the Hopi, Zuni, and Tewa natives, collectively known as Pueblo Indians, against Spanish rule. The seeds of this dramatic moment in the lives of the Pueblo people were sown in 1598 when Spaniard Juan de Oñate invaded their lands in the northern frontier regions of New Spain (Mexico) in 1598. Oñate's forces, with the help of Catholic priests and missionaries, brutally subjugated the Pueblos and forcibly converted them to Catholicism. Those elements sacred to their own beliefs, the *kiva* (room for ceremonial rituals) and *kachinas* (representations of spirit beings), were systematically destroyed. Rigid adherence to what they could believe and how they could marry, pray, and live their lives was strictly monitored. Resistance was met with imprisonment, torture, and mutilation through amputation.

Popé (also Po'pay), a religious leader from the Taos pueblo, launched a secret plan for rebellion which united more than 70 native villages. More than 2,000 Pueblo warriors attacked, sacked, and burned Spanish colonial headquarters at Santa Fe. Over 400 Spaniards were killed. Two-thirds of the Catholic priests in the region were killed, Catholic missions were razed, and Catholic ritual images were destroyed. The people of the pueblos reestablished their cultural and political primacy, returning particularly to use of kivas as places of worship and the veneration of kachinas. Even after the Spanish restored their control over the region more than a decade later, they had learned their lesson, adopting a tolerant approach to religious observance.

Heads Up: What You Need to Know

On the APUSH exam, you should know that Native American resistance to Spanish colonizing efforts in North America, particularly after the Pueblo Revolt, led to Spanish accommodation of some aspects of Native American culture in the Southwest.

Spanish Florida. Spanish *La Florida* was claimed by Juan Ponce de León in 1513 during an expedition to North America. Spanish Florida territory was much larger than today's state of Florida because it was once considered part of Cuba. Most of the indigenous populations of Spanish Florida resisted the conquest, but were weakened by diseases and battles.

As time progressed, there were few natives left to convert or enslave, there was a decline in natural resources (gold and silver), and there were hurricanes that resulted in environmental catastrophes. By the 17th century, Spain lost interest in Florida, but it was useful to Spain to defend the Caribbean from possible invaders. In 1763, Britain controlled Spanish Florida for a short time, and then returned it to Spain in 1784. By 1819, Spain agreed to transfer the region to the U.S. in exchange for payment of Spanish debts after a series of early-19th-century *Seminole Wars* (conflicts over recapturing runaway Native Americans and African American slaves who fled to Spanish Florida).

> **Did you know?** The French, who were responsible for much of the settlement of Canada and what we now know as the Great Lakes region, were also searching for wealth and motivated by the Jesuits' desire to convert the natives. Although their colonization experience differs slightly, it is similar to the British experience—their first attempt failed, but a successful colony (Quebec) was established under the leadership of Samuel de Champlain in 1608, 1 year after the founding of Jamestown. Unlike the British, French colonists were often fur traders and intermarried with native women to establish important economic and military alliances.

Haciendas. Haciendas were landed estates in Spanish America, usually owned by Spaniards or *Criollos* (Spaniards born in the Americas). The emergence of haciendas marked an uneven transition from mining and the indigenous enslavement associated with the encomienda system to an agricultural/pastoral system. Haciendas developed on land either expropriated from indigenous people or purchased legally after the land had been vacated by them through a combination of conflict and European epidemics. The agricultural haciendas were concentrated in central Mexico on the rich farmlands around Mexico City, while ranching and livestock raising on pastoral estates tended to be in the northern lands of Mexico and South America. The day-to-day labor was provided by indigenous workforces who were given a place to live and a source of food on the estate. Their debt to the *patron* (owner) was paid through labor, a system known as debt peonage. During seasonal planting and harvest times, additional local native workers were recruited. Playing one patron against another, workers had slightly more control over their wages than those living on the haciendas.

Britain's Settlements (c. 1607 to 1754)

While Britain's first attempts at establishing colonization in North America were unsuccessful, it was able to establish its first permanent settlement in 1607—Jamestown.

The Lost Colony of Roanoke Island

In 1585, Sir Walter Raleigh received permission from Queen Elizabeth to move several families (115 settlers) to **Roanoke Island** (North Carolina) to establish a colony. Raleigh sent his close friend, John White, to lead the expedition to North America. White established a community on Roanoke Island, but it was too late in the season to plant crops. White returned to Britain for desperately needed food and supplies, but was kept from returning to Roanoke Island for several years because Britain was at war with Spain. (In 1588, Spain tried to invade Britain.) When White finally returned in 1590, he found no one—the settlers had disappeared without a trace.

HISTORIOGRAPHY. *Historians have debated the disappearance of the Roanoke Island colonists. Some believe that because the settlers had violent conflicts with the natives, they were slaughtered or enslaved by various tribes. Others believe that since they were starving, they assimilated into friendly tribes, like the Croatan Indians, in order to survive. The only clue to the disappearance of the lost colony was the word "Croatan" that was carved on a door post.*

British Colonies

The primary reason Britain expanded to America in the 17th century was to make money through business ventures and mercantilism. Even though the colonists themselves drew from principles of their common background, the British colonies developed differently from each other.

> **TEST TIP: On the APUSH exam, it's important to be able to compare and contrast "colonialism" and "imperialism." Although these terms are interrelated, they have slightly different meanings. Both terms refer to a powerful nation taking control of a weaker nation or territory, but imperialism refers to the conquest (often by means of a military) and total control of another nation for territorial expansion and power. Imperialists apply their own foreign policies to the newly acquired region.**
>
> **Colonialism, on the other hand, refers to a more powerful nation starting a settlement (colony) in another nation or region for the purpose of exploiting natural resources, labor resources, and economic gain. Colonialism is the result of imperialism. Some historians say that imperialism is an "ideological concept" of power that drives colonialism, and colonialism is the "practice" of settling into another region or nation.**

Before we discuss the similarities and differences of each of the regions, let's take a look at how the colonies started through the three types of funding and governance that brought British settlers to America: joint-stock colonies, proprietorships, and royal colonies.

Colonial Governance		
Region	**Type of Governance**	**Description**
Jamestown (Virginia)	Joint-stock colony	In 1607, the first permanent British settlers formed a colony in Jamestown (Virginia). The expedition was funded by business investors from the Virginia Company (also known as London Company), a joint-stock venture. The colonies were operated by shareholders, who were expected to invest, share profits and losses, and recruit colonists and governors (some of whom were stockholders themselves). The investors were hoping to find gold and silver; the sole purpose was to make money.
Maryland and Pennsylvania	Proprietorship	By 1632, Maryland was settled as a refuge for Catholics. By 1640, Britain granted governing rights to a *proprietor* (a person appointed by the British monarchy to rule and govern the colony). The proprietor could be one person or a small group of people. The appointed proprietor could grant religious freedom, ban slavery, or impose other forms of legislation on the colonists.

Region	Type of Governance	Description
New York and the Carolinas (once proprietary colonies)	Royal colony	Royal colonies were owned and governed directly by the king or queen. Many colonies ended up being ruled by the British monarchy even if they started as joint-stock colonies or proprietorships.

British Colonial Geographic Regions

British settlement populations grew steadily, and a stream of immigrants from Western Europe swelled the colonial populations. On the APUSH exam, you should be familiar with the similarities and differences in the British colonial regions. Colonies had distinct economic, geographic, and governing characteristics. Britain developed permanent settlements in three geographic regions: southern, New England, and middle colonies.

Southern Colonies

First colony: Jamestown (Virginia)

Present-day regional states: Virginia, Maryland, North Carolina, South Carolina, and Georgia

Economy: Cash-crop farming (tobacco, cotton, and rice) and slavery

Geography: Fertile coastal plains, warm winters, and long, hot summers

Key Facts about Southern Colonies

Founded by a joint-stock company. Wealthy aristocrats and London businessmen were responsible for establishing the first British colony. Businessmen decided to form the joint-stock **Virginia Company** (also known as the London Company) in order to seek the riches they believed to be found in the New World. King James II granted the joint-stock company a charter for their colony in 1606. A group of gentlemen, their servants, and a few artisans began a voyage to North America with little experience in farming, agriculture, or overall survival. A common European belief at the time was that they would find "good" natives who would provide them with food and protection from harsh weather conditions and possible enemies. After all, the Spanish had made it appear as if wealth was easily attainable, and native populations could be easily conquered (which was never really true).

First settlers had a low survival rate. When settlers arrived at Chesapeake Bay (today's Virginia) in 1607, they were sorely disappointed—the natives didn't have large quantities of corn stored to give away to the early colonists. Many colonists refused to learn or participate in communal food production, so there was a high rate of disease, starvation, and death. Furthermore, the early colonists built a fort, named Jamestown after the British king, on a swamp that contained malaria-carrying mosquitos. Some of the native tribes that initially attempted to help the colonists became antagonized by their actions and stopped helping the colonists. Only 35 of the original 100 settlers survived.

The table below describes the actions carried out by influential people who changed the course of Virginia history.

Important Leaders	
Leader	**Impact**
John Smith (1580–1631)	The first important leader of Jamestown, Smith trained colonists to farm and work and applied military discipline to the principles of community cooperation. Smith not only fostered a more positive relationship with Powhatan, an important native leader, but he also established a "no work, no eat" policy in 1609, which ensured that the colonists wouldn't starve to death as long as they worked.
John Rolfe (1585–1622)	Rolfe was the husband of Pocahontas, the daughter of an important Native American *sachem* (tribal leader), who was known by his tribal name, Powhatan. Because Pocahontas' father was the leader of a large confederacy, Rolfe's marriage to Pocahontas created a political alliance that contributed to native tolerance of the British colonists. Rolfe was also known for introducing the cultivation of tobacco to Virginia. Tobacco became the colony's primary exporting crop. Since the region didn't possess the rich resources of gold and silver that the joint-stock company expected, tobacco became the source of Virginia's initial profits and economic sustenance.
Sir Edwin Sandys (1561–1626)	Sandys not only issued a charter calling for the first colonial assembly, but he also used his role as treasurer of the Virginia Company in 1618 to institute the policies of the headright system and indentured servitude, which created incentives to emigrate to, invest in, and provide labor for the colony.

Chesapeake colonies. Colonists in the Chesapeake Bay region, which originally included both Virginia and Maryland, suffered many hardships due to starvation and disease generated from a hot climate and swampy environment. Because of the Chesapeake's high mortality rates, it was sparsely populated. Conditions changed in 1612 when John Rolfe successfully cultivated the first tobacco for the export market. The Chesapeake then quickly developed rural agricultural economics based on the plantation system. While the region began to flourish economically and socially, labor to work tobacco farms remained scarce and class division was common. Landowners cultivating tobacco developed the headright system (see below) to gain the labor they needed in the Atlantic coastal tidewater region, but harsh working conditions and abuses of power rapidly polarized wealthy elites and the backcountry poor who had once been indentured servants. After a significant uprising of frontier farmers (see "Bacon's Rebellion" on the next page), Chesapeake planters then turned to African slavery as their labor source and encouraged the growth of ever more expansive and productive plantations. As a result of success in Virginia, other southern colonies, including North Carolina, began to export tobacco.

Heads Up: What You Need to Know

The APUSH exam frequently has a question about the importance of the tobacco plantation and slave system in the Chesapeake and Carolina colonies. The Chesapeake and North Carolina colonies grew prosperous by exporting tobacco—a labor-intensive product initially cultivated by white, mostly male, indentured servants and later by enslaved Africans. The cultivation of tobacco created an economically polarizing hierarchal society.

The headright system and indentured servitude. British settlers who paid for the journey of a poor laborer would gain that person as a servant for a particular period of time, usually 4 to 7 years; this was known as **indentured servitude.** Colonists who could pay their own way (and the way of others) were motivated by the **headright system (1618).** Settlers who came to Jamestown were granted 50 acres of land to farm, and those who had been there since 1616 were granted 100 acres. An additional 50 acres was granted for every slave or indentured servant brought to the colony. These were exploitative policies that provided the wealthy with free labor and large tracts of land until the 18th century.

House of Burgesses (1619). An early form of government was called the **House of Burgesses** (Virginia's first legislative assembly of elected representatives). The representatives were wealthy businessmen who began passing legislation that allowed them to hoard supplies, extend terms of service, control tobacco exports, and ensure that they could maintain power of the laws and courts.

Maryland (1632). Like Pennsylvania in the middle colonies, Maryland and Georgia began as proprietary colonies. Maryland was granted to Lord Baltimore (George Calvert) in 1632. Baltimore, who was a Catholic, promoted religious freedom through an *Act of Toleration* in 1649. The act allowed for the freedom of all Christians, but was intended to specifically protect Catholics, who were often persecuted in Britain. Once again, religious freedom had a skewed definition of religious tolerance—Jews and Muslims were unwelcome in the colony.

Bacon's Rebellion (1676). Bacon's Rebellion was between Virginia settlers and the ruling government of Virginia. Disappointed by the Virginia Company stockholders' greed and mismanagement, Britain's King James I took over the colony in 1624 and sent a series of royal governors to manage the colony. One of the most famous royal governors was William Berkeley.

Many *yeomen* farmers (small landowners who were former indentured servants) felt that Berkeley was not properly representing farmers. Farmers were frustrated with economic practices and felt that Berkeley was not adequately protecting them from Native American attacks. Since wealth was closely associated with the landownership that was needed to grow tobacco, wealthy landowners were allowed to possess sizeable partitions of "good" property located closer to the coast. Yeomen were forced onto the frontier, closer to the Native Americans.

In 1676, under the leadership of Nathaniel Bacon and after being denied permission to hunt down and fight Native Americans, the yeomen started an uprising. (Note: The farmers didn't differentiate between peaceful and hostile tribes, while Berkeley knew the differences between the two because he had been trading with some of the natives for extra income.) A civil war ensued for several months, which resulted in the burning of Jamestown and random attacks on some of the peaceful native tribes who happened to be nearby. When Bacon suddenly died from dysentery, the rebellion ceased, but 23 rebels were hung because the rebellion was seen as an act of colonial defiance against Britain.

Heads Up: What You Need to Know

On the APUSH exam, you should be familiar with the effects of Bacon's Rebellion (1676) because it was the first act of colonial rebellion. Since indentured servants participated in the uprising, the revolt caused a shift in the way colonists viewed labor and race relations. Indentured servitude became less popular and was replaced by free labor based on perceived racial differences (African slavery).

Some historians refer to this rebellion as the revolt that planted the seeds which inspired American self-government and sovereignty in 1765 and refer to Nathaniel Bacon as the "torchbearer" of the American Revolution.

The rise of chattel slavery (1676). The British king at the time, Charles II, revoked Berkeley's governance and recalled him to England. Bacon's Rebellion, however, sparked an important shift in colonial race and labor relations. Although African slaves had been brought to the colony as early as 1619, most lived and worked much in the same way as indentured servants, even socially mixing and intermarrying with poor whites.

After 1676, however, wealthy landowners feared future rebellions of indentured servants and began to invest in *chattel* slavery (slaves as personal property) for laborers. To protect their workforce and ensure the cooperation of poorer whites, wealthy landowners created laws that imposed many strict restrictions on black slaves, and they began soliciting the support of small property owners. This resulted in a rise in racial intolerance, social inferiority, and racial prejudice.

Georgia (1732). Georgia was granted to James Oglethorpe, a military leader and social visionary, who worked for prison reform in England, especially for debtors. Oglethorpe believed that England's working poor could become successful in the New World. Oglethorpe saw his colony as a refuge for those who were heavily in debt. King George II saw this colony as a possible military buffer for the other colonies, which could be threatened by the Spanish in Florida or the French in Louisiana. Oglethorpe settled with 114 colonists in what would become Savannah. In an effort to build a moral, classless society, he banned slavery, prohibited the sale of rum, and limited property ownership. Most of his restrictions were revoked within a decade because they slowed the economy and immigration.

New England Colonies

First colonies (1620–1691): Plymouth Colony (Massachusetts) and Massachusetts Bay Colony
Present-day regional states: Massachusetts, New Hampshire, Rhode Island, and Connecticut
Economy: Fisheries, shipbuilding, lumbering, commerce, and small-scale manufacturing
Geography: Ports on the Atlantic Ocean, mountains, rolling hills, rocky soil, cold winters, short summers

Key Facts about New England Colonies

Settlers were driven by religious beliefs. Unlike the stockholders of the Virginia Company, the founders of the New England colonies were driven to the New World by their religious beliefs. Fleeing from persecution in Europe, many people sought a safe place to freely practice their religion. New England colonists contained two primary religious groups: the **Pilgrims,** who wanted to separate from the Church of England, and the **Puritans,** who wanted to reform the Church of England. It is important to recognize that while these groups dominated New England society, not all of these colonists were blindly dedicated to Pilgrim or Puritan beliefs. If they did not obey Puritan law or voiced criticisms, however, they could be severely punished or exiled from their communities.

The Mayflower Compact (1620). The Mayflower Compact became the first written agreement for self-government in the colonies, allowing individuals to choose their own leaders and laws. A group of Pilgrims led by William Bradford left England on the *Mayflower,* a ship destined for northern Virginia. While at sea, the heads of each family wrote and signed a governing document for their new colony, *The Mayflower Compact.* Since some of the men were not Pilgrims (a few were adventurers or tradesmen), the stability of the group was protected from settlers who wanted to live by "their *owne libertie*" through the forming of a "Civil Body Politic," which created rules that all colonists had to agree to follow before disembarking. After 41 male passengers signed the compact, the group proceeded to build a town, which they called Plymouth.

Plymouth Colony. Plymouth Colony was established in present-day Massachusetts. In his diary, Bradford wrote about the difficulties that the Pilgrims faced, including a period of inclement weather, starvation, and death from diseases like *scurvy* (caused by lack of vitamin C). Since many were too sick to work or build shelters, they didn't leave the ship for several months. About 45 of the 102 original colonists died the first winter. The rest of the colonists survived with the help of Native Americans, including local tribes of

Wampanoag. Aided by **Squanto** (a Patuxet who learned to speak English when he was enslaved by a British sea captain), the colonists were able to form a long-lasting alliance with **Massasoit,** sachem (leader) of the Wampanoag Confederacy. Plymouth Colony merged with the Massachusetts Bay Colony in 1691 (see below).

Did you know? The **Wampanoags** initially saw Squanto's assistance as a betrayal and demanded that he be turned over to them for punishment (he was living with and serving as the Pilgrim's interpreter, guide, and advisor at the time). Tensions between the tribe and the Pilgrims grew and were only relieved when Massasoit became gravely ill. When one of the Pilgrims nursed him back to health, Massasoit concluded that the English were his friends. The moral of this story: good deeds matter!

King Philip's War (1675–1678). Also known as **Metacom's War,** this was an American Indian military confrontation in New England over land, resources, and political boundaries. In the 50 years following the legendary first Thanksgiving, relations between the Wampanoag Confederacy of tribes and waves of new colonists deteriorated. English settlements expanded along the coast and up the Connecticut River Valley, encroaching on traditional lands of various Algonquin tribes. By 1675, the British population had grown to about 80,000.

The death of John Sassamon, a *praying Indian* (native who was converted to Christianity), who had served as a mediator between the Wampanoag and the English, led to the arrest and hanging of three Wampanoag men who were accused of his murder. Metacom, the son of the Wampanoag chief, led his confederacy in attacks on settlements across the frontier, including Plymouth itself. Mohawks of the Iroquois Confederacy, rivals of the Algonquin people, allied themselves with the colonists and counterattacked against isolated Algonquin villages. The French were drawn in, joining with their Algonquin allies in counter-raids against New England settlements in Maine. In the end, 1,000 colonists were killed and 3,000 Native Americans lay dead, including Metacom. With organized town governments unaffected by the war, a low mortality rate, and a 3 percent rate of population increase, New England recovered. The same cannot be claimed for the Native Americans within Metacom's confederacy. Those natives who remained fled to the north and west, leaving most of the land in Massachusetts, Connecticut, and Rhode Island clear for settlement.

Massachusetts Bay Colony. The Massachusetts Bay Colony was funded and composed of Puritans who, like the Pilgrims, were suffering from religious oppression. After receiving a royal charter from Charles I, the group immigrated to a region north of Plymouth and settled in 1630. John Winthrop, an early governor of the colony, saw the settlement as a "city on a hill" or a holy society that would provide a religious example for the world. Winthrop's sentiments not only reflected the attitudes of most of the Puritan inhabitants, but they also became the guiding principles of religion and government for many of New England's colonies.

Puritans did not separate church and state. The Puritans came to America for religious freedom, but established a *theocratic* (religion-based) government. The Puritans supported democracy to a certain extent—unlike voting privileges in Virginia, which required property ownership, all church members were able to vote in town hall meetings. Families immigrated together, which was different from the Virginia settlers, who retained a majority of male immigrants until the early 18th century. In New England, women were educated so they could read the Bible (a requirement for all good Puritans) and were even allowed to vote in town meetings if their husbands were absent.

Salem Witch Trials (1692–1693). Puritans' tolerance of others was limited. Religious freedom to other religious groups was denied, church membership was required, and religious dissenters were heavily persecuted. In fact, two colonists who challenged the traditional Puritan practices, Roger Williams and Anne Hutchinson, were banned from the colony. Williams later established Rhode Island, instilling principles of religious freedom in his new colony. Starting in 1692, Puritans conducted a series of witch trials in Salem, prosecuting colonists accused of witchcraft. Although it began with the frivolous accusation by a few teenage girls, it produced mass hysteria in Massachusetts, which resulted in the deaths of at least 20 people who were executed (hanged) or died in prison.

Heads Up: What You Need to Know

On the APUSH exam, you should be familiar with the Salem Witch Trials. Compare and contrast the 17th-century trials with the 20th-century phenomenon of *McCarthyism* (vicious accusations by Senator Joseph McCarthy that communism infiltrated the U.S. government, which caused social and political panic—covered in Chapter 11). On free-response questions, you can use the example of Arthur Miller's dramatic play, *The Crucible*. Drawing from the history of Salem, Miller wrote the play in 1953 to compare the witch trials to the anti-communism panic of the Cold War McCarthy era.

Both events serve as a historical examples of the effects of religious extremism, intolerance, social mass hysteria, and the failure of government to provide citizens with legal due process.

Middle Colonies

First British settlement (1664): The Dutch granted the land to the powerful British military, and Dutch New Netherland became British New York.

Present-day regional states: Pennsylvania, New York, Delaware, and New Jersey

Economy: Large-scale farming (corn and grain production), manufacturing, and commerce

Geography: Ports on the Atlantic Ocean, open fertile plains, mild to cold winters, long summers

Key Facts about Middle Colonies

New York and Pennsylvania were part of the middle colonies and generally composed of ethnically diverse and religiously tolerant individuals. The middle colonies' wheat and grains often provided food for neighboring regions. Ethnic groups included the Dutch, British, Swedish, Germans, Scotch-Irish, and French as well as African slaves and Native American tribes full of Iroquoian and Algonquian speakers.

New Netherland (New York). New York was not established by the British; rather, it was first settled by the Dutch through the Dutch East India Company in 1614. Known originally as New Netherland, the colony soon prospered through a thriving fur trade with local Algonquian tribes. This inspired the formation of the Dutch West India Company in 1621 and its establishment of the colony's primary settlement (New Amsterdam) on Manhattan Island in 1624. Desiring the successful trade that the Dutch were enjoying in North America, England's King Charles II sent four ships to demand New Netherland's surrender in 1664. Unprotected, the Dutch colony immediately complied and Charles gave the colony to his brother James, the Duke of York (hence its new name New York). Although the royal governors in charge of the colony gave the colonists no legislative representation, Dutch settlers continued to influence architecture, culture, and trade. Fur and farms generated income and the thriving port of New York became central to the region's commercial interests.

Pennsylvania. Pennsylvania was settled by the **Quakers,** who were religiously tolerant individuals led by William Penn. Granted a royal charter in 1681, Penn established a colonial government that consisted of a governor, a member of his family, a Provincial Council, and a large representative General Assembly (the assembly had little actual power). Since the Quakers associated individual belief with salvation, the colony was open to all Christians and the colonists generally treated Native Americans with respect. The colonists bought land from the natives and honored their treaties. Unlike the Puritans, Quakers allowed women to take an active role in church activities, including preaching (something that got Anne Hutchinson excommunicated from the Puritans in Massachusetts).

The Thirteen Colonies

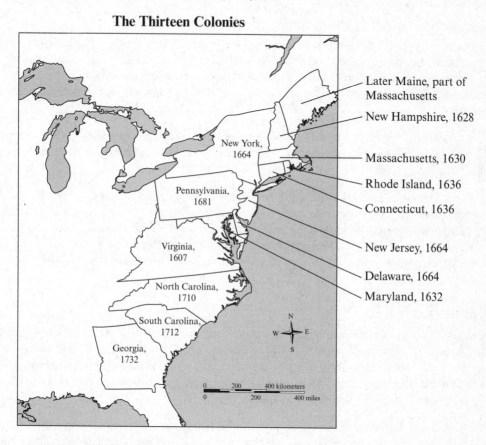

British Colonial Economics

The English Crown financed the colonial settlements, expecting to expand economic wealth and power through its investments.

Mercantilism

Britain was motivated by an economic system that dominated Europe called **mercantilism,** which moved imperialist nations away from an agricultural base and toward an economy supported by trade. Many European leaders believed the world contained only a particular amount of wealth and a nation's power was related to how much of that wealth it could obtain. The system was tied to government control of the economy and underscored the importance of overseas colonies, which were seen as important resources of raw materials and new markets for surplus goods.

The Spanish and British perfected mercantilism in the New World in different ways. In the 16th century, the conquistadors focused on collecting gold and silver from the Aztec Empire and then shipped these precious metals to Spain. Unable to find gold or silver in the lands it settled a century later, Britain sought to establish mercantilism through trade. Britain (the Mother Country) received agriculture and raw materials from its colonies (to make into manufactured products), and then sold the agriculture and goods throughout Europe and its other colonies, which included those in North America and the Caribbean. Raw materials such as tobacco, cotton, sugar, or fur were shipped to Europe and created a base of wealth for the English Crown.

Heads Up: What You Need to Know

The economic concept of **mercantilism** frequently appears on the APUSH exam. The British needed a robust economy to maintain their power and wealth. Mercantilism involved government regulations for economic and territorial dominance. Mercantilism was an economic system that provided Britain with increased wealth by exporting materials, goods, and agriculture from America to Britain.

On the APUSH exam, remember that the British government increasingly attempted to incorporate its North American colonies into a coherent, hierarchical, and imperial structure in order to pursue mercantilist economic aims.

In addition, you should be able to distinguish between U.S. economic practices across periods of time. The two main types of mercantile trade were *protectionism* (the government regulated trade by imposing tariffs on exported or imported goods) and *free trade* (commercial manufacturers freely traded with and sold to foreign nations). Although British mercantilism was a policy of protectionism, the modern-day economic practice of capitalism emphasizes free trade.

The Navigation Acts

In the 17th century, mercantilism was implemented through various Navigation Acts and triangular trade. The **Navigation Acts** were regulations passed in 1651, 1660, and 1663 that tightened British control over trade in the colonies. The Navigation Acts basically declared that trade could only be carried out in English ships with English crews and everything had to pass through English ports before it was sent anywhere else. Certain goods, especially tobacco, could only be exported to England.

Many of the colonists opposed the acts because they allowed Britain to set prices for imports and exports and repressed trade relations with other nations, like the Dutch (the first act is actually seen as a major cause of the Anglo-Dutch War in 1652). Virginia tobacco growers, who traded with the Dutch, deeply resented the acts, but New England shipbuilders were thrilled with the monopoly they were granted in their industry. Other colonists simply ignored the acts by becoming expert smugglers.

Triangular Trade

Operating from the 16th to the early 19th centuries, **triangular trade** was a commerce exchange process that allowed nations to pay for their imports through their exports. For example, Britain shipped goods to West Africa, where the goods were traded for slaves, who were shipped to the colonies in the West Indies. The slaves were then traded for sugar, rum, and other products (produced by other slaves) that were shipped back to Britain for sale on the European market. New England colonies produced some of the rum that was shipped to Africa in exchange for slaves.

Triangular Trade

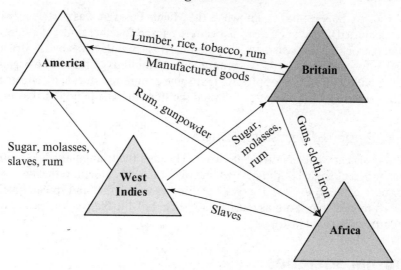

Triangular Trade Map

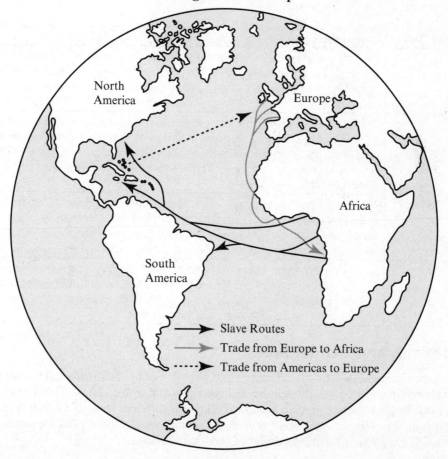

The Middle Passage

The route from Africa to the West Indies, known as the **Middle Passage,** was particularly horrific for Africans who were being transported as slaves. African slaves were packed together under the ship's deck with little room to move, breathe, or sleep for several weeks (months, if the weather was bad). Africans were denied light and fresh air, and many—an estimated 15 percent (or about 2 million) of those who began the journey—became ill or died. Conditions were so oppressive that some committed suicide by refusing to eat or by throwing themselves overboard. Sharks often followed the ships in anticipation of the desperate or the dead.

Triangular Trade Transferred Devastating Diseases

Triangular trade was also grave for Native Americans. Through the triangular trade route, Europeans brought smallpox, tuberculosis, whooping cough, measles, flu, and cholera to the New World. Since the natives had never been exposed to such diseases, the diseases were lethal and spread quickly as epidemics. Smallpox is believed to have wiped out as much as 90 percent of the Native American population and was recorded for generations in tribal histories.

British Colonial Societies

The colonial societies were shaped by the attitudes that colonists brought with them from Britain. Colonial societies had several distinct social classes.

Colonial Social Class	Characteristic
Gentry	The gentry were people of the wealthy upper class who owned large amounts of the best land. The gentry controlled the government representation, courts, and colonial publications. They dominated colonial society by intermarrying and passing their positions and wealth down to their sons.
Yeoman	Yeomen were farmers who owned small properties. After Bacon's Rebellion, yeomen were granted the right to vote and the gentry began to hold elections that competed for their vote. More prevalent in agricultural colonies, yeomen produced crops both to sustain their households and to export to Britain. Yeomen labor often came from their households, which (if they were successful) could have contained a slave.
Indentured servant	Indentured servants were people whose labor was promised to another for 4 to 7 years. After Bacon's Rebellion, the use of indentured servants declined. After they were freed, many became small-property owners, but some worked as manual laborers, tenant farmers, sailors, or hired servants. If they became "poor whites" and didn't own property, they couldn't vote in the assembly.
Slave	Slaves were those whose labor was promised to another for life because of their racial status. Although Native American and African slaves mixed with and shared the lifestyle of indentured servants before Bacon's Rebellion, slaves were on the lowest rung of the social class system and their rights were eventually taken away completely.

Colonial Family and Gender Roles

Northern colonial immigrants were often families that were driven by their Christian beliefs and duties as parents and church members. Even though they believed men and women had different roles to uphold (like work in the fields or tend the home), their social structure was different from that which developed in the South. In Virginia, for example, there was a shortage of women until around 1720. Up until that point, men and women worked together to share the duties of their households.

As the slave trade accelerated, however, many women no longer had to work alongside their husbands to tend crops in the fields. Since the need for young brides decreased, families could also keep their daughters at home longer, which meant they could teach the girls basic housekeeping skills. After Bacon's Rebellion, a husband's status depended on his property ownership and dependents, including family members, indentured servants, and slaves. Colonial women had few rights and could not vote.

British Colonial Slavery

Black chattel slavery became the primary source of labor in agricultural colonies after Bacon's Rebellion, but it is important to note that no form of labor was seen as ideal among the colonists. African slaves were expensive and had language barriers, but Native American enslavement could result in retaliation from local tribes. Colonists felt that indentured servants were temperamental, rebellious, and at best, a temporary solution to a permanent labor shortage. Native Americans, slaves, and indentured servants also often ran away from landowners, sometimes together.

Key Facts about Colonial Slavery

Racism. Racism was certainly always a factor in enslavement, but later in history racism developed through ideological discriminatory practices, racial divisions, and characteristics of white superiority. In the 17th century, the attitudes of the white lower-class colonists toward slavery were not the same as the attitudes of white Americans in the 18th to the 20th centuries. In the 17th century, pagan religious beliefs were often seen as a justification for slavery, not racism. African slaves often intermarried, socialized, worked beside, and developed friendships with indentured servants and Native Americans. African Americans could buy or were granted their freedom, were allowed a certain degree of autonomy to complete their tasks, and were even trusted with rifles during native attacks.

Changes after Bacon's Rebellion. After former indentured servants rebelled with Nathaniel Bacon in 1676, behaviors and legislation significantly changed because slavery provided the colonists with a stable labor force. Laws were passed that distinguished black slaves from white servants: Slaves were restricted in their movements, banned from using guns, denied trials by jury, and prohibited from interracial marriage. Free men of color were not allowed to hold a public office. Slave owners were also given the right to kill, whip, and control slaves, and children born to slave mothers automatically became slaves.

Slave resistance. African slaves found several ways to combat their oppression. They slowed their work pace, broke equipment, feigned illness, pilfered food and tools, ran away (or helped others), and committed arson. Their culture and religion, which combined African, American, and evangelical traditions, provided them with physical and emotional strength. Extended kinship groups and families also provided stability in the midst of subjugation, oppression, and mistreatment. These actions are often interpreted as determination among those identified as property to reclaim some part of their freedom and humanity.

The Stono Rebellion (1739)

Armed slave resistance was rare. One of the earliest resistances occurred in 1712 in New York, which had the largest slave population outside of the southern colonies. Denied the broader rights and freedoms under British rule than they had when the Dutch ruled New Netherland, 23 slaves armed with swords, guns, and hatchets gathered, set fire to a building near Broadway, and attacked whites arriving on the scene to put out the fire. Nine whites were killed and several more were wounded.

The most famous and largest revolt of colonial times was the **Stono Rebellion.** It took place in South Carolina, the colony perhaps most steeped in the culture of enslavement. It was an uprising led by approximately 20 South Carolinian slaves who were headed for Spanish Florida, where they had been promised freedom.

Marching south from the Stono River, the slaves recruited other slaves and attacked several whites (about 45 died), but were stopped by the militia and were either executed or sold to be shipped to the West Indies.

Consequences of the Stono Rebellion

The consequences of the Stono Rebellion were swift and created an even more restrictive system. Many whites in the region believed that part of the problem was the presence of Africans among those slaves born and raised within the slave system. They thought domestic slaves were more accustomed to bondage and complacent with their condition. A 10-year moratorium was imposed on further importation of slaves from Africa. South Carolinian legislators then passed the **Negro Act of 1740,** which severely tightened the control slave owners had over their slaves and strictly enforced the restrictions that were already in place. Several things were prohibited, including slave gatherings, teaching slaves to read, or allowing them to practice trades to earn their own money. A half-hearted attempt was made to ban brutal punishments by masters, but this was next to impossible to enforce because earlier laws prohibited blacks from giving testimony against whites in court. Despite the effort to cool the simmering rebellion, additional slave revolts occurred in South Carolina and Georgia during the next 2 years.

British Colonial Culture

The Tobacco Market

Changes in the tobacco market also influenced colonial attitudes, especially in Virginia. The **Tobacco Inspection Act (1730)** allowed for the destruction of poor-quality tobacco, which was often grown by yeomen, who did not have access to the high-quality soil and the labor forces of the gentry. The gentry had already been serving as middlemen in the tobacco market by agreeing to ship their poorer neighbors' crops to Europe to sell, which enabled them to take a monetary "cut" of the profits for themselves. The inspection act gave them an even greater monopoly of the market because it provided them with the ability to wipe out entire crops of their competitors' tobacco.

In the 1740s, things changed when Scottish merchants (or **factors**) set up trading stores loaded with imported goods that took tobacco for payment. This crushed the gentry's ability to control credit and opened the door for the yeomen (and free whites) to challenge their power.

Heads Up: What You Need to Know

On the APUSH exam, you should know that the presence of different European religious and ethnic groups contributed to a significant degree of pluralism and intellectual exchange, which was later enhanced by the first Great Awakening and the spread of European Enlightenment ideals.

The Great Awakening

Simultaneously, the **Great Awakening** (1730–1750), a religious revival led by ministers like George Whitefield and Jonathan Edwards, was encouraging colonists to begin to think differently. Whitefield, a minister of the Church of England, traveled from place to place in America as an itinerant preacher, drawing crowds so large he delivered his revival sermons in large outdoor tents. In England, Whitefield and fellow Anglicans John and Charles Wesley founded a "Methodist" reform movement within the Church of England that placed more emphasis on biblical revelation, assurance of salvation for the "saved" individual, and direct access to God for all Christians through the act of prayer. Methodism eventually split off from the Church of England, becoming its own denomination. Whitefield's sermons gave rise to the new denomination in America.

The Great Awakening ultimately created a more diverse, if more polarized, body of Christian faithful in the British colonies. Presbyterian and evangelical Baptist missionaries brought the revival south from New England into Virginia. Baptist converts would account for 10 percent of all southern Christians by the 1770s.

The debate of emotional revivalist spirit split the Congregational church into "Old Light" and "New Light" factions. The New Light ministers of the Great Awakening rejected the ritual, ceremony, and traditions of Old Light clergymen. The New Light ministers held emotional camp meetings that stressed the importance of personal salvation, individual thinking, and tolerance. This not only produced an *egalitarian* (equal rights) culture that separated common people from the social control of the wealthy, but it also increased the number of women and slaves in congregations and led to the rejection of religious and political authority.

The Great Awakening decreased support for the Anglican Church and divided other denominations.

> **Did you know?** The colonial gentry were always thinking of ways to sustain their elevated representative position—when their power was threatened, they used several strategies to regain power. One method was to become evangelical Christians themselves, and another method was to redirect the colonists' anger from the gentry to the British!

Quakers and Anglicans disapproved of the theatrical nature of the revivalists and grew in number, while the greatest gains were made by the new Baptist and Methodist denominations. The tenets of the Great Awakening set the stage for the republican principles of the American Revolution and the eventual separation of church and state.

British Colonial Government

Salutary Neglect

For the most part, the British practiced **salutary neglect** (Britain's unofficial policy to relax the enforcement of strict colonial laws) in their colonies. This means that Britain essentially ignored colonists and allowed them to govern themselves through town meetings and colonial assemblies.

Laws such as the Navigation Acts, designed to incorporate the colonies into the larger mercantile system of the British Empire, were often irregularly enforced or not enforced at all, partly due to the distance of the colonies from England itself. Allowed to develop largely on their own, the colonies formed regionally unique forms of local governance. These often included elements of democratic self-government, such as New England town meetings and the first elected colonial legislature (the House of Burgesses), which was dominated by Virginia's economic and political elites.

Dominion of New England

One exception to self-governance was the **Dominion of New England** (1686–1689), which was established by James II to break the power of the New England Confederation. It formed a colonial alliance among Rhode Island, Massachusetts, Connecticut, and New Hampshire. The tightening of British control appeared necessary because the Massachusetts Bay Colony seemed out of control (its charter was revoked when it failed to obey the orders of Charles II, James' predecessor).

King James sent an extremely unpopular governor, Sir Edmund Andros, to rule the colonial Dominion. Andros enforced the Navigation Acts (which were largely being ignored), severely restricted or abolished town meetings, and dismissed local legislatures. Andros heavily taxed the region, revoked land titles, and ignored the recommendations of a colonial advisory council.

Needless to say, Andros was unpopular with the colonists, who considered Andros arrogant and rude. In 1688, Britain experienced a **Glorious Revolution** (King James II was overthrown in favor of William and Mary of Orange). When news reached the colonies, a Boston mob overthrew Andros and sent Increase Mather (a minister) to appeal for a new Massachusetts charter, which was granted. The long-lasting consequences of the colonial Dominion, however, were associated with more secular forms of government (the region had been substantially influenced by the Puritans) and a growing resentment of imperialist power and rule.

Chapter Review Practice Questions

Practice questions are for instructional purposes only and may not reflect the format of the actual exam. On the actual exam, questions will be grouped into sets. Each set contains one source-based prompt (document or image) and two to five questions.

Multiple-Choice Questions

Questions 1–3 refer to the following image.

SR. NATHANIEL BACON.
From an Original at the Lord Viscount Grimston's, at Gorhambury.

Source: Thomas Chambers, "Sir Nathaniel Bacon," 1762.

1. Based on your knowledge of U.S. history, the image above best supports which of the following conclusions?

   A. Nathaniel Bacon was a poor farmer who was fed up with his mistreatment by the British king.

   B. Nathaniel Bacon was a member of Governor Berkeley's council who led an infamous colonial rebellion.

   C. Nathaniel Bacon was a governor of Jamestown who pardoned Indians and failed to protect frontiersmen.

   D. Nathaniel Bacon was an indentured servant who garnered wealth and property through slavery.

2. Based on your knowledge of U.S. history, which of the following best explains the cause of Nathaniel Bacon's behavior?

   A. Wealthy landowners were being pushed onto the frontier in search of good land to grow tobacco.
   B. The Tobacco Inspection Acts gave the gentry too much power.
   C. Slavery was being used instead of white indentured servitude as the primary labor source.
   D. Frontiersmen believed that the colonial governor only protected the rich and his own interests.

3. Based on your knowledge of U.S. history, which of the following best describes *indentured servitude* as it was practiced in North America?

   A. A promise for a specific period of labor in exchange for passage to the American colonies
   B. The intent to enslave someone for a lifetime
   C. Selling oneself for property or cash in order to pay for debts or escape prison
   D. The service of women in the colonies, who were enslaved in everything but name

Questions 4–6 refer to the following excerpt.

For we must consider that we shall be as a city upon a hill. The eyes of all people are upon us. So that if we shall deal falsely with our God in this work, we have undertaken, and so cause him to withdraw his present help from us, we shall be made a story and a by-word through the world. We shall open the mouths of enemies to speak evil of the ways of God, and all professors for God's sake. We shall shame the faces of many of God's worthy servants, and cause their prayers to be turned into curses upon us till we be consumed out of the good land whither we are a going.

—Source: John Winthrop, "City upon a Hill," 1630. A concept taken from a Christian biblical parable of Salt and Light, "You are the light of the world. A city set upon a hill cannot be hidden."

4. Winthrop's speech best exemplifies which of the following in American colonial development?

   A. The Quakers' belief in a tolerant society that would practice gender equality and a positive relationship with Native Americans
   B. The Pilgrims' reverence of the Mayflower Compact
   C. The Puritans' dedication to creating a religious society that would serve as an example for the world
   D. Virginians' respect for God and the Queen

5. Based on the views expressed in the excerpt, Winthrop would most likely have been associated with which of the following colonies?

   A. Virginia
   B. Pennsylvania
   C. Maryland
   D. Massachusetts

6. Based on your knowledge of U.S. history, which of the following most accurately describes British American northern and southern colonies?

A. New England had a mixed economy and was settled by religious people who formed family units in villages and towns.

B. New England and the middle colonies were dominated by an agricultural economy and were colonized by joint-stock companies intending to make a profit.

C. Virginia was known as the breadbasket of the New World, exported grain, and was more religiously tolerant than other regions in British America.

D. The colonies were settled by the people of England; therefore, the northern and southern colonies were not really different.

Answers and Explanations

Multiple-Choice Questions

1. **B.** To answer this question, you must look carefully at the image and draw from your knowledge of colonial history. Choice B mentions Governor Berkeley and identifies Bacon as a member of the council, suggesting that he is a property owner since only property owners could hold an official position. Bacon also appears to be a wealthy man in the image (which is reflected in his clothing). The portrait links Bacon to public office, which only a member of the gentry could hold in colonial America. Choice B also mentions the rebellion (Bacon's Rebellion of 1676), which is an important event in colonial history. Bacon led farmers and former indentured servants in a rebellion which targeted Indians rather than pardoned them, eliminating choice C. Bacon was neither a farmer nor an indentured servant himself, eliminating choices A and D.

2. **D.** Frontiersmen believed that the colonial governor only protected the rich and his own interests, choice D. Bacon's followers knew about Governor Berkeley's trade with friendly Native Americans. Bacon resented Berkeley's hesitancy to allow yeomen farmers to slaughter innocent tribes in retaliation for attacks on their region. This question could have been solved through the process of elimination. Yeomen were pushed to the frontier, not the wealthy elites, eliminating choice A. Based on colonial history, you know that the Tobacco Inspection Acts were implemented in 1730, eliminating choice B. If you know slavery became the primary labor source as a result of (not before) Bacon's Rebellion, choice C can also be eliminated.

3. **A.** Based on history, colonists practiced indentured servitude. Passage to the New World was given to persons in exchange for approximately 4 to 7 years of labor, choice A. Choice B describes slavery. Choices C and D were not labor systems that existed among the colonies.

4. **C.** Winthrop's speech exemplifies the Puritans' dedication to creating a religious society that would serve as an example for the world, choice C. Even if you are not familiar with John Winthrop as a Puritan leader, you can easily eliminate choices A and D because the text hints at shame if the audience doesn't live up to what Winthrop is suggesting (hinting that they are supposed to serve as an example). Since the excerpt fails to mention government, it is also unlikely that choice B is the answer.

5. **D.** John Winthrop was one of the leading founders of the Massachusetts Bay Colony, choice D, which was established by Puritans in order to serve as a religious example (a "city on a hill") to the world. Not doing so would be considered shameful for the Puritans, which Winthrop directly expresses in the excerpt. The Quakers of Pennsylvania (a middle colony) were also religious, but sought to live in harmony with others rather than serve as an example for God, eliminating choice B. The Virginians, choice A, sought to make money with their colony; Maryland, choice C, was a proprietary colony.

6. **A.** New England was characterized by religion, towns, and mixed economies of fishing, lumbering, and commerce, choice A. Known as the breadbasket of the New World, southern colonies like Virginia and the middle colonies, not New England, were dominated by agriculture and cash-crop farming, eliminating choices B and C. Choice D is incorrect because each of the colonial regions—southern, New England, and the middle colonies—had distinct governing, geographic, and economic features.

Chapter 6
Period Three: Revolutionary America (1754 to 1800)

Period Three explores the events of the American Revolution and the formation of a new nation.

- Pre-Revolutionary Events (1754 to 1775)
- The American Revolution (1775 to 1783)
- The Role of Women in the American Revolution
- The Formation of a New Nation (1783 to 1791)
- The United States Constitution (1787)
- The Early Republic (1789 to 1800)
- Foreign Affairs

Overview of AP U.S. History Period Three

Chapter 6 guides you through an understanding of what influenced American colonists to rebel and fight the British and how the United States progressed as a nation in its early years. The historical developments discussed in this chapter explore the study topics related to the American Revolution, including the pre- and post-revolutionary events that are specific to the APUSH exam.

Use the chart below to guide you through what is covered on the exam. The curriculum contained in this chart is an abridged version of the concept outlines with topic examples. Visit https://apstudent. collegeboard.org/apcourse/ap-united-states-history/ for the complete updated APUSH course curriculum descriptions and key concepts.

AP U.S. History Key Concepts (1754 to 1800)	
Key Concept	**Specific Content**
KEY CONCEPT 3.1: THE AMERICAN REVOLUTION **Britain's attempts to assert tighter control over its North American colonies and the colonial resolve to pursue self-government led to a colonial independence movement and the Revolutionary War.**	The competition among the British, French, and Native Americans for economic and political advantage in North America culminated in the French and Indian War (which became part of the Seven Years' War in Europe), in which Britain defeated France and allied with Native Americans. The desire of many colonists to assert ideals of self-government in the face of renewed British imperial efforts led to a colonial independence movement and war with Britain.

Continued

Key Concept	Specific Content
KEY CONCEPT 3.2: A NEW NATION **The American Revolution's democratic and republican ideals inspired new experiments with different forms of government.**	The ideals that inspired the revolutionary cause reflected new beliefs about politics, religion, and society that had been developing over the course of the 18th century. After declaring independence, American political leaders created new constitutions and declarations of rights that articulated the role of the state and federal governments while protecting individual liberties and limiting both centralized power and excessive popular influence. New forms of national culture and political institutions developed in the United States alongside continued regional variations and differences over economic, political, social, and foreign policy issues.
KEY CONCEPT 3.3: THE EARLY REPUBLIC **Migration within North America and competition over resources, boundaries, and trade intensified conflicts among peoples and nations.**	In the decades after American independence, interactions among different groups resulted in competition for resources, shifting alliances, and cultural blending. The continued presence of European powers in North America challenged the United States to find ways to safeguard its borders, maintain neutral trading rights, and promote its economic interests.

Significant Themes

Now that we've discussed the curriculum, let's discuss the significant themes related to this period. The theme-related study questions that follow will help you make mental connections to the context of the "big picture" of this time period. Keep in mind that these questions often overlap and apply to other themes of social, political, religious, geographic, ideological, technological, and economic developments.

Glance through the study questions before you start the review section. Take notes, highlight questions, and write down page number references to reinforce your learning. Refer to this list until you feel comfortable with your knowledge of the material.

Study Questions Related to Significant Themes for Period Three

Theme 1: American and National Identity

1. What were the British colonists' principles? (Hint: The British colonists' principles were based on the Enlightenment ideals that emphasized natural rights and equality. The foundation of the U.S. Constitution was based on these fundamental principles.)

2. How did slavery and the language of freedom affect the relationship between northern and southern states? What kinds of debates and compromises occurred as a result? (Hint: The language of the U.S. Constitution was created through a series of compromises between free states and slave states. References to "citizens" included only white male property owners. Abolitionism created growing divisions between the North and South.)

Theme 2: Politics and Power

1. How and why did salutary neglect end? (Hint: Salutary neglect was the failure of the British to strictly enforce laws; it ended as the result of the French and Indian War.)

2. Who were the key leaders in the independence movement and how did they object to the taxes imposed by the British? (Hint: The Sons of Liberty objected to British Parliament's taxation laws without colonial representation and formed boycotts, protested, and destroyed tea in the Boston Tea Party. Also see Thomas Paine's *Common Sense*.)

3. What were the key battles of the American Revolution and why were they important? (Hint: Battle of Trenton—inspired colonists; Battle of Saratoga—a turning point; and Battle of Yorktown—final defeat of the British.)

4. What were the problems with the Articles of Confederation? How were they fixed? (Hint: The Articles of Confederation was the first form of government for the 13 colonies. It was designed to impose a semblance of unity, but limited federal control so the new states didn't feel threatened. It was replaced with the U.S. Constitution.)

Theme 4: Culture and Society

1. What was "republican motherhood" and why was it important? (Hint: Republican motherhood was the term used to define women's roles in society during the Revolution—i.e., educating women not for personal enrichment, but for the ability to educate the next generation of republican citizens.)

2. What was the advice of George Washington in his Farewell Address? (Hint: Washington warned against divided political *factions* (parties), encouraged neutrality in foreign conflicts, and discouraged foreign alliances.)

Theme 6: Geography and the Environment

1. What role did Native Americans play in the events that led to the American Revolution? (Hint: The French and Indian War.)

2. How did Native Americans affect the new nation? (Hint: The Land Ordinance of 1785 set up a system of townships out of unsettled lands in the west, but it created a 10-year conflict (1785–1795) between Native Americans and the newly formed U.S. In 1787, the Northwest Ordinance banned slavery and the statehood process.)

Theme 7: America in the World

1. What was the British perspective of American colonists? (Hint: The British believed that they were protecting American colonists, providing them with economic opportunities for trade, and sharing British culture. They simply desired to pay the debts the colonists were accumulating, therefore, they did not believe it was unfair to tax the colonists.)

2. What were the domestic and global impacts of the American Revolution? (Hint: Think about the way the new government was formed, the retention of slavery as an economic system, and the French Revolution.)

3. What were some of the foreign policy decisions of George Washington? How did John Adams make things better or worse? (Hint: Washington urged his fellow citizens to seek out beneficial economic relationships with all countries, but not to become involved in politics. He urged Americans to stay neutral in foreign affairs. Adams signed the Alien and Sedition Acts, which allowed the government to imprison or deport foreigners—mostly those who spoke against the president or Congress.)

Important Events, Terms, and Concepts

The list below shows important events, terms, and concepts that you should be familiar with on the APUSH exam. These and other important terms are printed in boldface throughout the chapter. Because the APUSH exam requires you to pay attention to the historical context and connections rather than details, don't bother memorizing the terms now. Simply place a check mark next to each as you study. You can return to this list to review as often as necessary. After you finish the review section, you can reinforce what you have learned by working through the practice questions at the end of this chapter. Answer explanations provide further clarification into perspectives of U.S. history.

Event/Term/Concept	Year/Brief Description	Study Page
French and Indian War	**1754–1763.** A conflict between the British and French that also involved each country's colonists and Native American allies. It resulted in the end of salutary neglect (see Chapter 5) in the British colonies.	p. 109
Sugar, Stamp, and Quartering Acts	**1764–1765.** Legislation passed by the British to which the colonists objected, mainly because they were being taxed without representation in Parliament.	p. 111
Sons of Liberty	**1765–1776.** A secret society that often violently attacked British officials who attempted to enforce much-opposed British taxes. The Sons of Liberty were responsible for the Boston Tea Party in 1773.	p. 111
Battles of Lexington and Concord	**1774.** Battles that began the American Revolution.	p. 112
Continental Association	**1774.** Formed to organize non-importation and non-exportation agreements in objection to British policies.	p. 112
Declaration of Independence	**1776.** A document written by Thomas Jefferson to declare independence from Britain that included a list of grievances and rights according to Enlightenment principles of natural law and equality.	p. 113
First and Second Continental Congresses	**1774–1783.** The colonists sent representatives to these to object to British laws and petition for negotiation. After the Battles of Lexington and Concord, the representatives governed the colonies and managed the war.	pp. 112–113
Articles of Confederation	**1777 (ratified 1781).** First form of government for the newly independent states. Under the Articles, the states retained their sovereignty but were unified under the banner of a centralized general government authorized to conduct the war against Britain, deal with foreign governments, and handle territorial disputes with Native Americans. It was replaced by the U.S. Constitution in 1787.	p. 119

Event/Term/Concept	Year/Brief Description	Study Page
U.S. Constitution and the Bill of Rights	**1787.** The U.S. Constitution created a federal form of government in which power is distributed geographically between a central government and regional or state governments. (See Constitutional Convention, below.) **1791.** The Bill of Rights was the first 10 amendments to the Constitution, including freedom of speech, religion, and the press as well as the right to bear arms, protection from unlawful searches and seizures, and the right to reject citizen housing of soldiers.	pp. 120–121
Northwest Ordinance	**1787.** Provided a way for the federal government to add new states and territories and banned slavery above the Ohio River.	pp. 122–123
John Locke and Jean-Jacques Rousseau	Enlightenment philosophers whose preaching of natural rights, liberty, and checks on government inspired Americans to rebel against Britain and create a never-before-seen republican system of rule.	p. 110
Patriots and Loyalists	Colonists who held opposing viewpoints. Patriots supported the war of independence; Loyalists felt it was treasonous and supported the British.	p. 113
Federalists and Anti-Federalists	Opposing groups that arose during the ratification of the Constitution. These groups would eventually become the basis for the nation's first political parties.	p. 121
Constitutional Convention	**1787.** Held in Philadelphia after Shays' Rebellion, this convention was organized to improve the Articles of Confederation, which had not led to an effective federal government.	p. 119
Alien and Sedition Acts	**1798.** Legislation that limited and punished particular actions of immigrants and Jeffersonian Republicans. They were objected to as unconstitutional by the Kentucky and Virginia Resolves. The Acts were repealed in 1802.	p. 127
Abolition	Movement to end slavery that began in the late 18th century. Until the Revolution, few Americans fought vocally and openly for the abolition of slavery. As the 1760s dawned and Americans began denouncing English tyranny and proclaiming their own rights to liberty, many recognized the contradictions in their arguments, given the existence and acceptance of slavery, and started taking action.	pp. 117–119

Chapter Review

For Period Three, content knowledge focuses on the causes and consequences of the American Revolution, the philosophical influence of Enlightenment thinkers on the revolutionary movement, and the various experiments that the newly independent Americans undertook to create a government that rejected the tyranny and absolutism of the Old World. The chapter also covers disputes with Native Americans as the United States expanded its boundaries westward and diplomatic challenges at home and abroad.

Heads Up: What You Need to Know

As you study the topics related to the APUSH exam for this period, be sure that you can identify and describe the following:

1. Identify and describe the events leading to the conflict between the British and the colonists. For example, the French and Indian War, the Proclamation Act, and the British taxation laws.

2. Describe the philosophy that inspired the war. For example, the European Enlightenment.

3. Explain the significance of the major events and developments (who were the key leaders?). For example, the Battles of Lexington and Concord, the Second Continental Congress, the Declaration of Independence, the Battle of Saratoga, and the Treaty of Paris.

4. Identify and explain the domestic and international impacts of the war. For example, **Domestic:** The roles of women and slavery, the division of northern and southern states, the Articles of Confederation, and the Declaration of Independence. **International:** Treaty of Paris, spread of revolutionary ideas inspired a shift from monarchical regimes, the French Revolution, and British territorial losses.

The following diagram covers events from 1754 to 1783. It will help you conceptualize the time frame and understand how these events are interconnected.

American Revolution Timeline (1754 to 1783)

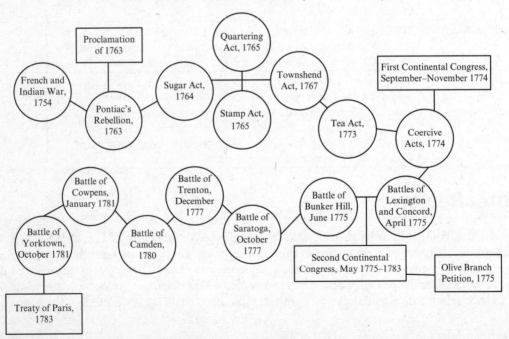

TEST TIP: Two major wars are covered in this chapter: the French and Indian War and the American Revolution, plus several additional armed conflicts with Native Americans. As a reminder, the AP U.S. History curriculum does not emphasize military history. You are not expected to acquire detailed knowledge about battles and tactics, generals and enlisted men, advances and retreats, etc. However, you should know about the overall strategies, turning points, advantages, and disadvantages that impacted the outcomes where noted in the AP U.S. History Key Concept outline. For the most part, the content and curriculum involving wars are about the social, economic, geographic, and political implications of the conflicts.

Pre-Revolutionary Events (1754 to 1775)

To understand the reasons for the American Revolution, it is important to first be familiar with the growing conflict between the colonies and Britain. The main developments surrounding these pre-war developments include the French and Indian War, European Enlightenment, the Proclamation Act, and taxation laws.

The French and Indian War (1754–1763)

British salutary neglect (British failure to strictly enforce laws) came to an end as a result of the **French and Indian War,** which was part of a global conflict that is referred to as the Seven Years' War (1756–1763) in European history. Britain and France had been engaged in conflict for European dominance and a larger imperial struggle for North American territory for over a century.

Causes and Consequences of the French and Indian War	
Causes	**Consequences**
After years of skirmishing between the French and British and their various Native American allies over territory and control of the fur trade, a showdown over claims to the Ohio River Valley (instigated by a young George Washington) prompted a conflict in the 1750s, the outcome of which would determine which of the two imperial powers would be dominant in North America. In search of new land to settle, Virginian traders and farmers moved west of the Appalachian Mountains just as the French were expanding south from Canada or east from the Great Lakes into the same region. Both nations claimed the land and built forts along the river, but since the British heavily outnumbered the French, they decided to force the French to leave. The Virginia militia, which was led by a young George Washington, was commissioned to gather information about a French stronghold, Fort Duquesne, in 1754. On the way to the fort, his troops and their Iroquois allies ran into a French scouting party, whom they obliterated at the Battle of Jumonville.	**Americans aided the British.** Professional British soldiers (with the help of the colonists and some of their Native American allies) ended up winning the war and capturing Lake Ontario, Quebec, Montreal, and Detroit. The British angered some of the colonists for three reasons: 1) the British recruited militias to fight with them in the French and Indian War, 2) the British demanded that the colonists pay their own war debts, and 3) the British limited the colonial settlements after the war. **Native American divisions.** The Native Americans were split in their loyalties; they did not fight only with the French, as the name of the war suggests. Some tribes viewed the French as important protectors and trading partners, and others were more loyal to the British. Regardless of their European allies, native villages and crops suffered greatly because battles often took place on their land. The same type of native division and destruction occurred during the American Revolution. **France was driven out of North American territories east of the Mississippi.** In 1763, the war ended with the **Treaty of Paris,** which granted the British large portions of French territory, including Canada and the Appalachian territory up to the Mississippi River. Native Americans' land was given away without their consent. As a result, many tribes felt betrayed by their European allies. **Britain had dominance and territorial gains in North America.** To keep Britain out of its lands in the west (Louisiana), France gave the Louisiana Territory to Spain. The Spanish then gave Florida to the British. **The French and Indian War sparked a turning point in the relationship between the British Empire and the British American colonies.** Britain had incurred a heavy financial debt to fight the war. The British began to take a much more active role in consolidating their empire and incorporating it into their mercantilist system. Parliament believed that the American colonists should pay their fair share of the war's cost. Parliament's attempts to enforce Crown policy on its existing American colonies from this point forward put Britain and its colonies on a collision course, which culminated in the American Revolution.

Heads Up: What You Need to Know

On the APUSH exam, you should be familiar with the **European Enlightenment** (also known as the Age of Reason). It changed the colonists' worldview and was one of the driving forces behind the American Revolution and the Declaration of Independence.

European Enlightenment

Although many 18th-century philosophers were quite different, the intellectual movement sparked by their collective work is known as the European Enlightenment (known as the **Age of Reason**). Enlightenment thinkers promoted the use of reason and knowledge to improve the conditions of society. They held that a nation's progress could be achieved through the application of science and rationality to complex social, political, economic, and cultural problems.

Before the Enlightenment, Europeans generally followed the unquestionable authority of the monarchy and the Church. Enlightened ideas sparked *humanism* (individual knowledge and critical thinking), *rationalism* (knowledge based on reasoning), and *empiricism* (truth determined by examining concrete, observable facts).

When writing the Declaration of Independence, Thomas Jefferson drew from Enlightenment thinkers like **John Locke** and **Jean-Jacques Rousseau,** who promoted *egalitarianism* (equality), liberty, a *social contract* (an agreement between a government and people), and *republicanism* (a government founded on the power of the people). In the Declaration, Jefferson stated that all citizens (meaning all white male property owners) were entitled to natural rights of life, liberty, and property. As Locke advocated, Jefferson rejected the "divine right" of a monarchical king to rule and declared the colonies free.

Did you know? In a letter to his friend William C. Jarvis, Jefferson wrote, "I know of no safe depositary of the ultimate powers of society, but the people themselves; and if we think them not enlightened enough to exercise their control with a wholesome discretion, the remedy is not to take it from them, but to inform their discretion by education." Jefferson expressed a commonly held belief among Enlightenment thinkers—ultimate sovereignty lies with the people and is superior to other forms of government that are based on absolutism and the "divine right of kings," but a sovereign nation cannot function if the people are uneducated and uninformed.

Proclamation Act (1763)

In 1763, a Native American Ottawan chief named Pontiac led a revolt of several western tribes that formed a confederation that was growing tired of infringements upon their land. Native attacks on white settlements caused frontier colonists to once again call on the British military to save them. **Pontiac's Rebellion** substantiated the British belief that the colonists would continue to cause problems that would cost Britain a substantial amount of money to solve. Britain reassessed its handling of colonial affairs and passed the **Proclamation Act of 1763,** which forbade colonists from moving west of the Appalachian Mountains. Although it was intended to prevent hostilities, the act simply angered white colonists, who believed they had a right to expand.

Taxation Laws (1764 to 1774)

To pay for the war and colonial expenses, Britain decided to create laws (acts) to increase colonists' taxes. The timeline of the acts in the table below will help you understand the sequence of events that led to the growing tensions between Britain and the colonies.

Taxation Laws and the Colonists' Response		
Legislation	**What It Did**	**Colonists' Response and Consequences**
Sugar Act (1764)	Taxed non-British imported sugar and molasses.	The Sugar Act, also known as the American Revenue Act, was enacted to boost Britain's economy and force colonists to trade with Britain. Because there was a simultaneous crackdown on the Navigation Acts (which made smuggling more difficult), merchants and shippers suffered most, especially in New England. Colonists objected to the new tax and boycotted British luxury imports. British merchants who were losing money then pressed Parliament to repeal the Sugar Act, which it did in 1766.
Quartering Act (1765)	Required colonists to provide food and housing to British soldiers.	Britain assigned an army in the colonies to protect the frontier. Parliament passed the Quartering Act to require colonists to shelter and feed the troops. Colonists strongly objected to having British troops in their homes. Some colonial leaders suggested that troops be housed on remote farms or in suburban public houses (which was denied). Others simply refused to comply with the army's demands or asked for funds to build barracks, which allowed them to circumvent the act until 1774 (see the Coercive Acts, below).
Stamp Act (1765)	Taxed a variety of documents (registration of legal papers and the purchase of newspapers, pamphlets, etc.); stamps were placed on the documents to show the tax had been paid.	The Stamp Act mostly irritated the *gentry* (high social class), publishers, and merchants because they were the ones who had to pay the tax. A Stamp Act Congress made up of nine colonies met in New York to object to the taxation. The Virginia Resolves, written by Patrick Henry, noted that Parliament had no right to tax the colonies without colonial representation. The **Sons of Liberty** (a secret society) also formed in Boston to attack British officials, especially stamp distributors and tax collectors who were often "tarred and feathered." Colonists boycotted British goods, and British merchants once again objected to the loss of income. In 1766, the British Parliament repealed the Stamp Act.
Townshend Acts (1767)	Taxed imports like paper, tea, glass, and paint, to pay royal officials in the colonies who had previously answered to colonial assemblies for their salaries.	A series of acts implemented by Charles Townshend, British chancellor of the Exchequer. Colonists hated this act because it gave the British the right to search their homes and businesses to look for smuggled goods. The colonists once again boycotted British goods, protested the legislation, and through the Daughters of Liberty, promoted the domestic production of cloth and "homemade" goods. In 1768, the boycott resulted in the British troops' occupation of Boston. British troops were called in to uphold the act and were verbally attacked by a mob and pelted with objects. In the confusion, the troops shot into the crowd and killed five rioters (known as the **Boston Massacre**). The public outcry and the fact that the British were still losing more money than they were making caused Parliament to repeal all taxation acts—except the tax on tea—in 1770.

Continued

Legislation	What It Did	Colonists' Response and Consequences
Tea Act (1773)	A tea monopoly that allowed only the British East India Company (which was almost bankrupt) to sell to the colonists.	Colonists protested the monopoly by preventing tea ships from entering harbors, burning tea, and locking warehouses. Members of the Sons of Liberty disguised themselves as Native Americans, boarded three ships in Boston Harbor, and dumped over 300 chests of tea into the water. This historical event became known as the **Boston Tea Party.**
Coercive Acts (1774)	Angered by the tea party, the British Parliament passed severe laws to punish the colonists.	Also known as the Intolerable Acts to the colonists, the Coercive Acts were considered a threat not just to Massachusetts, but to the liberty of all colonists. Britain closed the port of Boston until payment was received for the ruined tea, reduced the power of the Massachusetts legislature, expanded the Quartering Act, and allowed royal officials accused of crimes to be put on trial in England. The Coercive Acts inspired all of the 13 colonies to meet at the **First Continental Congress** (except Georgia, which wanted British help to manage hostile Native Americans). Representatives at the Congress created the **Continental Association,** an organization designed to lead the ongoing boycotts, and declared the Coercive Acts void. Colonists also supported the *Suffolk Resolves* (Massachusetts' declaration to stop exporting to Britain if the acts weren't repealed in a year) and formally petitioned King George III for assistance. The king responded by sending more troops to oppose the rebels.

The American Revolution (1775 to 1783)

Britain's road to Concord (April 18, 1775). British General Thomas Gage had been in North America since 1754. Gage served in the French and Indian War and during Pontiac's Rebellion. He returned to England in 1773, but was recalled to America when colonial tensions rose in 1774. Less than a year after he was appointed military governor of Massachusetts, he gathered British troops from all over the northern colonies to set up a *garrison* (fort) in Boston. In April 1775, he ordered 700 men to march to Concord, where it was rumored that the colonial militia was stockpiling weapons. Gage's intention was to seize the weapons and arrest the rebel leaders.

The war begins at the Battle of Lexington (April 19, 1775). Paul Revere, a patriotic supporter, learned of Gage's plan and warned the *colonial minutemen* (militiamen who were ready for battle at a "minute's" notice) that the *British Red Coats* (British soldiers) were coming. On the way to Concord, the British killed eight colonists at Lexington in a brief skirmish, which became the "shot heard round the world" that marked the beginning of the revolution. When they reached Concord, the British found nothing. The colonial militia, who had scattered after Lexington, regrouped to engage the British after they heard about the Battle of Lexington. The inexperienced militiamen used guerilla-fighting techniques to gain an unexpected victory at Concord against the soldiers (their success may also be attributed to their numbers—they more than doubled the amount of British soldiers).

The **Battles of Lexington and Concord** are considered the beginning of the American Revolution, but keep in mind they happened before the colonists declared war. The Battle of Lexington began as a skirmish. It was not originally intended to be a war to gain American independence.

TEST TIP: The American poet and philosopher Ralph Waldo Emerson wrote a poem about the start of the American Revolution called the "Concord Hymn" (1837). Use the line from his poem, "shot heard round the world," as an example in your free-response question about the outbreak of the American Revolution.

Second Continental Congress (May–July 1775). Frustrated by King George's failure to respond to their grievances and the military battles that had occurred at Lexington and Concord, representatives from the 13 colonies decided to meet in a Second Continental Congress in May 1775. Because the fighting continued, they agreed to place George Washington at the head of the Continental Army, but colonists still argued about how far they should press the British government. Many colonists had never been good at unifying and others felt rebellion was treasonous. In an effort to compromise and ease tensions, the Congress made one last appeal to King George in July 1775. Known as the **Olive Branch Petition,** the men asked to negotiate, but their efforts were rejected by Britain.

Siege of Boston (April 19, 1775–March 17, 1776). The **American Continental Army** (formed by the colonies after the outbreak of war) immediately began the **Siege of Boston,** which allowed colonists to eventually retake the city. During the siege, the **Battle of Bunker Hill** (June 17, 1775) was fought for control of the Charlestown Peninsula and the hills located across the harbor. Because it was technically a victory for the British, the conflict enabled them to evacuate the city, but the strength of the colonial forces once again surprised the British. As a result, the British suffered more casualties, fired Gage (he was replaced by William Howe in October), and began taking the Continental Army more seriously. The British even became convinced they could not defeat the unruly rebels without hiring foreign mercenaries (mostly German Hessians) to assist them.

Declaration of Independence (July 4, 1776). As a result of Britain's refusal to negotiate with American colonists, the Congress began to do more than just manage the colonial war effort—it began to run the colonies. The Congress also sent a minister to Britain's old enemy, France, to gather international support (Ben Franklin took over this job several months later) and moved slowly toward a **Declaration of Independence,** which was drafted by Thomas Jefferson and signed by the representatives on July 4, 1776.

Reasons for Colonial Success

When the war erupted in 1775, most people thought the British (and their colonial loyalists) would triumph over the American colonists. After all, Britain's well-organized military was one of the most powerful in the world. On the APUSH exam, you may need to explain the reasons why American colonists won, in spite of their military disadvantage over the mighty British army.

Heads Up: What You Need to Know

On the APUSH exam, it's important to note that colonists' loyalties were split throughout the war. At the start of the war, approximately one-third were **Patriots** (those who supported the revolutionaries), one-third were **Loyalists** (those who supported the British king), and the other third were neutral (they really didn't care about the conflict).

Even though Patrick Henry, a lawyer and politician, wrote a speech with a famous saying, "Give me liberty, or give me death," 10 years earlier when he responded to the Stamp Act in 1765, no real consensus about American independence existed until Thomas Paine's popular pamphlet *Common Sense* was published in January 1776. Paine made a clear argument for the creation of a republic, and more people began to side with the Patriots and support the war.

Americans were familiar with the land. Although Great Britain had one of the greatest militaries of the time period, the American Continental Army's objective was to hold on until the British submitted. While the British were trained to form lines and fire in unison, colonists tended to use trees and groundcover to hide until they were ready to attack. Note: Even though fighting the war at home was a military advantage, it was a major disadvantage after the war because of the physical destruction that it caused. Many colonists lost their homes, farms, properties, and businesses. Towns and families were torn apart when they were forced to choose sides (about 20 percent of the colonists continued to remain loyal to Britain; these Loyalists were called *Tories* by the colonists).

Americans were strongly motivated. The American Continental soldiers were much more passionate about their cause, while many British soldiers were merely following orders. For example, the winter of 1777–1778 was a low point when the colonists camped at **Valley Forge.** The American Continental soldiers suffered from food and supply shortages, poor housing, sickness, and disease. Yet, they refused to give up. George Washington's Continental Army came through the harsh conditions with an even greater dedication to continue.

Americans promised slaves freedom. Since both sides promised slaves their freedom in exchange for fighting, a number of African Americans enlisted as soldiers. African Americans responded to the Battles of Lexington and Bunker Hill, served as substitutes for the wealthy, and became gunners, sailors, and spies. The British were the first to begin the practice; however, Lord **Dunmore's Proclamation** convinced many neutral colonists in the South to join the Patriots when it freed slaves who ran to British lines to fight. Neither side was interested in equality or global emancipation. The British saw emancipation as a war aim that would allow them an advantage in a territory that was not their own. When they would run low on supplies in stockades or forts, British commanders often pushed out the very people who ran to their lines for protection or to enlist. Most colonists, including George Washington (a slave owner himself), rejected the use of freed slaves in the Continental Army until its numbers dwindled in 1777 and 1778.

American women supported the war efforts. While a few colonial women, like Deborah Sampson, dressed as men and served as soldiers and spies, most supported the war by staying at home to manage their family farms and businesses in the absence of their husbands. Some delivered food directly to troops in the field. Others worked as seamstresses, sewing uniforms and flags for the army, or followed their husbands in the army as nurses, washerwomen, and cooks.

Key Battles

No in-depth knowledge of military war history is required on the APUSH exam, but you should know some of the names and outcomes of key battles of the American Revolution.

Key Battles of the American Revolution			
Battle	Date	Description	Outcome
Battle of Trenton (New Jersey)	December 1776	Washington and his men crossed the frozen Delaware River on Christmas Day to crush the Hessian Army.	The American victory increased morale and inspired many Continental soldiers to enlist or re-enlist.
Battle of Saratoga (New York)	October 1777	The Battle of Saratoga was actually two significant battles. Although the British achieved a small victory, an 18-day battle weakened the British Army. When the Americans attacked again, the British were defeated.	Turning point in the revolution. The American victory convinced France to send them much-needed military and economic aid. France recognized the colonists and formally became their ally.

Battle	Date	Description	Outcome
Battle of Camden (South Carolina)	August 1780	This battle was part of the British "Southern Strategy" to defeat the Patriots by turning the war away from the northern ground where it was primarily fought (Boston, New York, etc.). Believing there were more Loyalists in the southern colonies who might persuade slaves to fight alongside the British, the British focused on the South. In the Battle of Camden, Americans were weakened by *dysentery* (a stomach infection), resulting in heavy losses.	A crushing defeat for the American Continentals. It resulted in British control of South Carolina.
Battle of Cowpens (South Carolina)	January 1781	American military southern campaign to reconquer South Carolina.	The American victory caused British General Charles Cornwallis to redirect British troops farther north, leading to the Battle of Yorktown.
Battle of Yorktown (Virginia)	October 1781	Americans surrounded British troops on land and French ships surrounded British troops at sea.	This was the final defeat of the British Army. The war ended October 19, 1781.

The Treaty of Paris (1783)

The war officially ended with the **Treaty of Paris** in 1783, when Benjamin Franklin, John Adams, and John Jay met with representatives of Britain. In the treaty, Britain agreed to cease all military attacks, withdraw all military troops, recognize American independence, and cede to the U.S. all territory from the Mississippi River to the Great Lakes. In return, Americans agreed to enforce the payments owed to British creditors and return property confiscated during the war so that Britain would not prosecute (or execute) the Loyalists (many of whom emigrated to England or Canada). It is important to note that most of the territory in the Treaty of Paris belonged to various Native American tribes rather than the British or the Americans. Many tribes felt betrayed by their respective allies. Conflicts over land sparked a series of domestic wars between native confederations and the U.S. in the 1780s and 1790s.

The Role of Women in the American Revolution

Heads Up: What You Need to Know

On the APUSH exam, it is important to understand that the effects of the American Revolution on women in the early republic were far-reaching, both in America and abroad. Make sure that you are familiar with the Daughters of Liberty and Republican Motherhood.

The Daughters of Liberty

The **Daughters of Liberty** searched for ways to support the revolutionary cause. Boycotts and non-importation movements, like those sparked by the Stamp Act and Townshend Acts, gave women an opportunity to support the cause since the purchase of consumer goods was often women's responsibility. Most active in the northern colonies, the Daughters of Liberty made homespun cloth and held "sewing bees" to make import of British textiles less vital. Women also went into their home gardens to create herbal concoctions used to replace British tea.

After the revolution began, many Daughters of Liberty, like Esther de Berdt Reed, continued to contribute to the cause. An ongoing problem faced by General Washington and his Continental Army was lack of funding to maintain their fighting efforts and money to pay soldiers since states could not be compelled to provide the funding Washington requested. At the urging of Reed, a group of Philadelphia's upper-class women organized themselves as the "Ladies Association of Philadelphia." The First Lady and her group made door-to-door appeals throughout the city, asking for donations that would be used to support Washington's army. Women in New Jersey, Maryland, and Virginia took up the challenge and formed their own associations. Washington suggested that a better use for the money would be for supplies and to buy cloth to manufacture uniforms. Not only did the association agree to Washington's request, they made the uniforms themselves, embroidering their names on the inside collar (also Washington's request) so the men would be aware of the support they received from mothers, wives, and daughters back home.

Republican Motherhood

Republican motherhood was not a term used in the 18th century; rather, it was coined in the 20th century to give form and definition to the cultural changes inspired by the American Revolution that influenced women's roles in the new nation. The same Enlightenment ideology that served as an inspiration for the egalitarian language of the Declaration of Independence influenced women who had actively supported the revolution to call for an expansion of their place in society. Although they were not advocating equality, they based their arguments for inclusion on the rhetoric of the revolution, which praised natural rights, called for civic activism, and promoted the sovereignty of the people.

Some ladies, including Abigail Adams, became advocates of education for women. They argued that women should receive education not for their own benefit or enrichment, but for that of their children, whom they were to teach the values of republicanism, virtuous citizenry, and self-reliance. Unfortunately, the few women who took the ideals of the revolution a step further and asked for an active role in the government were denied. Adams' appeal to "remember the ladies" in political representation was lost on male leaders like her husband John Adams, who became the second president of the United States. Men of this era considered a woman's citizenship as absorbed in the standing of her husband, father, or son; therefore, women were not given the right to influence the new government. Instead, they were tasked with republican motherhood, which encouraged them to learn democratic values in order to raise the next generation of good citizens, particularly sons who would uphold the principles of equality and freedom.

Women's responsibility for the civic virtue of the nation during this time period may have excluded direct political participation, but it opened pathways for women in succeeding generations for civic engagement through reform movements like abolition and women's rights.

Source: Jean Leon Gerome Ferris, "Betsy Ross," c. 1920. Showing the stars and stripes flag in 1777; General George Washington is seated at the left. The 13 stars represent the original 13 colonies. (Controversy surrounds the creator of the flag; it is sometimes attributed to Francis Hopkinson.)

The Formation of a New Nation (1783 to 1791)

The first attempts to establish a national government in the colonies (now called "states") were imperfect, but these foundations laid the groundwork for the Articles of Confederation and the United States Constitution.

HISTORIOGRAPHY. *Historians note that early leaders like Thomas Jefferson, John Adams, and George Washington felt that the success or failure of the American "experiment" in government would have global repercussions. Since behavior in the United States might serve as a model for other countries wishing to adopt democratic policies, political factions and divisions were initially discouraged. For example, George Washington saw them as a threat to the fledgling nation. Church and state were separated and titles of nobility were made impossible. Several states in the North even enacted gradual emancipation laws to free the enslaved.*

Individuals all over the world were inspired by the revolution's ideals and the new American republican government. For example, France (an important ally to the American Continental Army), was motivated to begin a revolution of its own in 1789—the French Revolution.

Abolition

Before we discuss the Articles of Confederation and the U.S. Constitution, it's important to understand **abolition.** The ideology of the American Revolution inspired support for a small abolitionist movement to end slavery promoted by free blacks, Quakers, and other religious sects in the colonies. It called for individual and collective political action. Enslaved African Americans, motivated by ideals of liberty and equality, began to hope that they would soon be free.

Source: John Bufford after William L. Champey, "Boston Massacre: March 5, 1770," c. 1856.

The situation was complicated by the awareness that 5,000–8,000 African Americans fought alongside the Patriots in their revolt against British tyranny and that just as many—if not more—had fought for freedom alongside the British. Some black Loyalists had even relocated to Nova Scotia or the British colony of Sierra Leone in Africa. The independence, bravery, and autonomy of these individuals threatened the stability of social and political hierarchies based on race.

Some slaves were granted freedom as a result of their owner's feelings of guilt and hypocrisy or their own military service. One American who clearly recognized the contradiction was Abigail Adams, wife of future president John Adams. She denounced the moral hypocrisy of fighting for freedom and liberty for oneself while so obviously denying it to others who were just as deserving. Dr. Benjamin Rush, himself a slave owner and a Founding Father, was forced to reconsider the practice of slavery based on the Enlightenment ideals he believed in and what he thought it meant to be a Christian. Rush wrote a scathing attack on slavery in 1773 entitled "An Address to the Inhabitants of the British Settlements in America, upon Slave-Keeping." He became an ally of Absalom Jones, a freed slave, abolitionist, and lay minister in the Methodist Church who founded the **Free African Society** in 1775. In 1784, the Free African Society was incorporated as the Pennsylvania Abolition Society, and Dr. Rush became one of its leading members, along with Thomas Paine.

In the aftermath of the revolution, other states put their ideals into action by ending slavery. The New York Manumission Society, formed in 1784, was the first anti-slavery group in that state. Yet, while many people in the northern states supported the abolition of slavery, most people in the southern states were adamantly against the emancipation of slavery.

In many southern states, the population of black Americans exceeded that of white Americans. Outnumbered, many white southerners feared freed slaves, who they believed might incite slave revolts (an anxiety that would continue until the Civil War). Furthermore, the southern economy was directly dependent upon the slave labor system for agricultural production. Patrick Henry of Virginia, for example, celebrated for his "give me liberty, or give me death" speech urging the House of Burgesses to send troops in support of the revolution, owned 65 slaves. Likewise, George Washington, president of the Constitutional Convention and first president of the United States, had over 300 slaves working his Mount Vernon estate.

TEST TIP: On the APUSH exam, remember that an important impact of the revolution was the growing sectional division between the northern and southern states that contributed to the Civil War almost a century later in 1861 (think about continuity and changes over time).

The Articles of Confederation (1777, ratified in 1781)

The first attempt to write a document to centralize government for the 13 colonies was called the **Articles of Confederation.** The 13 independent states were strongly divided and diverse. Many state representatives were concerned about the "tyrannical" power of monarchs (specifically George III, the British king). Representatives were convinced that a strong centralized government would threaten local power. Therefore, the Second Continental Congress that created the Articles and sent them to the states for ratification intentionally designed the Articles as weak. Even though the Articles were ultimately ineffective, they unified the states during the revolution, and Thomas Jefferson considered the Articles a "model" for a future government. Although the Articles gave Congress *sovereignty* (authority and power to negotiate), this first written document was generally created to ensure the independence of the states.

The Articles gave the federal government limited powers to conduct military engagements, negotiate treaties, resolve controversies among states, and settle territorial issues. However, the Articles quickly proved to be too limited to govern the country, especially after a farmers' rebellion in Massachusetts led by Daniel Shays made it clear that federal leaders didn't even have the power to contain a domestic uprising. A **Constitutional Convention** was called in 1787 to suggest possible improvements to the Articles of Confederation. Since white southerners linked their own freedom to the ability to own slaves (whom they identified as the "property" in the Declaration of Independence), state representatives had to compromise when discussing the creation of a new document.

Did you know? Shays' Rebellion (1786–1787) was directly connected to the writing of the **U.S. Constitution.** Taking place in rural Massachusetts, it was a revolt of 500 farmers who felt the wealthy men who controlled the state's government and tax collecting procedures were driving them into debt (taxes helped to pay for the war debt). Farmers borrowed money from merchants to pay their taxes, and when farmers couldn't pay the rich merchants, their farms were taken away from them in the state's courts. Since the central government was granted little power under the Articles of Confederation, it was difficult to raise an army to stop the violent protests. American leaders— fearing the vulnerability of the new country—began looking for ways to improve the ineffective central government.

The United States Constitution (1787)

Delegates met in Philadelphia in 1787 to repair the Articles of Confederation, but after many debates and counterproposals, the delegates decided to write a new document, the **U.S. Constitution.** The Constitutional Convention was presided over by George Washington, the only person who the argumentative delegates could agree on as fair and impartial. Confidentiality was strictly enforced so the public would not be aware of the debates until the final resolutions were agreed upon. The resulting U.S. Constitution, which established our current system of government, defined the scope and limits of government power. Several disputes, including those concerning slavery, divided the delegates. The Constitution was created through a series of compromises between slave states and free states, and those with large and small populations.

Key Facts about the United States Constitution

- Divided power between the states and the central government (*federalism*).
- Divided powers of government into three branches: *legislative* branch (creates laws), *executive* branch (executes laws), and *judicial* branch (interprets laws).
- Established checks and balances to ensure a balanced rule. No one branch would have too much power (only Congress could declare war, presidents could be impeached, etc.).
- Created a government to put the power in the hands of its citizens.
- Defined a system for electing representatives. Anti-Federalists opposed the Federalists because they worried that state and local communities would not have equal representation. How could one representative adequately represent thousands of people? To settle the differences, a **Great Compromise** (1787) was proposed to have proportional representation in the House of Representatives. The legislative branch of government would be made up of two houses: the **House of Representatives** and the **Senate.** The **Senate** would be composed of two individuals from each state (to appease states with small populations). The House of Representatives would be composed of a proportional number of individuals determined by population (to appease those with large populations).
- Legalized slavery (to appease the slaveholding delegates of the southern states) and slave trade could not be abolished until 1808. A fugitive slave clause required runaways to be returned to their owners.
- Considered each slave three-fifths of a person for the sake of state representation (the *Three-Fifths Compromise,* to appease delegates from states with large populations of slaves).

Federalist Papers (1787 to 1788)

Thirty-nine delegates signed the U.S. Constitution on September 17, 1787. To ensure ratification by the states, Alexander Hamilton, James Madison, and John Jay wrote the **Federalist Papers,** a large collection of 85 essays and articles that explained and justified the need for the provisions of the Constitution. The Federalist Papers outlined how the government should operate and why a powerful central government was the best choice. The Federalist Papers were published anonymously under the name "Publius." The authors, who later became known as Federalists, envisioned a large commercial republic, established a basis for judicial review, and suggested that a strong federal government was the best protection for individual rights. The authors also argued for checks and balances within the government's new system.

Federalists and Anti-Federalists

Even though Anti-Federalist papers were published to thwart the attempts of the Federalists, the Constitution was fully ratified by June 21, 1788. The Anti-Federalists lost the battle, but achieved success in 1791 when their objections were addressed through a list of 10 amendments created and added by James Madison, who was then serving in the House of Representatives. These amendments became known as the Bill of Rights and were soon ratified by the states.

Heads Up: What You Need to Know

The APUSH exam may require you to know the difference between the **Federalists** and the **Anti-Federalists,** so make sure you can compare and contrast the two. Use the table below to understand the differences. Try not to get confused by the key players. The Federalists are generally associated with Alexander Hamilton, John Adams, and, to some extent, George Washington. Anti-Federalists are often strongly connected to Thomas Jefferson. Keep in mind that James Madison, who began as a Federalist, soon switched sides to become Jefferson's protégé.

Comparing Federalist and Anti-Federalist Positions	
Federalists (Federal)	**Anti-Federalists (States)**
Key supporters who opposed the ineffective Articles of Confederation: John Adams, Alexander Hamilton, George Washington, and John Jay.	Key supporters who wanted the Articles of Confederation to be amended, not discarded: Thomas Jefferson, Samuel Adams, James Monroe, and Patrick Henry.
Advocated for a strong central government and favored limiting state power.	Advocated strong state and local governments and a weak national (federal) government. Argued that the Federalists took too much power away from the states (or "the people").
Favored a large republic to protect individual freedoms.	Favored a small republic to protect individual rights.
Supported a broad interpretation of the Constitution and initially believed the Bill of Rights was unnecessary.	Wanted a strict interpretation of the Constitution and supported the Bill of Rights.
Supported a national bank and believed the economy should be driven by manufacturing and industry (this was the start of American capitalism).	Rejected a national bank because they believed society and the economy should be driven by subsistence farming (this was based on an "agrarian myth" that was never really a widespread practice—even small farmers at least occasionally marketed cash crops).
Federalists mainly resided in urban and industrialized areas that were dominated by big business interests.	Anti-Federalists mainly resided in rural and agricultural areas.

The Bill of Rights (1791)

Although those who wrote the Constitution believed that it could stand on its own, there were others who considered a declaration of rights necessary to establish a new government. Upon the request of various states, the **Bill of Rights** (the first 10 amendments) was drafted to include the rights of states and citizens. The Bill of Rights balances the Constitution with specific prohibitions of the federal government. It includes the freedom of speech, religion, and the press as well as the right to bear arms, protection from unlawful searches and seizures, and the right to reject citizen housing of soldiers.

> TEST TIP: On the APUSH exam, you may be asked why the Bill of Rights was important to add to the Constitution. State representatives (Anti-Federalists) were afraid that a powerful federal government could abuse the individual rights of people. The Bill of Rights protected individual citizens. Think about how our nation today might be different without these protections (i.e., freedom of speech, freedom of the press, etc.).

The Early Republic (1789 to 1800)

The First Political Party System

The U.S. political system in the 21st century is dominated by two parties (the Democrats and the Republicans), but many early American leaders disliked partisanship because they believed political factions caused damaging divisions. As disparities continued between those who disagreed about the nature of power and government, however, political unions and disagreements began to spark the formation of the First Party System, which was made up of Federalists (led by Hamilton) and Anti-Federalists (led by Jefferson and Madison). The Anti-Federalists morphed into the **Democratic-Republican Party** in the early 1790s. Eventually "Democratic" was dropped from the party name, and the party soon became known as the "Republicans."

Until 1800, the Federalists dominated the government. Our first president, George Washington (1789–1797), did not belong to a political party, but when he became president, he appointed Hamilton to serve as the first Secretary of the Treasury, guiding the new economy through the establishment of the first national bank, the U.S. mint, protective tariffs, and free-trade policies with Britain. Hamilton also funded the national debt (which the states had accumulated fighting the war) and expanded domestic manufacturing.

The timeline below can help you visually understand how developments presented in this section are related to the Early Republic.

Timeline of the Early Republic

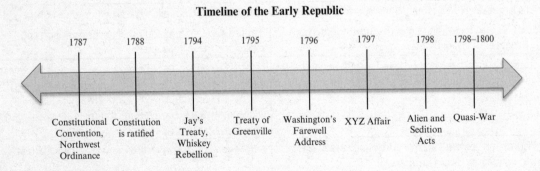

1787	1788	1794	1795	1796	1797	1798	1798–1800
Constitutional Convention, Northwest Ordinance	Constitution is ratified	Jay's Treaty, Whiskey Rebellion	Treaty of Greenville	Washington's Farewell Address	XYZ Affair	Alien and Sedition Acts	Quasi-War

Northwest Ordinance (1787)

After the Northwest Territory was granted to the U.S. in the Treaty of Paris, Congress considered the land part of the United States and was motivated to enact the **Northwest Ordinance.** The ordinance allowed the federal government to design the first organized territory of the United States by allowing for expansion through the creation of new territories and states. It also prohibited slavery above the Ohio River, which increased sectional tensions and set a precedent for the **Missouri Compromise** (a political compromise made in 1820 that allowed Missouri to be admitted to the Union as a slave state if Maine could be admitted as a free state to balance northern and southern interests). An imaginary line was also drawn across the Louisiana Territory to show a boundary between free and slave regions (see p. 154, Chapter 7).

Late 18th-Century States and Territories

Northwest Indian War (1785 to 1795)

The early 1790s led to tensions with Native Americans, who objected to the British giving away large portions of their land without their consent. The British considered the land they negotiated in the Treaty of Paris (1783) ceded to the English Crown by the French after their defeat in the French and Indian War (1754–1763). Yet much of this land was not included in the treaties that Europeans (of any nation) had negotiated with resident native tribes. Native Americans, especially those who had sided with the British in the American Revolution, felt betrayed. Native Americans considered the land their communal property and hunting grounds and became angry when white settlers' ever-increasing demand for expansion led to unauthorized "squatting" in their territories.

Members of the Wyandot (Huron), Shawnee, Delaware, and many other tribes formed a **Western Confederacy** that sought to militarily defend their lands. In 1785, the native confederacy engaged in a domestic war with a weak U.S. Army. In the early years of the conflict, the natives received ammunition and guns from the British, raided new settlements, and achieved several victories.

After suffering initial losses in what became an extended Northwest Indian War, the U.S. Army was forced to expand, which allowed it to become victorious. In 1792, President George Washington appointed a revolutionary veteran, General Anthony Wayne, to lead U.S. forces (known as the **Legion of the United States**) in defeating the native confederation. Victory finally came 2 years later at the **Battle of Fallen Timbers** (1794). The **Treaty of Greenville** (1795) ended the conflict, forcing tribesmen to turn over large sections of their region and calling for them *not* to align with any other nation (especially the British).

TEST TIP: Pay close attention to common issues with Native American land infringements. They increased tensions between white settlers and many tribes throughout U.S. history. To connect how they affected certain developments at certain times, look carefully at when, why, where, and how these conflicts arose. How do they seem to overlap both within the periods and between them? Link this to their results and see if you can identify any discernable patterns. Then examine what those patterns might mean within the larger context of history.

The Whiskey Rebellion (1794)

One of Hamilton's major mistakes was convincing Congress to impose a tax on whiskey to generate revenue in 1791. The first tax on a domestic product led to the **Whiskey Rebellion** in 1794, which was organized by farmers in Pennsylvania who often turned their surplus grain into liquor to earn extra money. As former war veterans, many believed they were upholding a "no taxation without representation" ideology and did not see the violence imposed on tax collectors as wrong. After negotiations with the rebels didn't work, President Washington was forced to lead the U.S. militia to stop the revolt. By the time the army reached Pennsylvania, the rebellion had disassembled.

TEST TIP: Be able to compare and contrast Shays' Rebellion (1786) and the Whiskey Rebellion (1794). Under the Articles of Confederation, the government had little power to prevent Shays' Rebellion, but under the U.S. Constitution, President Washington had the power to stop the Whiskey Rebellion.

Foreign Affairs

As the new leader of a young country with a brand-new form of government, George Washington was careful in the way he handled America's relationship with other nations. While the United States wanted to be recognized as a legitimate player in the world, it could not get involved in foreign affairs and wars. The United States was too heavily in debt from the war and had its own internal conflicts. Washington stressed neutrality in foreign affairs and continued to develop a friendly relationship with Great Britain.

Key Facts about Foreign Affairs in the Late 18th Century

The French Revolution (1789). The revolution in France overthrew a centuries-old monarchy in order to replace it with a republic. Many Americans supported the French Revolution because the ideals were similar to those of the American Revolution. The two revolutions certainly shared the ideas of the Enlightenment in its founding principles.

American revolutionaries were without question driven by their expectations regarding the rule of law and constitutionalism, ideas instilled by the very British government from which they won their independence. That is why a government consisting of separate branches and the issue of the Bill of Rights were so critically important. The limitations to government's authority over its people had to be imposed by checks and balances as well as further protections from abuse of authority that were clearly written and understood.

In American politics, the French Revolution became controversial, separating Federalists like Hamilton from Jefferson and his Republican supporters. Although Thomas Jefferson, the Secretary of State, looked favorably on aiding the French in the French Revolution, Washington was reluctant to assist France monetarily. France expected America's support, but Washington and his cabinet all believed neutrality was essential. The young nation was in no position to get dragged into a continental war.

> **Did you know?** One can see the fingerprints of Jefferson on the foundational document of the French Revolution, "The Declaration of the Rights of Man," drafted by Jefferson's compatriot Marquis de Lafayette. At the outbreak of the French Revolution, Jefferson was living in Paris in his capacity as U.S. Minister to France. His home was often open to Lafayette, along with his fellow moderate revolutionaries.

American and British tensions (1793). Britain and France were once again at war, and this caused the foreign sympathies of a divided U.S. government to become even more tenuous. Because they felt King Louis XVI had violated the rights of the people and were predisposed to bias against European monarchs in general, many Americans sympathized with France even though the king was executed by guillotine. Angered by the American Revolution, the refusal of many Americans to pay British debts, and what they viewed as American support for the French, the British began stopping U.S. ships and capturing American sailors (who were then forced to serve in the Royal Navy). Although this practice was nothing new (it had existed since the formation of the colonies), it intensified during this period. The British also confiscated goods headed for France. Jefferson and other **Republicans** (by then the "Democratic" part of their name had been dropped) wanted to declare war, but Hamilton and the Federalists chose to remain friendly with Britain in order to retain British trade alliances.

Jay's Treaty (1794). In 1794, Washington—who tended to side with the Federalists—sent the Supreme Court's Chief Justice (John Jay) to negotiate a treaty with the British. **Jay's Treaty** got the British to withdraw soldiers from the Northwest and set up a commission to settle border disputes. Washington, although still highly popular, came under heavy criticism for the treaty because it allowed the British to continue to board U.S. ships (they just had to pay for the goods they took) and failed to address American *impressment* (forcing someone to serve in the army or navy). Washington simply saw it as the price he had to pay for peace.

Washington's Farewell Address (1796). Preparing to leave the presidency, President Washington decided to make a valedictory address to the nation. What emerged was not just a farewell, but a presentation of the guiding principles he believed would take the nation forward into the future. He urged unity and cautioned citizens to identify as Americans first over local or regional identifications. The Union would make every part of the nation stronger, where petty differences would make it weaker and had the potential to tear the nation apart. He also warned against the growing influence of political parties, as men conspired to fulfill their own agendas instead of staying focused on the will of the majority. Washington considered parties a danger to the republic. Finally, he famously warned the nation to steer clear of foreign alliances. Well aware of the machinations used by the French and the British to try to draw the United States into their war during his administration, Washington urged his fellow citizens to seek out beneficial economic relationships with all countries, but to stay out of foreign politics. Europeans had been fighting each other for centuries, and for the United States to wade into those waters might spell disaster. He wished the country to remain neutral.

Heads Up: What You Need to Know

George Washington's **Farewell Address** is often a topic on the APUSH exam. When Washington left office in 1796, he delivered an important speech. Remember Washington's three main guiding principles from his farewell address for free-response questions: 1) a warning against the divisive nature of political factions (parties); 2) encouraging Americans to remain neutral in foreign conflicts; and 3) a warning about the dangers of forging permanent foreign alliances.

Washington's governance and effective leadership stand out in American history. His words have been used throughout history to support *bipartisanship* (agreement between two political parties) and *isolationism* (policies that are served by a nation's best interest; agreements with other nations are rejected).

Source: Constantino Brumidi, "Apotheosis of Washington," 1865. This classical Greek painting is in the rotunda dome of the U.S. Capitol Building today. Washington was held up as a godlike hero. The painting depicts George Washington seated amongst the heavens with the gods and angels (*apotheosis* refers to someone raised to a godlike status).

XYZ Affair (1797–1800). Conflicts with foreign nations continued in the early years of the republic. Trying to avoid war again in 1797, John Adams (the second U.S. president and a Federalist) sent three diplomats to France. The French foreign minister, Charles de Talleyrand, demanded a bribe before he would even see the men (not an uncommon practice in Europe). Offended, the Americans left, which created a **quasi-war** that lasted until 1800 when it was settled through the Treaty of Mortefontaine. The entire incident, known as the **XYZ Affair,** allowed Federalists to criticize Republicans for their support of France.

Alien and Sedition Acts (1798). In the middle of the tensions, Congress (which largely sided with Federalists) passed the **Alien and Sedition Acts,** a series of laws supported by Adams that limited the actions of Jefferson's Republicans and "perceived enemies" of the state (foreigners). They included legislation that postponed the citizenship of French and Irish immigrants and allowed the government to imprison or deport immigrants at will. Fines and imprisonment were imposed on those who spoke against the president or Congress. Jefferson and Madison responded with the **Kentucky and Virginia Resolves** (1788–1789), which declared the acts unconstitutional.

> **TEST TIP:** The Kentucky and Virginia Resolves become important again during South Carolina's Nullification Crisis in 1832. If you are called to write on either situation, make sure you remember their connection and discuss both.

Chapter Review Practice Questions

Multiple-Choice Questions

Practice questions are for instructional purposes only and may not reflect the format of the actual exam. On the actual exam, questions will be grouped into sets. Each set contains one source-based prompt (document or image) and two to five questions.

Questions 1–3 refer to the following image.

Source: Emanuel Leutze, *Washington Crossing the Delaware*, 1851.

1. Which of the following historical aspects of the American Revolution is portrayed in Leutze's painting?

    A. Washington's arrogance and instability as a leader
    B. The destruction of natural resources associated with General Howe's attack
    C. The Continental Army's dedication to a hopeful cause amidst cold and hardship
    D. The dawning of morning after a difficult battle in South Carolina

2. Based on your knowledge of U.S. history, which of the following most accurately describes the impact of the American Revolution?

    A. The republican language that was used to rouse the revolution held major benefits for African Americans and women.
    B. The establishment of a new democratic government inspired France and other nations around the world.
    C. New legislation connected church and state, and upheld nobility clauses.
    D. Sectional tensions were minimal since political leaders and colonists were focused on unification.

3. Based on your knowledge of U.S. history, which of the following best explains how Native Americans influenced events leading to the Revolutionary War?

    A. Pontiac's Rebellion increased tensions with the British.
    B. Native Americans were pushed farther west as fighting continued along the coast.
    C. Native American tribal regions allowed British troops to stockpile weapons.
    D. Native American leaders discouraged negotiations between the British and the colonists.

Questions 4–6 refer to the following passage.

> By referring the matter from argument to arms, a new arena for politics is struck; a new method of thinking hath arisen. All plans and proposals prior to the nineteenth of April, *i.e.* to the commencement of hostilities, are like the almanacs of the last year; which, though proper then, are superseded and useless now…
>
> I have heard it asserted by some, that as America hath flourished under her former connection with Great Britain, that the same connection is necessary towards her future happiness, and will always have the same effect. …I answer roundly, that America would have flourished as much, and probably much more, had no European power had anything to do with her. The commerce, by which she hath enriched herself are the necessaries of life, and will always have a market while eating is the custom of Europe.
>
> But she has protected us, say some. That she has engrossed us is true, and defended the continent at our expense as well as her own is admitted, and she would have defended Turkey from the same motive, viz. the sake of trade and dominion.
>
> —Source: Thomas Paine, *Common Sense,* 1776.

4. Which of the following best describes the colonial conflict that Paine is addressing in the excerpt from *Common Sense*?

    A. The frustration of the colonists with the British trade policies
    B. The tensions between different colonists, especially those arguing for either reconciliation or separation
    C. The British Parliament's concern that the Continental Army had already begun a military engagement
    D. The jealousy between British colonists in North America and those in other parts of the world

5. Based on your knowledge of U.S. history, which of the following most directly reflects a turning point in the negotiations for reconciliation between the British and the colonists?

   A. Battles of Lexington and Concord
   B. The Boston Massacre
   C. Trade boycotts
   D. Parliamentary legislation

6. The ideas expressed by Paine in the excerpt refer to which of the following British economic systems?

   A. Capitalism
   B. Monarchism
   C. Constitutionalism
   D. Mercantilism

Document-Based Question

1 question

60 minutes

Reading Time: 15 minutes (brainstorm your thoughts and organize your response)

Writing Time: 45 minutes

Directions: The document-based question is based on the seven accompanying documents. The documents are for instructional purposes only. Some of the documents have been edited for the purpose of this practice exercise. Write your response on lined paper and include the following:

- **Thesis.** Present a thesis that supports a historically defensible claim, establishes a line of reasoning, and responds to all parts of the question. The thesis must consist of one or more sentences located in one place—either the introduction or the conclusion.
- **Contextualization.** Situate the argument by explaining the broader historical events, developments, or processes that occurred before, during, or after the time frame of the question.
- **Evidence from the documents.** Support your argument by using the content of six of the documents to develop and support a cohesive argument that responds to the question.
- **Evidence beyond the documents.** Support your argument by explaining at least one additional piece of specific historical evidence not found in the documents. (Note: The example must be different from the evidence used to earn the point for contextualization.)
- **Analysis.** Use at least three documents that are relevant to the question to explain the documents' point of view, purpose, historical situation, and/or audience.
- **Historical development.** Use historical reasoning to show complex relationships among the documents, the topic question, and the thesis argument. Use evidence to corroborate, qualify, or modify the argument.

Based on the documents that follow, answer the question below.

Question 1: Evaluate the extent to which the Early Republic's political, economic, and geographic views shaped the writing and approval of the U.S. Constitution.

Document 1

Source: Thomas Jefferson, *Notes on the State of Virginia*, 1781. Written in response to France's Secretary of the French Legation to America about the natural resources and economy in Jefferson's home state, Virginia.

Those who labor in the earth are the chosen people of God, if ever he had a chosen people, whose breasts he has made his peculiar deposit for substantial and genuine virtue... Corruption of morals in the mass of cultivators is a phenomenon of which no age nor nation has furnished an example. It is the mark set on those, who not looking up to heaven, to their own soil and industry, as does the husbandman, for their subsistence, depend for it on the casualties and caprice of customers. Dependence begets subservience and venality, suffocates the germ of virtue, and prepares fit tools for the designs of ambition... While we have land to labor then, let us never wish to see our citizens occupied at a workbench, or twirling a distaff. Carpenters, masons, smiths, are wanting in husbandry: but, for the general operations of manufacture, let our work-shops remain in Europe... The loss by the transportation of commodities across the Atlantic will be made up in happiness and permanence of government. The mobs of great cities add just so much to the support of pure government, as sores do to the strength of the human body. It is the manners and spirit of a people which preserve a republic in vigor. A degeneracy in these is a canker which soon eats to the heart of its laws and constitution...

Document 2

Source: Daniel Shays' open letter to the public published in William Butler's *Hampshire Gazette*, November 15, 1786. Three years after the Treaty of Paris, Butler wrote an open letter on the front page of the *Hampshire Gazette* to keep the public aware of issues and challenges that faced the new republic.

Gentlemen,

BY information from the General Court, they are determined to call all those who appeared to stop the Court to condign punishment. Therefore I request you to assemble your men together, to see that they are well armed and equipped with sixty rounds each man, and to be ready to turn out at a minute's warning: likewise to be properly organized with officers.

I am your most obedient, and shall ever serve,

DANIEL SHAYS.

Document 3

> **Source: Alexander Hamilton, *The Federalist Papers*, No. 15, 1787.**
>
> ...the point next in order to be examined is the "insufficiency of the present Confederation to the preservation of the Union." It may perhaps be asked what need there is of reasoning or proof to illustrate a position which is not either controverted or doubted, to which the understandings and feelings of all classes of men assent, and which in substance is admitted by the opponents as well as by the friends of the new Constitution... It is true, as has been before observed that facts, too stubborn to be resisted, have produced a species of general assent to the abstract proposition that there exist material defects in our national system; but the usefulness of the concession...is destroyed by a strenuous opposition to a remedy, upon the only principles that can give it a chance of success. While they admit that the government of the United States is destitute of energy, they contend against conferring upon it those powers which are requisite to supply that energy. They seem still to aim at things repugnant and irreconcilable; at an augmentation of federal authority, without a diminution of State authority; at sovereignty in the Union, and complete independence in the members... This renders a full display of the principal defects of the Confederation necessary, in order to show that the evils we experience do not proceed from minute or partial imperfections, but from fundamental errors in the structure of the building...

Document 4

> **Source: U.S. Constitution, Article I, Section 2, Clause 3, 1787.**
>
> Representatives and direct taxes shall be apportioned among the several states which may be included within this Union, according to their respective numbers, which shall be determined by adding the whole number of free persons, including those bound to service for a term of years, and excluding Indians not taxed, three-fifths of all other persons. The actual enumeration shall be made within three years after the first meeting of the Congress of the United States, and within every subsequent term of ten years, in such manner as they shall by law direct. The number of representatives shall not exceed one for every thirty thousand, but each state shall have at least one representative...

Document 5

> **Source:** Benjamin Russell, "The Raising of the Sixth Pillar," *Massachusetts Centinel*, 1788. The illustration portrays the ratification of the Constitution. The five pillars depict the ratifying states: Delaware, Pennsylvania, New Jersey, Georgia, and Connecticut. Massachusetts was in the process of ratifying.
>
>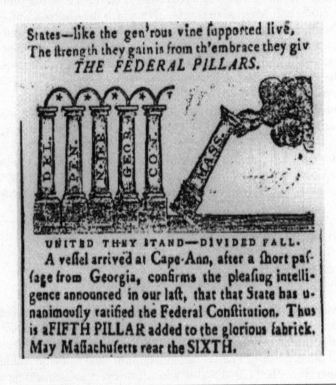
>
> States—like the gen'rous vine supported live,
> The strength they gain is from th'embrace they giv
> *THE FEDERAL PILLARS.*
>
> UNITED THEY STAND—DIVIDED FALL.
> A vessel arrived at Cape-Ann, after a short passage from Georgia, confirms the pleasing intelligence announced in our last, that that State has unanimously ratified the Federal Constitution. Thus is a FIFTH PILLAR added to the glorious fabrick. May Massachusetts rear the SIXTH.

Document 6

> **Source:** James Madison, *The Federalist Papers,* No. 51, 1788.
>
> To what expedient, then, shall we finally resort, for maintaining in practice the necessary partition of power among the several departments, as laid down in the Constitution? The only answer that can be given is, that as all these exterior provisions are found to be inadequate, the defect must be supplied, by so contriving the interior structure of the government as that its several constituent parts may, by their mutual relations, be the means of keeping each other in their proper places... In order to lay a due foundation for that separate and distinct exercise of the different powers of government, which to a certain extent is admitted on all hands to be essential to the preservation of liberty, it is evident that each department should have a will of its own; and consequently should be so constituted that the members of each should have as little agency as possible in the appointment of the members of the others. Were this principle rigorously adhered to, it would require that all the appointments for the supreme executive, legislative, and judiciary magistracies should be drawn from the same fountain of authority, the people, through channels having no communication whatever with one another...

Document 7

Source: Patrick Henry, *Foreign Wars, Civil Wars, and Indian Wars—Three Bugbears,* 1788.

In opposition to the new Constitution, Henry wrote an Anti-Federalist response to James Madison's Federalist Papers.

...If we admit this Consolidated Government, it will be because we like a great splendid one. Some way or other we must be a great and mighty empire, we must have an army, and a navy, and a number of things. When the American spirit was in its youth, the language of America was different. Liberty, Sir, was then the primary object... But now, Sir, the American spirit, assisted by the ropes and chains of consolidation, is about to convert this country to a powerful and mighty empire. If you make the citizens of this country agree to become the subjects of one great consolidated empire of America, your Government will not have sufficient energy to keep them together. Such a Government is incompatible with the genius of republicanism. There will be no checks, no real balances, in the Government...and yet who knows the dangers that this new system may produce; they are out of the sight of the common people: They cannot foresee latent consequences. I dread the operation of it on the middling and lower class of people. It is for them I fear the adoption of this system.

Answer Explanations

Multiple-Choice Questions

1. **C.** Choice C is the only possible choice. The colonists were fighting for a worthy cause of independence as they navigated the Delaware River's icy waters. The painting depicts Washington's prominent strength as he heads into battle with his Continental Army, making choice A incorrect. The men are navigating through an icy river and no other natural resources are depicted in the painting, so choice B is also incorrect. While choice D depicts the bright light of dawn in the background of dark tones, the context is not historically accurate; the crossing was in New Jersey, not South Carolina. Even if you are not familiar with this famous painting, you should be familiar with the colonists' dedication to their cause.

2. **B.** The new government established in America significantly impacted republican ideologies in other nations, choice B. France held its own revolutionary movement in 1789. African Americans and women had no legal rights (choice A), even though some slaves were freed and women were admired for their ability to become republican mothers. There were no nobility clauses, choice C, within the new government, which was based upon the "will of the people" and egalitarian language drawn from the Enlightenment that would not have supported an aristocracy. Some northern states gradually enacted emancipation laws, which increased regional tensions, making choice D incorrect.

3. **A.** The British were called on by the colonists to defeat the Native American Ottawa tribe led by their Native American chief, Pontiac; this increased Native Americans' tensions with the British, choice A. After this campaign, the British passed the Proclamation Act of 1763, which forbade the colonists to expand west of the Appalachian Mountains, making choice B incorrect. Always eager for expansion, this angered colonists and increased tensions between them and the British government. Choices C and D are not relevant.

4. **B.** Although you may have been tempted to select choice A (the frustration of the colonists with the British trade policies), Paine's passage addresses more than one reason for separation from the Mother Country. On the APUSH exam, you should be familiar with Paine's work, because he is one of the Founding Fathers of the U.S. Paine's argument must relate to more than just trade. The passage specifically responds to those colonists who argue for reconciliation, choice B. Choices C and D are incorrect because Paine is reflecting an American perspective, not a British one.

5. **A.** Paine's passage directly mentions the Battles of Lexington and Concord, choice A, by date, April 19, 1775. Paine describes the battles as "a commencement of hostilities." Choices B and C, the Boston Massacre and trade boycotts, occurred in 1767 when colonists boycotted trade and British troops shot protesters who were throwing objects at the soldiers. Choice D, the British Parliamentary legislation, is not relevant.

6. **D.** The only British economic system that fits the colonial period is mercantilism, choice D. Mercantilism was the system where royal monarchies controlled trade and economic profits. Mercantilism dominated economic trade during European expansion in North American in the 18th century. While both mercantilism and capitalism are economic systems geared toward making profits, capitalism (choice A) focuses on private enterprises. The key phrase in the question is "economic systems," eliminating the political systems listed in choices B and C.

Document-Based Question

DBQ Scoring Guide

To achieve the maximum score of 7, your response must address the scoring criteria components in the following table.

Scoring Criteria for a Good Essay	
Question 1: Evaluate the extent to which the Early Republic's political, economic, and geographic views shaped the writing and approval of the U.S. Constitution.	
Scoring Criteria	Examples
A. THESIS/CLAIM	
(1 point) Presents a historically defensible thesis that establishes a line of reasoning. (Note: The thesis must make a claim that responds to *all* parts of the question and must *not* just restate the question. The thesis must consist of *at least* one sentence, either in the Introduction or the conclusion.)	The essay provides a strong thesis with historical evidence about the development and implementation of the U.S. Constitution. This essay follows a historical line of reasoning by explaining the political, geographic, and economic tensions, and it also relates the thesis to the importance of the writing and passage of the U.S. Constitution. The essay argues that Shays' Rebellion served as a turning point in the governance of the nation and explains that compromises were necessary to ensure ratification by certain regions and political factions.

Scoring Criteria	Examples
B. CONTEXTUALIZATION	
(1 point) Explains the broader historical context of events, developments, or processes that occurred before, during, or after the time frame of the question. (Note: Must be more than a phrase or reference.)	The essay starts by contextualizing the time period, late 18th century. The essay then provides the general context of the developments surrounding the Constitution and outlines specific events that sparked the Constitutional Convention. The essay frames the context of these events by referencing the inadequacy of the Articles of Confederation and the reasons for the Articles' weakness. Further, the essay provides a broader historical understanding of the conflicts between northern and southern states, and well as conflicts between the Federalists and Anti-Federalists. This leads to the compromises made by these groups and a discussion of ratification.
C. EVIDENCE	
Evidence from the Documents **(2 points)** Uses at least *six* documents to support the argument in response to the prompt. OR **(1 point)** Uses the content of at least *three* documents to address the topic prompt. (Note: Examples must describe, rather than simply quote, the content of the documents.)	To receive the highest possible points, the response must address at least six documents that relate to the thesis. This essay utilizes all seven documents. Most of the documents are analyzed using purpose, but some require a knowledge of their context and the "big picture" events that surround them—making them relevant to the argument. For example, Document 2 relates to the ineffectiveness of the Articles of Confederation that led to the importance of the writing of the Constitution (Documents 3, 4, and 6), but then the essay goes on to discuss those who opposed the Constitution (Document 7).
Evidence Beyond the Documents **(1 point)** Uses at least one additional piece of specific historical evidence beyond those found in the documents relevant to the argument. (Note: Evidence must be different from the evidence used in contextualization.)	The body paragraphs provide specific examples of outside events that inspired the documents. The essay does this by discussing Shays' Rebellion, the Articles of Confederation, the political ideologies of the Federalists and Anti-Federalists, and the Three-Fifths Compromise.
D. ANALYSIS AND REASONING	
(1 point) Uses at least *three* documents to explain how each document's point of view, purpose, historical situation, and/or audience is relevant to the argument. (Note: References must explain how or why, rather than simply identifying.)	All seven documents utilize some element of analysis. For many of the documents, students have to use point of view to determine the author's position. They can then be examined for their purpose and applied to the argument.
(1 point) Uses historical reasoning and development that focuses on the question while using evidence to corroborate, qualify, or modify the argument. (Examples: Explain what is similar and different; explain the cause and effect; explain multiple causes; explain connections within and across periods of time; corroborate multiple perspectives across themes; or consider alternative views.)	The essay provides coherence throughout the argument and concrete examples that develop the thesis throughout the essay. It guides the reader through a chronological explanation to qualify and corroborate important events and ideologies during the American Revolutionary Era related to the U.S. Constitution. The essay ends by moving into a different time period (continuity and change over time), and concludes with the perspectives about the need for the Bill of Rights and future amendments.

Sample Response

Even though many early American leaders in the late 18th century rejected the division caused by political factions, the nation was not harmonious in the early years of the newly created republic. The United States suffered from several political, economic, and geographic tensions that distinctly affected how its government developed. Its Constitution, which outlines federal authority and guarantees citizens certain rights and privileges, was constructed through several compromises that adapted to a variety of needs and political ideologies. Although its interpretation is still debated, it remains an effective document that has been flexible enough to successfully serve the American people for over two hundred years.

After the revolution, the Articles of Confederation continued to serve as the governing document for the United States. However, as indicated by Daniel Shays' open letter (Document 2), unrest and rebellion soon arose from economic quarrels in the state of Massachusetts. In 1786, a group of farmers became disgusted with the policies of state leaders, who were driving them into debt. The farmers revolted in a series of events known as Shays' Rebellion. Since the federal government had difficulty raising an army to control the unrest, it demonstrated the deficiencies with the Articles of Confederation, leading directly to a call for a document to replace it.

The Constitutional Convention was then held in Philadelphia in 1787. Before an effective document could be written, however, several arguments developed among the delegates. For example, sectional divisions were common. Small states, located primarily in the North, were worried about representation. Pro-slavery states, located primarily in the South, wanted to ensure slavery (which their economies depended upon) would be allowed to continue (Document 4). Federalists and Anti-Federalists, whose political theories differed, also disagreed (Documents 3 and 6). Federalists, like Alexander Hamilton (Document 3), pushed for a great deal of central power through the federal government, supported manufacturing, and argued that northern and southern states could benefit from a central economy that promoted industry and marketing. Anti-Federalists, like Patrick Henry (Document 7), felt that liberty resided in local and state governments and worried about abuses of power. Like Thomas Jefferson (Document 1), they believed that the economy should be driven by subsistence farming and felt promoting urban industry would only result in a society that was greedy and corrupt.

Delegates knew that several compromises would be necessary to ensure the Constitution's acceptance by nine of the thirteen states, which was necessary for the document's ratification. The slave trade was allowed to continue until 1808, and questions of representation were addressed through the Senate (which provided for two delegates from each state) and the House of Representatives (which based representation on population). To further satisfy southern states, a clause was added that allowed slaves to be counted as three-fifths of a person. Federalists like Alexander Hamilton and James Madison (Documents 3 and 6) also published a series of essays that explained the benefits of a strong market economy and a government of the people that would contain a system of "checks and balances."

As the image regarding Massachusetts' ratification indicates (Document 5), their argument that a strong central government was necessary for a united country convinced many, but Anti-Federalists like Patrick Henry (Document 7), who eventually became Jeffersonian Democratic-Republicans, still worried over abuses of power. This led many states to call for amendments spelling out specific "freedoms." In 1791, James Madison (Document 6) wrote the Bill of Rights, ten amendments, which include freedom of the press, religion, and speech, the right to bear arms, and protection from unlawful searches and seizures. Because American citizens have demanded additional rights throughout U.S. history, other amendments have been added to the Constitution over time, including those that prohibit slavery and discrimination in citizenship, voting, and public spaces.

Chapter 7

Period Four: Early America (1800 to 1848)

Period Four explores the first half of the 19th century, when the new nation struggled to define itself, its territories, and its role as a democratic nation.

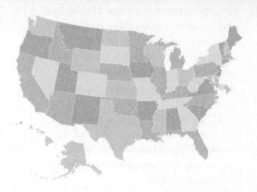

- The Jeffersonian Era (1800 to 1828)
- The War of 1812 (1812 to 1815)
- The Era of Good Feelings (1816 to 1825)
- Economics in the 19th Century
  - The Market Revolution (1815 to 1840)
  - The First Industrial Revolution (c. 1840 to c. 1870)
- Social and Political Tensions in the 19th Century
- Cultural Shifts in the 19th Century
- The Jacksonian Era (1828 to 1850)

Overview of AP U.S. History Period Four

Chapter 7 explains how America developed and expanded in these early years and covers the political, military, and economic conflicts that influenced the nation's culture, society, and geography. Topics include the Jeffersonian Era, the Era of Good Feelings, the Jacksonian Era, immigration, and tension between the northern and southern states. The presented historical developments will help you organize the curriculum and grasp specific topics that are related to the APUSH exam.

Use the chart below to guide you through what is covered on the exam. The curriculum contained in this chart is an abridged version of the concept outlines with topic examples. Visit https://apstudent. collegeboard.org/apcourse/ap-united-states-history/ for the complete updated APUSH course curriculum descriptions and key concepts.

AP U.S. History Key Concepts (1800 to 1848)	
Key Concept	Specific Content
KEY CONCEPT 4.1: POLITICAL AND NATIONAL PROGRESS **The United States began to develop a modern democracy and celebrated a new national culture, while Americans sought to define the nation's democratic ideals and change their society and institutions to match them.**	The nation's transition to a more participatory democracy was achieved by expanding suffrage from a system based on property ownership to one based on voting by adult white males, and it was accompanied by the growth of political parties. While Americans embraced a new national culture, various groups developed distinctive cultures of their own. Increasing numbers of Americans, many inspired by new religious and intellectual movements, worked primarily outside of government institutions to advance their ideals.

Continued

Key Concept	Specific Content
KEY CONCEPT 4.2: THE MARKET REVOLUTION **Innovations in technology, agriculture, and commerce powerfully accelerated the American economy, precipitating profound changes to U.S. society and to national and regional identities.**	New transportation systems and technologies dramatically expanded manufacturing and agricultural production. The changes caused by the market revolution had significant effects on U.S. society, workers' lives, and gender and family relations. Economic development shaped settlement and trade patterns, which unified the nation while also encouraging the growth of different regions.
KEY CONCEPT 4.3: EXPANSION **The U.S. interest in increasing foreign trade and expanding its national borders shaped the nation's foreign policy and spurred government and private initiatives.**	Struggling to create an independent global presence, the United States sought to claim territory throughout North America and promote foreign trade. The United States' acquisition of lands in the West gave rise to contests over the extension of slavery into new territories.

Significant Themes

Now that we've discussed the curriculum, let's discuss the significant themes related to this period. The theme-related study questions that follow will help you make mental connections to the context of the "big picture" of this time period. Keep in mind that these questions often overlap and apply to other themes of social, political, religious, geographic, ideological, technological, and economic developments.

Glance through the study questions before you start the review section. Take notes, highlight questions, and write down page number references to reinforce your learning. Refer to this list until you feel comfortable with your knowledge of the material.

Study Questions Related to Significant Themes for Period Four

Theme 2: Politics and Power

1. What kinds of events led to the demise of the Federalists and the election of Republicans? (Hint: Jeffersonian Era and the Hartford Convention when Federalists were viewed as disloyal to the Union.)

2. What led to the rise of the Whigs and Democrats? (Hint: The Corrupt Bargain of John Quincy Adams and Henry Clay led to the rise of the Whig Party and the emergence of the Second Party System.)

3. How did the federal government both stay constant and expand during this time? (Hint: Be sure to consider Thomas Jefferson's policies, the role of the Supreme Court, and economic nationalism. Even though Jefferson was instrumental in forming a political party, he claimed to dislike them; therefore, he cooperated with the Federalists. His goal was to draw Federalists into the Republican Party. John Marshall, a Federalist and Supreme Court Justice, repeatedly pitted himself against Jefferson. Marshall sought to increase the power of the federal government while Jefferson purchased the Louisiana Territory to expand an agrarian society.)

Theme 3: Work, Exchange, and Technology

1. What was the market revolution and how did it change the way the economy and society operated? What were some of the positive results of the market revolution? What were some of the negative results? (Hint: Think about industrialization and Henry Clay's plan, the American System, which encouraged industrial manufacturers and the agricultural industry to work cooperatively. Positive: New innovations, transportation, production, expansion, economic boom, and the rise of the middle class. Negative: Increased laborers (low wages for laborers and slaves) caused poor working conditions and abuses in factories and mills.)

2. How did workers' lives change? How and why did some workers begin to fight for their rights? (Hint: A new middle-class began to emerge, but laborers worked for low or minimal wages and long hours, causing extreme poverty and sectional division. Labor reform movements began to draw attention to the injustices that employers were imposing at factories and mills.)

3. What were some of the inventions that changed agricultural production in the South and the West? What did these sections of the country specialize in and how did that affect their people's worldviews? (Hint: The cotton gin, steel plows, and mechanical reapers made it possible to speed up the process of agricultural crops in the South. Expansion in the Northwest (at the time known as the West) and the shipment of goods was made possible by railroads, steamboats, and national roads. Southerners had a Jeffersonian agrarian mindset so demands for slave labor increased. The Northwest had an industrial mindset associated with trade in agricultural products like wheat, cattle, and grains.)

Theme 4: Culture and Society

1. What kinds of social, religious, economic, and political experiences shaped the American people during this era? (Hint: Political and economic corruption spread. As a result, reform, ideological, and philosophical movements began: The Second Great Awakening, Transcendentalism, abolition.)

2. What kinds of reform movements were developed during the early 19th century? (Hint: Temperance, education, prison, mental health, and abolitionist.)

Theme 5: Migration and Settlement

1. Why did Jefferson wrestle with the issue of buying the Louisiana Territory? How did this purchase affect exploration and settlement? (Hint: Jefferson believed in small government, states' rights, and an agrarian lifestyle. He wanted to expand farming and limit industrialization. Even though the purchase was not in the Constitution and he believed strictly in its power, Jefferson put aside his principles because he desired land needed for national growth and security.)

2. How did the market revolution affect patterns of migration and immigration? (Hint: Migration increased from Germany, Ireland, and China. Immigrants were drawn to America for opportunities to gain employment.)

3. How were Native Americans affected by Western migration? What did they do in response to continual encroachments on their land? (Hint: As westward expansion increased, native tribes were removed from their ancestral lands (Indian Removal Act). Even though a court decision (*Worcester v. Georgia*) ruled in favor of Native Americans remaining on their land, President Jackson disregarded the ruling, which led to the Trail of Tears in 1838.)

4. What was the Trail of Tears and what mark does it leave on American history? (Hint: The Trail of Tears was a series of forced removals of Native Americans from their territories. Native Americans were forced off their land, and thousands died as a result of their journey westward.)

Theme 6: Geography and the Environment

1. What role did Native Americans play in the events that led to the War of 1812? (Hint: Native Americans resented settler expansion and were militarily supported by the British. This caused American resentment of the British.)

Theme 7: America in the World

1. What were some of John Quincy Adams' key contributions as Secretary of State? (Hint: He became an important diplomat because he helped to create the Monroe Doctrine, one of the most important foreign policy documents in the U.S. to prevent new colonization in the Americas.)

2. Why was the Monroe Doctrine created? What were its basic characteristics and how did it affect the Western Hemisphere? (Hint: The Monroe Doctrine warned European nations that colonization would be considered an act of war. This made the New World (Western Hemisphere) completely separate from the Old World.)

Important Events, Terms, and Concepts

The list below shows important events, terms, and concepts that you should be familiar with on the APUSH exam. These and other important terms are printed in boldface throughout the chapter. Because the APUSH exam requires you to pay attention to the historical context and connections rather than details, don't bother memorizing the terms now. Simply place a check mark next to each as you study. You can return to this list to review as often as necessary. After you finish the review section, you can reinforce what you have learned by working through the practice questions at the end of this chapter. Answer explanations provide further clarification into perspectives of U.S. history.

Event/Term/Concept	Year/Brief Description	Study Page
Louisiana Purchase	**1803.** Jefferson's purchase of the Louisiana Territory from the French, which almost doubled the size of the U.S.	pp. 145–146
Marbury v. Madison	**1803.** The court decision that established the judicial review—that is, the ability of the Supreme Court to declare a law unconstitutional, making the law null and void.	p. 144
Embargo Act	**1807.** The U.S. ceased trading with Britain and France during the Napoleonic Wars because both foreign nations violated merchant ships. The embargo crippled the U.S. economy and contributed to the War of 1812.	p. 146
War of 1812	**1812–1815.** A military conflict between Britain and the U.S. (sometimes known as the "Second American Revolution").	pp. 146–150

Event/Term/Concept	Year/Brief Description	Study Page
Market Revolution	1815–1840. A period of great economic growth that led to political, social, and geographic changes in the country and the workforce.	pp. 151–152
Era of Good Feelings	1816–1825. A period in the U.S. when one political party dominated—the Republicans. Despite their efforts at the Hartford Convention, the Federalists were defeated, and only the Republicans existed. The Hartford Convention was an unsuccessful artifice for their self-preservation and not a measure inflicted on them.	p. 150
Missouri Compromise	1820. An agreement between pro-slavery and anti-slavery factions that temporarily calmed sectional divisions by allowing Maine to enter the Union as a free state and Missouri to enter as a slave state. No slavery was allowed north of the 36° 30' latitude line.	p. 154
Monroe Doctrine	1823. A policy that opposed European colonialism in the Americas. Any attempt to colonize the Western Hemisphere would be seen as a threat to the U.S. The doctrine would become very important later in the 19th century.	p. 151
Corrupt Bargain	1824. According to Andrew Jackson's followers, the bargain was a political arrangement between Henry Clay and John Quincy Adams that ensured Adams' victory as president in 1824, with Clay becoming his Secretary of State.	pp. 157–158
Nullification crisis	1828–1832. A political crisis during Andrew Jackson's presidency. South Carolina attempted to nullify the federal Tariff of 1832, which almost led to South Carolina's secession and a civil war.	p. 159
Indian Removal Act	1830. The law forced the removal of Native American tribes from their ancestral homelands in the southern states.	p. 159
Transcendentalists	1830s–1840s. A group of American philosophers led by Ralph Waldo Emerson who promoted individualism, self-reliance, a connection to nature, and intuition.	p. 157
Bank War	1829–1836. Andrew Jackson believed that too much economic power was in the hands of a private corporation. Jackson campaigned to destroy the Second Bank of the U.S. and replaced it with several state banks.	p. 159
Economic nationalism	Promoted by Henry Clay's American System, this is an economic philosophy that favored domestic control of the economy and labor and emphasized protective tariffs and other federally funded mandates to support the U.S. economy.	pp. 151–152

Chapter Review

The main topics discussed in this chapter include the Jeffersonian Era, the War of 1812, the Era of Good Feelings, the Market Revolution, political and social sectional tensions, cultural shifts, the Jacksonian Era, and the annexation of Texas.

The timeline below should help you visually identify the historical events that transpired during each presidency.

Early America (1800 to 1848)

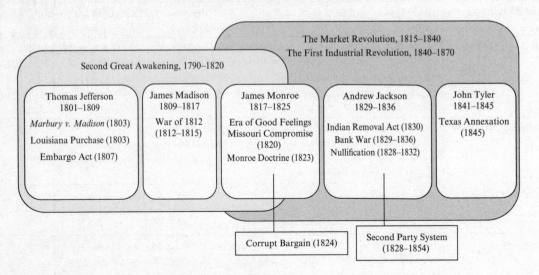

The Jeffersonian Era (1800 to 1828)

The Jeffersonian Era was an important turning point in American political history.

The Decline of the Federalist Party and the Rise of the Republican Party

As discussed in Chapter 6, before this time period Federalists steered the country under the leadership of the first president, George Washington, Alexander Hamilton, and the second president, John Adams. It was a time when a fundamental political debate developed over the nature of centralized power and whether or not liberty could exist if a federal government was allowed to dictate to citizens their individual states' rights. Two distinct factions continued to argue over states' rights and national centralized authority. Federalists called for national and economic unity to lead America to an industrialized future. Republicans called for states' independence and believed that yeomen farmers were a perfect model to lead America to a bright future.

Everything changed in 1800 when Vice President Thomas Jefferson, a Republican, defeated President John Adams, a Federalist, to become the third president of the United States. With Jefferson as president, many people expected a new revolution that would overturn much of what had been achieved under Federalist rule.

Early American political leaders wanted a peaceful transfer of power; however, since a transfer had never happened before, the transition was known as the **Revolution of 1800** (it led to the decline of the Federalist Party and ushered in a generation of Republican Party ruling). The election campaign had been vicious, but Jefferson called for reconciliation in his inaugural address, which was given in the nation's new capital, Washington, D.C. Jefferson attempted to unify the nation in his speech with the words "Every difference of opinion is not a difference of principle. We are all Republicans; we are all Federalists." Ultimately, Jefferson's goal was to draw Federalists into the Republican Party.

Key Facts about the Jeffersonian Era

Problems with the electoral system. While the election signaled to the rest of the world that a democratic government could work, it simultaneously revealed problems with the electoral system. According to the original Constitution, members of the Electoral College were allowed two votes (for different people) and there was no distinction between presidential and vice-presidential electoral votes. In other words, the person who got the most votes won, while the runner-up was made vice president. In the election of 1800, Jefferson and Aaron Burr (his running mate) tied. To break the tie, the vote went to the House of Representatives, which was largely composed of Federalist Party members. Alexander Hamilton, a champion of the Federalist Party, disliked Burr and was instrumental, surprisingly, in swinging the votes to Jefferson, his old enemy. In Hamilton's mind, Jefferson was the lesser of two evils.

Did you know? Alexander Hamilton had good reason for opposing Aaron Burr, whom he identified as corrupt. While some people praised Burr for his policies of economic and gender equality, others noted his arrogant tendency to put himself and his power above others. Burr not only plotted with radical Federalists to secede New England from the Union, but he was involved in plots to take Mexico from Spain in order to unite Mexico with the Louisiana Territory and place it under his rule.

Electoral reform—the Twelfth Amendment (1804). The Twelfth Amendment was added to the Constitution to prevent confusion in the future. From that point forward, electors were allowed to choose only one person for president and another for vice president (this system is still in place today).

Jefferson as president (1801–1809). Jefferson believed in small government, states' rights, and agricultural subsistence. He saw the yeoman farmer (a small, independent farmer who did not own slaves) as the backbone of America. According to Jefferson, farmers were the best example of creating a long-lasting American ideal that linked *agrarianism* (rural farming) to purity; and he connected the city, bankers, and industrialists to corruption. Jefferson pardoned those who had been arrested under the **Alien and Sedition Acts** of 1798 (laws that criminalized immigrants), cut federal expenses, kept a small staff, and reduced the national debt. Tending to solve governmental problems in an informal manner, Jefferson had frequent dinner parties that allowed political opponents to discuss heated issues in a relaxed atmosphere.

Jefferson cooperated with the Federalists. The Federalist influences did not disappear during Jefferson's presidency. Although Jefferson disliked Hamilton's national bank, Jefferson decided to keep the bank operating. Federalists also maintained about half of Adams' political appointments.

HISTORIOGRAPHY. *Scholars call Jefferson's agricultural ideals the **agrarian myth**. The agrarian myth is the belief that a rural farming society is superior to an urban city society. Although the myth was viewed as having the romantic appeal of a "good life" on the family farm, rural society was far from idyllic. Conditions of poverty, environmental disaster, overwork, hunger, and illiteracy were common. The agrarian myth was also never really an actuality in the American economy since even colonists exported cash crop agriculture to make money. People believed in it, though—a desire to "live off the land" made life appear to be pure. Many people believed that comfortable living was obtainable in the country and that the "evils" of the city would expose them* *to poverty, poor living conditions, greed, and disease. The agrarian myth continually pushed people toward westward expansion. Many historians believe that the Populist Movement during the late 19th century (Chapter 9) was motivated by the agrarian myth.*

Significant Supreme Court Cases

The election of 1800 may have swept a Federalist president out of office, but the one branch of government that remained firmly in the party's control was the Supreme Court. A month before he left the presidency in 1801, John Adams appointed John Marshall as Chief Justice. Marshall was a die-hard Federalist who opposed states' rights and continually sought ways to increase the power of the federal government. Marshall guided decisions handed down by the high court for the next 35 years. Carefully choosing cases that had clear implications for the power of the "national" government and the Court itself, Marshall made his mark on the political and legal history of the nation.

Marbury v. Madison (1803)

It was during this time period that the power of the judicial branch of the government increased. One of the landmark cases decided by the Court was **Marbury v. Madison.** Just days before Adams left office, Congress passed the **Judiciary Act** (1801), which created "midnight" appointments for Federalist candidates. When Jefferson's Secretary of State James Madison failed to allow one of the men, William Marbury, to take his position after the presidency changed hands, Marbury sued. The resulting Court case, *Marbury v. Madison* (1803), established the *judicial review process* (a system of checks and balances enabling the Supreme Court to declare legislation null and void) by declaring parts of the Judiciary Act of 1789 unconstitutional.

McCulloch v. Maryland (1819)

Two other significant Court cases under Marshall's term were *McCulloch v. Maryland* and *Gibbons v. Ogden.* In **McCulloch v. Maryland** (1819), the state of Maryland challenged Hamilton's Second National Bank (the charter of the first one had expired and was renewed in 1816). Marshall struck down Maryland's claim that the Bank was unconstitutional (Maryland argued that Congress was not expressly granted the authority to establish a bank in a state without that state's permission) and denied Maryland's right to tax a federal bank. These issues were over the supremacy clause of the Constitution, as well as implied powers. Marshall vindicated the use of implied powers.

Gibbons v. Ogden (1824)

In the **Gibbons v. Ogden** (1824) case, Marshall firmly established Congress' authority over interstate commerce by denying New York the ability to grant certain individuals the sole right to navigation privileges in waterways connected to other states (this had created a steamboat monopoly that other people were complaining about). Regulation of commercial activity within a state (*intrastate*) was reserved to the states, but commercial activity between two or more states (*interstate*) was the exclusive purview of Congress.

Heads Up: What You Need to Know

On the APUSH exam, you should be familiar with the *Marbury v. Madison* case. It is a landmark case that is the foundation of U.S. constitutional law. In the judicial review process, the Supreme Court becomes the primary interpreter of Constitution law when legislative and executive actions are subject to review using the following judicial process: 1) Citizen(s) contest federal or state laws, 2) the decisions of federal or state courts are appealed, 3) the Supreme Court reviews the case and interprets how the U.S. Constitution applies to the law, and 4) the Supreme Court applies the Constitution to make a decision.

The Louisiana Purchase (1803)

Republicans felt that building a strong nation required territorial expansion and landownership. The United States made a deal with France to purchase a vast amount of unexplored wilderness from the Mississippi River to the Rocky Mountains. To give perspective about the immense scale of land (see the map that follows), today these states include Arkansas, Colorado, Iowa, Kansas, Louisiana, Minnesota, Missouri, Montana, Nebraska, New Mexico, North Dakota, Oklahoma, South Dakota, Texas, and Wyoming. This was one of Jefferson's greatest achievements because it almost doubled the size of the United States. The land also provided transportation routes along the Mississippi River, valuable natural resources, and fertile soils for farming.

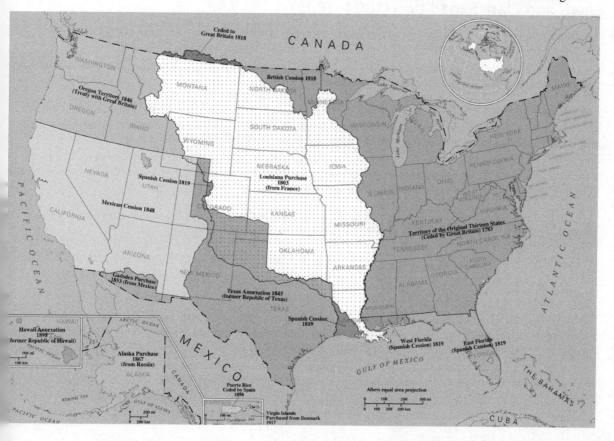

Heads Up: What You Need to Know

The APUSH exam frequently refers to the **Louisiana Purchase,** which almost doubled the size of the United States. Be sure you know that the territory, ceded to Spain after the French and Indian War, was back in French hands by 1800. France's objective in acquiring it was to establish a presence in the western frontier after it controlled a slave revolt in one of its colonies (St. Domingue) that later progressed into the Haitian Revolution.

By 1803, Napoleon Bonaparte found defeat inevitable in St. Domingue and needed funds to cover his European wars. He offered to sell the entire territory to the U.S. for a ridiculously low price (about 3 cents an acre). At that time, Robert Livingston was U.S. Minister (or Ambassador) to France. Jefferson sent Secretary of State James Monroe to help Livingston negotiate with Napoleon. They jumped at the chance to purchase the land for $15 million on Jefferson's behalf.

Issues of constitutionality were often brought up because Jefferson doubted his power as president to buy new regions. Remember, as a Republican, Jefferson believed in the strict interpretation of the Constitution. However, Jefferson wanted to expand farming and stop the concentration of wealth in the big cities' industrial manufacturing. Ultimately, the deal was just too good to pass up!

Lewis and Clark Expedition (1804–1806)

As soon as the Louisiana Purchase was finalized, Jefferson sent a team of 44 explorers (the Corps of Discovery) to study the wilderness. Military Captain Meriwether Lewis and William Clark were the co-leaders, and their primary mission was to find a water route across North America. The team traveled for 3 years through uncharted territory and faced nearly every hardship imaginable.

Lewis and Clark were assisted by many Native Americans, who served as guides and provided sustenance and advice. The most well-known native was **Sacagawea,** a Shoshone woman. She served as an interpreter and helped the explorers form important indigenous contacts. Along their journey westward, Lewis chronicled the expedition in a daily journal to report the climate, geography, plants, and Native American observations. Together, Lewis and Clark traveled down the Ohio River, up the Missouri River, and across the Continental Divide until they reached the Pacific Ocean in 1805 (today's Oregon).

The War of 1812 (1812 to 1815)

After gaining independence in the late 18th century, the United States was a minor power in world affairs. The new nation was struggling to gain its foothold in the world, but no longer had protection from the powerful British army.

When James Madison became president in 1809, he inherited many problems from Jefferson's administration, and both men were weak at enforcing foreign and domestic policies. Jefferson had implemented the **Embargo Act** of 1807 to fight British *impressment* (Britain taking American merchant ships and sailors, then forcing them to join the British Royal Navy) during the Napoleonic Wars (for Britain, this lasted from 1803 to 1815). The United States, however, lacked the military power to stop the British. Because the embargo prohibited trade between the U.S. and any foreign port, the embargo severely damaged the American economy and led to several protests in commercial shipping districts.

Continued tensions between the United States and Britain eventually led to the **War of 1812.**

Causes and Consequences of the War of 1812		
Event/Causes	Explanation	Consequences
Impressment: The British capture of American men, goods, and ships (1803–1812)	When Britain and France battled over European ports in 1806, American merchant ships were appropriated in the British blockades (about 1,500 ships were seized).	In December 1807, Jefferson's **Embargo Act** was created in response to British impressment. The trade embargo crippled the American economy. Britain continued seizing American ships, goods, and men. Madison replaced the Embargo Act with the **Non-Intercourse Act of 1809,** which allowed for trade, but limited trade with Britain or France. The Non-Intercourse Act was eventually phased out through another bill, **Macon's Bill Number 2,** stating that the U.S. would trade with any nation that respected its neutrality. Napoleon of France agreed to the bill, but then changed his mind. In the meantime, Britain continued to seize American ships, which served as one of the reasons for declaring war.
Chesapeake-Leopard Affair (1807)	The Chesapeake-Leopard Affair added tensions between Britain and the U.S. The *Chesapeake* (an American ship) was attacked by the *Leopard* (a British warship) off the Virginia coast. The British ship was searching for British deserters aboard the *Chesapeake*. After a short battle, the captain of the *Chesapeake* surrendered.	The British removed four deserters, who were put on trial (the one who was a British citizen was hanged). The captain of the ship was court-martialed. Americans were outraged by the incident, which led to future calls for war.
Battle of Tippecanoe (1811)	President Madison also had problems on the home front in the Northwest with Native Americans who resented settler expansion. Many settlers who expanded west were confronted by threats of Native American raids. The Shawnee chief, **Tecumseh,** unified many Native American tribes to resist white settlers who had violated treaty boundaries. The governor of the Indiana Territory, William Henry Harrison (later elected president), decided to attack Native Americans and burned down their villages. Many Native Americans were forced to flee to Canada.	Tecumseh and his brother, the Prophet, joined the British to align against the United States. The Battle of Tippecanoe contributed to American resentment of the British because the British supplied Native Americans on the frontier with weapons.

Continued

Event/Causes	Explanation	Consequences
Madison pressured into war by the War Hawks (1810–1812)	The Speaker of the House, Henry Clay, the young Republican congressman, led a group called the "War Hawks," who criticized President Madison and pressed him to go to war. They considered British assistance to the Native Americans a threat on the frontier and were offended by Britain's continued disrespect for American autonomy.	Madison eventually asked Congress for a declaration of war. Opposition occurred across party lines. None of the Federalists voted for war, but 80 percent of the Republicans voted for war. Since the Republicans had the majority of votes in Congress, the measure passed. The war that followed is often called the "Second American Revolution" because the U.S. was essentially fighting Britain once again to establish U.S. legitimacy and autonomy. Note: Communication across continents took weeks in the early 19th century. Britain's King George III was preoccupied with France, but had made a decision to stop impressment. If the communication had arrived before the declaration of war, the war might have never occurred.

The United States military and economy were not prepared for war when it began. Believing in small government, Jefferson had severely cut military expenses during his administration (1801–1809). Jefferson didn't believe that a strong army and navy were necessary and saw the expense as excessive. After the war began in 1812, U.S. forces tried to invade Canada but failed. This negatively affected soldier and citizen morale and deeply divided the citizens' support for both the government and the war. Fortunately, the U.S. was able to recover and ultimately became victorious.

Key Facts about Events of the War of 1812

The Creek War (1813–1814). The Creek War was a regional conflict with Native Americans over the Mississippi Territory (today's Alabama and Georgia). White settlers in the region appealed to the federal government for help, and U.S. troops were sent to defeat the Native Americans. The result was the cession of the territory.

Battle of York (1813). After several failed military campaigns, U.S. troops crossed Lake Ontario, took control of the Great Lakes region and York (today's Toronto), and burned several government buildings. This battle led to British retaliation in Washington the following year.

The U.S. Capital attacked (1814). When the Napoleonic Wars were winding down in 1814, the British were able to allocate more military resources to fight the United States. In a devastating shock to the U.S., the British overran and burned Washington, D.C. President Madison and many congressmen received word that British forces were marching to the nation's capital, so they fled the city before the enemy arrived. The President's wife, Dolley Madison, quickly gathered important treasures before departing, including a portrait of George Washington (now hanging in the White House), Cabinet papers, and the presidential silverware. The British invaded and set fire to the executive mansion (not yet called the White House), several government buildings, and some private homes. Smoke and flames engulfed the city. The White House and many other buildings were later rebuilt by 1817.

Source: Everett, "The War of 1812—British Forces Burning Washington, D.C.," 1814.

Battle of Horseshoe Bend (1814). General Andrew Jackson (a future president) and his troops won this battle and slaughtered the *Red Sticks,* Upper Creek warriors who united with Tecumseh's confederation to fight U.S. expansion.

Hartford Convention (1814–1815). The convention was a series of anti-war meetings held in Hartford, Connecticut, and led by the New England Federalist Party. The Federalists argued about the federal government's increasing power and the war. Discussions at the meetings included the Embargo of 1807, the Louisiana Purchase, and the Three-Fifths Compromise. Radicals called for New England's secession.

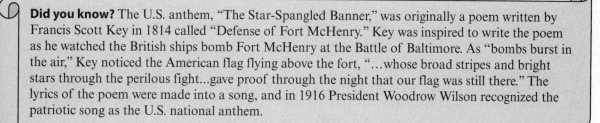

Did you know? The U.S. anthem, "The Star-Spangled Banner," was originally a poem written by Francis Scott Key in 1814 called "Defense of Fort McHenry." Key was inspired to write the poem as he watched the British ships bomb Fort McHenry at the Battle of Baltimore. As "bombs burst in the air," Key noticed the American flag flying above the fort, "…whose broad stripes and bright stars through the perilous fight…gave proof through the night that our flag was still there." The lyrics of the poem were made into a song, and in 1916 President Woodrow Wilson recognized the patriotic song as the U.S. national anthem.

The war ends with the Treaty of Ghent (1814). British and American leaders met in Ghent, Belgium, to sign the Treaty of Ghent (also called the Treaty of Peace and Amity) on Christmas Eve 1814. The news of the Treaty of Ghent took several months to reach the States. No one in North America knew about the peaceful settlement. In January 1815, Andrew Jackson engaged the British in the **Battle of New Orleans** to prevent them from seizing the city. His victory caused the British to retreat from the Louisiana Territory. Jackson's victory boosted his reputation, ultimately making him a war hero and creating a huge wave of patriotism and nationalism throughout the U.S.

Heads Up: What You Need to Know

The APUSH exam may require you to understand the implications of the close timing of the final events of the War of 1812. The Battle of New Orleans actually occurred *after* the war was over. The Federalist actions at Hartford might have been received more positively if they had occurred at the beginning of the war, but since they took place around the same time as the Treaty of Ghent and the Battle of New Orleans, they made the Federalists appear to be disloyal to the U.S. The war essentially ended the political power of the Federalists and directly contributed to the demise of the First Party System, which you must know for the exam.

TEST TIP: Some students conclude that nothing changed as a result of the War of 1812 because there were no territorial changes and no policy changes. However, on the APUSH exam, be prepared to respond to questions about the historical results of the war: (1) The treaty restored territories that both countries had before the war. (2) The victory legitimized the United States to the world, and showed the world that the U.S. was a strong nation. (3) Americans began to show a greater sense of patriotism. (4) The signing of the treaty ended the conflict regarding the causes of the war. (5) A peaceful, cooperative relationship began between the United States and Britain. (6) The power of Native Americans was weakened.

The Era of Good Feelings (1816 to 1825)

The Era of Good Feelings was the political mood of the United States when people felt inspired, patriotic, and unified.

Because the Federalists were so unpopular after the Hartford Convention, Republican James Monroe (the fifth president) easily won the election of 1816. Like James Madison, Monroe was a Virginia politician and a protégé of Thomas Jefferson. He served in the Continental Army, advocated for Jefferson's policies of small government, and helped to establish the Republican Party. His term ushered in an **Era of Good Feelings,** so-named because of the existence of only one political party—the Republicans.

Several positive foreign policy developments occurred during Monroe's term, generally through the efforts of his Secretary of State, John Quincy Adams. For example, the U.S. and Britain signed the **Treaty of 1818** (also known as the London or Anglo-American Convention). The international agreement allowed New England fishermen to access British fisheries and established the northern border of the Louisiana Territory. It also allowed for joint occupation and settlement in the Oregon Territory.

Adams also oversaw the U.S. acquisition of Florida in 1819 after Andrew Jackson exceeded his authority by destroying Native American villages and attacking a Spanish fort. The result was the **Adams-Onís Treaty** (also known as the Transcontinental Treaty), in which Spain transferred Florida to the U.S.

The Monroe Doctrine (1823)

Adams' crowning achievement was writing the **Monroe Doctrine.** Designed to respect the United States' sphere of influence in the Western Hemisphere, the doctrine promoted a clear separation between the New World and the Old World. It stated two principles: (a) any European attempt at colonization in the Western Hemisphere (the "New World") would be viewed as an act of aggression, and (b) the U.S. would not interfere with Europe's existing colonies and would stay away from conflicts in Europe (the "Old World"). The doctrine primarily concerned the Latin American nations that were fighting to gain independence from Spain and noted that they were to be left alone. If the U.S. felt the liberty of these nations was in jeopardy or its own interests were threatened, it would be obligated to intervene.

When it was written in 1823, the doctrine was largely a symbolic gesture because the U.S. did not have the military strength to support any intervention. Fortunately, Britain (its trading partner and military superior) honored the doctrine. Note: The doctrine became especially significant in the 1890s, when the U.S. had gained the military force to support it. By then, imperialism and expansionism had become important U.S. foreign policy goals (see Chapter 9).

Heads Up: What You Need to Know

The Monroe Doctrine is an important foreign policy strategy that frequently appears on the APUSH exam. In continuity and change questions about the doctrine, you can use the example of the Spanish-American War. The doctrine was invoked in 1898 by President William McKinley when the United States cited Spain's colonial involvement in Cuba as a threat to its security. Spain's defeat was a turning point in history because it sparked U.S. imperialism in the Western Hemisphere. Years later, when the Dominican Republic was bankrupt in 1904, President Theodore Roosevelt issued the Roosevelt Corollary to the Monroe Doctrine. This allowed Roosevelt to take a "Big Stick" approach to foreign policy in the Western Hemisphere and insert the U.S. into economic issues between Latin America and Europe. It also allowed the U.S. to intervene in any internal or external tensions in the region and to ensure U.S. financial interests would remain secure.

Economics in the 19th Century

During the Era of Good Feelings, the Republicans decided to embrace some of the Federalists' policies, mainly because the country was growing and needed support for an increasingly important manufacturing segment of the economy.

The Market Revolution (1815 to 1840)

America was growing at a rapid pace and was rich in natural resources. The United States needed to develop an economic plan that no longer depended on Britain and other foreign nations for commerce. Inspired by some of Hamilton's economic programs, Henry Clay created an economic plan called the **American System** (known as **economic nationalism** or the **National System**), whereby American industrial manufacturers and the agricultural industry would work together to promote commerce. Clay's plan advocated the following:

1. **Protective tariffs.** Protected American manufacturers from foreign competition by charging taxes on imported goods, thus raising the prices of European goods. Clay believed that by placing tariffs on foreign products, the sales of U.S. goods would increase.

2. **Internal improvements.** Encouraged the building of a better transportation infrastructure (roads, railroads, and canals) that was necessary for manufacturers to transfer goods to commercial markets.

3. **The Second National Bank.** Considered necessary to establish a system of stable currency (state banks often made their own money at this time, a practice that often caused financial instability and inflation). A Second National Bank would provide a system of lending supported by the government rather than private institutions or individuals. The first bank's charter expired in 1811, and Congress renewed it in 1816.

Congressional support of the American System stimulated the economy and contributed to the **Market Revolution,** a period of incredible economic and technological growth in the United States. Goods and trade goods were both stimulated in local and regional markets and drawn into national and global markets.

The First Industrial Revolution (c. 1840 to c. 1870)

The Industrial Revolution was a major economic turning point in the Market Revolution. On the APUSH exam, you should be familiar with the significance of the Industrial Revolution—its causes and consequences.

THE PROGRESS OF THE CENTURY.
THE LIGHTNING STEAM PRESS.   THE ELECTRIC TELEGRAPH.   THE LOCOMOTIVE.   THE STEAMBOAT.

Source: Currier and Ives, "The Progress of the Century," c. 1876. Depicts the extraordinary inventions of the 19th century that revolutionized America. (Background: People using the steam press, steamboat, and locomotive.)

The Industrial Revolution was important because it created a massive change in how people discovered and used energy to make life easier and more efficient. Industrialization spurred new innovations to increase human efficiency and gave rise to mechanized and commercial productivity. The Industrial Revolution progressed in phases as inventions were created. This chapter discusses the first phase of the Industrial Revolution (c. 1840–c. 1870), and Chapter 9 discusses the second phase of the Industrial Revolution (1870–1914).

Inventions

Invention	Inventor	Importance
Spinning jenny	James Hargreaves (1760)	Allowed for spinning multiple threads together, thus reducing the amount of work needed to produce cloth.
Steam engine	James Watt (1765)	The steam engine was the first type of engine to power machinery in factories. The steam engine used coal to create steam and drive industry.
Steamboat		Steamships ran on the same principle as steam engines, using coal to create steam for faster and more efficient transportation over long distances.
Steam locomotive	Richard Trevithick (1804)	The early steam locomotive changed the world from manual and animal-pulled transportation to high-pressure steam for engine power to transport people and goods throughout the country. The first practical locomotive was built in 1812.
Cotton gin	Eli Whitney (1794)	Invented by one of the most famous of the industrial inventors, the cotton gin picked out the seeds in cotton fibers much faster and inexpensively than the process could be done by hand. In the South, it significantly sped up cotton production and led to an increased demand for land to grow it on and slaves to pick it. This influenced the northern textile industry, reducing the cost of the raw materials for clothing. Even the poorest populations could then afford to wear manufactured cloth.

Key Facts about the Impact of the Market Revolution and the First Industrial Revolution

Mass production of goods. Technological developments and inventions from the Industrial Revolution—like steam power, the cotton gin, steel plows, and mechanical reapers—made it possible to mass-produce goods at an increased rate of speed; both commercial items and agricultural crops were produced with machines. Because transportation advances (national roads, canals, and railroads) made shipping to remote areas easier, farmers and industrialists felt more comfortable expanding into the West.

Regional product specialization. Certain regions of the country became associated with producing specific products. For example, the South was known for cotton and plantation-style agriculture, the North was associated with manufacturing and trade in factories, and the West (now the Midwest) focused on producing grains, wheat, and cattle.

Increased unskilled labor. In the North, unskilled laborers were able to be managed in a task system that allowed them to mass-produce goods. The need for skilled artisans decreased, and the need for cheap laborers increased—a new managerial class (or "middle class") was created to supervise the laborers.

Demand for slave laborers. The textile (clothing) industry was booming since the Embargo Act increased demand in the U.S. The cotton mills in the North needed cotton to produce the domestic cloth, and even though slave trade had been abolished in 1808, the need for slave labor in the South increased.

Increased migration and immigration. Hoping for the chance to make their fortunes, or at least possess their own farms, people began moving farther south and west. Immigrants, especially those of Irish descent, were drawn to the opportunities in the cities and often worked as laborers in manufacturing plants for low wages.

TEST TIP: The Era of Good Feelings was characterized as a period of great economic success. As transportation systems linked major industrial cities and ports, the national market prospered and American citizens thrived. It's important to know for the APUSH exam, however, that there was a swift downturn in the economy that caused debt and poverty called the Panic of 1819 (1819–1822). This was the first economic depression that the U.S. experienced. When the Second Bank of America realized that it had extended too many loans and too much credit, it quickly tried to restrict credit lending. But it was too late. The primary causes of the economic collapse included debts from the War of 1812, increased westward expansion, and failed bank loans.

HISTORIOGRAPHY. *Although the Market Revolution and the American System were often seen as positive developments in America, some historians point out that they did not go unchallenged. People began to associate the new values that came with commercialism as corrupt, particularly if they were residing in a rural area which was contrasted with the demands of the city. The criticism was no less harsh in urban environments. People noticed that tensions increased in families as working-class women and children were forced to take employment that required them to work for long hours under terrible conditions just so they could earn enough money to eat. Slums multiplied and access to medical treatment was limited to the wealthy or the new middle class. Members of the old artisan guilds began to organize into cohesive groups to object to exploitative labor practices (these groups became the basis for labor unions that would form later). Nativist organizations like the **Know Nothing Party** complained about a wide range of immigrants, including the Germans, Irish, and Chinese.*

Social and Political Tensions in the 19th Century

The protective tariffs of the American System also increased sectional tensions. Many southerners and small farmers initially supported Clay's economic nationalism because the internal improvements that came with it enabled them to access better markets for their goods. However, cash-crop producers soon began to feel that the high tariffs were only in place to benefit northern industrialists. Countries that were heavily taxed for exporting their products to the U.S. began to place high tariffs on U.S. products exported to them. This meant that southern states suffered an economic downturn when tariffs for shipping cotton and other crops overseas increased. Southerners were also required to pay higher prices for manufactured items because northerners were protected from significant competition by the tariffs, which allowed them to increase prices for manufactured goods.

The Missouri Compromise (1820)

In 1819, when Missouri requested permission to enter the Union, tensions grew. Missouri was expected to easily enter the Union as a slave state, but New York Congressman James Tallmadge opposed slavery and suggested a Constitutional amendment that would prohibit any more slave states in the Louisiana Territory. Fearing that the North would take away all of its political power, the South vehemently objected. To diffuse the situation, Henry Clay proposed the **Missouri Compromise** of 1820, which disallowed slavery above **36° 30' north** (an imaginary territorial boundary line based on longitude and latitude). To balance legislative representation, Maine entered the Union as a free state when Missouri was designated a slave state.

Cultural Shifts in the 19th Century

Although not directly influenced by the Market Revolution, several cultural shifts in religion, class hierarchy, literature, and art emerged during this period.

Religious Movements

People who lived in rural communities believed that corruption and greed were the result of commercialism and the nation's growing industrialization. This belief was one of the reasons religious fervor continued to spread throughout the United States.

Source: J. Maze Burbank, "Methodist Camp Meeting" [of a Religious Revival in America], c. 1839.

The popularity of Protestant evangelical religions rose out of the **Second Great Awakening** (1790–1850), which caused membership in various denominations to surge at an unprecedented rate.

The Second Great Awakening was a 19th-century religious movement resulting in thousands of conversions to evangelical religions. *Itinerant* (traveling from town to town) preachers, like **Charles Finney,** would bring their message to people in a series of emotionally charged religious revivals to recruit new believers. Some of these meetings would last several days or even a week. Similar to the First Great Awakening in the 1730s and 1740s, this second round of religious demonstrations promoted personal salvation and emotionalism. It was initially influenced by the egalitarian principles of the revolution; therefore, ministers often encouraged democratic church practices. At first, they allowed African Americans and women to preach and become active members of congregations. Methodist and Baptist church populations grew in popularity, and congregations were once again split in their level of support for the revivals.

Did you know? Many historians believe that evangelical Christianity, spread through the First and Second Great Awakenings, had a particular effect on the culture of southern states. Although it began as a religion of the common people, Evangelicalism was taken over by the southern elite, who eventually used it to uphold a *patriarchal* society (society controlled by men). By the 1820s, women were no longer able to preach and extreme emotionalism was discouraged. Slaves were required to receive permission from their owners to attend church and were then segregated during worship. Additionally, during the sectional debates over slavery that occurred just prior to the Civil War, religion was used to defend both pro-slavery arguments in the South and anti-slavery arguments in the North.

Reform Movements

The Market Revolution also contributed to the birth of middle-class America. Reform movements began to emerge that called for women's rights, temperance, improvements in prisons, and the abolition of slavery. Although these first crusades would not become as powerful as the succeeding organized movements, the initial movements allowed people to object to the inequalities they observed in society.

19th-Century Reform Movements		
Reform Movement	**Primary Leaders**	**Description**
Temperance movement	Various Christian denominations, women	Sparked by the religious movement, the temperance movement was a social and political movement against alcohol consumption. Fines were imposed for selling alcohol without a license and for public intoxication. This movement influenced alcohol laws and the prohibition of alcohol. (Note: From 1917 to 1933, the Eighteenth Amendment was ratified to prohibit the manufacturing, transportation, and sale of alcohol.)
Education reform	Horace Mann (1796–1859)	Horace Mann transformed U.S. education by promoting a public school system that would be accessible to all children living in his home state of Massachusetts. He campaigned for higher standards for teacher training, overhauled the existing education system, and was later elected to the U.S. House of Representatives. The work he did in Massachusetts influenced other states—especially in the North—to support public education.
Movement for the fair treatment of the mentally ill and prisoners	Dorothea Dix (1802–1887)	Dix was an activist who advocated for people with mental and physical disadvantages, such as patients in mental institutions and prisoners in jails across America and Europe. Dix became a supporter of female nurses and was instrumental in changing social attitudes about people with mental illnesses.
Abolitionist movement	William Lloyd Garrison (1805–1879)	Garrison was a journalist and social reformer who founded an anti-slavery newspaper in 1831 called *The Liberator*.
	Frederick Douglass (1818–1895)	Douglass was born into slavery and escaped slavery as a young man. He became one of the greatest leaders and voices for the abolitionist movement.

Philosophical Movements

Another popular movement during the 19th century was **Transcendentalism.** As a philosophy, Transcendentalism emerged from the ideals of *Romanticism* that emphasized "intuitions of the mind" (Immanuel Kant) rather than scientific empiricism. Transcendentalism suggested that the universe, mankind, and all forms of nature are interconnected.

Transcendentalism inspired American literary works in the U.S., including the writings of **Ralph Waldo Emerson** (poet and essay writer), **Henry David Thoreau** (poet, writer, philosopher, and close friend of Emerson), and **Margaret Fuller** (journalist and women's rights advocate). Transcendental philosophy adopted the American tendency to value individualism and self-reliance, which already existed as part of Jefferson's yeoman agrarian myth and motivated people to settle the western frontier. Like Romanticism, this movement also rejected the rational thinking of the Enlightenment and encouraged intuition as the guiding force in decision-making. Transcendentalists also encouraged people to immerse themselves in nature and lead simple lives.

TEST TIP: Literature, art, and music often reflect the historical mood of a nation. On the APUSH exam, use the works of Emerson, Thoreau, or Fuller as evidence in your essay responses about the mid-19th-century literary movement of transcendentalism. For example, Thoreau and Emerson's interests in nature support some ideas of agrarianism (i.e., Thoreau's novel *Walden, or Life in the Woods*, exemplifies the beauty of nature as humans separate from the modern "industrial" world).

Thoreau also wrote *Civil Disobedience*, which argued that people have a social obligation to do what is morally right despite unjust government laws, such as slavery. In other words, the government should not have authority over one's conscience. In support of abolition, Thoreau refused to pay government taxes because the government supported slavery (he was jailed as a result). As you will see in Chapter 8, the issues of abolition and sectional divisions intensified by 1861.

The Jacksonian Era (1828 to 1850)

The Era of Good Feelings ended with the presidential election of 1824.

The Election of 1824

Five candidates ran for president: John Quincy Adams (Secretary of State), Henry Clay (Speaker of the House), William H. Crawford (Secretary of the Treasury), John C. Calhoun (Secretary of War), and Andrew Jackson (war hero). Early in the race, Crawford suffered a paralytic stroke and Calhoun couldn't get the support he needed to continue to run, so both men dropped out. The remaining three candidates were political rivals whose campaigns were highly competitive. By 1823, candidates were arguing over sectional tensions and the financial Panic of 1819, which had generated more divisions over economic nationalism. Jackson was victorious with the popular vote. No candidate won the Electoral College, so the House of Representatives had to decide who would become president—Adams was chosen.

The Corrupt Bargain

When John Quincy Adams became the winner and announced that Henry Clay would serve as his Secretary of State (a position that many considered a step toward the presidency), Jackson accused Clay of conspiring with Adams to swing the House votes in Adams' favor. Since both Clay and Adams supported economic nationalism and Jackson was an "old school" Jeffersonian Republican who supported states' rights, the decision became known as the **Corrupt Bargain.** It directly contributed to Jackson's election in 1828—other important factors were Adams' uneventful presidency and his failure to use the spoils system to garner political support.

The Second Party System (1828 to 1854)

As the result of the tension in society, separate political ideologies began to emerge. Simultaneously, many states begin eliminating property requirements for voting, allowing universal white male suffrage into their electoral system. A rise of new political parties began to emerge in the **Second Party System:** the Jacksonian Democrats and the Whigs.

The Second Party System Comparing Democrats and Whigs	
Democratic Party (States' Government Rights)	**Whig Party (Federal Government Rights)**
Leader: President Andrew Jackson, who supported the "common man."	**Leader:** John Quincy Adams, who united the Whigs in their hatred for Andrew Jackson. Whigs thought Jackson abused his power as president—they called him "King Andrew."
Principles: Promoted traditional principles of Jeffersonian Republicans, including a small national government.	**Principles:** Promoted political and economic nationalism, a strong national government, and modernization.
Region: Rural regions—more likely to be southerners or those who supported states' rights (small farmers, skilled and unskilled laborers, etc.).	**Region:** Urban regions—more likely to be northerners or those who were involved in industry (merchants, business professionals, etc.).
Economics: Disliked federal interference in economic and social matters.	**Economics:** Supported federal funding of economic and moral legislation, especially banks and transportation.
Position on abolition: Most supported slavery.	**Position on abolition:** Most supported abolition (anti-slavery).

The Election of 1828

The election of 1828 was vicious. Still bitter over the Corrupt Bargain, Andrew Jackson proudly proclaimed he was the champion of the common man who would fight government fraud. Jackson accused his opponent, presidential incumbent John Quincy Adams, of misusing public funds—Adams responded by branding Jackson an adulterer and a murderer. Jackson easily won the election of 1828 (178 to 83 electoral votes), garnering most of his support in the South and West (New Englanders primarily voted for Adams).

Jacksonian Controversies

Sectional division would continue to be a dominant theme during Jackson's presidency. Jackson overused the *spoils system* (appointing government offices to political supporters), was unwilling to compromise, and had a harsh personality that garnered him many political enemies. Political opponents referred to him as "King Andrew" because of his authoritarian behavior, which was similar to a monarchical despot's.

The most important events of Jackson's presidency are listed in the table below. Note: Related themes and events are grouped together in the same category.

Important Jacksonian Era Events

Event/Theme	Explanation	Significance/Consequence
Indian Removal Act (1830) **_Worcester v. Georgia_** (1832) **Trail of Tears** (1838)	The Indian Removal Act allowed for the forcible relocation of 125,000 Native Americans (Chickasaw, Choctaw, Cherokee, and other tribes) from their ancestral homelands to federal territory west of the Mississippi River—this was done to make room for white settlers in the southern states.	Christian missionaries and Native Americans protested. The Cherokee Nation sued for their right to remain on their land in **_Worcester v. Georgia_** (1832). The Supreme Court ruled in favor of Native Americans, stating that the state government of Georgia did not have the power to enforce the law. However, Jackson disregarded the Supreme Court's decision. Jackson's refusal to honor the Court's decision led to the **Trail of Tears** in 1838. By the end of the decade, very few Native Americans remained in the Southeast. The Trail of Tears was a series of forced relocations from Native American territories. The journey west over thousands of miles was difficult and led to the deaths of thousands of Native Americans.
Bank War (1829–1836) **Panic of 1837** (1837–mid-1840s)	Jackson vetoed the renewal of the charter of the Second Bank of the U.S. (BUS) in 1832 (4 years before it was due to expire). Jackson believed that the bank was an abuse of federal power that favored business interests. Nicholas Biddle (the bank's president) made the issue a primary concern in the election of 1832. Biddle, his ally Henry Clay, and Jackson "warred" over the future of the BUS.	These events not only furthered sectionalism, they caused a financial panic. When Jackson defeated Clay in 1832, Jackson ordered the withdrawal of all federal money from the BUS and deposited it into state banks that supported the Democrats. These "pet banks" began printing huge amounts of paper money that would soon become useless. Biddle also called in all BUS loans, which couldn't be paid. This resulted in an economic collapse known as the **Panic of 1837.**
Nullification crisis (1828–1832) **Force Bill** (1833) **Compromise Tariff** (1833)	The nullification crisis was a sectional crisis that occurred when Congress passed a very high protective tariff that infuriated many southerners. The South Carolina legislature objected through the publication of "The South Carolina Exposition and Protest." Written anonymously by John Calhoun, it claimed states had the right to nullify federal legislation if they determined a law was unconstitutional. In 1832, Congress passed another tariff (known as the **Tariff of Abominations** in the South), which South Carolina declared unconstitutional. The state threatened to secede if forced to collect the tariff.	The nullification crisis caused more tensions among southern and northern states. South Carolina was surprised to find that Jackson, a die-hard advocate of states' rights, became angry and wanted to use military force against the state. The congressional solution to avoid civil war was the "Olive Branch and the Sword." This included a **Force Bill** (1833) that allowed the federal government to use military force to collect the tariff if necessary. Henry Clay and John Calhoun also convinced Congress to pass the **Compromise Tariff of 1833.** The tariff stated the government would gradually lower rates, and South Carolina accepted the compromise. Unfortunately, this tariff was ultimately replaced by the Black Tariff of 1842, which set rates even higher than those in the Tariff of Abominations.

> **Did you know?** Henry Clay was known as a "Great Compromiser" because of the work he did to avoid contentious sectional issues between slave states and free states. Clay played a major role in the creation and passing of the Missouri Compromise (1820), the Compromise Tariff (1833), and the Compromise of 1850. Unfortunately, his Congressional leadership skills were not enough to get him elected to the presidency. He ran for president five times but lost every election!

The Annexation of Texas (1845)

One issue that Jackson avoided was the annexation of Texas, especially after his offer to buy the region was rejected by the Mexican government in 1829.

Key Facts about the Annexation of Texas

Americans invited to settle in Mexico (1824). Mexico invited Americans to settle in its northern frontier (what is now Texas) as early as 1824, shortly after it gained its independence. Many living in the southern states jumped at the opportunity for expansion, especially yeomen farmers who desired better land to produce cash crop agriculture. To earn generous Mexican land grants, white settlers had to do little more than agree to become Catholic, follow Mexican law, and pay a minimal surveying fee.

Americans swarmed the region and rejected Mexican culture (1830). Instead of becoming a stabilizing force in Mexico's borderlands, Americans soon began rejecting Mexican culture, religion, and law. Encouraged by colonizers like Stephen Austin, people immigrated to the territory in massive numbers, often bringing their slaves with them (even after Mexico outlawed slavery in 1829). By 1830, white settlers and their slaves quadrupled Mexicans living in the region. When immigration was halted, people entered the country illegally, easily avoiding Mexican troops stationed along the border.

Americans residing in Mexico appealed for annexation (1835). In 1835, Santa Ana became dictator of Mexico, which motivated Mexican Texans to declare their independence and appeal to the U.S. for annexation. Since Texas wanted to join the Union as a slave state and Jackson was already fighting intense sectional division in the country in the nullification crisis, the president avoided recognizing Texas' "Lone Star Republic" until the last day of his presidency. His successor, **Martin Van Buren** (a Democrat who had won the election of 1836 simply because the Whigs ran too many candidates), also avoided annexation because he viewed it as a political disaster. Van Buren had no desire to wage a war with Mexico.

Texas became a U.S. state (1845). Texas would not become part of the United States until the presidency of **John Tyler,** who rose to the office after the death of **William Henry Harrison.** Winning on a Whig Party ticket, Harrison died of pneumonia only 32 days after entering the White House. Tyler had once been a Jacksonian Democrat and had recently joined the Whig Party as Harrison's running mate. When he began vetoing issues related to high tariffs and a new national banking system, the Whigs expelled him and almost all of his cabinet resigned. To garner political support in the South, Tyler fought hard to seek approval for the controversial annexation of Texas, to which Congress finally agreed. After numerous negotiations and treaties, Texas became a state in December 1845, 6 months after Tyler left office.

Chapter Review Practice Questions

Multiple-Choice Questions

Practice questions are for instructional purposes only and may not reflect the format of the actual exam. On the actual exam, questions will be grouped into sets. Each set contains one source-based prompt (document or image) and two to five questions.

Questions 1–3 refer to the following political cartoon.

Source: "King Andrew the First," 1833. Image depicts President Andrew Jackson as an absolute monarch. The political cartoon was created in response to Jackson's order to remove federal deposits from the Bank of the United States.

1. The cartoon's portrayal of President Andrew Jackson was intended to

   A. Suggest that executive power was being abused
   B. Call for the support of President Jackson
   C. Promote the idea of a Republican monarchy in the United States
   D. Forge a unified front during war

2. Based on your knowledge of U.S. history, who were the most likely supporters of this published cartoon?

   A. The Federalists
   B. Jacksonian Democrats
   C. The Whig Party
   D. The Second Party System

3. Based on your knowledge of U.S. history, which of the following best describes why the Second Party System developed in the U.S.?

   A. The nullification crisis created additional sectional division.
   B. Christian missionaries and the Native Americans themselves resisted the Indian Removal Act.
   C. Many states had eliminated property taxes from their voting qualifications.
   D. The Hartford Convention made the Federalists unpopular.

Questions 4–6 refer to the following excerpt.

And be it further enacted. That in all that territory ceded by France to the United States, under the name of Louisiana, which lies north of thirty-six degrees and thirty minutes north latitude, not included within the limits of the state, contemplated by this act, slavery and involuntary servitude, otherwise than in the punishment of crimes, whereof the parties shall have been duly convicted, shall be, and is hereby, forever prohibited: Provided always, That any person escaping into the same, from whom labour or service is lawfully claimed, in any state or territory of the United States, such fugitive may be lawfully reclaimed and conveyed to the person claiming his or her labour or service as aforesaid.

—Source: Excerpt from the Missouri Compromise (1820), an act to authorize the people of the Missouri territory to form a constitution and state government, and for the admission of such state into the Union on an equal footing with the original states, and to prohibit slavery in certain territories.

4. Based on your knowledge of U.S. history, which of the following best represents a condition of this act of legislation?

   A. Kentucky was considered a border state with both free and enslaved persons.
   B. Maine was admitted to the Union as a free state.
   C. Certain states were allowed to enact gradual emancipation acts.
   D. People participating in the Underground Railroad would be severely punished.

5. The excerpt best reflects an example of

   A. An attempt to thwart the growing sectional division between the North and the South
   B. The general attitude of the country toward emancipation and slavery
   C. A legislative solution to the status of lands gained through the Mexican-American War
   D. The behavior of the Republicans during the Era of Good Feelings

6. Based on your knowledge of U.S. history, which of the following was another legislative policy supported by Henry Clay?

   A. The Tallmadge Amendment
   B. The annexation of Texas
   C. The Indian Removal Act
   D. The Compromise of 1850

Document-Based Question

1 question

60 minutes

Reading Time: 15 minutes (brainstorm your thoughts and organize your response)

Writing Time: 45 minutes

Directions: The document-based question is based on the seven accompanying documents. The documents are for instructional purposes only. Some of the documents have been edited for the purpose of this practice exercise. Write your response on lined paper and include the following:

- **Thesis.** Present a thesis that supports a historically defensible claim, establishes a line of reasoning, and responds to all parts of the question. The thesis must consist of one or more sentences located in one place—either the introduction or the conclusion.

- **Contextualization.** Situate the argument by explaining the broader historical events, developments, or processes that occurred before, during, or after the time frame of the question.

- **Evidence from the documents.** Support your argument by using the content of six of the documents to develop and support a cohesive argument that responds to the question.

- **Evidence beyond the documents.** Support your argument by explaining at least one additional piece of specific historical evidence not found in the documents. (Note: The example must be different from the evidence used to earn the point for contextualization.)

- **Analysis.** Use at least three documents that are relevant to the question to explain the documents' point of view, purpose, historical situation, and/or audience.

- **Historical development.** Use historical reasoning to show complex relationships among the documents, the topic question, and the thesis argument. Use evidence to corroborate, qualify, or modify the argument.

Based on the documents that follow, answer the question below.

Question 1: Analyze the origins and effects of the shift in the American economy from 1815 to 1840.

Document 1

Source: John Rutherford, "Facts and Observations in Relation to the Origin and Completion of the Erie Canal," 1825.

Rutherford examined the importance of the Erie Canal in New York and quantified its success in a book containing maps, charts, and statistics.

On the 2nd of March, 1811, Mr. Gouverneur Morris and the other commissioners made a long and very luminous report on the subject, showing very clearly the advantages of an interior route, in preference to that by Lake Ontario; and proposing the construction of a canal with an uniform descent of the water of Lake Erie at the rate of six inches to a mile, to a reservoir near Hudson's River...

The report was followed by a law which was passed on the 8th of April, reciting that

"Whereas a communication by means of a canal navigation between the great Lakes and Hudson's River, will encourage commerce and manufactures, facilitate a free and general intercourse between parts of the United States, and tend to the aggrandizement and posterity of the country, and consolidate and strengthen the union, that Gouverncur Morris, Stephen Van Rensselaer, DeWitt Clinton, Simeon De Witt, William North, Thomas Eddy, Peter B. Porter, Robert R. Livingston, and Robert Fulton, be appointed commissioners for the consideration of all matters relating the said inland navigation."

Document 2

Source: Henry Clay, "In Defense of the American System," 1832. Senator Clay's economic plan for higher tariffs to protect American industries played an important role in the 19th-century American economy.

This transformation of the condition of the country from gloom and distress to brightness and prosperity, has been mainly the work of American legislation, fostering American industry, instead of allowing it to be controlled by foreign legislation, cherishing foreign industry. The foes of the American System, in 1824, with great boldness and confidence, predicted, 1st. The ruin of the public revenue, and the creation of a necessity to resort to direct taxation. The gentleman from South Carolina, (General Hayne,) I believe, thought that the tariff of 1824 would operate a reduction of revenue to the large amount of eight millions of dollars. 2d. The destruction of our navigation. 3d. The desolation of commercial cities. And 4th. The augmentation of the price of objects of consumption, and further decline in that of the articles of our exports. Every prediction which they made has failed—utterly failed.

Document 3

Source: Charles Sellers, American historian, *The Market Revolution: Jacksonian America, 1815–1846*, 1991. An economic analysis of historical developments after the War of 1812. As the market and class conflicts grew, tensions grew between the federal and democratic forces.

As pent-up demand galvanized commodity production, as masters of slave and capital followed a flood of pioneer farming folk across the Appalachians into the heart of the continent, Americans first realized that they were indeed undergoing a market revolution…the enterprising began to envision limitless growth through the extension of the internal market across a continental domain.

Postwar boom dramatized sectional interdependence, as agricultural exports, cotton above all, flooded from South and West, to pay for a returning flood of European imports, and plantations bought more northeastern manufactures…

Document 4

Source: Seth Luther, Pamphlet, "Address to the Working-Men of New England," 1832. Seth Luther, a Massachusetts carpenter, was a labor reformer in the 1830s and 1840s focusing on issues pertaining to the exploitation of children. Luther was instrumental in helping to pass the nation's first law to control child labor—enacted by Massachusetts in 1842.

A member of the United States Senate seems to be extremely pleased with cotton mills. He says in the Senate, "Who has not been delighted with the clockwork movements of a large cotton manufactory? He had visited them often, and always with increased delight." He says the women work in large airy apartments, well warmed. They are neatly dressed, with ruddy complexions, and happy countenances… We would respectfully advise the honorable Senator to travel incognito when he visits cotton mills… In that case we could show him, in some of the prisons in New England called cotton mills, instead of rosy cheeks, the pale, sickly, haggard countenance of the ragged child—haggard from the worse than slavish confinement in the cotton mill. He might see that child driven up to the "clockwork" by the cowskin [whip], in some cases… We could show him many females who have had corporeal punishment inflicted upon them; one girl eleven years of age who had her leg broken with a billet of wood; another who had a board split over her head by a heartless monster in the shape of an overseer of a cotton mill "paradise."

Document 5

> Source: Eli Whitney, American inventor, "Cotton Gin Patent," March 14, 1794. The cotton gin revolutionized the production of cotton by speeding up the process to remove seeds from cotton fiber.

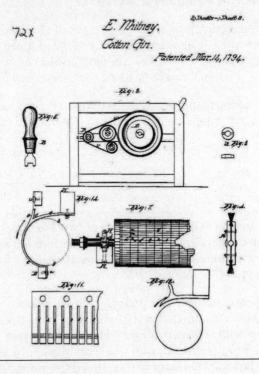

Document 6

> Source: John James Audubon, "The Squatters of the Mississippi," 1833. Naturalist and ornithologist John Audubon is known for his studies of American birds. In his quest to study birds, he encountered "miserable beings" living in the swamps of the Mississippi.

The individuals who become squatters choose that sort of life of their own free will. They mostly remove from other parts of the United States after finding that land has become too high in price, and they are persons who, having a family of strong and hardy children, are anxious to enable them to provide for themselves. They have heard from good authorities that the country extending along the great streams of the West is of all parts of the Union the richest in its soil, the growth of its timber, and the abundance of its game; that, besides, the Mississippi is the great road to and from all the markets in the world; and that every vessel borne by its waters affords to settlers some chance of selling their commodities, or of exchanging them for others. To these recommendations is added another, of even greater weight with persons of the above denomination, namely, the prospect of being able to settle on land, and perhaps to hold it for a number of years, without purchase, rent, or tax of any kind. How many thousands of individuals in all parts of the globe would gladly try their fortune with such prospects I leave to you, reader, to determine.

Document 7

Source: John H. Winston, Broadside circulating in Stokes County, North Carolina, 1836. The North Carolina Collection, Wilson Library, UNC-Chapel Hill.

Answer Explanations

Multiple-Choice Questions

1. **A.** The image was a political cartoon of President Andrew Jackson as a despotic monarch, thus suggesting that executive power was being abused, choice A. It was designed to draw the public's attention to the policies of a president who abused his veto and constitutional power. Jackson disregarded the judicial branch, possessed an authoritarian personality similar to despots', and vetoed a great number of congressional legislation. The cartoon was published when Jackson acted without congressional approval to remove federal deposits from the Bank of the United States (notice he holds a "veto" in the cartoon). Choices B and C are contrary to the cartoon's intended meaning. Choice D is irrelevant.

2. **C.** The cartoon would most likely be promoted by Whigs (choice C), Jackson's political opponents who viewed Jackson as abusing his presidential power. The Whig Party (named for the English antimonarchist party) was a political party that supported the authority of Congress over the president. It favored modernization and economic protectionism to stimulate industry. Although the Whigs had their roots in the Federalist Party, choice A, this party no longer existed. Jacksonian Democrats, choice B, were in opposition to the Whigs and would not have supported this cartoon. The Second Party System, choice D, is not a political party and would not have had supporters.

3. **C.** The Second Party System is not specific to a particular party. It is a term used by historians to name the political system from 1828 to 1854 of Jacksonian Democrats and Clay's Whig Party (Republicans). The origin of the splitting of the Republicans after the Era of Good Feelings into two parties, the Jacksonian Democrats and Whigs, is associated with universal white male suffrage (many states' elimination of property taxes from their voting qualifications, choice C), objections to economic nationalism, and the Corrupt Bargain. Choice A, the nullification crisis, occurred in 1832 when South Carolina declared that federal tariffs were unconstitutional, and therefore, null. Choice B, resistance to the Indian Removal Act, is not relevant, and choice D, the Hartford Convention, transpired in 1814 when the Federalist Party met to discuss the problems arising from the federal government's power.

4. **B.** The only choice that directly refers to the Missouri Compromise of 1820 is choice B. In 1819, the U.S. had 11 free states and 11 slave states, creating an even balance in the U.S. Senate. The compromise allowed Missouri (a slave state) to be admitted to the Union if Maine (a free state) could also be admitted to the Union, choice B. An imaginary line was also drawn across the Louisiana Territory. Since the text mentions the prohibition of slavery, it cannot be choice A, which indicates a mixed population. It also says nothing about gradual emancipation, nor insinuates that this is a clandestine operation, eliminating choices C and D.

5. **A.** Remember to choose the *best* answer to the question. One of the main stipulations of the compromise was that Maine had to enter the Union as a free state to "balance" Missouri's entrance as a slave state, thus an attempt to thwart the growing sectional division between the North and the South, choice A. While the Missouri Compromise was created during the Era of Good Feelings (choice D) and reflected attitudes about slavery in the country (choice B), it is a document intended to quell increasing sectional divisions about power and new territories. The Mexican-American War (choice C) did not take place until 1848, and tensions about slavery were addressed through popular sovereignty and other strategies, not this type of compromise.

6. **D.** Congressman Henry Clay was known as the "Great Compromiser." In the Missouri Compromise, Clay proposed admitting Maine to the Union to create a balance of Senate power. Clay was also responsible for temporarily quieting sectional division through the Compromise of 1850 when he defended a similar conflict over territorial expansion of territories acquired during the Mexican-American War, choice D. The Tallmadge Amendment of 1819, choice A, was a bill that requested Missouri be admitted as a free state. The Texas annexation in 1845, choice B, incorporated Texas into the Union. Choice C, the Indian Removal Act of 1830, authorized the president to grant unsettled lands west of the Mississippi River in exchange for ancestral Native American lands.

Document-Based Question

DBQ Scoring Guide

To achieve the maximum score of 7, your response must address the scoring criteria components in the table that follows.

Scoring Criteria for a Good Essay	
Question 1: Analyze the origins and effects of the shift in the American economy from 1815 to 1840.	
Scoring Criteria	**Examples**
A. THESIS/CLAIM	
(1 point) Presents a historically defensible thesis that establishes a line of reasoning. (Note: The thesis must make a claim that responds to *all* parts of the question and must *not* just restate the question. The thesis must consist of *at least* one sentence, either in the introduction or the conclusion.)	The essay provides coherence throughout the argument by uniting various points in a clear thesis statement. It provides strong topic sentences and transition statements to contextualize and connect the origin and effects of the Market Revolution. The essay guides the reader through a historical chronological explanation of important events and reasons for the shift in the American economy during the early 19th century.
B. CONTEXTUALIZATION	
(1 point) Explains the broader historical context of events, developments, or processes that occurred before, during, or after the time frame of the question. (Note: Must be more than a phrase or reference.)	The essay first identifies the Market Revolution and discusses the political influence of Clay and the American System. It then moves into a notation of technological advances, geographic expansion, increased sectionalism, and the cultural and gender effects of the need for labor.
C. EVIDENCE	
Evidence from the Documents **(2 points)** Uses at least *six* documents to support the argument in response to the prompt. OR **(1 point)** Uses the content of at least *three* documents to address the topic prompt. (Note: Examples must describe, rather than simply quote, the content of the documents.)	To receive the highest possible points, the response must address at least six documents that relate to the thesis. The essay also adds examples that historically contextualize and unify the information contained in the documents. For example, Documents 2 and 3 reference the Market Revolution and Documents 1 and 5 reference the industrial projects (Erie Canal and cotton gin) that helped in economic growth, while Document 4 provides an example of the labor abuses caused by industrialization. Documents 6 and 7 reference the expansion to the south and west territories.
Evidence Beyond the Documents **(1 point)** Uses at least one additional piece of specific historical evidence beyond those found in the documents relevant to the argument. (Note: Evidence must be different from the evidence used in contextualization.)	The body paragraphs provide specific examples of outside events that inspired the documents. The essay does this by discussing the tensions surrounding political divisions, sectionalism, the rise of the managerial class, immigration, and the cultural effects of using women and children to work in the cities. The essay concludes by discussing the booms and busts created by the market and political division as well as the increased sectional tensions due to expansionism.

Continued

Scoring Criteria	Examples
D. ANALYSIS AND REASONING	
(1 point) Uses at least *three* documents to explain how each document's point of view, purpose, historical situation, and/or audience is relevant to the argument. (Note: References must explain how or why, rather than simply identifying.)	All seven of the documents utilize some element of analysis and explanation of the documents' point of view. For example, Document 4 provides the perspective of a labor reformer, Seth Luther, calling attention to employers' abuses of women and children. On the other hand, Documents 1 and 5 describe the contributions of technological inventions that made commerce and productivity possible.
(1 point) Uses historical reasoning and development that focuses on the question while using evidence to corroborate, qualify, or modify the argument. (Examples: Explain what is similar and different; explain the cause and effect; explain multiple causes; explain connections within and across periods of time; corroborate multiple perspectives across themes; or consider alternative views.)	The essay provides a coherent and well-organized argument and uses the historical reasoning of continuity and change over time and the cultural, political, and geographic effects of the changes. The essay clearly identifies and describes a turning point in the American economy. It provides corroboration and qualification that demonstrate the effects of the economic shift and argues that the Market Revolution was generated through the united action of Congress during the Era of Good Feelings.

Sample Response

After the War of 1812, the actions of several key congressmen caused the American economy to experience a significant change, which led to important economic, geographic, and cultural changes. The turning point in the American economy was known as the Market Revolution, which took place from 1815–1840, a time that was during and beyond the Era of Good Feelings. Ushering in a historic surge in geographic growth and expansion, the Market Revolution increased regional sectionalism, political division, and the need for unskilled labor for industrial work. It generated a new managerial class and sparked arguments about the roles of women and children in the workplace.

The Era of Good Feelings led to the Federalists' demise after the Hartford Convention meetings when the Federalists met to discuss their dissatisfaction of the War of 1812. The secrecy of the convention backfired when the war had already ended. The Federalists appeared disloyal to the U.S. and became unpopular. When the war ended, Republicans felt free to embrace some of the Federalists' economic policies. Riding the tide of nationalism and patriotism, Henry Clay was one of several young congressmen who promoted the American System (also known as the National System or economic nationalism), a series of policies designed to stimulate the economy. As Clay himself noted, the American System brought prosperity to much of the nation (Document 2). The system used protective tariffs to shield domestic manufacturers from foreign competition; funded internal improvements that linked markets through roads, railroads, and canals; and stabilized currency and lending practices through a second national bank.

Other factors contributed to the economic growth. States funded their own transportation projects—like New York's Erie Canal (Document 1)—with the intention to encourage commerce and improve access to remote areas. New inventions and technology, like steam power and Eli Whitney's cotton gin (Document 5), were applied to improve production. As historian Charles Sellers stated in Document 3, all of this combined to create a "market revolution" that split regional production and encouraged interdependence and expansion. The South became known for cotton and other cash-crop plantations, the North for manufactured goods, and the West for grains and wheat.

One distinctive impact of the Market Revolution was migration. People began to seek opportunities in regions farther south and west, where land was abundant, available, and inexpensive, as hinted in the advertisements (Document 7). If people had little or no money, they became the "squatters" that Audubon mentions in Document 6, providing for themselves by settling on land that no one else claimed and attempting to make their fortunes in fertile regions before they were forced to move on.

Another impact of the economic transformation was an increase in the demand for unskilled workers. While slaves labored in the South, northerners sought cheap wage laborers for their mills and factories. Immigration increased as work became available in the cities. Because wages remained low, women and children often had to be employed in order to meet a family's financial needs. As a result, abuses occurred and reformers like Seth Luther felt compelled to contradict the praises of legislators by drawing attention to the vicious nature of factory work (Document 4). The nature of the family began to change as women and children worked outside the home. A new "middle" class also began to emerge because factories required managers, who were paid more and had the ability to buy the domestic goods that were becoming more and more available each day.

Unfortunately, the Market Revolution also led to extreme poverty and increased sectional division. Boom cycles in the market were followed by busts and panics, which often destroyed lives and threw families, both rural and urban, into extreme debt. In the South (and sometimes even the West), protective tariffs were viewed negatively because they appeared to protect only northern manufacturers. The protective tariffs limited the profits on cotton exports and kept prices for domestic goods high. South Carolina even challenged tariffs in 1828 and 1832, stating they were unconstitutional. This led to a nullification crisis that some consider a precursor to the Civil War. Thus, while the economic benefits of the American System and the Market Revolution cannot be denied, it is important to remember that the economic growth did not come without a price to Americans.

Period Five: The Civil War and Reconstruction (1844 to 1877)

Period Five explains the sectional tensions leading to the Civil War:

- Western Expansion
- U.S. Immigration and Migration
- The Mexican-American War (1846 to 1848)
- The California Gold Rush (1848)
- The Escalation of North and South Sectional Tensions
  - The Abolitionist Movement
- The Civil War (1861 to 1865)
- The Reconstruction Era (1865 to 1877)

Overview of AP U.S. History Period Five

Chapter 8 reviews key conflicts associated with American western expansion and the growing regional tensions in social, political, and ideological viewpoints as well as clashes with other peoples, such as Native Americans and Mexicans. As the country grew, free soilers and slave owners battled over the legality of slavery in the new territories. Historical developments include western expansion, the end of the Second Party System, the Civil War—its causes, leadership, and major events—and Reconstruction. The chapter concludes by offering a description of the short-lived biracial cooperation that characterized the end of the period and the violence that was used to redeem the South.

Use the chart below to guide you through what is covered on the exam. The curriculum contained in this chart is an abridged version of the concept outlines with topic examples. Visit https://apstudent.collegeboard.org/apcourse/ap-united-states-history/ for the complete updated APUSH course curriculum descriptions and key concepts.

AP U.S. History Key Concepts (1844 to 1877)	
Key Concept	**Specific Content**
KEY CONCEPT 5.1: WESTERN EXPANSION AND IMMIGRATION **The United States became more connected with the world, pursued an expansionist foreign policy in the Western Hemisphere, and emerged as the destination for many migrants from other countries.**	Popular enthusiasm for U.S. expansion, bolstered by economic and security interests, resulted in the acquisition of new territories, substantial migration westward, and new overseas initiatives. In the 1840s, Americans continued to debate questions about rights and citizenship for various groups of U.S. inhabitants.

Continued

Key Concept	Specific Content
KEY CONCEPT 5.2: SECTIONAL DIVISIONS **Intensified by expansion and deepening regional divisions, debates over slavery and other economic, cultural, and political issues led the nation into civil war.**	Ideological and economic differences over slavery produced an array of diverging responses from Americans in the North and the South. Debates over slavery came to dominate political discussion in the 1850s, culminating in the bitter election of 1860 and the secession of several southern states.
KEY CONCEPT 5.3: CIVIL WAR AND RECONSTRUCTION **The Union's victory in the Civil War and the contested reconstruction of the South settled the issues of slavery and secession, but left unresolved many questions about the power of the federal government and citizenship rights.**	The North's greater manpower and industrial resources, the leadership of Abraham Lincoln and others, and the decision to emancipate slaves eventually led to the Union military victory over the Confederacy in a devastating Civil War. Reconstruction and the Civil War ended slavery, altered relationships between the states and the federal government, and led to debates over new definitions of citizenship, particularly regarding the rights of African Americans, women, and other minorities.

Significant Themes

Now that we've discussed the curriculum, let's discuss the significant themes related to this period. The theme-related study questions that follow will help you make mental connections to the context of the "big picture" of this time period. Keep in mind that these questions often overlap and apply to other themes of social, political, religious, geographic, ideological, technological, and economic developments.

Glance through the study questions before you start the review section. Take notes, highlight questions, and write down page number references to reinforce your learning. Refer to this list until you feel comfortable with your knowledge of the material.

Study Questions Related to Significant Themes for Period Five

Theme 1: American and National Identity

1. How was the definition of citizenship altered and debated during this time period? (Hint: Think about how this era affected not only African Americans, but also women and immigrants. As African Americans began to challenge dominant beliefs about rights and citizenship, women also intensified their calls for equality. For immigrants, examine nativism and their role in the voting system as well as the rise of political bosses and machines. Discuss how the focus of the women's movement changed after the passage of the Fifteenth Amendment. You could also consider middle-class women's roles in the reform movements mentioned in Chapter 7.)

2. What specific legislation was designed to guarantee citizenship and rights to African Americans after the Civil War? (Hint: Important things to consider are the Thirteenth, Fourteenth, and Fifteenth Amendments, as well as the Civil Rights Acts of 1866 and 1875. Be sure to note how African American citizenship was initially defended by the federal government through specific legislation like the Reconstruction Act, the creation of the Freedmen's Bureau, and Grant's Enforcement Acts, as well as Radical Republican support of free labor ideology.)

3. How were progressive acts "reversed" in the South? (Hint: Analyze the role of violence and white vigilante groups like the Ku Klux Klan, including specific attacks like the Colfax Massacre. Also examine the attack on black rights through both the rise of Lost Cause mythology that associated Reconstruction with corruption, and the political abandonment of black voters by the Republican Party as it began to change. Focus on specific judiciary decisions as well, including the Slaughterhouse cases, *U.S. v. Cruikshank,* and *Plessy v. Ferguson.*)

Theme 2: Politics and Power

1. What were the events that led up to the Civil War? (Hint: Analyze specific pieces of legislation, judicial decisions, literature, and individual actions, noting how they increased Antebellum sectional tensions—states' versus federal rights. Things to consider include the Compromise of 1850, the Dred Scott decision, *Uncle Tom's Cabin,* the Kansas-Nebraska Act, the caning of Charles Sumner, the Lincoln-Douglas debates, and John Brown's attack on Harpers Ferry. Be sure to also note national divisions during the election of 1860 and the consequences of Lincoln's victory.)

2. What were the specific actions of the abolitionists and why were they considered a threat to the South? (Hint: Both before and during the Civil War, abolitionists were seen as a huge threat—economically, politically, and socially—to southerners' way of life. Explore not just the work of key figures like William Lloyd Garrison, Frederick Douglass, and Harriet Tubman, but political conflicts associated with nullification, western expansion, free soilers, and Lincoln's election—all of which were often associated with abolitionists, even if those assumptions were incorrect.)

3. How and why did the Second Party System end? (Hint: Examine the reasons why sectional divisions between northern and southern Whigs and Democrats became too difficult to reconcile. Also explore the rise of additional political parties, including the free soilers, who eventually composed much of the Republican Party—note other individuals who were drawn to that party, focusing on those who were not necessarily abolitionists.)

4. What was the difference between Presidential and Radical Reconstruction? (Hint: Note the difference between the early policies of Abraham Lincoln, Andrew Jackson, and the Radical Republicans. Be sure to mention the significance of Lincoln's Ten Percent Plan, Jackson's actions, the Black Codes, the Reconstruction Act, and the Thirteenth, Fourteenth, and Fifteenth Amendments, as well as other pieces of Radical legislation that seemed to challenge traditional southern hierarchies. Also note how those were received by both northern and southern populations.)

5. How, when, and why did Reconstruction end? (Hint: Analyze the motivations for and the consequences of the Compromise of 1877, noting the continued marginalization of African Americans and immigrants after Reconstruction as you read additional chapters. For example, African Americans and others continued to be marginalized. Be sure to address *why* this happened.)

Theme 4: Culture and Society

1. How did Reconstruction change the dynamics between black and white Americans? What were the economic, social, and cultural effects of emancipation? (Hint: It is important to consider the challenges to social and racial hierarchies in the South during Reconstruction in reference to the passage of particular legislation and the ways it was revoked—much of this is referenced in the hints for Questions 2 and 3 of Theme 1.)

2. How and why did the women's movement split? (Hint: Define the Fifteenth Amendment and examine the reaction of various individuals within the women's movement to universal black male suffrage.)

Theme 5: Migration and Settlement

1. Explain the role of western expansion. What was Manifest Destiny and how did it affect American, Native American, and Mexican life? (Hint: Define Manifest Destiny and note the way it encouraged racist attitudes and practices in relation to frontier expansion—after you read Chapter 10, you can also discuss how this related to imperialist practices in the early 20th century. Note the role of Manifest Destiny in the annexation of Texas, the Mexican-American War, the development of Native American reservations, and the destruction of many aspects of Native American culture and life.)

2. Who were the free soilers and what did they believe and promote? (Hint: Examine the sectional division of pro- and anti-slavery portions of the Whigs and Democrats who unified under specific premises. Relate this to expansion and acquisitions of territory through the Treaty of Guadalupe Hidalgo.)

Theme 6: Geography and the Environment

1. How did geography affect political tensions between the North and the South? (Hint: Consider why southerners insisted on their right to expand with their slaves and how this affected their general political stance. Be sure to note why they would have rejected the Wilmot Proviso and the arguments of the free soilers. Also note the importance of tensions created by the Compromise of 1850, especially those associated with newly acquired western territories and the Fugitive Slave Act. Be sure to also discuss the Kansas-Nebraska Act, focusing on both its consequences and how it related to the Missouri Compromise.)

Theme 7: America in the World

1. What were the origins and consequences of the Mexican-American War? (Hint: Note the border tensions caused by immigration and territorial conflicts associated with Texas as well as the state's eventual annexation. Connect the Treaty of Guadalupe Hidalgo to an increase in sectional tension, the rise of the Free Soil Party, and Antebellum political unrest.)

2. What were international relations like before, during, and after the Civil War? How did foreign nations feel about the United States, especially during the military conflict between the North and the South? (Hint: Analyze U.S. politicians' and citizens' respect for and relationship with the Mexican government to discuss foreign relations prior to the Civil War. For an examination of international relations during and after the war, think about Union and Confederate attempts to garner support for their causes. Be sure to mention hopes associated with the winning of particular battles, especially Antietam, and the way reunification affected America's foreign reputation.)

Important Events, Terms, and Concepts

The list below shows important events, terms, and concepts that you should be familiar with on the APUSH exam. These and other important terms are printed in boldface throughout the chapter. Because the APUSH exam requires you to pay attention to the historical context and connections rather than details, don't bother memorizing the terms now. Simply place a check mark next to each as you study. You can return to this list to review as often as necessary. After you finish the review section, you can reinforce what you have learned by working through the practice questions at the end of this chapter. Answer explanations provide further clarification into perspectives of U.S. history.

Event/Term/Concept	Year/Brief Description	Study Page
Manifest Destiny	**1845.** The term coined by journalist John O'Sullivan to describe the belief that God preordained white U.S. settlers to expand the nation's territory to the Pacific Ocean.	p. 178
Wilmot Proviso	**1846.** A legislative act to ban slavery in any land gained from Mexico during the Mexican-American War. It passed the House of Representatives but not the Senate, so it did not become law.	p. 188
Mexican-American War	**1846–1848.** A conflict between the U.S. and Mexico, which began over a contested border with Texas and resulted in the U.S. acquisition of new territories in the West.	p. 180
Kansas-Nebraska Act	**1854.** A controversial legislative act that repealed the Missouri Compromise, allowing people in states to decide whether or not to allow slavery. Slavery could be decided through popular sovereignty or the people's vote.	p. 189
Republican Party	**1854.** The Republican Party was formed by former Free Soil Party members and anti-slavery Whigs. The Republicans were a pro-business party that prohibited slavery in new western territories.	p. 182
Dred Scott decision	**1857.** A landmark Supreme Court decision that proclaimed African Americans were not citizens. The Court ruled that it was a constitutional right to own slaves and that the decision could not be banned anywhere in the U.S.	p. 190
Abraham Lincoln	**1861–1865.** An Illinois Republican senator whose presidential election caused several southern states to secede, which started the Civil War. Known as one of the most important presidents of the U.S., he guided the nation through one of its most difficult periods of sectional divisions.	pp. 184, 193
Emancipation Proclamation	**1863.** An executive order that declared "All persons held as slaves…shall be then, thenceforward, and forever free" in the Confederate states.	pp. 192–193
Freedmen's Bureau	**1865.** A federal agency created to provide food, shelter, clothing, schools, etc., for newly emancipated slaves.	p. 199
Reconstruction Act	**1867.** Congress divided the "rebel" southern states into five military districts and enacted strict requirements for southern states to reenter the Union. The act ended Johnson's Presidential Reconstruction.	p. 200
Thirteenth, Fourteenth, and Fifteenth Amendments	**1865–1869.** A series of amendments to the Constitution that prohibited slavery, gave all people born in the U.S. the rights of citizenship (except Native Americans), and enabled all men—including African Americans—to vote.	pp. 199–200
Compromise of 1877	**1877.** An informal deal that settled the disputed 1876 election. The deal was made between southern Democrats and President Rutherford B. Hayes to ensure his uncontested election and allow Democrats to regain control of the South.	pp. 204–205

Chapter Review

Chapter 8 covers events associated with the Civil War: resources, motivations, outcomes, and the leadership of the Union and Confederate armies. After the Union's victory, African Americans had hopes for a brighter future that was sparked by new legislation and opportunities during Reconstruction, but the consequences of northern apathy severely limited definitions of American freedom and citizenship. The chapter concludes by describing the violence of southern redemption and summarizes the end of Reconstruction.

Western Expansion

Migrations of American pioneer families in the 1840s began to swell in western territories and interest in westward expansion continued to rise. The Louisiana Purchase expanded the U.S. territory in 1803, and the American System and Market Revolution provided Americans with the infrastructure and opportunities that drove them to the western frontier.

Many people adhered to the belief that God had preordained white U.S. settlers to dominate the continent by extending the country all the way to the Pacific Ocean. This was called **Manifest Destiny** (1845), a term first used by newspaper editor John O'Sullivan to justify the annexation of Texas. Manifest Destiny was also used to legitimize the Mexican-American War and the usurpation of Native American land.

U.S. Immigration and Migration

In the 1840s and 1850s, opportunities created by booms in the economy continued to draw immigrants and increase populations in cities, which eventually pushed American migration farther westward. Immigrants arrived with high hopes but were often politically and economically exploited and forced to live in extreme poverty. Native-born Americans feared immigrants would take away their jobs and some were prejudiced against those of Jewish or Catholic faiths. In rural regions, many people could not afford the best land to farm. People sought cheap land in the new western territories. Southerners hoped for the western expansion of slavery, which would provide them with the advantages needed for economic and social upward mobility. As tensions grew and cities became more and more crowded, white settlers began to move west. Unfortunately, the westward movement infringed on Native American and Mexican lands, which contributed to unrest and armed conflicts.

Key Facts about Immigration in the 1840s and 1850s

Ireland's Great Famine (1845–1849). Ireland experienced a period of mass starvation caused by a disease that destroyed potato crops. This was a turning point in Ireland's history because potatoes were the staple food for many people. The period is known as the Great Famine or the Irish Potato Famine because approximately 1 million people died and another 1 million left Ireland. Ireland lost between 20 and 25 percent of its population when people emigrated to the U.S. and other countries. Irish immigrants often settled in urban centers, like New York, filled the need for cheap labor in factories, and worked as servants for the wealthy.

German Confederation revolution (1848–1849). Uprisings swept across Europe in 1848, causing instability and chaos. In the German states, revolutionaries demanded a democratic government, but their efforts were quickly crushed by their leaders' military troops, resulting in land seizures, unemployment, and severe hardship for citizens. The turbulence caused more than a million German speaking people to immigrate to the U.S. around the same time period as the Irish. Fleeing anti-Semitic persecution, some Jewish Germans contributed to this number. Many Germans often found hope in the opportunities available through farming in the Midwest or shopkeeping in small towns and cities.

The rise of political bosses and machines. Some German immigrants arrived with particular skills and the money they needed to gain a favorable reception among U.S. citizens who were against the arrival of the newcomers. Unfortunately, their Irish counterparts did not receive the same opportunities. The Irish were often treated poorly, lived in poverty, and found themselves in need of assistance to gain citizenship and basic access to resources. For this reason, many Irish immigrants traded their votes to politicians who provided them with favors. Congregating in the tenements of major cities, many vulnerable Irish people supported "political bosses" like the infamous William Tweed, a former immigrant himself who rose to power through a system of corrupt patronage. Tweed was elected to the 7th ward of Tammany in New York (a Democratic Party political organization which became synonymous with political greed). Supported by immigrants, he used the Tammany Hall Democratic political machine to take control of the New York legislature and steal massive sums of money from the city.

The rise of nativism. Political bosses, crowding, and job competition in major cities caused many native-born Americans to develop anti-immigrant feelings. Because many Germans were Jewish and almost all the Irish were Catholic, this led to a Protestant-based *nativist movement* (the policy of protecting the interests of native-born Americans) that assumed immigrants were immoral and incompatible with U.S. society (some Protestants were anti-Semitic and others feared that the Catholic pope would gain political power in the U.S.). The rise of nativism was evident on shopkeeper signs that read "No Irish Need Apply."

Know-Nothing Party (1849). The continued hostility toward Irish Catholics led to the formation of the Know-Nothing Party. They were called Know Nothings because when asked about their political polities, they replied by saying "I don't know." The group was a "secret" political organization, and believed that foreign-born citizens should be banned from political office. The Know Nothings influenced political elections and anti-immigrant legislation.

Heads Up: What You Need to Know

The U.S. had several periods of immigration, which were often influenced by various events in different time periods. Keep this in mind as you are taking the APUSH exam and look for context clues that will help you determine which wave of immigration a question or document might concern.

Another wave of immigration occurred after the Civil War during the Second Industrial Revolution (c. 1880 to 1920). (Note: The Market Revolution is sometimes associated with the first wave of immigration.) Rather than being connected to the development of the Know-Nothing Party, this second wave is more clearly linked to labor tensions, social reform, and the development of unions. Both waves, however, are linked to political machines and discrimination, which were prevalent in the U.S. well into the 20th century.

The Mexican-American War (1846 to 1848)

As tensions were beginning to rise with Mexico, a tenuous situation was developing over a land dispute in the Pacific Northwest, a fur-trading region. Britain and the U.S. had jointly occupied the Oregon Territory since 1818. The possession of the land was being disputed by both countries. In the election campaign of 1844, Democratic candidate James Polk used a specific slogan to promise that he would settle the border dispute with Britain in the Pacific Northwest: "Fifty-four forty or fight!" The possibility of war with two different countries on two different fronts was unthinkable—luckily, the war with Britain was averted through the **Oregon Treaty** (1846). The treaty established a northern U.S. border at the 49th parallel, instead of the annexation of the whole territory at 54° 40' north (line of latitude between the 54th and 55th parallels north that forms the boundary between Alaska and Canada).

Although the war with Britain was prevented, a war with Mexico would soon follow.

> **TEST TIP:** The two main causes of the Mexican-American War were a Texas border dispute and U.S. President Polk's desire to expand America to the Pacific Ocean "from sea to shining sea."

In 1845, Mexico became furious with the United States about the annexation of Texas. This prompted a border dispute with Mexico regarding the location of the southern border of Texas—the territory between the Nueces and the Rio Grande rivers. In addition, American President James Polk and expansionists desired to expand farther into Mexican lands. Polk secretly tried to negotiate with Mexico to buy its northern territories, but an angry Mexican government refused the offer of Polk's representative, John Slidell. After repeated conflicts between the Mexican and American armies in disputed territory along the Rio Grande, Polk asked Congress to declare war on Mexico and sent in troops under General Zachary Taylor to occupy the land he wanted. Because Mexico's government and military power were weak and unstable when the war broke out with the U.S. in 1846 (Mexico was still struggling to rebuild after its many wars to gain independence from Spain in 1821), the U.S. had achieved an easy victory by 1848.

The **Mexican-American War** ended with the **Treaty of Guadalupe Hidalgo** (1848), which confirmed Texas as a U.S. territory (establishing a distinct border at the Rio Grande) and granted Mexico's northern territories—including Alta California and Santa Fe de Nuevo Mexico (now called California, New Mexico, Arizona, Nevada, and Utah)—to the United States for $15 million.

The California Gold Rush (1848)

When Mexico ruled Alta California, few Americans traveled across the Sierra Nevada through its rugged trails. By the 1840s, however, white settlers began to move westward from Missouri. When the Mexican-American war broke out, these settlers fought to make California part of the United States.

The discovery of gold by James W. Marshall in 1848 changed the political, social, and economic history of the state. "Gold fever" became a national phenomenon. When gold was discovered at Sutter's Mill in California, many settlers headed to the territory in search of fortune. The influx of gold, migrants, and immigrants into the region contributed to its rapid growth and annexation as a state in 1850. The population increased from 15,000 in 1847 to 92,000 in 1850, and 380,000 in 1860 (see "Compromise of 1850" on p. 189).

Source: The first Fort Laramie at the Oregon Trail as it looked prior to 1840 by Alfred Jacob Miller (painted from memory, 1858–1860).

The Impact of Westward Expansion on Native Americans

Western expansion had a devastating impact on Native Americans. This was mostly because Manifest Destiny was based on the racist premise that whites were superior to other races. The discovery of gold in California and the acquisition of Texas, the Oregon Territory, and, later, the entire Southwest led to clashes between various Native American tribes and U.S. federal troops (and migrants) throughout the 1850s. White hunters also carelessly destroyed herds of buffalo (a major source of food and clothing for Native Americans), shooting them for sport or making a profit from their valuable hides. Warfare and malnutrition forced many Native Americans to give up their ancestral homelands and live on U.S. Indian reservations.

Did you know? Territorial wars with Native Americans were nothing new for the U.S. army. The U.S. battled Tecumseh and his allies in the War of 1812 (pp. 146–150). The American military participated in three conflicts with the Seminoles for land in Florida: the First Seminole War (1816–1819), the Second Seminole War (1835–1842), and the Third Seminole War (1855–1858). Collectively known as the Florida or **Seminole Wars,** they resulted in the devastation of the Seminoles. The few who were left in this region were eventually relocated to a reservation in Florida.

United States Territorial Expansion

TERRITORIAL ACQUISITIONS. 1783-1853

OREGON COUNTRY BRITISH CLAIMS EXTINGUISHED 1846

LOUISIANA PURCHASE FROM FRANCE 1803

MEXICAN CESSION 1848

UNITED STATES 1783

GADSDEN PURCHASE FROM MEXICO

TEXAS ANNEXED 1845

FLORIDA PURCHASE FROM SPAIN 1821

The Escalation of North and South Sectional Tensions

Key Facts about the Escalation of North and South Sectional Tensions

The Free Soil Party (1848). A group of anti-slavery Whigs and Democrats gathered together to form the **Free Soil Party** in 1848. The party was short-lived, but its basic premise was that free men on free soil would provide a better foundation for the U.S. economy than an economy based on slavery. The Free Soil Party believed that the expansion of slavery should be prohibited.

The Republican Party (1854). After the passage of the **Kansas-Nebraska Act** in 1854, members of the Free Soil Party merged with other anti-slavery Whigs to establish the Republican Party. Like the Whigs, Republicans were pro-business, and supported high tariffs, stable banking, and infrastructure developments like railroads. Republicans also wanted to offer free land to western farmers and ban slavery in any new territory.

Did you know? Republicans were rapidly gaining popularity in the North, but were soon attacked by southern politicians and newspaper writers. Republicans were accused of being a "motley group" because they seemed to offer something for everyone. The Republican Party attracted Free Democrats, Protestants, industrialists, the Free Soil Party, African Americans, factory workers, farmers, and abolitionists.

Bleeding Kansas (1854–1861). The term "Bleeding Kansas" was used to describe the violent turmoil that took place between pro-slavery and anti-slavery groups when Kansas was becoming a new U.S. territory. In 1854, the Kansas-Nebraska Act was passed which allowed Kansas and Nebraska to determine slavery status by popular sovereignty. The act divided the nation because it suggested that Kansas would become a slave state and Nebraska would become a free state. Sectional tensions emerged, and Kansas became flooded with violent confrontations (see also "Key Events Leading to the Civil War," pp. 188–190).

The Lecompton Constitution. This was the second of four proposed constitutions for Kansas. James Buchanan was elected president in 1856, mainly because he had little to do with the fighting in Kansas. Unfortunately, this meant he misunderstood the volatile feelings associated with the conflict. Buchanan supported the passing of a pro-slavery constitution in Lecompton, Kansas, even though an anti-slavery document was also created in Topeka, Kansas, to govern the state. The competing constitutions demonstrated the failure of popular sovereignty because supporters of one document boycotted the election of the other. Recognizing the Lecompton Constitution's fraudulence, both Congress and Kansas' territorial governor, a pro-slavery Buchanan appointee named Robert Wagner, refused to uphold the proposed constitution. Since Stephen Douglas (the primary proponent of popular sovereignty and a northern Democrat) was an outspoken opponent of the document, southern Democrats were further alienated from the party.

The caning of Charles Sumner (1856). Agitated by the situation in Kansas, Radical Republican Charles Sumner attacked slaveholders in Congress in one of his speeches. Sumner especially mocked fellow senator Andrew Butler, who was from South Carolina. Two days later, Representative Preston Brooks, a relative of Butler's, beat Sumner mercilessly with a cane, almost killing him. The violence had moved into the halls of Congress, and the incident revealed the magnitude of the divided nation.

FORCING SLAVERY DOWN THE THROAT OF A FREESOILER

Source: John Magee, "Forcing Slavery Down the Throat of a Freesoiler," 1856. Depicts Republican resentment for the violence against anti-slavery settlers from the Kansas-Nebraska Act. The bearded free soiler is bound to the Democratic platform and restrained by Democrats: Buchanan, Cass, Douglas, and President Pierce.

Lincoln-Douglas debates (1858). Abraham Lincoln and **Stephen Douglas** participated in a series of seven debates in Illinois that were part of an election campaign for the U.S. Senate. Since the debates concerned sectional issues, they gained national attention. Douglas held fast to the replacement of the Missouri Compromise with popular sovereignty, which put the ability to permit or ban slavery in the power of a state's people instead of banning it from a specific region. Lincoln saw popular sovereignty and the Dred Scott decision as a departure from traditional U.S. practices (the Supreme Court had used the Scott case to pronounce that owning slaves was a white man's constitutional right, regardless of what anyone else—including the federal government or a state's voters—might determine). Lincoln pressed Douglas about the Northwest Ordinance of 1787, which had banned slavery in a large portion of the country shortly after the Revolutionary War, and the Compromise of 1850, which gave those who wanted to object to the Fugitive Slave Act little freedom to reject the return of runaway slaves to their former owners.

The Freeport Doctrine (1858). Douglas' viewpoint in the Freeport Doctrine suggested that slavery was in the hands of the majority and could be banned or approved (regardless of the Dred Scott decision) through a voting process. This made Douglas very unpopular in the South, even though he also supported a state's right to *permit* slavery. Lincoln suggested that African Americans be treated equally because of what was stated in the Declaration of Independence. Lincoln observed that the country was headed for a calamity if the division in the nation continued. When Lincoln stated "a house divided cannot stand," Douglas replied that the Founding Fathers had set up the states to be independent, and states could essentially do as they pleased through the voting process. Lincoln lost the Illinois state Senate election of 1858, but the debates brought him national attention. Lincoln impressed the Republicans with his political views and great speaking abilities.

The Election of 1860. The four most important candidates in the presidential election of 1860 were Lincoln, Douglas, Vice President John Breckinridge, and Tennessee senator John Bell. In the North, the Republicans supported Lincoln and the Democrats supported Douglas. Southern Democrats chose Breckinridge because he supported the expansion of slavery and wanted to annex Cuba as a slave state. Bell, a wealthy slave owner, was promoted by the Constitutional Union Party, which favored implementing the Constitution rather than fighting over slavery.

Even though Lincoln and Douglas did not appear on ballots in many southern states, Lincoln was pronounced the victor, with 40% of the popular vote and 180 votes from the Electoral College.

TEST TIP: On the APUSH exam, you should be familiar with the initial southern Confederate states that seceded from the U.S. When Lincoln won the presidency in 1860, southerners did not want to be part of the United States and viewed Lincoln as a threat. South Carolina seceded from the Union and Mississippi, Florida, Alabama, Georgia, Louisiana, and Texas (against the wishes of its famous founder, Sam Houston) soon followed. These states joined together to form a "Confederacy" and elected Jefferson Davis as its president. Lincoln did not want to start a war, but he made it clear that he would not permit secession.

Results of the Election of 1860

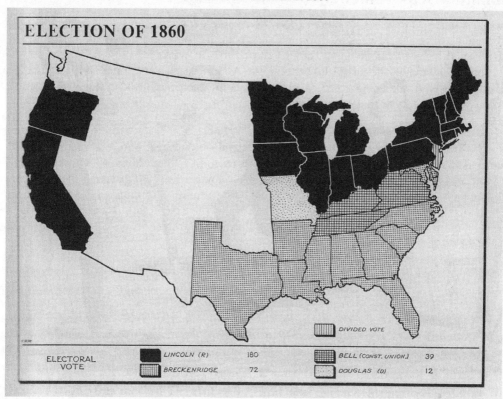

Attempts at compromise. In his inaugural address, Lincoln tried to calm tensions by claiming he was not an abolitionist and stating that he had no intention of outlawing slavery in states where slavery was already legal. Still, Lincoln insisted he could not honor the southern states' secession as a legitimate political act and viewed it as an act of rebellion. This kept several Border States in the upper southern region from seceding at that time.

States like Virginia, Kentucky, Maryland, North Carolina, and Tennessee were not as dependent on slavery as those in the Deep South. Border States were composed of a large number of former Whigs, many of whom were pro-Union and believed secession was akin to treason. The **Crittenden Compromise (1860),** a legislative act written by Kentucky senator John Crittenden, tried to appease the South through six constitutional amendments that could not be repealed. The amendments guaranteed the continued existence of slavery in the South and extended the imaginary line of the Missouri Compromise (at 36° 30' N latitude) to the west. The amendments were strongly opposed by Lincoln and other Republicans. Hence, the compromise was rejected.

The Abolitionist Movement

The **abolitionist movement** was a campaign to end slavery in the United States. It had extensive roots in the U.S. and could be traced as far back as with the Quakers in the 1600s and the Great Awakening in the 1730s and 1740s. The language of freedom and equality during the American Revolution sparked calls for emancipation. Recall that in the early 19th century, the Atlantic slave trade ended in the United States and the Second Great Awakening (p. 155) inspired people to become involved in various reform organizations, including those that opposed slavery.

As sectional tensions rose dramatically in the 1830s and 1840s, anti-slavery sentiments continued to grow in the North. Arguing that slavery was an immoral institution that hurt both blacks and whites, abolitionists held meetings that featured the horrific stories of escaped slaves, which were often firsthand accounts told by the slaves themselves. By publishing slave narratives and inserting themselves into political dialogues, both black and white abolitionists drew attention to the abuses embedded within the South's "peculiar institution." Abolitionists worked toward the destruction of slavery and were seen as a threat by prominent southerners. As a result, the abolitionist movement was one of the key factors that led to the Civil War.

HISTORIOGRAPHY. *When thinking and writing about history, historians must be able to set aside their own personal assumptions, beliefs, and biases. To capture and analyze the motivations and responses of particular individuals during the Civil War, historians must be able to objectively describe individuals in "historical terms" and within the context of a specific historical period or situation. It is important to remember that southerners promoted states' rights arguments to defend their lifestyle, culture, and exploitative labor practices. Even though many Confederate soldiers did not own slaves, most were white men who associated slavery with their own ability to gain financial and social advantages. Southerners fought hard to retain their way of life. Therefore, the war was about slavery, slave owners' ability to expand, and the power of slaveholding states in the federal government (not states' rights). It is also important to recognize that while some northerners were motivated by abolition and morality, most were more likely to be concerned with preserving the Union than freeing slaves.*

Notable Abolitionists	
Leader	Impact
William Lloyd Garrison (1805–1879)	Editor of the abolitionist newspaper *The Liberator*, Garrison was often considered a radical by those calling for moderate terms of freedom (like colonization or gradual legislation). He was known for his uncompromising stance against slavery, was founder of the American Anti-Slavery Society, and unapologetically demanded immediate emancipation.
Frederick Douglass (1818–1895)	An escaped slave from Maryland, Douglass was the most vocal and famous black abolitionist of his time. A gifted speaker, Douglass traveled throughout the North and even to Britain to tell his story and encourage others to support the abolition of slavery. He published his own abolitionist newspaper, *The North Star*, became a prominent statesman, recruited black soldiers for the Union Army, and even supported equal rights for women.
Harriet Tubman (1822–1913)	Tubman was born a slave and was nicknamed "Moses" for her ability to lead slaves to freedom. Tubman helped John Brown recruit men for his attack on Harpers Ferry and worked as a Union spy during the Civil War.
Sarah Moore Grimké (1792–1873)	Along with her sister Angelina, Sarah Grimké was one of the first white women to speak against slavery in public (before it was deemed appropriate for women to do so). The sisters were born in Charleston and influenced by the injustices they saw on their father's plantation.

Heads Up: What You Need to Know

African American abolitionists **Harriet Tubman** and **Frederick Douglass** frequently appear on the APUSH exam. Formerly enslaved, they became leaders in the fight to free slaves from bondage.

Tubman was famous for leading many slaves to freedom using the **Underground Railroad,** which provided secret assistance to runaway slaves who were trying to make their way north. Tubman was also a women's rights advocate and Civil War soldier. Her famous quotes, "My people must go free" and "I would fight for my liberty so long as my strength lasted," illustrated her fortitude and fearless efforts to free slaves. Historians have used Tubman's speeches to document the slaves she rescued in Maryland. During the 13 trips she conducted, she led dozens of slaves to freedom.

Douglass' autobiography, the *Narrative of the Life of Frederick Douglass,* is an ideological example of the opposition to slavery. His work is considered one of the most influential writings about the firsthand experiences of slavery. Another example you might want to use in free-response questions is a speech Douglass gave in New York in 1851. When Douglass was asked to speak at a July 4th celebration, he criticized the hypocrisy of Independence Day when thousands of slaves were still being oppressed, asking, "What to the Slave is the Fourth of July?" White Americans were free, but African Americans continued to be enslaved and were considered only three-fifths of a person!

The Civil War (1861 to 1865)

The Civil War—one of the bloodiest wars in American history—was the result of over 40 years of tensions between northerners and southerners. Several factors led to increased tensions during the mid-19th century as party lines became deeply divided between northern and southern states.

Causes of the Civil War

Conflicts over slavery in newly acquired territories from the Mexican-American War were only some of several events that contributed to increased sectional and political divisions in the 1840s and 1850s. Congress was divided, economic class differences were widening, the abolitionist movement was gaining momentum, and Abraham Lincoln was elected president in 1860, all of which produced fears in white southerners who believed their lifestyle, power, and economy would be destroyed.

Southern Democrats served constituents who hoped to expand their financial opportunities through landownership and slavery, supported the war. Southern Whigs, who valued industry, trade, and northern business networks, opposed the war and wanted to remain in the Union. Abolitionists criticized the South's militancy and its unapologetic efforts to claim new territory for slavery. Others harbored doubts over Polk's aggressive decision to dispatch troops in the Mexican-American War without consulting Congress, seeing his actions as just another attempt to gain new land for slave owners.

Compare and Contrast Northern and Southern Viewpoints

The table that follows compares and contrasts the differing viewpoints that contributed to the increased tensions between northerners and southerners.

Compare and Contrast Northern and Southern Viewpoints		
Differing Viewpoints	**Northern**	**Southern**
Views about the war	It was a "war of rebellion."	It was a "war of states' rights."
Views about social and economic practices	Although many northerners were farmers, the northern economy was diversified and industrialized. Northerners often embraced a modern society and economy. Some promoted a free labor ideology that valued independence and market participation.	The southern economy was dependent on agriculture and slave labor for cotton and tobacco farming. Cultural beliefs were a "way of life," and southerners felt unjustly criticized by northerners for their provincial attitudes and rural habits.
Views about government authority— federal versus states' rights	The U.S. Constitution made the federal government supreme. Rejected nullification	Supported the doctrine of nullification whereby states could nullify federal laws Supported states' rights
Views about the expansion of slavery	Northerners did not want to expand slavery westward. Supported no more slave states in the Union; California was admitted as a free state in 1850.	Cotton exhausted the soil in the "Old South." Southerners supported slavery expansion because it was the key to economic survival. New slave states were admitted to the Union (Missouri, Kansas, and Texas).

Key Events Leading to the Civil War

The key events leading to the Civil War that you should be familiar with for the APUSH exam are listed in the table below.

Key Events Leading to the Civil War			
Key Event	**Brief Summary**	**Description**	**Result**
Wilmot Proviso (1846)	Prohibited slavery in states gained from the Mexican-American War	The proviso, written by Pennsylvania congressman David Wilmot, was a legislative act that prohibited slavery in any territory that might be gained from Mexico.	The proviso was supported by several legislators from free states, but ultimately did not become law because it was rejected in the Senate. The Wilmot Proviso deeply angered southerners, who saw it as an attempt to thwart their economic and political power.

Key Event	Brief Summary	Description	Result
Compromise of 1850	A resolution to resolve the dispute of slavery	After the Mexican-American War, the question was, which new territories would allow slavery? The Compromise of 1850 was an effort to resolve sectional strife by introducing a set of bills written by Henry Clay, John Calhoun, and Daniel Webster.	As a result of the Compromise of 1850, 1) California was admitted as a free state; 2) the slave trade was banned in Washington, D.C.; 3) Texas surrendered land to New Mexico; 4) New Mexico and Utah were permitted to use *popular sovereignty* (states' self-government so each state could vote for or against slavery); and 5) a Fugitive Slave Act was passed, which became a problem because it was more severe than previous legislation. The act assigned heavy fines to northerners who refused to actively assist in the capture and return of runaways, which angered many northerners. Although people generally tolerated the existence of slavery, some resented being forced to aid the enslavers.
Uncle Tom's Cabin (1852)	A novel written about the brutality and harsh reality of slavery	*Uncle Tom's Cabin* (1852) was written by Harriet Beecher Stowe, who was inspired by the new Fugitive Slave Act. It is a novel about the long-suffering African American slaves.	This book was one of the causes of the Civil War because it stressed the horrors of slavery and intensified the moral argument abolitionists used to defend their cause. The book was popular in both Europe and the United States. President Lincoln saw it as one of the reasons why northern sympathies turned against the South. It is rumored that Lincoln described Stowe as "the little lady who started a war."
Kansas-Nebraska Act (1854)	Legislation that allowed Kansas and Nebraska to determine slavery status by popular sovereignty	Before the Kansas-Nebraska Act, Kansas and Nebraska were blocked from slavery by the Missouri Compromise of 1820 (no slavery west of the Mississippi River). The act was written by Stephen A. Douglas, a northern Democratic senator from Illinois who wanted political support to build a transcontinental railroad. The railroad would benefit his state by stretching from Chicago to California. Southerners would not allow the railroad unless they could eliminate the Missouri Compromise.	The act voided the Missouri Compromise and became one of the main causes of the Civil War. Legislators believed that Kansas would become a slave state and Nebraska would be a free state. But Kansas soon became flooded with aggressive pro- and anti-slavery migrants, and demonstrations and fights ensued when each side started using guns and guerrilla warfare to defend its positions. The conflict became known as Bleeding Kansas, and federal troops had to be sent in to stop the fighting. The violence in Kansas showed that Americans were unable to peacefully resolve their sectional divisions about slavery. The act also led to the fall of the Second Party System by splitting (and thus destroying) the Whig Party.

Continued

Key Event	Brief Summary	Description	Result
Dred Scott decision (1857)	*Sanford v. Dred Scott* was a controversial U.S. Supreme Court decision that denied emancipation to an African American slave.	Dred Scott, an African American slave who was brought to the North by his master, attempted to bring a claim for his freedom after his master died. Scott had lived in a free state for 2 years that banned slavery according to the Missouri Compromise.	The Dred Scott case was a landmark decision by the U.S. Supreme Court that determined that no African American slaves could claim U.S. citizenship. According to the Court's ruling, Scott, or any other African American, had no right to petition the Court for freedom. The Court was led by Justice Roger B. Taney, a southerner and a supporter of slavery, who held that Congress had no right to prohibit slavery anywhere in the U.S. The Missouri Compromise was deemed unconstitutional, which outraged many northern congressmen and abolitionists.
Harpers Ferry (1859)	An attack in West Virginia on a U.S. military arsenal by radical abolitionists	Believing that slaves would rise up to assist him in an armed revolt, radical abolitionist John Brown attacked the federal arsenal at Harpers Ferry, West Virginia. The slaves did not rebel and Brown's efforts were soon defeated.	Although Brown was judged and executed for treason by the U.S. government, his attack seemed to prove to southerners that people from the South, their lifestyle, and their culture were in immediate danger. Although most northerners saw Brown as an unstable religious zealot, some abolitionists considered him a martyr. Note: John Brown was also involved in the altercations in Kansas before Harpers Ferry. After anti-slavery forces attacked the free soil city of Lawrence in 1856 (known as the Sack of Lawrence), Brown and his radical followers slashed to death five pro-slavery settlers at Pottawatomie Creek.

Heads Up: What You Need to Know

The APUSH exam may require you to make connections between several events leading up to the Civil War in order to explain what contributed to the end of the Second Party System. Make sure you understand the implications of the rise of new parties and the Kansas-Nebraska Act. Northern Whigs, who voted against the act, joined the Republican Party, and southern Whigs, who supported the act, joined the Democratic Party. The Democratic Party was also split along northern-southern lines over the election campaign of 1860. Southerners walked out of the Second National Convention because Douglas was chosen to run as president. Keep in mind that neither Douglas nor Lincoln even appeared on southern ballots during the election of 1860.

The Civil War Erupts

As the final efforts at compromise began to dwindle, all hope of avoiding war faded away. The Civil War began with the attack at Fort Sumter and lasted 4 bloody years. The average age of the soldiers who fought in the war was 25, and the conflict took the lives of over 620,000 soldiers, well over the number who have been killed in any other U.S. military engagement (World War II is the second highest at approximately

405,000). By the time Confederate General Robert E. Lee surrendered at Appomattox Court House, Virginia, one in three men were dead, countless others were sick or missing limbs, and the landscape and infrastructure of the South were completely destroyed.

Fort Sumter (April 12, 1861). The Battle of Fort Sumter started the Civil War. When South Carolina left the Union in December 1860, U.S. (Union) troops were sent to Fort Sumter in Charleston Harbor, South Carolina, to man the federal outpost. The men stationed there began to run out of supplies in March, so Lincoln told the Confederate (southern) Army that he intended to send supplies—not reinforcements—to his troops at the *garrison* (fortress for troops). Before ships with the supplies could arrive, Confederate leaders claimed the fort as their own. Confederates began firing at the fort, but the U.S. commander, Robert Anderson, refused to turn it over. Only a mule was killed, but the devastation caused by Confederate shelling eventually forced Anderson to surrender. As a result of the attack, Lincoln called for 75,000 Union soldiers to respond to the rebellion. Feeling betrayed by Lincoln's "militant" action, several upper southern states seceded (Arkansas, Virginia, and North Carolina). Many people in Tennessee and western Virginia held pro-Union sympathies, but Tennessee decided to join the South in 1861. West Virginia determined its own fate by separating from the rest of Virginia, forming its own state, and remaining in the Union.

Did you know? The war wasn't universally supported in either the North or the South. Not all northerners believed in abolition, and not all southerners believed in state secession. The military draft was resisted in both regions and caused violent riots in New York City in 1863. The **Copperheads**, an extreme group of Peace Democrats from Ohio, Indiana, and Illinois, publically protested against Lincoln and emancipation. Many southern political leaders (including Confederate Vice President Alexander Stephens) also became angry with Confederate President Jefferson Davis when he began to implement basic war measures, including the impressment of crops and slaves to assist the army.

When the war started, there were split loyalties among northern and southern families, friends, and neighbors. For example, First Lady Mary Todd Lincoln had relatives who fought for the South. The Confederate President's wife, Varina Davis, had a brother who fought for the Union. Both sides suffered the loss of family unity.

Border States. One of Lincoln's primary concerns was keeping Kentucky, Missouri, Delaware, and Maryland in the Union. These states were not only in a strategic location (close to Washington, D.C.), but were composed of slaveholders who would have been more than happy to fight and manufacture goods and military supplies for the South—some of the upper southern states that had already seceded provided the Confederate Army with similar advantages.

The map below is a visual depiction of sectional divisions: U.S. Union States, Confederate States, and Border States.

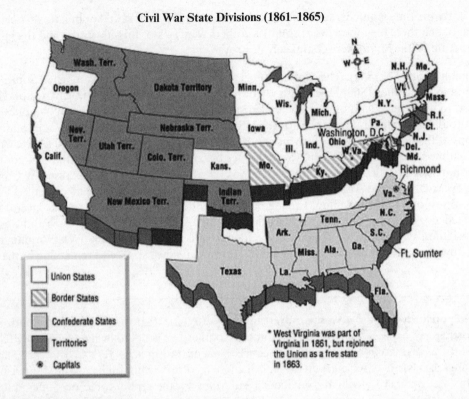

Civil War State Divisions (1861–1865)

* West Virginia was part of
Virginia in 1861, but rejoined
the Union as a free state
in 1863.

Legend:
- Union States
- Border States
- Confederate States
- Territories
- Capitals

Heads Up: What You Need to Know

The APUSH exam may require you to recognize the importance of the **Border States** and their relation to the *writ of habeas corpus* (a constitutional right that does not allow the government to hold people without officially charging them with a specific crime). Border States were highly contentious regions during the war, and these states were often battered with guerrilla warfare and infighting. Lincoln kept the Border States under control through unconventional methods, including martial law and the suspension of habeas corpus. Lincoln's actions were not unusual—Jefferson Davis also suspended habeas corpus in southern regions that contained a strong Unionist sentiment, like east Tennessee. However, in the charged atmosphere of the Civil War, both leaders were heavily criticized for this practice.

HISTORIOGRAPHY. *Historians recognize that Lincoln's views on slavery evolved as the Civil War progressed. While he possessed moral objections to slavery—which he was not afraid to express publically—he was not a radical abolitionist. Like many northerners, Lincoln initially believed it would be better to end slavery through legislation that prohibited its expansion. He encouraged colonization and gradual emancipation, and his original goal during the Civil War was only to preserve the Union. As the war continued, however, Lincoln met with Frederick Douglass and received firsthand reports about the horrors of slavery and the bravery of black Union soldiers, which altered his position. By 1865, Lincoln had not only issued the* **Emancipation Proclamation,** *but also spoke frequently about the importance of ending slavery through military emancipation and legislation.*

Emancipation

Contrary to what many people believe, emancipation did not occur with a single document nor can it be attributed solely to Abraham Lincoln. It happened gradually through the efforts of the U.S. government, the Union Army, and the slaves. As northern armies entered the South, slaves ran to Union lines, worked for the federal army, and fought for their freedom. The Union Army was initially ordered to return fugitive slaves to their owners when Confederates came to their camps to claim their "property," but some soldiers and generals refused to comply. Northerners resented aiding the South and felt the slaves could be put to work in their own camps instead of assisting the enemy. While Lincoln first wanted to abolish slavery through compensated emancipation, he was motivated by the actions of several Union generals, the war itself, and the courage of black soldiers to develop stronger anti-slavery legislation as the war progressed. Therefore, the combined actions of several individuals led to the freedom of African Americans.

The following chart is a chronological list of significant people and events that led to emancipation.

Important Leaders of Emancipation	
Leader	**Importance**
Benjamin Butler (May 1861)	Butler was a commanding officer at Fort Monroe in Virginia when three slaves fled to the fort for asylum. When approached by a Confederate officer under a flag of truce demanding their return, Butler declared the slaves were "contraband of war" and stated he had no constitutional duty to return the slaves to their owners. This policy was eventually adopted by the federal government.
John C. Fremont (August 1861)	Fremont, an explorer who later became a politician, was the commander of the Western Armies. He declared that all slaves in Missouri were free while stationed in St. Louis. Fearing the secession of the Border States, the federal government dismissed Fremont and rescinded his order, but his actions set an important precedent.
David Hunter (May 1862)	Hunter was a Union general in South Carolina when he began enlisting black soldiers into the Union Army and declared that all slaves working for Confederates in Georgia, Florida, and South Carolina were free. Lincoln ordered him to disband the black unit he was forming and rescinded his order since only the president had the power to make such a declaration.
William Tecumseh Sherman (1861–1865)	Sherman was a general in the Union Army who was involved in the Port Royal experiment at the Sea Islands. Sherman gave former slaves land that their Confederate masters had abandoned while fleeing the Union Army. Sherman paid them for the crops they harvested. In 1862, Sherman requested northern teachers for the slaves. In 1865, after talking with former slaves in Savannah, he issued Field Order Number 15, which confiscated a strip of coastline from Charleston to the Sea Islands and gave the land to black families in 40-acre segments. Sometimes broken-down Union mules were given to the families to use for farming.
Abraham Lincoln (January 1863)	Lincoln issued the **Emancipation Proclamation** in September 1862 (effective January 1863 if the Confederacy did not end the "rebellion"). The proclamation was implemented as a war measure to deny Confederates the labor and service of slaves. This legislation freed slaves in the Confederacy, but the proclamation did not include the Border States, where slavery remained legal. Still, it strengthened the Union cause by adding a moral element to abolish slavery, which encouraged foreign countries to turn away from recognizing or aiding the South.
Frederick Douglass (1863)	Douglass was instrumental in recruiting African American soldiers for the **54th and 55th Massachusetts Infantry,** two all-black units that were commanded by white officers. Black soldiers were paid less than their white counterparts, often suffered discrimination and injustices in the Union Army, and were viciously attacked and killed by Confederate soldiers. Motivated to fight for their freedom, they were not deterred by these disadvantages and were regularly commended for their bravery. Their service motivated Lincoln to push vigorously for emancipation during the war and was often considered grounds for citizenship by Radical Republicans.

Politics and War

Legislation

During the war, when southern Democrats seceded and could no longer protest against Republican measures in Congress, several legislative acts supporting Republican agendas were passed. These acts were highly influential when the war was over and would eventually lead to the growth of the economy, industry, and agriculture in the North and West.

1861	The **Morrill Tariff** increased import tariffs, which were used to protect domestic production and prices from foreign competition.
1862	The **Homestead Act** granted farmers western land at little or no cost. This contributed to westward expansion. The **Pacific Railway Act** was one of the most significant acts passed. It approved the building of a transcontinental railroad from the Missouri River to the Pacific Ocean that would be completed in 1869. It was a symbolic representation of the nation reuniting and also encouraged expansion.
1863–1864	Two **National Bank Acts** attempted to give the federal government control over the economy and the banking system without forming another Bank of the United States (the Second Bank of the United States had been highly unpopular in the Jacksonian Era). The legislation established a system of national banks that operated alongside state banks and set a uniform national currency.

Election of 1864

Unlike Davis, who had been elected for a 6-year term, Lincoln had to run for reelection. His political leadership was often attacked on several fronts—the Radicals in his own party believed he was not moving quickly enough to eliminate slavery and defeat the rebels. Some northern Democrats supported the war, but others—like his opponent General George McClellan—believed it was being mishandled. These **Peace Democrats** wanted to approach the Confederates to negotiate political terms for peace.

Lincoln won the election by a huge majority, partly because **William T. Sherman,** a general in the Western Theater of the Civil War (see "Important Battles of the Civil War," pp. 195–197), who had recently achieved a victory at the **Battle of Atlanta,** an event that significantly increased northern morale. Lincoln was also highly popular with Union soldiers, some of whom were able to vote. Those who couldn't find a way to vote often recommended him to their friends and families in the letters they sent home.

Civil War Military Strategies

The North had several advantages over the South when the war began. Its population and soldiers were more than double those of its Confederate counterparts. On the APUSII exam, you may be asked to compare and contrast the northern and southern Civil War military advantages and disadvantages. As you will see in the table below, resources and mobilization made a difference in the outcome.

Civil War Military Strategies	
North **The United States of America, called the "Union"**	**South** **The Confederate States of America, called the "Confederacy"**
Leaders: President Abraham Lincoln, General Ulysses S. Grant, and General William Tecumseh Sherman	Leaders: President Jefferson Davis, General Robert E. Lee, General Stonewall Jackson, General Pierre Gustave Toutant Beauregard
The North had a greater number of soldiers because the North was populated with 19 million people in 22 states.	The South had a lesser number of soldiers because the South was populated with almost 6 million people in 11 states; however, one-third of the population were slaves.
Slaves fled to the Union lines to become soldiers. Free black men were recruited to join the Union Army. Native Americans served in the Union Army.	Slaves were highly discouraged from becoming soldiers (it was not legal for slaves to be armed until the war was almost over). Some slaves accompanied their masters as servants, and others were impressed to build roads and work at the battle lines. Native Americans served in the Confederate Army.
The North was industrialized and produced 90 percent of all manufacturing of goods, weapons, uniforms, supplies, and transportation (railroad).	The South had a limited ability to manufacture weapons, uniforms, and supplies. Efforts to build industrial facilities (although many) were often thwarted by the Union Army. Union soldiers routinely destroyed Confederate railroads, armories, and foundries.
The North had a large navy.	The South had no navy.
The North was supported by the U.S. government so it had economic advantages.	Southerners' government was newly formed and it was adjusting to its role as a new government. The South had to print its own money because it had limited economic capital.
The North fought in unfamiliar southern states and faced guerrilla warfare and ambushes.	The South fought a defensive war in its own region. It was highly dedicated to defending Southerners' homes and property.
The North was slow to start but was soon victorious at the Battle of Antietam, Battle of Gettysburg, Battle of Vicksburg, Sherman's March to the Sea, and the Battle of Appomattox Court House, which ended the war.	Southerners were arrogant and confident. The South won many early battles—First Bull Run, Seven Days' Battle, Second Bull Run, and the Battle of Fredericksburg—but lost to the North in later battles.

Did you know? *Guerilla warfare* is a "hit-and-run" military tactic that was commonly used by the Confederates since they were familiar with their homeland. Small groups of armed soldiers or civilian combatants would hide behind brushes and trees, waiting to sabotage the enemy or raid enemy camps. This type of warfare was used against the United States in the Vietnam War (1961) and in the Middle East (Afghanistan and Iraq) by insurgents in the 21st century.

Important Battles of the Civil War

The Battle of Atlanta was not the only influential military engagement of the war. Areas where major battles of the Civil War took place were called theaters. There were three theaters of the Civil War: the Eastern Theater, the Western Theater, and the Trans-Mississippi Theater. The following table breaks down the significance of other important battles.

Important Battles of the Civil War		
Battle	**Description**	**Outcome**
Battle of Bull Run Manassas, Virginia (July 1861)	The first major battle of the Civil War, also known as the Battle of Manassas. It was a short distance from Washington, D.C. Thinking it would be entertaining, "tourists" from the city came out to watch, only to panic during the Union's unorganized retreat. The Confederates, led by P. T. Beauregard and Thomas Jackson, were victorious.	Bull Run revealed that Union troops were inexperienced and leadership was poor—the war would neither be short nor easy to win. Jackson, standing like a "stone wall" in the fighting, received a nickname that stuck with him until his death in 1863: "Stonewall Jackson."
Battle of Antietam Sharpsburg, Maryland (September 1862)	A bloody day in American history. Although Union troops stopped General Lee's Confederate Army from advancing into Maryland, Union General George McClellan's hesitancy to pursue the Confederates worked against him. Instead of destroying the Confederates, he allowed them to retreat to Virginia, where their army regrouped.	Technically, Antietam is considered a draw, but it is seen as a turning point in the war for the Union because it significantly damaged General Lee's hopes for a northern invasion and foreign support. It also allowed Lincoln to issue the Emancipation Proclamation. Lincoln removed the ineffective General McClellan because he failed to pursue the Confederates.
Battle of Vicksburg Vicksburg, Mississippi (June 1863)	The final part of the year-long Vicksburg Campaign (1862–1863). Union General Grant designed this campaign to capture Vicksburg, an important Confederate stronghold. After a 40-day siege of the city, the Confederates began to run out of supplies and eventually surrendered.	The siege was another turning point of the war. It was part of the Union's Anaconda Plan, which was a blockade of southern ports and a simultaneous advance down the Mississippi River that was designed to split the Confederacy in two. It essentially cut off several states, including Texas and Louisiana, from the rest of the South and limited western Confederate communication and access to resources.
Battle of Gettysburg Gettysburg, Pennsylvania (July 1863)	The largest battle ever fought in North America and also the bloodiest—it resulted in the most casualties of any Civil War conflict, including the loss of several generals on both sides. Confederate General Lee invaded the North for the second time, pushing into Pennsylvania to get the fighting away from Virginia. His defeat was so drastic that he offered his resignation as commander of the Army of Northern Virginia, which Davis refused.	Gettysburg is often considered the most important engagement in the war because it dashed southern attempts to shift the battlefield and change the course of the war, which might have allowed the Confederates to negotiate favorably for peace. It ended a losing streak for the Union Army. Many historians see it as the beginning of the end for the Confederacy.
Sherman's March to the Sea Atlanta to Savannah, Georgia (November–December 1864)	This was more a military campaign than a battle. Along the way, northern soldiers raided plantations, stole food and supplies, and burned properties. Union soldiers also destroyed transportation and communication networks and participated in several skirmishes and battles.	Sherman's intention was to obliterate the South's infrastructure and economy. It was hugely successful. The march's value can be placed in its psychological impact on Confederate civilians. Sherman's "total war" strategy severely affected morale. Many southerners were hungry, desperate, and tired of war. It was a significant turning point in Union victory.

Battle	Description	Outcome
Battle of Appomattox Court House Appomattox Station, Virginia (April 1865)	The final battle of General Lee's Confederate Army. By the time the battle was fought, Lee's army was exhausted from the 10-month Siege of Petersburg. His men were attempting a retreat, which was cut off by Union forces. Grant suggested Lee surrender even before the fighting began.	General Grant's victory led to Lee's surrender on April 9, 1865, at a common home in Appomattox Court House (which was a village in Virginia, not a building). The surrender of other Confederate armies soon followed, marking the end of the Civil War a month later.

Lincoln's Assassination (April 14, 1865)

John Wilkes Booth, an actor and Confederate sympathizer, assassinated President Lincoln in Ford's Theater just 5 days after Lee's surrender. His death was heavily mourned. A bloody civil war had just come to an end, and Northern citizens wondered who would guide the country through its reunification. The enslaved grieved the man they saw as the "Great Emancipator." The future looked uncertain as Americans faced several daunting questions: What was the appropriate level of Confederate punishment? Which branch of the federal government should rule? How should the newly freed slaves be integrated and protected?

The Reconstruction Era (1865 to 1877)

Vice President Andrew Johnson became president after Lincoln's assassination. The war was over, but homes, farmlands, and cities were devastated. It was a time for healing and reconstruction. Politicians ultimately came up with two plans to rebuild the nation.

The first, known as **Presidential Reconstruction** (1865–1866), was implemented by President Johnson. Since it was largely unsuccessful, a second attempt, **Radical Reconstruction** (1868–1876), was created by Radical Republicans in Congress, who sought black voters to maintain power, introduced biracial cooperation to legislators, and passed legislation designed to protect African Americans' social and political rights. For the first time, blacks had a voice in American history. However, Republican efforts also failed—southerners responded negatively to their policies and accused them of corruption, patronage, and favoritism. Legislation lacked the enforcement it needed to make a real difference and soon northerners became tired of protecting black citizens in the South. This opened the door for violence, which allowed "un-reconstructed" white southerners to take control of state governments. As early as 1866, paramilitary groups including the Ku Klux Klan (see pp. 202–203), began to form in the South and by 1870, their power extended to almost every southern state. Before true reform could take hold, southerners eliminated the economic, political, and social power of black Americans and dashed the hopes of many former slaves.

Key Facts Leading to Presidential Reconstruction

Lincoln's Ten Percent Plan (1863). This plan was formally called the Proclamation of Amnesty and Reconstruction Plan. During the war, Lincoln and Congress wrestled with ideas for reunification. The Union Army had taken over several regions of the South, so Lincoln introduced a plan in these areas that was supposed to ease "rebellious" states into Reconstruction. Lincoln allowed a Confederate state to rejoin the Union if 10 percent of its citizens took an oath of loyalty and agreed to free its slaves. Radical Republicans viewed the lenient policy as a way for wealthy plantation owners to easily regain control of the South.

Wade-Davis Bill (1864). Radical Republicans and others in Congress proposed an alternative plan to the Ten Percent Plan, the **Wade-Davis Bill.** This was a stricter plan that disenfranchised all high-ranking Confederates and required 50 percent of the state's white males to take a loyalty oath to be readmitted to the Union. It abolished slavery and renounced secession. Lincoln failed to sign the bill because he wanted a policy that was flexible. The bill never became law.

Johnson and the Ten Percent Plan (1865). After Lincoln's death, President Johnson inherited a Conservative Republican Congress—its majority was less adamant about calling for federal control of the states than some of the more radical members of the Republican Party. Moderate and conservative Republicans also believed that emancipating the slaves was a significant step toward freedom and had no intention of writing legislation that would promote social or legal equality. Johnson was actually a southern Democrat from Tennessee who believed that secession was illegal. In his view, the Confederacy never really existed; therefore, policies toward reunification should be lenient. As long as slavery was abolished, Johnson felt no qualms about upholding states' rights, regardless of the oppressive nature of states' individual practices. Johnson began enforcing the Ten Percent Plan, and although he required plantation owners to personally appeal to him, he pardoned almost all who asked. In 1865, he revoked **Sherman's Field Order No. 15** and gave confiscated land back to former plantation owners in the Sea Islands that had been given to, or bought by, their former slaves.

Black Codes (1865–1866). Soon after the war, southerners were running state legislatures. The Black Codes were passed. These laws restricted African Americans' freedom, and forced blacks to live under oppressive conditions.

> TEST TIP: On the APUSH exam, it is important to know the consequences of the Black Codes passed by the Democratic southern states after the Civil War. The Black Codes reestablished slavery in all but name in southern states. Despite gaining freedom, 4 million African Americans faced conflicts and struggles for almost 100 years after the Civil War. African Americans couldn't vote, testify in court, serve in state militias, or own property. Vagrancy laws—which were applied to people who appeared jobless or homeless—even forced black men and children to work for whites without pay. Through the Black Codes, southern states found a new scheme to suppress emancipation. Although the Black Codes were revoked during the Radical Reconstruction, they were replaced by the Jim Crow laws in the early 19th century, which served the same purpose. (Note: Many African Americans could not vote because poll taxes and literacy tests were used to prevent blacks from voting. Blacks did not regain the ability to vote until the Voting Rights Act of 1965.)

Radical Reconstruction (1867 to 1877)

When Alexander Stephens, Vice President of the Confederacy, was elected to the U.S. Senate, most Republicans, including the moderates, were appalled that it seemed so easy for southern politicians to regain the power they had before the war. Republicans blamed Johnson for this and wanted to remove him from office because of his policies. Johnson was put on trial for impeachment, but some Republican congressmen questioned the legality of the proceedings. Johnson escaped a guilty verdict in the Senate by one vote. Congress refused to seat Stephens, however, and tossed out Johnson's reconstruction plan, which allowed radicals to introduce their own plan for Reconstruction.

Shortly after Congress refused to impeach Johnson, Republicans announced they had chosen former Union general **Ulysses S. Grant** as their presidential candidate for 1868. During Grant's campaign against Horatio Seymour, he made no promises and gave few speeches. The Republicans were still able to present Grant as a war hero who only sought peace, and described Seymour and other Democrats as secessionists and traitors, a political tactic that became known as "waving the bloody shirt." Grant also benefitted from new black voters in the South and easily won the election with over 200 electoral votes.

A series of reconstruction acts are listed in the table below.

Radical Reconstruction Acts		
Legislative Act	**Description**	**Impact**
Thirteenth Amendment (1865)	Even before the Civil War ended, Congress passed the Thirteenth Amendment, abolishing slavery and involuntary servitude in the U.S.	Slavery was abolished in the U.S. in all states by December 6, 1865.
Freedmen's Bureau Bill (1865)	Congress created a federal agency, the Freedmen's Bureau, designed to provide food, shelter, clothing, schools, medical services, and legal assistance to former slaves. When it expired in 1866, Congress had to override Johnson's veto to extend the bill.	There were many successes of the bill. Although it was always underfunded and understaffed, the Freedmen's Bureau assisted many African Americans to marry, become educated, and receive legal services. An all-black school, Howard University, was established as a result of the Freedmen's Bureau Bill (it now accepts all races and genders). One of the failures of the bill was that Confederate land that was given to slaves during the war was restored to its original white owners. The bill was dismantled in 1872 when southern states pressured Congress to abolish it.
Civil Rights Act of 1866	First act by Congress to state that all citizens born in the U.S., regardless of race or color (except non-taxed Native Americans), had equal legal rights. It was passed by overriding Johnson's veto.	The act prohibited southern states from authorizing the Black Codes and protected the newly freed slaves by providing them with the right to draw up contracts and sue. This act gave slaves the right to refuse labor to whites and move to find better employment. The spirit of this act continues in modern civil rights laws, but at the time, it failed to eradicate many elements of the Black Codes. Southerners often engaged in discriminatory practices such as vagrancy laws that threatened jailing blacks who were unemployed in southern states.

Continued

Legislative Act	Description	Impact
Reconstruction Act (1867)	Tired of Johnson's policies, Congress wrote the Reconstruction Act of 1867.	The act was passed in spite of Johnson's veto and split the South into five military districts. In order to re-enter the Union, states were required to ratify the Fourteenth Amendment, register male African Americans to vote, have a legislature free from ex-Confederates, and write a state constitution that guaranteed African American rights.
Tenure of Office Act (1867–1887)	Restricted the power of the president and prevented presidents from removing particular office holders without the approval of the Senate.	Since Johnson believed the act was unconstitutional, he felt free to fire Edwin M. Stanton, Lincoln's Secretary of War. The House used the act to try to impeach Johnson, but ultimately impeachment was not successful. Johnson narrowly escaped impeachment because the next man in line for president was Ben Wade, a Radical Republican, whom moderates didn't trust. Johnson, with only a short time left in his term, agreed to cooperate if he was acquitted.
Fourteenth Amendment (1868)	The Fourteenth Amendment granted U.S. citizenship rights—including life, liberty, property, and due process—to all persons born or naturalized in America (except Native Americans, who were considered citizens of other nations). States were not allowed to abridge these "privileges and immunities."	The amendment was passed by Congress in 1866, but it wasn't ratified until 1868 because until Radical Reconstruction began (1867), some southern states still had considerable influence in Congress. The amendment expanded the protection of civil rights to slaves. Later in the century, the protections would be legally revoked. The Fourteenth Amendment was used by corporations and states to continue oppressive practices.
Fifteenth Amendment (1869; ratified in 1870)	The Fifteenth Amendment guaranteed voting rights to all men.	The amendment granted all male citizens the right to vote regardless of race, color, or servitude. For the first time, African American men were allowed to vote, but discriminatory practices continued in southern state governments to prevent African Americans from exercising their right to vote. Almost 100 years later, in 1965, the Voting Rights Act was passed to overcome the barriers of state and local discriminatory practices.
Civil Rights Act of 1875	Called the "Enforcement Act," this Congressional act banned discrimination in public places, like railroad cars, hotels, and theaters.	By 1883, the Supreme Court ruled this act unconstitutional. This outraged many people because they felt it opened the door to segregation and injustices, especially in southern states (which it did). "The world has never witnessed such barbarous laws entailed upon free people" (Henry McNeal Turner, 1883). African Americans had to wait until 1964 before Congress passed a law to forbid discrimination in public places.

Of Course He Wants to Vote the Democratic Ticket,
Harper's Weekly, *October 21, 1876.*

Source: A. B. Frost, "Reconstruction Voting," 1876. Intimidation practices used by the Democratic Party to suppress southern black voters.

TEST TIP: The APUSH exam may require you to be familiar with the Fifteenth Amendment, not only as it related to black male suffrage, but also to the women's movement (see Chapter 9). Be aware that the amendment split opinions of women who had been fighting for voting rights. Women who supported the amendment as a step in the right direction formed the American Woman Suffrage Association (AWSA) led by Lucy Stone. Women who didn't support the amendment formed the National Woman Suffrage Association (NWSA) led by activist Susan B. Anthony. Members of the NWSA resented being left out of the legislation and felt white women should have been given the right to vote before black men.

On the APUSH exam, you should be familiar with three key figures in the 19th-century women's rights movement: Lucy Stone, Susan B. Anthony, and Elizabeth Cady Stanton all played key roles in women's right to vote.

Post-War African American Freedoms

For African Americans, freedom meant more than just having control over their own labor—it meant that they no longer had to live under the conditions of slavery. Their physical bodies were now their own and they could live, move, and worship where they chose without white supervision.

Key Facts about Post-War African American Freedoms

Education and religion. When the Freedmen's Bureau and philanthropic northern missionaries established schools, former slaves of all ages rushed to learn. Black colleges, like Fisk University in Tennessee and Howard University in Washington, D.C., were established in 1866 and 1867. In addition, black Baptist and Methodist churches grew rapidly throughout the South. The ministers of these churches played important roles in the social and political development of black communities. These leaders not only served as spiritual advisors, but they also became active political leaders and office holders.

Marriage and family. Black couples were eager to become legally married because it had often been forbidden while they were enslaved. Black men could also claim social and political rights as the result of becoming heads of households (white men had been doing this since the Revolutionary Era). Irritating their former white owners (who needed labor for their fields after the war), black women refused to work in the fields and called for the same way of life as white women, who advocated *separate domestic spheres* (separate roles and privileges) for men and women. Black women who were forced to work to help support their families would frequently choose domestic labor like laundering, cooking, or housekeeping instead of physical labor like harvesting or farming.

Politics. African Americans embraced their new rights as citizens. After the passage of the Fifteenth Amendment, they formed **Union Leagues,** organizations closely associated with Republicans, that held political meetings and helped register black voters. During Radical Reconstruction, over 2,000 African Americans were elected to various political offices. From 1872–1873, **Pinckney B. S. Pinchback** briefly served as the governor of Louisiana. Although whites retained majorities in all state legislatures except South Carolina (where there was a black majority), fourteen African Americans were elected to the House of Representatives and two were elected to the Senate: **Hiram Revels** in 1870 and **Blanche K. Bruce**—a former slave—in 1875, both from Mississippi.

Post-War Southern Resistance and Redemption

Southerners became intensely angry with Radical Republicans and those who supported them. Democrats publically criticized *carpetbaggers* (northern entrepreneurs who moved to the South for economic gain) and *scalawags* (southern-born Republicans, often Unionists during the war). Southerners portrayed them as greedy and corrupt, lower-class individuals who took advantage of the dire circumstances of the region, seizing properties, money, and power as they rose in political status. The real truth is that although some were opportunists, most carpetbaggers and scalawags were middle-class individuals who embraced a new political, social, and economic order. Many were dedicated to the rebuilding of the South, and several were northern educators and missionaries who traveled south to help the newly freed African Americans.

Eventually, many Radicals in Congress died and northern opinions split. Calling themselves the "redeemers" of the South, southern Democrats began using violence to regain power. Simultaneously, the Supreme Court made progressive legislation useless, and white citizens throughout the country began to value the nation's reunification more than its reconstruction. As a result, black Americans were forced into a system of rigid segregation and second-class citizenship.

Key Facts about Southern Resistance and Redemption

The Ku Klux Klan. Founded in Tennessee in 1866, the Ku Klux Klan was a terrorist group that used physical violence and murder to rebel against northern policies. Members were often former Confederate soldiers and easily recognizable in local communities, even though they operated at night and hid their faces behind white hoods while committing crimes. The group was responsible for abusing and killing large numbers of African Americans and Republicans.

> **Did you know?** The violence committed by the KKK inspired Congress to pass the **Enforcement Acts** in 1870 and 1871 to protect black voters and Republican office holders from violence. Otherwise known as the Ku Klux Klan Acts, this legislation allowed the president to enforce the Fifteenth Amendment by prohibiting states or groups from interfering with voting. It enabled him to use federal troops to uphold the act and employ Federal Marshals to prosecute misconduct. Initially, Grant used it against Klansmen throughout the South, and after several high-profile cases, the violence was temporarily relieved. Attacks resumed sporadically in various states, however, and returned full force after the court case of *U.S. v. Cruikshank* in 1876, which stifled prosecution under the acts, and the **Compromise of 1877**, which ended federal control in the South. The KKK continues to exist in the 21st century.

Colfax Massacre (1873). Members of the KKK and other white vigilante groups took part in the Colfax Massacre, a confrontation between white supremacists and black veterans over control of the Louisiana city's courthouse on Easter Sunday. After the black men ran out of ammunition during the shooting, 50 of them tried to surrender but were shot down by the whites who formed a paramilitary group. Up to 100 African American townspeople were then murdered in a killing spree that white citizens later called a riot (the total number was difficult to determine because some of the bodies were dumped in a local river).

Supreme Court Cases

Ulysses S. Grant won the presidential election of 1872, but by then, northerners were growing tired of Reconstruction. The Republican Party split and certain factions of it became more sympathetic to southern Democrats' accusations of greed and corruption. At the same time, several landmark Supreme Court cases overturned a lot of the progressive actions of the Radical Republicans. Their rulings met with little opposition.

Post-War Important Supreme Court Cases	
Case	Summary
Slaughterhouse Cases (1873)	A legal dispute involving butchers in Louisiana. These cases resulted in a Supreme Court ruling that stated the Fourteenth Amendment only applied to the federal government, not the states. This essentially allowed various southern states to enact the **Jim Crow laws** (1890). These state and local laws created and enforced racial segregation.
U.S. v. Cruikshank (1876)	The Supreme Court used these cases to reject the prosecution and conviction of three white men who had been arrested for their role in the **Colfax Massacre,** citing the violation of their constitutional rights (the right to bear arms and the right to assembly). This made the **Enforcement Acts,** which had been used to charge the men, useless. It encouraged unrestrained violence in the South.
Plessy v. Ferguson (1896)	This case upheld segregation laws in the South by determining that if "separate but equal" facilities were provided for African Americans, states did not have to allow black citizens access to the same places as whites. It marked the final "undoing" of Radical Reconstruction by reversing the **Civil Rights Act of 1875.**

Heads Up: What You Need to Know

It is important to remember that these Supreme Court cases had wide-reaching effects. For example, the APUSH exam may ask how the Fifteenth Amendment was disempowered. Keep in mind that when the Supreme Court began ruling against the radicals' legislation, many southern states rewrote their constitutions. Poll taxes and literacy tests became mandatory requirements in some southern states for voting. Often a "grandfather clause" allowed someone to vote if his grandfather had voted before 1865, which excluded the formerly enslaved. Southern efforts stifled the political voices of both African Americans and many poor whites, who also had difficulty meeting the new requirements.

The End of Reconstruction

HISTORIOGRAPHY. *Historians place the end of the Reconstruction Era at different times. The dates often depend on how they interpret the meaning of the era. Some consider the U.S. as a whole, including the political challenges of marginalized groups in the West, like Chinese immigrants or Native Americans. Others note the memories of Union veterans, who may have reconciled with reunification, but never forgot their sacrifices enough to accept the full inclusion of the South. For the purpose of the APUSH exam, the end of the Reconstruction Era is connected to the Compromise of 1877, a political marker that sparked changes in many southern states that led to a fairly universal white rejection of black rights. Be aware, however, that other interpretations exist. Change happened gradually and varied in different regions. Many African Americans hoped for and continued to instigate reforms in education, cultural pride, grassroots movements, and legal precedents throughout the late 19th and early 20th centuries, long before what most people consider the Civil Rights Era (1950s to 1960s).*

Election of 1876. The presidential election of 1876 was one of the most controversial elections in U.S. history. Samuel Tilden, a Democrat from New York, received 184 Electoral College votes, while Rutherford B. Hayes, a Republican from Ohio, received 185 Electoral College votes. To complicate matters, Tilden won the popular vote. In three states (Florida, Louisiana, and South Carolina), 20 electoral votes remained uncounted. After a heated legal battle, the votes were awarded to Hayes, who was proclaimed the winner. The Democrats—who used violence and corruption to prevent Republicans from voting in the election—protested the Hayes victory, ironically citing fraud.

Compromise of 1877. Although it has never been proven, many scholars believe an informal deal was struck between Republican President Hayes and southern Democrats, who wanted to regain control in the states that remained under federal jurisdiction (the same states whose votes had been contested). The **Compromise of 1877** promised the following:

- The removal of all U.S. troops from Louisiana, South Carolina, and Florida
- The appointment of at least one southern Democrat to Hayes' cabinet
- The construction of another transcontinental railroad, the Texas and Pacific Railway Company, which would run through the South
- The acceptance of Hayes as president without a Democratic filibuster to block his inauguration
- An agreement to protect black rights in the states in question

As soon as Hayes was made president (without a filibuster), he ordered U.S. troops in the three states to return to their barracks, freeing the Democrats to regain political control. Hayes also appointed a southerner to be postmaster general. Plans for the railroad fell through, however, and it is unlikely that southern Democrats ever had any intention of keeping their promise to protect African American rights. The compromise allowed southern Democrats to "redeem" the entire South. Southerners then imposed social segregation, passed voting restrictions, and implemented systems of sharecropping to restrict the legal and financial position of African Americans. Southern whites retained this system of social, political, and economic oppression for almost 100 years.

Chapter Review Practice Questions

Practice questions are for instructional purposes only and may not reflect the format of the actual exam. On the actual exam, questions will be grouped into sets. Each set contains one source-based prompt (document or image) and two to five questions.

Multiple-Choice Questions

Questions 1–3 refer to the following painting.

Source: John Gast, *American Progress,* 1872. The painting was commissioned to be published in a popular travel guide.

1. Which of the following most directly reflects the image?

   A. White settlers' desire to become one with Native American culture
   B. The belief that American progress was associated with western expansion
   C. A rejection of the limitations of urban life
   D. Technological advances that made it possible to access global markets

2. Based on your knowledge of U.S. history, which of the following best describes the definition of Manifest Destiny?

   A. The American assumption about the holy nature of God
   B. The belief that the United States had been destined to expand to the Pacific Ocean
   C. The belief that support should be given to slave immigrants in California
   D. The belief that support should be given to Native Americans and Chinese immigrants in California

3. Based on your knowledge of U.S. history, Manifest Destiny contributed to the continuity of which of the following developments in the late 19th century?

   A. An armed conflict with British settlers in the Oregon Territory
   B. The peaceful annexation of Texas into the Union
   C. Additional conflicts with various Native American tribes
   D. Controversy surrounding the Lecompton Constitution

Questions 4–6 refer to the following excerpt.

Four score and seven years ago our fathers brought forth on this continent, a new nation, conceived in Liberty, and dedicated to the proposition that all men are created equal. Now we are engaged in a great civil war, testing whether that nation, or any nation so conceived and so dedicated, can long endure. We are met on a great battlefield of that war. We have come to dedicate a portion of that field, as a final resting place for those who here gave their lives that that nation might live… But, in a larger sense, we cannot dedicate—we cannot consecrate—we cannot hallow—this ground. The brave men, living and dead, who struggled here, have consecrated it, far above our poor power to add or detract… It is rather for us to be here dedicated to the great task remaining before us—that from these honored dead we take increased devotion to that cause for which they gave the last full measure of devotion—that we here highly resolve that these dead shall not have died in vain—that this nation, under God, shall have a new birth of freedom—and that government of the people, by the people, for the people, shall not perish from the earth.

—Source: Abraham Lincoln, *Gettysburg Address* speech delivered on November 19, 1863, at the dedication of the Soldiers' National Cemetery.

4. The excerpt from Lincoln's speech best expresses which of the following motives for entering the Civil War?

   A. To preserve the Union
   B. To free the slaves
   C. To protect states' rights
   D. To generate sympathy for the dead

5. Based on your knowledge of U.S. history, which of the following best explains why the Battle of Gettysburg was viewed as a turning point in the Civil War?

   A.   It was instrumental to Lincoln winning the 1864 election.
   B.   Lee's victory enabled Confederates to hope for a successful peace settlement.
   C.   The battle stimulated a series of Union victories that motivated the Army of the Potomac.
   D.   It resulted in a successful southern attempt to shift the battlefield from North to South.

6. Based on your knowledge of U.S. history, which Civil War battle led directly to General Lee's surrender to General Grant?

   A.   The Battle of Atlanta
   B.   The Siege of Vicksburg
   C.   The Battle of Appomattox Court House
   D.   Sherman's March to the Sea

Document-Based Question

1 question

60 minutes

Reading Time: 15 minutes (brainstorm your thoughts and organize your response)

Writing Time: 45 minutes

Directions: The document-based question is based on the seven accompanying documents. The documents are for instructional purposes only. Some of the documents have been edited for the purpose of this practice exercise. Write your response on lined paper and include the following:

- **Thesis.** Present a thesis that supports a historically defensible claim, establishes a line of reasoning, and responds to all parts of the question. The thesis must consist of one or more sentences located in one place—either the introduction or the conclusion.

- **Contextualization.** Situate the argument by explaining the broader historical events, developments, or processes that occurred before, during, or after the time frame of the question.

- **Evidence from the documents.** Support your argument by using the content of six of the documents to develop and support a cohesive argument that responds to the question.

- **Evidence beyond the documents.** Support your argument by explaining at least one additional piece of specific historical evidence not found in the documents. (Note: The example must be different from the evidence used to earn the point for contextualization.)

- **Analysis.** Use at least three documents that are relevant to the question to explain the documents' point of view, purpose, historical situation, and/or audience.

- **Historical reasoning.** Use historical reasoning to show complex relationships among the documents, the topic question, and the thesis argument. Use evidence to corroborate, qualify, or modify the argument.

Based on the documents that follow, answer the question below.

Question 1: Analyze the developments that contributed to both sides of sectional tensions leading to the Civil War.

Document 1

> **Source: Frederick Douglass, "The Meaning of July 4 for the Negro," 1852. Excerpt from speech given in New York to celebrate Independence Day.**
>
> What, to the American slave, is your 4th of July? I answer; a day that reveals to him, more than all other days in the year, the gross injustice and cruelty to which he is the constant victim. To him, your celebration is a sham; your boasted liberty, an unholy license; your national greatness, swelling vanity; your sounds of rejoicing are empty and heartless; your denunciation of tyrants, brass fronted impudence; your shouts of liberty and equality, hollow mockery; your prayers and hymns, your sermons and thanksgivings, with all your religious parade and solemnity, are to him, mere bombast, fraud, deception, impiety, and hypocrisy—a thin veil to cover up crimes which would disgrace a nation of savages. There is not a nation on the earth guilty of practices more shocking and bloody than are the people of the United States, at this very hour.

Document 2

> **Source: Kansas-Nebraska Act, 1854. An act to organize the territories of Kansas and Nebraska, Section 14.**
>
> ...it being the true intent and meaning of this act not to legislate slavery into any Territory or State, nor to exclude it therefrom, but to leave the people thereof perfectly free to form and regulate their domestic institutions in their own way, subject only to the Constitution of the United States...

Document 3

> **Source: Chief Justice Roger Taney, "The Opinion of Chief Justice Taney in the *Dred Scott v. Sandford* case," March 6, 1857.**
>
> A free negro of the African race, whose ancestors were brought to this country and sold as slaves, is not a "citizen" within the meaning of the Constitution of the United States.
>
> When the Constitution was adopted, they were not regarded in any of the States as members of the community which constituted the State, and were not numbered among its "people or citizens." Consequently, the special rights and immunities guaranteed to citizens do not apply to them. And not being "citizens" within the meaning of the Constitution, they are not entitled to sue in that character in a court of the United States, and the Circuit Court has no jurisdiction in such a suit.

Document 4

Source: Lincoln-Douglas Debates, 1858. Known as the "Great Debates of 1858," these senatorial debates were a series of seven debates between Republican Abraham Lincoln and Democratic Senator Stephen A. Douglas.

I will say here, while upon this subject, that I have no purpose directly or indirectly to interfere with the institution of slavery in the states where it exists. I believe I have no lawful right to do so, and I have no inclination to do so. I have no purpose to introduce political and social equality between the white and the black races…but I hold that notwithstanding all this, there is no reason in the world why the negro is not entitled to all the natural rights enumerated in the Declaration of Independence, the right to life, liberty and the pursuit of happiness.

—Abraham Lincoln

He tells you that I will not argue the question of whether slavery is right or wrong. I tell you why I will not do it. I hold that under the Constitution of the United States, each state of this Union has a right to do as it pleases on the subject of slavery… It is none of our business whether slavery exists in Missouri or not.

—Stephen A. Douglas

Document 5

Source: John Magee, "Southern Chivalry: Argument versus Club's," 1856. The caning of Charles Sumner. The Miriam and Ira D. Wallach Division of Art, Print Collection: The New York Public Library Digital Collection.

SOUTHERN CHIVALRY — ARGUMENT versus CLUB'S.

Document 6

> **Source: John Brown, radical abolitionist, addresses the Virginia Court when he was about to receive the sentence of death, 1859.**
>
> This Court acknowledges too, as I suppose, the validity of the law of God. I saw a book kissed, which I suppose to be the Bible, or at least the New Testament, which teaches me that, "All things whatsoever I would that men should do to me, I should do even so to them." It teaches me further, to "Remember them that are in bonds, as bound with them." I endeavored to act up to that instruction. I say I am yet too young to understand that God is any respecter of persons. I believe that to have interfered as I have done, as I have always freely admitted I have done, in behalf of his despised poor, I have done no wrong, but right. Now, if it is deemed necessary that I should forfeit my life, for the furtherance of the ends of justice, and mingle my blood further with the blood of my children, and with the blood of millions in this Slave country, whose rights are disregarded by wicked, cruel, and unjust enactments, — I say; let it be done.

Document 7

> **Source: South Carolina's Ordinance of Secession, December 20, 1860.**
>
> A geographical line has been drawn across the Union, and all the States north of that line have united in the election of a man to the high office of President of the United States, whose opinions and purposes are hostile to slavery. He is to be entrusted with the administration of the common Government, because he has declared that that "Government cannot endure permanently half slave, half free," and that the public mind must rest in the belief that slavery is in the course of ultimate extinction...
>
> The guaranties of the Constitution will then no longer exist; the equal rights of the States will be lost. The slaveholding States will no longer have the power of self-government, or self-protection, and the Federal Government will have become their enemy...
>
> We, therefore, the People of South Carolina, by our delegates in Convention assembled, appealing to the Supreme Judge of the world for the rectitude of our intentions, have solemnly declared that the Union heretofore existing between this State and the other States of North America, is dissolved, and that the State of South Carolina has resumed her position among the nations of the world, as a separate and independent State; with full power to levy war, conclude peace, contract alliances, establish commerce, and to do all other acts and things which independent States may of right do.

Answer Explanations

Multiple-Choice Questions

1. **B.** Always look for the "best" answer among the choices listed. Although the rural setting of the painting might represent a rejection of the limitations of urban life (choice C), the central figure depicts Columbia, a goddess-like personification of United States liberty. She is leading settlers westward, extending a telegraph line and carrying a school textbook under her arm. This suggests that expansion was an American "divine right," making choice B correct. This American attitude helped to fuel western settlement, but it also led to the removal and demise of many Native Americans. Based on the prevailing attitudes in the late 19th century, most white settlers never had any desire to become one with Native American culture (choice A). The railroad is depicted in the background of the painting, but not in a featured place of importance. Therefore, technological and global markets (choice D) are not the focus here.

2. **B.** Although you might be tempted to select choice A because of the "holy" goddess-like image, Manifest Destiny was the belief that God had preordained the United States to expand westward, choice B. The concept of Manifest Destiny rationalized the acquisition of territories. It was coined by journalist John O'Sullivan when he defended the annexation of Texas in 1845: "The fulfillment of our manifest destiny is to overspread the continent by Providence for the free development of our yearly multiplying millions." Choices C and D are incorrect because there was no consensus that support should be given to Native Americans, Chinese, or slaves.

3. **C.** The correct answer can be reached through the process of elimination. There was no armed conflict with British settlers in Oregon (choice A), the annexation of Texas led to the very intense, "un-peaceful" Mexican-American War (choice B), and the Lecompton Constitution was associated with sectional tension rather than Manifest Destiny (choice D). This leaves choice C as the only possible answer; Manifest Destiny contributed additional conflicts with various Native American tribes, choice C.

4. **A.** Lincoln's speech suggests that the preservation of the Union, choice A, which may *include* a "new birth of freedom," was the North's primary motive for entering the war. While Lincoln's speech references equality, only 10 states freed slaves. It wasn't until the Thirteenth Amendment in 1865 when the abolishment of slavery was enacted, making choice B incorrect. Choice C, to protect states' rights, is also incorrect, as evidenced by Lincoln's indication that the nation should not cease to exist. Choice D, to generate sympathy for the dead, is far from the praise he bestowed upon them.

5. **C.** This question requires students to know about some of the basic facts of the Battle of Gettysburg in order to determine why it was viewed as a turning point in the Civil War. Since the Confederacy lost the battle, choices B (Lee's victory enabled Confederates to hope for a successful peace settlement) and D (it resulted in a successful southern attempt to shift the battlefield from North to South) are incorrect. Slavery wasn't abolished by the Thirteenth Amendment until after Lincoln's reelection, which makes choice A (it was instrumental to Lincoln winning the 1864 election) impossible. The answer must be choice C, the battle stimulated a series of Union victories that motivated the Army of the Potomac.

6. **C.** The key words in the question are "directly" and "battle" (Sherman's March, choice D, is technically considered a military action). Although all of the choices heavily contributed to the Union's victory, Lee surrendered at Appomattox Court House in April 1865, which makes the Battle of Appomattox Court House the one that was *directly* responsible for Lee's surrender to Grant, choice C. The Battle of Atlanta (choice A) boosted morale and helped gather support for Lincoln's reelection. The Siege of Vicksburg was a turning point in the war (choice B), but neither immediately led to the war's end. The potential answer may have been different if the question had used the words "contributed to" or "was a factor in."

Document-Based Question

DBQ Scoring Guide

To achieve the maximum score of 7, your response must address the scoring criteria components in the table that follows.

Scoring Criteria for a Good Essay	
Question 1: Analyze the developments that contributed to both sides of sectional tensions leading to the Civil War.	
Scoring Criteria	**Examples**
A. THESIS/CLAIM	
(1 point) Presents a historically defensible thesis that establishes a line of reasoning. (Note: The thesis must make a claim that responds to *all* parts of the question and must *not* just restate the question. The thesis must consist of *at least* one sentence, either in the introduction or the conclusion.)	The essay provides coherency throughout the argument by uniting various points in a clear thesis statement. It guides the reader through a chronological explanation of important events and reasons for political northern and southern ideologies. This essay uses the Missouri Compromise as a starting point and develops issues related to expansion. It argues that sectional tensions increased through the effects of several specific events: the Mexican-American War territorial slavery issue, the abolitionist movement, the Kansas-Nebraska Act, and the election of Lincoln in 1860.
B. CONTEXTUALIZATION	
(1 point) Explains the broader historical context of events, developments, or processes that occurred before, during, or after the time frame of the question. (Note: Must be more than a phrase or reference.)	The essay provides strong topic sentences and transition statements to historically contextualize and connect all of the events it mentions. It also overlaps the effects of certain pieces of legislation or actions, demonstrating the complexity of regional animosity. The essay also adds examples that historically contextualize and unify the information contained in the documents, including the Missouri Compromise, the Mexican-American War, and the Compromise of 1850.
C. EVIDENCE	
Evidence from the Documents **(2 points)** Uses at least *six* documents to support the argument in response to the prompt. OR **(1 point)** Uses the content of at least *three* documents to address the topic prompt. (Note: Examples must describe, rather than simply quote, the content of the documents.) **Evidence Beyond the Documents** **(1 point)** Uses at least one additional piece of specific historical evidence beyond those found in the documents relevant to the argument. (Note: Evidence must be different from the evidence used in contextualization.)	To receive the highest possible points, the response must address all seven of the documents and relate the documents to the thesis. Most of the documents are analyzed for purpose, but since sectional division is the primary topic, point of view becomes relevant to all of them. The essay provides a number of specific examples and legislative laws that influenced the argument. For example, Documents 1, 4, and 6 relate to northern tensions, and Documents 2, 3, and 7 relate to southern tensions. The body paragraphs provide specific examples of outside events that inspired the documents. The essay does this by discussing the tensions surrounding political division, sectionalism, violent emotion and attacks, expansionism, and cultural threats.

Scoring Criteria	Examples
D. ANALYSIS AND REASONING	
(1 point) Uses at least *three* documents to explain how each document's point of view, purpose, historical situation, and/or audience is relevant to the argument. (Note: References must explain how or why, rather than simply identifying.)	For all seven of the documents, the response utilizes some element of analysis and explanation of the documents' point of view. Point of view is used to provide the author's position on the subject as well as identify where the author stands on the issues that are being discussed. They are then applied to the argument.
(1 point) Uses historical reasoning and development that focuses on the question while using evidence to corroborate, qualify, or modify the argument. (Examples: Explain what is similar and different; explain the cause and effect; explain multiple causes; explain connections within and across periods of time; corroborate multiple perspectives across themes; or consider alternative views.)	The essay provides a coherent and well-organized argument and uses the historical reasoning of causation throughout the response. The essay simultaneously identifies and analyzes the causes of the Civil War. To bring the essay together, the essay first identifies attempts to compromise. It then moves into a notation of increased sectionalism and violence, noting the role of expansion and the implicit threats (real or imagined) that each region believed it was experiencing. The essay concludes by discussing the election of 1860 and the secession of the southern states. It leads into the Civil War and refers to emancipation while hinting at the progressive legislation of Radical Reconstruction.

Sample Response

Throughout the early 19th century, several political compromises had been reached that controlled sectional tension between northern and southern American states. One of these was the Missouri Compromise (1820), which established an imaginary line at 36° 30' that generated an understood separation between territories that entered the Union as states that either allowed or prohibited slavery. As the country began to expand farther west in the 1840s and 1850s, however, the Missouri Compromise and the sectional divisions it held in check began to disintegrate. Northerners began to resent the slavery that continued to exist throughout the country and southerners began to feel as if their lifestyle, political power, and economy were severely threatened. Simultaneous, overlapping events increased the animosity these individuals had for each other's cause. By the time Abraham Lincoln was elected president in 1860, politicians from both regions found it impossible to compromise and the nation exploded into civil war.

One of the primary causes of the Civil War was the abolitionist movement. As Frederick Douglass noted in his speech (Document 1), former slaves and their advocates found it intolerable that the U.S. continued to celebrate its status as a nation based on equality when millions of people still remained in physical bondage. Abolitionists in the North, like Douglass and William Lloyd Garrison, spoke publically about the hardships and immorality of slavery. The presence of abolitionists upset southerners like Preston Brooks, the man who caned Charles Sumner (Document 5), a radical northern politician who spoke against the expansion of slavery into new territories like those received from the Mexican-American War. Although not all southerners owned slaves, the culture and economy of the South was based on its "peculiar institution" for economic and social stability. If slavery was not allowed to expand with the rest of the country, the southerners felt they would be limited in their ability to gain and obtain prosperity.

In 1854, the Kansas-Nebraska Act contributed to sectional anger (Document 2). Emotions were still high from the passage of the Compromise of 1850, which introduced the concept of popular sovereignty, a procedure designed by Illinois senator Stephen Douglas to allow incoming states to vote for their slave or free status. When the Kansas Territory applied for statehood, it was flooded with both pro- and anti-slavery settlers, who began violent conflicts (known as "Bleeding Kansas") for control of the state. Congress became involved in the struggle, especially after President Buchanan endorsed the Lecompton Constitution, a pro-slavery document that was disputed in Kansas and the Senate. The violence extended to the legislative halls of Washington. Brooks caned Sumner 3 days after Sumner gave a speech against the expansion of slavery into Kansas. In the speech, Sumner insulted both southern honor and one of Brooks' relatives. Although he was ousted from the House of Representatives where he held a seat, Brooks remained highly popular in the South. He was soon reelected in the South Carolina district he represented.

The Kansas-Nebraska Act was not the only event that reversed the Missouri Compromise. In 1857, the Supreme Court determined a former slave suing for his freedom, Dred Scott, had no legal jurisdiction in the U.S. In his opinion, Chief Justice Roger Taney not only determined African Americans were not legal citizens, but he also noted that they were only designated as property by the Constitution (Document 3). Since the Constitution explicitly stated that the government could not infringe on any citizen's right to property, Congress had no legal ability to prohibit slavery in any state. Thus, Taney determined the Missouri Compromise was null and void, which severely angered northerners, who were growing tired of the South's demands that they uphold slavery. Again, tensions had already increased because of the Compromise of 1850, which also included a strict Fugitive Slave Act that attempted to force many to cooperate with slave catchers by strictly fining those who did not. Scott's case convinced northerners that the South would continue to infringe on their own moral code by compelling them to allow slavery in states that had banned it for decades.

While Douglas held to his belief that popular sovereignty was the legitimate way to determine the country's future, others envisioned a different future. Abraham Lincoln, Douglas' opponent for the 1858 Illinois senate seat, was a "free soiler," someone who believed that while slavery should continue in the South, it should be prohibited in all new states or territories (Document 4). Free soilers merged with other groups, especially the anti-slavery Whigs whose party had been destroyed by the Compromise of 1850, to form the Republican Party. Radical abolitionist John Brown, in an effort to create a slave uprising, attacked a federal arsenal at Harpers Ferry in 1859. Brown, like many zealots, believed that nothing but violence would solve the conflict and did not regret his actions (Document 6). Even though he was tried and executed, southerners were further convinced that their lifestyle and values were endangered. Southerners were determined to defend them wholeheartedly.

When Lincoln won the election of 1860 as the new party's candidate, radical southern politicians were further outraged. Even though Lincoln had clearly stated he would not interfere with the southern right to hold slaves, South Carolina almost immediately seceded from the Union (Document 7). Before Lincoln was sworn into office in March 1861, six other states followed, including Mississippi, Alabama, and Louisiana. The southern Confederacy was joined by four Border States in April after fighting began at Fort Sumter in Charleston Harbor. This began a bloody, 4-year Civil War, which would eventually emancipate African American slaves and attempt to begin the long process of ensuring their civil rights

Period Six: The Gilded Age (1865 to 1898)

Period Six explores a period of inspired technological and communication advances that resulted in rapid economic growth—the Gilded Age.

- The Second Industrial Revolution (c. 1870 to c. 1914)
- Economics of the Gilded Age
- Politics and Government of the Gilded Age
  - The Populist Movement
- Social Changes of the Gilded Age
  - Social and Economic Theories
  - Women's Roles
  - Immigration
  - Labor Unions
- Geographic Regions of the Gilded Age
  - Southern Region
  - Western (Midwest) Region
  - Native American Conflicts
- International Relations of the Gilded Age

Overview of AP U.S. History Period Six

Chapter 9 covers transitions in American history associated with the Gilded Age beginning in 1878. Legal, technological, and communication developments caused a Second Industrial Revolution that changed U.S. culture, society, and the economy. The historical topics covered in this chapter help to explain how conflicts continued to grow between nativists and immigrants, labor and management, Native Americans and western migrants, and wealthy businessmen and social reformers.

Note: Period Six of the AP U.S. History key concepts begins in 1865. However, the history topics covered from 1865 to 1877, the Reconstruction Era, are discussed at the end of Chapter 8 following the Civil War.

Use the chart below to guide you through what is covered on the exam. The curriculum contained in this chart is an abridged version of the concept outlines with topic examples. Visit https://apstudent. collegeboard.org/apcourse/ap-united-states-history/ for the complete updated APUSH course curriculum descriptions and key concepts.

AP U.S. History Key Concepts (1865 to 1898)	
Key Concept	**Specific Content**
KEY CONCEPT 6.1: THE RISE OF CAPITALISM **Technological advances, large-scale production methods, and the opening of new markets encouraged the rise of industrial capitalism in the United States.**	Large-scale industrial production—accompanied by massive technological change, expanding international communication networks, and pro-growth government policies—generated rapid economic development and business consolidation. A variety of perspectives on the economy and labor developed during a time of financial panics and downturns. New systems of production and transportation enabled consolidation within agriculture, which, along with periods of instability, spurred a variety of responses from farmers.
KEY CONCEPT 6.2: URBAN AND RURAL TRANSFORMATION **The migrations that accompanied industrialization transformed both urban and rural areas of the United States and caused dramatic social and cultural changes.**	International and internal migration increased urban populations and fostered the growth of a new urban culture. Larger numbers of migrants moved to the West in search of land and economic opportunity, frequently provoking competition and violent conflict.
KEY CONCEPT 6.3: CULTURAL AND INTELLECTUAL MOVEMENTS **The Gilded Age produced new cultural and intellectual movements, public reform efforts, and political debates over economic and social policies.**	New cultural and intellectual movements both buttressed and challenged the social order of the Gilded Age. Dramatic social changes during the period inspired political debates over citizenship, corruption, and the proper relationship between business and government.

Significant Themes

Now that we've discussed the curriculum, let's discuss the significant themes related to this period. The theme-related study questions that follow will help you make mental connections to the context of the "big picture" of this time period. Keep in mind that these questions often overlap and apply to other themes of social, political, religious, geographic, ideological, technological, and economic developments.

Glance through the study questions before you start the review section. Take notes, highlight questions, and write down page number references to reinforce your learning. Refer to this list until you feel comfortable with your knowledge of the material.

Study Questions Related to Significant Themes for Period Six

Theme 1: American and National Identity

1. How were immigrants incorporated into or rejected from U.S. national identity? (Hint: Explain how the immigrant population changed and why particular immigrants who had formerly been rejected in American society became more acceptable. Think about how Asian immigrants—especially the Chinese—were treated in the West and how legislation began to either include or exclude certain groups. Your answer could be extended after reading about further immigration restrictions in Chapter 10.)

2. What were the competing visions of an ideal American economy and society? Who held them and what was their motivation for acting on them? (Hint: Consider the differences between the living and working conditions of workers, middle-class individuals, and the wealthy in many regions throughout the country. Discuss the conflicts that arose between workers and industrialists in the North and those between sharecroppers and landlords in the South. Note the role of the Populists in relation to this question, explaining their complaints, the cyclical system of debt in which those complaints originated, and how they proposed to solve these issues.)

Theme 2: Politics and Power

1. How was economic, legal, and political power distributed during the Gilded Age? (Hint: Focus on wealth inequalities during this period. Examine the excesses of the rich, the development of powerful corporations, and many government officials' partial ownership of the corporations and railroads they refused to regulate or control.)

2. How did accusations of corruption affect the government and citizens' faith in it? (Hint: Discuss the Crédit Mobilier and Whiskey Ring scandals within the Grant administration during Reconstruction, which caused people across the nation—especially southerners—to complain about both government excesses and the carpetbaggers and scalawags they thought were taking advantage of the South. To extend your analysis, be sure to also note the complaints of the Populists and discuss why they considered the unregulated abuses of corporations and railroads the cause of their cyclical debt.)

3. Were any political measures taken to curb the power of businesses and the wealthy? (Hint: Be sure to discuss the Pendleton Act, the Interstate Commerce Act, and the Sherman Antitrust Act, noting both their goals and effectiveness.)

4. How did the Populist Movement form? (Hint: Analyze southern and western farmers' problems with perpetual debt due to the crop-lien system. Important developments to note include the rise of the Granger Movement, various alliances, the Subtreasury Plan, the People's Party, and the Omaha Platform.)

Theme 3: Work, Exchange, and Technology

1. How and why did business power increase so much during this period? What are vertical and horizontal integration? (Hint: Explore the role of the government in the regulation of business during this era. It is important to note the rise of the railroad industry, the protection of private contracts because of a prevalent free-labor ideology, and laissez-faire economic policies. Key figures like Andrew Carnegie and John Rockefeller will also help you define vertical and horizontal integration and their role in business consolidation.)

2. How did work change? What was the role of women and children in the workforce? (Hint: Be sure to focus on how scientific management and industrial growth affected work tasks and workers' self-esteem and value to employers. Discuss the roles of women and children in industrial labor and cotton mills and the abuses that came with this practice as well as their inability to qualify for certain labor organizations.)

3. How did labor unions fit into the new economy and society? (Hint: Analyze workers' complaints, especially noting their work hours, wages, and low standard of working and living conditions. Discuss the differences among various labor organizations, including the Knights of Labor, the American Federation of Labor, and the Industrial Workers of the World. Connect these things to the Great Railroad Strike, the Homestead Steelworkers Strike, the Haymarket Square Riot, and the Pullman Railroad Strike.)

4. What was the government's position when tensions between labor and management arose? Provide some examples of how conflicts escalated and/or were solved. (Hint: Discuss the use of the Sherman Antitrust Act and government troops to quell strikes and destroy unions. Focus on the results of particular conflicts, including the Haymarket Square Riot and the Pullman Railroad Strike, especially focusing on the role of police, the jailing of Eugene Debs, and the actions of President Grover Cleveland.)

Theme 4: Culture and Society

1. How can increases in immigration, migration, and urban populations be related to changes in American culture? (Hint: Discuss the poverty associated with immigration and the swelling of cities, which created new social reform organizations often run by women, who became more visible in the public sphere. Note the changing immigrant population, the formation of ethnic neighborhoods in urban centers, and the spread and meshing of many cultures along the frontier.)

2. How were changes in American society related to Social Darwinism, the Gospel of Wealth, or the Social Gospel? (Hint: Be sure to compare and contrast these intellectual theories, noting how they were used by some to explain the wealth gap and by others to defend the need for social reform. Key figures to include are Andrew Carnegie and Jane Addams.)

3. How did the women's movement progress? (Hint: Analyze how gender roles changed, especially for middle-class educated women, who often worked in reform organizations. Consider the role of Jane Addams, the Settlement House Movement and its role in the formation of New Women, and how women fulfilled ideals of true womanhood through their public work. Note their work to improve public hygiene and in temperance organizations, while discussing their call for the vote in order to fulfill what they considered their civic duties.)

Theme 5: Migration and Settlement

1. What drove the advance of western migration during the Gilded Age? How did ideals related to individualism relate to this? (Hint: Explore both the role of the Second Industrial Revolution and Manifest Destiny in western expansion, relating this to the need to push the frontier farther west to open additional markets and to provide land for white settlers.)

2. What was the effect of western migration on American Indians? (Hint: Be sure to mention physical, cultural, and legislative tensions and consequences associated with frontier expansion and the demand for land by white settlers. Key events include various conflicts with the U.S. Army, like those that occurred at Little Bighorn and Wounded Knee, as well as the Nez Percé's unsuccessful fight against removal and the cultural attack on tribal autonomy instigated through the Dawes Act.)

3. How were Asian immigrants persecuted or discriminated against in the West? (Hint: Consider the role of Chinese immigrants in the West and the nativism that encouraged the passage of the Chinese Exclusion Act of 1882.)

4. Who were the "new immigrants" and how were they different from those who immigrated in the past? (Hint: Be sure to contrast these individuals with the Irish and German immigrants mentioned in previous chapters. They came from different countries and were criticized for different reasons.)

Theme 7: America in the World

1. How was the conception of the frontier redefined during this era? (Hint: Be sure to relate this to Frederick Jackson Turner's thesis and imperialism, both of which encouraged the expansion of American opportunity for power, masculine strength, and economic gain.)

2. How did the Second Industrial Revolution affect the need for international relations and global expansion? (Hint: Link this to the growth of industrialism and the need for additional markets and natural resources. After reading Chapter 10, you can extend your answer by focusing on examples in relation to Cuba, Teddy Roosevelt's use of the Monroe Doctrine to intervene in Latin America, and the accession of Hawaii.)

Important Events, Terms, and Concepts

The list below shows important events, terms, and concepts that you should be familiar with on the APUSH exam. These and other important terms are printed in boldface throughout the chapter. Because the APUSH exam requires you to pay attention to the historical context and connections rather than details, don't bother memorizing the terms now. Simply place a check mark next to each as you study. You can return to this list to review as often as necessary. After you finish the review section, you can reinforce what you have learned by working through the practice questions at the end of this chapter. Answer explanations provide further clarification into perspectives of U.S. history.

Event/Term/Concept	Year/Brief Description	Study Page
Pacific Railroad	**1869.** The first transcontinental railroad. It was instrumental in the expansion of trade markets and transportation during the Second Industrial Revolution.	p. 222
Liberal Republicans	**1872.** A political party that supported the policies of many southern Democrats and severely opposed the reelection of Ulysses S. Grant and his Radical Republican supporters.	p. 225
Chinese Exclusion Act	**1882.** The first legislative act in U.S. history that banned the immigration.	p. 232
New South	**1886.** A term used by reformers to refer to the modernization of society. It was developed by journalist Henry Grady to reject the values of the Old South and promote a modern industrial region that would allow its people to reap the rewards of economic success.	p. 236
Frontier Thesis	**1893.** Also known as the "Turner Thesis" because it was developed by Frederick Jackson Turner. The theory pointed to frontier expansion as the most important factor of American democracy, egalitarianism, and economic vitality.	p. 238
Social theories	**Late 19th century.** Intellectual theories that were used to explain and manage economic inequalities during the Gilded Age: Social Darwinism (applies biological concepts of "survival of the fittest" to society); Gospel of Wealth (describes the social responsibility of the wealthy class); Social Gospel (movement that applied Christian values to social problems).	pp. 229–230
Crop-lien system	**1860s–1930s.** A system of credit lending that bound sharecroppers and tenant farmers to merchants, landlords, and bankers who financed their rent and equipment by imposing liens on farmers' crops. The system kept small farmers in perpetual debt.	p. 226

Continued

Event/Term/Concept	Year/Brief Description	Study Page
Populist (People's) Party	**1875–1896.** An agrarian political party popular in the South and West that called for bimetallism, federal regulation, and open election practices.	pp. 226–229
Mugwumps	**1884.** Republican political activists who were angered by what they viewed as financial corruption. The Mugwumps switched parties to support Democratic presidential candidate Grover Cleveland in the 1884 election.	p. 225
Jane Addams	**1889.** Established Hull House, one of the first settlement houses in the U.S. Addams was a social worker and "New Woman" who began the settlement house movement in Chicago.	pp. 230–231
Scientific management theory	**Late 19th century.** Known as "Taylorism," this is a theory invented by Frederick Taylor that analyzes and synthesizes workflow for efficiency. Designed to improve labor management and productivity in factories.	p. 223
Labor organizations	Various labor organizations that unionized skilled and unskilled workers formed during this time period. Organizations negotiated with employers and organized strikes, boycotts, and violent protests to obtain better wages and working conditions for laborers. Examples include Knights of Labor, American Federation of Labor (AFL), and the Industrial Workers of the World (IWW).	pp. 233–235

Chapter Review

The information discussed in this chapter covers several overlapping topics associated with the rapid economic growth of the Gilded Age, including the Second Industrial Revolution, increasing formation and power of corporations, tensions between labor and management, and the search for new markets and means of production. Changes in American culture and society will also be covered, including the rise of the middle class and differences in opinions that led to reform organizations, the protection of free labor, and individual rights.

Heads Up: What You Need to Know

On the APUSH exam, it is important to be familiar with the **Gilded Age** (c. 1878 to c. 1900). The Gilded Age was a wave of rapid growth, industry, and immigration. It coincided with Britain's Victorian Era and the Belle Époque in France. After the Civil War, vast wealth was abundant, but the new prosperity was not shared among all citizens. The term "Gilded Age" was coined by American writer Mark Twain. In his novel *The Gilded Age: A Tale of Today* (1893), Twain satirized the post–Civil War social problems of materialism, greed, and corruption and the ruthless bankers, crooked politicians, and underhanded land speculators who took advantage of the vulnerable. Twain believed that the American culture of the late 19th century was deceptively appealing, but political and social immorality hid beneath a thin layer of glitz and glamour.

The Second Industrial Revolution (c. 1870 to c. 1914)

A period of rapid industrialization and intense economic growth emerged after the Civil War. Several factors contributed to industrialization, including technological and communication advances, new forms of transportation, government subsidies, government incentives for immigrants to settle in the U.S., innovations in production and management, and the pursuit of new markets. As Americans began to focus on consumerism and production, urban culture and society changed. Unions and rural cooperatives called for protection and businessmen called for global markets. As the period progressed and the dream of being an independent small farmer became increasingly problematic, Americans began to think differently about their rights and obligations as citizens and workers.

HISTORIOGRAPHY. *It is important to remember history does not have clear chronological markers of delineation that begin and end with specific dates. Historians only categorize developments into eras in order for us to be able to contextualize and think about related events and individuals within specific time periods. Every chapter you study will note progressions relating to things that have happened in the past. When thinking about any period of history, you should always consider what situations, developments, and processes happened before, during, and after its events.*

For example, the Second Industrial Revolution is associated with a period that spans several decades (1870–1914). While it can be identified by its unique characteristics, the economic growth that occurred was influenced by the Market Revolution, a steady flow of immigrants throughout the 19th century, and Americans' continuous pursuit of a more efficient means of production and financial gain. The Second Industrial Revolution also sparked changes in domestic and foreign politics, society, and culture that carried over into the 20th century.

Inventions

Several important technological inventions helped to shape the Second Industrial Revolution.

Second Industrial Revolution Inventions	
Technology	**Importance**
Transportation Railroad (1869) Automobile (1903–1908)	**Railroad.** Advances in the production of iron and steelmaking contributed to the building of large bridges and the transcontinental railroad lines. After 1870, railroads became one of the most important features of the Second Industrial Revolution when the transcontinental railroad expanded across the entire country, greatly increasing access to national markets. **Automobile.** The first gas-powered automobile was developed by Karl Benz of Germany in 1885. In the U.S., Henry Ford developed the Model A in 1903, but the Model T became the first mass-produced automobile in 1908. **Assembly line.** Henry Ford introduced the assembly line, which organized workers through specialized labor. (Note: This sort of division of labor existed before Ford—see Taylorism—but he made the process more efficient by including a *moving* conveyor belt.) This meant that workers would become skilled in one task and then repeat the task over and over again. It was monotonous work, but the assembly line was so successful that the workers in Ford's factories produced a car every 90 seconds on average.
Telecommunication Telegraph (1844) Telephone (1876)	Innovations in communication advanced the development of businesses and corporations throughout the U.S. and the world. The telegraph was invented by Samuel Morse before the Civil War, enabling people to send messages across the country. Alexander Graham Bell invented communication through a wire—the telephone. Although other inventors worked on this discovery, Bell is credited for the first official patent. A year after his invention, many businesses wanted this new form of modern communication.

Continued

Technology	Importance
Electricity (1882)	Thomas Edison advanced electrical discoveries, creating inventions like the light bulb and the phonograph. Electricity was used to power factory machines, mass-produce goods, and provide light for longer days of manufacturing. New business organizational models were created based on mass production using electricity.
Agriculture	In the South and West, canning machines and the mechanical reaper increased agricultural production (Cyrus McCormick invented the mechanical reaper in 1831). Farmers also started using ammonia as fertilizer to promote plant nutrition.

Heads Up: What You Need to Know

On the APUSH exam, it is important to recognize the significance of the railroad industry during the Second Industrial Revolution. The first transcontinental railroad, known as the **Pacific Railroad,** was completed in 1869 and made shipping goods faster and cheaper. The railroad expanded markets and led to the growth of related industries, especially coal and steel. In 1883, railroad companies created *time zones* (uniform time zones based on region) to standardize their shipping schedules, which are still in use today. Supported by private investment and federal land grants (or subsidies), railroads were some of the first U.S. corporations. The railroad owners were often seen as "robber barons" who were allowed to operate with little government regulation.

Transcontinental Railroad Growth (1870 to 1890)

Source: United States Senate, Select Committee on Interstate Commerce, 1886.

Key Facts about the Second Industrial Revolution

New production methods. Electric motors, lighting, steam engines, and more accurate machine tools improved working conditions and changed methods of production in factories. Advances in technology caused the decline of a need for skilled labor in large industrial cities.

Taylor's scientific management theory. Business owners and their managers began to apply Frederick Taylor's *Principles of Scientific Management* (called Taylorism) to optimize workers' efficiency and productivity while minimizing the sequence of motions to complete tasks. Using specific logical steps, the system analyzed and synthesized workflow to develop standard practices that would eliminate wasted time and materials. Unfortunately, this management system caused conflicts between supervisors and their workers (workers were no longer connected to what they were making through the craft industry).

The rise of corporations. Many wealthy entrepreneurs shifted their business models in order to increase their profits during this period. Entrepreneurs formed trusts (corporations) that were managed by a single individual or a board of stockholders that dominated a single industry. These corporations used vertical and horizontal integration to control all of the steps involved in production. With **vertical integration,** corporations controlled the entire supply chain of a specific industry. With **horizontal integration,** a corporation bought and merged with smaller companies of the same industry. The integrations allowed corporations to establish fixed prices, secure markets, and eliminate competition. Andrew Carnegie (1835–1919), a Scottish-born immigrant, established U.S. Steel (the world's first billion-dollar corporation), and John D. Rockefeller (1839–1937) established the first oil refinery, Standard Oil Company. Carnegie and Rockefeller were well-known corporate owners who used both vertical and horizontal integration.

Economics of the Gilded Age

Key Facts about Economics of the Gilded Age

The American dream. An ideology was born out of the 19th-century American notion that economic and social successes were based on hard work and perseverance. The ability to negotiate one's own prosperity and labor was highly valued during the Gilded Age.

TEST TIP: On the APUSH exam, remember the American dream as an example of the social climate during the Gilded Age. The American dream was supported by literature and fine art. For example, fiction writer Horatio Alger wrote "rags-to-riches" stories suggesting that hard work and good luck would enable any individual to succeed in the new economy. The heroes of Alger's novels overcame humble beginnings and adversities to achieve great economic successes, similar to real-life entrepreneur Andrew Carnegie. Unfortunately, the American dream was just that—a dream. Stories like Andrew Carnegie's were uncommon and success was generally the result of access to goods, political and social connections, and wealth, which few working-class Americans had.

Laissez-faire economics. *Laissez-faire* economics (the policy of a "hands-off" approach to the economy) was supported by the U.S. government. Because of the dedication to free labor ideology and individualism, politicians strongly supported the "sanctity of the contract" and felt the government should have no regulatory role in the economy. This meant businesses were protected much more than people. Many government officials overlooked the growing wealth gap and the economic desperation of the working class. The government believed that if an employee did not want to work under the conditions specified by employers, the employee could just refuse the terms. At the time, there was no government interest in controlling monopolies or establishing labor laws. Workers were often exploited, especially before unions formed to object to abusive practices.

Heads Up: What You Need to Know

On the APUSH exam, you should be familiar with Adam Smith's *The Wealth of Nations* and his economic theories. Some say his work on capitalism is one of the most groundbreaking contributions to political economics. Smith argued that **mercantilism** (the prevailing economic theory discussed in Chapter 5) was based on a flawed understanding of the natural laws of human nature—Smith believed that humans were self-interested individuals, so mercantilism could never produce real economic progress. Smith argued for two important economic concepts: *laissez-faire capitalism* and the *invisible hand*. These concepts changed the way people understood economics, the role of government, and the relationship between business owners and their employees.

Laissez-faire capitalism: An economic theory in which the government did not interfere in the natural system of the economy. Smith believed that if the government did not interfere, the economy would self-regulate and everyone would benefit.

The invisible hand: The invisible hand is a metaphor that describes the unintended economic benefits of self-interest when people are free to buy, sell, and compete without government interference. It is based on a set of invisible natural laws that contribute to a nation's economic stability and prosperity. It may seem greedy to think about wealthy people pursuing self-interest, but Smith argues that the unintentional effect is an economic benefit for everyone.

Politics and Government of the Gilded Age

Since politicians were often investors in major corporations and big businesses, unrestricted corruption was common during the Gilded Age.

Key Facts about Politics and Government of the Gilded Age

Political corruption. President Grant's two administrations (1869–1877) were heavily criticized for numerous scandals. One of the most famous scandals was Crédit Mobilier (1872–1873), a company that sold or gave shares of Union Pacific stock to congressmen who were overseeing the railroad's federal funding package. Another infamous scandal was the Whiskey Ring (1875), which allowed well-placed officials to divert tax revenues from whiskey distillers and distributors to government agents and Republican politicians in Chicago, Milwaukee, Cincinnati, and New Orleans.

Source: Joseph Keppler, "The Bosses of the Senate," 1889. Cartoon depiction of the U.S. Senate being controlled by the corporate businessmen of steel, copper, oil, iron, coal, and sugar—the giant money bags who monopolized the economy through political control.

Political divisions. In 1872, the **Liberal Republican Party** was formed in Cincinnati to object to Republican corruption and oppose President Grant's reelection. Although the party disbanded after the election, Liberal Republicans endorsed newspaper editor Horace Greeley for president, joined with Democrats in criticizing Radical goals in the South, and pressed for the reunification of the country.

Another Republican division occurred during the presidential election of 1884 when Republican candidate James G. Blaine was accused of financial corruption. Republican activists who rejected the financial corruption supported Democrat Grover Cleveland in the 1884 election and were known as **Mugwumps** (named after the Native Algonquian word for "chief," implying they were holding themselves above party lines).

Political legislative acts. Although the political system failed to regulate the rapidly growing economy, lawmakers did pass several key pieces of legislation. Most of the legislative acts were ineffective during this era, but they set important precedents for the future.

Legislative Act	Impact
Pendleton Act (1883)	The act reformed the government civil service system by requiring that government positions be awarded based on a merit system of competitive examination. In the past, people were routinely given government jobs based on their political connections (called the *spoils system*). A Civil Service Commission was established to oversee the Pendleton Act, but it was not effective because it applied to only 10 percent of the available positions. By 1980, however, the act expanded to more than 90 percent of federal employees.

Continued

Legislative Act	Impact
Interstate Commerce Act (1887)	This act was the result of *Illinois v. Wabash*, a Supreme Court case that declared states could not regulate commerce beyond their boundaries. It required railroads to charge universal shipping rates, set reasonable prices, and forbade railroads from offering reduced rates to favored customers. Unfortunately, the act didn't give the government the power to enforce its requirements or set rates of its own.
Sherman Antitrust Act (1890)	While this act outlawed practices that reduced free trade, at first it was only applied to limit the power of unions to prevent strikes. It was not meant to reduce trusts or control monopolies until Teddy Roosevelt convinced the Justice Department to use it to do so in 1904 (see Chapter 10).

> **TEST TIP:** The Sherman Antitrust Act is a landmark legislative law that frequently appears on the APUSH exam. The act reduced economic competition and outlawed trade *monopolies* (exclusive control of a product or service) and price-fixing. It was enacted to promote economic competition, but some historians believe that this act led to a manipulation of prices.

The Populist Movement

The **Populist Movement** (called the People's Party) was a political alliance of agrarian reformers who protested the impact of industrialization. In the 1870s and 1880s, farmers experienced an economic depression due to a *drought* (a long period of no rainfall). Southern and western farmers faced falling crop prices and increasing costs to produce and ship agriculture.

Key Facts about the Causes of the Populist Movement

Farmers became frustrated because they did not have legislative support to defend against high railroad freight charges, high tariff rates, government corruption, and the perpetual debt that resulted from sharecropping. Farmers wanted citizen advocates to be involved in proposing and voting for Senate bills, instead of the Senate representatives. Farmers who felt underrepresented by their lack of market power organized cooperatives in cotton and wheat, which eventually led to their political objections and protests against the systematic benefits awarded to large agricultural producers.

Causes of the Populist Movement	
Issue	**Description**
Economic dependency	The *crop-lien system* (a southern credit system from landowners and local merchants) worked against small farmers because farmers had to borrow money from landlords and merchants for seed and supplies. As costs continued to increase, small farmers were often in more debt at the end of a growing season than at its beginning.
High interest rates	Farmers paid high interest rates on loans from merchants, bankers, and landlords. Populists felt that the rates were unregulated and contributed to the perpetual debt created by the crop-lien system. Many farms were forced into foreclosure.
Falling crop prices	The drought and the global expansion of the market caused a drop in agricultural prices. The decline in crop prices hurt the farmers' ability to pay off their debts.

Issue	Description
Protective tariffs	High tariffs protected manufacturers, but farmers believed that the tariffs kept them from being competitive in the global market.
Inflated railroad freight charges	The cost of transporting crops was extremely high because biased freight charges were being charged by the railroads. Railroads gave corporations large discounts on shipping charges, making it impossible for small farmers to compete.
Overproduction	Speculation and the promise of economic freedom in the West attracted more farmers than the market could sustain. The supply soon exceeded the domestic and international demand.
Environment	It was not easy to produce healthy agricultural crops in many regions. The environmental impact of poor soil conditions, drought, locust swarms, and grasshopper plagues threatened crops and made it difficult to grow and sustain crops.

The Evolution of the Populist Party (the People's Party)

Through the years, farmers formed various alliances to gain support and nominate government representatives. These early coalitions and farmers' unions paved the way for the Populist Party. The chart below traces the development and timeline of these groups.

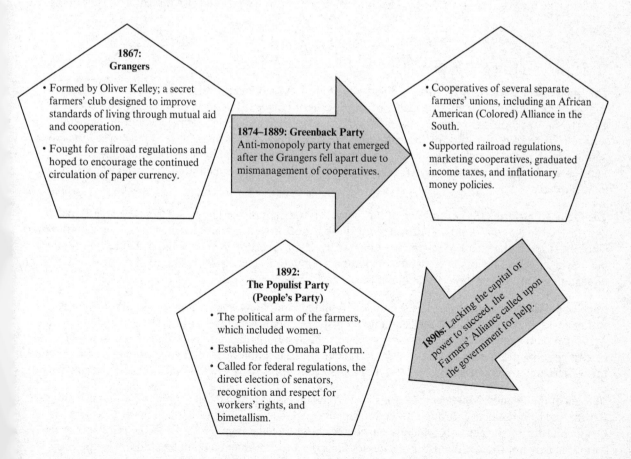

1867: Grangers
- Formed by Oliver Kelley; a secret farmers' club designed to improve standards of living through mutual aid and cooperation.
- Fought for railroad regulations and hoped to encourage the continued circulation of paper currency.

1874–1889: Greenback Party
Anti-monopoly party that emerged after the Grangers fell apart due to mismanagement of cooperatives.

- Cooperatives of several separate farmers' unions, including an African American (Colored) Alliance in the South.
- Supported railroad regulations, marketing cooperatives, graduated income taxes, and inflationary money policies.

1890s: Lacking the capital or power to succeed, the Farmers' Alliance called upon the government for help.

1892: The Populist Party (People's Party)
- The political arm of the farmers, which included women.
- Established the Omaha Platform.
- Called for federal regulations, the direct election of senators, recognition and respect for workers' rights, and bimetallism.

Heads Up: What You Need to Know

On the APUSH exam, you should be able to compare and contrast some of the key issues between the Populist Party and the railroads, bankers, politicians, or corporations. The Populist Party focused on several issues—railroad freight charges, inflation, and decreasing crop prices—but one of the most important Populist demands was for *free silver* (the unlimited coinage of silver), which they thought would decrease the value of the money they owed to the banks.

To understand the reasons for the Populists' demand, you must understand the context of this issue. The Populists objected to the *gold standard,* which held that a sound national currency was backed by gold. The Populists were upset when the mining of silver was discontinued in 1873 and wanted the dollar to be supported by silver as well as gold. Populists thought *bimetallism* (two metals, gold and silver) would increase the money supply and create an inflationary economy that would allow them to raise their prices and pay off their debts more quickly.

Bankers, however, did not want money devalued because they wanted the full value of the money that was owed to the bank. This was the same reason that the Grangers originally wanted *greenbacks* (paper money that was distributed to the Union during the Civil War) to continue flowing into the economy. Note: The desire for free silver also gained the support of miners in the West.

The Rise and Fall of the Populist Party

The Subtreasury Plan (1890). Frustrated with the animosity of bankers and merchants toward agrarian cooperatives, Charles Macune, the leader of the Southern Farmers' Alliance, proposed the creation of government warehouses to store crops until market prices were favorable. Farmers would immediately receive 80 percent of the value of the crops through federal loans. If farmers weren't able to sell the crops within a year, the government would auction the crops. Although the plan never became a law, the Subtreasury Plan led the Farmers' Alliance into politics and was instrumental in the formation of the People's Party.

The Omaha Platform (1892). Adopted at the formal convention of the People's Party (Populist Party) in Omaha, Nebraska, the Omaha Platform merged the cooperative concerns of agrarians, miners, and urban laborers. It was a statement of resolutions that set the basic tenets of the party and called for graduated income taxes, secret ballots in elections, corporation regulations (especially for railroads), the direct election of senators, 8-hour workdays, and bimetallism.

Populist political success (1892). The Populists circulated pamphlets, traveled on speaking tours, and campaigned throughout the southern and western states. Alliance members in the West included African Americans and women. Speakers, secretaries, treasurers, and organizers were often women, some of whom rose to national prominence. Populist efforts resulted in the election of several governors and congressmen in the western and midwestern U.S. In 1892, Populists even supported a presidential candidate, James Weaver.

The end of the Populist Movement (1896). The 1896 Democratic presidential candidate, William Jennings Bryan, rose to prominence through his endorsement of free silver. This caused the Populists to join the Democrats during the election, which is considered the end of the Populist Party. While the Populist Party was ultimately not successful, historians do not consider the movement a complete failure. In the early

20th century, Progressive politicians adopted and ultimately passed many of the statutes from the Populists' political platform.

HISTORIOGRAPHY. *Most historians believe the Populists were unsuccessful for two reasons: racist divisions and their inability to appeal to northern industrial laborers. In the South, their efforts were hindered by the segregation of the alliances, which limited the party's political power—most southern Populists supported Democrats, uniting under white supremacy rather than agrarian concerns. In the North, the increased conflict between capitalists and laborers had become intense, but urban workers worried that agrarian demands would increase food prices and were more likely to support Republicans, who imposed high tariffs to protect the manufacturers that employed the workers.*

Social Changes of the Gilded Age

Industrialization created enormous and unprecedented amounts of wealth for elite classes and divided social classes into the rich and the poor. Other social classes (the working class and the middle class) were beginning to take shape during this period. The government did little to ensure the basic needs of every citizen, and the wealthy were often critical of the poor.

Social and Economic Theories

The government's attitude toward social reform was similar to its attitude toward the economy—it did little to ensure that the basic needs of every citizen were being met. Several intellectual theories developed during this period to explain the financial inequalities that resulted from the Second Industrial Revolution. The belief in free labor and *heroic individualism* (an American philosophical ideal that places high value on individual beliefs and rights, equating their protection with success and progress) caused some upper- and middle-class Americans to criticize the working class.

Heads Up: What You Need to Know

On the APUSH exam, you should be familiar with some of the causes and consequences related to key social developments and legislative statues during the Gilded Age. For example, theories like Social Darwinism, the role of the New Woman in America, the impact of immigration, the effects of discrimination, and the rise of labor reform movements greatly affected the way U.S. citizens thought about society and the economy.

Social Darwinism. Social scientist William Graham Sumner popularized three theories in the American social sphere: *Social Darwinism* (social "survival of the fittest), *ethnocentrism* (judging another culture based on one's own culture), and *laissez-faire economics* (the government policy of a hands-off approach to the economy). Social Darwinism brought an unpleasant aspect to American society, but it appealed to the wealthy and owners of large corporations to justify their wealth. Many Americans saw themselves as superior to other races, ethnicities, and economic classes in society. Some ignored institutional disadvantages and implied that their successes were linked to inherently stronger characteristics, or their desire to work harder than others (see "The American dream," p. 223). Social Darwinism was often cited by the upper and middle classes as the reason for the massive gap between the rich and poor.

Gospel of Wealth. The "Gospel of Wealth" was an article written by Andrew Carnegie in 1889. The article suggested that the most intelligent, able-minded citizens held a concentration of wealth; hence, the "best" individuals in society should manage money for everyone's benefit. The article was a benevolent form of Social Darwinism. Yet Carnegie still advocated for the poor and believed that the wealthy had a moral responsibility to help the less fortunate, stating, "Successful men should help lift the unsuccessful into more productive lives...a man who neglects this duty and dies rich, dies disgraced."

Social Gospel. The Social Gospel movement was linked to a Protestant intellectual movement. It applied one's Christian faith to the social problems of inequality and poverty. The movement called on Christians to assist others who were less fortunate. It was an inspiration for many middle-class reformers who rejected Social Darwinism.

Women's Roles

During the Gilded Age, women began working at an unprecedented rate and became more visible in society. Unlike their Antebellum counterparts, women became dissatisfied with the limitations of the *cult of domesticity* (also known as *true womanhood*), which described the limits of a woman's role—managing household duties; practicing religion; remaining pure in heart, mind, and body; and staying submissive to her husband. The cult of domesticity had developed from ideals of *republican motherhood* (a term used to define an educated woman's role to instill values in her family to make a strong American republic, 1783 to 1830), which encouraged women to reflect qualities like morality, purity, and submissiveness while staying within the boundaries of the home.

Key Facts about Women's Roles

The New Woman. Women in the middle and upper classes received college educations and began to exhibit personal, social, and economic independence. The term *New Woman* was named by Sarah Grand, but popularized by British-American writer Henry James to describe an educated, career-minded feminist. New Women pushed the limits of a male-dominated society.

Maternal commonwealth. The New Woman feminist ideal was transferred to the public sphere. Women used their intellect and skills to pursue a *maternal commonwealth* (maternal values of caretaking that helped to shape the public) to care for the less fortunate in society and work for the common good.

Did you know? Middle-class African American women were also instrumental in changing gender roles during the Gilded Age and the Progressive Era. During the Reconstruction Era, some African American women had the opportunity to be educated in all-black colleges. When their fathers' and husbands' political power declined, women became determined to project a positive public image of black citizens. Black women frequently worked alongside white women in the temperance and suffrage movements and appealed to white officials to assist in African American communities.

The Settlement House Movement. One of the most famous women of the Gilded Age was **Jane Addams,** a college-educated woman who was known as the "mother of social work." After a visit to England, Addams was inspired to begin Hull House in Chicago (1889), a settlement house that provided a home for the poor and destitute, who were often immigrants. The middle-class volunteer women who ran the house not only provided residents with food and shelter, but also taught them basic skills, how to speak English (often immigrants), and how to assimilate into the American culture. Although settlement houses were intended to offer support to poor women and children, the volunteers also reached out to teenage boys and men. Since the volunteer women lived among the residents (which was an unprecedented form of social work at the time) and unmarried women were usually highly chaperoned, they sometimes recruited middle-class men to supervise male residents. By 1900, there were approximately 100 settlement houses throughout the U.S. with middle-class women managing all of them. The Hull House remained Addams' home for her entire life.

TEST TIP: On the APUSH exam, cite the work of the late-19th-century New Woman Jane Addams in your free-response essay for questions about the roles of the 19th-century New Woman. Addams not only established settlement houses, but she also advocated for women's suffrage and fought for the rights of women, children, and the poor. She helped to sponsor several laws: limiting the hours of work for women, eliminating child labor, creating juvenile courts for minors, making attendance at public schools mandatory, and helping to ensure safe working conditions in factories. Addams believed in the Christian virtue of good deeds and believed that society needed to help immigrants adjust to the American way of life while respecting their traditions and beliefs.

Women helped to improve public sanitation. Rapid industrialization and urbanization created issues with public hygiene that many government officials chose not to address. As people began to migrate or immigrate to major industrial centers, cities began to deteriorate from soiled streets, poor sewage systems, and polluted living conditions. Residents of slums and tenements were exposed to infectious diseases like typhus, cholera, and tuberculosis, which wealthy citizens soon worried would spread to their neighborhoods. Middle-class women who worked in settlement houses began noticing the poor sanitation conditions in poor neighborhoods. Some of these women decided to make improvements, which led to public hygiene campaigns throughout the nation. Jane Addams was even appointed Chicago's garbage inspector, a position she used to greatly improve the city's garbage collection system.

The Woman's Christian Temperance Union (WCTU).
Temperance is giving up all alcoholic beverages. Although alcohol consumption had always been prevalent in the U.S., the hardships of the Civil War caused alcohol consumption to rise. This made some people believe that alcohol was the reason for the "degeneration" of society. Many middle-class reformers—including women—criticized the Irish and German Catholics, blaming their cultural drinking practices for social problems. The Woman's Christian Temperance Union was formed in 1874 in Cleveland, Ohio. Led by Frances Willard in 1879, its primary objective was a nationwide ban on alcohol (some local and state agencies had already prohibited the sale of alcohol in specific regions), but the WCTU also conducted missionary work, supported women's suffrage, labor reform laws, and prison reform laws, and held national and international conventions.

Source: Thomas Edison, "Kansas Saloon Smasher," Thomas Edison Motion Picture Studios, 1895. Satirical still photograph of teetotaler women.

The Women's Suffrage Movement. Women were not allowed to vote until the Nineteenth Amendment was passed in 1920. However, during the Gilded Age, some states allowed women to vote. Due to the difficulty of frontier life and the influence of the Populist Movement, women were granted the right to vote in four western states: Wyoming (1869), Colorado (1893), Idaho (1896), and Utah (1896). The passage of the Fifteenth Amendment may have split the suffrage movement in the rest of the country, but many women continued to actively pursue voting rights because they associated voting with the ability to improve society. In 1890, the two most influential organizations for women (the NWSA and the AWSA) united under the **National American Woman's Suffrage Association** (NAWSA). Over the next two decades women began to grow in numbers in the struggle for women's rights.

Heads Up: What You Need to Know

Susan B. Anthony (1820–1906) was a famous activist in the women's suffrage movement. On the APUSH exam, you should be familiar with her contributions to women's suffrage. Anthony and Carrie Chapman Catt led the NAWSA, and encouraged suffragettes to recruit other women, petition legislatures, and campaign for their cause through newspaper ads, posters, banners, and parades. In 1856, Anthony campaigned for anti-slavery and encountered many hostile mobs. Anthony worked tirelessly for women's rights, and in 1920 the Nineteenth Amendment, which allowed women the right to vote, was named the Susan B. Anthony Amendment.

Immigration

New opportunities for industrial employment led to an increase in immigration from different regions of the world and gave rise to labor unions to support the working class.

New immigrants. Before 1880, immigrants were primarily of British or western European descent. Due to civil unrest and programs in various countries, however, new nationalities of immigrants began to arrive on the East Coast. New immigrants were generally of Russian, Polish, Jewish, or Italian descent and often settled in industrial cities, serving as resources for cheap labor. Many formed ethnic neighborhoods where they established their own shops, theaters, and newspapers. Others lived in tenements and slums or headed west. U.S. natives opposed their presence even though some middle-class reformers, such as Jane Addams, attempted to help them assimilate and ease their poverty.

Asian discrimination. Chinese immigrants (predominantly men) migrated to California in the early 19th century to work in agriculture and the garment industry. By the 1850s, Asians were laboring in mines and later became instrumental in the construction of transcontinental railroads. Discriminatory attitudes increased as the Chinese presence grew in the West. Responding to citizens' demands for job protection and "white purity," Congress passed the **Chinese Exclusion Act** (1882), which prohibited immigration of all Chinese laborers. Unfortunately, the act subjected resident Chinese workers to harsh documentation procedures, unwarranted raids, and legal prosecution.

Source: Joseph Keppler, "Welcome to All," 1880. Depicts America as a land of refuge. Immigrants have an optimistic outlook as they are being welcomed aboard the U.S. ark to travel to America—the land of opportunity. The sign reads "free education, free land, free speech, free ballot, and free lunch." Most immigrants did not realize they would face a difficult life in America.

Labor Unions

The Second Industrial Revolution replaced human workers with machinery and tools of the industrial system. Scientific management, corporate corruption, and poverty caused resentment and bitterness among the working class and business management. To protect their interests, the working class began to organize and form labor unions to lobby for higher wages, shorter hours, and improved working conditions.

Some of the most important unions are listed below.

The Formation of Labor Unions		
Union	Characteristics	Significance
Knights of Labor (1869)	Led by Terence Powderly during its peak in the 1880s, the Knights of Labor began as a secret organization. It welcomed all kinds of skilled and unskilled workers, including immigrants, women, and African Americans.	The Knights of Labor demanded 8-hour workdays and negotiated with employers for better working conditions. Members of the union were idealistic and worked to counter the violent image of other early organizations, like the Molly Maguires (an Irish secret society). The Knights of Labor favored a reasonable approach to negotiations, but were not averse to organizing strikes and boycotts to temper the effects of employer exploitation and retaliation.
American Federation of Labor (AFL) (1886)	The AFL was a union of skilled workers led by Samuel Gompers, a former leader of the Cigar Makers Union.	The AFL became the largest union in the U.S. in the early 20th century. Management was more likely to work with the AFL because the AFL negotiated contracts for higher wages and better working conditions, rather than organizing labor strikes. Because the union did not include unskilled whites, women, blacks, or immigrant workers, it had little effect on industries that were not "craft" oriented.

Continued

Union	Characteristics	Significance
Industrial Workers of the World (IWW) (1905)	The IWW, also known as the "Wobblies," was led by "Big Bill" Haywood and Mary "Mother" Jones. It included all laborers, even unskilled African Americans.	The IWW was a radical union. It practiced revolutionary unionism that used violence to obtain its goals. Its overall philosophy was to create solidarity among the working class in order to overthrow the power of employers and the wage system so that workers could take charge of their own work decisions. Many members were influenced by socialism and anarchy.

TEST TIP: On the APUSH exam, you may be required to distinguish between the Knights of Labor, the AFL, and the IWW. Be sure to note the similarities and differences among the organizations, relating them to their primary leaders. It is also important to understand the goals of each organization, as well as the impact of key strikes receiving public support for their causes.

Labor Conflicts

The table that follows describes the causes and consequences of important labor conflicts during the Gilded Age.

Labor Disputes		
Union Strike	**Causes**	**Consequences**
Great Railroad Strike (1877)	The first national strike walkout, which began in West Virginia when workers for the Baltimore and Ohio Railroad protested against a 10 percent wage cut (the second wage cut in 8 months).	It inspired strikes by railroad laborers in several states, who burned property and violently fought with national guardsmen, state and local militias, and private armies hired by the railroads. Although the strike drew attention to poor working conditions and wages, it also highlighted the growing division between classes during the Gilded Age. The Commune of 1871 (a workers revolt in Paris) caused the government and the general public to fear social unrest, which resulted in the laborers' suppression rather than genuine concern for their needs.
Haymarket Square Riot (1886)	In the 1880s, the McCormick plant in Chicago began using machinery to reduce its dependency on skilled labor. When unions were banned and wages were cut in 1885, the workers went out on strike. The following year, tensions were high when Illinois labor organizers called for strikes and demanded 8-hour workdays for workers. During the strike, police fatally shot two McCormick laborers when they tried to prevent strikebreakers from entering the factory. A rally was organized to protest the deaths and a bomb went off, killing seven people, including a policeman.	The press used the bombing incident to associate labor activism with violence and radicalism, linking it to immigrants who advocated for socialism and anarchy. Several immigrants became scapegoats for the bombing deaths—four immigrant laborers were hanged and one committed suicide in prison before the governor pardoned the rest in 1893. The riot essentially ended the Knights of Labor, which supported the unskilled laborers in the strikes. The AFL was established soon after, creating a new kind of labor union that pioneered "business unionism" by organizing only skilled laborers and embracing negotiated contract agreements.

Union Strike	Causes	Consequences
Homestead Steelworkers Strike (1892)	Frustrated with the strength of the steelworkers union in his Pennsylvania mills, Andrew Carnegie and his manager Henry Frick refused to employ men at the Carnegie Steel Company who belonged to labor unions. Frick was determined to break the union. When workers went out on strike, the steelworkers were locked out, barracks were built for strikebreakers, and the *Pinkerton Detective Agency* (which served as a private security guard agency) was hired to guard the mills. In July 1892, a gunfight occurred between the opposing groups on a nearby river, killing nine workers (and seven Pinkerton detectives), and injuring dozens of people.	The Pennsylvania governor sent thousands of militiamen to calm the situation and eventually forced the strikers to relent to management's terms. The Carnegie Steel Company had more than a hundred strikers arrested. The union was crushed, public opinion remained on the side of business, and corporations were reassured of government support. After a short time, steelworkers were forced to work longer hours for lower wages. The volatile situation also inspired a New York anarchist who attempted to assassinate Frick. Frick survived being shot and stabbed.
Pullman Railroad Strike (1894)	The strike began after the mistreatment of railroad employees living in Pullman City, a Chicago neighborhood controlled by the railroad. Wages decreased, but housing and the cost of living increased. Facing starvation, several thousand workers went on a "wildcat" strike (without a union to back them).	Eugene Debs, leader of the American Railway Union (ARU), sent organizers to Pullman to recruit many of the workers. When the company would not negotiate, the ARU refused to allow any passenger or freight trains with Pullman cars to move, stopping traffic in much of the country. Debs was arrested and President Grover Cleveland sent federal troops into the city to break up the strike, using the Sherman Antitrust Act to justify his actions.

Source: "The Condition of the Laboring Man at Pullman."

Geographic Regions of the Gilded Age

Southern Region

Sharecropping and tenant farming. Since the Civil War devastated the infrastructure, economy, and resources of the South, many southerners struggled to regain their financial footing. During Reconstruction, southern plantation owners came up with a system to regain control of a compliant labor force while receiving economic benefits. They negotiated contracts with small farmers (black and white) who had become impoverished by the limited opportunities available after the war. The plantation owners agreed to rent the farmers land in exchange for shares in the farmers' crop production. Because few people had cash to buy agricultural products, plantation landowners and local merchants supplied the seed and equipment that was needed to farm, stating that they could just be repaid with another share of the farmers' harvest. Landowners always found ways to cheat farmers out of profits, so sharecroppers and tenant farmers remained in a constant cycle of debt.

Southerners call for a New South. The destruction of the southern agricultural system left the majority of its people in dire poverty. Fed up with a stagnant economy, progressive southerners, like newspaperman Henry Grady, began to call for a New South to reinvigorate the southern states. Southerners believed their region could enrich itself like the North, through industry and commerce, and called for sectional reconciliation, urbanization, and modernization. Despite its advances in lumber, coal, iron, and textile production in the late 19th century, most historians conclude that the southern economy remained well behind its northern counterpart. Many of the South's natural resources were shipped to the North, and northern investors often obtained a large share of the profits from the cotton mills and other industries that they sponsored.

Western (Midwest) Region

Chicago and the Great Lakes Region. The geographic region we now call the Midwest (then called the West) underwent significant development after the Civil War. Even during the *Antebellum Era* (before the Civil War), transportation advances allowed Chicago to serve as an import and export center. As industrialization increased, the Great Lakes region (Illinois, Indiana, Michigan, Minnesota, New York, Ohio, Pennsylvania, and Wisconsin) played an even more essential role in the national economy, serving as a link between northern and western markets. The Great Lakes region became a key production center for iron, steel, and machinery and enabled agriculture, lumber, and manufactured goods to be shipped in and out of the U.S. interior.

Western farming. The 1862 **Homestead Acts** (Chapter 8) also inspired western migration. Immigrants, day laborers, and *exodusters* (African Americans who migrated from states along the Mississippi River to Kansas) followed wagon trains on trails to Santa Fe, California, and Oregon, attempting to make a better life for themselves by working and applying for land. Farming was much more difficult than most people were led to believe. Agricultural crops were often in high demand, but environmental influences such as excessive heat, droughts, and *locusts* (species of grasshoppers) made raising crops difficult. Competition with large corporations and declines in global and domestic markets kept western farmers in heavy debt. Corn, wheat, and cotton production flourished, however, and after 1890, government aid helped offset a few of the risks.

Native American Conflicts

White settlers continued to infringe on Native American land, which caused increased tensions and battles on the western frontier. The growing farming, cattle, and mining industries made things worse. Soon the U.S.

government was revoking treaties and encouraging the army to use military force to control Native American tribes who rebelliously refused to move to reservations.

The chart that follows identifies several key events related to important Native American struggles of the Gilded Age.

Native American Conflict		
Event	**Description of Conflict**	**Impact**
The Battle of the Little Bighorn (June 1876)	Also known as "Custer's Last Stand," this was a battle between the Plains Indians (Sioux and Cheyenne), led by Sitting Bull and Crazy Horse, and the U.S. Army's 7th Calvary, led by George Custer. It was one of the last efforts for Native Americans to preserve their way of life.	Taking place in the Dakota Territory as part of the Great Sioux War, it was a triumphant victory for the Native Americans, who killed Custer and over 250 Army soldiers. Although the U.S. Army lost the battle and Custer's soldiers led several vicious attacks on Native Americans, Custer and his men eventually became heroic figures that inspired many Americans to continue fighting against Native Americans. Eventually, the tribes were defeated. In 1877, Native Americans were forced onto reservations and land was annexed to the U.S.
Nez Percé Removal (1877)	Several bands of the peaceful Nez Percé Native Americans decided to fight the federal government's confiscation of Native American ancestral lands in Oregon. Some of the tribe members attempted to flee to Canada to avoid forced removal, but were pursued by the U.S. Army. Those who didn't die in the fighting or on the treacherous journey were eventually sent to a reservation in Oklahoma.	In 1879, Chief Joseph became desperate to help the starving and diseased people of his tribe. As one of the leaders of the coalitions that ruled the tribe, he surrendered in a famous speech in which he appealed to the humanity of his enemies and petitioned for mercy using traditional American egalitarian language.
Dawes Act (1887)	A legislative act signed by President Grover Cleveland that divided Native American reservation land into small allotments for individuals within the tribe.	The law changed the legal status of Native American colonies from "tribes" to "individuals." Native Americans were not granted land or citizenship unless they agreed to live individually, obey state and federal laws, and "adopt the habits of civilized lives." The act not only destroyed tribal authority, but it placed tribal land in the hands of federal managers. The U.S. then resold the remaining land to U.S. speculators, railroads, and American settlers. The act was terminated in 1934.
Wounded Knee Massacre (1890)	When several tribes gathered to observe the Ghost Dance near Wounded Knee Creek in South Dakota, the U.S. government sent in troops to prevent an uprising. A scuffle with a deaf Native American caused a gun to discharge, and the Army opened fire on the crowd, killing more than 150 Native Americans.	The incident marked the end of Native American resistance, and although now remembered as a tragedy, reaction to it was generally favorable when it occurred. Congress awarded 20 Medals of Honor to soldiers who participated, and their commander, although considered incompetent by his superiors, was promoted.

International Relations of the Gilded Age

Missionaries and sailors had been traveling abroad for decades, but it wasn't until the 1880s that American citizens started giving significant thought to international relations. After the Civil War, Americans focused on reconstruction, financial progress, and western expansion. As the 19th century progressed, however, Americans began to search for new opportunities and new economic markets.

America's frontier was redefined (1893). Historian Frederick Jackson Turner delivered a speech in Chicago to the American Historical Association, arguing that American democracy was deeply linked to important qualities of the American frontier (the **Frontier Thesis**). Emphasizing equality, individualism, and opportunities for economic success, Turner theorized that the frontier shaped American character and calmed social unrest. Turner also suggested the frontier was disappearing and that progress would stagnate and die without international expansion.

America's trade market was redefined. When U.S.-manufactured goods and agricultural production increased, supply often exceeded demand of the domestic market. American businessmen moved into international markets dominated by Britain and other foreign nations and sought new regions for their products, especially in Latin America, the Pacific, and Asia. Republicans retained high tariffs, which protected American producers. As you will see in 20th-century U.S. history (Chapter 10), the American economy unfortunately began to depend on global trade, which made businesses vulnerable to recurrent booms and busts, banking panics, and economic depressions, just like they had been in the 19th century.

Did you know? In 1863, Napoleon invaded Mexico and established the Austrian Maximilian I as king. Under pressure from the U.S. government, Napoleon withdrew his troops in 1866, allowing Mexican rebels to overthrow and execute the king. The incident indirectly caused the federal government to pay closer attention to violations of the Monroe Doctrine (p. 151). After the Civil War, the U.S. was distracted by domestic affairs, but by 1895, foreign policy began to change. As American investments in Latin American trade increased, it became necessary to enforce the Monroe Doctrine. When a border dispute arose between Venezuela and British-controlled Guyana, the U.S. intervened in the negotiations in order to keep Europe out of the Western Hemisphere. The incident signified that American global power was increasing and began a trend of U.S. involvement in Latin American affairs.

Chapter Review Practice Questions

Practice questions are for instructional purposes only and may not reflect the format of the actual exam. On the actual exam, questions will be grouped into sets. Each set contains one source-based prompt (document or image) and two to five questions.

Multiple-Choice Questions

Questions 1–3 refer to the following image.

PACIFIC CHIVALRY.
Encouragement to Chinese Immigration.

Source: Thomas Nast, "Pacific Chivalry: Encouragement to Chinese Immigration." *Harper's Weekly,* 1869.

1. The image most directly reflects which of the following?

    A. The railroad managers' mistreatment of slaves in the West
    B. The manipulation and abuse of Chinese immigrants in the West
    C. The railroad practices in the West that were offensive to the general public
    D. The main reason that workers revolted during the building of the transcontinental railroad

2. Based on your knowledge of U.S. history, which of the following most directly describes the political results of the conditions shown in the image?

    A. Legislative demands made by the Populist Party for urban laborers, who were often immigrants
    B. Legislative regulations for railway freight by the Interstate Commerce Commission
    C. Legislative demands from the Know Nothing Party outlined in anti-immigration pamphlets
    D. Legislative acts banning a specific group of immigrants from entering the United States

3. Which of the following best describes why transcontinental railroads were considered important to the U.S. economy during the late 19th century?

   A. The railroad owners were considered well-intentioned benefactors of the Gilded Age economy.
   B. The railroad industry made transportation and shipping goods more expensive but also more accessible, so the wealthy were able to utilize the railroads to their advantage.
   C. The railroad industry helped to develop standardized shipping by creating temporary time zones.
   D. The railroad industry boosted industries like coal and steel.

Questions 4–6 refer to the following excerpt.

   We have witnessed for more than a quarter of a century the struggles of the two great political parties for power and plunder, while grievous wrongs have been inflicted upon the suffering people. We charge that the controlling influences dominating both these parties have permitted the existing dreadful conditions to develop without serious effort to prevent or restrain them… They propose to drown out the outcries of a plundered people with the uproar of a sham battle over the tariff, so that the capitalists, corporations, national banks, rings, trusts, watered stock, the demonetization of silver and the oppressions of the usurers may all be lost sight of. They propose to sacrifice our homes, lives, and children on the altar of mammon; to destroy the multitude in order to secure corruption funds from the millionaires…we seek to restore the government of the Republic to the hands of "the plain people," with which class it originated. We assert our purposes to be identical with the purposes of the National Constitution; to form a more perfect union and establish justice, ensure domestic tranquility, provide for the common defense, promote the general welfare, and secure the blessings of liberty for ourselves and our posterity.

   —Source: Preamble for the Omaha Platform: Launching the Populist Party, 1892.

4. Based on your knowledge of U.S. history, the speech best reflects which of the following causes for the agrarian revolt in the late 19th century?

   A. American political greed and corruption
   B. Americans' demands for open and direct elections
   C. Americans' growing concern for social welfare legislation
   D. Americans' outcry against the oppressive working conditions of women and children in industrial cities

5. Which of the following demands were expressed in the excerpt of the Preamble for the Omaha Platform?

   A. The return to the gold standard
   B. The rejection of income tax laws
   C. The commencement of 8-hour workdays
   D. The appeal for industrial mining

6. Based on your knowledge of 19th-century U.S. history, which of the following best describes the success of the Populist Party?

   A. The Populist Party was divided by racism, regionalism, and bimetallism; Populists were not united on a single issue, and failed in their objectives.
   B. The Populist Party was not considered successful since other political parties rejected its issues.
   C. The Populist Party achieved limited success in the Gilded Age, but the issues became reform policies in the 20th century.
   D. The Populist Party elected several governors and senators in the Midwest, which made it popular throughout the nation.

Document-Based Question

1 question

60 minutes

Reading Time: 15 minutes (brainstorm your thoughts and organize your response)

Writing Time: 45 minutes

Directions: The document-based question is based on the seven accompanying documents. The documents are for instructional purposes only. Some of the documents have been edited for the purpose of this practice exercise. Write your response on lined paper and include the following:

- **Thesis.** Present a thesis that supports a historically defensible claim, establishes a line of reasoning, and responds to all parts of the question. The thesis must consist of one or more sentences located in one place—either the introduction or the conclusion.
- **Contextualization.** Situate the argument by explaining the broader historical events, developments, or processes that occurred before, during, or after the time frame of the question.
- **Evidence from the documents.** Support your argument by using the content of six of the documents to develop and support a cohesive argument that responds to the question.
- **Evidence beyond the documents.** Support your argument by explaining at least one additional piece of specific historical evidence not found in the documents. (Note: The example must be different from the evidence used to earn the point for contextualization.)
- **Analysis.** Use at least three documents that are relevant to the question to explain the documents' point of view, purpose, historical situation, and/or audience.
- **Historical reasoning.** Use historical reasoning to show complex relationships among the documents, the topic question, and the thesis argument. Use evidence to corroborate, qualify, or modify the argument.

Based on the documents that follow, answer the question below.

Question 1: Evaluate the rapid industrial and economic growth during the Gilded Age and explain how this growth impacted political and social organizations in the U.S.

Document 1

Source: *Massachusetts Bureau of Statistics of Labor, Thirteenth Annual Report,* 1883. Business owner commenting on his employees.

I regard my people as I regard my machinery. So long as they do my work for what I choose to pay them, I keep them, getting out of them all I can. What they do or how they fare outside my walls I don't know, nor do I consider it my business to know. They must look out for themselves as I do for myself.

Document 2

Source: Ida Tarbell, excerpt from *The History of the Standard Oil Company,* 1904. A book about 19th-century corporate oil tycoon John D. Rockefeller, one of the wealthiest men in America.

To know every detail of the oil trade, to be able to reach at any moment its remotest point, to control even its weakest factor—this was John D. Rockefeller's ideal of doing business. It seemed to be an intellectual necessity for him to be able to direct the course of any particular gallon of oil from the moment it gushed from the earth until it went into the lamp of a housewife. There must be nothing—nothing in his great machine he did not know to be working right. It was to complete this ideal, to satisfy this necessity, that he undertook, late in the (18)70s, to organize the oil markets of the world, as he had already organized oil refining and oil transporting. Mr. Rockefeller was driven to this new task of organization not only by his own curious intellect; he was driven to it by that thing so abhorrent to his mind—competition. If, as he claimed, the oil business belonged to him, and if, as he had announced, he was prepared to refine all the oil that men would consume, it followed as a corollary that the markets of the world belonged to him.

Document 3

Source: C. Jay Taylor, "Our Religious Landlords and Their Rookery Tenants," 1895. Contrasting the outward piety of New York City's wealthy landlords and their indifference to the living conditions of their tenants in the slums.

OUR RELIGIOUS LANDLORDS AND THEIR ROOKERY TENANTS.

Document 4

Source: Andrew Carnegie, essay on "The Gospel of Wealth," 1889. Millionaire and philanthropist Andrew Carnegie argued that the wealthy have a moral duty to be charitable. When he died, he donated 90 percent of his fortune to charity.

In former days there was little difference between the dwelling, dress, food, and environment of the chief and those of his retainers. The Indians are today where civilized man then was. When visiting the Sioux, I was led to the wigwam of the chief. It was just like the others in external appearance, and even within the difference was trifling between it and those of the poorest of his braves. The contrast between the palace of the millionaire and the cottage of the laborer with us today measures the change which has come with civilization.

This change, however, is not to be deplored, but welcomed as highly beneficial. It is well, nay, essential for the progress of the race that the houses of some should be homes for all that is highest and best in literature and the arts, and for all the refinements of civilization, rather than that none should be so. Much better this great irregularity than universal squalor. Without wealth there can be no Mæcenas. The "good old times" were not good old times. Neither master nor servant was as well situated then as today. A relapse to old conditions would be disastrous to both—not the least so to him who serves—and would sweep away civilization with it. But whether the change be for good or ill, it is upon us, beyond our power to alter, and therefore to be accepted and made the best of. It is a waste of time to criticize the inevitable.

Document 5

Source: Jane Addams, "The Subjective Necessity for Social Settlements," 1893. Excerpt from a speech in which she explains why reformers must add the social function to democracy because dependence of classes on each other is reciprocal.

The Settlement then, is an experimental effort to aid in the solution of the social and industrial problems which are engendered by the modern conditions of life in a great city… It is an attempt to relieve, at the same time, the over accumulation at one end of society and the destitution at the other; but it assumes that this over accumulation and destitution is most sorely felt in the things that pertain to social and educational privileges… Its residents must be emptied of all conceit of opinion and all self-assertion, and ready to arouse and interpret the public opinion of their neighborhood. They must be content to live quietly side by side with their neighbors, until they grow into a sense of relationship and mutual interests. Their neighbors are held apart by differences of race and language, which the residents can more easily overcome. They are bound to see the needs of their neighborhood as a whole, to furnish data for legislation, and to use their influence to secure it. In short, residents are pledged to devote themselves to the duties of good citizenship and to the arousing of the social energies, which too largely lie dormant in every neighborhood given over to industrialism. They are bound to regard the entire life of their city as organic, to make an effort to unify it, and to protest against its over-differentiation.

Document 6

> **Source: Samuel Gompers, excerpt from speech regarding the future of the labor movement, 1890. Gompers was the president of the American Federation of Labor (AFL).**
>
> You know that it is the theory of our government that we can work or cease to work at will… It is true that we can cease to work when we want to, but I deny that we can work when we will, so long as there are a million idle men and women tramping the streets of our cities, searching for work. The theory that we can work or cease to work when we will is a delusion and a snare. It is a lie.
>
> What we want to consider is, first, to make our employment more secure, and, secondly, to make wages more permanent, and, thirdly, to give these poor people a chance to work. The laborer has been regarded as a mere producing machine…but the back of labor is the soul of man and honesty of purpose and aspiration… We live in the later part of the nineteenth century. In the age of electricity and steam that has produced wealth a hundred fold, we insist that it has been brought about by the intelligence and energy of the workingmen, and while we find that is now easier to produce, it is harder to live. We do want more, and when it becomes more, we shall still want more. And we shall never cease to demand more until we have received the results of our labor.

Document 7

> **Source: Mother Jones, "Civilization in Southern Mills," March 1901. Mary Harris "Mother" Jones was a labor activist and a champion of the working class. Jones was also a founder of the Industrial Workers of the World (IWW) labor union, called the "Wobblies."**
>
> I visited the factory in Tuscaloosa, Ala., at 10 o'clock at night. The superintendent, not knowing my mission, gave me the entire freedom of the factory and I made good use of it. Standing by a siding that contained 155 spindles were two little girls. I asked a man standing near if the children were his, and he replied that they were. "How old are they?" I asked. "This one is 9, the other 10," he replied. "How many hours do they work?" "Twelve," was the answer. "How much do they get a night?" "We all three together get 60 cents. They get 10 cents each and I 40."
>
> I watched them as they left their slave-pen in the morning and saw them gather their rags around their frail forms to hide them from the wintry blast. Half-fed, half-clothed, half-housed, they toil on, while the poodle dogs of their masters are petted and coddled and sleep on pillows of down, and the capitalistic judges jail the agitators that would dare to help these helpless ones to better their condition.

Answer Explanations

Multiple-Choice Questions

1. **B.** The image depicts the Pacific Railroad's mistreatment of Chinese immigrant laborers, choice B, not slave laborers, choice A. Notice the sign posted in the background. It shows that the Chinese were taxed more than Anglo-Americans. Many Chinese immigrants who migrated to California laid train tracks for the transcontinental railroad. By 1870, 90 percent of the workers were Chinese, but the Chinese were subject to discrimination and abuse by railroad managers. Choices C and D are incorrect because the American abuse and manipulation of Chinese and other immigrants was supported by the general public, leading to the Chinese Exclusion Act, and Chinese workers did not revolt when building the railroad.

2. **D.** The animosity toward Chinese immigrants in the West eventually led to the passage of the Chinese Exclusion Act in 1882, which banned Chinese immigrants, choice D. Although Chinese men often worked as miners, the Chinese had nothing to do with the Populist Party, choice A, or the biased freight charges of the railroad, choice B. The anti-immigrant, anti-Catholic sentiments of the Know Nothing Party, choice C, were closely associated with the Antebellum Era and the Irish, not the Chinese during the Gilded Age.

3. **D.** The railroad industry helped to boost the U.S. economy in many industries such as coal, steel, and iron, choice D. The men who ran the railroads were often considered corrupt, greedy "robber barons," eliminating choice A. The transcontinental railroads made shipping cheaper and easier, which allowed both small and large producers better access to markets. Therefore, choice B (the railroad industry made transportation and shipping goods more expensive but more accessible, so the wealthy were able to utilize the railroads to their advantage) is incorrect. Although the railroads established time zones that are still in use today, choice C is not the best answer for this time period.

4. **A.** The excerpt best reflects the greed and corruption embedded into the capitalistic system that allowed greedy and corrupt men to establish and maintain power at the expense of "plain people," choice A. While open and direct elections, choice B, are mentioned in the excerpt, they are not the focus of the selected text, which is focused on "capitalists," "corruption," and "the blessings of liberty" that Populists believed were being denied. An agrarian-based, rather than an urban movement, the Populists are also unconcerned with social welfare (choice C) or the specific working conditions of women and children (choice D), neither of which they mention here.

5. **C.** Populists supported fair working conditions, which included an 8-hour workday, choice C. Since the Populists rejected the gold standard (choice A) and industrial corporations (choice D), you can eliminate choices A and D. Populists supported, not rejected, graduated income tax laws, eliminating choice B.

6. **C.** The Populist Party achieved limited success in the Gilded Age, but the issues became reform policies in the 20th century, choice C. Populists were not divided by bimetallism, choice A, nor were they popular throughout the U.S., choice D. Their issues were adopted by other parties, not rejected, eliminating choice B.

Document-Based Question

DBQ Scoring Guide

To achieve the maximum score of 7, your response must address the scoring criteria components in the table that follows.

Scoring Criteria for a Good Essay	
Question 1: Evaluate the rapid industrial and economic growth during the Gilded Age and explain how this growth impacted political and social organizations in the U.S.	
Scoring Criteria	**Examples**
A. THESIS/CLAIM	
(1 point) Presents a historically defensible thesis that establishes a line of reasoning. (Note: The thesis must make a claim that responds to *all* parts of the question and must *not* just restate the question. The thesis must consist of *at least* one sentence, either in the introduction or the conclusion.)	A strong thesis must follow a line of reasoning while explaining the political and social impacts of the rapid growth in the U.S. during the late 19th century, the Gilded Age. The argument should also discuss several organizations, groups, and alliances and their different attitudes toward the industrial and economic changes that occurred. The essay is arranged topically and develops these topics with clear examples and evidence of organizations (leading businesses, labor unions, and reform movements).
B. CONTEXTUALIZATION	
(1 point) Explains the broader historical context of events, developments, or processes that occurred before, during, or after the time frame of the question. (Note: Must be more than a phrase or reference.)	The essay develops the thesis with examples and evidence to develop the context of industrial and economic growth during the Gilded Age. The essay starts with a general discussion of the reasons that led to the Second Industrial Revolution, and notes the effect of the transcontinental railroad on industrialization and urbanization. In the context of the Gilded Age, the essay goes on to relate the topic to specific groups and their reactions during this time period.
C. EVIDENCE	
Evidence from the Documents **(2 points)** Uses at least *six* documents to support the argument in response to the prompt. OR **(1 point)** Uses the content of at least *three* documents to address the topic prompt. (Note: Examples must describe, rather than simply quote, the content of the documents.)	Remember to aim for the most possible points. To accomplish this, you must address at least six documents. The essay utilizes all seven documents. Most of the documents are analyzed using purpose and applying them to other facts that one should know if writing about industrialization and urbanization during the Gilded Age. For example, Documents 1, 2, 3, and 4 refer to the wealthy corporate perspectives of the Gilded Age, and Documents 5, 6, and 7 show how labor and reform movements paved the way to offer help to employees, immigrants, the poor, and the less fortunate.
Evidence Beyond the Documents **(1 point)** Uses at least one additional piece of specific historical evidence beyond those found in the documents relevant to the argument. (Note: Evidence must be different from the evidence used in contextualization.)	The essay needs to provide specific examples of outside events that inspired the documents. The essay does this by discussing scientific management, Social Darwinism, New Women, and exploitative business and labor practices. It also distinguishes between the labor unions, the AFL and the IWW.

Scoring Criteria	Examples
D. ANALYSIS AND REASONING	
(1 point) Uses at least *three* documents to explain how each document's point of view, purpose, historical situation, and/or audience is relevant to the argument. (Note: References must explain how or why, rather than simply identifying.)	The essay provides as least three references from the documents' point of view and historical situation. For example, the artist of Document 3 demonstrates the contrasting perspectives of wealthy building owners to "walk by" the poor tenants without regard to the less fortunate. Documents 2 and 4 describe the perspectives of two of the wealthiest men in 19th century America, Rockefeller and Carnegie. The essay goes on to distinguish the two men by showing that Carnegie also was an advocate to help the less fortunate.
(1 point) Uses historical reasoning and development that focuses on the question while using evidence to corroborate, qualify, or modify the argument. (Examples: Explain what is similar and different; explain the cause and effect; explain multiple causes; explain connections within and across periods of time; corroborate multiple perspectives across themes; or consider alternative views.)	This essay provides both supporting and dissenting viewpoints to show coherence to the overall argument. The essay ends with showing the changes and continuities over time by shifting to a different time period—the Progressive Era. The suggestion is that the unfettered capitalism that was prevalent in the Gilded Age did not continue in the future. It mentions the agrarian side of the issues, relating them to the Populists, while hinting at important changes during the Progressive Era.

Sample Response

Due to government subsidies, technological advances, and scientific business management, the U.S. economy grew rapidly during the Gilded Age. Transcontinental railroads—like the Pacific Railroad—not only encouraged western migration and opened the nation to new markets, but the railroad also led to the growth of related industries, including coal, iron, and steel. Industrial manufacturing increased in urban centers (especially New York and Chicago) and people fled the rural agrarian countryside to search for employment in cities. At the same time, thousands of immigrants flocked to the U.S., hoping to secure job and income opportunities. The rapid growth in industrialization and urbanization resulted in a wide gap in wealth, causing different reactions among the various social classes, ethnicities, and races. Since the government failed to regulate the abusive business practices of large corporations, many in the upper and middle classes dismissed the effects of urban poverty, and used intellectual and ideological theories to justify the financial benefits of ignoring impoverished populations. The working-class citizens, however, objected to corporate abuses and corruption by forming labor unions (Documents 6 and 7), and social reformers established institutions that sought to help the poor (Document 5).

The use of Frederick Taylor's principles of a business scientific management system standardized tasks and synthesized workflow, reduced the need for skilled laborers, and caused many employers to treat their employees as simply "cogs" in the industrial machine who could be easily replaced (Document 1). Many wealthy employers and factory managers adhered to the tenets of Social Darwinism, suggesting the "fittest" rose to the top of society, which Andrew Carnegie hinted at in his "Gospel of Wealth" (Document 4). As Taylor's illustration indicates, the wealthy ignored the impoverished in immigrant neighborhoods, charged exorbitant rent payments for cramped apartments in the tenements, and made themselves rich at the expense of the less fortunate while explaining their actions through social and ideological justifications (Document 3). Although Carnegie was an advocate of Social Darwinism, he did not overlook the obvious struggles of the poor and pressured those with financial wealth to help the needy. Carnegie benevolently financed philanthropic projects, and like the middle-class social reformers who worked in Jane Addams' settlement houses, he encouraged others to do the same. New Women, like Jane Addams, were an example of charitable social work (Document 5). Addams lived with and cared for the destitute, teaching people important basic U.S. assimilation skills while encouraging local legislators to assist the poor, immigrants, women, and children.

Ironically, Carnegie's business practices in steel production were responsible for the wide gap in wealth. Carnegie discouraged the unionization of his employees, and like John D. Rockefeller of Standard Oil (Document 2), he used vertical and horizontal integration to increase his wealth. Carnegie dominated the market by buying out all of his competitors and investing in every step of the production process. Since the federal government believed it had no regulatory role in stopping these giant corporations from monopolizing entire industries, wealthy businessmen were able to set prices, secure markets, control the economy, and dictate the terms of employment.

A belief in free labor dominated the American culture. Legislators protected manufacturers and their contracts rather than employees. As a result, work conditions remained harsh and wages were low, often requiring an entire family, including women and children, to work to support a household. Union leaders like Samuel Gompers of the American Federation of Labor and Mother Jones of the Industrial Workers of the World (Documents 6 and 7) shared the same cause to support laborers, but they responded differently to working-class issues. The AFL, as Gompers indicates in his speech (Document 6), may have been stubbornly determined to fight for secure employment and wages, but his organization of skilled workers was more likely to work with corporations to negotiate contracts and terms of employment. The IWW, on the other hand, sought to unite the working class in an attempt to overthrow exploitative practices of the producing class, as indicated by Jones' implicit attack against capitalism and its supporters (Document 7). The IWW was more likely to boycott and strike against their employers.

The government itself often backed corporations, disregarding the needs of common laborers as it had during the Homestead Steelworkers Strike (1892) and the Pullman Railroad Strike (1894). Therefore, the economic benefits of the Gilded Age's industrialism remained in the hands of the privileged few. The period of unfettered capitalism did not last long, however. The protests that began with common workers (agrarians) and Populists developed into federal reforms during the Progressive Era, when politicians and reformers "busted" the power of the trusts and worked hard to regulate society and the economy.

Chapter 10

Period Seven: The Rise to Global Power (1890 to 1945)

Period Seven explores progression, expansion, economic depression, and global conflicts.

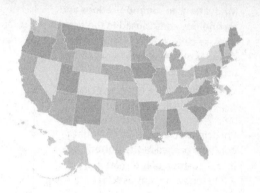

- U.S. Imperialism
- The Spanish-American War (1898)
- The Progressive Era (1890 to 1920)
- World War I (1914 to 1918)
- The Interwar Period (1919 to 1938)
  - Cultural Changes
  - Economic Changes
  - The Great Depression (1929 to 1939)
  - The New Deal
- World War II (1939 to 1945)
- Post–World War II

Overview of AP U.S. History Period Seven

In the 20th century, the United States became a global superpower. The corruption of the Gilded Age ended, and the Progressive Era brought a series of political, economic, and social reform programs. Americans experienced rapid growth and expansion opportunities, but were later challenged by a devastating economic decline and the involvement in two catastrophic global wars.

Use the chart below to guide you through what is covered on the exam. The curriculum contained in this chart is an abridged version of the concept outlines with topic examples. Visit https://apstudent.collegeboard.org/apcourse/ap-united-states-history/ for the complete updated APUSH course curriculum descriptions and key concepts.

AP U.S. History Key Concepts (1890 to 1945)	
Key Concept	**Specific Content**
KEY CONCEPT 7.1: ECONOMIC GROWTH AND DECLINE	The United States continued its transition from a rural, agricultural economy to an urban, industrial economy led by large companies.
Growth expanded opportunity, while economic instability led to new efforts to reform U.S. society and its economic system.	In the Progressive Era of the early 20th century, Progressives responded to political corruption, economic instability, and social concerns by calling for greater government action and other political and social measures.
	During the 1930s, policymakers responded to the mass unemployment and social upheavals of the Great Depression by transforming the U.S. into a limited welfare state, redefining the goals and ideas of modern American liberalism.

Continued

Key Concept	Specific Content
KEY CONCEPT 7.2: MODERNITY AND GLOBAL COMMUNICATION **Innovations in communications and technology contributed to the growth of mass culture, while significant changes occurred in internal and international migration patterns.**	Popular culture grew in influence in U.S. society, even as debates increased over the effects of culture on public values, morals, and American national identity. Economic pressures, global events, and political developments caused sharp variations in the numbers, sources, and experiences of both international and internal migrants.
KEY CONCEPT 7.3: GLOBAL CONFLICTS AND U.S. WORLD POWER **Participation in a series of global conflicts propelled the United States into a position of international power while renewing domestic debates over the nation's proper role in the world.**	In the late 19th century and early 20th century, new U.S. territorial ambitions and acquisitions in the Western Hemisphere and the Pacific accompanied heightened public debates over America's role in the world. World War I and its aftermath intensified ongoing debates about the nation's role in the world and how best to achieve national security and pursue American interests. U.S. participation in World War II transformed American society, while the victory of the United States and its allies over the Axis powers vaulted the U.S. into a position of global, political, and military leadership.

Significant Themes

Now that we've discussed the curriculum, let's discuss the significant themes related to this period. The theme-related study questions that follow will help you make mental connections to the context of the "big picture" of this time period. Keep in mind that these questions often overlap and apply to other themes of social, political, religious, geographic, ideological, technological, and economic developments.

Glance through the study questions before you start the review section. Take notes, highlight questions, and write down page number references to reinforce your learning. Refer to this list until you feel comfortable with your knowledge of the material.

Study Questions Related to Significant Themes for Period Seven

Theme 1: American and National Identity

1. How did the definitions of democracy and freedom change for various groups, including women, immigrants, and African Americans? (Hint: Consider African American service in both world wars, the new voting base and black communities created by the Great Migration, and the work of black women and key figures like W. E. B. Du Bois and A. Philip Randolph. Note how immigration restrictions continued to single out particular individuals, setting quotas and bans that limited entry and thus national inclusion. Women's service in both world wars (especially in manufacturing, the military, and the public sector) also affected demands for inclusion.)

2. How were basic American rights suspended during World War I? Why was this justified and how was it enacted? Who was affected by it and how did it change the way Americans began to think about their rights and obligations as citizens? (Hint: Analyze this in relation to the Espionage Act (1917) and the Sedition Act (1918), as well as the no-strike pledges given by many unions. Discuss attacks on Socialists, those who criticized the government, and union organizations like the IWW, whose

members were often jailed. Also examine the rise of vigilante community groups like the American Protection League, which questioned the loyalties of ethnic minorities and targeted people who spoke out against the draft or seemed "disloyal.")

Theme 2: Politics and Power

1. Who were the imperialists and the anti-imperialists? (Hint: In order to discuss the imperialists and anti-imperialists, focus on expansion that began with the Spanish-American War, noting who objected to U.S. involvement and who supported it. Be sure to consider why these things mattered to Americans who desired new markets and to those who believed American men were becoming "soft." Examine key figures like William McKinley, William Jennings Bryan, and Theodore Roosevelt, mentioning the influence of yellow journalists and Mahan's *The Influence of Sea Power on History,* the Rough Riders, the Anti-Imperialist League, and the war in the Philippines.)

2. What is the definition of Progressivism? (Hint: Concentrate on the Progressives' desire for regulation, order, and reform, exploring political, economic, and social agendas of Progressives like Theodore Roosevelt and Woodrow Wilson, as well as New Women like Jane Addams. Be sure to include Roosevelt's Square Deal, maternal welfare policies and legislation, and both Wilson's and Roosevelt's "attack" on trusts. Include William Howard Taft's economic policies as well, and note why Roosevelt felt the need to create the Progressive Party during his last campaign for the presidency. Be sure to note the difference between political Progressives, social Progressives, and the Progressive Party.)

3. How did the regulation of the American economy change during the Progressive Era? Who were the muckrakers and what was their role in sparking these changes? (Hint: Focus on Theodore Roosevelt's attack on corporations as part of his Square Deal, noting specifics like his use of the Sherman Antitrust Act to destroy the National Securities Company and the way he distinguished "good" and "bad" trusts. Carry this through Taft's and Wilson's policies, which include a continuation of destroying corporate monopolies and the creation of regulatory agencies like the Federal Reserve and the Federal Trade Commission—be able to define the importance of the latter. Also note the role of muckrakers like Ida Tarbell and Upton Sinclair, who exposed abuses and led to the passage of key pieces of legislation—link Sinclair to the Pure Food and Drug Act.)

4. What were the First and Second New Deals? How did FDR's policies arise and transform the nation? How do other groups fit into these policies? (Hint: Think about Democratic support, conservative resistance, and labor unions, as well as those struggling economically. Consider the difference between the motivating factors behind the First New Deal, which was intended to provide relief, recovery, and reform, and the Second New Deal, which was designed to provide security. Include specific programs like the Emergency Bank Act, Civilian Conservation Corps, Agricultural Adjustment Act, Federal Emergency Relief Association, Tennessee Valley Authority, National Industry Recovery Act, Federal Housing Administration, Work Progress Administration, the Social Security Act, and the National Labor Relations Act (also known as the Wagner Act). Define them as pieces of legislation and analyze their success or failure while discussing their connection to other programs or each other.)

5. What was the Red Scare of 1919 and the Palmer Raids and why are they important? (Hint: Think of this first Red Scare in relation to the Bolshevik Revolution in Russia. Link it to fears of labor unrest and the Espionage Act and Sedition Act, which allowed for the persecution of Communists and Socialists in America, who were often also labor activists. When defining the Palmer Raids, concentrate on the role of A. Mitchell Palmer and J. Edgar Hoover as well as the suspension of legal rights, including the ability to search without warrants. Note how the Palmer Raids changed the way Americans thought about and defended their civil rights.)

Theme 3: Work, Exchange, and Technology

1. How did FDR's administration mobilize for World War II? What impact did this have on the economy? (Hint: Consider the amount of financial support produced by the federal government for mobilization. Examine not only government subsidies and contracts with private industry, but also attempts at regulation through the War Production Board, the Office of Price Administration, and the Fair Employment Commission. Be sure to connect high employment and increased wages to the end of the Depression, linking this not to the war itself, but to the government's willingness to go into heavy debt to mobilize for it. Also note the importance of African Americans and women in the mobilization process and the change in labor dynamics due to the need for mass production.)

Theme 4: Culture and Society

1. How did leisure time and people's spending habits and behavior change after World War I? What dangers were associated with unregulated spending and markets? (Hint: Explore this in relation to shifts in culture and attitudes during the 1920s, discussing the Jazz Age, the rise of materialism, flappers, and the technological advances that allowed for consumerism. Especially note changes in production that made goods inexpensive and accessible as well as the importance of entertainment, "mad" investment, "buying on the margin," and the falling economic conditions people failed to recognize. Link these things to the stock market crash of 1929 and the Great Depression, noting the suffering of Americans as a result of overproduction, loose economic policies, and wealth inequality.)

2. How did various perceptions of the government's social responsibility shift during the Progressive Era? How can this be compared to both the efforts of the Populists (see Chapter 9) and Franklin Roosevelt's efforts to alleviate suffering caused by the Great Depression? (Hint: Connections between all of these can be made by examining how Progressives, Populists, and FDR refocused people's expectations of the government. Concentrate on how government spending was called for to alleviate the poverty, inequality, and suffering of American citizens. Focus on New Women's and Progressive politicians' call for legislation that addressed the employment of women and children, poor living conditions in urban centers, and immigrant assimilation. Think about how many of the demands of the Populists—especially those addressing regulation and agricultural assistance—were carried out during the Progressive Era. Also, note how FDR's New Deal legislation intended to address poverty by creating programs like the Work Progress Administration and the Civilian Conservation Corps to employ individuals and focused on taking care of the elderly and poor through Social Security and direct assistance.)

3. How did politicians and political spokesmen like FDR, Huey Long, and Father Charles Coughlin use the radio to their benefit? (Hint: Discuss how Roosevelt used fireside chats to calm worries about the Depression and later, World War I, and garner support for his programs and legislation. Contrast this with Huey Long and Father Coughlin, who used the radio to generate a political base that was critical of the New Deal and, in Long's case, allowed him to promote his own agenda, which included the "Share Our Wealth" plan. Be sure to mention Coughlin's anti-Jewish rhetoric and support of Hitler, noting how he was ultimately censored by the Vatican and the American people.)

Theme 5: Migration and Settlement

1. How did responses to migration within and to the United States affect the country during this period? Explain the role of nativism. (Hint: Note the race riots that occurred as a result of the first wave of the Great Migration. After reading Chapter 11, connect this to the white flight to suburbia and

conservative politics after its second wave. Note the objections to immigration in the first half of the period, while noting the U.S.'s leniency during and after World War II as a result of expanding definitions of national inclusion, the Holocaust, and the Bracero Program, which filled a need for labor during the war.)

2. What is the Great Migration and how did it affect American culture and society? (Hint: Define the Great Migration not only in terms of African American movement from the South to the North, but also as a result of particular oppressions like Jim Crow laws, white violence, and the convict lease system. Discuss the problems that continued in the North, including housing and employment discrimination, race riots, and eventually white flight to suburbia. Also focus on the positives, like the ability to vote and the development of black communities in urban centers like New York and Chicago. Explain how the New Negro Movement, Harlem Renaissance, and the ability to form a voting base increased black pride and affected politics, noting how these things connect to the Civil Rights Movement of the 1950s and '60s.)

Theme 6: Geography and the Environment

1. What is the difference between preservation and conservation? What was Theodore Roosevelt's role in changing the way the government used its natural resources? (Hint: Examine conservation as one portion of Roosevelt's Square Deal, focusing on the influence of John Muir and the different ways preservationists and conservationists viewed the public use of nature. Be sure to discuss Roosevelt's anger over the Ballinger-Pinchot Affair and its connection to preservation, conservation, and the political or economic abuse of natural resources.)

Theme 7: America in the World

1. Compare and contrast foreign policy during the various eras of this period. A chart might be useful here—don't forget to mention expansionism or isolationism and key policies of the Spanish-American War, World War I, and World War II. (Hint: Focus on contrasting the expansionism and imperialism of the Spanish-American War with the isolationism and desire to "stay out of Europe's fight" that were associated with late entries into both world wars. Be sure to compare and contrast neutrality policies prior to the world wars and explore Wilson's and FDR's actions during each war as well as their ideas about what to do when victory was achieved, especially noting the difference between and reasons for Congressional support of the League of Nations and the United Nations.)

2. How did attitudes about expansion change after the United States won the Philippine-American War in 1903? (Hint: Contrast the drive for new markets and masculine prowess through war with the stories of atrocities heard by the American public during the Philippine-American War. Discuss the role of the Anti-Imperialist League in the rejection of military imperialism and the new focus on economic and political dominance of countries in the Western Hemisphere.)

3. How do the Roosevelt Corollary, dollar diplomacy, Wilson's foreign policy, and the Good Neighbor Policy differ? (Hint: Consider the role of political and economic influence during the Progressive Era for the first two, focusing on the different ways Teddy Roosevelt and Taft asserted strength in the Western Hemisphere, contrasting both of their policies with Wilson's moral diplomacy. Discuss FDR's dedication to the Good Neighbor Policy in relation to the domestic concerns of the Depression, which created the need to continue isolationism.)

4. How did the Germans (and international events as a whole) challenge neutrality in both world wars? What promoted the United States' hesitancy to enter these wars? What changed to pull the U.S. into each world

war? How was the loyalty, patriotism, and cooperation of the American people generated during each? (Hint: Focus on the United States' involvement in trade with various nations before both World War I and World War II. Contrast Wilson's and Roosevelt's attitudes toward each war and the German perception that both U.S. presidents were unfairly assisting particular countries rather than remaining neutral. Be sure to include specifics like U-boat activity, the sinking of the RMS *Lusitania*, and the Zimmermann Telegram when discussing World War I and the various Neutrality Acts and the Lend-Lease Act when discussing World War II. To note how support was generated for each, discuss the way propaganda was managed through the Committee on Public Information and the Office of War Information.)

Important Events, Terms, and Concepts

The list below shows important events, terms, and concepts that you should be familiar with on the APUSH exam. These and other important terms are printed in boldface throughout the chapter. Because the APUSH exam requires you to pay attention to the historical context and connections rather than details, don't bother memorizing the terms now. Simply place a check mark next to each as you study. You can return to this list to review as often as necessary. After you finish the review section, you can reinforce what you have learned by working through the practice questions at the end of this chapter. Answer explanations provide further clarification into perspectives of U.S. history.

Event/Term/Concept	Year/Brief Description	Study Page
New imperialism	**1870–1914.** A new wave of territorial expansion that was led by the United States, Europe, and Japan. Powerful countries acquired underdeveloped countries (territories) for political and economic control.	pp. 255–256
Spanish-American War	**1898.** A military conflict in Cuba that stimulated arguments about imperialism and resulted in U.S. territorial acquisition in the Pacific.	pp. 258–260
Progressive Era	**1890–1920.** A period when politicians, reformers, and other forward-looking individuals sought to regulate the economy and improve labor and society.	pp. 260–270
Trust-busting	**1900s.** A Progressive political tactic that attempted to regulate and often destroy corporations that abused the economy for purposes of economic gain. It was a common practice for President Teddy Roosevelt's administration to prosecute corporate trusts that violated federal antitrust laws, like the Sherman Antitrust Act (1890), which had rarely been enforced.	p. 266
Roosevelt Corollary vs. dollar or moral diplomacy	**1909–1921.** Different forms of Progressive foreign policies, advocated by Roosevelt, Taft, and Wilson. While Teddy Roosevelt tended to use military force and negotiation to influence other nations, Taft used U.S. economic strength and Wilson used morality to legitimize his decisions.	pp. 266, 268, 270
Great Migration	**1910–1940.** The exodus of African Americans from the South to the North in an attempt to escape violence and the limitations of segregation.	pp. 263–264
Federal Reserve	**1913.** The American creation of a centralized banking system. Its purpose was to manage the flow of currency in order to solve the problems of inflation and deflation.	p. 269
Red Scare	**1917–1920 (First Red Scare), 1947–1957 (Second Red Scare).** The pervasive fear of the rise of Communism.	p. 276
Treaty of Versailles	**1919.** The peace treaty ending World War I. The U.S. did not sign the treaty because the U.S. had strong isolationist sentiments after WWI and rejected some of the treaty's conditions.	pp. 274–275

Event/Term/Concept	Year/Brief Description	Study Page
Stock market crash	**1929.** A financial crash that was the result of the wild speculation, over purchasing, and greed of the 1920s. It contributed to the Great Depression that followed.	pp. 279–280
Great Depression	**1929–1939.** A period of global economic crisis that caused massive unemployment as well as physical and psychological hardship.	pp. 280–283
New Deal	**1933–1938.** A series of legislative acts designed by the Franklin Roosevelt administration. The New Deal attempted to relieve suffering caused by the Depression and stimulate recovery. Ultimately, it transformed the relationship between U.S. citizens and their government.	pp. 284–288
Japanese American internment	**1942–1945.** After Japan's attack on Pearl Harbor, Hawaii, in 1942, anti-Asian sentiment spread throughout the U.S. During World War II, thousands of Japanese Americans were forcibly relocated to concentration camps in the western U.S.	p. 294
Neutrality and isolationism	The foreign policies of both Woodrow Wilson and Franklin Roosevelt before U.S. entry into both world wars.	pp. 270, 275
Good Neighbor Policy	A foreign policy that encouraged interaction between the U.S. and Latin America.	pp. 290–291

Chapter Review

The information discussed in Chapter 10 builds on historical events from preceding chapters. As Americans redefined their freedoms, rights, and privileges, the country not only moved into an age of modernism, but also emerged as a global superpower with a strong military force. This shifted American interactions both domestically and abroad.

Let's begin with America's worldview, which shifted toward acquiring territories in other parts of the world.

U.S. Imperialism

In the late 19th century, America turned its attention to overseas territorial expansion through a new wave of imperialism. While some people reacted positively and embraced Western ideas brought to them by U.S. soldiers and citizens, others tried to shield themselves from Western invaders in the hope of retaining their traditions. Some nations even started rebellions, but the U.S. ultimately achieved dominance in the Western Hemisphere through its military, economic, and political might.

The concept of imperialism frequently appears on the APUSH exam. Before we discuss the reasons for U.S. expansion and the territories that the U.S. acquired, you should be familiar with key terms and types of imperialism.

Imperialism Key Terms	
Term	**Definition**
Imperialism	Imperialism is when a stronger, more dominant nation takes control of another nation—usually through military force—for territorial, economic, or political gain.
Colonial imperialism	Colonial imperialism is when a dominant nation takes control of a territory, and the weaker territory is made part of the stronger nation's empire.

Continued

Term	Definition
Protectorate imperialism	Protectorate imperialism is similar to colonial imperialism, but the difference is that the dominant imperialist nation allows the native ruler to remain in power. The weaker nation is a sovereign territory, but is dependent on the dominant imperialist nation for "protection." The imperialist nation controls all major decisions.
Sphere of influence	The sphere of influence is when a dominant imperialist nation gains exclusive economic, government, and cultural power in a region through military force or diplomacy. This allows the imperialist nation to acquire all economic rights to trade from the weaker nation.
Open Door Policy	In 1898, the United States persuaded Europeans to agree to an Open Door Policy. Secretary of State John Hay's *Open Door Note* outlined foreign policy changes designed to keep France, Germany, Britain, Italy, Japan, and Russia from dominating trade in China. In 1895, China lost a war with Japan and was politically and economically unstable. European imperial nations were eager to divide China into European colonies. Under Hay's "open door" strategy, all nations would have access to trade in China. It specified that no European powers should control the Chinese region. The policy called on spheres of influence to be enforced to establish equal trading rights to all nations. Although the U.S. had no sphere of influence at the time in China, it did not want to be excluded from future investments there. The policy was rooted in the desires of anti-imperialists who wanted access to Chinese trade markets in the future without sacrificing China's independence.

Key Facts about U.S. Imperialism

The inspiration for territorial acquisitions included some of the following reasons.

Frontier expansion. Supporters of Turner's Frontier Thesis, which described how American democracy was inextricably linked to the American frontier, saw the acquisition of other nations as a way to expand U.S. power.

Global market expansion. Politicians and wealthy businessmen wanted to expand American markets and trade overseas. Senator Albert J. Beveridge, for example, suggested Americans should become "master organizers of the world," stating in 1897 that "the trade of the world must be and shall be ours."

Overseas expansion. In his book *The Influence of Sea Power upon History* (1890), Alfred Thayer Mahan stated for a strong navy to secure international markets overseas. Mahan argued that the British controlled the seas and this paved the way to world dominance. Mahan theorized that the key to world dominance and economic success in international politics was maritime dominance. Mahan's book was used by various U.S. politicians to justify imperialism, including ex-naval officer and future president Theodore Roosevelt.

Did you know? Religion and racism played important roles in the new wave of imperialism. Americans developed a sense of racial, cultural, and religious superiority and felt it was their duty to civilize underdeveloped regions in Africa, the South Pacific, and Latin America. Underdeveloped nations were considered "uncivilized." During U.S. expansion, women also found opportunities to travel and extend their experiences in other countries. Women frequently embraced missionary work to establish schools and other religious institutions throughout the South Pacific.

U.S. Territorial Acquisitions

HISTORIOGRAPHY. *Historians often refer to Rudyard Kipling's 1899 poem "The White Man's Burden" when referencing imperialist motives of the United States and its colonization of the Philippine Islands. Kipling was a friend of President Roosevelt's and believed that the United States was called to humanitarian action in underdeveloped territories. According to Kipling, the "white empire" of the United States was called to take up the moral responsibility to advance modern civilizations in colonized territories.*

United States Territorial Acquisitions, 1857–1903

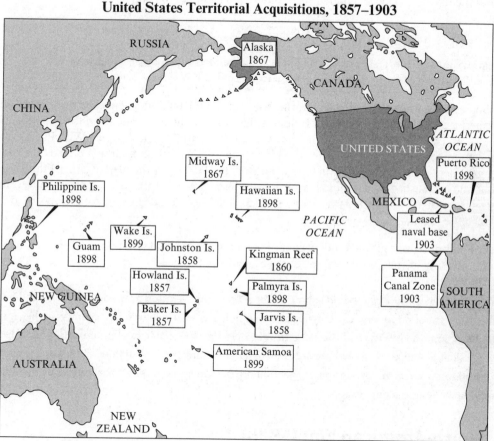

Source: Late-19th-Century U.S. Territorial Acquisitions—Pacific Region and Caribbean.

Alaska (1867)

Secretary of State William Seward negotiated to buy Alaska from the Russian Empire. Although he saw the region as an important site for coaling stations of Pacific merchant ships, his $7.2 million purchase was met with disapproval. Seward's decision to purchase Alaska was mocked for having no purpose and the purchase became known as "Seward's ice box." In the late 19th century, however, attitudes about the purchase began to change. The rise in production stimulated by the Second Industrial Revolution caused growing interest in foreign trade, which led to calls for territorial expansion through imperialism.

The Islands of Hawaii (1898)

The U.S. acquired Hawaii because of its location in the Pacific and its proximity to China and Japan. Hawaii was the only territory located in the Pacific, and sugar was a rich commodity grown on the independent islands. In 1893, Hawaii became a U.S. protectorate when concerns over taxes and import duties led American interests in the kingdom to overthrow the Hawaiian monarch, Queen Liliuokalani. Riding high on a wave of imperialism and expansion, Congress annexed the region as a territory in 1898 at the request of President William McKinley. American missionaries brought about changes to Hawaii's political, economic, and religious life. By 1959, Hawaii entered the United States as the 50th state.

The Islands of the Philippines, Guam, and Puerto Rico (1898)

Under the provisions of the Treaty of Paris (1898), which ended the Spanish-American War, the U.S. acquired the Philippines, Guam, and Puerto Rico from Spain.

In the Philippines, the Filipinos had been fighting the Spanish for their independence since 1896. After the Spanish-American War, the U.S. promised Filipinos that it would help liberate them from the Spanish Empire; however, U.S. politicians became hungry for economic and political power. With President McKinley determined to take possession of the Philippines, the American military entered into a long military engagement with Filipino nationalists from 1899 to 1902. With the help of other Filipinos, the U.S. won the war and established a provisional governor, William Howard Taft, to modernize the territory and its inhabitants. Unfortunately, reports of atrocities by U.S. Army soldiers decreased American support for imperialism in the region.

In 1946, the Philippines was granted independence from the United States, but Guam and Puerto Rico remain "unincorporated" territories of the United States even today.

> TEST TIP: On the APUSH exam, you should know that some Americans rejected overseas expansion. Anti-imperialists included writers, social reformers, entrepreneurs, and politicians who believed the country should focus on its domestic affairs. Some people worried about the costs involved in maintaining foreign interests, while others fretted about the possibility of allowing non-whites access to national resources. The Anti-Imperialist League was formed to show opposition to overseas expansion; it distributed pamphlets asserting that territorial acquisition was incompatible with American democracy.

The Spanish-American War (1898)

In 1895, revolutionaries in Cuba overthrew their Spanish rulers. Sensationalist journalists pressured McKinley to enter the war, and imperialists like Theodore Roosevelt (who was not yet president) saw the conflict as an opportunity to build U.S. masculine strength and character. Other imperialists supported the war because they understood the possibilities that Cuba's economic markets could provide the U.S.

The Rise of Yellow Journalism

In 1895, revolutionaries in Cuba overthrew their Spanish imperialist rulers. *Yellow journalists* (journalists who wrote stories that twisted facts to influence the public), like those hired by Joseph Pulitzer's *New York World* and William Randolph Hearst's *New York Journal,* encouraged U.S. politicians to enter the war. Journalists attacked politicians when politicians hesitated to assist the fledgling nation of Cuba.

For example, the American battleship *Maine* was destroyed in a Cuban harbor and nearly 260 soldiers were killed. Yellow journalists twisted the facts, as illustrated on the front page of the *New York Journal* below, and blamed Spain. The journalists based their stories on sensational headlines rather than well-researched news. Reporters cast Cuba as a helpless woman who needed to be rescued by the U.S. military, and calls for war grew even stronger.

Source: *New York Journal*, "Destruction of the War Ship Maine Was the Work of an Enemy." February 17, 1898.

Key Events of the Spanish-American War

Imperialists like Assistant Secretary of the Navy Teddy Roosevelt also saw the war with Spain as an opportunity to build U.S. strength and character. Fearing America's men were growing "soft," some people believed that the war would allow U.S. soldiers to achieve the heroic glory they needed to become good American leaders.

Key Events of the Spanish-American War		
Event	**Description**	**Results**
U.S.S. *Maine* (February 15, 1898)	The U.S.S. *Maine*, a ship stationed in Havana Harbor to observe the Cuban circumstances, exploded, killing nearly 260 U.S. soldiers.	When the Navy blamed the destruction of the ship on a submerged mine, most Americans assumed the Spanish were responsible. Many historians, however, believe the explosion could have been caused by a boiler accident. Regardless, the American deaths led to a public outcry for war.
Teller Amendment (April 20, 1898)	The amendment was proposed by Henry Teller, a Colorado Republican, in response to President McKinley's request for war. The amendment established conditions on military involvement in Cuba.	The amendment demanded Spain's immediate withdrawal from Cuba (which resulted in its declaration of war on the U.S.), forbade the U.S. annexation of Cuba, and stressed humanitarian reasons for intervention. It eased concerns of anti-imperialists and isolationists.

Continued

Event	Description	Results
Rough Riders (1898)	Rough Riders was a nickname given to the first U.S. Volunteer Cavalry. When U.S. Assistant Navy Secretary Teddy Roosevelt heard America had entered the war, he resigned his post as Assistant Secretary to form the Rough Riders and lead them in the Battle of San Juan Hill.	Rough Riders were made up of a diverse group of men from the American Southwest, including cowboys, miners, gamblers, policemen, and veterans. Roosevelt pitched them as the "best" American men for fighting and often exaggerated their exploits. Rough Riders discredited the help of others, especially African American buffalo soldiers, who helped to seize San Juan Hill during the Spanish-American War.
Battle of Manila Bay (May 1, 1898)	The Battle of Manila Bay in the Philippines was the most decisive battle of the Spanish-American War. U.S. Commodore George Dewey easily destroyed the Spanish fleet off the coast of the Philippines. While Spanish losses were from 300 to 400 casualties, American losses amounted to only 6 casualties.	The Battle of Manila ended the short war in Cuba and led to the Paris Peace Conference between the U.S. and Spain. (Note: Cubans were not allowed to negotiate their own terms.) The Spanish granted Cuba independence, and the U.S. acquired the Philippines, Guam, and Puerto Rico as territories.
Platt Amendment (1901)	The amendment, drafted by Senator Oliver Platt of Connecticut, was added to the new Cuban Constitution to withdraw U.S. troops from Cuba based on conditions in the amendment.	The conditions of the Platt Amendment defined terms of U.S. and Cuba's relations. It banned Cuba from making treaties with any nation, established U.S. rights to Guantanamo Bay and other naval bases in Cuba, and authorized the U.S. military to intervene in Cuba when it felt U.S. interests were threatened. It was viewed as a betrayal by Cuban resistance fighters. As part of a "good neighbor" policy, the amendment was withdrawn in 1934 (except for U.S. rights to a naval base in Cuba).

The Progressive Era (1890 to 1920)

In the late 19th century, **Progressivism** (age of reform) swept across the nation. Reform movements applied new strategies to improve society, government, the environment, and the economy. **Progressives** valued equal rights and aimed to eliminate the corruption of the Gilded Age that developed during the vast industrial growth. Progressives were often businessmen, labor activists, middle-class reformers, women, and government officials. They were motivated to act by *muckrakers* (journalists who exposed abuses in government, society, and industry) and fought to regulate the economy, protect women and children, weaken the power of political bosses, and improve the rights and conditions of workers.

TEST TIP: Think like a historian as you review the material in this chapter. Compare the actions and conduct of post–Civil War (and Gilded Age) Americans to early-20th-century Americans. What remained the same and what changed? Compare the continuities and changes of foreign policies, political trends, and reform movements.

For example, post–Civil War Americans enthusiastically pursued industrial growth. Industry contributed to innovations in transportation, settlements, the growth of cities, and increased productivity. Because wealthy corporate bosses and political leaders applied old approaches to control society, immigrants, and the working class, political corruption and industrial abuses of power were commonplace. This led to changing attitudes in America, with a rise of labor unions and an appeal for government intervention—it was the birth of Progressivism.

Progressive Era—Women and Children

The increasing visibility of women and children in the workplace led many women social reformers, especially New Women who worked in settlement houses or led volunteer organizations, to call for protective legislation (see Chapter 9).

Muller v. Oregon (1908). A Supreme Court decision that limited women's factory work to 10 hours per day. Although the famous case was intended to protect a "special group" that was considered too physically weak to work more hours, many women saw it as sexually discriminatory and resented the limitation. These women believed that only they had a right to determine how they earned a living.

Maternalist welfare reform policies. Laws that provided state assistance to benefit widows and children had once come from a highly corrupt paternal system that was associated with Civil War veterans' pensions and political patronage, but middle-class women began to push for improvements through voluntary organizations and social clubs in the early 20th century. As women appealed to male politicians for change, women organized informal networks that allowed for protective legislation in many cities and states. By 1912, their appeals eventually reached the national level with the establishment of the **Children's Bureau,** a federal agency that sought to protect children and their mothers. At times, the agency was staffed entirely by women.

Progressive Era—African Americans

In the South, the failure of Populism increased support for policies of white supremacists, which were established by *Redeemers* (southern Democrats who had "redeemed" the South from Radical Republicans in the Reconstruction Era) and encouraged by Progressive businessmen who advocated for a new industrial South. After the Civil War, *Lost Cause* myths (legends and fiction that romanticized slavery and slave ownership in the Antebellum period while honoring the Confederacy and its soldiers) united white southerners with their northern counterparts, causing northerners to become insensitive to the effects of systematic discrimination and violence in the South. After the Compromise of 1877, southern Democrats slashed state budgets—which had been inflated during Reconstruction—as well as property taxes, leaving little money for public schools, hospitals, or mental asylums. Although wealthy southerners benefited from these practices, poor whites and African Americans suffered greatly.

African American Discrimination

African Americans faced oppression during the Progressive Era. New laws endorsed regional discrimination, permitted white citizens to abuse black citizens, and provided blacks with few individual, financial, or social opportunities. Some of the worst discriminatory abuses are listed in the table that follows.

African American 20th-Century Discrimination	
Discrimination	Impact
Vagrancy laws	Based on the Vagrancy Act of 1866, any African American who was unemployed or appeared homeless was punished. The law added severe criminal sentences for small crimes, and enabled the convict lease system to flourish. State and local prisoners (mostly African Americans) were forced to work for public corporations, including railroads and mines, with no compensation. Terrible conditions in the labor camps often resulted in disease and death.

Continued

Discrimination	Impact
Sharecroppers and tenant farmers	African American sharecroppers and tenant farmers occupied the lowest rung of a stagnant southern agricultural economy. Black farmers were routinely cheated out of fair settlements on their crops, and if they protested, they were violently attacked by white vigilantes.
Segregation	Segregation was implemented through **Jim Crow laws** (state and local segregation laws in all public facilities enacted after Reconstruction, which lasted from 1890 to 1965). Racial segregation existed in most southern states through the reinterpretation of the Fourteenth Amendment in the Slaughterhouse cases, and the enforcement of *Plessy v. Ferguson* (see Chapter 8).
Disfranchisement	*Disfranchisement* (being deprived of the right to vote) eliminated the votes of most poor white males and all black males through a series of laws and new constitutions passed in southern states from 1890 to 1906. These laws included stipulations for poll taxes, literacy tests, and a registrar's approval of the voter's "understanding" of the U.S. Constitution. Grandfather clauses exempted whites whose relatives had voted before 1865. Southern demagogues, who appealed to white voters through vicious speeches and racial threats (like Tom Watson and Ben Tillman) continued to be elected.
Lynching	Lynching became rampant throughout the South as a "social correction." African Americans were brutally attacked and executed. African Americans were often falsely accused of sexually assaulting white women. Unfortunately, some lynchings were celebrated in white southern communities, with picnics and advertisements. Many African American activists, including Ida B. Wells and W. E. B. Du Bois, spoke out against this vicious practice.

African American Resistance

Key Facts about African American Resistance

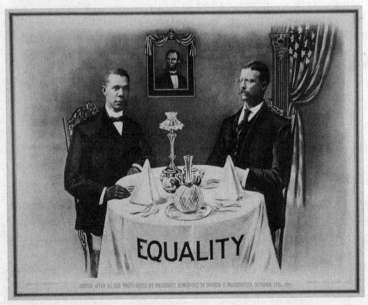

Source: Everett, "Booker T. Washington Dines at the White House [with President Roosevelt]," October 17, 1901. Washington was the first African American to dine at the White House.

Booker T. Washington. A former slave who had risen to success with the aid of a white benefactor, Booker T. Washington sought to better the conditions of African Americans in the South.

His 1895 **Atlanta Compromise** promoted growth through industrial education and cooperation with white employers. Although he was often criticized for being too "soft" and accommodating, the **Tuskegee Institute** he established in Alabama offered many black southerners the ability to acquire jobs and provide for a better standard of living. Washington's goal was to build a large black middle class that would earn the respect of whites and end violence.

W. E. B. Du Bois. Washington's philosophical opposite, Du Bois was an educated northerner who advocated classical educations for a **Talented Tenth,** the top 10 percent of the African American population that could lead the rest to equality. Du Bois helped found the Niagara Movement in 1905 (civil rights organization in Niagara Falls), and the **National Association for the Advancement of Colored People** (NAACP) in 1909.

TEST TIP: The National Association for the Advancement of Colored People (NAACP) is an important African American organization that you should be familiar with for the APUSH exam. Its continuities and its mission have changed from the 20th to the 21st centuries. The NAACP was originally founded by W. E. B. Du Bois to discuss solutions to the civil rights challenges facing African Americans, particularly the actions of southern states' lynchings, disenfranchisement of blacks, and segregation. In the 21st century, the NAACP focuses on national initiatives and public efforts to ensure political, educational, social, and economic equal rights for African Americans.

African American Women. When African American men were denied the right to vote, many African American women took up the responsibility of political activism. Drawing from religious and social networks, these women paralleled the work of the New Women of the Gilded Age and Progressive Era. Black women helped the poor, taught lessons in housekeeping and "respectability," spoke out against gambling and alcohol, and established black clubs to assist migrants to industrial cities. Like many in the small black middle class, however, their definitions of racial uplift often conflicted with those of working-class African Americans.

The Great Migration

In search of a better life, black southerners began moving to the North as early as 1879, but in 1910, 90 percent of African Americans still lived in the South. However, increasingly difficult conditions caused more than one million African Americans to migrate to the North from 1910 to 1920. The first wave of this **Great Migration** lasted until c. 1930, and another wave of migration occurred from 1941 to 1970, when World War II sparked another industrial boom.

Heads Up: What You Need to Know

The APUSH exam may require you to know the difference between *de jure segregation* and *de facto segregation* and how these terms related to the Great Migration. Although African Americans had escaped segregation established by law in the South (known as *de jure* segregation), many were disappointed when they discovered *de facto* segregation in the North (segregation that was established by fact). Even though their living standards improved, African Americans struggled to be treated fairly and were limited to menial jobs and inadequate housing.

Key Facts about the Great Migration

African Americans were inspired to leave the South because of fears of violence, crop damage caused by boll weevils and other pests, and the Second Industrial Revolution (which increased industrial and economic opportunities for many working-class citizens).

Religious exodus. Some African Americans viewed their journey north as a religious exodus because they were escaping conditions of poverty or white oppression. When cruel landlords or plantation owners attempted to use threats and physical force to prevent migration, black families became even more determined to leave the South.

Urban cities. As migrants arrived in northern industrial centers, urban populations soared, straining the resources of established black communities. As a result, black churches and social institutions changed, directing much of their energy to assisting those in need of food, clothing, employment, or temporary living arrangements.

Cultural renaissance. Many African Americans experienced discrimination when they attempted to find jobs and housing. African Americans often settled in the slums of large cities, and this caused an evolution of the African American culture. For example, many artists and activists flourished in New York's Harlem, where they cultivated black pride and celebrated black traditions. Some of the best American poets and writers of this period were African American, including Langston Hughes, Claude McKay, and Zora Neale Hurston.

Race riots. When African Americans began sharing space with whites, competing for low-wage jobs, and becoming more assertive, racial tensions soared. The Ku Klux Klan publically resurfaced in the 1920s, and several race riots occurred in both the North and South.

20th-Century African American Race Riots	
City	**Description**
East St. Louis, Missouri (1917)	When black workers were hired to replace white strikers at an aluminum ore company, white mobs poured into the streets on both May 28 and July 2, 1917, and attacked African Americans. People were pulled off streetcars, homes were burned, and people were shot and lynched. The police did not stop the violence.
Chicago, Illinois (1919)	On July 27, 1919, Eugene Williams, a black teenager, was swimming in a white section of Lake Michigan. The teen was stoned to death by a group of white youths; the police refused to arrest the murderer. Attacks from black and white mobs began on Chicago's South Side and continued for about a week. Thirty-eight people were killed (blacks and whites) and over 500 were injured.
Elaine, Arkansas (1919)	The Elaine Massacre occurred when black sharecroppers attempted to unionize. Two white men were shot when they confronted unionizers at a church, which caused the sheriff to call for a "posse" to find the black perpetrators. A white mob formed, destroying property and attacking African Americans on sight. While hundreds of blacks were killed, only five white men died in the fighting.
Tulsa, Oklahoma (1921)	Black World War I veterans had witnessed more positive race relations in France than in the U.S. When veterans returned to the U.S., they were more assertive and willing to fight for injustices. When Dick Rowland was accused of accosting a white woman in an elevator, black veterans tried to prevent his lynching. White mobs started a riot in the black section of town, and burned the neighborhood to the ground.
Rosewood, Florida (1923)	Claiming that a black drifter beat and sexually assaulted a white woman in Sumner, Florida, a white mob attacked and lynched a resident of Rosewood, a self-sufficient all-black town. When other black residents rose up to defend themselves, a greater mob formed. The mob violently murdered African Americans and destroyed the entire town.

Progressive Era—Immigration

Divisions along lines of class and race also impacted the definition of American citizenship and nationhood, which began to exclude certain immigrants (this also transferred to other U.S. territories in the Western Hemisphere). Discrimination not only inspired calls for immigration restrictions, but was also used to justify war and expansion.

The rise of "new immigrants" stirred a sharp change in attitudes toward immigrants. Americans began to view these immigrants as belonging to a low level in the hierarchy of classes and believed some immigrants were racially inferior. This kind of discrimination gave strength to anti-immigration organizations, like the **Immigration Restriction League** (1894), that called for immigration limits.

The timeline below can help you understand how immigration laws advanced in the early 20th century.

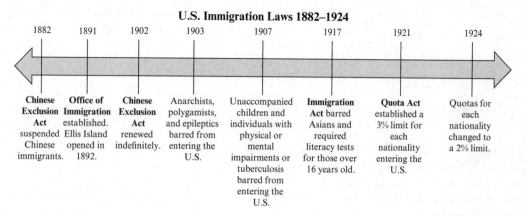

U.S. Immigration Laws 1882–1924

1882	1891	1902	1903	1907	1917	1921	1924
Chinese Exclusion Act suspended Chinese immigrants.	**Office of Immigration** established. Ellis Island opened in 1892.	**Chinese Exclusion Act** renewed indefinitely.	Anarchists, polygamists, and epileptics barred from entering the U.S.	Unaccompanied children and individuals with physical or mental impairments or tuberculosis barred from entering the U.S.	**Immigration Act** barred Asians and required literacy tests for those over 16 years old.	**Quota Act** established a 3% limit for each nationality entering the U.S.	Quotas for each nationality changed to a 2% limit.

Progressive Era—Government

This section covers the domestic and foreign priorities of U.S. presidents during the Progressive Era.

William McKinley's Presidency (1897 to 1901)

Republican president William McKinley chose a war hero and governor of New York, Teddy Roosevelt, as his vice presidential running mate when he ran for his second presidential term in 1900. The U.S. victories in the Spanish-American War allowed the pair to easily win the election against anti-imperialist William Jennings Bryan, who ran as the Democratic candidate, just like he had in 1896. While Bryan traveled the country on a limited budget, McKinley was backed by large business interests. McKinley did little campaigning, only occasionally appearing to speak on his front porch.

McKinley was assassinated in 1901, and Roosevelt ascended to the presidency.

Theodore "Teddy" Roosevelt's Presidency (1901 to 1909)

Progressive politicians existed on the national, state, and local levels, but Theodore Roosevelt was the first Progressive president. With Roosevelt in office, Progressivism soon became a widespread movement.

Roosevelt's Domestic Policies

Roosevelt's domestic policies promoted a **Square Deal** (protection from unfair business practices) for the American people aimed at controlling corporations, promoting conservation of the environment, and protecting consumers.

Roosevelt's Domestic Policies	
Corporate trusts	Roosevelt confronted the abuses of consolidation by distinguishing greedy corporations that manipulated the economy from those that served public interests. One of his earliest acts was to file suit against J. P. Morgan's Northern Securities Company, which controlled most of the country's railroad freight. Using the Sherman Antitrust Act as justification for his **"trust-busting,"** Roosevelt encouraged the attorney general to break up the monopoly. The government won the case, and the company was dissolved.
Environmental conservation	An avid hunter and outdoorsman, Roosevelt worked with preservationists like John Muir to set aside millions of acres of land as national forests and parks. Roosevelt and his advisors believed more in conserving natural resources for public consumption than banning their use completely, but they still encouraged the regulation of logging and mining while authorizing the protection of wildlife and the environment on government lands.
Consumer protection	When Upton Sinclair's *The Jungle* revealed the mishandling of the meat-packing industry, Roosevelt encouraged Congress to pass the Pure Food and Drug Act (1906). It placed restrictions on manufacturing and allowed for government inspections of the production and labeling of food and drugs.

Roosevelt also became personally involved in labor strikes. In 1902, when Pennsylvania and West Virginia coal miners went out on strike, the president was concerned the public would have no heat for their homes that winter. Roosevelt called both sides to the White House and threatened to nationalize the mines if they did not reach an agreement.

Roosevelt's Foreign Policies

Roosevelt's foreign policy was to "speak softly and carry a big stick." In 1904, he added the **Roosevelt Corollary** to the Monroe Doctrine, which allowed the U.S. to assertively enforce the formerly weak doctrine with a growing military power. Any nation that was observed as a foreign aggressor justified U.S. military intervention.

Panama Canal (Completed in 1914)

During the Roosevelt administration in 1904, the United States was formally given control to oversee the construction of the Panama Canal. The Panama Canal continues to be important to the United States' international maritime trade and economy because it is an artificial waterway that connects the Atlantic Ocean with the Pacific Ocean for U.S. imports and exports.

The Panama Canal gave the U.S. quicker passage to the Atlantic Ocean from the Pacific Ocean for the Navy, but it also allowed trade to become much more efficient. When Colombia refused to sell a 6-mile strip of land that the U.S. needed to build the canal, Roosevelt used the Roosevelt Corollary to intervene in Latin American (and Caribbean) foreign affairs. Roosevelt resorted to underhanded dealings and supported a rebel uprising in Panama so that its newly independent government would support the project when Colombia rejected it.

U.S. Trade Through the Panama Canal

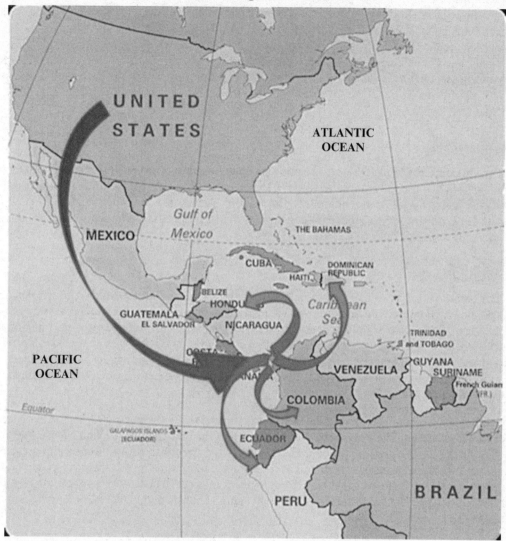

Source: U.S. Government Export, 2011.

TEST TIP: Be sure to know other important legislative acts during the Progressive Era as well as the differences among the Progressive policies of Roosevelt, Taft, and Wilson. Some of the Populists' demands also came to fruition in this era: the Hepburn Act (1906), which gave the Interstate Commerce Commission the power to examine and regulate railroad freight; and the Sixteenth and Seventeenth Amendments, which established both a graduated income tax and the direct election of senators.

William Howard Taft's Presidency (1909 to 1913)

Although highly popular, Roosevelt chose not to pursue a third term in the 1908 election and handpicked his successor in his good friend and secretary of war, William Howard Taft. The former governor of the Philippines easily defeated William Jennings Bryan, who was running as the Democratic candidate for the third and final time. Unfortunately, the 300-pound Taft was not as charismatic as Roosevelt. Taft tended to fall asleep during meetings and was often uncomfortable in the political spotlight. Although Taft continued to break up corporate monopolies, he soon disappointed Progressives by lowering protective tariffs and environmental restrictions.

Taft's Foreign Policies

Instead of relying on force or negotiation as Roosevelt had, Taft was more likely to employ **"dollar diplomacy"** policies that used the guarantee of U.S. loans and investments to control foreign nations. This did not mean Taft shied away from sending U.S. troops abroad. For example, when fighting broke out in Nicaragua in 1912, he sent U.S. troops to the region in order to support the insurgents and seize the custom house.

Taft's Domestic Policies

In 1909, Taft became involved in a controversial scandal, the **Ballinger-Pinchot Affair.** Gifford Pinchot, who had managed financial reserves under Roosevelt as head of the U.S. Forestry Service, became angry with Richard Ballinger, Taft's secretary of the interior, for behavior Pinchot considered corrupt. Pinchot accused Ballinger of having personal connections with private trusts and offering Alaskan coal fields to private mining companies. After a Congressional investigation, Taft concluded Ballinger had acted properly and fired Pinchot. When Roosevelt heard about the incident, he was furious and decided to run against Taft in the next election.

Although Republicans were loyal to Taft, Roosevelt was undeterred in the pursuit of his former friend's defeat. Roosevelt set up his own **Progressive Party,** which was then nicknamed the **Bull Moose Party** because he claimed to be "fit as a bull moose" and ready to fight for the American people. Roosevelt repeated the sentiment after a would-be assassin shot him, but failed to kill him, while he was giving a speech in front of a Milwaukee hotel shortly before the election. Democrats nominated **Woodrow Wilson,** New Jersey's governor and former president of Princeton University, and Socialists nominated labor activist and union leader Eugene Debs.

The following diagram explains the differences between the platforms of the candidates.

The Election of 1912

Taft (Republican)	Roosevelt (Progressive)	Wilson (Democrat)	Debs (Socialist)
Platform supported conservative policies of traditional Republicans and portrayed Roosevelt as too radical and Progressive.	New Nationalism platform, which wanted to regulate, but not crush, big business. Supported women's suffrage, a minimum wage, and social welfare programs.	New Freedom platform, which favored small businesses over corporations and promoted economic regulations that would ensure free trade.	Platform included tax reform, a minimum wage, the direct election of presidents, and social welfare programs.

Because Taft and Roosevelt split the Republican vote, Wilson won the election by a landslide, capturing 435 electoral votes. Roosevelt received 88 electoral votes and Taft received 8 electoral votes. Although Debs did not get any electoral votes, he received the highest percentage of the popular vote for any Socialist candidate.

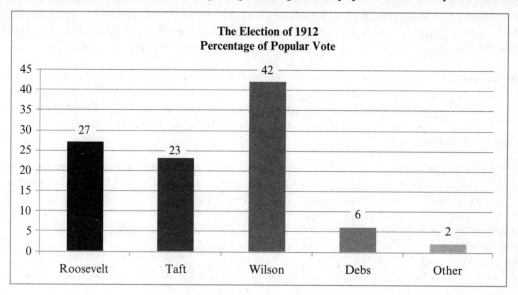

The Election of 1912
Percentage of Popular Vote

Woodrow Wilson's Presidency (1913 to 1921)

Wilson's Domestic Policies

Wilson's **New Freedom** platform called for stronger antitrust laws, the protection of unions, and government intervention that would encourage the growth and support of small businesses. Wilson developed agencies and policies that were welcomed by corporations because they stabilized the market and created order without succumbing to Socialist demands. Wilson also promoted fair labor practices and a responsible foreign policy.

The most important legislative acts of Wilson's administration are listed in the following table.

Year	Legislation
1913	**Federal Reserve.** Established 12 regional banks that were overseen by a central federal board appointed by the president. The reserve replaced a national bank and allowed President Wilson to reclaim control of the nation's economy from wealthy entrepreneurs and private bankers who had to "save" the country after the Panic of 1907.
1914	**Federal Trade Commission.** A federal agency that could investigate and prohibit unfair business practices to discourage price-fixing and monopolies. **Clayton Act.** This act exempted labor unions from antitrust laws and ensured their right to strike.
1916	**Keating-Owens Act.** Known as the Wick's Bill, it prohibited the sale of interstate goods produced by factories that employed youth under the age of 14. **Adamson Act.** Federal law that established 8-hour workdays for railroad workers. **Warehouse Act.** Allowed the government to give loans to farmers on security of their crops kept in federal warehouses as collateral.

Wilson's Foreign Policies

Moral diplomacy was Wilson's system of foreign policy that rejected imperialism and supported countries that promoted democracy and peace. Wilson advocated for U.S. influence through moral righteousness, missionary efforts, and free trade rather than military force or economic control. However, unlike some of his predecessors, Wilson was not afraid to use military force when necessary. Wilson sent troops into Haiti, the Dominican Republic, and Mexico when he felt American interests and lives were threatened.

When World War I began in Europe in 1914, Wilson encouraged Americans to remain neutral, and U.S. citizens agreed. The U.S. was isolated from the war in Europe, so it was easier for the U.S. to stay out of the military conflict, especially because diverse groups of Americans (Jewish, Irish, and German) held ethnic loyalties to one country or another. As you will see in the next section, remaining neutral became challenging for Wilson.

Did you know? Wilson was highly committed to American neutrality and won the 1916 election by promising to keep the U.S. out of the Great War. Simultaneously, he felt politically and morally obligated to remain diplomatically involved in the conflict. On January 22, 1917, over 2 months before the U.S. even entered World War I, the president addressed Congress, stating he was committed to helping Europe achieve **"Peace Without Victory"** through a truce that would at least stop the bloodshed.

World War I (1914 to 1918)

After years of dormant political and social tensions, the nations of Europe entered into a "Great War," called World War I. The United States was isolated from Europe and wanted to remain neutral, but after 2 years of **neutrality,** the U.S. entered World War I in 1917. Before we discuss the developments that led to the U.S. involvement in the war, let's cover the reasons for the global conflict in Europe.

The Causes of World War I in Europe

In Europe, an extreme form of nationalism was emerging in France, Russia, and especially Germany that led to the outbreak of war in 1914. On the APUSH exam, the acronym MAIN will help you remember the main causes of the war.

Militarism. European nations had advanced military technology and were ready for war. Unfortunately, when the war started, the new technologies and outdated military tactics (trench warfare) led to unthinkable casualties and bloodshed.

Alliances. European nations were entangled in secret pacts that divided nations, and there were no international organizations like the United Nations to help settle their disputes. *Triple Alliance:* Germany, Austria-Hungary, and Italy. *Triple Entente:* France, Russia, Britain (the U.S. joined in 1917).

Imperialism. In 1914, Europe was the world power, but European nations desired to control the remaining free territories of the world to increase trade markets. This led to rivalries among nations.

Nationalism. The surge of extreme *nationalism* (strong allegiance to one's nation) in Europe stirred strong emotions and animosities about other nations.

Why the U.S. Entered World War I

War propaganda. News circulated that cast Russians as autocratic Anti-Semites and Germans as atrocious barbarians, which influenced American public opinion about the war. (Note: The propaganda continued after the U.S. entered the war.)

Heads Up: What You Need to Know

The APUSH exam will likely require you to know the reasons it became challenging for the U.S. to remain neutral about World War I:

- War propaganda
- U.S. merchant ships were blockaded.
- The *Lusitania* was attacked (1915).
- The Zimmermann Telegram (1917)

U.S. merchant ships were blockaded. German blockades made it difficult for the U.S. to trade with Britain and France. Although the U.S. should have stopped trading with all nations, Wilson worried over the economic cost of such a policy. Wilson continued to allow economic activity in Britain and France, but this made American merchant ships susceptible to attacks by German *U-boats* (underwater boats; similar to submarines).

The *Lusitania* was attacked (1915). Germany's military torpedoed a British civilian ocean liner en route from New York to England. More than 1,100 passengers and crew members were killed, including 128 American passengers. U.S. citizens were angered by the attack and this created public support for the war, but the U.S. still did not enter the war for almost 2 years. Germans justified the destruction of the ship because they believed the ship was carrying ammunition for the British.

The Zimmermann Telegram (1917). The British intercepted a telegram that was sent from Germany to the German foreign secretary of Mexico. Germany's intention was to lure Mexico into the war by promising to return to it the southwest territory of the U.S. that Mexico lost in 1848 during the Mexican-American War (Chapter 8). The fear of a substantial military conflict on U.S. soil was enough to convince both Wilson and U.S. citizens to enter the European war.

HISTORIOGRAPHY. *Many U.S. historians identify World War I as a "Progressive War" because it was managed bureaucratically and the rhetoric of social and political justice was used to legitimize its causes. As the U.S. mobilized for war, the U.S. government increased citizens' expectations. The **War Industries Board** was established to coordinate the purchase of war supplies and ammunition. Agencies were set up to take control of railroad transportation, fuel, food, and labor. In the name of cooperation, vigilante organizations of private citizens, like the American Protective League, attacked those who failed to support the military draft, and ethnic loyalties were criticized and discouraged. It was a time when women and African Americans lobbied for their rights, citing patriotism, and participation in the war effort was used as justification for national inclusion.*

The U.S. Enters World War I (1917)

Source: "U.S. at War: Wilson," *The Chicago Daily Tribune.* President Wilson asked Congress for a declaration of war on April 2, 1917. Wilson's petition to "make the world safe for democracy" was incredibly successful; the measure was quickly passed in both legislative houses.

Support for the war was generated through several tactics, illustrated in the following diagram.

Wilson's Strategies for Public Support of World War I

PROPAGANDA

Muckraker George Creel led the **Committee on Public Information** (CPI), an agency charged with generating public support for the war. CPI used newspapers, advertisements, radio, and cinema to deliver its public information messages.

ESPIONAGE AND SEDITION ACTS

In 1917 and 1918, legislatures passed laws that heavily fined and jailed people suspected of aiding the enemy, obstructing the war efforts, or committing acts of disloyalty. Pacifists, like Socialist Eugene Debs, were jailed for speaking against the U.S. involvement in the war.

NO-STRIKE PLEDGES

The AFL worked with industry leaders to create a labor force that was dedicated to American production. In return for agreements not to strike, workers received higher wages and 8-hour workdays. Because the IWW refused to participate, its members were often persecuted.

Key Facts about the U.S. Impact on World War I

The U.S. entered the war late (1917). During the final year of fighting, the U.S. entered the war. After slowly gathering support for the Selective Service Act (in response to the war, the act gave the president power to draft citizens into the military), America sent approximately 1 million soldiers overseas.

Hundred Days Offensive (1918). In 1915 and 1916, both sides (the Triple Alliance and Triple Entente) of the conflict engineered massive offensives to try to break through the enemy lines. When the U.S. joined the war, General John Pershing and his American Expeditionary Forces (the American Army) were a welcome sight to the war-weary British and French troops on the front lines. Thousands of fresh American troops arrived on the Western Front. It was only a matter of time before Germany would surrender. The American troops participated in several key battles, including the Hundred Days Offensive, which ended the war.

Germany surrendered (November 11, 1918). German war efforts fell apart and many German soldiers deserted the military. A revolution formed by Socialists and anarchists erupted in Munich. On November 9, 1918, German Kaiser Wilhelm II abdicated and fled to Holland. German citizens had put all of their faith in the kaiser in 1914, and they felt betrayed by his failure to deliver a quick and easy victory as promised. Instead of taking responsibility for the defeat, the blame was given to the new democratic leaders of Germany, the Marxist **Social Democrats (SPD)**. The SPD were unfairly blamed for Germany's defeat and surrender in 1918.

Did you know? In 1918–1919, just as the war was winding down, a global pandemic spread and killed more people than the fighting in World War I (about 20 to 40 million people died). The Spanish influenza (*La Grippe* in Spanish) was one of the deadliest outbreaks in history. It lasted almost 1 year and was brought to the U.S. by infected soldiers. Despite attempts to halt its progression, over 25 percent of American citizens were affected and about 3 percent died from the flu.

Post–World War I

The consequences of World War I changed the course of world history. Aside from the millions of people who were killed or wounded, the impact of the war included the following:

- The world balance of power shifted, new nations were formed, and territories changed the face of Europe.
- Political resentments formed, especially in Germany, about the Treaty of Versailles, which planted the seeds for World War II in 1939.
- The Communist Party was formed in Russia, which impacted the U.S. after its creation (e.g., the First and Second Red Scares and McCarthyism in the 1950s).

Wilson's Peace Settlement: Fourteen Points

Before discussing the Treaty of Versailles, it is important to understand what led up to the treaty. President Wilson was an idealist who envisioned a world organization to protect nations and prevent future wars. Wilson proposed Fourteen Points to preserve post-war world peace and diplomacy in a speech presented before the U.S. Congress on January 8, 1918.

Wilson felt that the balance of power and secret treaties had caused World War I and wanted to prevent Europe from returning to old habits. At that time, no other world leader had ever declared such a proposal for global cooperation and world peace. For the APUSH exam, you do not have to memorize each of the Fourteen Points, but it's important to understand some of the key ideas of Wilson's main points:

- Free and open trade
- Freedom of the seas
- National self-determination for people. Wilson believed that citizens should have the right to determine who controls the government.
- Public treaties to slow down the production of weaponry
- Open diplomacy ("transparency") rather than secret alliances
- Arms reduction
- A new international institution to secure peace—the League of Nations

Wilson had a vision for a safer world, but his proposal failed. Wilson could not enforce all of the points, especially since he did not really believe in *self-determination* (the right for a nation to determine its own government) for people in Africa and Asia.

Although parts of the Fourteen Points became a blueprint for the Treaty of Versailles, the plan failed for several reasons. Some nations were not interested in democracy. The idea of national self-determination inflamed Eastern Europe, Asia, and the Middle East. But probably the most important reason the Fourteen Points failed was that the British and French wanted to punish Germany for aggressive acts during World War I. This was a critical point in history because the Treaty of Versailles was one of the primary causes of the start of World War II.

Treaty of Versailles (1919)

After the war, the Allied Powers (U.S., Britain, France, and Italy) made most of the decisions at the Paris Peace Conference. At the Paris Peace Conference, the **Treaty of Versailles** was established to restore the European balance of power and promote peace, but Europeans were not interested in peace—they wanted to get even with Germany. Germany was forced to give up colonial territories to Britain and France and was forced to pay for all of the damages of World War I. Most importantly, Germany was forced to accept complete responsibility for starting the war in **Article 231.**

Heads Up: What You Need to Know

On the APUSH exam, it's important to remember the Treaty of Versailles and the resentments that were formed during the Paris Peace Conference.

Germany's resentment. Germany and Austria-Hungary were not invited to take part in the peace conference, and the terms of the Treaty of Versailles humiliated and angered the Germans. Because Allied forces suffered a great deal of destruction and blamed Germany for the war (especially Britain and France), they did not accept President Wilson's Fourteen Points of "peace." Instead, the Allied forces severely limited the German military, reassigned German colonies, and forced Germany to pay for war reparations. The last condition was a significant cause of economic hardship in Germany and a significant factor of World War II.

Japan's and Italy's resentment. Japan and Italy were disrespected and treated condescendingly at the peace table. In fact, Italy's premier walked out of the conference.

Why are these resentments important to remember? U.S. President Wilson had great foresight about world peace, but the European powers did not listen. The Treaty of Versailles caused growing resentment and led to extreme nationalism in Germany. This set the stage for the next war 20 years later—World War II.

The Interwar Period (1919 to 1938)

The interwar period is the time between World War I and World War II. In the 1920s, the United States started a period of modernity and mass consumerism, but domestic concerns about differing views of politics, race, and religion started civil unrest in America.

The League of Nations (1920 to 1946)

As President Wilson had proposed, the League of Nations (1920–1946) was formed after World War I, but Germany and Russia were not allowed to join at the time. The League was created with the purpose of preventing aggression that might cause another great war.

For the APUSH exam, it's important to know that Wilson did not receive support from the U.S. Senate to approve the League of Nations (or the Treaty of Versailles). Opposition was led by senators like Henry Cabot Lodge who were dedicated to **isolationism** and worried that participation in a global peacekeeping organization would commit America to European wars. The United States refused to become a member of the League of Nations.

In 1919, Wilson had a massive stroke and this limited his ability to negotiate with Congress. (Note: Some historians believe that his failed peace negotiations in France caused the stroke.) The U.S. never became a member of the League, which affected foreign affairs. The U.S. retreated from world affairs and entered a period of isolationism. As a result, the League failed to prevent World War II and was replaced by the United Nations in 1946, at which time the United States became a member.

Warren Harding's Presidency (1921 to 1923)

After the political disappointments of world affairs during World War I, Americans wanted to change domestic social reforms and reject Progressive ideas. Americans sought Republican presidents like Warren Harding, who believed in small government, provided huge tax cuts for the wealthy and big businesses, and promised a "return to normalcy" in the United States. Harding's victory signaled the beginning of a new era for America, but unfortunately, Harding was not well qualified, and because he was a heavy drinker, his administration was blamed for corruption and scandals.

Key Issues of the 1920s		
Issue	**Description**	**Results**
The Bolshevik Revolution (1919–1920)	In 1917, a **Bolshevik Revolution** led by Vladimir Lenin (Russia's leader from 1917 to 1924) overthrew Czar Nicholas II, which caused a **Red Scare** in the U.S. Coupled with working-class and African American unrest in the U.S., the revolution sparked fears of Communism and led Attorney General A. Mitchell Palmer to believe labor strikes were part of a global conspiracy to overthrow established governments.	Attorney General Palmer ordered federal agents like **J. Edgar Hoover** to search offices of radical organizations and without warrants arrest those who seemed suspicious. Although the **Palmer Raids** hindered public support for unions and Socialists, the raids also encouraged Americans to define and defend their civil liberties.
Prohibition (1920)	Believing that "strong drink of alcohol" was the root of all social problems, temperance reformers convinced legislators to pass the **Eighteenth Amendment,** which banned the sale, production, or transportation of alcohol. The amendment was ratified in 1919 and went into effect in 1920.	Prohibition was impossible to enforce, especially since most Americans desired to drink alcohol. Smuggling alcohol was easily achieved through the Caribbean and Canada. Government officials and police officers were simply bribed to look the other way. Illegal bars called "speakeasies" were located in every city, and organized crime used the law to conduct a profitable black market.
Women's suffrage (1920)	Women fought for the right to vote for almost a century. Finally, women were granted the right to vote through the **Nineteenth Amendment,** which was ratified on August 18, 1920.	By the end of World War I, 15 states allowed women to vote and both the Democrats and the Republicans openly supported the issue. Millions of women proudly voted for the first time during the presidential election of 1920.
Teapot Dome Scandal (1921–1922)	Harding's secretary of the interior, Albert Fall, received bribes to lease Navy oil reserves in Wyoming and California to private corporations.	Fall went to prison, and the scandal deeply damaged the reputation of both the Harding administration and the federal government.

THE STEAM ROLLER

Source: "The Steam Roller of progress crushes the opposition." Women gain the right to vote in 1920.

Calvin Coolidge's Presidency (1923 to 1929)

When Harding died in office in 1923, his vice president, **Calvin Coolidge,** erased all hints of scandal from the White House and ran a successful election campaign of his own in 1924, benefitting from a split in the Democratic Party. The Coolidge administration was dedicated to maintaining economic gain while running an efficient national government and lowering both the national debt and income taxes.

Herbert Hoover's Presidency (1929 to 1933)

Coolidge was followed by **Herbert Hoover,** who won the presidential election of 1928. Hoover was a wealthy businessman who had been in charge of national and international food rations during World War I. Because he was an orphan who obtained financial benefits through hard work and education, Hoover recognized social issues but believed that private institutions, not the government, were responsible for addressing them.

Cultural Changes

The 1920s became known as the "Roaring Twenties" because they were a period of economic prosperity and dramatic cultural changes in Western society. It was the first time that more people lived in cities than in rural farming regions of the U.S. After World War I, many young people became disillusioned with traditional art forms and culture and a new "modern" culture was born.

Key Facts about Cultural Changes

Modern art and music. After World War I, many young people became disillusioned with traditional art forms and culture, so the 1920s inspired changes in music, art, and literature. This period was called the *Jazz Age* because it reflected the style of the African American music that became widely popular. Dance halls, the radio, and phonograph records popularized jazz and young people often just wanted to listen to music and dance.

Surrealism became a popular art form in the early 1920s. Surrealism was a cultural movement that depicted bizarre and impossible scenes that seemed contrary to reality. This art form was symbolic of the sudden cultural changes people were experiencing during the Roaring Twenties. Artists painted depictions of dreams, irrational scenes, and juxtapositions of scenes that seemed to have no connection. Because of a worldwide depression and two world wars, American artists also began painting a unique form of *realism* that depicted American regional scenes from 1925 to 1945.

Source: Grant Wood, "American Gothic," 1930. Wood's famous painting chronicled the history of traditional Midwestern moral values during the Great Depression. The rigid, upright characters are a symbol of the down-to-earth qualities of pride and fortitude that represented Americans who were overcome by hardship. The horizontal roof line is symbolic of the inseparable stability that God can provide during difficult socioeconomic times.

Modern literature. Writers like F. Scott Fitzgerald, Sinclair Lewis, and Ernest Hemingway grew disillusioned with conformity, traditional middle-class values, and materialism. Modern literature stressed the alienation of human beings from society and the isolation of the human mind. Known as the **Lost Generation,** writers often left the United States and wrote as expatriates.

> **TEST TIP:** In the aftermath of World War I, post-war sentiments about a lost generation and the madness of war were mounting. American writer Ernest Hemingway famously wrote *The Sun Also Rises*. It was based on the men and women who came of age during World War I. This *Lost Generation* (a phrase coined by Gertrude Stein) represented people who lacked motivation or purpose, without hope for a better future due to the horrific atrocities they experienced during World War I. Use Hemingway's novel as an example for World War I free-response questions.

Modern women. The most familiar symbol of the Roaring Twenties was the "flapper." Women known as *flappers* cut their hair, shortened their skirts, and rejected social restrictions by drinking, smoking, and dancing publically. The sale of alcohol was prohibited according to the Eighteenth Amendment, but this only drove the liquor trade underground, and people bought and sold alcohol illegally.

Religious restrictions. While there was a dramatic change toward the freedoms of modernity, there was also a rise in religious fundamentalism. Fundamentalism rose in response to these cultural shifts. For example, because fundamentalists interpreted the Bible literally and advocated the teaching of creationism in schools, biology teacher John Scopes was put on trial for teaching evolution in Tennessee. Prosecuted by William Jennings Bryan and defended by Clarence Darrow, Scopes was found guilty but received the minimum penalty (a fine of $100), which demonstrated Americans' increasing tolerance for secularism.

> **Did you know?** Consumerism and technological advances led to social and cultural changes. The economy was on a strong upswing during the Roaring Twenties. Mass production and the easy approval of credit enabled people to purchase goods formerly reserved for the middle and upper classes. New domestic technologies such as the icebox, telephone, and radio were manufactured quickly and inexpensively. Model-T automobiles manufactured in Henry Ford's factories flew off assembly lines as people began overspending to purchase luxury items. Advertisements pushed consumers to buy merchandise they didn't need, and merchandise became symbols of status and pride. Furthermore, radio broadcasts and films not only changed the way Americans were entertained, but they also transformed how the news was delivered and received.

Economic Changes

The **stock market crash of 1929** caused millions of people to lose their savings overnight. People panicked, made poor judgments, and felt resentful.

The Causes of the Stock Market Crash

The 1920s are often remembered for wild speculation, the rapid expansion of the U.S. stock market, and the purchase of stocks in excess of their real value. Several factors contributed to the stock market crash on October 29, 1929 (known as **Black Tuesday**), that led to the Great Depression.

Stock Market Crash	
Buying "on the margin"	People, as well as corporations, borrowed money from banks for call loans, set up by stockbrokers to allow buyers to purchase stock for a small margin of their value, sometimes as low as 10 percent. Investors then borrowed the rest of the money, hoping to pay it back when the stock prices increased and they sold their shares. Unfortunately, lenders could call for repayment at any time, and often did when prices fell.
"Mad" investments in the stock market	As early as 1927, standard rules of rational behavior and investments did not seem to apply. People did not buy to invest, but to acquire wealth as quickly and easily as possible. People were becoming greedy.
Falling economic conditions	Stocks were not just overbought and overvalued, stocks continued to rise even though production was falling. The competition among manufacturers increased and caused an oversupply of goods— the supply of goods exceeded the demand. This caused a collapse in prices and forced many manufacturers out of business, especially in agriculture. As factories closed, unemployment increased.

In August 1929 the stock market reached its peak, but it began to naturally decline in September and October. On October 29 it crashed, causing thousands of people to lose billions of dollars in a single day.

HISTORIOGRAPHY. *While it is tempting to paint President Herbert Hoover as the "bad guy" of the Great Depression, historians note that the president viewed the stock market crash as a natural consequence of the booms and busts of a capitalist market system. Hoover thought it would help the country overcome negative financial attitudes and behaviors. Hoover could have responded to the crisis more effectively, but he believed that private industry would quickly recover as it had during the recession of 1921. Sadly, additional circumstances prevented a quick recovery. His actions resulted in public outcry, the election of Franklin Roosevelt (who promised to end the suffering that was the result of the crash and the depression that followed), and a global depression that was devastating to the people of many nations.*

The Great Depression (1929 to 1939)

It is easy to identify the stock market crash as a contributing factor to the Great Depression, but it is important to recognize that it was not the single cause of the economic devastation that followed. The incredible amount of consumer debt and number of bank failures that resulted from consumer carelessness is what actually led to the economic crisis that caused the Great Depression. When the stock market failed, people could not pay off their loans, purchases, and credit installments. Home values depreciated and people lost their possessions, including their homes. People tried to withdraw their savings from their bank accounts, but banks collapsed because government regulations at the time did not insure the money in bank accounts. The banks did not have enough money for millions of people to withdraw their money (often because they had invested the money themselves or given it to other customers in the form of loans), and people did not have enough money to pay off their debts.

Source: National Archives and Records Administration, November 16, 1930. A common scene from the Great Depression. The unemployed lined up in Chicago at a "soup kitchen" established to feed the hungry and homeless. Before the Social Security Act, soup kitchens across America, like this one owned by mobster Al Capone, were the only source of meals for jobless people.

Causes of the Great Depression	
Consumer overspending	Massive gaps in wealth continued—the top 1 percent of the country owned most of the assets. The economy was based on an unstable economic foundation of consumer overspending. A culture of spending exceeded average incomes. With rapid advancements in technology, most companies were now using machines instead of human labor to lower their labor costs. People were working less and didn't have the money to spend, yet they kept buying. How did people buy goods with no money? Financing was available through *credit installment plans* (early forms of credit cards). Consumers continued buying and investing using credit installment plans to pay for products, but fell into massive debt that they could not repay when the crisis hit.
Agricultural overproduction	Agricultural overproduction throughout the post-war period flooded the domestic market and caused prices to fall. American farmers began to suffer from financial downturns long before the average U.S. citizen.
Failure of the Revenue Act of 1926	Tax breaks for the rich and high tariffs failed to stimulate the economy and hinted to the world the U.S. was selfishly intent on protecting its own markets. The Revenue Act of 1926 did not lead business owners to reinvest their tax credits to benefit consumers or workers, and the Hawley-Smoot Tariff of 1930 raised import duties to their highest levels, which caused other countries to retaliate with excessive import taxes of their own. The result was heavily strained domestic and global markets.
Increased interest rates	The international economic system was based on the **gold standard.** The gold standard meant that every nation's currency was backed up by gold reserves. The United States had emerged from World War I with the strongest economy in the world, so it was able to store up more gold. However, by the end of the 1920s, the other nations' economies had recovered from war reparations. The U.S. Federal Reserve feared that investors from other countries would buy up gold and take it back to their nations, so the Federal Reserve raised interest rates. Other nations were forced to take their currencies off of the gold standard, and interest rates dramatically increased. The increased interest rates caused two massive shocks to the stock market in 1928 and 1929.
Bank failures	Bank failures and panics occurred when people lost confidence in their banks and rushed to withdraw funds in 1930 and 1931. Unfortunately, many banks used the deposits of customers' money to invest in the stock market or government securities. Even if they did invest the deposits, banks rarely held onto reserves and were much more likely to lend money out to other customers. Banks began to call in loans and sell their assets in a desperate attempt to get the cash they needed. Many closed and people lost their entire savings.
American mindset	A negative psychology developed in America, causing some people to lose hope when they experienced hardship or had goods, homes, or land repossessed. Faced with hunger and desperation, people often became overwhelmed at the amount of poverty in society, became cynical, and believed economic relief was impossible.

Hoover's Response to the Great Depression

By the time the market reached its bottom in 1932, 13 million people were unemployed and at least one-fourth of U.S. households had no income. Hoover saw government aid and welfare policies as "handouts." He was unaware of the degree of hardship Americans were experiencing and advocated policies of American individualism and tradition, suggesting that people just reduce their spending or work harder.

When Hoover realized U.S. companies were firing people even though he asked businesses not to lay off employees, he raised income taxes. The increase in taxes was intended to provide revenue for government projects that would provide employment opportunities and state and local assistance, especially for organizations that did not have the resources to effectively meet people's needs. Hoover's minimal efforts did little to provide relief and frustrated U.S. citizens who were angered by his inaction and the taxes that often drained what was left of their meager finances. When thousands of people became homeless, the makeshift shanty camps they built to live in were named **Hoovervilles** to mock the president.

The Dust Bowl

Source: Dorothea Lange, "Migrant Mother," 1936. This famous photograph symbolizes the distress suffered by a destitute family during the Great Depression.

Mechanization, overproduction, and careless farming led to significant harm of the environment in the western United States. During 1934, 1936, and 1939, severe drought created waves of dry storms that swept the Great Plains. Caused by the erosion of topsoil and native grasses that had once trapped moisture, the dust storms blackened the sky with sickening clouds of dust and traveled across several states, including Texas, Oklahoma, and New Mexico.

The storms destroyed farms and family homes, forcing millions of people to leave the region, which became known as the **Dust Bowl.** Looking for work and shelter, migrants often strained local and state resources that were already struggling. As a result, many New Deal agencies were dedicated to mitigating both the Dust Bowl's causes and effects. For example, the Civilian Conservation Corps (CCC) helped farmers achieve modern growing techniques that conserved soil, Congress passed additional legislation to protect the environment, and the situation justified the continuation of Agricultural Adjustment Administration (AAA) payments.

The Veteran Bonus March

Although Harding vetoed legislation for soldier bonuses, Congress granted bonuses in 1924 through the **World War Adjusted Compensation Act** (known as the **Bonus Act**). Although veterans could not receive full payment until 1945, bonuses were partially redeemable and used as collateral for loans. In the summer of 1932, almost 20,000 unemployed veterans and their families gathered in Washington to lobby for early payment (this gathering became known as the **Bonus March**). The government refused to help them, and Hoover ordered General Douglas MacArthur to remove the veterans and their families from the public property. When the veterans and their families resisted, the veterans were driven out of the camps, and their shelters and belongings were burned.

TEST TIP: On the APUSH exam, you may be asked to write about the Bonus March in a free-response question. Be sure to address the important role that World War I veterans played in politics. Hoover's treatment of the former soldiers was just one example of how disconnected he was from the plight of common people. Hoover's attitude was also a contributing factor to his landslide loss to Franklin Roosevelt in the presidential election of 1932. Although Roosevelt was opposed to bonus payments during his campaign, he recognized the veterans' ability to negatively sway public opinion. In 1933, when a smaller group of veterans gathered to protest again, Roosevelt provided them with a campsite in Virginia, sent the First Lady to calm them, and offered the veterans jobs with the Civilian Conservation Corps (CCC). Congress' overriding of Hoover's veto for early bonuses in 1936 saved Roosevelt, and he easily won reelection. Many of the veterans were siding with his political opponents until they heard the news of their benefits, then they rallied to vote for Roosevelt.

Franklin D. Roosevelt's Presidency (1933 to 1945)

In an effort to remain president, Hoover supported a limited number of legislative acts in 1932 that would provide at least a small measure of emergency assistance. It was too little, too late. **Franklin Delano Roosevelt** (often called FDR), his Democratic opponent, was overwhelmingly victorious over Hoover.

Did you know? Franklin Roosevelt was a fifth cousin of President Teddy Roosevelt. Franklin's wife, Eleanor Roosevelt, was the niece of Teddy Roosevelt. Teddy Roosevelt's younger brother, Elliot, was Eleanor Roosevelt's father. He died when Eleanor was 10 years old. President Teddy Roosevelt gave the bride away when Eleanor married Franklin Roosevelt.

The Election of 1932

Roosevelt led an upbeat campaign that promised to provide people with a **New Deal** that would give them the government aid they so desperately needed. Roosevelt's optimistic speeches gave U.S. citizens hope for the future, a renewal of faith in their traditions, and the ability to restore some measure of economic stability. Roosevelt clearly won the election, with 472 electoral votes to Hoover's 59 electoral votes. The map that follows shows that only six states (in gray) voted for Hoover.

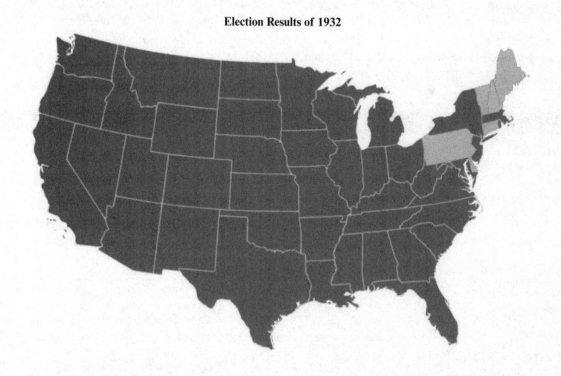

Election Results of 1932

The New Deal

Historians characterized Roosevelt's New Deal in two stages: the **First New Deal** (1933–1934) and the **Second New Deal** (1935–1938). The *first hundred days* (refers to the legislative accomplishments of a first-term president during the first 100 days in office) of Franklin Roosevelt's presidency were occupied with emergency legislation that focused on the 3R's: relief, recovery, and reform. Roosevelt's policies expanded the range and power of the federal government and ushered the United States into a new era of Democratic values that lasted until the 1970s.

Heads Up: What You Need to Know

On the APUSH exam, it's important to be familiar with some of the most important New Deal relief, recovery, and reform programs that the Roosevelt administration designed to help the country gain economic stability after the Great Depression—these programs still exist today!

- Established the **Federal Communications Commission** (FCC). Regulates all broadcasting and communications.
- Established the **Securities and Exchange Commission** (SEC). Protects security markets (the stock market) and investors. Regulates brokerage firms, securities exchanges, and investment funds.
- Created the **Federal Housing Administration** (FHA) to reduce homelessness. The FHA insures home loans and sets the standards for financing and construction.
- Established the **Federal Deposit Insurance Corporation** (FDIC) to insure up to $250,000 of bank deposits. The FDIC was established to prevent bank failures and help restore public confidence in banks.
- Repealed **Prohibition,** which lifted restrictions so that the sale of alcohol was permitted. This repeal generated federal revenue through taxation.

Roosevelt's First New Deal Legislative Acts		
Legislation	**Details**	**Results**
Emergency Banking Act (March 1933)	FDR called a special session of Congress to temporarily stabilize the banking system and declared a 3-day bank holiday to give failing banks some relief. The act authorized the Federal Reserve to issue currency and gave FDR the power to reopen banks and control foreign exchange.	Federal funds were appropriated to keep banks from collapsing and when the banks reopened, people brought back their deposits. In June, the **Glass-Steagall Act** established more permanent reforms by creating the Federal Deposit Insurance Corporation (FDIC) and banned banks from investing depositors' money for their own profit.
Civilian Conservation Corps (March 1933)	The Civilian Conservation Corps provided government jobs to young men (ages 18–25) who were required to send a large portion of their paychecks home to support their families. These men often worked in national parks and forests and helped farmers learn to grow crops more efficiently without damaging the environment.	The Civilian Conservation Corps secured jobs for men who were often denied access to social or cultural opportunities. These men learned new skills, became educated, and received regular medical checkups. The men planted trees, fought forest fires, prevented soil erosion, and built trails, roads, and ranger stations.

Legislation	Details	Results
Federal Emergency Relief Act (May 1933)	The Federal Emergency Relief Act authorized direct financial assistance for those in need. It embodied the massive government economic relief that Hoover had resisted throughout his presidency.	The Federal Emergency Relief Act provided $500 million in aid to local institutions and states. It funded soup kitchens, paid teachers' salaries, provided the poor with blankets and Christmas gifts, and staffed nursery schools.
Agricultural Adjustment Act (May 1933)	Reduced agricultural production by paying farmers not to grow crops on their land, and it offered loans to farmers above the market value of their harvests. Local agents were hired to set production quotas and monitor reductions.	Although the act was helpful to large growers and landowners, the act hurt tenant farmers and sharecroppers, whose landlords failed to "share" federal funds. Many small farmers moved to the North, urban centers, or the West Coast in search of better opportunities.
Tennessee Valley Authority Act (May 1933)	A federal project designed to build dams in the Tennessee River Basin that would provide many rural areas with hydroelectricity, flood control, and fertilizer manufacturing.	Projects like this had previously been rejected because U.S. policymakers did not want to give the federal government permission to compete with private industry. The Tennessee Valley Authority Act marked the first time there was a federally owned corporation.
National Industry Recovery Act (June 1933)	Modeled after WWI's industrial board, the National Industry Recovery Act encouraged businesses to set prices and end competition in order to become exempt from antitrust laws. It also recognized workers' rights to organize and set minimum wages and maximum hours of labor.	The National Industry Recovery Act was not very effective because its economic practices were difficult to enforce. In 1935 and 1936, this act and the Agricultural Adjustment Act were declared unconstitutional by the Supreme Court.

The Second New Deal

The second stage of Roosevelt's relief, recovery, and reform programs was a second burst of legislative programs known as the Second New Deal (1935–1938). Immediately after relief was underway, the next stage of Roosevelt's plan concentrated on goals that provided Americans with a sense of security to improve the government's relationship with its citizens. For the APUSH exam, the three most important programs were the Works Progress Administration, the Social Security Act, and the National Labor Relations Act (known as the Wagner Act).

Legislation	Description
Works Progress Administration (1935)	Established by the Emergency Relief Appropriation Act, the program provided government jobs to build highways, dams, bridges, and public edifices. The WPA hired unemployed artists, sculptors, and writers to work on federal projects. In the first year alone, more than 3 million people secured public jobs.
Social Security Act (1935)	Created a system for old-age benefits for workers, but also provided unemployment insurance, benefits to victims of industrial accidents, and benefits to mothers, children, the blind, and the disabled. States were given federal grants for immediate relief. The working public was taxed to provide revenue for all programs.

Continued

Legislation	Description
National Labor Relations Act (1935)	When the National Recovery Act (NRA) was declared unconstitutional, the National Labor Relations Act (known as the Wagner Act) replaced it and entrusted the National Labor Relations Board with even more power. If workers were denied the right to unionize, employers could be jailed or fined. The Wagner Act created FDR's support among the working class, especially among union members.
Rural Electrification Act (1936)	Provided inexpensive loans for the installation of and access to electricity in rural farming communities.
Adjusted Compensation Payment Act (1936)	Known as the **Bonus Act,** it was passed by Congress over Roosevelt's veto and provided World War I veterans with early bonus payments that veterans had been seeking since 1932. Since the president felt it favored a particular group of veterans and neglected to contribute to general relief efforts, he did not support the bill.
U.S. Housing Authority (1937)	The U.S. Housing Authority created the **Housing Act** to improve public housing conditions. This federal agency provided loans to states to build low-cost housing units. Like the FHA, it was intended to combat homelessness.

Roosevelt and Domestic Relations

Many people shifted their voting statuses from Republican to Democrat during the Roosevelt era. The New Deal reduced unemployment, attempted to initiate economic recovery, and allowed many groups previously denied government benefits access to relief. Because of this, and FDR's willingness to appease labor leaders, Democrats became the leading political party of the era. Citizens who were formerly loyal to the Republican Party shifted their votes to the Democratic Party, supporting policies that provided them with direct assistance to get relief from the Great Depression. Citizens included immigrants, ethnic minorities, liberals, and members of unions.

Key Facts about Roosevelt's Domestic Relations

Labor relations. Although Roosevelt was often viewed as the "champion of labor," he was more concerned with generating working-class consumers who would stimulate the economy than manufacturers that had true negotiating power. Roosevelt's alliance with John Lewis (founder of a coalition of union members called the **Congress of Industrial Organizations**) was intended to gain political support. Although Roosevelt publically supported minimum wages and the right to collective bargaining, he hesitated before supporting the Wagner Act in 1935. Roosevelt only supported the act to quell the unrest between laborers and employers that developed when the economy began to recover.

Heads Up: What You Need to Know

Regardless of Roosevelt's motivations, the president saw union members as important constituents. Anti-unionism was no longer popular. In 1937, the Congress of Industrial Organizations (CIO) had 280 formal organizers and successfully led highly publicized strikes at both General Motors and U.S. Steel. By 1940, millions of Americans were union members.

For the APUSH exam, you should know the following about unions during this time frame:

- Benefits were generally reserved for working-class white men. Fair practices in hiring and employment did not include women or blacks until the middle of World War II—although both groups were included in collective labor organizations, they usually played minimal roles.

- A rise in union support actually ended the American Federation of Labor (AFL) because it insisted on categorizing laborers by trades. Many of its leaders refused to recognize new unions at the AFL's national convention in 1935, which led to a fatal split in the organization.

- In 1955, the AFL merged with the CIO to create the AFL-CIO, which is one of the most influential labor unions in the U.S. today.

The Supreme Court. An economic downturn in 1937 caused a recession in the U.S. The Supreme Court nullified both the National Recovery Act (NRA) and the Agricultural Adjustment Act (AAA). Fearing other programs were in jeopardy, Roosevelt hinted that some of the Supreme Court's members were getting too old to make effective decisions. When Roosevelt asked Congress to appoint one new judge for every justice over 70, his political opponents accused him of attempting to "pack" the court in his favor.

Political opponents. Political divisions continued to exist between urban and rural branches of political parties, and northerners and southerners frequently disagreed about how the government should operate. Many Republicans called Roosevelt a Socialist and suggested he was abusing his presidential power. Southern Democrats criticized his wife, Eleanor, and other New Deal liberals for sympathizing with African Americans and providing them with benefits that undermined white racial control in their constituencies. As a result, Roosevelt's suggestions for progressive legislation were continually challenged, especially after 1938, when the liberal influence in Congress had significantly diminished.

Did you know? Eleanor Roosevelt, the First Lady, was dedicated to many social, political, and racial causes. Some people said they were getting "two presidents" instead of one. Mrs. Roosevelt helped African Americans, minorities, and the poor. She was a champion for civil rights, humanitarian causes, and greater freedoms, while criticizing discrimination and the mistreatment of the less fortunate. Her work, along with other activists, caused tensions in the Democratic Party, especially among southern Democrats, who were usually elected by white segregationists. After the president's death, the new president, Woodrow Wilson, appointed Mrs. Roosevelt as the U.S. delegation head of the United Nations, where some called her the "First Lady of the World."

Huey Long. Powerful Louisiana Governor Huey Long was inspired to become president and launched promises for a radical redistribution of wealth called the **Share Our Wealth Plan.** Long promoted it as a more effective relief program than the New Deal. In order to gather political support, Long promised the impossible—a plan that included a $5,000 income-free pension, education, radios, and cars for all Americans, which he stated could be funded through the taxation of the rich. Although Long was prepared to run for the presidency, he was assassinated in Baton Rouge by the son-in-law of a political opponent. Since the southern demagogue was known for his shady personal and political dealings, no one was surprised. Long's enemies had formed cooperatives sworn to kill him, and Long traveled with numerous armed bodyguards, who immediately killed the assassin.

Charles Coughlin. Catholic priest Father Charles Coughlin became famous through a nationally syndicated radio program that he used to denigrate both President Roosevelt and the New Deal. Millions of people listened to Coughlin blame the international Depression on the Ku Klux Klan, Jewish bankers, FDR, and anyone with wealth or influence. Coughlin's anti-Semitic views ultimately ended his career—when he spoke approvingly of Hitler and Mussolini in 1939, he lost popularity. The Vatican censured his political speeches and his radio show was cancelled.

> TEST TIP: APUSH exam free-response questions might ask you to draw assumptions about or compare and contrast the New Deal's level of successes or failures. Relevant issues to include in your essay might include the specific examples of relief legislative acts that were offered to everyday citizens and specific oppositional complaints of the legislative acts. Remember that the New Deal increased the federal government's power, transformed citizens' expectations, improved labor relations, and provided Americans with effective regulation and security.
>
> The New Deal, however, did *not* end the Great Depression. In 1939, 20 percent of American citizens were still unemployed and the country experienced another recession. FDR's attention was actually shifted away from New Deal policies by European events and Keynesian economics. Both events inspired the "massive deficit spending" that occurred during World War II, which is what really ended the Depression.

World War II (1939 to 1945)

When World War II erupted in Europe, the financial hardship of the Great Depression caused American citizens and politicians to insist on neutrality. Americans knew that the U.S. economy was impacted by the global economy, and citizens empathized with European allies, but most Americans were hesitant to get involved in another foreign war if the conflict did not directly threaten the U.S. People feared an influx of refugees and the possibility of depleting military resources.

The Road to World War II

Before we discuss the U.S. involvement in World War II, it's important to understand the main reasons for the outbreak of the global conflict. Tensions were rising between military powers in both Europe and the Pacific throughout the 1930s.

Cause	Description
Great Depression	The global economy created economic, social, and political instability in Europe and Asia. People were desperately looking for relief, and tensions were rising from old resentments.
World War I resentments	Germany, Italy, and Japan resented their unfair treatment at the Versailles Peace Conference after World War I.

Cause	Description
Extreme ideologies	The strengthening of extreme nationalistic thinking throughout European nations changed the political ideological climate: Fascism in Germany, totalitarianism and Fascism in Italy, Socialism in the Soviet Union, and imperialism in Japan.
Appeasement	By 1933, Adolf Hitler and the Nazi Party started to build military strength in Germany, but European leaders failed to enforce the Treaty of Versailles that restricted Germany from remilitarizing. Nations like Britain and France hoped to keep peace at any cost in order to prevent war. Germany invaded the Rhineland in 1935 to take back its territory lost during World War I, but still the European leaders said nothing.
Munich Conference	Hitler demanded that Czechoslovakia surrender Sudetenland (a region that was taken away from Germany in World War I), but Czechoslovakia refused. In 1939, Hitler met with European leaders at the Munich Conference. The British Prime Minister believed that this small appeasement would satisfy Hitler. In order to avoid war, Hitler was given Sudetenland if he would agree to stop expansion into and invasions of other nations. Instead, Hitler invaded Czechoslovakian territories and then attacked Poland in 1939.
Japan's expansion	Japan had been experiencing industrialization, but after the Great Depression, the Japanese economy crashed. A new conservative group of militaristic leaders rose to power; they centralized Japan through the *Imperial Way Faction* (Japanese imperialism that was fueled by Social Darwinism). The increased growth of Japan was not supported by its natural resources or land. Japan sought out imperialistic expansion by invading Manchuria (a northern region of China) in 1931. Then in 1937, Japan formed an alliance with Germany.
Holocaust	Germany's persecution of Jews had begun long before the war, but during the war Hitler's anti-Semitic Nazi Party destroyed Jewish synagogues, businesses, and homes. Hitler's belief in Fascism convinced many German citizens that Jews were an inferior race. Hitler's terrifying Nazi destruction and propaganda did not stop on the battlefields. As Germany fought against its enemies, Hitler and his henchmen enacted the Final Solution to the "Jewish problem," attempting the genocide of Jews in Europe. Hitler set up death camps across Nazi-occupied Europe that engineered the death of more than 6 million Jews, along with other "undesirables" such as homosexuals, gypsies, the disabled, Slavs, and others.

Timeline of World War II

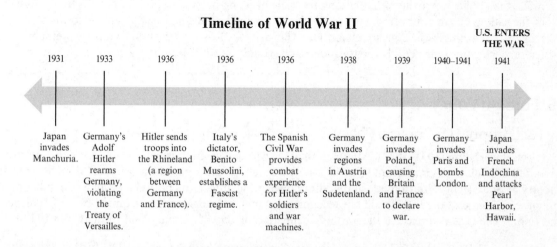

1931	1933	1936	1936	1936	1938	1939	1940–1941	**U.S. ENTERS THE WAR** 1941
Japan invades Manchuria.	Germany's Adolf Hitler rearms Germany, violating the Treaty of Versailles.	Hitler sends troops into the Rhineland (a region between Germany and France).	Italy's dictator, Benito Mussolini, establishes a Fascist regime.	The Spanish Civil War provides combat experience for Hitler's soldiers and war machines.	Germany invades regions in Austria and the Sudetenland.	Germany invades Poland, causing Britain and France to declare war.	Germany invades Paris and bombs London.	Japan invades French Indochina and attacks Pearl Harbor, Hawaii.

Did you know? Although Hitler had forcefully annexed Austria and the Sudetenland in 1938, international leaders hoped their leniency for his actions at the Munich Conference would appease Hitler's lust for power. It did not—on March 15, 1939, the German Army invaded the rest of Czechoslovakia and a few months later, Hitler invaded Poland, causing Britain and France to declare war. The same year, Hitler signed a **Nazi-Soviet Nonaggression Pact** with Stalin (also called the Molotov-Ribbentrop Treaty). Stalin feared that capitalistic nations would team up against the Soviet Union, so he made a pact with Hitler. Germany and Russia agreed to divide the conquered Eastern European nations into "spheres of influence," but not to attack each other. On June 22, 1941, however, Germany invaded the Soviet Union and broke the pact.

Heads Up: What You Need to Know

The following descriptions will help you understand why the United States was against the extreme political ideologies of totalitarianism, Fascism, and Communism.

Totalitarianism is a single-party dictatorship that requires citizens to completely submit to the ruling government (activities, beliefs, and values). Opposition is not permitted and anyone who disagrees with the ruling government can be killed or imprisoned. Totalitarian governments are anti-Democratic. For example, Russia was led by Stalin (1925–1953) and China was led by Mao Zedong (1949–1976).

Fascism is a form of radical, extreme nationalism and is extremely militaristic so that people are controlled by fear. All Fascist nations are totalitarian and do not accept democracy, which is considered a sign of moral weakness. Fascists believe in national or racial supremacy over all other nations (or races). Citizens are not allowed individualism. For example, Italy and Germany were Fascist nations from 1919–1945.

Communism is a socio-economic system of government of a "classless" society. It stresses social equality rather than political equality. All decisions are made by a one-party state and the party is the custodian of the nation. Communism eliminates social classes, capitalism, unequal wealth, and all forms of religion. For example, the Soviet Union (today known as the Russian Federation) was a Communist nation during this time period. Today, China, Cuba, Laos, North Korea, and Vietnam are Communist.

U.S. Foreign Policy

Key Facts about U.S. Foreign Policy

U.S. rejects imperialism (1931–1932). Although the U.S. was dedicated to isolationism during the interwar period, the U.S. felt it was important to make a statement about the Japanese invasion of Manchuria in 1931. Secretary of State Henry Stimson issued the **Stimson Doctrine,** informing both the Empire of Japan and the Republic of China that the U.S. would not recognize any territorial acquisition acquired by imperialistic force. (Note: The U.S. also rejected the Soviets' occupation of Latvia, Estonia, and Lithuania in 1940.)

Good Neighbor Policy (1933). In U.S. relations with Central and South America, FDR furthered isolationist policies by rejecting the interventionist policies of his Progressive predecessors. The Good Neighbor Policy was actually established by Hoover, who gave a speech in 1928 that emphasized America's commitment to being a "good neighbor" to other nations in the Western Hemisphere. As a result, most of the Platt Amendment, a bill that outlined the conditions for withdrawing from Cuba after the Spanish-American War, was dissolved in 1934, and during World War II and the Cold War, the U.S. gathered support for its interests by financially aiding several Latin American countries, including the Dominican Republic and Brazil.

The Neutrality Acts (1935–1937). When tensions rose in Europe and Asia, the U.S. was determined to stay out of the conflict, just like it had before World War I. Therefore, Congress passed a series of Neutrality Acts between 1935 and 1937 that legislators believed would safeguard isolationism.

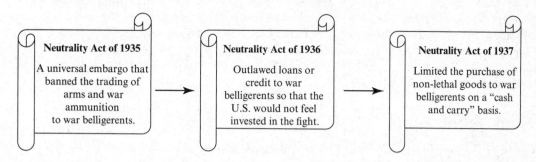

Neutrality Act of 1935

A universal embargo that banned the trading of arms and war ammunition to war belligerents.

Neutrality Act of 1936

Outlawed loans or credit to war belligerents so that the U.S. would not feel invested in the fight.

Neutrality Act of 1937

Limited the purchase of non-lethal goods to war belligerents on a "cash and carry" basis.

The Neutrality Acts were perceived as a sign of American weakness by other countries. The acts did not clearly define "belligerent" and did not differentiate nations that were either victims or aggressors. As a result, the U.S. tended to favor its former allies and punished weaker nations that had few resources.

The U.S. Enters World War II

In 1939, after Hitler invaded Poland, there was widespread unrest in Europe. President Roosevelt, who was sympathetic to British Prime Minister Winston Churchill's declaration of war on Germany, then called for another Neutrality Act that allowed for the sale of arms to Britain and France on a cash-and-carry basis. The bill passed, ending the embargo. Several events occurred in 1941, causing the United States to enter the war on December 7, 1941.

Key Facts about the U.S. Entering World War II

Lend-Lease Act (March 1941). The United States had become isolationist, but Roosevelt established policies that situated the U.S. on the edge of involvement. Roosevelt convinced Congress to pass the **Lend-Lease Act,** motivated by the desire to provide relief to the British, who were on the verge of collapse after the devastating attacks of the *Luftwaffe* (German Air Force) during the Battle of Britain. Despite objections by isolationists, Roosevelt signed the act into law. The U.S. leased military arms, ammunition, and naval destroyers to Britain in exchange for 99-year leases to eight British military bases in the Western Hemisphere. The lease program became known as "an arsenal of democracy." Secret U.S. and British talks started about the U.S. engaging in the war.

Atlantic Charter (August 1941). The U.S. collaborated with Britain to draft the **Atlantic Charter,** an agreement that defined post-war goals, including a commitment to human rights, mutual disarmament, free trade, and no territorial expansion without the consent of the nations concerned. Most importantly, Roosevelt and British Prime Minister Winston Churchill became both political and personal friends.

Pearl Harbor attacked (December 7, 1941). Japan had slowly been gaining power by conquering small islands in the Pacific, and while U.S. military leaders and politicians expected another attack in the region, they believed it would be minor. Therefore, the U.S. was shocked when a massive assault began on December 7 on American warships docked in Hawaii at Pearl Harbor. Basing their assessments on racist assumptions, many U.S. officials did not believe that the Japanese were capable of organizing such a destructive attack. The next day, President Roosevelt asked Congress for a declaration of war, which was granted immediately. By December 11, Germany and Italy, Japan's Axis allies, declared war on the U.S.

The U.S. extends the Lend-Lease Act to the Soviet Union. Because Hitler despised Slavic people and considered them inferior, he launched a brutal air and ground campaign, which was intended to crush the Soviet Red Army and exploit its resources. Hitler demonstrated little mercy to civilians. In desperate need of assistance, the Russians hoped that the U.S. would send troops to their region as soon as the U.S. entered the war. Instead of directly helping the Soviet Union, the U.S. sent aid through the Lend-Lease Act. Nazi forces found themselves bogged down in the Russian winter, and the Soviets survived the Battle of Stalingrad. The U.S. and the Soviet Union were key allies throughout the war, but Stalin resented Roosevelt's choices, which caused tensions during and after the war.

The Home Front

Key Facts about the Home Front During World War II

Four Freedoms. On January 6, 1941, Roosevelt addressed Congress about **Four Freedoms** that people of all nations should be allowed to enjoy and suggested that Americans had a responsibility to uphold these freedoms. These freedoms encapsulated Democratic ideals and motivated many throughout the war: freedom of speech, freedom of worship, freedom from want (poverty), and freedom from fear.

Source: Norman Rockwell, "Four Freedoms," 1943. This classic wartime poster from the American artist celebrated Democratic and patriotic values of small-town American life.

Fireside chats. During World War II, U.S. citizens looked for leadership from the president that had brought them through the harrowing events of the Great Depression. To inspire Americans to support the war, Roosevelt continued the radio addresses he had begun in 1933 to communicate with U.S. citizens. During these "fireside chats," Roosevelt spoke directly to the people to give them encouragement and information about domestic policy, the war abroad, and hope for the future.

Source: J. Howard Miller, "We Can Do It!" 1942. Iconic World War II image of "Rosie the Riveter," which symbolized American working women and inspired the morale of workers.

Propaganda. From 1941 to 1945, the **Office of War Information** was established to create war propaganda. The propaganda was disseminated both at home and abroad. Films, posters, and sensational catchphrases like that in the poster, "We Can Do It!" were used to gather support for the war. Because the Committee on Public Administration (CPI) excessively used propaganda during World War I, Congress failed to properly fund the Office of War Information, and the office suffered from mismanagement. Eventually, private advertisers took over the promotion of the war, leading Americans—including soldiers—to connect consumerism with the benefits of democracy. This trend continued after the war.

American labor changed. Changes in labor dynamics caused all Americans to "do their part" for the war effort. Unions vowed not to strike as businesses raised wages and set reasonable work hours. When the Selective Service began to draft male soldiers, women and African Americans stepped up to provide the factory labor the country needed. In 1942, Mexican agricultural workers were recruited through the Bracero Program (a series of agreements that encouraged Mexicans to work in the U.S.).

War agencies created. When the U.S. entered the war, FDR created several federal agencies to manage the war efforts. This extended the power of the federal government (which grew 400 percent during World War II) and led to increased spending, especially in the form of military contracts. As a result, unemployment dropped from 14 percent to 2 percent in less than 3 years (1940–1943) and manufacturing production increased substantially, effectively ending the Great Depression.

U.S. World War II Agencies	
War Production Board	The War Production Board, established in 1942, supervised the production of weapons and supplies used in the war: Automobile plants made tanks and planes, ribbon factories made parachutes, and other domestic manufacturers made everything from mosquito netting to weapons. The government granted large subsidies to big business to keep profits high and production up. Over $180 billion was spent on supplies, weapons, and ammunition.
Office of Price Administration	The Office of Price Administration (OPA), established in 1941, attempted to combat inflation by setting prices and controlling rent. It rationed products that soldiers needed or that were important for winning the war (rubber, gasoline, sugar, coffee, etc.). When employment rose, Americans soon associated their increased ability to purchase products with patriotism and freedom. A black market developed for products, and people soon questioned the effectiveness of the OPA.
Fair Employment Practices Commission	The Fair Employment Practices Commission (FEPC) was established in 1941, when African Americans, led by black activist A. Philip Randolph, threatened to march on Washington to object to unfair labor and hiring practices in factories. The order banned discrimination in defense industries and government factories and set up the FEPC to enforce compliance. This was seen as a major victory for the African American community. By 1944, over 1 million black Americans were employed in U.S. industries.

Discrimination. During World War II, national inclusion expanded as people rallied together to fight in the war, buy war bonds, and work in factories. Americans of Irish or Jewish descent, for example, became much more accepted than they had been in the past. Furthermore, even though the U.S. had committed several discriminatory acts against blacks and other minorities, the United States condemned Germany for the atrocities inflicted on the Jewish population in Europe, the **Holocaust** (the persecution and genocide of over 11 million people whom the Nazis considered "inferior," including 6 million Jews).

Japanese American internment. In February and March of 1942, 117,000 Japanese American citizens were interned through Executive Order 9906. Even those who were U.S. citizens were forced to relocate to isolated camps in the West, where they were incarcerated behind barbed wire and questioned about their loyalties to the U.S. Some Japanese Americans sued the government, questioning the constitutionality of its actions, but the Supreme Court denied any wrongdoing in cases like *Hirabayashi v. United States* (1943) and *Korematsu v. United States* (1944).

African Americans in the military. Almost 2 million African Americans served in the U.S. military during World War II. Black Americans who enlisted encountered discrimination and racism in the armed services both domestically and abroad because they were still subject to the Jim Crow laws. Only menial duties were available to African Americans, like physical labor and cooking. African Americans rarely received promotions and were treated badly by many white soldiers. In southern training camps, black northerners were subjected to segregation and extreme prejudice. Institutional racism continued even after the war. For example, black veterans' access to the benefits of the G.I. Bill was much more limited than that of their white counterparts. The African Americans' experiences inspired many to call for more aggressive action for civil rights both during and after the war (see Chapter 11).

Did you know? Several military units of African Americans were valuable in the fight against the enemy on all fronts of World War II. For example, the all-black Tuskegee Airmen broke barriers when these military fighter pilots were deployed to fight air missions in Europe. Their dive-bombing missions destroyed enemy aircraft and brought many military successes to the U.S.

Source: Office of War Information poster of the Tuskegee Airmen, "Keep us Flying," 1943.

Zoot Suit Riots. White sailors and marines stationed in California took offense at the attitudes and flashy clothing ("zoot suits") of second-generation Mexican-American youths in California urban centers like Los Angeles, San Jose, and San Diego. Because the soldiers considered the Mexican-Americans to be juvenile delinquents, criminals, and draft dodgers, animosity and racial tension ran high. In June 1943, violent altercations broke out between the two groups in Los Angeles. After the fighting subsided, Governor Earl Warren appointed a committee to investigate the riots. It heavily criticized the military, the police department, and the media for racial propaganda.

Key U.S. Events of World War II

The U.S. fought on two fronts: Europe and the Asian-Pacific (called the European Theater and the Asian-Pacific Theater).

The European Theater

After the Soviet Union was attacked by Germany in June 1941 and the United States was attacked by Japan in December 1941, Britain, the Soviet Union, and the United States formed an alliance—the "Big Three."

> **TEST TIP: It is important to have a general idea of the key players of World War II.**
>
> - **The Allied Powers** (called the *Allies*). The "Big Three" Allies included Great Britain, the United States (joined in 1941), and the Soviet Union (joined in 1941 after Germany's betrayal). Other Allied nations included Belgium, the Netherlands, Denmark, Norway, Greece, Yugoslavia, Poland, nationalist China, Canada, Australia, New Zealand, and France (until 1940).
>
> - **The Axis Powers**: Germany, Italy (joined from 1940 until 1943), Japan, Hungary, Bulgaria, Finland, and Romania.

The Allies' military strategies in Europe were primarily conceived by the United States and Britain. Roosevelt focused on three European war strategies: (1) securing key European fuel reserves in North Africa, (2) battling the German submarine fleet in the Atlantic, and (3) liberating Italy from Fascism.

The year 1943 proved to be the major turning point in the war. In the West, American and British troops took part in the invasion of Italy and major victories in northern Africa. In the East, the Soviets blockaded the German Nazi southern entryway to the Caspian Sea and the Baku oil fields that the Nazis so desperately needed. On both the European Western and Eastern fronts, the Allies began to push back against the Nazis, who suddenly seemed less than invincible.

Key U.S. Battles of World War II (European Theater)	
Battle	**Description**
Invasion of Normandy (June 1944)	The northern Africa strategy was a success. Italy proved to be very weak and easy to remove from the war. However, the invasion from the west through the beaches of Normandy, France, in 1944 was extremely difficult and almost failed. Known as **D-Day,** it is often considered the largest amphibious (land and sea) invasion in history. Hitler's forces had entrenched themselves in concrete bunkers on the ocean's coast in France. Commanded by U.S. General Dwight D. Eisenhower, Allied forces (composed of 200,000 American, British, and Canadian troops) landed at Normandy with the intension to liberate the German-occupied territory. The invasion succeeded, and the Allies created a foothold in France that eventually allowed for significant progress throughout Europe.
Battle of the Bulge (December 1944)	The last major German offensive occurred when Hitler organized a surprise attack on Allied forces in Belgium, France, and Luxembourg. The battle caught the Allied forces completely off guard, and the U.S. incurred high casualties. It is considered the largest and most vicious of the U.S. altercations during the war. After the attack, the Allies regrouped to strike devastating blows on the German Army's armory and soldiers, which allowed them to push into Germany by early 1945.

On the European front, the United States drove through France into Germany, defeating the German Army on May 8, 1945. During this period, European Allied leaders met to discuss the post-war settlement (see pp. 297–298).

The Asian-Pacific Theater

Conflict between the U.S. and Japan. A second strategy in World War II involved the Asian-Pacific Theater and Japanese expansion. The U.S. and Britain responded to early Japanese aggression with the Atlantic Charter, which froze oil sales to Japan. When attempts to negotiate with the United States failed, Japan began to consider the U.S. an enemy. Japan then organized and completed a successful attack on U.S. battleships stationed at Pearl Harbor on December 7, 1941, hoping to severely damage the U.S. Pacific fleet and discourage America's Navy from preventing any other military strikes planned for Southeast Asia. At Pearl Harbor, U.S. losses were substantial. Four battleships sank (all eight in the harbor were severely damaged) and over 2,000 Americans died. Because no aircraft carriers were in Pearl Harbor that day and the Japanese failed to hit important fuel resources and repair shops, however, the U.S. Pacific fleet was able to recover much more quickly than the Japanese expected. Six battleships were returned to service and America rallied around the attack, declaring war on Japan the next day.

Japan attacked U.S. territories. On the same day as Pearl Harbor, Japan attacked the U.S. territories of the Philippines, Guam, and Wake Island. In response, U.S. General Douglas MacArthur and Admiral Chester Nimitz developed *island hopping,* a military strategy to invade small islands and secure military bases. Their plan was to use the American Navy to take out small satellite islands supporting Japanese expansion. When this was finished, the United States would directly attack Japan.

The struggle in the Philippines. The U.S. defeats in the Pacific resulted in high casualties and vicious warfare. By January 1942, the **Bataan Peninsula** in the Philippines was one of the few remaining U.S. strongholds in Southeast Asia. The battle for its control resulted in a massive defeat for the Americans and Filipinos, resulting in the surrender of almost 80,000 soldiers, who were led on a massive death march that covered over 60 miles. The men were treated brutally, fed little, and sporadically killed—although statistics vary, scholars believe 500–1,000 Americans and 6,000–9,000 Filipinos died during the death march. Thousands of others perished from disease, mistreatment, or starvation in prisoner of war camps.

Key U.S. Battles of World War II (Asian-Pacific Theater)	
Battle	**Description**
Battle of the Coral Sea (May 1942)	The first battle in which aircraft carriers engaged with each other. This battle resulted in a strategic Allied victory. Although the battle resulted in heavy damage for the carriers and planes of both sides, it marked the first time a Japanese advance had been checked.
Battle of Midway (June 1942)	Seen as the turning point for the U.S., this battle prevented the Japanese from obtaining Midway Island, which was located just north of Hawaii and could provide Japan with an airstrip from which to launch future attacks on Southeast Asia, Hawaii, and even the U.S. West Coast. It allowed the U.S. to take an offensive position in the Pacific and significantly weakened the Japanese Navy.
Battle of Guadalcanal (August 1942 to February 1943)	The battle for the airfield on Guadalcanal marked a turning point for U.S. forces. After months of fighting, the Japanese were forced off the island.

Battle	Description
Battle of Iwo Jima (February to March 1945)	U.S. forces landed on the Japanese-controlled Iwo Jima and recaptured the stronghold. Even though the island was filled with tunnels and bunkers that were difficult to penetrate, U.S. numbers and air power ensured victory, especially because Japanese forces could not be reinforced and found it difficult to retreat. At Iwo Jima, the Japanese lost 20,000 men, and the Americans lost 6,000 men.
Battle of Okinawa (April to June 1945)	One of the bloodiest in the Asian-Pacific Theater, this battle was part of the island-hopping campaign toward the end of the war. Because it was located in close proximity to Japan, Okinawa provided Americans with a staging ground and landing strips from which to launch a possible invasion. At Okinawa, the Japanese lost 110,000 men, and the Americans lost over 82,000 men.

The End of World War II

The war in Europe ended on May 8, 1945 (known as **V-E Day**). The Big Three of the Grand Alliance— Franklin Delano Roosevelt (U.S.), Winston Churchill (Britain), and Joseph Stalin (Soviet Union)—wanted to weaken Germany and prevent a resurgent Germany from rising up to cause a World War III. When it became apparent that Germany would lose the war, the three men met in Yalta, which was located in the Crimea. At the **Yalta Conference** (February 4–11, 1945), the Big Three agreed to split up Europe between Soviet spheres of influence and British spheres of influence.

Source: Encyclopedia Britannica online. From left to right: Winston Churchill (United Kingdom), Franklin D. Roosevelt (United States), and Joseph Stalin (Union of the Soviet Socialist Republics).

On April 12, 1945, Roosevelt died, less than a month before the end of the war in Europe. Roosevelt, Stalin, and Churchill were considered the central leaders of the Allies, and Roosevelt's death caused a considerable amount of anxiety throughout the world.

The Allied leaders met again at the Potsdam Conference in August 1945 after Roosevelt's death. Harry S. Truman, Roosevelt's former vice president, assumed the presidency and joined Churchill and Stalin to discuss the future, which included making decisions about reparations, territorial boundaries, and how to judge war criminals. At the **Potsdam Conference** (July 17–August 2, 1945), President Truman learned about the possibility of the first successful detonation of an atomic bomb. Although he did not tell the Allies about this revelation, Truman's decision to use the bomb would prove to be one of the most significant events in world history.

The U.S. Bombs Hiroshima and Nagasaki in Japan

After World War II was over in Europe, the war continued to drag on for months with Japan. The U.S. eventually defeated Japan, but at an extreme cost. The United States secured military bases on one island after the next in the Pacific, but after the contests in Iwo Jima and Okinawa, the U.S. came to an important conclusion about what the Japanese were willing to do in order to win. Since Japanese culture was based on the *Bushido code* (Japanese people gave all loyalty to the emperor), Truman's military advisors believed that the Japanese were willing to fight to the death to honor the will of their Japanese leadership. Many U.S. officials thought there would be no end to the war unless the emperor announced an official decree of surrender.

President Truman stated that dropping the atomic bomb on Japan was an absolute necessity to reduce the number of Allied casualties that might have resulted from a continuation of warfare. Some of Truman's advisors believed that the Japanese emperor was still being advised that Japan could win the war. The U.S. thought the war could continue for several months and worried that a land invasion of Japan could lead to about 1 million deaths of American soldiers, and even higher numbers of Japanese civilian and military casualties. Therefore, the atomic bombs could serve as a tactic to shock the Japanese leadership into a surrender.

The United States dropped a bomb on the city of Hiroshima, Japan, on August 6, 1945. Colonel Paul Tibbets' B-29 bomber *The Enola Gay* dropped "Little Boy" on the Japanese city. The bomb immediately annihilated 90 percent of the landscape and killed almost 100,000 Japanese citizens. Three days later, Nagasaki experienced the devastation of another bomb, which vaporized another 70,000 Japanese citizens. Thousands more died of radiation over the next several months. The bombs had the desired effect—the Japanese surrendered on August 14, 1945 ("V-J Day").

HISTORIOGRAPHY. *Although the atomic bombs ended the war, the release of the bombs had long-lasting effects on the Japanese people and significantly contributed to the Cold War. Some historians argue that it was wrong to drop the bombs because they killed so many people. This group of historians argue that the Japanese military was defeated by 1945, although they agree that the emperor had to issue a surrender before soldiers would concede. Historians from this school of thought assert that the emperor wanted to surrender. The problem was that the Americans would only accept an "unconditional surrender" in which the emperor would have to completely remove himself from office. This move would have undermined the Japanese culture and the respect for their emperor. The emperor's advisors were split. Three generals believed the war could be won, and three generals wanted to surrender. According to this school of thought, the U.S. could have offered Japan a "conditional surrender" to allow the emperor to remain in a symbolic position of power, but this negotiation would have undermined the first group of generals who claimed that they could win the war. However, there was another underlying issue—the problem was that the U.S. was motivated to use the atomic bombs to scare the Russians from invading Southeast Asia and many politicians were tired of fighting an expensive war that had sacrificed the lives of American citizens.*

TEST TIP: When studying World War II, be sure to focus on the major causes and effects of the war, such as changes in government and society, mobilization, economics, and world power. Although details like battles and specific legislation are good to use as evidence to support your position, they are not as important as knowing what caused the war, how the war changed the U.S., and its long-term results (some of these are discussed in the next chapter).

Post–World War II

The Establishment of Global Organizations

Many European nations, such as Germany and France, were completely destabilized after World War II. The end of the war led to a global reorganization that was significantly different from the end of World War I. The leaders of the United States, Britain, and France decided that the cause of World War II was an "economic" problem. These world leaders came together to form international institutions to regulate the global economy, especially in the developing world. Three major institutions were established after World War II: the **United Nations,** the **International Monetary Fund,** and the **World Bank.**

The United Nations (UN). The United Nations was formed in 1945 to replace the failed League of Nations. The UN was established as an organization that promoted international diplomacy. It included a large global parliament called the General Assembly. After the war, the power of the UN was held by a Security Council, a group of four principal nations: the United States, the Soviet Union, China, and Great Britain. The goal of the Security Council was to mediate and make military decisions when necessary to keep the peace around the world. To avoid conflicts, each nation was allowed to cast one vote during the decision-making process. The UN also had the ability to help refugees, settle global disputes through an International Court of Justice, and provide healthcare benefits for people in numerous countries. During the Cold War, however, the conflict between the United States and the Soviet Union often paralyzed the Security Council.

International Monetary Fund and the World Bank. Although the UN was important for peacekeeping, the real power was set at the **Bretton Woods Conference** in New Hampshire (United States). This is where the International Monetary Fund (IMF) and the World Bank were established to unite countries economically. The UN believed that if countries shared a common economic interest, they would be less likely to engage in war. The goal of the IMF was to lay down the ground rules for economic aid to countries, but countries had to comply with the rules (fight inflation, industrialize to build their economies, and lower tariffs). If the countries could accomplish this, they were able to receive financial aid for development from the World Bank. This economic influence led to the power of the American and northern European countries over the developing world. During the Cold War, this economic influence was used by the United States as a strategy in negotiating with the Soviet Union. The idea was to advance countries into a global market of trade.

Chapter Review Practice Questions

Practice questions are for instructional purposes only and may not reflect the format of the actual exam. On the actual exam, questions will be grouped into sets. Each set contains one source-based prompt (document or image) and two to five questions.

Multiple-Choice Questions

Questions 1–3 refer to the following political cartoon.

THE BIG STICK IN THE CARIBBEAN SEA

Source: William Allen Rogers, "The Big Stick in the Caribbean Sea," 1904. President Theodore Roosevelt enforcing his concept of the Monroe Doctrine.

1. Which of the following historical aspects of Roosevelt's foreign policy is portrayed in Rogers' political cartoon?

    A. Roosevelt's determination to bend the will of all small countries to his dreams for America
    B. Roosevelt's bullying tactics with foreign and domestic trusts
    C. Roosevelt's commanding presence in foreign nations, which enabled him to manipulate them
    D. Roosevelt's assertive approach to foreign policy, which was to "speak softly and carry a big stick"

2. Based on your knowledge of U.S. history, which of the following best describes the difference between the Roosevelt Corollary and Taft's dollar diplomacy?

    A. The Roosevelt Corollary was supported by the people, while dollar diplomacy was supported by Congress.
    B. The Roosevelt Corollary focused on the use of military force and negotiation, while dollar diplomacy focused on coercion through foreign investment.
    C. The Roosevelt Corollary focused on Latin American nations, while dollar diplomacy focused on those torn by war and poverty.
    D. The Roosevelt Corollary was established to maintain control, while dollar diplomacy was established for intervention.

3. Based on your knowledge of U.S. history, which of the following policies of Franklin Delano Roosevelt reversed the Roosevelt Corollary?

   A. The First New Deal
   B. The Good Neighbor Policy
   C. The Second World War
   D. Dollar diplomacy

Questions 4–6 refer to the following passage.

We entered this war because violations of right had occurred which touched us to the quick and made the life of our own people impossible unless they were corrected and the world secured once and for all against their recurrence. What we demand in this war, therefore, is nothing peculiar to ourselves. It is that the world be made fit and safe to live in; and particularly that it be made safe for every peace-loving nation which, like our own, wishes to live its own life, determine its own institutions, be assured of justice and fair dealing by the other peoples of the world as against force and selfish aggression. All the peoples of the world are in effect partners in this interest, and for our own part we see very clearly that unless justice be done to others it will not be done to us. The programme of the world's peace, therefore, is our programme; and that programme, the only possible programme, as we see it, is this:

   I. Open covenants of peace, openly arrived at, after which there shall be no private international understandings of any kind but diplomacy shall proceed always frankly and in the public view.
   II. Absolute freedom of navigation upon the seas, outside territorial waters, alike in peace and in war, except as the seas may be closed in whole or in part by international action for the enforcement of international covenants.
   III. The removal, so far as possible, of all economic barriers and the establishment of an equality of trade conditions among all the nations consenting to the peace and associating themselves for its maintenance...

—Source: Woodrow Wilson, excerpt from a speech given to Congress on January 8, 1918.

4. Which of the following most directly reflects the circumstances surrounding Wilson's Congressional address?

   A. Wilson was discussing the impact of the First World War on the Navy.
   B. Wilson was presenting his Fourteen Points for world peace after the conclusion of the First World War.
   C. Wilson was presenting the reasons why the U.S. entered the war and ideas for withdrawing from the war.
   D. Wilson was discussing the terms of the Treaty of Versailles, which eventually ended the war.

5. Based on your knowledge of U.S. history, which of the following best demonstrates why African Americans might have been disappointed in Wilson's speech?

   A. The speech reflected Wilson's imperialistic foreign policy, which contradicted his ideas for peace.
   B. The speech focused on making the world safe for all nations, yet the U.S. was often not a safe place for African Americans.
   C. The speech did not mention the segregated army or African American service.
   D. The speech reflected the U.S. demands for the war without mentioning the demands of other countries.

6. Which of the following was the direct result of Wilson's speech during the negotiations of the Treaty of Versailles?

   A. Wilson was not successful; the leaders of Britain and France were more interested in punishing Germany than in developing a significant plan for world peace.

   B. Wilson was somewhat successful; although the leaders of Britain and France ultimately rejected most of Wilson's ideas, they formed the League of Nations, which provided collective security.

   C. Wilson was moderately successful; Congress supported many of Wilson's ideas, including the League of Nations, which influenced the leaders of Britain and France to accept some terms of peace.

   D. Wilson was successful; both Congress and world leaders supported Wilson's ideas, which enabled him to play a key role in peace negotiations.

Document-Based Question

1 question

60 minutes

Reading Time: 15 minutes (brainstorm your thoughts and organize your response)

Writing Time: 45 minutes

Directions: The document-based question is based on the seven accompanying documents. The documents are for instructional purposes only. Some of the documents have been edited for the purpose of this practice exercise. Write your response on lined paper and include the following:

- **Thesis.** Present a thesis that supports a historically defensible claim, establishes a line of reasoning, and responds to all parts of the question. The thesis must consist of one or more sentences located in one place—either the introduction or the conclusion.

- **Contextualization.** Situate the argument by explaining the broader historical events, developments, or processes that occurred before, during, or after the time frame of the question.

- **Evidence from the documents.** Support your argument by using the content of six of the documents to develop and support a cohesive argument that responds to the question.

- **Evidence beyond the documents.** Support your argument by explaining at least one additional piece of specific historical evidence not found in the documents. (Note: The example must be different from the evidence used to earn the point for contextualization.)

- **Analysis.** Use at least three documents that are relevant to the question to explain the documents' point of view, purpose, historical situation, and/or audience.

- **Historical reasoning.** Use historical reasoning to show complex relationships among the documents, the topic question, and the thesis argument. Use evidence to corroborate, qualify, or modify the argument.

Based on the documents that follow, answer the question below.

Question 1: Evaluate the extent to which the Great Depression impacted Americans.

Document 1

Source: Herbert Hoover, "Statement on Public vs. Private Financing of Relief Efforts," February 3, 1931. Hoover's philosophy of limited government "handouts" made it clear that the government would not provide direct aid during the economic crisis of the Great Depression.

This is not an issue as to whether people shall go hungry or cold in the United States. It is solely a question of the best method by which hunger and cold shall be prevented. It is a question as to whether the American people on one hand will maintain the spirit of charity and mutual self-help through voluntary giving and the responsibility of local government as distinguished on the other hand from appropriations out of the Federal Treasury for such purposes. My own conviction is strongly that if we break down this sense of responsibility of individual generosity to individual and mutual self-help in the country in times of national difficulty and if we start appropriations of this character we have not only impaired something infinitely valuable in the life of the American people but have struck at the roots of self-government. Once this has happened it is not the cost of a few score millions, but we are faced with the abyss of reliance in future upon government charity in some form or other. The money involved is indeed the least of the costs to American ideals and American institutions.

Document 2

Source: Franklin D. Roosevelt, "Inaugural Address," March 4, 1933. Roosevelt's first inaugural address sought to ease the nation's fears about the stagnant economy by reassuring people that he would implement economic reform programs and people would be "put to work."

Our greatest primary task is to put people to work... Hand in hand with this we must frankly recognize the overbalance of population in our industrial centers and, by engaging on a national scale in a redistribution, endeavor to provide a better use of the land for those best fitted for the land. The task can be helped by definite efforts to raise the values of agricultural products and with this the power to purchase the output of our cities. It can be helped by preventing realistically the tragedy of the growing loss through foreclosure of our small homes and our farms. It can be helped by insistence that the Federal, State, and local governments act forthwith on the demand that their cost be drastically reduced. It can be helped by the unifying of relief activities which today are often scattered, uneconomical, and unequal. It can be helped by national planning for and supervision of all forms of transportation and of communications and other utilities which have a definitely public character. There are many ways in which it can be helped, but it can never be helped merely by talking about it. We must act and act quickly.

Document 3

Source: Governor Huey Long, "Speech on Public Radio," April 1935. Long criticized Roosevelt's New Deal and formed the Share-Our-Wealth Society.

We find not only the people going further into debt, but that the United States is going further into debt... Instead of his promises, the only remedy that Mr. Roosevelt has prescribed is to borrow more money if he can and to go further into debt. The last move was to borrow $5 billion more on which we must pay interest for the balance of our lifetimes, and probably during the lifetime of our children. And with it all, there stalks a slimy specter of want, hunger, destitution, and pestilence, all because of the fact that in the land of too much and of too much to wear, our president has failed in his promise to have these necessities of life distributed into the hands of the people who have need of them.

Document 4

Source: Harris and Ewing, "Bonus Army Camp," 1932. The photograph depicts the aftermath of destruction following President Herbert Hoover's forced evacuation orders.

Document 5

Source: Anonymous, "Letter to Franklin Roosevelt from an African American Man," October 19, 1935.

Dear Mr. President

Would you please direct the people in charge of the releaf work in Georgia to issue the provisions + other supplies to our suffering colored people. I am sorry to worrie you with this Mr. President but hard as it is to believe the releaf officials here are using up most everything that you send for them self + their friends. They give out the releaf supplies here on Wednesday of this week and give us black folks, each one, nothing but a few cans of pickle meet and to white folks they give blankets, bolts of cloth and things like that. I dont want to take to mutch of your time Mr president but will give you just one example of how the releaf is work down here the witto Nancy Hendrics own lands, stock holder in the Bank in this town and she is being supplied with Blankets cloth and gets a supply of cans goods regular this is only one case but I could tell you many.

Please help us Mr. President because we cant help our self and we know you is the president and a good Christian man we is praying for you. Yours truly cant sign my name Mr President they will beat me up and run me away from here and this is my home.

Document 6

Source: Caroline Henderson, "Letter to a friend in Maryland," June 30, 1935. Letter from an Oklahoma farmer's wife.

Contrary to many published reports, a good many people had left this country either temporarily or permanently before any rains came. And they were not merely 'drifters,' as is frequently alleged. In May a friend in the southwestern county of Kansas voluntarily sent me a list of the people who had already left their immediate neighborhood or were packed up and ready to go. The list included 109 persons in 26 families, substantial people, most of whom had been in that locality over ten years, and some as long as forty years. In these families there had been two deaths from dust pneumonia. Others in the neighborhood were ill at that time. Fewer actual residents have left our neighborhood, but on a sixty mile trip yesterday to procure tract repairs we saw many pitiful reminder of broken hopes and apparently wasted effort. Little abandoned homes where people had drilled deep wells for the precious water, had set trees and vines built reservoirs, and fenced in gardens—with everything now walled in half buried by banks of drifted soil, told a painful story of loss and disappointment.

Document 7

> **Source: Father Charles Coughlin, "Sermon," 1937. Coughlin was a political leader and supporter of Roosevelt's New Deal.**
>
> All we who twenty years ago entered a war to fight its battles to make the world safe for democracy, tonight we stand aghast because its last fortification, its last tower of strength, the Supreme Court of America, who has been a protector of the rights of the poor, who has been the protector of the rights of the rich, who has been the protector of the liberties of all, is now assailed and is now the target for those who blame it for our misdemeanors and who blame it for the Depression and the following misery which eventuated from it.
>
> Somebody must be blamed, of course. But those in power always forget to blame themselves. They always forget to read the Constitution of the United States of America that says, "Congress has the power to issue and regulate the value of money." And blinding their eyes to that as they protect the private issuance of money and the private fixation of money, we are going merrily on our way.

Answer Explanations

Multiple-Choice Questions

1. **D.** Theodore Roosevelt's foreign policy via the Roosevelt Corollary was associated with the ability to intervene in foreign affairs if U.S. interests were threatened: Speak softly and carry a big stick, choice D. Roosevelt added this assertive approach to the Monroe Doctrine, which strengthened U.S. power in the Western Hemisphere. Since Roosevelt is actually pictured with a "big stick" carried across his shoulder, this approach is directly referenced—he is not depicted as bullying or manipulating other countries (choices B and C), nor does the image suggest any sort of bending or superior will (choice A).

2. **B.** The Roosevelt Corollary was focused on direct, aggressive intervention in foreign affairs. Taft, Roosevelt's successor, was more likely to focus on indirect guidance through foreign investment and loans, hence the name "dollar diplomacy." These policies are accurately described in choice B: The Roosevelt Corollary focused on the use of military force and negotiation, while dollar diplomacy focused on coercion through foreign investment.

3. **B.** President Roosevelt's Corollary was renounced by FDR's attempts to gain power in the Western Hemisphere by becoming a "good neighbor" to other nations in the region, choice B. While the Good Neighbor Policy directly references the federal government's approach to Latin America (like the Roosevelt Corollary), the First New Deal (choice A) deals with domestic concerns and the Second World War (choice C) occurred in Europe. Dollar diplomacy (choice D) is incorrect because it is a foreign policy of the Taft administration, not the Roosevelt administration.

4. **B.** Wilson's speech is associated with his Fourteen Points proposal, which sought "peace without victory," choice B. Although Wilson mentions the seas, he is not directly speaking about the U.S. Navy, but global concerns; therefore, choice A is incorrect. Wilson is also discussing terms of peace, rather than withdrawal, eliminating choice C. Since the war is not over yet (see the date of the speech), he cannot be discussing the Treaty of Versailles (choice D).

5. **B.** African Americans placed their hopes in Wilson's rhetoric, but were sadly disappointed by the actions of his administration, which did not support or advocate for civil rights, choice B. Ultimately, African American support for World War I contributed to black pride in the 1920s and more aggressive movements for fair treatment. Wilson's approach to foreign policy was not imperialistic (choice A), nor would African Americans have expected him to mention army segregation (choice C). At this time, Wilson also presented his views, rather than a collective vision sponsored by many nations (choice D).

6. **B.** Choice A (Wilson was not successful; the leaders of Britain and France were more interested in punishing Germany than in developing a significant plan for world peace) is a true statement, but it is not the best answer among the choices listed. Although Wilson's proposal with Fourteen Points was rejected by world leaders in peace negotiations, European leaders did organize a plan for peace, the League of Nations, choice B (even though it was a weak organization). The U.S. Congress, however, did not accept the League of Nations or the Treaty of Versailles, eliminating choices C and D.

Document-Based Question

DBQ Scoring Guide

To achieve the maximum score of 7, your response must address the scoring criteria components in the table that follows.

Scoring Criteria for a Good Essay	
Question 1: Evaluate the extent to which the Great Depression impacted Americans.	
Scoring Criteria	**Examples**
A. THESIS/CLAIM	
(1 point) Presents a historically defensible thesis that establishes a line of reasoning. (Note: The thesis must make a claim that responds to *all* parts of the question and must *not* just restate the question. The thesis must consist of *at least* one sentence, either in the introduction or the conclusion.)	The essay provides coherency throughout the thesis argument by uniting various points in a clear thesis statement. The thesis argument evaluates various reactions to the hardship produced by the Great Depression. To receive the highest possible score, it is important to delineate the different groups, and the degree to which they were impacted. The sample essay focuses on a range of historical people, including politicians, their opponents, average Americans, minorities, and other national figures.
B. CONTEXTUALIZATION	
(1 point) Explains the broader historical context of events, developments, or processes that occurred before, during, or after the time frame of the question. (Note: Must be more than a phrase or reference.)	The essay provides a strong contextual understanding of the events during the time frame of the topic question and the documents are all contextualized using facts about events during the time period. The essay starts by discussing the broad context of the stock market crash of 1929 and its immediate aftermath. It then outlines various responses to the economic crisis that followed. Support is given through the contextualization and evaluation of the original documents, which directly reference evidence.

Continued

Scoring Criteria	Examples
C. EVIDENCE	
Evidence from the Documents **(2 points)** Uses at least *six* documents to support the argument in response to the prompt. OR **(1 point)** Uses the content of at least *three* documents to address the topic prompt. (Note: Examples must describe, rather than simply quote, the content of the documents.)	To receive the highest possible points, the response addresses all seven of the documents and relates the documents back to the thesis. The writer uses all seven documents to compare and contrast the perspectives of American leaders, their opponents, and citizens. Documents 1, 2, and 3 provide perspectives from political leaders and their opponents, Document 4 provides a perspective from a select group (in this case Bonus Marchers) and Documents 5, 6, and 7 provide perspectives from average American citizens whose lives were dramatically changed by the economic depression.
Evidence Beyond the Documents **(1 point)** Uses at least one additional piece of specific historical evidence beyond those found in the documents relevant to the argument. (Note: Evidence must be different from the evidence used in contextualization.)	The essay provides ample evidence from related events surrounding the Great Depression. For example, Document 2 shows that Roosevelt's main solution to the Great Depression was to "put people to work," but Roosevelt needed programs to employ people. The essay goes further by providing examples to aid in setting up these programs (i.e., the Federal Emergency Relief Administration, hydroelectricity program, Securities and Exchange Commission, Federal Deposit Insurance Corporation, etc.).
D. ANALYSIS AND REASONING	
(1 point) Uses at least *three* documents to explain how each document's point of view, purpose, historical situation, and/or audience is relevant to the argument. (Note: References must explain how or why, rather than simply identifying.)	Most of the documents are analyzed using purpose and the writer applies this purpose to other facts related to the Great Depression. All seven of the documents utilize some element of analysis. Most use purpose and application. For example, the body paragraphs provide specific examples of outside events that influenced the speakers in the documents (i.e., Huey Long in Document 3 was critical of Roosevelt's program and started a "Share Our Wealth" program). The essay specifically discusses how political developments and attitudes affected average Americans and how aid was ultimately distributed.
(1 point) Uses historical reasoning and development that focuses on the question while using evidence to corroborate, qualify, or modify the argument. (Examples: Explain what is similar and different; explain the cause and effect; explain multiple causes; explain connections within and across periods of time; corroborate multiple perspectives across themes; or consider alternative views.)	The essay provides a coherent and well-organized argument and uses the historical reasoning of causation throughout the response. The essay is developed by following a chronological path that includes clear topic sentences, which are created to describe various policies and the level of their effectiveness or ineffectiveness. The essay argues that although the New Deal did not end the Great Depression, it was the most significant response to the economic crisis. The essay ends by moving into a different time period, but keeps the era relevant to the thesis statement. The suggestion is that although the Great Depression did not end until World War II, the New Deal was significant because it created the infrastructure necessary to nurture post-war growth.

Sample Response

When the U.S. stock market crashed in 1929, the nation was thrown into a Great Depression that devastated many American families. As the industrial infrastructure collapsed, many people lost their jobs, possessions, and homes. Unable to feed their children and with little faith in the financial system, U.S. citizens rushed to withdraw savings from local banks, which contributed to their failure and added to the devastation. Responses to this economic crisis varied. Veterans protested (Document 4), labor unions formed, and Americans clamored to fight unemployment or demand assistance. Unfortunately, politicians found it difficult to find appropriate responses to their needs. Aid was often ineffective, sporadically distributed, or heavily criticized. Although the most successful programs were part of Franklin Roosevelt's New Deal, even they did not end the Depression.

The Republican government that was in power when the Great Depression began initially rejected federally funded aid. Republicans viewed programs that provided direct relief as "handouts" that would damage individualistic traditions and democracy. Herbert Hoover, president when the economic crash occurred, believed an economic balance would soon follow through the recovery of private enterprise. Hoover advised people to "tighten their belts," appealed to large companies to retain their workers, and asked local and state charities to meet the needs of the destitute (Document 1). Because he failed to understand the level of hunger and devastation the American people were suffering, however, Hoover's statements about "mutual self-help" and national character rang hollow. He incurred further unpopularity through his mistreatment of Bonus Marchers (Document 4), unemployed World War I veterans who traveled to Washington to appeal for the early payment of federally promised military compensation. Hoover not only refused to help them, but he also ordered the U.S. Army to remove them from public property. The attacks on and burning of the former soldiers' camps horrified many and made him highly unpopular.

In 1932, Hoover was easily defeated by Franklin Roosevelt in the presidential election. The optimistic FDR promised a "New Deal" for the country, which would allow individuals to regain both their sustenance and their pride. Roosevelt began enacting his inaugural promises almost immediately. He not only granted a bank holiday to allow the banks to recover, but he also enacted programs that "put people to work" through the Civilian Conservation Corps (CCC)—which required young men working on forestry and agricultural projects to send money home (Document 2). Roosevelt appealed to Congress for acts that would grant direct aid through the Federal Emergency Relief Administration (FERA), pay farmers to leave land fallow (AAA) to fight agricultural overproduction, and design a federal project that would bring hydroelectricity to rural areas that had never had it before (TVA). During FDR's first administration, the Securities and Exchange Commission (SEC) and Federal Deposit Insurance Corporation (FDIC) were also established to ensure that the financial system was regulated properly, and federally sponsored government works projects through the WPA furthered employment. During his second administration, old-age pensions were established through the Social Security Act and his reputation as "champion of labor" was reaffirmed through the Wagner Act, which guaranteed the right of the unions that were sprouting up all over the U.S. to organize and strike.

The New Deal was not without its critics. Many Republicans and southern Democrats in Congress criticized FDR, stating he had too much executive power. Like Huey Long, the Louisiana senator who developed an alternative "Share Our Wealth" program, they chastised him for driving the country further into debt through billions of dollars of federal aid (Document 3). Long suggested the redistribution of wealth, an impossible task he claimed could be accomplished through a taxation of the rich, which would "guarantee" the employment and housing of all Americans. In 1937, after the NRA (legislation related to set pricing and limited business competition) and the AAA had been declared unconstitutional, Roosevelt claimed the Supreme Court was antiquated and needed to be reinvigorated with younger justices. This opened him up to "court packing" accusations like those evident in the speech of

Father Charles Coughlin, a Michigan priest who blamed Congress, wealthy Jewish bankers, and greed for the Depression (Document 7). New Deal benefits were also seen as faulty because they were unevenly distributed. Since local and state agencies controlled who received benefits, African Americans and other minorities were often turned away when they appealed for aid. Eleanor Roosevelt and liberal New Deal activists attempted to rectify the problem, but their assistance could only penetrate so far. Poor white and black sharecroppers suffered tremendously because many landlords did not pass AAA benefits to their tenants but instead hoarded large government checks and relief supplies for themselves (Documents 5 and 6).

Even with all its inadequacies, the New Deal *did* help average Americans to regain a sense of accomplishment through the limited economic recovery it provided. The Great Depression did not end until the government poured enormous amounts of money into private industries through subsidies and federal contracts, but the Roosevelt administration in the 1930s changed the expectations of common citizens and shifted the political allegiances of many people who received direct aid. The New Deal can also be considered the most significant response to the Depression because it set up the national infrastructure necessary for the extensive post-war growth that greatly benefited the lives of future generations of Americans.

Chapter 11

Period Eight: The Post-War Era and the Cold War (1945 to 1980)

Period Eight explores the post-war culture, Civil Rights Movement, political scandals, and conflicts in the Cold War, Korean War, and Vietnam War.

- The Cold War (1947 to 1991)
- The Korean War (1950 to 1953)
- The Vietnam War (1955 to 1975)
- The U.S. and Cuba
- U.S. Domestic Policy
- The Atomic Age
- The Civil Rights Era (1950s to 1960s)
- The Rise of the Christian Right
- Domestic Political Discontent (1970s)

Overview of AP U.S. History Period Eight

After World War II, the United States was a global superpower, having advanced in politics, military power, science, and technology. In 1945, British Prime Minister Winston Churchill said, "America at this moment in history stands at the summit of the world."

Chapter 11 covers the economic growth of the United States in the 1950s, the African American struggle for equal opportunities and rights, and various cultural and military conflicts associated with the Cold War. The countercultural movement of the 1960s, including the role of Beat poets and non-conformists, is discussed, as well as the political scandals, international conflicts, and domestic challenges that caused many Americans to lose faith in the federal government in the 1970s. To help you organize and remember the material, a detailed review explains important events, individuals, concepts, and historical trends.

Use the chart below to guide you through what is covered on the exam. The curriculum contained in this chart is an abridged version of the concept outlines with topic examples. Visit https://apstudent.collegeboard. org/apcourse/ap-united-states-history/ for the complete updated APUSH course curriculum descriptions and key concepts.

AP U.S. History Key Concepts (1945 to 1980)	
Key Concept	**Specific Content**
KEY CONCEPT 8.1: THE COLD WAR **The United States responded to an uncertain and unstable post-war world by asserting and working to maintain a position of global leadership, with far-reaching domestic and international consequences.**	United States policymakers engaged in a *cold war* (a nonviolent, constant state of political hostility) with the authoritarian Soviet Union, seeking to limit the growth of Communist military power and ideological influence, create a free-market global economy, and build an international security system. Cold War policies led to public debates over the power of the federal government and acceptable means for pursuing international and domestic goals, while protecting civil liberties.
KEY CONCEPT 8.2: CIVIL RIGHTS AND LIBERALISM **New movements for civil rights and liberal efforts to expand the role of government generated a range of political and cultural responses.**	Seeking to fulfill Reconstruction-Era promises, civil rights activists and political leaders achieved some legal and political successes in ending segregation, although progress toward racial equality was slow. Responding to social conditions and the African American Civil Rights Movement, a variety of movements emerged that focused on issues of identity, social justice, and the environment. Liberalism influenced post-war politics and court decisions, but it came under increasing attack from the left as well as from a resurgent conservative movement.
KEY CONCEPT 8.3: POST–WORLD WAR II TRANSFORMATION **Post-war economic and demographic changes had far-reaching consequences for American society, politics, and culture.**	Rapid economic and social changes in American society fostered a sense of optimism in the post-war years. New demographic and social developments, along with anxieties over the Cold War, changed U.S. culture and led to significant political and moral debates that sharply divided the nation.

Significant Themes

Now that we've discussed the curriculum, let's discuss the significant themes related to this period. The theme-related study questions that follow will help you make mental connections to the context of the "big picture" of this time period. Keep in mind that these questions often overlap and apply to other themes of social, political, religious, geographic, ideological, technological, and economic developments.

Glance through the study questions before you start the review section. Take notes, highlight questions, and write down page number references to reinforce your learning. Refer to this list until you feel comfortable with your knowledge of the material.

Study Questions Related to Significant Themes for Period Eight

Theme 1: American and National Identity

1. How did the definitions of freedom and national inclusion change during this period? (Hint: Analyze how these concepts expanded during this time period, not only for African Americans, but also for other ethnic minorities, like Latinos and Native Americans. Explore how feminists and gay activists were also inspired by the Civil Rights Movement and discuss how conservative white Americans sought to expand their own rights and privileges. Be aware that this question overlaps somewhat with the following question, which expands its concepts.)

2. List the events that inspired debates about Americans' civil, social, and political rights during this time. What are the characteristics of certain individuals' claims in these debates? (Hint: While an answer to this question might explore African American claims to increased civil and social rights, which include desegregation and an end to public and private discrimination, it should also focus on white claims for the restoration of "law and order" through Nixon's Silent Majority, Sunbelt conservatives' objection to federally ordered busing in the North based on "colorless" arguments that focused on individual merit, and the Religious Right's political activism in the name of its own agenda, which included countering claims for civil rights by feminists, ethnic minorities, and the gay community.)

Theme 2: Politics and Power

1. How did the Cold War affect domestic politics? (Hint: Concentrate on the role of Joseph McCarthy and the actions of the House Un-American Activities Committee or HUAC, which destroyed the lives of suspected Communists through false or exaggerated reports of suspected activities. Also note Eisenhower's Highway Act and the Soviet use of African American civil rights conflicts, which drew negative attention to the "non-democratic" practices of the U.S. government. The latter drew support for civil rights legislation in the Truman and Kennedy administrations in particular.)

2. America had a long history of segregation and inequality—why were changes enacted after WWII? What influenced these changes? (Hint: Be sure to list specific events that sparked changes in civil rights legislation. For example, note the work of the National Association for the Advancement of Colored People in challenging legal precedents like *Plessy v. Ferguson* and demonstrations for the implementation of *Brown v. Board of Education* and *Morgan v. Virginia* through the actions of the Little Rock Nine, James Hood and Vivian Malone, and the Freedom Riders. Be sure to also note the Montgomery Bus Boycott, the sit-ins that began in North Carolina, voting registration work in Mississippi, and the Birmingham Campaign of 1963.)

3. Who were the Religious Right and why were they important? (Hint: Explore the political response of conservative evangelicals like Jerry Falwell and Pat Robertson to the countercultural movement. Be sure to mention their political demands—which included anti-liberal policies, their connection to New Right conservatives in the Sunbelt, the role of migration, and the Moral Majority and Christian Coalition's influence on the Republican Party.)

4. Compare and contrast Richard Nixon with Jimmy Carter. How did each man come to power? What were their primary objectives, policies, constituencies, presidential challenges, etc.? Why did each man decline in power and what effect did that have on American society and politics? (Hint: Concentrate on Nixon's appeal to conservatives who were dissatisfied with liberal policies like LBJ's Great Society, which seemed to offer "handouts" to the poor. Discuss the Watergate scandal and the way it led to Carter's victory over Nixon's successor, Gerald Ford. Also note both men's foreign policy successes, especially those associated with *détente* (the easing of hostility between countries), including Nixon's visit to China, Carter's Camp David Accords, and both men's participation in the SALT agreements.)

5. What was the major oil crisis that occurred in the 1970s? How did it originate? How did it affect the American economy, people's individual lives, and national energy policies? (Hint: Discuss how U.S. support for Israel led to the OPEC embargo and the resulting energy crisis, noting the length of gas lines, Carter's appeal to the American people to reduce their consumption, and concern for the security of oil-producing allies, like Afghanistan, in the future.)

Theme 3: Work, Exchange, and Technology

1. What were some of the key characteristics of the post-war economic "boom"? (Hint: Consider the increase in production, government intervention in the economy through the continuation of industrial subsidies, population increases, and the avocation of consumer spending through television, radio, and magazine advertisements, as well as the rise in middle-class "real wages.")

2. How did technological advances affect industrial and military expectations after World War II and during the Cold War? (Hint: Examine the development of the Sunbelt in terms of government funding for factories, arms facilities, and industrial complexes that focused on technology. Be sure to also connect this to the growth of atomic testing, nuclear power, and post-war booms in production and space travel due to the government's belief that the U.S. had to "compete" with the Soviets in order to prove its industrial, technological, and military might.)

Theme 4: Culture and Society

1. Compare and contrast the way various people reacted to the Civil Rights Movement. (Hint: Be sure to consider political as well as social and cultural movements. Investigate the impact of both black and white Americans' support of the nonviolent resistance techniques of Martin Luther King Jr.'s Southern Christian Leadership Conference, the Student Nonviolent Coordinating Committee, and the Congress of Racial Equality, as well as how the movement changed in the late 1960s. Be sure to note the impact of important figures like Malcolm X, Robert Williams, and Stokely Carmichael and the promotion of black nationalism and self-defense by groups like the Black Panthers. Also note the role of white Americans in the South like George Wallace and Orval Faubus, who participated in segregationist political schemes that had to be addressed by the federal government, particularly focusing on events linked to Faubus' objection to the Little Rock Nine and Wallace's "stand at the schoolhouse door." Note Sunbelt conservatives' merit-based politics that were used to justify objections to federally ordered busing throughout the country.)

2. What were the features of post-war culture? How did the post-war culture, the economic boom, and the Atomic Age characterize American lives in the 1950s? (Hint: Note the guilt, fear, and final embrace of the Atomic Age, which permeated popular culture and promoted conformity through consumerism, specific gender roles, traditional values, and nuclear families. Discuss the creation of the affluent society through the economic boom and the benefits for white families provided by the GI Bill, which included higher education and access to home ownership for veterans, as well as white flight from the cities and the development of suburbia. Be aware that the benefits of the 1950s post-war economic boom were not equally distributed—discriminatory practices limited housing and employment for black families and veterans.)

3. Who challenged post-war values? What were the features of the countercultural movement they created? (Hint: Explore the initial role of Beat writers and poets like Allen Ginsberg and Jack Kerouac in the rejection of post-war suburban culture, conformity, and materialism. Examine how their ideas can be connected to a movement in the 1960s, made up of people who supported gender equality, alternative lifestyles, and the experimentation of art, music, sexuality, and drugs.)

Theme 5: Migration and Settlement

1. What caused the Sunbelt to grow and how did it affect U.S. political and social development? (Hint: Concentrate on demographic shifts as the result of both black and white Americans in search of jobs during and just after World War II, which continued through the 1970s. Also note the production boom stimulated by government subsidies and technology. Be sure to explore how these shifts affected

suburbanization, conservative political shifts (especially for white Americans during the late 1960s and 1970s), and busing controversies. Important concepts to include are reactions to the Great Society and civil rights legislation as well as the Silent Majority and the rise of the New Right.)

2. How did attitudes toward immigration shift during this period? Why did a transformation occur? (Hint: Link this to the Immigration and Nationality Act that ended quotas established in the 1920s and drew a large number of Latino and Asian immigrants—both legal and illegal—into the country. Be sure to mention increased labor activism, including that of Cesar Chavez in the 1970s, as well as the objection to illegal immigrants that has continued into the 21st century.)

Theme 7: America in the World

1. What kinds of relations did the U.S. have with smaller countries after World War II? What was its relationship with its former allies and new nations? (Hint: Discuss Stalin's desire for security and his falling out with Harry S. Truman, FDR's successor. Analyze the role of containment, especially in relation to American beliefs about the domino effect theory and what came to be known as the Iron Curtain. Other important things to examine include the use of the Truman Doctrine and the Marshall Plan to support our allies and the formation of the North Atlantic Treaty Organization and the Warsaw Pact. To extend this argument, consider how the U.S. became involved in the Korean and Vietnam wars, especially in relation to fears about the "loss" of China and the support of France in Indochina.)

2. How did the U.S. aid war-torn countries that were attempting to recover after World War II? What was its motivation for doing this? (Hint: This question connects to some aspects of the previous one, but the answer should specifically focus on America's dedication to economically aiding European governments that rejected Communism and advocated democratic principles, even though they might not necessarily be democracies. Be sure you understand that this principle is extended throughout the 20th century to Asia and Latin America, which is explored both in this chapter and in Chapter 12.)

3. Compare and contrast the Korean and the Vietnam wars. How did each start? What were their key events and outcomes? How did average Americans respond to them? How did they influence Cold War foreign and domestic policies? (Hint: A chart might be useful to help you organize this information. For example, consider the role of containment in each war; examine how Japanese, Soviet, and French occupation complicated issues of nationalism in Korea and Vietnam; and discuss the separation of Korea and Vietnam into northern and southern territories with different governments, one advocating Communism and the other focusing on democratic principles. Be aware, however, that while neither South Korea nor South Vietnam had democratic governments, their leaders were not Communists, so they were supported by the U.S. government and military. Make sure you explore the role of China and the United Nations in the Korean conflict and the domestic and political crises created by Vietnam, while noting that neither conflict ended with a clear victory for the U.S. military.)

4. Describe post-war events in Latin American during this period and note their effect on international relations and U.S. foreign policy. (Hint: Focus on events in Cuba that are associated with Castro, the Cuban Revolution, and the Bay of Pigs invasion. Note how these led to the Cuban Missile Crisis, which sparked events that almost brought the U.S. into a nuclear war with the Soviets. Discuss the role of the Kennedy administration in both the creation and resolution of the missile crisis, noting the placement of ballistic missiles in Italy and Turkey and the diplomatic agreement reached with Soviet leader Nikita Khrushchev. While the Cold War did not cool during Johnson's administration, the crisis itself could be traced to less aggressive diplomatic discussions related to nuclear warheads and the promotion of détente and arms agreements under the Nixon and Carter administrations.)

Important Events, Terms, and Concepts

The list below shows important events, terms, and concepts that you should be familiar with on the APUSH exam. These and other important terms are printed in boldface throughout the chapter. Because the APUSH exam requires you to pay attention to the historical context and connections rather than details, don't bother memorizing the terms now. Simply place a check mark next to each as you study. You can return to this list to review as often as necessary. After you finish the review section, you can reinforce what you have learned by working through the practice questions at the end of this chapter. Answer explanations provide further clarification into perspectives of U.S. history.

Event/Term/Concept	Year/Brief Description	Study Page
Kennan's "Long Telegram"	1946. A telegram from George Kennan (a U.S. ambassador in Moscow) to Harry Truman that indicated the Soviets were bent on global expansion and the U.S. was the only country that could stop them.	pp. 318–319
Truman Doctrine	1947. Truman's foreign policy of anti-Communist containment that was implemented through economic aid and a defense of the principles of democracy. The American policy funded anti-Communist groups in Greece and Turkey.	p. 319
Marshall Plan	1948–1952. Formally known as the European Recovery Program, the Marshall Plan financially assisted democratic European countries after World War II. The purpose of the plan was to increase trade in the West and prevent the expansion of Communism in Europe.	p. 319
Korean War	1950–1953. A Cold War military conflict between the Soviets in North Korea and UN forces in South Korea that resulted in a resolution that left the opposing parties in relatively the same place they started.	pp. 321, 323
Brown v. Board of Education of Topeka	1954. A Supreme Court case that overturned *Plessy v. Ferguson*, which ordered the desegregation of schools.	p. 322
Gulf of Tonkin Resolution	1964. A Congressional act that gave the president the power to attack a nation that posed a military threat, like Vietnam.	p. 322
Vietnam War	1955–1975. A Cold War military conflict between the North Vietnamese Army (NVA), led by nationalist and Communist Ho Chi Minh, and South Vietnamese forces (the Army of the Republic of Vietnam or ARV). The United States military supported and advised the South Vietnamese. After Americans withdrew from the conflict, the NVA invaded South Vietnam, imprisoning and killing those who had cooperated with the U.S. and uniting the country under Communism.	pp. 321–323
Martin Luther King Jr. (1929–1968)	Leader of the Civil Rights Movement. Inspired by Gandhi, King was active in civil rights from 1955 to 1968. He was known for promoting nonviolent forms of civil rights protests and received the Nobel Peace Prize in 1964 for fighting racial inequality through nonviolence. King was assassinated in 1968.	p. 331
Civil Rights Act	1964. Following the increasing numbers of civil rights protests, President John F. Kennedy introduced legislations that would afford individuals of all races, religions, and nationalities equal rights. After Kennedy's assassination, President Lyndon Johnson called upon Congress to pass the Civil Rights Act of 1964.	p. 334
Great Society	1964–1965. The domestic policy of President Lyndon Johnson that sought to declare a "War on Poverty" and eliminate racial discrimination.	p. 337
Watergate scandal	1973. A political scandal that forced Richard Nixon to resign rather than face impeachment.	p. 340

Event/Term/Concept	Year/Brief Description	Study Page
Silent Majority	A coalition of white political supporters of states' rights and small government that influenced the election of Richard Nixon and contributed to the death of liberal policies.	p. 337
Détente	**1972–1980.** *Détente* means "the easing of hostility [between countries]". The name was given to the foreign policy principle that encouraged improved relations during the Cold War between the U.S. and the Soviet Union.	p. 317
Camp David Accords	**1978.** The 1978 meeting of leaders Egyptian President Anwar Sadat, Israeli Prime Minister Menachem Begin, and U.S. President Jimmy Carter. They agreed that Egypt would never again invade Israel if Israel turned over the Sinai Peninsula to Egypt.	p. 341
Iran Hostage Crisis	**1979–1981.** An international crisis in which 52 Americans were held in Iran for 444 days. It contributed to the unpopularity of Jimmy Carter and the election of Ronald Reagan in 1980.	p. 341

Chapter Review

After World War II, dormant political energies were present around the world. The U.S. attempted to contain the Soviet Union and its Communist ideology by building up military power and encouraging other nations to support a free-market economy, but American ideology ostracized both individuals and nations who held dissenting social or political opinions. The resulting Cold War with the Soviet Union included antagonistic military confrontations, especially in Korea, Vietnam, and some Latin American, Asian, and African countries. The Cold War challenged non-conformists and inspired some Americans to question the power of a McCarthyism federal government and its actions, which appeared inappropriate. Domestically, Americans led a civil rights movement to battle discrimination, sparking other equal rights movements: LGBT (lesbian, gay, bisexual, transgender), environmental, feminist, Latino, and Native American.

HISTORIOGRAPHY. *As you read this chapter, keep in mind that scholars view history on a collective continuum—history is rarely evaluated by specific defined eras or periods. Time period categories are identified in order to explain and discuss historical trends and developments. The events, theories, debates, influences, motivations, and reactions often overlap and expand within time periods. When studying the topics in this chapter, it is important to recognize that the U.S. had a long history of nurturing fears associated with what many Americans considered subversive uprisings. Long before the "red scare" of McCarthyism, the Civil Rights Movement, or the busing protests of the 1970s, any form of resistance to oppression was seen as a threat to the delicate balance of the nation's moral, social, and political foundations.*

The Cold War (1947 to 1991)

The Cold War was between two world superpowers—the United States and the Soviet Union—and their major differences in ideologies and economics. After World War II, the shaky alliance between U.S. President Harry S. Truman and Soviet Premier Joseph Stalin disintegrated, primarily because Truman had a different vision of the post-war world than Stalin. Disagreements began to affect the development of global relations, resulting in a cold war that was characterized by military aggression, weapons development, unstable international relations, and intense competition. Tensions mounted into the Cold War when the unprecedented prospect of a nuclear war between these two superpowers was evident. These tensions continued until 1972 when a period of *détente* (an easing of strained relations) improved the U.S. and Soviet relations.

Heads Up: What You Need to Know

The key events about the Cold War to remember for the APUSH exam are as follows: U.S. post-war containment (Kennan's "Long Telegram," the domino effect, the Truman Doctrine, the Marshall Plan); the Berlin Blockade and the Airlift Crisis; the Warsaw Pact; the Iron Curtain; and China's fall to Communism.

Post–Word War II Key Events

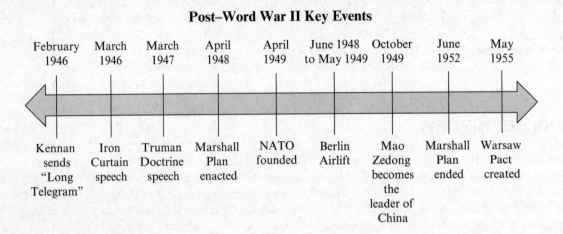

February 1946	March 1946	March 1947	April 1948	April 1949	June 1948 to May 1949	October 1949	June 1952	May 1955
Kennan sends "Long Telegram"	Iron Curtain speech	Truman Doctrine speech	Marshall Plan enacted	NATO founded	Berlin Airlift	Mao Zedong becomes the leader of China	Marshall Plan ended	Warsaw Pact created

U.S. Containment

Russia had experienced devastation during World War II, and Stalin wanted a victory settlement that would guarantee secure borders for Russia. Before U.S. President Franklin Roosevelt died, he promised Russia a specific region in Eastern Europe. After the war, however, Stalin sought territorial expansion in other regions to promote and spread Communism, which he considered an ideal form of government and the basis of his own power and stability.

Fearing the spread of Communism, Truman embraced an active foreign policy, which rejected Communism and promoted democratic forms of government. This was a shift away from the presidents of former eras who advocated for U.S. isolationism after major military conflicts. Truman adopted the strategy of **containment** (the idea that Communism could not be allowed to spread to other nations). Containment was intended to limit the Soviets' post-war power and Communist influence in Europe. The U.S. implemented containment through economics and the threat of the atomic bomb, which the Soviets didn't successfully develop until 1949.

The divide between the U.S. and Soviet worldviews was envisioned as an **Iron Curtain.** The Iron Curtain was described by Britain's Winston Churchill as a boundary that symbolically separated Europe into two competing ideologies: Western democracy and Eastern Soviet totalitarian Communism.

Key Facts about U.S. Containment

Kennan's "Long Telegram." The idea of containment was developed by American diplomat George Kennan, who had lived in Russia during the 1930s and 1940s. Kennan argued in his "Long Telegram" to Truman that Stalin was not looking to take over the world like Hitler, but Stalin was dangerous because he wanted to spread Communism in strategic areas to protect Russian nationalism. Kennan suggested that the United States surround Russia with military bases in Western Europe. Kennan argued that the United States should use propaganda, secret services, and the military to remove the threat of potential Soviet Union Communist allies in the developing world.

Domino effect theory. Containment was heavily motivated by a political theory known as the **domino effect.** Western leaders believed that if one country fell to Communism, its neighbors would all soon follow. The metaphor suggested that the Communists wanted to overtake one country at a time—and each country would topple like a stack of dominoes tipping over.

Truman Doctrine (1947). The fear at the time was that the Soviets were secretly coordinating with Communist groups to interfere in the political and economic conflicts in Greece and Turkey. In a speech that supported a policy known as the **Truman Doctrine,** President Truman asked Americans to monetarily aid Greece and Turkey in order to help free people resist subjugation by "armed minorities" or "outside pressures." The Truman Doctrine was a U.S. plan that called for Congress to fund anti-Communist groups in Greece and Turkey. Although the U.S. didn't militarily intervene, $400 million was provided to support the two nations' economies and militaries.

Marshall Plan (1948). After World War II, the United States offered economic aid to war-torn countries in Western Europe through the European Recovery Program (better known as the **Marshall Plan,** named after Secretary of State George C. Marshall, who promoted the plan). The economic assistance plan helped to rebuild the infrastructure and stimulate European economies from the devastation of World War II. The main strategy of the Marshall Plan was to develop a marketplace for industry and global trade. One of the goals of the United States was to prevent what happened at the Treaty of Versailles after World War I. If European nations were stable, then they might be less likely to turn to Fascism and Communism. The Soviet Union was offered this assistance but rejected the help because the offer came with conditions that required democratic governments and capitalist trade. Because Eastern European countries did not qualify to share the $12.4 billion that Britain, France, West Germany, and other democratic nations received from the U.S. from 1948 to1952, the Soviet Union created a similar plan known as the Molotov Plan.

Heads Up: What You Need to Know

In the aftermath of World War II, the United States and the Soviet Union superpowers continued to compete for allies in the developing world—democracy versus Communism. On the APUSH exam, you should be aware that many of the underlying political, social, and economic world conflicts from the 1950s through the 1990s were prompted by democratic or Communist ideological beliefs. The United States and its Western allies feared that Communism would take over the world via the domino effect theory. China fell to Communism in 1949, and several other countries also fell to Communist rule. Today, only five countries remain Communist states: China, North Korea, Cuba, Laos, and Vietnam.

Key Events Leading to the Cold War

Several events in 1948 and 1949 sparked increased tensions in the post-war period. The most important are listed below.

Berlin Blockade and Airlift Crisis (1948–1949). Immediately after Germany's defeat in World War II, Germany was divided into four Allied-occupation zones. Eastern Germany went to the Soviet Union, while Western Germany went to the United States, Great Britain, and France, with Berlin as the capital city. The city of Berlin was also split into sectors: East Berlin was occupied by the Soviet Union, and West Berlin was occupied by the United States, Great Britain, and France.

As tensions developed, Stalin began to distrust the United States and its post-war actions in Europe. He refused to allow supplies to pass through the Russian section of Berlin. Water, food, goods, and railroads were blocked. The U.S. and its allies (Britain, Canada, and Australia) responded by using airplanes to deliver food, fuel, and supplies into West Berlin for a year. Stalin had no more leverage, and near the end of 1949 he gave in, having gained nothing but turning Germans against Soviet rule. When Stalin finally lifted the supply blockade, ill feelings remained between the Russian dictator and the United States.

NATO (1949). The United States led the effort to form **NATO (North Atlantic Treaty Organization).** This was a group of northern European and North American countries that promised to respond to any Soviet aggression into Western Europe. Ten Western nations joined NATO, and Russia viewed its formation as an offensive act.

Warsaw Pact (1955). Russia responded to NATO by forming its own version of the international alliance, known as the **Warsaw Pact.** The Warsaw Pact was an Eastern European military defense pact between Communist nations to defend against the threat of Western democratic invasions. These nations connected with common ideological backgrounds to provide them with political and military assistance if their security was threatened. The Soviet Union was the leader. The pact unified the Soviet Union with many other Eastern European nations: Poland, East Germany, Czechoslovakia, Hungary, Romania, Albania, and Bulgaria. In the 1990s, the Warsaw Pact officially disbanded after several countries had withdrawn from all military interventions.

> **TEST TIP:** On the APUSH exam, using organizations like NATO as an example in your DBQ response can help show historical connections over time. Although NATO was organized in 1949, it continues today as an intergovernmental military and political organization to safeguard and resolve international conflicts. NATO was originally organized by the United States and other democratic nations as a response to Communist threats.

China falls to Communism (1949). The Communist Party of China (later called the People's Republic of China) was established in 1949 after the Chinese Civil War (1945–1949). Mao Zedong was the leader of the Communist revolution that forced the collapse of China's nationalist government. The Soviets tested their first successful nuclear bomb in 1949, and North Korea invaded South Korea in 1950. This led to the United States coalition of the United Nations landing in South Korea to push the North Koreans back past the 38th parallel. By the early 1950s, the Americans and Western Europeans believed that Joseph Stalin and his ally Mao Zedong were setting up a line of dominoes in Southeast Asia. This further convinced the Truman administration that policies of containment were essential in the fight for global democracy.

Most Cold War conflicts were embodied in strained foreign relations, competitive technological and scientific advances, weapons programs, and economic assistance. Unfortunately, supporters of democratic or Communist forms of government also participated in armed conflicts, especially in Third World countries that were attempting to cast off imperialistic rule after World War II.

The Korean War (1950 to 1953)

Key Facts about the Korean War

Korea was liberated from Japan in 1945 just after World War II, but the country was divided by differing political ideologies. This division eventually caused the Korean War, which pitted the United States against the Soviet Union.

Korea divided into North Korea and South Korea. Korea had been ruled by Japan since 1910, but after Japan surrendered in World War II, Korea became available for new leadership. The country was divided into southern (occupied by the United States during the Second World War) and northern (occupied by the Soviet Union) territories. North Korea (Democratic People's Republic of Korea) began advocating Communism, and South Korea (Republic of Korea) began advocating democracy. Both had separate governments and claimed to be the "real" rulers of Korea.

South Korea invaded (1950). When Communist North Korea invaded democratic South Korea in an effort to impose Communism, this started the first military conflict of the Cold War. Truman saw the invasion as an act of aggression and convinced the United Nations' Security Council to condemn the act (coincidentally this occurred when the Soviets had been boycotting the council).

U.S. supports South Korea. The United Nations stepped in to support South Korea and the U.S. used its policy of containment to block Communism from taking over South Korea (the majority of the UN forces belonged to the U.S.). The United States aided South Korea, and China aided North Korea. The U.S. troops were led by **Douglas MacArthur,** whose aggressive advances caused China to fear for its own safety. Chinese forces entered the war and pushed UN fighters back to the **38th parallel north** (the original border between North Korea and South Korea). The Korean War ended in a stalemate, but eventually a cease fire was reached even though nothing changed. Determining a winner for the war is difficult since participants basically ended up where they started. More than 2.5 million people were killed during the Korean War.

> **TEST TIP:** The APUSH exam may contain a question about the importance of the Korean War in relation to civil rights. The war began in 1950, 2 years after Truman desegregated the U.S. military through Executive Order 9981. In Korea, African American combat troops were integrated into the rest of the Army, and for the first time African American men held elite military positions as aviators, technical specialists, and officers. This does not mean they did not face racial discrimination from other soldiers, but many were accepted by their white counterparts and were able to increase their opportunities by remaining in the Army after the war ended.

The Vietnam War (1955 to 1975)

Although Vietnam had been a French colony since 1880, Japan took control of Vietnam during World War II. In the 1950s, the French returned to occupy Vietnam.

Key Facts about the Vietnam War

North Vietnam falls to Communism (1945). After the war, **Ho Chi Minh** led a movement against the French for independence in North Vietnam, called the Democratic Republic of Vietnam. Ho Chi Minh was a *nationalist* (an individual who wanted political independence for his nation) and was upset by French rule. He believed Communism offered his people the best solution for their problems. France, however, wished to retain Vietnam as a colony, so an armed conflict began (the **Indochina War**). Ho Chi Minh's soldiers (the **Viet Minh**) lacked modern weaponry and would hide out in forests and engage in *guerrilla warfare* (sudden attacks) on the French Army troops in order to weaken them and steal their weapons. The U.S. helped France fund the war, but in 1954, the French negotiated a treaty with the Viet Minh that divided Vietnam at the **17th parallel north** (the demilitarized zone that established the dividing line between North Vietnam and South Vietnam). The Indochina War (which is sometimes known as the "first" war because a second conflict followed with the U.S.) became one of the longest and most costly battles against colonization that occurred in the 20th century.

The U.S. enters the Vietnam War (1955). The United States' first involvement in Vietnam began in 1955 when military advisors were sent to Vietnam. Initially, Ho Chi Minh appealed to President Truman for assistance, believing the U.S. would support a revolutionary movement of independence. Because Ho Chi Minh was a Communist, however, Truman offered assistance to France (a European ally) instead of the Viet Minh. This upset the North Vietnamese and sparked a dedicated fight to unify the entire nation of Vietnam under a Communist regime that was modeled after the Soviet Union or China. The French agreed to leave Vietnam, which gave the Vietnamese the ability to reunite the country through a national election, but the United States feared Vietnam would fall to Communism.

Under President Kennedy's administration in the 1960s, over 3,200 U.S. military troops were sent to Vietnam. The U.S. established an ally in South Vietnam and decided to support its regime, which at that time was led by Ngo Dinh Diem, who was corrupt and not well liked by the Vietnamese.

Gulf of Tonkin (1964). Diem was assassinated in a South Vietnamese military coup in 1963, but the U.S. continued to support a number of ineffective South Vietnamese presidents and tensions in the country still ran high. A big change in U.S. foreign policy in relation to Vietnam occurred when Lyndon Johnson became president of the United States. In 1964, Johnson claimed that the North Vietnamese attacked two U.S. battleships in the **Gulf of Tonkin.** Johnson asked Congress for an escalation of combat troops; after this declaration, the number of American troops in Vietnam rose to 500,000 soldiers. Note: In 2005 and 2006, when many government documents were declassified, the American public learned that the Johnson administration was operating under faulty conclusions during this time period and may have even falsified information that led to support for this action and the unlimited power Johnson was given to conduct the Vietnam War as a result.

The U.S. involvement in Vietnam escalates (1965–1969). Johnson's goal was not necessarily to go to war with North Vietnam, but to send U.S. military advisors into the region to prevent the spread of Communism. Johnson later sent American troops to bolster South Vietnam's military defenses against the North Vietnamese Army (whom U.S. soldiers disparagingly called the *Viet Cong*).

The U.S. drafts soldiers. Most of the American soldiers who fought in Vietnam were working-class men who were either *drafted* (forced military service) or enlisted to avoid the draft. Soldiers were motivated to join the armed forces for a variety of reasons, including patriotism, educational opportunities, and military benefits. As the war escalated and U.S. soldiers were increasingly deployed, soldiers and their families began to resent the numerous ways middle- and upper-class men found to "dodge" the draft, which included receiving medical exemptions from family doctors and enrolling in college. As a result of this and their war experiences, when soldiers returned from military service, many of these Vietnam veterans participated in anti-war protests.

The U.S. struggles with warfare disadvantages. The U.S. found itself in an unprecedented dilemma between the North Vietnamese and South Vietnamese. American troops were militarily limited because, just like the French, the U.S. had difficulty conducting a serious ground assault in a jungle war against the Viet Cong. In small villages, U.S. soldiers found it nearly impossible to determine who the enemy was and often directed their frustration at people who later turned out to be innocent. At other times, they trusted individuals who turned out to be aiding the North Vietnamese. In the meantime, the Soviet Union and China supplied the NVA with ammunition, supplies, and political advice, and casualties continued to grow.

The U.S. anti-war movement at home. The war, and all of its brutality, was televised, and the counterculture of the 1960s produced heavy protests in the U.S. Although protests appeared sporadically and were often conducted by several different organizations that did not communicate with each other, the **anti-war movement** compelled Johnson to limit the escalation of the war and caused him not to seek another presidential term in 1968. Anti-war protests also pressured President Richard Nixon to end the war.

Compare and Contrast the Korean War and Vietnam War

The following table shows the similarities and differences between the wars in Korea and Vietnam.

Korean War	Both Wars	Vietnam War
First conflict to extend containment policies to Asia.	The U.S. did not formally declare war on either country.	Women in the Army served in traditional ways as nurses and support staff. Attitudes and roles were beginning to change toward women.
First time the U.S. Army was desegregated.	Both Korea and Vietnam had long histories of imperialism.	
Most Americans supported the war.	U.S. containment policies influenced the U.S. involvement in both countries.	Many people didn't support the Vietnam War—even war veterans protested the U.S. involvement when they returned home.
	No clear U.S. victory was achieved in either country.	The war negatively affected foreign policy during the Cold War and beyond. Leaders remembered the nightmare of Vietnam.
	Both presidents (Truman and Johnson) were determined to fight because they feared criticism. (Truman was criticized when China fell to Communism.)	

The U.S. and Cuba

In the late 1950s, the Cuban government was led by the military dictatorship of **Fulgencio Batista.** During his two terms in office (1933–1944 and 1952–1959), Batista established his power through patronage (the granting of political positions and favoritism to those who support a particular leader) and built up support with the Cuban military, elite landowners, and foreign investors (especially U.S. industrialists who were attracted to Cuba's prosperous sugar plantations). Batista used his power to benefit himself and his associates. He enriched himself through a corrupt government, created massive poverty, and controlled the media, the legislature, and the education system. Although Batista was clearly an oppressive dictator, he was against Communism. Therefore, an economic relationship with Cuba benefitted U.S. citizens, and the United States wanted to continue diplomatic relations with Cuba under his regime.

Multiple revolutionary groups in Cuba, however, sought to end Batista's control of the country, including Cuban nationalist **Fidel Castro,** who orchestrated a revolutionary movement through guerrilla warfare in 1958. When Castro became the new dictator of Cuba, Cubans welcomed the change of regimes because he improved education and healthcare. However, like Batista, Castro soon began to brutally persecute and imprison anyone who opposed his regime. This caused thousands of Cubans to flee from Cuba to the U.S.

Although he denied being Communist, Castro resented foreign control of Cuba's economy and began to trade with the Soviet Union while rejecting U.S. economic support. Castro turned to Soviet leader **Nikita Khrushchev** for military and economic support. Although Communist organizations had existed in Cuba since 1902, they were weak institutions. Castro's interaction with the Soviet Union inspired him to transform his ruling party (the United Party of the Cuban Socialist Revolution or the PURSC) into the Communist Party of Cuba in 1965. Because of existing U.S./Soviet Union Cold War tensions, and Cuba's close proximity to the United States, the U.S. then developed a strained relationship with Cuba.

> TEST TIP: On the APUSH exam, you may be asked why Cuba was so important to the United States. The answer is geography. The island of Cuba is less than 100 miles from the United States. Not only was the U.S. interested in agricultural exports and trade with Cuba, but the U.S. was threatened that a foreign power might seize Cuba and maximize control just a short distance from the U.S. The U.S. was comfortable with Cuban sovereignty as long as it did not collaborate with a powerful foreign nation—like the Soviet Union—which could use its ports to attack the U.S.

Key Facts about the U.S. and Cuba

Bay of Pigs Invasion (1961). U.S. President Dwight D. Eisenhower coordinated a plan with the CIA to secretly overthrow the Castro regime. The covert operation was called Operation Mongoose. The plan included an invasion at the **Bay of Pigs** in Cuba by an American-sponsored paramilitary group. When Eisenhower's term came to an end, he handed off the plan to his successor, President John F. Kennedy. The soldiers landed at the Bay of Pigs with the intention of overthrowing Fidel Castro. However, the invasion failed. The U.S. provided less air support than Kennedy had promised to the Cuban soldiers on the ground because Castro's military forces found out about the plan and organized a successful counter-offensive. The U.S. continued to support forces that objected to Castro's government.

Cuban Missile Crisis (October 1962). In response to the attempted invasion at the Bay of Pigs, Castro allowed Soviet leader Nikita Khrushchev to place nuclear ballistic missiles in Cuba to stop any future attacks from the United States. Although the **Cuban Missile Crisis** almost brought the U.S. into a nuclear war, President Kennedy saw Khrushchev's actions as a threat to the balance of power in the Western Hemisphere and believed it was important to publically object to a Soviet-Cuban alliance.

The Soviets' continued involvement in Cuba was only one of the reasons for the 13-day standoff between Kennedy and Khrushchev. America's aggressive pursuit of a nuclear arsenal had enabled the U.S. to produce and deploy many more destructive weapons than the Soviet Union (even though the Kennedy administration claimed otherwise). When the U.S. placed ballistic missiles in Italy and Turkey, which made them capable of reaching Moscow and Leningrad, Khrushchev looked favorably on Castro's request for missiles in Cuba. The placement of missiles in Cuba allowed the Soviets to threaten the U.S. in the same way that they were threatened.

Cuban Missile Crisis

Source: Map of the Western Hemisphere showing the full range of the nuclear missiles from Cuba to the U.S.

Kennedy's public announcement about the crisis. This sobering Cold War occurrence became so intense that Kennedy was forced to notify the American public—and the Soviet Union—in a televised speech. Kennedy had to announce to the public that his administration knew of the placement of Soviet missiles in Cuba and that he would impose a *quarantine* (blockade) on Cuba until the nuclear ballistic missiles were removed.

The aftermath of the crisis. The crisis was eventually solved with diplomacy that led to an agreement that the U.S. would never again invade Cuba if the Soviet Union dismantled all nuclear ballistic missiles in Cuba. Kennedy stated he would stop intervening in Cuban affairs and authorized the removal of U.S. missiles in Turkey. The incident caused each side to think carefully before commencing such a dangerous confrontation in the future. Believing that the Soviet Union was capitulating to U.S. pressure, Castro was enraged by the agreement. American allies in Europe were also angered by the event because they were not notified of the tensions that led to the crisis until after it had occurred.

HISTORIOGRAPHY. *If the APUSH exam calls for you to write about the Cuban Missile Crisis, be sure you understand the historiographical context of the situation. Although the Kennedy administration has been traditionally praised for its avoidance of nuclear war, many historians now criticize Kennedy for overreacting to* *a situation that the U.S. had largely created. It is important to understand that the Soviets had been living with the threat of nuclear weaponry in neighboring countries for years. U.S. thermonuclear warheads were installed in Britain and aimed at the Soviet Union as early as 1959, and blockades were considered acts of war. Therefore, both Castro's requests and Khrushchev's actions were neither as unreasonable nor as internationally "illegal" as Kennedy claimed.*

U.S. Domestic Policy

The post-war boom of the late 1940s and 1950s created a thriving economy and population. However, the Cold War pervaded U.S. culture and inspired domestic policies that both prepared for a devastating nuclear conflict and represented America as the defender of global freedom and democracy. Since Communism and Socialism were viewed as evil forms of government that sought to repress the people they ruled, anyone who dissented from traditional American values or political opinions was considered a threat to American society. Many innocent Americans were financially and socially ruined as a result of the U.S. government's persecution.

McCarthyism (1947 to 1956)

Although concerns about Communism had existed in the U.S. since the Russian Bolshevik Revolution (1917), the Cold War intensified government efforts to rid the country of perceived Communist threats.

Key Facts about McCarthyism

House Un-American Committee (1938). In the late 1940s, people who held government positions were subjected to loyalty tests. The House Un-American Committee (HUAC), which was established to investigate private citizens suspected of Communist subversive activities, intensified its efforts after World War II. The committee directed its efforts toward those who criticized America, its politics, or had been members of the Communist Party in the past.

The rise of McCarthyism. An anti-Communist climate created fear of disloyalty in America and contributed to the rise of "Red Scare" politicians, like Senator Joseph McCarthy from Wisconsin. In 1950, Senator McCarthy declared that he had a list of more than 200 State Department employees who were members of the Communist Party. Senator McCarthy began accusing people mercilessly and was initially given the political authority to blame people for subversive activities. An investigation was launched, but no proof of any Communist activity was found. However, over 2,000 government employees lost their jobs as a result of these investigations.

Senator McCarthy's downfall came in 1954 when he aggressively attacked members of the armed services. The investigative hearings (called the **Army-McCarthy Hearings**) were broadcast on national television. As McCarthy intimidated witnesses, the hearings revealed to the public that Senator McCarthy was nothing more than a powerful bully. Army lawyer Joseph Welch responded to McCarthy by saying, "Have you no sense of decency, sir?" By the time the hearings concluded, two-thirds of the Senate voted to censure Senator McCarthy, saying that his acts were "reprehensible and unbecoming of a U.S. senator." Senator McCarthy died just a couple of years later, in 1957.

Did you know? Both the HUAC and McCarthy accused American citizens of disloyalty by passing secret documents to the Soviets. **Julius and Ethel Rosenberg** were convicted of conspiracy to commit espionage with little evidence, through the words of a single informer. The Rosenbergs were executed for treason in 1953. In the 1950s, African Americans and the Hollywood film industry were specifically targeted for Communist wrongdoings because many activists, writers, and artists had supported Socialism during the 1920s and 1930s, when Communism seemed to bolster their hope for a better, more equal society. A Hollywood "blacklist" of "Communist sympathizers" was instituted, which barred actors, musicians, writers, and directors from filmmaking.

The Atomic Age

The dropping of atomic bombs on Japan during World War II created guilt, fear, and apprehension in the lives of many Americans during the post-war period. Although Americans initially celebrated the achievement, many atomic scientists soon began to feel remorse when they saw the massive destruction in Japan. Some theologians, public figures, and intellectuals recommended international control of atomic energy. Writers often promoted a vision of an earthly paradise based on this control or suggested morality and behavior would be negatively altered by what they called the **Atomic Age.**

The Atomic Age and the Cold War contributed to several cultural and economic developments.

Key Facts about the Cultural and Economic Developments of the Atomic Age

Atomic energy. When U.S. fears became evident, politicians reassured the public that atomic energy had positive effects and destructive weapons were necessary for national security. This became especially important in 1952 after the successful test of a *hydrogen bomb* (a bomb with atomic energy), which was even more powerful than the atomic bombs used in WWII. Americans soon grew complacent and accepted a new age, which had a distinct place for dangerous forms of energy and weapons.

Source: Civil Defense Nuclear Fallout Poster, "Radioactive Fallout," 1955. The propaganda poster from a Civil Defense training class to "take cover" from radioactive fallout during the Atomic Age. It was an age for foreboding and fear.

Shifts in popular culture. As public fears of atomic bombs decreased, the Atomic Age and Cold War began to impact popular culture. Subliminal messages of super patriotism, ultimate power, intolerance, anti-Communism, militarism, and suspicion were embedded in many Hollywood films, TV programs, comic books, and toys. The cultural influence was visible to the general public as late as the 1980s (e.g., Tom Clancy novels and films like *Rambo* and *The Manhattan Project*).

The nuclear family. Images of a "nuclear" family, which consisted of a homemaking wife and a wage-earning father with two to three children and a family pet, were also embedded in American culture. This **culture of**

conformity encouraged Americans to fulfill their civic duty through familial responsibilities. Women who had worked during WWII quit their jobs to make room for returning veterans. Voices of dissent or protest were considered "un-American," so few people spoke out on behalf of the rights of common laborers or African Americans in the late 1940s and early 1950s.

The baby boom. When families were being reunited after the war, the birth rate soared. A record number of babies—about 77 million—were born from 1946 to 1963, causing this period to be known as the **baby boom,** and those born during this period, "baby boomers."

The affluent society. The government subsidizing of private industries continued, and the Marshall Plan opened new international markets, which caused the U.S. economy to flourish. Benefits for veterans, including educational opportunities, low-interest loans, and unemployment programs, were provided through the Servicemen's Readjustment Act of 1944 (better known as the **GI Bill**). As a result, the poverty level dropped 8 percent in 1950, and by 1960, 60 percent of Americans were considered "middle class." Because Americans enjoyed new cars, new homes, and other consumer goods, the 1950s were sometimes labelled as having an "affluent society."

The Beat Generation. Not all Americans in the post-war era felt fulfilled through traditional values and consumerism. In the mid-1950s, a group of artists and intellectuals began expressing frustration and anger at society's attempt to force self-control and conformity on those who sought a different lifestyle. In 1955, Allen Ginsberg's poem "Howl" became a quintessential example of non-conformity. Part of the **Beat Generation,** Ginsberg and writers like Jack Kerouac and Norman Mailer became popular with a group of young adults who became disparagingly known as "beatniks" or "hipsters." The work of the beatniks broke the rules of traditional literature and conveyed the sentiments of those who rebelled against the ideals and moral codes stressed by their parents, organized society, and the government (which saw conformity as a way to combat totalitarianism). Many scholars believed that their work influenced alternative lifestyles that had a direct influence on the development of the **Counterculture Movement** of the late 1960s (p. 339).

Federal-Aid Highway Act (1956). Federal legislation was created to allocate $25 billion of defense funds for a public works project that would construct over 40,000 miles of interstate highways. The **Federal-Aid Highway Act** (also known as the National Interstate Defense Highway Act) was signed into law by President and former World War II General Dwight D. Eisenhower. Ninety percent of the highways were funded by the federal government, which generated income by taxing gasoline. The highways were built to connect U.S. Air Force bases to ensure the easy transportation and rapid mobilization of U.S. troops if the nation entered into another war.

Americans moved to suburbs. The Highway Act made travel cheap and accessible, and the baby boom caused the geographic and population composition of the country to change. New roads allowed young families to easily travel from home in the suburbs to work in the cities. Suburbs rose on the outskirts of cities and people began to migrate as they became dissatisfied with their urban lifestyles. Unfortunately, because of discriminatory housing policies, suburban living reinforced racial divisions and poverty in inner cities.

Heads Up: What You Need to Know

On the APUSH exam, make sure that you are familiar with the significant effects that the Highway Act had on the U.S. economy. It directly contributed to the financial boom of the 1950s for the following reasons:

- It led to an increase in federal construction employment and the production of important supplies like gravel, tar, and asphalt.

- It eased travel, which created a desire for new automobiles and produced a "car culture" that stimulated the manufacturing of cars, tires, and oil. Auto repair shops and gas stations sprouted up across the nation, employing mechanics and attendants who served the public in a new way.

- It sparked an interstate trucking industry. The transportation of goods became easier, and the new trucking industry was able to distribute goods much quicker. Delivery times were reduced, agriculture was less likely to spoil, and consumers paid less for goods and services.

- It inspired roadside businesses for food, entertainment, and lodging. Hotels were built along the highways (a practice that continues today) and both local restaurants and fast-food chains, like McDonald's, rose in popularity.

- It inspired tourism, as families traveled along highways for vacations and outings, which made short trips less expensive for middle- and working-class Americans.

The Civil Rights Era (1950s to 1960s)

The fight against racial discrimination was not new in the 1950s and 1960s. Political activism began just after Reconstruction and continued through the Progressive Era. During World War II, African Americans began to speak out against the discrepancy between the democracy that the U.S. government said it was fighting for and the oppression of black American citizens in the military and on the home front. Activists like A. Philip Randolph embarked on a **Double V Campaign** that would ensure victory at home and abroad. African Americans moved to northern cities after the war to pursue work in industrial factories. This added to a powerful northern black voting base that increased during the first wave of the Great Migration and caused many politicians—including Truman, Kennedy, and Johnson—to include civil rights platforms in their election campaigns.

HISTORIOGRAPHY. *Historians rarely reduce the Civil Rights Movement to a single historical event. The Civil Rights Movement identifies events of the 1950s and 1960s as the culmination of the lengthy period of African American resistance described above, but the struggle against racism and segregation started in early America.*

TEST TIP: On the APUSH exam, be sure to use examples of literature, art, and music as evidence to support mid-20th-century cultural shifts. For example, in the 1950s and 1960s, American culture was represented in American literature. Ralph Ellison famously wrote "The Invisible Man" in 1952—an American short story that addressed the social and ideological issues that faced 20th-century black Americans. Ellison's novel depicts a young African American man whose skin color renders him with an invisible identity. Harper Lee wrote a Pulitzer Prize–winning novel, *To Kill a Mockingbird,* in 1960 that was loosely based on Lee's observations of racial inequality in the South. Although the book has been taught in American public schools for decades to help students learn about prejudices, local and state oppositions have called for the removal of the book in the classroom curriculum, even today in the 21st century.

The Civil Rights Movement

Black Americans used several tactics to combat segregation and disfranchisement in the United States. The **NAACP** (pp. 331, 333) and the **Congress of Racial Equality** (CORE) had been fighting for African American rights for several years. Both organizations continued to play a pivotal role in the Civil Rights Movement, but new institutions of resistance were also established in the 1950s and 1960s.

Civil Rights Organizations	
Organization	**Description**
Southern Christian Leadership Conference (SCLC) (1957)	The SCLC was founded by Martin Luther King Jr. after the Montgomery Bus Boycott in 1957. The organization used nonviolent protests, religious and interracial networks, and the media as tools to promote change.
Student Nonviolent Coordinating Committee (SNCC) (1960)	In 1960, Bob Moses and Ella Baker founded SNCC (pronounced "snick") to assist black and white youths who were staging sit-ins, freedom rides, and other forms of nonviolent protests. SNCC played an essential role in grassroots voter registration drives, which were often challenged by white community leaders.
The Council of Federated Organizations (COFO) (1961)	In the summer of 1961, the NAACP, SCLC, CORE, and SNCC joined forces to form the COFO, an interracial movement designed to coordinate local networks in order to promote voter rights, register black voters, and distribute funds. The organization played a key role in the fight for African American political rights in Mississippi.
Black Panthers (1966)	Originating in California, the Black Panthers was a militant organization. The group of black Americans, mostly men, believed in armed self-defense against white violence, especially acts of aggression that were perpetrated by the police. The Black Panthers upheld ideals of black nationalists like Malcolm X and Robert F. Williams, who called for a separation from white culture, African American economic freedom, and black unity and pride.

Heads Up: What You Need to Know

For the APUSH exam, it is important to understand the changes in the black resistance movement after 1965. Frustrated by white resistance to desegregation, as well as the continuation of systemic poverty and discrimination, many nonviolent activists turned to more aggressive forms of protest. A good example is the shift in the goals of the Student Nonviolent Coordinating Committee (SNCC). After the passage of the **Voting Rights Act** in 1965 (prohibiting racial discrimination in voting), the organization became more militant, influenced by leaders like **Stokely Carmichael,** who felt that although some progress had been made, discrimination in housing and employment still prevented African Americans from enjoying the privileges of full citizenship. Carmichael had once participated in nonviolent protests, but eventually joined the Black Panthers, promoted black nationalism, and changed the once interracial SNCC to an "all-black" organization.

Leaders of the Civil Rights Movement

During the 1960s, several leaders played important roles in the Civil Rights Movement. **Martin Luther King Jr.,** a Baptist minister, is probably the most well-known civil rights activist. King was an effective civil rights leader with strong oratory skills. In August 28, 1963, King delivered his famous "I Have a Dream" speech at the March on Washington. He was honored with the Nobel Peace Prize in 1964 for his dedication to nonviolent protests.

A. Philip Randolph was an activist for civil rights and the labor movement. He organized the Brotherhood of Sleeping Car Porters labor union for the Pullman Company, was one of the original organizers of the March on Washington, and was heavily involved in the Double V Campaign during World War II.

John Lewis, a civil rights leader who was disappointed with the Kennedy administration and often called for more militant action, was asked by Randolph to cut parts of his own speech during the March on Washington because his message was considered too aggressive for the movement being led by King at that time. Lewis continued in King's organization and was even savagely beaten on "Bloody Sunday," but he was also angered by the censorship of his opinions. Lewis was president of the Student Nonviolent Coordinating Committee and today is a U.S. Congressman in Atlanta, Georgia.

Roy Wilkins was the director of the National Association for the Advancement of Colored People (NAACP) and worked with both Randolph and King. He participated in the March on Washington in 1963 and the Selma to Montgomery march in 1965.

> **TEST TIP:** The APUSH exam may require you to write about the complex relationships between various civil rights organizations and their leaders. It's not important to memorize each of the leaders, but it is important to remember that there were several key leaders of the Civil Rights Movement. King was the most famous, and when he was assassinated in 1968, his death severely wounded the movement. However, King was not the only leader of civil rights, and the movement continued after his death.
>
> Although King was praised for calling attention to the pending Civil Rights Bill and called for fair employment, wages, and hiring practices, his "I Have a Dream" speech was criticized by other civil rights leaders for not being radical enough. Other divisions of the movement, like those of the Student Nonviolent Coordinating Committee, sympathized with more radical forms of human rights strategies.

Civil Rights U.S. Supreme Court Cases

The NAACP, which had been fighting African American oppression in the American judicial system since 1910, continued to challenge oppressive laws in the courts.

Important Civil Rights Supreme Court Cases	
School Desegregation Cases	
Mendez v. Westminster (1946)	The ruling was that forced segregation of Mexican students from public schools in California was deemed unconstitutional because Mexican students are considered "white."
	Governor Earl Warren (later the Chief Justice of the Supreme Court that would decide *Brown v. Board of Education*) was inspired to sign a law in California that repealed all segregationist school provisions in the state.
McLaurin v. Oklahoma State Regents (1950)	The ruling reversed a lower court decision upholding the "separate but equal" status at the University of Oklahoma when a black graduate student attempted to receive his Doctorate in Education. The Court's decision held that the isolation of an African American student made the student's education "unequal" in the eyes of the law.
Brown v. Board of Education of Topeka (1954)	This is an important case to memorize for the APUSH exam; it established that it was unconstitutional to have separate public schools for black and white students. This landmark case completely overturned *Plessy v. Ferguson*, which established "separate but equal" schools for black students, determining that segregation had an extremely negative effect on African American students' self-esteem.
Brown II (1955)	The ruling was that the desegregation of schools must be carried out with "deliberate speed," which supported *Brown v. Board of Education*'s order for segregation but continued to be vague about a timeline. The phrase "with deliberate speed" was open to interpretation and gave white southerners a loophole for resistance, suggesting they didn't need to move to desegregate immediately. This case made court-ordered desegregation, the kind supported by *Brown v. Board of Education*, difficult to enforce.
Public Travel and Transportation Cases	
Morgan v. Virginia (1946)	The ruling made segregation on commercial interstate buses illegal. The case was instigated by Irene Morgan, a black woman who refused to give up her seat to a white person when she was traveling on a Greyhound bus from Virginia to Maryland in 1945. This action was similar to **Rosa Parks'** actions in Montgomery 10 years later, which prompted the **Montgomery Bus Boycott,** a black community action led by **Martin Luther King Jr.** and others who challenged the public segregation of city buses.
Browder v. Gayle (1956)	As a result of the **Montgomery Bus Boycott,** this ruling decided that segregation on buses was unconstitutional.
Boynton v. Virginia (1960)	Extended *Morgan v. Virginia* by outlawing racially segregated interstate bus terminals.
	These three cases inspired the **Freedom Riders,** an interracial group of students who traveled from Washington, D.C., to Mississippi in 1961 on two buses, stopping at public terminals along the way. Sponsored by SNCC and CORE, they met resistance in Alabama—one of the buses was firebombed in Anniston, students were beaten in Birmingham, and students experienced mob violence in Montgomery. President Kennedy provided students with a federal escort (the National Guard) so that they could complete their journey.

Civil Rights Desegregation in Schools

White resistance to school desegregation was prevalent in the South, where superintendents often chose to close schools completely rather than submit to federal orders to integrate classrooms.

Key Facts about Desegregation in Schools

The University of Alabama (1956). When an African American woman, **Autherine Lucy,** was admitted to the University of Alabama, riots broke out on campus and she was suspended. In 1963, Alabama governor **George Wallace** vowed to support "segregation now, segregation tomorrow, and segregation forever" in his inaugural address, and any southern politician who did anything less risked reelection. To symbolically uphold his stance, Wallace stood in the doorway of a building at this university to prevent two black students from entering. Wallace was immediately forced to step aside by the National Guard under the executive order of President Kennedy.

The Little Rock Nine (1957). In Little Rock, Arkansas, nine black students—hand-selected by the NAACP for their excellent attendance, grades, and citizenship—were stopped from entering the city's Central High School by white segregationists, who were supported by Arkansas' National Guard (and deployed by Governor Orval Faubus). When President Eisenhower, who did not personally support desegregation or civil rights, saw that the military was being used to disobey a Supreme Court order, he was furious and sent federal troops to Arkansas to escort and protect the black students.

The University of Mississippi (1962). Brutal riots occurred on the campus of the University of Mississippi—with the full consent of Governor Ross Barnett—as a response to the registration of a black student, James Meredith. Two people were shot, and white mobs burned property. Federal Marshals were sent to quell the violence, but they were attacked. Despite enduring extreme harassment and hatred, Meredith graduated in 1963. His actions inspired other black students to enroll in the University of Mississippi.

Source: "A Court-Ordered Integration at Little Rock Central High School," 1957. Insults were shouted to Elizabeth Eckford as she marched away from a line of National Guardsmen who banned her from attending school at Little Rock Central High School.

Civil Rights Desegregation in Public Places

All-white voting primaries, *grandfather clauses* (old rules that continued to apply), poll taxes, and fraud were used to legally disfranchise African American male voters in the late 19th and early 20th centuries. Throughout the 20th century, discrimination and intimidation continued in the South as court cases and legislation that challenged segregation were struck down by biased white politicians, judges, and juries. The 1950s and 1960s, however, provided black Americans with a specific historical context and greater opportunities to publically challenge these injustices.

Key Facts about Civil Rights Desegregation in Public Places

The Birmingham Campaign (1963). The Southern Christian Leadership Conference (SCLC) became involved in local activism efforts to integrate Birmingham, Alabama, which Martin Luther King Jr. identified as the most segregated city in the country. King organized a nonviolent protest march from the 16th Street Baptist Church (a primary African American meeting location) to City Hall. The march turned into a vicious attack on African Americans by the local police. The police used water hoses and dogs to terrorize participants and bystanders, which included women and children.

In September, white supremacists bombed the church, resulting in the deaths of four innocent African American girls. Both the bombing and the televised broadcast of the police violence earlier in the year generated widespread support for the **Civil Rights Act of 1964,** which outlawed discrimination in public accommodations.

Mississippi Freedom Summer (1963). Known as the Mississippi Summer Project, the Council of Federated Organizations (COFO) began recruiting northern and local college students—both black and white—to participate in SNCC and CORE voter registration drives in Mississippi. The work expanded into the summer of 1964, which became known as the "Freedom Summer." The recruiting angered local Ku Klux Klan members and white segregationists, who responded with violence.

In June, two white northerners, Michael Schwerner and Andrew Goodman, and a local African American, James Chaney, were murdered in Mississippi. The deaths contributed to splits in the movement because they caused many volunteers to question the effectiveness of nonviolent actions and interracial cooperation.

National Democratic Convention (1964). The Council of Federated Organizations (COFO) was instrumental in helping **Fannie Lou Hamer,** a grassroots activist, in forming the **Mississippi Freedom Democratic Party,** which challenged the state's all-white delegation at the Democratic National Convention in Atlantic City. Drawing attention to the absence of black voters in party activities, Hamer delivered a powerful televised speech discussing African American poverty and the violence committed against the black community. When Lyndon Johnson attempted to calm her with an offer of an "honorary" presence at the convention, she refused. By the time the party met again in 1968, the national Democrats demanded equal representation in all states.

Selma to Montgomery March (1965). Members of the Student Nonviolent Coordinating Committee (SNCC) and the Southern Christian Leadership Conference (SCLC) organized a voter's rights march in Alabama from Selma to Montgomery, which was supposed to occur on March 7 (the date became known as "Bloody Sunday"). When marchers, led by Martin Luther King Jr., attempted to cross the Edmund Pettus Bridge, they were blocked and attacked by policemen armed with clubs and tear gas.

Although Alabama state officials tried to block a second march, the protestors regrouped and completed the march on March 21 under the protection of National Guard troops. The struggle inspired President Johnson to sign the **Voting Rights Act of 1965,** which prohibited racial or language discrimination in voting and ended literacy tests.

Did you know? The Civil Rights Act of 1964, which outlawed discrimination based on race, color, sex, or national origin, was first called for by President John F. Kennedy in June 1963, about 6 months before Kennedy was assassinated. His vice president and successor, Lyndon Johnson, advocated for the bill in Kennedy's honor. It was enacted by Congress the following June, with a vote of 73–27.

Civil Rights Support and Resistance

White responses to the African American Civil Rights Movement were mixed.

Civil Rights Support

Throughout the '50s and '60s, journalists published and televised politicians' racist statements, mob acts of violence, and the brutal conditions that remained in the Jim Crow southern states. The funeral of **Emmett Till** was even televised in 1955. Till was a 14-year-old African American boy who was lynched for allegedly flirting with a white woman at a grocery store. Till's mother insisted on an open casket, which revealed the damage done to his body when he was beaten, shot, hung, and thrown in a river to drown. Media attention garnered massive support for the Civil Rights Movement among northern politicians, ministers, college students, and white middle-class citizens, who helped through direct participation or votes.

Civil Rights Resistance

HISTORIOGRAPHY. *Segregationist politics had a long history in the U.S. South—it did not originate with objections to* Brown v. Board of Education *by Orval Faubus, George Wallace, and other southern Democrats. Although white supremacists' rhetoric and ideological views can be traced to the Antebellum Era, it is also important to recognize the role of* **States' Rights Democrats** *(or* **Dixiecrats***) in the white response to the Civil Rights Movement. The Dixiecrats used vicious language—based on the states' rights arguments that inspired the Civil War—that foreshadowed the brutal, uncompromising policies and language of those who rejected black voters, students, and human rights in the 1950s and 1960s.*

Split in the Democratic Party. The split in the Democratic Party became significant during the New Deal Era because it threatened the racial hierarchy established by Jim Crow laws in the South. The Democratic split occurred when northern Democratic Party members argued for the funding of African American programs and the protection of black labor rights. Some even worked toward a more equal society through biracial coalitions. After World War II, Democrats like President Truman appealed to black voters through legislation that encouraged fair employment and desegregation, which further angered southern Democrats.

The Dixiecrats. When the Democrats chose Truman as their presidential candidate in 1948, 35 southern delegates walked out of the convention. These Dixiecrats held their own convention, electing South Carolina's **Strom Thurmond** as their candidate. Thurmond lost the election, but several states were dominated by Dixiecrat politicians, including Louisiana, Mississippi, South Carolina, and Alabama. Political splits in the movement caused the Dixiecrats to dissolve into a lobbying organization by 1952, but their influence on southern politics remained significant. For example, Thurmond may not have been elected president, but he continued to serve as South Carolina's U.S. senator from 1954 to 2003.

George Wallace. Throughout the Civil Rights Era, southern politics was dominated by segregationist and white supremacist rhetoric that rejected liberal programs, criticized the government for corruption and irresponsibility, and accused northern politicians of influencing people who chose segregationist values. In 1964 and 1968, George Wallace used segregation and states' rights to gain popularity on a national level. Wallace ran for president, blaming the government for street crimes, urban riots, and ineffective policies. Wallace won 14 percent of the vote, which showed that many Americans agreed with his political point of view.

Heads Up: What You Need to Know

On the APUSH exam, use Governor George Wallace of Alabama as an example of the resistance to civil rights desegregation. Wallace was known for his southern Dixiecrat, pro-segregation politics and was once photographed standing in front of the University of Alabama to prevent black students from attending school. His famous quote, "segregation now, segregation tomorrow, segregation forever," can be used in free-response essays.

While campaigning for the presidential primaries in 1972, Wallace was shot by Arthur Bremer, who was more interested in fame than expressing dissatisfaction with Wallace's politics. Wallace survived the assassination attempt, but was left confined to a wheelchair for the rest of his life.

The Impact of Migration on Civil Rights

The production boom after World War II stimulated demographic shifts in population that had important social consequences. Government subsidies for private industries created jobs in the South and West (known collectively as the **Sunbelt**). Both black and white Americans moved to the Sunbelt states for jobs (for African Americans, this was considered part of the second wave of the Great Migration). The relocation of a large portion of the population had social and political consequences on white resistance to black civil rights.

Heads Up: What You Need to Know

The APUSH exam sometimes has questions that ask you to connect the presidency of Richard Nixon to the rise of the New Right (the conservative coalition made up of Sunbelt industrialists and Dixiecrats—southern Democrats who once supported segregationists and conservative business interests). The New Right's platform blamed liberalism for causing, rather than solving, problems and criticized programs like President Johnson's **Great Society,** which sought to end poverty and inequality through government assistance. In the 1968 election, Nixon labelled neoconservatives the **Silent Majority** and claimed he would fulfill their calls for "law and order," ensure states' rights, and end the chaos caused by the Vietnam War, busing, and African American activism. The support of the New Right helped Nixon become president in both 1968 and 1972.

	Characteristics	Consequences
Suburbanization	As black populations grew in urban centers and the Highway Act made travel easier to and from workplaces, white families relocated to the suburbs, where discriminatory housing practices produced a *de facto segregation* (racial, ethnic, or other segregation) that reinforced discriminatory color lines.	Second- and third-generation white immigrants often found inclusion in suburban neighborhoods, but suburbanization had devastating effects on urban businesses and black families. As chain stores and retail centers moved closer to middle- and upper-class suburban consumers, city centers deteriorated and African Americans, banned from the housing divisions, often became locked in inner-city poverty.
Political shifts	As white populations in the Sunbelt grew and civil rights legislation increased, objections to liberal policies led to shifts in the geopolitical composition of political parties.	People living in the South and West, once die-hard Democrats, began voting for conservative Republicans like Barry Goldwater and Richard Nixon. The trend had long-lasting effects—it contributed to the election of Ronald Reagan and the rise of the New Right. This merit-based ideology of individual rights contributed to the discriminatory busing protests. It also transformed the South into the conservative region it is today.
Busing controversies	Many states refused to integrate school systems, so the Supreme Court ordered states to begin busing procedures that would ensure desegregation in 1971. To protest the ruling of *Swann v. Charlotte-Mecklenburg Board of Education*, several grassroots organizations formed.	Restore Our Alien Rights (ROAR) in Boston and similar organizations in Charleston, Charlotte, and Atlanta objected to federal busing through vicious protests. Black students were often subjected to angry slurs and racial violence, committed by white mobs of both adults and teenagers.

Social Movements

African American demands for social and civil equality inspired several other social movements.

Social Movements (1960s and 1970s)

FEMINISM

Betty Friedan's *The Feminist Mystique* (1963) was a best-selling book that sparked a new stage of feminism throughout the U.S. As the first president of the **National Organization for Women** (NOW), Friedan drew attention to women's issues and supported the **Equal Rights Amendment**, which outlawed gender discrimination.

LATINO WORKERS

In 1962, **Cesar Chavez** co-founded the **United Farm Workers** union in order to protect the rights of Hispanic agricultural workers. The UFW supported and led agricultural strikes and other boycotts throughout California. Chavez's support of nonviolent protest improved the working conditions of many people.

AMERICAN INDIAN MOVEMENT (AIM)

AIM drew attention to the heavy unemployment, educational deficits, and racism faced by Native Americans. AIM criticized federal legislation and called for the reinstatement of tribal land. The organization led to the enactment of several important laws, including the **Indian Civil Rights Act** (1968) and the **Indian Self-Determination and Educational Assistance Act** (1975).

GAY LIBERATION MOVEMENT

The Stonewall Riots (1969), in which LGBT individuals fought back against the police who were trying to harass and arrest them, are often considered the beginning of the **Gay Liberation Movement.** The gay pride movement was made up of local and national organizations that fought for social and legal acceptance of living openly as a lesbian or gay person in the U.S.

STUDENT MOVEMENTS

Student organizations emerged around the country on college campuses to protest for student rights and free speech. One of the most well-known was the **Students for a Democratic Society** (SDS), which criticized the U.S. government through the **Port Huron Statement** and laid out a radical vision for a better future. The SDS blamed ineffective leadership for racial inequality, the Vietnam War, the nuclear arms race, and poverty, while calling for a new system of government.

TEST TIP: The APUSH exam may require knowledge about immigration issues that affected Cesar Chavez's fight for Hispanic workers. In 1965, the Immigration and Naturalization Act ended the quota system of the 1920s and gave immigration priority to individuals with U.S. relatives. Also known as the Hart-Celler Act, the legislation ushered in a period of intense immigration (both legal and illegal), which greatly increased the Latino population in America. At least 25 percent of these new immigrants were Mexicans, looking for employment opportunities, which they often found as migrant farm workers. Chavez's activism was stimulated by their mistreatment. Since illegal immigrants were also often used to break United Farm Workers' strikes, Chavez and other Latino activists were initially opposed to illegal immigrants. Chavez's position changed in the mid-1970s when he came to believe that illegal immigrants were being mistreated by both the growers and the government.

Did you know? In the late 1960s, the demand for equality by numerous groups encouraged the growth of the **Counterculture Movement,** which had been influenced by the Beat Generation's rejection of traditional moral codes and standards of behavior. The movement encouraged a subculture of young people, who held Progressive views of racial and gender equality. Young people wanted to bypass social and cultural lines of authority and experiment with religion, art, music, sexuality, drugs, and communal lifestyles.

The Rise of the Christian Right

Anti-war protests, the countercultural "hippie" lifestyles, feminism, urban riots, and social unrest made many conservative Christians feel that their worldview was being threatened. In the 1970s, church-attending Americans began to develop their own political subculture, which coincided with the development of Sunbelt conservatism and Nixon's Silent Majority. The Religious Right adopted the merit-based, individualistic ideology of the New Right and began to put their faith in the Republican Party.

The rise of the new Christian Right. With Sunbelt migration, evangelical Protestantism spread, especially in white communities. Large churches sprang up in the South and West, and there was a nationwide call for a return to moral values, traditional gender roles, and small government—all part of the platform of the new Christian Right. Believing that a liberal government encouraged immorality, Christian evangelical pastors and televangelists broke their practice of separating religion from politics and began encouraging church congregations to use their voting power to support new Christian Right beliefs.

The rise of religious political organizations. In 1979, Baptist minister Jerry Falwell founded the **Moral Majority,** a political organization that mobilized Christians to further conservative legislation and the politicians whom they supported. The organization led to the formation of other Christian organizations in the 1980s, like Pat Robertson's **Christian Coalition,** which played a key role in the election of Ronald Reagan.

Christian Right politics. The Christian Right supported several anti-liberal policies, including anti-abortion laws and legislation that supported the teaching of creationism and prayer in schools. The Christian Right also supported politicians who denied rights or privileges to minority groups, including African Americans, feminists, and homosexuals.

Domestic Political Discontent (1970s)

During the 1970s, many U.S. citizens were cynical about American politics and government, believing them to be corrupt and ineffective. Americans thought the "glory days" of the United States were lost and complained about politicians and an unpromising future.

Key Events That Led to Political Discontent in the 1970s

Event	Details	Impact
Watergate scandal (1972–1974)	Watergate was a political scandal that caused President Nixon to resign. In 1972, five men were accused of breaking into the **Watergate Complex** in Washington, D.C., which served as the headquarters for the Democratic National Committee. FBI investigations revealed that President Nixon and his administration not only knew about the activities, but attempted to cover up the president's involvement. Because Nixon lied about his involvement, he was forced to resign in 1974 to avoid impeachment.	Nixon's successor, Gerald Ford, pardoned him before charges could be officially issued. Ford had only recently become vice president because Spiro Agnew, Nixon's former vice president, had resigned due to bribery accusations. The scandals caused many Americans to distrust politicians, whom they believed were corrupt and dishonest. Some people stopped voting and others changed their voting parties. In 1974, Americans elected a group of young Democrats, known as the Watergate Babies, to Congressional seats and local and state offices.
President Gerald Ford (1974–1977)	President Ford took office under difficult circumstances. He presided over one of the worst economies in U.S. history and chose to pardon his predecessor, Nixon, which made Ford highly unpopular. Ford's first economic program sought to increase taxes, while his second suggested cutting them, which caused many people to criticize him for "flip-flop" policies that did little to make life better for struggling Americans.	Despite Ford's challenges, he was able to succeed in foreign policy. Ford signed the Helsinki Accords, a global agreement signed by many countries to improve relations between the Soviets and the West, and sent a military expedition to fight the genocidal Khmer Rouge in Cambodia. Regardless, Ford lost the 1976 election to a Democrat, **Jimmy Carter.** Carter was an evangelical from Georgia who promised to improve the country and its government.
Stagflation (1973–1980)	In the 1970s, the post-war boom began to naturally deteriorate and international competition increased. This caused manufacturers to lay off employees and raise prices. High inflation combined with high unemployment created *stagflation* (an economic condition in which inflation is high, unemployment is high, and the economy slows).	Stagflation had devastating effects on the U.S. economy. Stock market prices plunged as a recession hit the country from 1973–1975. At the beginning of 1975, inflation reached 11 percent, unemployment was at 9 percent, and the Gross National Product was at a –2 percent growth rate. Many Americans struggled in the economic decline. Job losses mounted, interest rates increased, and prices increased on basic goods, especially oil.
Oil embargo (1973)	In October 1973, an oil embargo was issued by the **Organization of the Petroleum Exporting Countries** (OPEC) for the U.S. backing of Israel in the Yom Kippur War (Arab-Israeli War in 1973). The price of oil per barrel immediately skyrocketed 400 percent. Although the price of oil later decreased, oil prices remained high throughout the 1970s.	President Carter appeared on national television to encourage people to conserve energy. The oil crisis caused restrictions in the sale of gasoline. Gasoline lines were long, and people could buy gas only on certain days. While the oil crisis did not cause the recession, it did make inflation worse by increasing energy costs. Its repercussions also made U.S. policymakers more aware of global energy sources, which have had a long-term impact on foreign policies.

Event	Details	Impact
Iran Hostage Crisis (1979)	In 1979, Iranian Islamist students stormed the U.S. Embassy in Tehran, taking 52 Americans hostage. The Islamists held revolutionary beliefs and were angry with the U.S. for providing the ousted Shah (Muhammad Reza Pahlavi) with medical assistance in New York after his exile (he was suffering from cancer). The hostages were held for 444 days.	The international crisis contributed to Carter's unpopularity, which was already high because of the economic and energy crises. Although Carter engaged in many diplomatic negotiations to ensure the hostages' release, the hostages were not freed from captivity until January 1981—moments after Reagan was sworn in as president.

Jimmy Carter's Presidency

Jimmy Carter was a religious man who encouraged peace throughout his presidency and attempted to continue principles of *détente* (improved relations between the U.S. and the Soviet Union) begun by his predecessors. President Carter, however, was not afraid to engage the opposition during the Cold War.

Key Facts about Carter's Foreign Policy

China (1979). President Carter continued Nixon's work by engaging in positive relations with China. Nixon had visited Communist China in 1972 and when Carter became president, he invited Deng Xiaoping, the Chinese Vice Premier, to the United States. During Deng Xiaoping's diplomatic visit, the United States agreed to recognize the Government of the People's Republic of China, a Communist institution, as the sole government of China, which it had refused to do prior to Carter's administration.

Nuclear arms treaties. Carter signed the SALT II agreement, an extension of SALT I (an arms control treaty that Nixon signed with Soviet premier Leonid Brezhnev).

The Carter Doctrine (1979). When the Russians invaded Afghanistan in 1979, Carter withdrew the U.S. ambassador from Moscow and asked the Senate to postpone its review of the SALT II agreement. Before Carter left office in 1980, he declared that any attempt by foreign nations to gain power in the Persian Gulf was an "assault on the vital interests" of the United States, which the U.S. would defend with military force. The principle, known as the Carter Doctrine, moved the U.S. away from détente and back toward containment.

Camp David Accords (1979). Although Jimmy Carter was not remembered as a successful president in domestic affairs, he was a well-respected champion of human rights and peaceful relations. In 1978, he invited Israeli Prime Minister Menachem Begin and Egyptian President Anwar Sadat to Camp David, where they spent 12 days working out a peace treaty between the two nations. The peace treaty was signed in 1979.

Nobel Peace Prize (2002). After Carter left the presidency, he and his wife Rosalynn formed the Carter Center in 1982, which still operates today. It is an organization that promotes positive relations through practical assistance to needy countries. Carter has received many awards for his active role in global peace campaigns, including the Nobel Peace Prize in 2002.

Chapter Review Practice Questions

Practice questions are for instructional purposes only and may not reflect the format of the actual exam. On the actual exam, questions will be grouped into sets. Each set contains one source-based prompt (document or image) and two to five questions.

Multiple-Choice Questions

Questions 1–3 refer to the following photograph.

Source: Warren Leffler, "Governor George Wallace being confronted by Deputy U.S. Attorney General Nicholas Katzenbach at the University of Alabama," June 11, 1963.

1. Which of the following best explains the conditions depicted in the photograph?

    A. The observance of the principles of fair media coverage during the struggle for civil rights
    B. The African American struggle for changes in education legislation during the Civil Rights Era
    C. The federal enforcement of regulations that were unconstitutional
    D. The rejection of federally enforced desegregation laws by locally elected segregationist politicians

2. Based on your knowledge of U.S. history, which of the following is another example of the conditions depicted in the photograph?

    A. Martin Luther King Jr.'s leadership during the Birmingham Campaign
    B. Orval Faubus' actions toward the Little Rock Nine
    C. Lyndon Johnson's endorsement of the Voting Rights Act of 1965
    D. The Supreme Court's decision in *Brown v. Board of Education*

3. Which of the following does NOT represent a continuation of Wallace's political agenda?

   A. Wallace's "segregation now, segregation tomorrow, segregation forever" speech
   B. Nixon's rejection of liberal policies, the advocating of states' rights, and the advocating of small government
   C. Objections to federally ordered busing in white communities
   D. The New Right's demand for merit-based, individualistic policies that supported conservative legislation

Questions 4–5 refer to the following passage.

Now is the time to make real the promises of democracy. Now is the time to rise from the dark and desolate valley of segregation to the sunlit path of racial justice. Now is the time to lift our nation from the quicksands of racial injustice to the solid rock of brotherhood. Now is the time to make justice a reality for all of God's children.

It would be fatal for the nation to overlook the urgency of the moment. This sweltering summer of the Negro's legitimate discontent will not pass until there is an invigorating autumn of freedom and equality. Nineteen sixty-three is not an end, but a beginning. Those who hope that the Negro needed to blow off steam and will now be content will have a rude awakening if the nation returns to business as usual. There will be neither rest nor tranquility in America until the Negro is granted his citizenship rights. The whirlwinds of revolt will continue to shake the foundations of our nation until the bright day of justice emerges.

—Source: Martin Luther King Jr., "I Have a Dream," August 28, 1963. Speech presented at the March on Washington for Jobs and Freedom. King calls for an end to racism in the United States.

4. The ideas expressed by King in the excerpt best reflect which of the following?

   A. The continuing African American dedication to complete equality
   B. The acknowledgment of civil rights progress since the Montgomery Bus Boycott
   C. The awareness of interracial assistance as well as resistance
   D. The religious motivations for African American discontentment

5. Based on your knowledge of U.S. history, how did events connected with King's speech demonstrate a continuance of the struggle for African American civil rights?

   A. The speech reflects hopes of equality witnessed during the Reconstruction.
   B. The speech echoed the 1940s march that protested job discrimination in wartime factories.
   C. The speech praises the civil rights progress that has occurred over time.
   D. The speech hints at specific citizenship rights that were connected to the court battles of the NAACP.

Document-Based Question

1 question
60 minutes

Reading Time: 15 minutes (brainstorm your thoughts and organize your response)
Writing Time: 45 minutes

Directions: The document-based question is based on the seven accompanying documents. The documents are for instructional purposes only. Some of the documents have been edited for the purpose of this practice exercise. Write your response on lined paper and include the following:

- **Thesis.** Present a thesis that supports a historically defensible claim, establishes a line of reasoning, and responds to all parts of the question. The thesis must consist of one or more sentences located in one place—either the introduction or the conclusion.
- **Contextualization.** Situate the argument by explaining the broader historical events, developments, or processes that occurred before, during, or after the time frame of the question.
- **Evidence from the documents.** Support your argument by using the content of six of the documents to develop and support a cohesive argument that responds to the question.
- **Evidence beyond the documents.** Support your argument by explaining at least one additional piece of specific historical evidence not found in the documents. (Note: The example must be different from the evidence used to earn the point for contextualization.)
- **Analysis.** Use at least three documents that are relevant to the question to explain the documents' point of view, purpose, historical situation, and/or audience.
- **Historical reasoning.** Use historical reasoning to show complex relationships among the documents, the topic question, and the thesis argument. Use evidence to corroborate, qualify, or modify the argument.

Based on the documents that follow, answer the question below.

Question 1: Evaluate the extent to which differing views about the Cold War impacted the development of U.S. foreign policy from 1945 to 1980.

Document 1

Source: George Kennan, excerpt from "Telegram to President Harry Truman," February 22, 1946.

Much depends on health and vigor of our own society. World communism is like a malignant parasite which feeds only on diseased tissue.... Every courageous and incisive measure to solve internal problems of our own society, to improve self-confidence, discipline, morale and community spirit of our own people, is a diplomatic victory over Moscow worth a thousand diplomatic notes and joint communiqués...

We must formulate and put forward for other nations a much more positive and constructive picture a sort of world we would like to see than we have put forward in the past. It is not enough to urge people to develop political processes similar to our own. Many foreign peoples, in Europe at least, are tired and frightened by experiences of past, and are less interested in abstract freedom than in security. They are seeking guidance rather than responsibilities. We should be better able than Russians to give them this. And unless we do, Russians certainly will.

Document 2

Source: President Harry Truman, "Address before a joint session of Congress," March 12, 1947. Speech to plead for aid to Greece and Turkey.

To ensure the peaceful development of nations, free from coercion, the United States has taken a leading part in establishing the United Nations. The United Nations is designed to make possible lasting freedom and independence for all its members. We shall not realize our objectives, however, unless we are willing to help free peoples to maintain their free institutions and their national integrity against aggressive movements that seek to impose upon them totalitarian regimes...

I believe that it must be the policy of the United States to support free peoples who are resisting attempted subjugation by armed minorities or by outside pressures.

I believe that we must assist free peoples to work out their own destinies in their own way.

I believe that our help should be primarily through economic and financial aid which is essential to economic stability and orderly political processes.

Document 3

Source: Notes regarding Truman's meeting with Congressional leaders from the Elsey Papers, June 27, 1950.

Upon finishing his statement, the President gave a brief summary of what lay behind this Government's decisions. The communist invasion of South Korea could not be let pass unnoticed, he said, this act was very obviously inspired by the Soviet Union. If we let Korea down, the Soviets will keep right on going and swallow up one piece of Asia after another. We had to make a stand some time, or else let all of Asia go by the board. If we were to let Asia go, the Near East would collapse and no telling what would happen in Europe. Therefore, the President concluded, he had ordered our forces to support Korea as long as we could—or as long as the Koreans put up a fight and gave us something we *could* support—and it was equally necessary for us to draw the line at Indo-China, the Philippines, and Formosa.

Document 4

Source: John F. Kennedy, "Televised Address," October 22, 1962. The president's speech to the American people regarding the Soviet Arms buildup in Cuba.

For many years, both the Soviet Union and the United States…have deployed strategic nuclear weapons with great care, never upsetting the precarious status quo which insured that these weapons would not be used in the absence of some vital challenge. Our own strategic missiles have never been transferred to the territory of any other nation under a cloak of secrecy and deception; and our history—unlike that of the Soviets since the end of World War II—demonstrates that we have no desire to dominate or conquer any other nation or impose our system upon its people…

…missiles in Cuba add to an already clear and present danger…this sudden, clandestine decision to station strategic weapons for the first time outside of Soviet soil—is a deliberately provocative and unjustified change in the status quo which cannot be accepted by this country…

…We are prepared to discuss new proposals for the removal of tensions on both sides, including the possibilities of a genuinely independent Cuba, free to determine its own destiny. We have no wish to war with the Soviet Union—for we are a peaceful people who desire to live in peace with all other peoples.

Document 5

Source: "Photograph of Anti-war Protests," January 19, 1968. Photograph taken in front of the White House while protesters are defending Eartha Kitt, a singer who had also protested the Vietnam War.

Document 6

Source: "Strategic Arms Limitation Talks (SALT) Agreement," May 26, 1972. Excerpt of the SALT agreement signed by Richard Nixon and Leonid Brezhnev limiting the development of both offensive and defensive strategic arms.

Article I

The Parties undertake not to start construction of additional fixed land-based intercontinental ballistic missile (ICBM) launchers after July 1, 1972.

Article II

The Parties undertake not to convert land-based launchers for light ICBMs, or for ICBMs of older types deployed prior to 1964, into land-based launchers for heavy ICBMs of types deployed after that time.

Article III

The Parties undertake to limit submarine-launched ballistic missile (SLBM) launchers and modern ballistic missile submarines to the numbers operational and under construction on the date of signature of this Interim Agreement...

Document 7

> **Source: Jimmy Carter, "State of the Union Address," January 23, 1980. President Carter speaking about economic and possible military action against the Soviet Union.**
>
> The region which is now threatened by Soviet troops in Afghanistan is of great strategic importance: It contains more than two-thirds of the world's exportable oil. The Soviet effort to dominate Afghanistan has brought Soviet military forces to within 300 miles of the Indian Ocean and close to the Straits of Hormuz, a waterway through which most of the world's oil must flow. The Soviet Union is now attempting to consolidate a strategic position, therefore, that poses a grave threat to the free movement of Middle East oil.
>
> This situation demands careful thought, steady nerves, and resolute action, not only for this year but for many years to come. It demands collective efforts to meet this new threat to security in the Persian Gulf and in Southwest Asia... And it demands consultation and close cooperation with countries in the area which might be threatened... Let our position be absolutely clear: An attempt by any outside force to gain control of the Persian Gulf region will be regarded as an assault on the vital interests of the United States of America, and such an assault will be repelled by any means necessary, including military force.

Answer Explanations

Multiple-Choice Questions

1. **D.** This question requires you to read and carefully analyze all of the answer choices. While the media reporters, choice A, and a representative of the federal government are present, choice C, the photograph is neither reflecting a demand for fair media coverage nor advocating Wallace's position. In 1954, *Brown v. Board of Education* ruled that segregation was unconstitutional. While it is part of the fight for African American education, choice B, it is not associated with the passing of legislation—it is the enforcement of that legislation. The photograph reflects Alabama Governor George Wallace and the segregationists' rejection of federal law in the South, choice D.

2. **B.** The only example of a segregationist attempting to defy federal laws referenced in the photograph is Arkansas Governor Orval Faubus' attempt to prevent black students from entering school at Little Rock Central High School, choice B. The other choices all reflect federal support for civil rights or protests "against" segregation.

3. **A.** The key words in the question are "NOT" and "continuation." Wallace's states' rights political agenda encouraged a belief in small government and the "discontinuation" of liberal policies that protected minority groups, which he saw as "special privileges." Wallace's "segregation now, segregation tomorrow, segregation forever" comment, choice A, is from his inauguration speech, which occurred *before* Wallace stood on the doorstep of the university, so it does NOT represent a continuation of his political agenda. This issue was also observed in Nixon's policies, choice B, and the New Right's political agendas, choice D, as well as the arguments put forward by white citizens who protested against the busing orders, choice C.

4. **A.** The excerpt reflects the persistent dedication to African American equal rights regardless of the gains made during the movement, choice A. The speech also points out that citizens who expect black Americans to be content with a few legislative gains, choice B, should not think their assistance or resistance, choice C, is enough to make the African American community discontinue its complaints about discrimination. While King's speech contains religious language, the purpose of the speech is not an inspiration for discontent, choice D.

5. **B.** King's speech was given in 1963 during the March on Washington for Jobs and Freedom, which was based on a similar march planned by A. Philip Randolph to protest job discrimination in wartime factories, choice B. The 1940s march was prevented by FDR's Executive Order 8802. While the speech does hint at equality, choice A, and progress, choice C, it neither reflects hopes nor praise for either. Rather, it demands fair citizenship rights—which were not connected to court battles, choice D.

Document-Based Question

DBQ Scoring Guide

To achieve the maximum score of 7, your response must address the scoring criteria components in the table that follows.

Scoring Criteria for a Good Essay	
Question 1: Evaluate the extent to which differing views about the Cold War impacted the development of U.S. foreign policy from 1945 to 1980.	
Scoring Criteria	**Examples**
A. THESIS/CLAIM	
(1 point) Presents a historically defensible thesis that establishes a line of reasoning. (Note: The thesis must make a claim that responds to *all* parts of the question and must *not* just restate the question. The thesis must consist of *at least* one sentence, either in the introduction or the conclusion.)	The essay provides coherency throughout the argument by uniting various points about the Cold War in a clear thesis statement. It guides the reader through the similarities and differences of important events and reasons for the U.S. foreign policy response to the Cold War.
B. CONTEXTUALIZATION	
(1 point) Explains the broader historical context of events, developments, or processes that occurred before, during, or after the time frame of the question. (Note: Must be more than a phrase or reference.)	The essay provides strong topic sentences and transition statements to historically contextualize and connect all of the events it mentions. A good response provides some historical context in each body paragraph. This essay discusses post–World War II military conflicts, cultural references, and nuclear arms negotiations, and places them in historical context. It also discusses both the public and political perspectives and actions. To conclude, it looks ahead to the Reagan administration and the end of the Cold War.

Continued

Scoring Criteria	Examples
C. EVIDENCE	
Evidence from the Documents **(2 points)** Uses at least *six* documents to support the argument in response to the prompt. OR **(1 point)** Uses the content of at least *three* documents to address the topic prompt. (Note: Examples must describe, rather than simply quote, the content of the documents.)	To receive the highest possible points, the response addresses all seven of the documents and relates the documents back to the thesis. Documents 1, 2, 3, and 7 address reasons that the U.S. implemented foreign containment of Communism during this time period. Document 4 shows the dangers of the Cold War. Document 5 provides a pictorial illustration of the public protests objecting to American wars, while Document 6 shows the continued negotiations with the Soviet Union to limit the construction of nuclear arms.
Evidence Beyond the Documents **(1 point)** Uses at least one additional piece of specific historical evidence beyond those found in the documents relevant to the argument. (Note: Evidence must be different from the evidence used in contextualization.)	The sample essay argues that U.S. administrations from 1945 to 1980 were influenced by the general public and suggests that foreign policy began with containment, then switched to improved relations through détente before returning to containment. It also hints at specific strategies used to promote anti-Communist and pro-democratic principles in a global context.
D. ANALYSIS AND REASONING	
(1 point) Uses at least *three* documents to explain how each document's point of view, purpose, historical situation, and/or audience is relevant to the argument. (Note: References must explain how or why, rather than simply identifying.)	The essay analyzes at least four of the documents using point of view, purpose, historical context, or audience. The essay notes the relevance of each speaker to the argument while comparing and contrasting different points of view and adding specific details to note the context and importance of their words.
(1 point) Uses historical reasoning and development that focuses on the question while using evidence to corroborate, qualify, or modify the argument. (Examples: Explain what is similar and different; explain the cause and effect; explain multiple causes; explain connections within and across periods of time; corroborate multiple perspectives across themes; or consider alternative views.)	The essay provides a coherent and well-organized argument and uses the historical reasoning of continuity and change over time and comparison. The thesis refers to different attitudes and beliefs of various Americans about the Cold War, including both specific politicians and the general public. It also notes how these things either stayed the same or changed over time to corroborate the evidence.

Sample Response

Sparked by post–World War II tensions between the United States and the Soviet Union, the Cold War developed during a time when global foreign policy was becoming more inclusive and less isolationist. From 1945 to 1980, American policymakers both influenced and were influenced by the public whose opinions about international conflicts (and the way to handle those conflicts) changed throughout the period. U.S. presidents shifted from policies of containment to détente, then back again, encouraging anti-Communism and the "defense of democracy" through economic aid and sanctions, military engagements, nuclear arms defense strategies, treaties, and public threats.

After World War II, many Americans feared the power of atomic energy, but because of the telegram of George Kennan (Document 1), which President Harry S. Truman received when Stalin was attempting to reassure his own security through the occupation of several Eastern European states, the federal government felt it imperative to reassure the public that weapons of mass destruction were necessary for the security of the U.S. as well as the defense of its citizens' lifestyle. A U.S. ambassador stationed in Moscow, Kennan told Truman that the Soviets intended to aggressively expand their power, depicted democracy negatively, and could only be stopped by American interests and power. The Truman administration adopted a U.S. policy of containment, which was intended to stop the growth of Communism and was made evident in the Truman Doctrine that became clear in a speech he gave before Congress in 1947, pleading for economic aid to Greece and Turkey (Document 2), struggling countries whose governments were faltering. Truman's speech sparked the European Recovery Program (also known as the Marshall Plan), which extended aid to European countries in order to "help free people to maintain sovereign states." These countries included Britain, France, and what would become West Germany.

While most containment policies were implemented through economic aid, some involved military conflicts, especially those associated with revolutionary governments in Asia and Latin America. When Communist forces invaded South Korea in 1950 and the United Nations condemned their actions, the Truman administration readily joined the fight (Document 3), as evidenced by the records of their meetings. Truman viewed the invasion as an act of aggression that could lead to the domino effect in Asia, a Cold War belief that if one country fell, its neighboring countries would soon follow. A similar principle was used to support both the Kennedy administration's involvement in the Cuban revolution and Johnson's decision to continue to deploy troops to Vietnam, a vicious war that lasted much longer than the 3 years Americans fought in Korea.

As Kennan's telegram suggests, part of containment involved promoting the "health and vigor" of U.S. society and culture. Civic duty was encouraged through self-control and social norms supported by the nuclear family and traditional gender roles. This was promoted through television, advertisements, and films and was associated with patriotism and moral codes. Not everyone responded to a culture of conformity, however, and the Cuban Missile Crisis in 1962 shocked the world into realizing how dangerous the Cold War could be. President Kennedy was forced to appear on television to inform the American public that there was evidence the Soviets had placed strategic nuclear missiles in Cuba (Document 4), which were capable of destroying cities in the eastern U.S. Although he claimed the country was full of "peaceful people who desire[d] to live in peace with all other peoples," the U.S. had employed the same strategies in the Cold War, pointing missiles at the Soviet Union from Britain as early as 1959. The Kennedy administration had also recently placed ballistic missiles in Italy and Turkey, which increased Soviet antagonism. Fortunately, Kennedy engaged in diplomatic negotiations that prevented nuclear war.

As reports of atrocities in Vietnam mounted, the dangers of nuclear weapons became more visible, and the Civil Rights Movement made public protests more acceptable, people began to speak out against the actions of the federal government in the Cold War. Public objections to nuclear arms and anti-war protests (like the one pictured in Document 5 in 1968) pressured politicians to change their foreign policy. In 1972, Nixon began policies of détente, which sought to improve relations with the Soviet Union. He first visited China and then signed the SALT I agreements with Leonid Brezhnev (Document 6), which recognized negotiations to decrease the production and dissemination of nuclear weapons. The arms limitation talks were continued by the Carter administration. Although Carter signed SALT II, which suggested further decreases in arms, the Soviet invasion of Afghanistan caused him to encourage Congress to stall their approval of it (Document 7). In his state of the union address, just before he left office, the president noted a policy that would become known as the Carter Doctrine, which suggested that the U.S. would use economic and military force to combat threats to its interests in the Persian

Gulf. His actions were motivated by the energy crisis the country had just experienced since the region in question controlled much of the world's oil.

The Cold War containment policies that Carter seemed to be returning to had begun with the Truman administration just after World War II, in 1946. Even though public objections had influenced U.S. foreign policy, ultimately economic sanctions and military engagement became stronger than the call for peaceful coexistence with the USSR. Furthermore, aggressive anti-Communist practices did not end in 1980—they actually culminated in Ronald Reagan's characterization of the Soviet government as an "evil empire" that sought to destroy democracy, which was surprisingly similar to the characterization of Communists promoted by Joseph McCarthy in the 1950s. Thus, the influence of this period remained, even until the end of the Cold War in 1991.

Chapter 12

Period Nine: The Globalization Era (1980 to the Present)

Period Nine explores the following 21st-century main topics:

- Ronald Reagan's Presidency (1981 to 1989)
- The Digital Revolution
- Globalization
- George H. W. Bush's Presidency (1989 to 1993)
- Bill Clinton's Presidency (1993 to 2001)
- George W. Bush's Presidency (2001 to 2009)
- The War on Terror (2001 to the Present)
- Barack Obama's Presidency (2009 to 2017)

Overview of AP U.S. History Period Nine

In the late 20th century, the New Right flourished and the dissatisfaction with Democratic leadership spread throughout the country, causing a surge of conservativism. This culminated in the Reagan Era. Learning from the Republicans, Democrats refocused their platform by adopting more conservative principles and appealing to the middle class. The political advances of several Republican presidents were followed by Democratic leaders like Bill Clinton and Barack Obama, the first African American president.

In the 21st century, globalization, digital communications, computers, and the Internet transformed daily life and expanded America's political, cultural, and financial roles. Even though the Cold War ended, the U.S. remained engaged in international military conflicts, especially after 9/11, when terrorism emerged as a threat to both national security and energy resources.

Use the chart below to guide you through what is covered on the exam. The curriculum contained in this chart is an abridged version of the concept outlines with topic examples. Visit https://apstudent. collegeboard.org/apcourse/ap-united-states-history/ for the complete updated APUSH course curriculum descriptions and key concepts.

AP U.S. History Key Concepts (1980 to the Present)	
Key Concept	**Specific Content**
KEY CONCEPT 9.1: CONSERVATIVE MOVEMENT A newly ascendant conservative movement achieved several political and policy goals during the 1980s and continued to strongly influence public discourse in the following decades.	Conservative beliefs regarding the need for traditional social values and a reduced role for government became more prevalent in U.S. politics after 1980.

Continued

Key Concept	Specific Content
KEY CONCEPT 9.2: THE IMPACT OF TECHNOLOGY **Moving into the 21st century, the nation experienced significant technological, economic, and demographic changes.**	New developments in science and technology enhanced the economy and transformed society, while manufacturing decreased. The U.S. population continued to undergo demographic shifts that had significant cultural and political consequences.
KEY CONCEPT 9.3: REDEFINING FOREIGN POLICIES **The end of the Cold War and new challenges to the U.S. forced the nation to redefine its foreign policy and role in the world.**	The Reagan administration promoted an interventionist foreign policy that continued in later administrations, even after the end of the Cold War. Following the terrorist attacks on September 11, 2001, U.S. foreign policy efforts focused on fighting terrorism around the world.

Significant Themes

Now that we've discussed the curriculum, let's discuss the significant themes related to this period. The theme-related study questions that follow will help you make mental connections to the context of the "big picture" of this time period. Keep in mind that these questions often overlap and apply to other themes of social, political, religious, geographic, ideological, technological, and economic developments.

Glance through the study questions before you start the review section. Take notes, highlight questions, and write down page number references to reinforce your learning. Refer to this list until you feel comfortable with your knowledge of the material.

Study Questions Related to Significant Themes for Period Nine

Theme 1: American and National Identity

1. How did the definition of freedom and citizenship both contract and expand during this period? (Hint: Think about questions of economic inequality and labor rights during the Reagan administration. Discuss concerns about Internet regulation and privacy as well as concerns about global trade and markets. Note Clinton's and Obama's attempts to create a universal healthcare system and the debates that continue about healthcare, immigration, and foreign and domestic policy abuses linked to the War on Terror.)

Theme 2: Politics and Power

1. What led to the election of Ronald Reagan and why are these factors important? (Hint: Draw on your knowledge about the lack of faith in the Carter administration as the result of the oil crisis and the Iran Hostage Crisis, linking them to the rise of the New Right, which included the Religious Right and Sunbelt conservatives. Also focus on Reagan's optimism and pride in the country, as well as his aggressive Cold War stance and suggestions for foreign policy.)

2. Which historical trends and events led to the end of the Cold War and the demise of the USSR? (Hint: Think about external and internal pressures in the Soviet Union, which include Gorbachev's *glasnost* and *perestroika* policies, the Reagan Doctrine, and the Reagan administration's massive spending to build a nuclear arsenal and defense system.)

3. How did the Democratic Party change in the 1990s? What was the role of Bill Clinton in this change? (Hint: Consider the changing role of liberalism, which became less directed toward social change and more directed toward establishing security for the middle class. Note Clinton's membership in the Democratic Leadership Council and his centrist political policies, which caused him to support traditionally Republican domestic policies, such as welfare reform, anti-Communist foreign policy, free trade, tax cuts, and deregulation.)

Theme 3: Work, Exchange, and Technology

1. What kinds of economic challenges and changes can be related to the Reagan administration? (Hint: Link Reagan's attempt to bring the country out of the stagflation of the 1970s through supply-side economics. Discuss how "Reaganomics" was supposed to work, as well as its level of success.)

2. How did the American workforce change during this period? (Hint: This is an open-ended question that could have many different answers—be sure to list as many factors as you can. Consider several aspects of the American economy during this time, especially shifts from an industrial to a service economy, the booming and busting of technologically driven companies, the destruction of labor unions through Reagan's actions against the air traffic controllers, etc.)

3. How did technology influence the U.S. labor force and the American economy? (Hint: Focus on the computer boom in Sunbelt districts, especially the West, as well as the development and crash of the dot-com industry in the 1990s and early 2000s.)

4. What contributed to the wealth gap evident in this era? (Hint: Analyze the deregulation and tax cuts promoted by presidents Reagan, George W. Bush, and Clinton, specifically linking them to the decline of real wages and the rise of debt for middle-class Americans, especially those of Latino or African American descent. Be sure to mention the influence of Reaganomics, the Tax Equity and Fiscal Responsibility Act of 1982, the Economic Growth and Tax Relief Reconciliation Act, and the housing market crash.)

Theme 4: Culture and Society

1. How did the conservative Christian Right influence the culture and the political trends and events of this period? (Hint: Discuss the ability of the Christian Right to affect the elections of both Reagan and George W. Bush, as well as discussing the level of support each president gave to the agendas of political evangelicals, including legislation that addressed abortion restrictions, the teaching of creationism in schools, aggressive foreign policies, and limitations on the rights of LGBT and black Americans.)

2. How have technological advances influenced U.S. society and culture in the 1990s and beyond? (Hint: Note the creation of the Internet and the dot-com industry, which has helped generate a global economy and increased access to specific goods and markets.)

Theme 5: Migration and Settlement

1. How have demographic changes in the U.S. South and West continued to influence political and cultural issues? (Hint: Sunbelt conservatives linked with evangelicals to influence politics in these areas. Be sure you can discuss how a once "solid South" had transformed into a Republican stronghold by the 1980s.)

Theme 7: America in the World

1. What was the role of the U.S. in global affairs in the 1980s? What was Reagan's Cold War policy and how did it affect other nations? (Hint: Examine the Reagan Doctrine and how it extended the Truman Doctrine. Discuss aggressive arms buildup, the Star Wars program, massive government investment in technology, and the insertion of U.S. military advisors and funds into regimes or revolutionaries who were fighting Communism. Be sure to consider both the successes and the limitations of Reagan's Cold War policies, including his role in ending the Cold War and the consequences of the Iran-Contra Affair.)

2. How did America's foreign policy change after September 11, 2001? Why is this important? (Hint: Examine how terrorist attacks on the World Trade Center and the Pentagon transformed the U.S. domestic and foreign policy, noting the importance of the wars in Afghanistan and Iraq, Bush's declaration of an "axis of evil," and the civil and human rights concerns generated by both the wars and the PATRIOT Act. Discuss how some military conflicts have been resolved while others continue.)

Important Events, Terms, and Concepts

The list below shows important events, terms, and concepts that you should be familiar with on the APUSH exam. These and other important terms are printed in boldface throughout the chapter. Because the APUSH exam requires you to pay attention to the historical context and connections rather than details, don't bother memorizing the terms now. Simply place a check mark next to each as you study. You can return to this list to review as often as necessary. After you finish the review section, you can reinforce what you have learned by working through the practice questions at the end of this chapter. Answer explanations provide further clarification into perspectives of U.S. history.

Event/Term/Concept	Year/Brief Description	Study Page
Reaganomics	**1980–1988.** Reaganomics was also known as "supply-side" or "trickle-down" economics. It is the belief that cutting taxes and deregulating private industry helps to stimulate the economy by creating jobs and surplus income for average American citizens.	pp. 359–360
Iran-Contra Affair	**1985–1987.** A political scandal during the Reagan administration that involved top officials violating an arms embargo in Iran to fund the anti-Communist revolutionary Contras, who were fighting against the Sandinistas in Nicaragua.	p. 362
"Star Wars"	**1984–1993.** The Strategic Defense Initiative was commonly known as Star Wars. It was a short-lived space-based defense program intended to thwart Soviet efforts to destroy the U.S. during a nuclear war by deflecting intercontinental ballistic missiles.	p. 362

Event/Term/Concept	Year/Brief Description	Study Page
Operation Desert Storm	**1991.** Operation Desert Storm was also known as the First Gulf War. It was the military engagement in Kuwait that defeated Saddam Hussein's efforts to conquer the country. It lasted only 100 hours, but the bombing continued for several weeks.	p. 364
NAFTA (North American Free Trade Agreement)	**1994.** NAFTA is a free-trade agreement for the Western Hemisphere that was signed during the Clinton administration. The agreement encourages trade and investment among the U.S., Canada, and Mexico by reducing restrictions like international tariffs and increasing trade.	p. 363
Dot-com boom and bust	**1995–2000.** The dot-com industry was stimulated by public access to the World Wide Web (the Internet). It resulted in an economic boom that began with the start-up of several online businesses. By 2000, however, many companies proved unstable and unsupportable, so the industry crashed, beginning a long road to recovery that lasted several years.	p. 363
9/11	**2001.** On September 11, 2001, coordinated terrorist attacks on U.S. soil occurred, beginning a War on Terror that prompted many anti-terror changes in American foreign and domestic policies.	p. 367
Osama bin Laden (1957–2011)	Osama bin Laden was a Saudi Arabian Muslim who was the leader of the international terrorist group Al-Qaeda, whose objective is to overthrow un-Islamic regimes. Bin Laden was a radical jihadist who instigated the U.S. 9/11 terror attacks. Although he went into hiding for many years, he was found and executed by the American military during the Obama administration in 2011.	p. 367
USA PATRIOT Act	**2001.** The USA PATRIOT Act is legislation that expanded the domestic power of law enforcement agencies and airport security in the interest of national security to "provide appropriate tools required to intercept and obstruct terrorism."	p. 368
Terrorism	The use of violence by religious and secular groups against non-military citizens in order to achieve a political goal. The most current examples have been the Muslim groups Al-Qaeda, ISIS, Hamas, and Hezbollah. In the past, the Irish independence movement (Irish Republican Army, or IRA) also used this means against the British for independence. During Reconstruction in the United States, southern Democrats used terrorism through vigilante groups like the Ku Klux Klan to gain power and prevent African Americans from obtaining civil and social rights.	pp. 367–368
Developing countries vs. developed countries	The United Nations classifies countries into two categories based on economic status and industrialization: developing countries (sometimes called Third World countries) and developed countries. Developing countries are largely in the Southern Hemisphere. These countries have low industrialization and tend to have authoritarian governments. Developed countries are sovereign countries that have advanced industrialization; they tend to have democratic governments.	p. 363
Barack Obama	**2009–2017.** Elected in 2008, Barack Obama was the first African American president of the United States. He was instrumental in the passing of a universal healthcare bill that provided medical insurance for all U.S. citizens.	p. 369

Chapter Review

The election of 1980 sparked an ascent of the New Right, a conservative political movement that led to a victory for Republicans and a temporary reduction of political power for Democrats. Although Republicans argued that the size and scope of government should be reduced, social programs remained popular in America. Both liberal and conservative politicians debated over the need for federal assistance, the role and responsibility of the U.S. government, and the value of free-trade agreements. After the advent of digital communications, America expanded its political, cultural, and financial roles in the world. The U.S. continued to be an important world leader, but after terrorist attacks, foreign policy efforts focused on fighting global terrorism. Additionally, climate change and consumption became clear issues of domestic and foreign policies.

Ronald Reagan's Presidency (1981 to 1989)

Americans became disillusioned with the Democratic presidential incumbent Jimmy Carter (Chapter 11) and his administration and foreign policy. By 1980, America faced economic inflation, racial divisions, increases in crime, and a liberal modern society that seemed to depart from a traditional value system. Republican candidate Ronald Reagan was a highly popular figure and was elected in 1980 (and reelected in 1984).

The Rise of Conservatism

The resurgence of conservatism changed the political and social mood in America in the 1980s to the 2000s. Many Americans wanted to return to the traditional values they believed supported economic prosperity, social order, and global power.

Key Facts about the Rise of Conservatism

Several factors contributed to the rise of conservatism in 1980, including Reagan's charisma and the growth of the New Right and the Christian Coalition.

Americans were influenced by Reagan's rhetoric. He became an important force in shaping the U.S. political atmosphere for decades. Reagan was a former actor and California's governor. He used his charm and persuasive oratorical abilities to win the hearts of many Americans. During his campaign, Reagan stressed nationalistic pride in America's abilities and authority. This was a distinct contrast to Carter's pessimistic language, which had always emphasized self-discipline and humanitarianism.

Americans were influenced by the Christian Right. Another important cause of conservatism was the rise of the religious Christian Right, right-wing Christian factions that supported extreme conservative policies. Conservative Christians believed that liberal politics bred immoral behavior and felt that Reagan was on their side of the culture war against the rising immoral values in America (those of feminists, gay rights activists, welfare recipients, etc.). While Reagan claimed to support anti-abortion legislation and promoted prayer and creationism in schools, his administration failed to address most Christians' concerns. Regardless, religious conservatives supported Reagan.

> **TEST TIP:** When considering the AP history reasoning skill of continuity and change over time, the mood of America in the 1980s was similar to the mood during the 18th century when Thomas Jefferson fought for Anti-Federalist "states' rights." For the APUSH exam, keep in mind that federal versus states' rights is a common theme throughout U.S. history.

Americans desired economic prosperity. Some working-class people in the *Rust Belt* (a Democratic Midwestern region that had suffered greatly from economic decline in the 1970s) became Reagan supporters. Drawn by Reagan's positive attitude, anti-Communist stance, and dedication to rebuilding the economy, people switched their political allegiance and voted Republican for the first time.

Reagan and Economics

Reaganomics

One issue that convinced many people to vote for Reagan in 1980 was his belief in *supply-side economics* (improving the economy by helping private business owners so that the rich could expand their businesses, produce more goods, and hire more people). Supply-side economics became known as **Reaganomics.** This economic theory is often advocated as a response to a financial decline related to unemployment, like that which occurred in the 1970s.

Reaganomics: Reagan's System of Economics

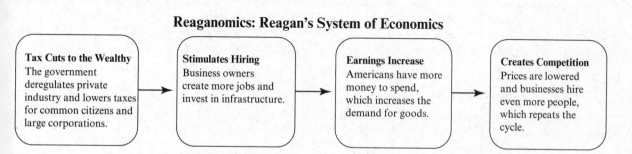

| **Tax Cuts to the Wealthy** The government deregulates private industry and lowers taxes for common citizens and large corporations. | **Stimulates Hiring** Business owners create more jobs and invest in infrastructure. | **Earnings Increase** Americans have more money to spend, which increases the demand for goods. | **Creates Competition** Prices are lowered and businesses hire even more people, which repeats the cycle. |

Source: Milt Priggee, "Trickle Down Theory…Reality," 2010. Reprinted with permission, www.miltpriggee.com.

Heads Up: What You Need to Know

On the APUSH exam, it is important to be familiar with Reaganomics, supply-side economics, and trickle-down economics, which are essentially the same economic theory with different names. The enactment of federal fiscal policies based upon its assumptions has demonstrated important historical and economic trends, but it is important to note that these concepts did not originate with Ronald Reagan. Herbert Hoover advocated for some of the same policies during the Great Depression, and Donald Trump's 21st-century economic policies are similar. Many economists in the 1980s believed that cutting taxes would cause people to invest in the American economy and stimulate more work. The idea was that this would force the government to cut its spending. These theories convinced the average American citizen that economic stability was achieved by giving more money to the wealthy.

HISTORIOGRAPHY. *Historians have concluded that trickle-down economics did not improve the economy. With the exception of George W. Bush (2001 to 2009), Republican presidents have generally approved large tax cuts, while Democrats like Bill Clinton raised taxes. As depicted in the following diagram, businesses actually decreased during the years that taxes were lowest, prices increased, worker productivity and "real wages" (those attributed to a middle-class standard of living) fell, and both the wealth gap and the average citizen's debt substantially increased.*

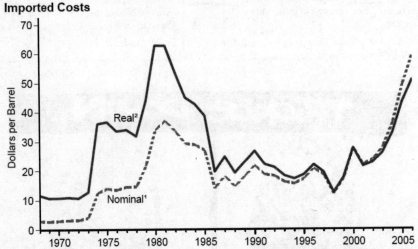

Source: Oil prices 1968–2006 (peak is 1980 with a steep decline over the 1980s during Reaganomics).

Reagan and Labor Unions

Although Reagan had once been president of the Screen Actors Guild, he was not supportive of labor unions during his presidency. In 1981, the Professional Air Traffic Controllers Organization (PATCO) went on strike for better wages, more productive work environments, and fewer hours. Reagan announced that the actions of the trade union were illegal and dangerous to national security and ordered them back to work within 48 hours. Ninety percent of the 13,000 strikers refused to comply, so Reagan fired them and banned them from federal service for life (although after 1986 they were allowed to reapply). The Federal Aviation Administration (FAA) was faced with the task of training enough air traffic controllers to replace those who were fired. It took almost 10 years before the air traffic staffing returned to normal. Reagan's move broke the power of the union and dealt a death blow to organized labor. (Note: In 1987, another union was formed for air traffic controllers—the National Air Traffic Controllers Association.)

Did you know? Labor unions had been struggling ever since the passage of the **Taft-Hartley Act** in 1947, which restricted the activities and power of labor unions. The Taft-Hartley Act weakened the strength of the **Wagner Act** (a part of FDR's New Deal legislation), which protected workers who wanted to organize or join a labor union, and placed restrictions on institutions encouraging "unfair labor practices." Unionism was dealt a further blow when the economy shifted from a manufacturing industry to a service industry. Massive employment layoffs occurred as the result of the domestic crises in the 1970s, especially in the Rust Belt. Reagan's actions in 1981 toward the air traffic controllers sent a clear message to organized labor: The federal government would no longer side with common workers in disputes. This established a clear precedent for U.S. workers that significantly decreased their ability to negotiate for improved working conditions and better wages.

Reagan and Tax Reform

During Reagan's administration, he lived up to his campaign promises to cut taxes through the **Economic Recovery Tax Act** (1981), which reduced marginal tax rates by 25 percent. Many of these tax cuts were undone by the **Tax Equity and Fiscal Responsibility Act** of 1982, which rescinded tax cuts due to the recession. During Reagan's second term in office, the **Tax Reform Act** (1986) simplified tax procedures and attempted to shift the tax base from individuals to corporations by eliminating tax shelters and loopholes. Fiscal spending, however, was not cut. Since the American people had come to expect the government to provide for their needs, Reagan's administration found it difficult to cut expensive programs like Social Security and Medicare. As a result, from 1980 to 1988, the national debt tripled in size.

Reagan and Foreign Policy

Another reason for increased federal spending was Reagan's Cold War foreign policy, which emphasized the accumulation of military arms and defense.

Reagan and Communism. Reagan considered the Soviet Union an "evil empire," and rejected *détente* (the easing of strained relations). He spoke harshly about Communist and Socialist nations and offered economic aid to anti-Communist regimes in Latin America and the Middle East.

Reagan Doctrine. Reagan was an advocate of interventionist policies that emphasized financial incentives, military assistance, and covert operations in nations that rejected *left-wing governments* (governments that support Socialist ideologies). Reagan's foreign policies became known as the **Reagan Doctrine.** Under Reagan's orders, the U.S. military assisted in conflicts in Beirut and Grenada. Reagan also authorized the U.S. military to provide ammunition and tactical training to Guatemalan forces to fight left-wing guerrillas who were taking over the region. The U.S supported a bloody military coup in Guatemala, and José Efraín Ríos Montt became the country's leader. Montt was later convicted for engaging in genocide and human rights violations.

Reagan and the Iran-Contra Affair (1986). Reagan's pre-occupation with eradicating Communism around the world led to two secret government operations. The U.S. made a deal to train and fund Nicaraguan Contra fighters (who were known drug dealers) to fight the Cuban-backed (Communist) Sandinistas. The U.S. also traded missiles to Iranian terrorists in exchange for freeing seven American hostages. This political scandal threatened Ronald Reagan's presidency and raised serious questions about the limits of the executive branch of government.

Reagan and the nuclear arms race. Reagan used the *arms race* (a competition between nations to make and hold the most weapons) to increase pressure on the Soviet Union during the Cold War. Reagan promoted the deployment of NATO's Pershing II missile in Europe (specifically West Germany) and attempted to defend the U.S. from the Soviets by developing a Strategic Defense Initiative program, a missile defense system to protect the U.S. against ballistic missiles, commonly known as SDI or **"Star Wars."** The SDI program pursued the technological development of a space-based anti-missile system to thwart nuclear attempts that target the U.S. with intercontinental ballistic missiles (ICBMs). The project received approval, but was ultimately discontinued in 1993.

Reagan demanded the removal of the Berlin Wall (1989). In the early 1980s, the Soviet leaders were replaced due to the deaths of previous presidents. For years, the Communist Party had been dominated by older people who had become isolated from the younger Russian generation's modern ideas. **Mikhail Gorbachev,** the new Russian president, used *perestroika* (increased awareness of the economy) to provide some economic freedoms for new Russian businesses. Gorbachev also introduced *glasnost* (transparency and openness to the public) to open up more freedom of thought.

In 1987, Reagan traveled to Berlin, Germany, where he gave a famous speech that encouraged Gorbachev to tear down the **Berlin Wall,** the primary symbol of both the Iron Curtain and the Cold War. As illustrated in the following image, in 1989 in the midst of progressive politics in Eastern European nations, East German borders were opened. By November, demolition on the wall had begun and Germany had initiated its reunification process, which was completed in 1990.

Source: "November 10, 1989, Tearing down the Berlin Wall," www.year1989.pl.

The Digital Revolution

In the interest of national defense and security, the Reagan administration invested heavily in technology and the computer industry. This investment had several repercussions in the years to come, which significantly influenced American economics, society, and culture.

Events and trends that can be linked to the rise of the **Digital Age** (also called the Information Age) are illustrated in the chart that follows.

Technology	Although economic slumps continued in the early 1980s for much of the country, universities and regions that received federal subsidies for research and development in the computer industry flourished. As the computer industry advanced in Silicon Valley, Los Angeles, and Boston, knowledge about and the availability of technology increased.
Internet	Although the history of computers and the Internet can be traced to the 1950s, advances in an accessible global network advanced considerably in the 1980s. Tim Berners-Lee invented the World Wide Web in 1989, which was released to the general public in 1991. This "internet" ushered in several important sociocultural and economic changes for average citizens, including the ability to access information and goods quickly and the increase of isolation and anonymous social or political criticism.
Dot-com industry	The Internet made access to global markets and services cheaper and more efficient. American investors were drawn to new dot-com companies, which experienced exponential growth between 1995 and 2000. Unfortunately, this speculative bubble burst in early 2001; many large companies like Google and Amazon survived, but smaller firms buckled, and the online industry remained unstable for almost a decade.
Culture	Popular culture reflected the nation's growing interest in the benefits and limitations of computers. Books, television programs, and films contained plots or characters associated with space travel, lasers, robots, or other automated devices. One of the first movies that reflected this shift in culture was George Lucas' *Star Wars* series.

Globalization

Globalization has been a positive step for the United States, but it has also had some significant disadvantages that have required responses from local political and social leaders. But what is globalization? Many students think that globalization is international trade. Although this is partly true, it is a limited view of globalization.

Through telecommunication, global connections and interactions with **developed countries** (industrialized nations) and **developing countries** (low industrialization) became much easier. Although global markets were not new (they have existed in the United States since the colonial period and in other nations much longer), trade expanded and competition increased. Under President Bill Clinton's administration in 1994, the North American Free Trade Agreement **(NAFTA)** went into effect. NAFTA grew from a trade agreement the United States negotiated with Canada in 1989 and the inclusion of Mexico in that agreement in 1991. As a result, it produced a regional bloc of countries that agreed to lower tariffs and allow for the easier movement of products, business, and economic services among these countries.

Heads Up: What You Need to Know

Globalization is a key concept that frequently appears on the APUSH exam. Globalization is about international trade, but it is also about the process of connecting economic and political developments throughout the world. Globalization eliminates boundaries to trade, cultural exchange, and information. This can be accomplished by nations lowering tariff taxes in order to spread trade, technology, labor, and information across international boundaries. The assumption behind globalization is that when boundaries are removed, a mutual exchange across boundary lines is stimulated.

George H. W. Bush's Presidency (1989 to 1993)

The end of the Cold War can be attributed to several factors, including geopolitical trends in many Eastern European nations. In the late 1980s, many Americans also believed that Reagan's anti-Communist stance and military buildup significantly influenced the collapse of the Soviet Union, which included some of those nations. This belief boosted Republican popularity.

In the 1988 presidential election, Reagan's vice president, George H. W. Bush, depicted his Democratic opponent, Michael Dukakis, as not only soft on crime and hard on taxes, but as a weak military defense leader. Many Americans viewed a strong military leadership as being necessary to U.S. global prowess. President Bush won by a landslide, capturing the votes of the Electoral College in 40 states.

Bush's Key Domestic and Foreign Policies	
Domestic Policies	**Foreign Policies**
Bush promised "no new taxes" during his campaign but was forced to raise taxes when faced with a massive national debt.	When Communist governments collapsed in Germany, the Warsaw Pact dissolved in many Eastern European nations like Czechoslovakia, Poland, and Yugoslavia, and other Eastern European nations followed suit.
Bush signed the **Americans with Disabilities Act** (1990), which provided many Americans with necessary accommodations.	Bush refused to impose sanctions on the government of China when thousands of students were arrested or killed while demonstrating for democracy in **Tiananmen Square,** Beijing, in June 1989.
Bush signed the **Oil Pollution Act** (1990) in response to a massive oil spill in Prince William Sound, Alaska, by the *Exxon Valdez*.	When Iraqi leader Saddam Hussein failed to respond to criticism and sanctions imposed by 35 countries of the United Nations for his 1990 invasion of Kuwait, Bush authorized **Operation Desert Storm,** an American-led ground-force effort to retake the small, oil-rich country. This **Gulf War** (1990–1991) did not last long—fewer than 150 U.S. soldiers were killed in the conflict.

TEST TIP: The APUSH exam may contain a question about the impact of the First Gulf War on the Second Gulf War, which was connected to the presidency of George H. W. Bush's son, George W. Bush (2001 to 2009). The First Gulf War was short, but many historians link it to a larger conflict with Iraq under the leadership of Saddam Hussein in the 21st century. George H. W. Bush was heavily criticized for removing troops in the Middle East before the implications of Hussein's regime were fully addressed. Historians connect the Second Gulf War, a much longer conflict that lasted from 2003 to 2011, to the way the First Gulf War was resolved.

Bill Clinton's Presidency (1993 to 2001)

In 1990, the stock market declined and the unemployment rate climbed, causing a national recession. The recession, along with President Bush's reversal of his position on taxes, made Bush an unpopular candidate in the 1992 election. Ross Perot, an eccentric Texan billionaire, entered the race as an independent presidential candidate. Perot criticized President Bush for his fiscal policies and alienated much of the conservative base. This split the Republican votes and ensured the victory of Arkansas Governor William (Bill) Jefferson Clinton.

Clinton's election shifted the Democratic Party. Clinton's election signaled that the Democratic Party was moving in a different direction. Clinton was a key member of the **Democratic Leadership Council,** a group of radical politicians who wanted to entice working- and middle-class male voters to shift their position on domestic, economic, and foreign policies. Formed in 1985, the council supported conservative legislation—especially anti-Communist foreign policies, free-trade agreements, and deregulation—and criticized welfare and affirmative actions. This allowed Clinton to promote himself as a bipartisan proponent of the middle class, contributing to his victory in the election and dedicating the Democrats to a less liberal political platform.

Clinton's healthcare reform. Clinton attempted to balance the budget and cut taxes, but he also appointed a healthcare reform team to garner bipartisan support for a plan that would provide medical insurance for all Americans. Led by his wife, Hillary Clinton, the team did not strive to abolish private healthcare. Rather, the goal was to include the government in negotiations for lower premiums and require employers to provide healthcare for all employees. The plan was rejected by private insurance companies and small business lobbies, who claimed it was socialistic.

Heads Up: What You Need to Know

On the APUSH exam, you may see questions about the continuities and changes over time regarding healthcare. Be sure you can connect the Clinton administration's attempts at healthcare reform to the **Affordable Care Act** of 2010, commonly known as **Obamacare.** The Affordable Care Act has prompted a highly controversial political debate that has sparked many arguments about the appropriate role of the federal government in the nation's healthcare. The act expanded coverage and reformed private insurance markets of the 21st century.

The rise of a Republican Revolution. During the Clinton presidency, Republicans remained strong—they captured majorities in the Senate and House of Representatives in the 1994 elections for the first time since the 1950s. Republican success is often called the **Republican Revolution,** or Gingrich Revolution, in reference to Speaker of the House Newt Gingrich, who emerged as an important political leader.

Republicans' contract with America. Gingrich promoted a conservative agenda, known as the **Contract with America,** which was developed by Republicans for the election campaign. The contract demanded a return to traditional family values, a balanced budget, tax cuts (especially in capital gains), deregulation, welfare reform, and increased funding for law enforcement and prisons. However, the contract proved more difficult to implement than many Republicans had hoped. While some of the Republican proposals became successful pieces of legislation, others were vetoed by Clinton or defeated in Congress.

Republicans call for Clinton's impeachment. In 1994, Kenneth Starr was chosen to head a legal team to investigate Clinton's **Whitewater scandal** (real estate investments made during his term as Arkansas governor, which made the president appear corrupt). President Clinton was never prosecuted because there was not enough evidence, but Starr was later made part of an investigation of Clinton's extramarital relationship with a young White House intern named Monica Lewinsky. President Clinton was charged with impeachment for lying about his affair with Lewinsky under oath in a sexual harassment case brought against him in 1999 by Paula Jones, a former employee. President Clinton's impeachment failed in the Senate, which could not gather the two-thirds vote needed to remove him from office.

George W. Bush's Presidency (2001 to 2009)

Republicans had attempted to harm Clinton—and by extension, the Democrats—by accusing the president of corruption and immorality, but Clinton's political scandals failed to damage his or his party's reputation. By the turn of the 21st century, American technological progress and the expansion of the dot-com industry had caused the economy to flourish and created a national surplus.

The Presidential Election of 2000

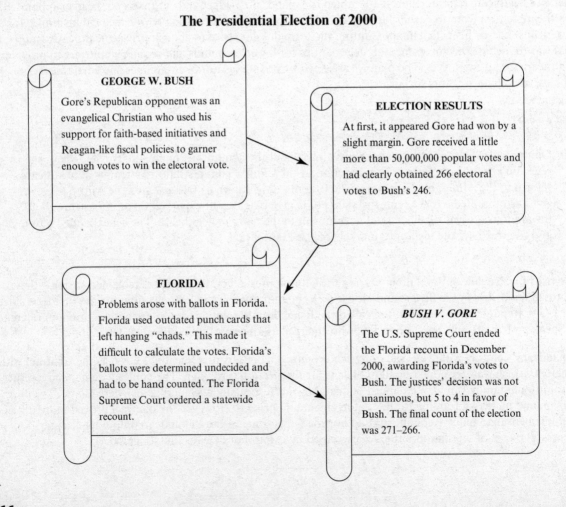

The Presidential Election of 2000

GEORGE W. BUSH

Gore's Republican opponent was an evangelical Christian who used his support for faith-based initiatives and Reagan-like fiscal policies to garner enough votes to win the electoral vote.

ELECTION RESULTS

At first, it appeared Gore had won by a slight margin. Gore received a little more than 50,000,000 popular votes and had clearly obtained 266 electoral votes to Bush's 246.

FLORIDA

Problems arose with ballots in Florida. Florida used outdated punch cards that left hanging "chads." This made it difficult to calculate the votes. Florida's ballots were determined undecided and had to be hand counted. The Florida Supreme Court ordered a statewide recount.

BUSH V. GORE

The U.S. Supreme Court ended the Florida recount in December 2000, awarding Florida's votes to Bush. The justices' decision was not unanimous, but 5 to 4 in favor of Bush. The final count of the election was 271–266.

Democratic Vice President Al Gore and Republican George W. Bush competed for the office of president in 2000. Although many citizens were not necessarily drawn to the personality of Vice President Gore, they continued to vote Democratic in the election of 2000. On election night, no clear winner emerged. It was too close to call until votes from Florida were re-tabulated. Fewer than 600 votes separated the two candidates. The issue went all the way to the Supreme Court and even though Gore won the popular vote, Bush narrowly won the electoral vote over Gore, 271 to 266.

Bush's Domestic Policies

President Bush, a former Texas governor who was the son of 41st President George H. W. Bush, was well known for his support of legislation that promoted the Christian Right's agenda, including the call for legislation that made late-term abortions illegal, limited stem cell research, and restricted same-sex marriage. Bush also engaged in campaign-funding reform, tax reform, and education reform.

Key Domestic Policies of George W. Bush	
Policy	**Description**
Economic Growth and Tax Relief Reconciliation Act (EGTRRA) (2001)	The act reduced income tax rates and expanded the tax code to include shelters in estate, gift, and retirement plan taxes. Like Reagan's tax policies, EGTRRA (pronounced "egg-tra") was designed to stimulate a "trickle down" economy boom in employment and investment. Although it offered a minimal one-time rebate to all citizens in 2001, the tax reform mainly benefited the rich, increasing the wealth gap in the U.S. even further. Investors chose to place their surplus monies in the growing real estate and/or stock market, rather than finance American industry.
No Child Left Behind Act (NCLB) (2002)	The act was a bipartisan law that was intended to ensure that public schools provided students with an appropriate education. This law linked school funding to test scores and improvement. Unfortunately, standards were often difficult to measure and resulted in teacher complaints and scoring scandals. NCLB was replaced by the **Every Student Succeeds Act (ESSA)** in 2015.
Bipartisan Campaign Reform Act (BCRA) (2002)	Also known as the **McCain-Feingold Act,** this act increased the role of private or corporate supporters ("soft money") in political campaigns by strictly enforcing limits placed on advertisements and national parties, which often back a single candidate rather than an issue.

The War on Terror (2001 to the Present)

On September 11, 2001—commonly known as **9/11**—the terrorist organization **Al-Qaeda** hijacked three U.S. commercial airplanes and used them as weapons to attack the Twin Towers of the **World Trade Center** in New York City and the Pentagon in Washington, D.C. A fourth hijacked plane was commandeered by passengers who fought back against the hijackers, causing the plane to crash before it could hit its target. As a result of the attacks, President Bush declared a "War on Terror," which marked several changes in U.S. foreign policy.

Bush's War on Terror Foreign Policies	
War in Afghanistan (2001 to Present)	Shortly after 9/11, Bush ordered an American offensive (combat and air support) to dismantle the **Taliban** in Afghanistan. The Taliban is a radical Islamic group that has governed the region through rigid religious restrictions. Taliban groups in the region were known to support terrorists like **Osama bin Laden,** the leader of Al-Qaeda. Although the U.S. anticipated a short military engagement in Afghanistan, American forces remain in the region. The War in Afghanistan is the longest war in U.S. history.

Continued

USA PATRIOT Act (2001)	In the interest of national security, the USA PATRIOT Act ("Uniting and Strengthening America by Providing Appropriate Tools Required to Intercept and Obstruct Terrorism") broadened the power of U.S. law enforcement by allowing for domestic or electronic searches without individual permission or a warrant. The act also increased airport security measures, began issuing color-coded warnings of possible attacks, and authorized the detainment and questioning of immigrants or suspected abettors at secret detention centers.
Axis of evil (2002)	In Bush's State of the Union address, he described North Korea, Iraq, and Iran as the "axis of evil" because they supported and funded terrorists and were attempting to build nuclear arsenals that could destroy the U.S. and its allies. The speech was reminiscent of both the Axis Powers of World War II and Reagan's branding of the Soviets as an "evil empire." Bush's speech was designed to gather public support for the War on Terror.
Operation Iraqi Freedom (2003)	In 2002, the Bush administration claimed Saddam Hussein (a tyrannical dictator of Iraq) had begun building weapons of mass destruction, which led to American military intervention in Iraq. Hussein's regime was defeated in 5 weeks. Hussein was captured in 2003 and put on trial by Iraq's interim government (the U.S. helped to install the interim government). He was executed in 2006 for his crimes against humanity; however, his defeat did not end corruption or infighting in Iraq. Insurgency, instability, and violence between *Sunni* and *Shiite* Muslims continues, and politicians (including President Barack Obama and President Donald Trump) have found it difficult to end the war, which has resulted in approximately 500,000 deaths and cost the U.S. $6 trillion. (Note: Sunnis and Shiites both follow the Islamic religion and believe in Allah as the supreme God, but the difference is that Sunnis believe Bakr, Umar, and Uthman are the true leaders of Muhammad, and Shiites believe that Ali is the true leader based on his blood lineage. Today, 90 percent of Muslims are Sunni. Most Shiites live in Iran and Iraq.)
Human rights concerns	Abuses of the PATRIOT Act made by the CIA, U.S. military, and FBI led to political and public debates regarding the violation of human and civil rights. While some Americans were most concerned with privacy violations, others criticized the abuses and torture of suspects and Iraqi prisoners. Prisoners of war were held at detention camps in **Guantanamo Bay** and **Abu Ghraib.** Public outcry has led to the curbing of military practices and some revisions in policy, but since its power was extended in 2011, the act remains a source of political conflict.

Did you know? The United States strengthened its enemies by inadvertently contributing to the expansion of terrorism in the Middle East. As the result of civilian casualties in Iraq and Afghanistan and the placement of radical leaders in American military prisons where they have formed relationships, terrorism and *jihad* (Islamic holy war) have grown in popularity. Although Osama bin Laden was executed by the U.S. in 2011 during an Obama administration military raid, extreme Islamist groups have gained members and overtaken many countries in the Middle East, starting civil war in Syria and growing more powerful than Al-Qaeda. The most infamous organization is the **Islamic State of Iraq and Syria** (ISIS), otherwise known as simply the **Islamic State** (IS).

Barack Obama's Presidency (2009 to 2017)

By 2007, the U.S. engagement in foreign wars had become questionable and expensive. Although Bush was reelected in 2004, Republican domestic and international policies grew increasingly unpopular. In 2008, younger voters turned to the Democrats, who offered a more racially diverse and middle-class vision of success for America's future. **Barack Obama,** the first African American president, was elected in 2008.

President Obama's domestic and foreign programs often reacted against or reversed Republican policies in education and healthcare. Obama revitalized issues that Democrats had been attempting to pass since the Clinton administration. Although Obama intended to end America's participation in military conflicts in the Middle East, U.S. foreign policy remains tenuous. In 2015, President Obama negotiated a United States and Iran deal called the Joint Comprehensive Plan of Action. The main purpose was to remove sanctions against Iran in exchange for Iran halting the production of its nuclear arms. The deal was condemned by many Republicans and by Israeli Prime Minister Benjamin Netanyahu.

Chapter Review Practice Questions

Practice questions are for instructional purposes only and may not reflect the format of the actual exam. On the actual exam, questions will be grouped into sets. Each set contains one source-based prompt (document or image) and two to five questions.

Multiple-Choice Questions

Questions 1–3 refer to the following passage.

> I came to the National Security Council six years ago to work in the administration of a great president... I observed the president to be a leader who cared deeply about people and who believed that the interests of our country were advanced by recognizing that ours is a nation at risk in a dangerous world, and acting accordingly...
>
> We sought to achieve the democratic outcome in Nicaragua that this administration still supports, which involved keeping the contras together in both body and soul. We made efforts to open a new relationship with Iran and recover our hostages. We worked on the development of a concerted policy regarding terrorists and terrorism and a capable—and a capability for dealing in a concerted manner with that threat...
>
> There were many problems. I believe that we worked as hard as we could to solve them, and sometimes we succeeded and sometimes we failed—but at least we tried. And I want to tell you that I for one will never regret having tried.
>
> —Source: Lieutenant Colonel Oliver North, U.S. Marine Corps,
> "Statement to the Joint Iran-Contra Congressional Committee," July 9, 1987.

1. Which of the following best explains the purpose of North's statement?

   A. North's promotion for the revolutionary fighters (Contras) and their cause
   B. The scapegoating of Reagan by the National Security Council for his knowledge of events in Iran and Nicaragua
   C. North's acknowledgment of the growing public outcry regarding U.S. foreign policies in the 1980s
   D. North's belief that his actions were instrumental in the U.S.'s fight in the Cold War

2. Based on your knowledge of U.S. history, how does North's statement corroborate U.S. foreign policies of the 1980s?

   A. The administration's policies were specifically associated with international terrorism.
   B. The administration's policies were implicitly associated with the Reagan Doctrine.
   C. The administration's policies were criticized by North, hinting at controversial practices.
   D. The administration's policies were newly developed and North focused on trial and error.

3. Based on your knowledge of U.S. history, which of the following best describes how U.S. foreign policy changed after Reagan left office?

   A. The United Nations was consulted more frequently as a tool to avoid military engagement.
   B. Southeast Asia and Europe became primary U.S. foreign relations concerns.
   C. Trade embargos were implemented when foreign relations failed to bend to U.S. desires.
   D. At the beginning of the 21st century, a War on Terror became the primary goal of U.S. policymakers.

Questions 4–5 refer to the following two diagrams.

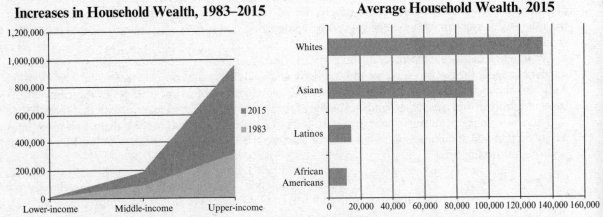

Source: Statistics gathered from House Resolution 159, 114th Congress, Session 1, March 18, 2015.

4. Which of the following best describes the trends in the U.S. economy from 1983 to 2015?

   A. The dominance of minorities and immigrants in the economy
   B. The unequal distribution of wealth among white Americans
   C. The growing disparity between the rich and poor in the U.S.
   D. The rejection of fiscal policies that broadened the American economy

5. Based on your knowledge of U.S. history, which of the following events best describes a direct cause for the trends depicted in the charts?

   A. The dot-com industry's decline in the early 2000s
   B. Reagan's inability to reform domestic programs like Social Security and Medicare
   C. George W. Bush's Economic Growth and Tax Relief Reconciliation Act (EGTRRA)
   D. Clinton's support and signing of the North American Free Trade Agreement (NAFTA)

Answer Explanations

Multiple-Choice Questions

1. **D.** North's statement is a defense of his behavior during the Cold War (Iran-Contra Affair), choice D. It reflects his own perceptions, not those of the public, choice C. Instead of blaming Reagan, choice B, North's statement praises him and aligns with the foreign policy of the era in which North was speaking (the 1980s). North's statement makes no comment, however, on the cause of the Contras, choice A, which appears to be irrelevant to his justification of the administration's actions.

2. **B.** Rather than criticizing the work of the National Security Council or Reagan's policies, choice C, North implicitly references the Reagan Doctrine, choice B, which advocated the funding and training of anti-Communists as a defense for the administration's actions. Although North acknowledges the "problems" they faced and discusses international terrorism, choice A, North was placing these things in the context of the Cold War policy of the 1980s, which was associated with Reagan, instead of making them the focal point of his discussion. Since the policies North is referencing had been followed by the Reagan administration since 1985, they were not newly developed, choice D.

3. **D.** After 9/11, the Middle East and the War on Terror replaced Cold War concerns, choice D. The War on Terror did not commence immediately after the end of the Reagan years, but it is the best answer among the choices listed. U.N. resolutions (like that which instigated the fighting in Korea), choice A, and trade embargoes, choice C (Jefferson even employed these), were not new tools of foreign policy. Southeast Asia and Europe were primary concerns during the Cold War, which included the Reagan Era, choice B.

4. **C.** The graphs do not reflect statistics for just white Americans, choice B. Many ethnic divisions are noted in the second graph, which indicates that white and Asian Americans greatly surpassed their Hispanic and African American neighbors in average household wealth. This also demonstrates that minorities and immigrants were NOT dominant in the economy, choice A. Neither graph reflects the rejection of fiscal policies that seek to increase the economy, choice D, but the first graph does note the growing wealth gap between various groups and classes of Americans, choice C.

5. **C.** Although Reagan's inability to reform social programs, choice B, may have increased the national debt and the dot-com industry bust, choice A, made life difficult for many Americans in the early 2000s, neither is a direct cause of the widening wealth gap. One might argue that some citizens recovered more quickly from U.S. recessions during this period than others, or that Clinton's support for NAFTA, choice D, removed industrial jobs as a means of support for many lower-income Americans, but neither of these is explicitly linked to these statistics. The best answer is choice C, George W. Bush's Economic Growth and Tax Relief Reconciliation Act (EGTRRA). Tax reform throughout the era in question increased surplus income for the rich, who failed to invest it in American industry, as many policymakers had hoped.

Chapter 13

Full-Length Practice Exam

This chapter contains a full-length practice exam that will give you valuable insight into the types of questions that may appear on the APUSH exam. As you take this practice exam, try to simulate testing conditions and time limits for each of the following sections:

Section	Questions	Time
Section I: Part A—Multiple-Choice Questions	55 questions	55 minutes
Section I: Part B—Short-Answer Questions	3 questions	40 minutes
Section II: Part A—Document-Based Question	1 question	60 minutes
Section II: Part B—Long-Essay Question	1 question	40 minutes

Answer Sheet for Multiple-Choice Questions

1 Ⓐ Ⓑ Ⓒ Ⓓ
2 Ⓐ Ⓑ Ⓒ Ⓓ
3 Ⓐ Ⓑ Ⓒ Ⓓ
4 Ⓐ Ⓑ Ⓒ Ⓓ
5 Ⓐ Ⓑ Ⓒ Ⓓ
6 Ⓐ Ⓑ Ⓒ Ⓓ
7 Ⓐ Ⓑ Ⓒ Ⓓ
8 Ⓐ Ⓑ Ⓒ Ⓓ
9 Ⓐ Ⓑ Ⓒ Ⓓ
10 Ⓐ Ⓑ Ⓒ Ⓓ
11 Ⓐ Ⓑ Ⓒ Ⓓ
12 Ⓐ Ⓑ Ⓒ Ⓓ
13 Ⓐ Ⓑ Ⓒ Ⓓ
14 Ⓐ Ⓑ Ⓒ Ⓓ
15 Ⓐ Ⓑ Ⓒ Ⓓ
16 Ⓐ Ⓑ Ⓒ Ⓓ
17 Ⓐ Ⓑ Ⓒ Ⓓ
18 Ⓐ Ⓑ Ⓒ Ⓓ
19 Ⓐ Ⓑ Ⓒ Ⓓ
20 Ⓐ Ⓑ Ⓒ Ⓓ
21 Ⓐ Ⓑ Ⓒ Ⓓ
22 Ⓐ Ⓑ Ⓒ Ⓓ
23 Ⓐ Ⓑ Ⓒ Ⓓ
24 Ⓐ Ⓑ Ⓒ Ⓓ
25 Ⓐ Ⓑ Ⓒ Ⓓ
26 Ⓐ Ⓑ Ⓒ Ⓓ
27 Ⓐ Ⓑ Ⓒ Ⓓ
28 Ⓐ Ⓑ Ⓒ Ⓓ
29 Ⓐ Ⓑ Ⓒ Ⓓ
30 Ⓐ Ⓑ Ⓒ Ⓓ

31 Ⓐ Ⓑ Ⓒ Ⓓ
32 Ⓐ Ⓑ Ⓒ Ⓓ
33 Ⓐ Ⓑ Ⓒ Ⓓ
34 Ⓐ Ⓑ Ⓒ Ⓓ
35 Ⓐ Ⓑ Ⓒ Ⓓ
36 Ⓐ Ⓑ Ⓒ Ⓓ
37 Ⓐ Ⓑ Ⓒ Ⓓ
38 Ⓐ Ⓑ Ⓒ Ⓓ
39 Ⓐ Ⓑ Ⓒ Ⓓ
40 Ⓐ Ⓑ Ⓒ Ⓓ
41 Ⓐ Ⓑ Ⓒ Ⓓ
42 Ⓐ Ⓑ Ⓒ Ⓓ
43 Ⓐ Ⓑ Ⓒ Ⓓ
44 Ⓐ Ⓑ Ⓒ Ⓓ
45 Ⓐ Ⓑ Ⓒ Ⓓ
46 Ⓐ Ⓑ Ⓒ Ⓓ
47 Ⓐ Ⓑ Ⓒ Ⓓ
48 Ⓐ Ⓑ Ⓒ Ⓓ
49 Ⓐ Ⓑ Ⓒ Ⓓ
50 Ⓐ Ⓑ Ⓒ Ⓓ
51 Ⓐ Ⓑ Ⓒ Ⓓ
52 Ⓐ Ⓑ Ⓒ Ⓓ
53 Ⓐ Ⓑ Ⓒ Ⓓ
54 Ⓐ Ⓑ Ⓒ Ⓓ
55 Ⓐ Ⓑ Ⓒ Ⓓ

Section I

Part A—Multiple-Choice Questions

Multiple-choice questions are grouped into sets. Each set contains one source-based prompt (document or image) and two to five questions.

55 questions

55 minutes

Questions 1–3 refer to the following passage.

> For the increase of shipping and encouragement of the navigation of this nation, wherein, under the good providence and protection of God, the wealth, safety, and strength of this kingdom is so much concerned; be it enacted by the King's most excellent majesty, and by the lords and commons in this present parliament assembled, and by the authority thereof, That from and after the first day of December 1660, and from thenceforward, no goods or commodities whatsoever shall be imported into or exported out of any lands, islands, plantations or territories to his Majesty belonging or in his possession…in Asia, Africa, or America, in any other ship or ships, vessel or vessels whatsoever, but in such ships or vessels as do truly and without fraud belong only to the people of England or Ireland…and whereof the master and three fourths of the mariners at least are English; under the penalty of the forfeiture and loss of all the goods and commodities which shall be imported into or exported out of any of the aforesaid places in any other ship or vessel…

> —Source: The "Navigation Act of 1660." British decree that prohibited colonies from trading directly with other European nations.

1. Which of the following best describes the underlying political and economic ideals that inspired the Navigation Act?

   A. Alexander Hamilton's motivation for a capitalistic society
   B. Thomas Jefferson's motivation for an independent nation
   C. The mercantilism practice of the English Crown
   D. The impressment practice of the English Crown

2. Based on your knowledge of U.S. history, which of the following best expresses the purpose of the Navigation Act?

   A. To create colonial dependence on Britain by limiting the trade of imports and exports
   B. To create tensions between the colonists and the British by prohibiting trade
   C. To create dependence between the colonists and the Dutch, with whom they had been trading for decades
   D. To create tensions between merchant sailors and commanders, who feared attacks by British ships

3. Which of the following best describes the result of the Navigation Act?

    A. Colonists authorized economic and trade support.

    B. Colonists resented limitations on trade and rebelled through smuggling.

    C. New England shipbuilders rebelled in an effort to combat a decrease in the demand for their vessels.

    D. British governors convinced colonial assemblies to support the Navigation Act.

Questions 4–6 refer to the following map.

Mississippi Territory, 1814

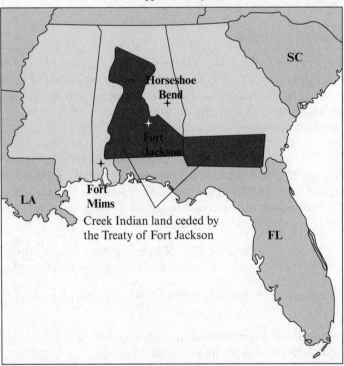

4. Which of the following North American military conflicts does the map reflect?

    A. The War of 1812

    B. The Trail of Tears

    C. The French and Indian War

    D. The American Civil War

5. Based on your knowledge of U.S. history, which of the following best explains why the Creek Indians surrendered their land?

    A. The Battle of Fort Jackson

    B. The movement of white settlers into the Mississippi Territory

    C. The defeat of the Creek Indians at the Battle of Horseshoe Bend

    D. The withdrawal of British soldiers during the Creek War in 1813

6. Which American general became a war hero and future U.S. president as a result of his successes during the Creek War and other military conflicts?

   A. William Henry Harrison
   B. Andrew Jackson
   C. George Washington
   D. Theodore Roosevelt

Questions 7–9 refer to the following passage.

   I am aware that many object to the severity of my language; but is there not cause for severity? I will be as harsh as truth, and as uncompromising as justice. On this subject, I do not wish to think, or to speak, or write, with moderation. No! no! Tell a man whose house is on fire to give a moderate alarm; tell him to moderately rescue his wife from the hands of the ravisher; tell the mother to gradually extricate her babe from the fire into which it has fallen; —but urge me not to use moderation in a cause like the present. I am in earnest—I will not equivocate—I will not excuse—I will not retreat a single inch— AND I WILL BE HEARD.

   —Source: William Lloyd Garrison, newspaper article about abolitionism, 1831.

7. The excerpt most directly reflects

   A. The northern call for civil war
   B. The American support of emancipation through colonization
   C. The uncompromising demand for immediate emancipation
   D. Lincoln's terms for the Border States

8. Based on your knowledge of U.S. history, which of the following was the name of William Lloyd Garrison's famous newspaper?

   A. *The North Star*
   B. *The Abolitionists*
   C. *The Missouri Gazette*
   D. *The Liberator*

9. Which one of the following actions did NOT contribute to the sectional divisions that caused the Civil War?

   A. The abolitionists added a moral element to the slavery debates.
   B. The abolitionists influenced domestic and foreign support by publishing pro-slavery documents.
   C. The abolitionists had meetings where escaped slaves told horrific stories about slavery.
   D. The abolitionists spoke out against legislation that did not uphold their values.

Questions 10–12 refer to the following political cartoon.

Source: Thomas Nast, "The Union as It Was—the Lost Cause, Worse than Slavery," *Harper's Weekly,* October 24, 1874. Depicts harassment by the Ku Klux Klan and the White League.

10. The political cartoon most directly reflects

    A. The persecution of African Americans before the Civil War

    B. The family divisions due to conditions in the South

    C. The northern Republican criticisms of "Redeemer" attempts to regain political power

    D. The low economic status of the members of the White League rebels

11. Which of the following represents the intimidation tactics suggested by the political cartoon?

    A. The execution of the Enforcement Acts

    B. The attack on the courthouse and the subsequent "riots" in Colfax, Louisiana

    C. The campaign led by Ulysses S. Grant for peace and stability

    D. The caning of Charles Sumner by a southern Congressional representative

12. Based on your knowledge of U.S. history, which of the following represents the end of the Progressive rights that African Americans had gained during Reconstruction?

    A. The pardoning of wealthy white southern planters by Andrew Johnson
    B. The enactment of the Black Codes restricting African American freedoms
    C. The Enforcement Acts exercised by President Ulysses S. Grant
    D. The Supreme Court case *Plessy v. Ferguson*

Questions 13–15 refer to the following passage.

> Faithfully pointing the Things of a BAD and DANGEROUS TENDENCY in the late and present religious Appearance in the Land…I shall first mention Itinerant Preaching. This had its Rise (at least in these Parts) from Mr. WHITEFIELD, though I could never see, I own, upon what Warrant, either from Scripture or Reason, he went about Preaching from one Province and Parish to another…
>
> The next Thing I shall take Notice of, as what I can't but think of dangerous Tendency, is that Terror so many have been the Subjects of, Expressing itself in strange Effects upon the Body…I am clearly in the Sentiment that the great Stress that has been laid upon such Terrors as have evidently been produced by the mechanical influence of awful Words and frightful Gestures has been a great Disservice to the interest of Religion…
>
> —Source: Boston clergyman Charles Chauncy, "Seasonable Thoughts on the State of Religion," 1743.

13. The excerpt most directly reflects which of the following mid-18th-century developments?

    A. The tensions between Old and New Lights during the First Great Awakening
    B. The disadvantages of religious teachings during the Second Great Awakening
    C. The violent objection to Puritan control of the Massachusetts Bay Colony
    D. The shift from religious to secular legislation in New England

14. Based on your knowledge of U.S. history, how did the events described in the passage influence colonial society?

    A. The events encouraged colonists to bring together church and state.
    B. The events caused colonists to reject tenets of individualism, toleration, and egalitarianism.
    C. The events opened the door for an evangelical culture that challenged the power of the gentry.
    D. The events had no direct influence on colonial society.

15. The ideas expressed in the excerpt most directly contributed to which of the following mid-18th-century developments?

    A. The split of northern and southern religious denominations as a result of sectional tensions
    B. The spread of Evangelicalism throughout the U.S. that lasted through the 19th century
    C. The use of religion for pro-slavery arguments by religious southern evangelicals
    D. The Second Great Awakening that sparked social reform movements

Questions 16–18 refer to the following graph.

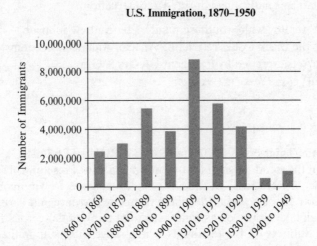

16. Which of the following is the main cause for the immigration trend after 1920?

    A. The demographic growth related to the Great Migration
    B. Prohibitions associated with the Chinese Exclusion Act
    C. Nativist legislation that increased immigration restrictions and established quotas
    D. The reestablishment of white supremacist vigilante groups like the Ku Klux Klan

17. The increase in immigration from 1880 to 1920 is most directly associated with which of the following developments in the United States?

    A. Immigrants shied away from labor organizations in order to "blend" into American society.
    B. Employers worked to end the wealth gap, allowing many immigrants to become successful property owners.
    C. Working-class racial tensions decreased as laborers united in common causes.
    D. Immigrants were drawn to urban centers to work, but often experienced exploitation and poverty.

18. Which of the following historical events best explains the lowest immigration trend from 1930 to 1939?

    A. The collapse of the U.S. economy in 1929
    B. A global economic depression
    C. World War I
    D. World War II

Questions 19–21 refer to the following passage.

> …the Nullification Crisis has usually been presented as an isolated event. Viewed in proper perspective, the confrontation between Andrew Jackson and the Carolina nullifiers was the central occurrence in the broader transition of South Carolina from the enthusiastic nationalism of 1816 to the extreme sectionalism of 1836…
>
> —Source: William W. Freehling, historian, *Prelude to Civil War*, 1965. An account of the nullification crisis from 1816 to 1836 that almost led to South Carolina's succession.

19. Which of the following best supports Freehling's interpretation of the nullification crisis?

   A. The nullification crisis had little effect on the people of South Carolina.
   B. The tensions over slavery developed in the North and South after 1816.
   C. The War of 1812 boosted American hopes and sparked sentiments of patriotism.
   D. Farmers and landowners resented high tariffs in the rural North and Deep South.

20. Which of the following best describes the impact of the event Freehling references in the excerpt?

   A. Tariffs were permanently lowered, which ended South Carolina's objection to Jackson's presidency.
   B. President Andrew Jackson, wanting to maintain peace, reacted meekly to the conflict.
   C. After the passage of the Force Bill, the nation was prevented from civil war only by a Congressional compromise.
   D. A generation of common South Carolinians rejected their legislators for almost forcing them to secede.

21. In the context of early-19th-century U.S. history, the nullification crisis provided evidence for which of the following developments?

   A. Sectional tension between the North and the South
   B. The rejection of the Republican election of Abraham Lincoln
   C. The objection to the Era of Good Feelings
   D. The South's growing antipathy toward John C. Calhoun

Questions 22–24 refer to the following passage.

   Our policy is directed not against any country or doctrine but against hunger, poverty, desperation and chaos. Its purpose should be the revival of a working economy in the world so as to permit the emergence of political and social conditions in which free institutions can exist. Such assistance, I am convinced, must not be on a piece-meal basis as various crises develop. Any assistance that this government may render in the future should provide a cure rather than a mere palliative. Any government that is willing to assist in the task of recovery will find full cooperation, I am sure, on the part of the United States government. Any government which maneuvers to block the recovery of other countries cannot expect help from us. Furthermore, governments, political parties or groups which seek to perpetuate human misery in order to profit therefrom politically or otherwise will encounter the opposition of the United States.

   —Source: George Marshall, "The Marshall Plan," 1947. Speech presented to the Harvard Alumni Association.

22. Which of the following best expresses Marshall's main goal?

   A. To defend U.S. economic aid as a propaganda tool
   B. To reject economic assistance offered by Soviet interests
   C. To advocate economic assistance for European recovery
   D. To work toward unity and cooperation with all foreign governments

23. Based on your knowledge of U.S. history, the Marshall Plan was primarily established in order to

    A. Promote Western democracy during the Cold War
    B. Justify targeting the Soviets for global destruction
    C. Defend U.S. capitalism and global privilege
    D. Establish an unbiased and nonpolitical recovery program

24. Based on your knowledge of U.S. history, one of the domestic results of the Marshall Plan was

    A. A rise in the employment of African Americans and women
    B. The enactment of the Servicemen's Readjustment Act of 1944 (GI Bill)
    C. The increase in German and Eastern European cultural exchange
    D. The beginning of new international markets for U.S. goods

Questions 25–26 refer to the following passage.

> And now I will state the Question betwixt me as a Governor and Mr. Bacon, and say that if any enemies should invade England, any Councellor Justice of peace or other inferior officer, might raise what forces they could to protect his Majesties subjects, But I say again, if after the Kings knowledge of this invasion, any the greatest peer of England, should raise forces against the kings prohibition this would be now, and ever was in all ages and Nations accompanied treason.
>
> —Source: Sir William Berkeley, his most Sacred Majesties Governor and Captain General of Virginia, "The Declaration and Remonstrance of 1676." Berkeley saw the rebellion as a direct challenge to his authority.

25. Governor Berkeley's speech reflects his position about which of the following colonial conflicts?

    A. The mob violence of the Stono Rebellion
    B. The armed uprising of angry yeomen and frontiersmen
    C. The battle between farmers and large landowners over tobacco inspections
    D. The violent objection of indentured servants to extensions in service

26. Based on your knowledge of U.S. history, why was this conflict considered a turning point in colonial history?

    A. It ushered in the shift from indentured servitude to slavery as the main form of labor.
    B. It represented the first abuse of authority by a royal governor.
    C. It drew attention to the unnecessary slaughter of peaceful Native Americans.
    D. It suppressed the rights of black slaves through the Negro Act of 1740.

Questions 27–29 refer to the following political cartoon.

Source: "Dividing the National Map," 1860. Depicts strong national divisions, as a map of the U.S. is being torn apart by four candidates of presidential campaigns.

27. The political cartoon most directly reflects

    A.   The infighting among candidates of the 1860 election

    B.   The regional fighting between Radical Republicans and President Andrew Jackson

    C.   The character of southern Democrats

    D.   The division of the country among the various presidential candidates of 1860

28. Based on your knowledge of U.S. history, which of the following was a result of the 1860 election?

    A.   Southerners who were sympathetic to pro-slavery politicians attacked Fort Sumter.

    B.   President Buchanan's objection to the election was published in a southern newspaper.

    C.   South Carolina seceded from the Union.

    D.   John Wilkes Booth created an assassination plan.

29. Which of the following best reflects Abraham Lincoln's attitude toward the South and slavery during the 1860 election?

    A.   Lincoln promised not to interfere with slavery in states where slavery already existed.

    B.   Lincoln advocated a free-soil policy and promised to end slavery in the U.S.

    C.   Lincoln's Emancipation Proclamation freed slaves in Confederate states.

    D.   Lincoln was morally opposed to slavery, but believed it should not be banned anywhere in the U.S. due to the constitutional rights of slaveholders.

Questions 30–31 refer to the following image.

Source: The bloody massacre perpetrated in King Street Boston on March 5th 1770 by a party of the 29th Regt.

30. The event shown in the image most directly reflects which of the following?

    A. An actual event based on the British slaughtering of innocent American colonists

    B. A loyalist perception of an event based on a mob attack of British soldiers

    C. A patriot's point of view of a historical event on the killing of five colonists

    D. The Continental Congress' perception of an event that began the war

31. Which of the following describes the importance of the event depicted?

    A. It was part of the colonists' growing animosity toward Britain and was prompted when Parliament asked colonists to pay for Britain's military debt.

    B. It was part of the colonists' growing animosity toward Britain and was prompted when several royal governors refused to honor requests for Native American land.

    C. It was part of General Gage's frustration during British occupation after the Battle of Lexington.

    D. It was part of the British Crown's frustration with the colonists' treatment of British soldiers after the passage of the Proclamation of 1763.

Questions 32–33 refer to the following passage.

No voting qualification or prerequisite to voting, or standard, practice, or procedure shall be imposed or applied by any State or political subdivision to deny or abridge the right of any citizen of the United States to vote on account of race or color...

—Source: Voting Rights Act of 1965. U.S. legislation that prohibited racial discrimination in voting.

32. Based on your knowledge of U.S. history, which of the following presidents signed the Voting Rights Act into law?

   A. John F. Kennedy
   B. Lyndon B. Johnson
   C. Dwight D. Eisenhower
   D. Richard Nixon

33. What was the historical context that preceded the Voting Rights Act that may have generated public and Congressional support?

   A. The televised beating of peaceful protestors who took part in the freedom rides in Anniston, Alabama
   B. The televised media coverage of the murder of three students in Jackson, Mississippi
   C. The televised funeral of murder victim Emmett Till
   D. The televised beating of peaceful protestors who marched in Selma, Alabama

Questions 34–35 refer to the following image.

Source: Charles Willson Peale, "Mary Gibson Tilghman and Sons, William Gibson and John Lloyd Tilghman," 1789.

34. This portrait best reflects which early-American ideology?

    A. Good citizenship, which started with the proper and obedient behavior of children
    B. Republican motherhood, which advocated the education of women so they could raise good citizens
    C. The bravery of widowhood, which noted women and children who lost fathers at war so children could grow up in a free country
    D. The family structure of the wealthy class, which encouraged the strength of the nation through privilege, as depicted in the clothing of the mother and her children

35. Based on your knowledge of U.S. history, which of the following best describes male politicians' response to women like Abigail Adams, who advocated to "remember the ladies"?

    A. Politicians supported egalitarian ideals by passing legislation that guaranteed women the rights they deserved as American citizens.
    B. Politicians connected women's roles to dependency and scoffed if women demanded even limited rights.
    C. Politicians supported women's ability to become educated in order to mother good republican citizens, but most politicians considered women's citizenship absorbed into the standing of their husbands or fathers.
    D. Politicians connected to the role of the wife in the family, who was expected to help her husband emotionally and financially.

Questions 36–38 refer to the following passage.

To all to whom these Presents shall come, we the undersigned Delegates of the States affixed to our Names send greeting…

    I. The Stile of this Confederacy shall be "The United States of America."
    II. Each state retains its sovereignty, freedom, and independence, and every power, jurisdiction, and right, which is not by this Confederation expressly delegated to the United States, in Congress assembled.
    III. The said States hereby severally enter into a firm league of friendship with each other, for their common defense, the security of their liberties, and their mutual and general welfare, binding themselves to assist each other, against all force offered to, or attacks made upon them, or any of them, on account of religion, sovereignty, trade, or any other pretense whatever…

—Source: Articles of Confederation, Article I, "Style," Article II, "States Rights," and Article III, "Mutual Defense," 1777–1781.

36. Based on your knowledge of U.S. history, the three Articles of Confederation were written in response to

    A. The need for a strong federal government to uphold civil liberties
    B. The Albany Plan, which sought to unify the colonies during the French and Indian War
    C. A call for states' rights that would guarantee regional security
    D. A wartime demand for a central government that could conduct military engagements and negotiate treaties

37. Which of the following events revealed the limits of the Articles of Confederation?

    A. Shays' Rebellion in rural Massachusetts
    B. Infighting among the colonies during the American Revolution
    C. The First Continental Congress
    D. The Continental Army's hardship at Valley Forge

38. Which of the following best describes the result of the ineffectiveness of the Articles of Confederation?

    A. The Articles were incorporated into state constitutions.
    B. The Articles were ineffective as a centralizing force and had to be completely replaced.
    C. The Articles needed to be modified to clarify civil rights and liberties.
    D. Although ineffective, the Articles were not modified for many years because federal politicians feared losing support for their state legislature policies.

Questions 39–40 refer to the following passage.

   The District Court's conclusion that assignment of children to the school nearest their home serving their grade would not effectively dismantle the dual school system is supported by the record, and the remedial technique of requiring bus transportation as a tool of school desegregation was within that court's power to provide equitable relief.

   —Source: *Swann v. Charlotte-Mecklenburg Board of Education,* 1971. U.S. Supreme Court Case dealing with busing students to promote integration.

39. Which of the following best explains the reason for the Supreme Court decision?

    A. The blatant disregard for *Brown v. Board of Education* throughout most of the South
    B. The desire to encourage public school attendance in lieu of the rise of private institutions in the 1960s
    C. The appeal for states' rights by the Dixiecrats
    D. Nixon's demand for a Silent Majority to restore "law and order"

40. The busing protests that occurred as a result of this Supreme Court decision were organized by which of the following?

    A. Militant African Americans who fought for their rights through aggressive protests and demonstrations
    B. Liberal legal organizations like the NAACP and the ACLU
    C. Business leaders who viewed the busing as harmful to the education of the next generation of children
    D. Southern citizens who violently opposed the forced desegregation of schools

Questions 41–43 refer to the following image.

Source: Thomas Nast, "Uncle Sam's Thanksgiving Dinner," *Harper's Weekly,* November 20, 1869.

41. Nast's political cartoon depicts which of the following social values during the Gilded Age?

   A. The belief that immigrants should be rejected and excluded from American national identity
   B. The belief that the peaceful integration of immigrants would lead to a national identity
   C. The belief in the White Man's Burden, which sought to encourage imperialism and civilize inferior races
   D. The belief that immigration quotas and regional developments were critical to expansionism

42. Which of the following best expresses Nast's underlying point of view?

   A. Nast wanted to criticize nativist beliefs that sought to pass discriminatory legislation and limit citizenship.
   B. Nast wanted to express how immigrants made positive contributions to the national economy.
   C. Nast wanted to show that the government had endless immigrant assistance programs.
   D. Nast wanted to describe the typical ethnically diverse American heritage.

43. Which of the following describes the changes in American attitudes about immigrants between 1880 and 1920?

   A. Immigrants were targeted by white supremacist groups in lynchings and other forms of violence.
   B. The Know Nothing Party rose in power and prestige.
   C. The enforcement of immigrant quotas and discriminatory legislation limited the influx of new immigrants.
   D. Labor organizations and political parties banned immigrant participation and barred immigrants from receiving civil rights.

Questions 44–46 refer to the following passage.

The recent alarming development and aggression of aggregated wealth, which, unless checked, will invariably lead to the pauperization and hopeless degradation of the toiling masses, render it imperative, if we desire to enjoy the blessings of life, that a check should be placed upon its power and upon unjust accumulation, and a system adopted which will secure to the laborer the fruits of his toil; and as this much-desired object can only be accomplished by the thorough unification of labor, and the united efforts of those who obey the divine injunction that "In the sweat of thy brow shalt thou eat bread," we have formed the Noble Order of the Knights of Labor with a view of securing the organization and direction, by cooperative effort, of the power of the industrial classes...

—Source: Preamble to the Constitution of the Knights of Labor, January 3, 1878.

44. The concerns expressed by the excerpt were a response to

   A. The increase in immigration from 1880 to 1920, which provided employers with cheap labor in the North

   B. The violence associated with anarchists and other militant labor organizations like the Industrial Workers of the World (IWW)

   C. The abuses of employers during the Gilded Age that relegated workers to replaceable components of the industrial system

   D. The denial of benefits intended for farmers and miners

45. The attitudes expressed by the writers of this excerpt contributed to which of the following 19th-century historical developments?

   A. The formation of labor organizations that used negotiations and strikes to obtain better working conditions and higher wages

   B. The unification of Populists with labor unionists to form a large advocacy group to change legislation

   C. The "class wars" that resulted in armed conflicts

   D. The regulation of industry and production motivated by sympathetic Gilded Age legislation

46. Based on your knowledge of U.S. history, which of the following contributed to the downfall of the Knights of Labor?

   A. The Great Railroad Strike

   B. The Haymarket Square Riot

   C. The Homestead Steelworkers Strike

   D. The Pullman Strike

Questions 47–49 refer to the following passage.

...they have deprived the Indians of their lives and souls, for the millions I mentioned have died without the Faith and without the benefit of the sacraments. This is a well-known and proven fact which even the tyrant Governors, themselves killers, know and admit. And never have the Indians in all the Indies committed any act against the Spanish Christians, until those Christians have first and many times committed countless cruel aggressions against them or against neighboring nations. For in the beginning the Indians regarded the Spaniards as angels from Heaven. Only after the Spaniards had used violence against them, killing, robbing, torturing, did the Indians ever rise up against them...

—Source: Bartolomé de las Casas, "A Brief Account of the Devastation of the Indies," 1542. Spanish missionary de las Casas arrived in the New World and lived according to the *encomienda* (living off the labor of the Natives). He later changed his heart and campaigned against the abuses of Native enslavement.

47. The attitude expressed by de las Casas suggests which of the following?

    A. The tensions in the New World associated with the Spanish monarchy's economic gain
    B. The rejection of slavery in the New World by religious organizations like the Jesuits
    C. The European debate regarding the appropriate management and treatment of Natives in the New World
    D. The feelings of resentment caused by European exploration and world power

48. Which of the following best describes one of the primary reasons for the European exploration of North America?

    A. The European desire to stabilize the economy with gold, silver, and precious metals
    B. The European quest for a western trade route to India
    C. The persecution of Catholics in Europe
    D. The inability to regulate European agriculture

49. Which of the following describes the impact of Spanish exploration on U.S. history?

    A. The Spanish settled in the Louisiana Territory and the U.S. purchased the territory to triple its size.
    B. Spanish gold funded much of the Revolutionary War.
    C. Dutch, Spanish, and British explorers battled for control of the Spanish-American Southwest.
    D. The Spanish settled in Florida and Texas, and U.S. conflicts arose to control those regions.

Questions 50–52 refer to the following image.

Source: Haskell Coffin, "Joan of Arc Saved France," 1918. World War I poster.

50. The war poster most directly depicts

   A. The end of isolationist foreign policies and the beginning of U.S. global intervention
   B. The U.S. government's attempt to gather financial and emotional support for the war
   C. Propaganda to appeal to mothers to support the war through consumer savings
   D. A propaganda attempt to harness citizen groups and shame those who did not support the war

51. Which of the following best represents the purpose for creating this war poster?

   A. As an appeal to women to work in factories
   B. A plea to persuade women to support the draft
   C. A promotion of women's political power as a wartime necessity
   D. A plea to convince women that their consumer power was important to war mobilization

52. Based on your knowledge of U.S. history, which of the following best represents a continuity of U.S. government propaganda posters in the years after the war?

   A. Posters created by the Committee on Public Information (CPI), which depicted Germans as barbarians
   B. Posters produced by the Office of War Information (OWI), which encouraged women to join the military
   C. Government press releases that shamed those who protested against the war
   D. Advertising commercials that aired during World War II marketing particular products as patriotic

Questions 53–55 refer to the following passage.

Our slaves are black, of another and inferior race... They are happy, content, unaspiring, and utterly incapable, from intellectual weakness, ever to give us any trouble by their aspirations. Yours are white, of your own race; you are brothers of one blood. They are your equals in natural endowment of intellect, and they feel galled by their degradation. Our slaves do not vote. We give them no political power. Yours do vote, and, being the majority, they are the depositories of all your political power. If they knew the tremendous secret, that the ballot-box is stronger than "an army with banners," and could combine, where would you be?... You have been making war upon us to our very hearthstones. How would you like for us to send lecturers and agitators North, to teach these people this, to aid in combining, and to lead them?

—Source: James Henry Hammond, "The Mudsill Speech," March 4, 1858. Hammond, a plantation owner from South Carolina, explains his "mudsill theory," whereby the menial class is necessary to perform duties so that the higher class can move civilization forward.

53. Which of the following best summarizes the author's argument?

    A. The objection of labor coalitions and political legislation in the North

    B. African American slaves are happy and committed to their masters.

    C. Antebellum tensions between northern and southern legislators

    D. The intention of granting voting rights to African Americans

54. The attitudes expressed by Hammond most likely

    A. Reflect the beliefs of northern and southern legislators

    B. Reflect the racist justification for oppression by white slave owners in the South

    C. Promote a class revolution for white workers

    D. Suggest industrial managers in the North should incorporate slavery into their factories

55. Based on your knowledge of U.S. history, which of the following events was the result of a differing worldview?

    A. The nullification crisis

    B. The American System

    C. The American Civil War

    D. The Bank War of the Jacksonian Era

IF YOU FINISH BEFORE TIME IS CALLED, CHECK YOUR WORK ON THIS SECTION ONLY. DO NOT WORK ON ANY OTHER SECTION IN THE TEST.

Part B—Short-Answer Questions

3 questions

40 minutes

Reading Time: 10 minutes (brainstorm your thoughts and organize your responses)

Writing Time: 30 minutes

Directions: Write your responses on lined paper. The short-answer questions will *not* require that you develop and support a thesis statement. Some short-answer questions include texts, images, graphs, or maps. Use complete sentences—bullet points or an outline is unacceptable. Write answers for the first and second questions and then answer EITHER the third or fourth question (not both). Answer **all** parts of the questions to receive full credit.

Question 1. Use the passages below to answer all parts of the question that follows.

Passage 1

Source: Richard Hofstadter, *Age of Reform,* 1955. Hofstadter is a historian who traces events of the Populist Movement, the Progressive Era, and the New Deal.

Concerning the great corporations, the Progressives felt that they were a menace to society and that they were all too often manipulated by unscrupulous men; on the other hand, many Progressives were quite aware that the newer organizations of industry and finance were a product of social evolution which had its beneficent side and that it was here to stay… As for the bosses, the machines, the corruptions of city life, they too found these things grave evils; but they were ready, perhaps all too ready, to admit that the existence of such evils was in large measure their own fault. Like the Populists, the Progressives were full of indignation, but their indignation was more qualified by a sense of responsibility, often even of guilt, and it was supported by a greater capacity to organize, legislate, and administer.

Passage 2

Source: Theodore Roosevelt, "New Nationalism," August 31, 1910. Speech presented at the dedication of the John Brown Memorial Park. Roosevelt argued for the great causes of equality, liberty, and self-government, which Americans had fought and died for during the Civil War.

…our government, national and state, must be freed from the sinister influence or control of special interests. Exactly as the special interests of cotton and slavery threatened our political integrity before the Civil War, so now the great special business interests too often control and corrupt the men and methods of government for their own profit. We must drive the special interests out of politics… For every special interest is entitled to justice, but not one is entitled to a vote in Congress, to a voice on the bench, or to representation in any public office. The Constitution guarantees protection to property, and we must make that promise good. But it does not give the right of suffrage to any corporation.

1. Using the passages, answer (a), (b), and (c).

    (a) Briefly explain ONE historical event or development that caused the frustration referenced in the passages.

    (b) Briefly explain how ONE specific historical event or development (not explicitly stated in the passages) could support Hofstadter's interpretation.

    (c) Briefly explain how ONE specific historical event or development (not explicitly stated in the passages) could support Roosevelt's interpretation.

Question 2. Use the image below to answer all parts of the question that follows.

Source: J. S. Pughe, "Putting his Foot Down," 1899. Image of the U.S. Open Door Policy depicting Uncle Sam holding a "Trade Treaty with China" while standing among the foreign rulers of Germany, Italy, England, Austria, Russia, and France.

2. Using the image, answer (a), (b), and (c).

    (a) Briefly describe ONE perspective about America's role in global expansionism supported by the image.

    (b) Briefly describe ONE specific historical event or development that led to the change in foreign policy depicted in the image.

    (c) Briefly explain ONE way in which the historical change depicted in the image was challenged between 1899 and 1917.

Choose EITHER Question 3 or Question 4.

3. Answer (a), (b), and (c).

   (a) Briefly describe ONE specific historical similarity between the women's rights movement in the period 1820–1864 and in the period 1865–1890.
   (b) Briefly describe ONE specific historical difference between the women's rights movement in the period 1820–1864 and in the period 1865–1890.
   (c) Briefly explain ONE specific historical effect of the women's rights movement in either the period 1820–1864 or in the period 1865–1890.

4. Answer (a), (b), and (c).

   (a) Briefly describe ONE specific historical similarity between the consumerism of the 1920s and the 1940s.
   (b) Briefly describe ONE specific historical difference between the consumerism of the 1920s and the 1940s.
   (c) Briefly explain ONE specific historical effect of the consumerism of the 1920s or the 1940s.

IF YOU FINISH BEFORE TIME IS CALLED, CHECK YOUR WORK ON THIS
SECTION ONLY. DO NOT WORK ON ANY OTHER SECTION IN THE TEST.

Section II

Part A—Document-Based Question

1 question
60 minutes

Reading Time: 15 minutes (brainstorm your thoughts and organize your response)
Writing Time: 45 minutes

Directions: The document-based question is based on the seven accompanying documents. The documents are for instructional purposes only. Some of the documents have been edited for the purpose of this practice exercise. Write your response on lined paper and include the following:

- **Thesis.** Present a thesis that supports a historically defensible claim, establishes a line of reasoning, and responds to all parts of the question. The thesis must consist of one or more sentences located in one place—either the introduction or the conclusion.

- **Contextualization.** Situate the argument by explaining the broader historical events, developments, or processes that occurred before, during, or after the time frame of the question.

- **Evidence from the documents.** Support your argument by using the content of six of the documents to develop and support a cohesive argument that responds to the question.

- **Evidence beyond the documents.** Support your argument by explaining at least one additional piece of specific historical evidence not found in the documents. (Note: The example must be different from the evidence used to earn the point for contextualization.)

- **Analysis.** Use at least three documents that are relevant to the question to explain the documents' point of view, purpose, historical situation, and/or audience.

- **Historical reasoning.** Use historical reasoning to show complex relationships among the documents, the topic question, and the thesis argument. Use evidence to corroborate, qualify, or modify the argument.

Based on the documents that follow answer the question below.

Question 1: Evaluate the extent to which differing views about civil and social resistance affected the development of the African American struggle against institutional oppression during the 20th century.

Document 1

> **Source: Booker T. Washington, "Atlanta Compromise Speech," September 18, 1895. Presented at the Cotton States and International Exposition in Atlanta, Georgia (a predominantly white audience).**
>
> Our greatest danger is that in the great leap from slavery to freedom we may overlook the fact that the masses of us are to live by the productions of our hands, and fail to keep in mind that we shall prosper in proportion as we learn to dignify and glorify common labour, and put brains and skill into the common occupations of life; shall prosper in proportion as we learn to draw the line between the superficial and the substantial, the ornamental gewgaws of life and the useful. No race can prosper till it learns that there is as much dignity in tilling a field as in writing a poem. It is at the bottom of life we must begin, and not at the top. Nor should we permit our grievances to overshadow our opportunities.

Document 2

> **Source: Gertrude Bustill Mossell, "The Work of the Afro-American Woman," 1908. Mossell wrote about a century of female black leaders, praising their achievements.**
>
> The emancipation of the Negro race came about at the entrance to that which has been aptly termed the Woman's Century; co-education, higher education for women, had each gained a foothold. The "Woman's Suffrage" movement had passed the era of ridicule and entered upon that of critical study. The Woman's Christian Temperance Union had become a strong factor in the reform work of the nation. These facts made the uplifting of the womanhood of this race a more hopeful task than might otherwise have been... Trammeled by their past condition and its consequent poverty, combined with the blasting influence of caste prejudice, they have yet made a fair showing. The men of the race, in most instances, have been generous, doing all in their power to allow the women of the race to rise with them.

Document 3

> **Source: W. E. B. Du Bois, "The Talented Tenth," from *The Negro Problem: A Series of Articles by Representative Negroes of Today,* 1903. Du Bois' essay refers to the "tenth portion" of the African American population that should be accorded the best educational and leadership opportunities.**
>
> The Negro race, like all races, is going to be saved by its exceptional men. The problem of education, then, among Negroes must first of all deal with the Talented Tenth; it is the problem of developing the Best of this race that they may guide the Mass away from the contamination and death of the Worst, in their own and other races. Now the training of men is a difficult and intricate task. Its technique is a matter for educational experts, but its object is for the vision of seers. If we make money the object of man-training, we shall develop money-makers but not necessarily men; if we make technical skill the object of education, we may possess artisans but not, in nature, men. Men we shall have only as we make manhood the object of the work of the schools—intelligence, broad sympathy, knowledge of the world that was and is, and of the relation of men to it—this is the curriculum of that Higher Education which must underlie true life. On this foundation we may build bread winning, skill of hand and quickness of brain, with never a fear lest the child and man mistake the means of living for the object of life...

Document 4

> **Source: Marcus Garvey, "The True Solution of the Negro Problem," November 25, 1922. Speech presented at the Universal Negro Improvement Association to explain a worldwide movement toward black liberation.**
>
> As far as Negroes are concerned, in America we have the problem of lynching, peonage and disfranchisement. In the West Indies, South and Central America we have the problem of peonage, serfdom, industrial and political governmental inequality. In Africa we have, not only peonage and serfdom, but outright slavery, racial exploitation and alien political monopoly. We cannot allow a continuation of these crimes against our race. As four hundred million men, women and children, worthy of the existence given us by the Divine Creator, we are determined to solve our own problem, by redeeming our Motherland Africa from the hands of alien exploiters and found there a government, a nation of our own, strong enough to lend protection to the members of our race scattered all over the world, and to compel the respect of the nations and races of the earth.

Document 5

Source: A. Philip Randolph, "Why We Should March," *Survey Graphic,* November 1942. Randolph supported the "Double V," victory for democracy at home and abroad. Randolph spearheaded a march on Washington to urge President Roosevelt to combat racial discrimination and end segregation in the military.

Though I have found no Negroes who want to see the United Nations lose this war, I have found many who, before the war ends, want to see the stuffing knocked out of white supremacy and of empire over subject peoples. American Negroes, involved as we are in the general issues of the conflict, are confronted not with a choice but with a challenge both to win democracy for ourselves at home and to help win the war for democracy the world over.

There is no escape from the horns of this dilemma. There ought not to be escape. For if the war for democracy is not won abroad, the fight for democracy cannot be won at home. If this war cannot be won for the white peoples, it will not be won for the darker races.

Document 6

Source: Walter Albertin, "Martin Luther King Jr. at a Press Conference: Why We Can't Wait," 1964.

Document 7

Source: Stokely Carmichael, "Black Power: The Politics of Liberation in America," 1969. Carmichael was a civil rights activist who originated the black nationalist slogan, "black power."

The only time I hear people talk about nonviolence is when black people move to defend themselves against white people. Black people cut themselves every night in the ghetto—don't anybody talk about nonviolence. Lyndon Baines Johnson is busy bombing the hell of out Vietnam—don't nobody talk about nonviolence. White people beat up black people every day—don't nobody talk about nonviolence. But as soon as black people start to move, the double standard comes into being.

You can't defend yourself. That's what you're saying…it is clear to me that we have to wage a psychological battle on the right for black people to define their own terms, define themselves as they see fit, and organize themselves as they see it.

IF YOU FINISH BEFORE TIME IS CALLED, CHECK YOUR WORK ON THIS SECTION ONLY. DO NOT WORK ON ANY OTHER SECTION IN THE TEST.

Part B—Long-Essay Question

1 question

40 minutes

Directions: Write your response on lined paper. You must demonstrate your ability to use specific, historical evidence and write an effective essay to support your argument. Your essay is considered a first draft and may contain some grammatical errors that will not be counted against you. However, to receive full credit, your essay must demonstrate historically defensible content knowledge and the following:

- **Thesis.** Provides a thesis that is a historically defensible claim, establishes a line of reasoning, and responds to all parts of the question—rather than merely restating or rephrasing the question. The thesis must consist of one or more sentences and must be located in one place—in the introduction or the conclusion.

- **Contextualization.** Describes how the historical context is relevant to the question. Relates the topic to broader historical events, developments, or processes that occurred before, during, or after the time frame. (Note: Must include more than a phrase or reference.)

- **Evidence.** Supports and develops the argument by identifying specific and relevant historical examples of evidence related to the topic of the question.

- **Historical reasoning.** Uses historical reasoning (comparison, causation, or continuity/change over time) to structure the argument that addresses the question.

- **Analysis.** Demonstrates a complex understanding of the historical development that focuses on the question to corroborate, qualify, or modify the argument. (For example, analyze multiple variables, explain similarities/differences, explain cause/effect, explain multiple causes, explain both continuity and change, explain connections across periods of time, corroborate multiple perspectives across themes, or consider alternative views.)

Choose ONE of the three long-essay questions below. The three questions focus on the same reasoning skill but apply to different time periods. This allows students to choose which time period they are best prepared to write about. Write ONE essay on the topic of EITHER Question 2, Question 3, or Question 4 that follows.

Question 2. Evaluate the extent to which increased European migration fostered change in the relationship between colonists, colonial governments, and the British monarchy from 1609 to 1754.

Question 3. Evaluate the extent to which internal U.S. migration fostered changes in American political alliances and citizen expectations from 1815 to 1880.

Question 4. Evaluate the extent to which internal U.S. migration fostered changes in American political alliances and citizen expectations from 1910 to 1990.

IF YOU FINISH BEFORE TIME IS CALLED, CHECK YOUR WORK ON THIS SECTION ONLY. DO NOT WORK ON ANY OTHER SECTION IN THE TEST.

Answer Key for Multiple-Choice Questions

1. C	12. D	23. A	34. B	45. A
2. A	13. A	24. D	35. C	46. B
3. B	14. C	25. B	36. D	47. C
4. A	15. A	26. A	37. A	48. B
5. C	16. C	27. D	38. B	49. D
6. B	17. D	28. C	39. A	50. B
7. C	18. B	29. A	40. D	51. D
8. D	19. C	30. C	41. B	52. D
9. B	20. C	31. A	42. A	53. C
10. C	21. A	32. B	43. C	54. B
11. B	22. C	33. D	44. C	55. C

Answer Explanations

Section I

Part A—Multiple-Choice Questions

1. **C.** The Navigation Acts (1651–1663) were shaped by a belief in mercantilism, choice C, a form of economic nationalism that held that only a limited amount of wealth existed in the world. Most European nations protected their economies by limiting trade through *protectionism* (government-imposed tariffs on exported and imported goods). Choice A, Alexander Hamilton's motivation for a capitalistic society, is incorrect; Hamilton was the first Secretary of the Treasury and supported free-trade policies, but the rise of capitalism did not transpire until the 19th century. Choice B, Thomas Jefferson's motivation for independence, and choice D, impressment (the British forcing colonists to serve in the British military), are not relevant to mercantilism and trade.

2. **A.** The act was designed to create colonial economic subordination to Britain by limiting the import and export of certain colonial goods, choice A. It is important to remember to choose the *best* answer to the question. Although the Navigation Act resulted in tensions between colonists and the British Empire, choice B, that was not the intention when the act was created. Instead of encouraging trade with and dependence on the Dutch (choice C), the acts were designed to eliminate dependence on any country other than Britain, the mother country. The question has little or nothing to do with tensions between sailors and commanders, choice D, and is focused much more on trade than human beings.

3. **B.** The colonists wanted to continue trade with the Dutch, so many of them became skillful smugglers, choice B. Before you select your answer, read the question and answer choices carefully. The Navigation Acts from 1651 to 1663 were unpopular in the British colonies; therefore, choices A (colonists authorized economic and trade support) and D (British governors convinced colonial assemblies to support the Navigation Act) can be eliminated. Choice C is incorrect because the Navigation Acts stimulated New England shipbuilding, which helped the region's economy to grow.

4. **A.** When evaluating maps, always look for clues in the title and labels to determine the context of the chronological time period. With this information, you should have been able to narrow down your answer to choice A or B. The date of this map of the Mississippi Territory is 1814, and the label "Horseshoe Bend" should lead you to events that led to the end of the War of 1812, choice A. The Trail of Tears, choice B, was in 1838 during the Indian Removal Act. Choice C, the French and Indian War, was in 1754, and choice D, the American Civil War, was fought from 1861 to 1865.

5. **C.** General Jackson's victory at Horseshoe Bend, choice C, was a virtual slaughter of the Red Stick (Upper Creek) Indians and marked a turning point for the United States in the War of 1812. The battle ended the Creek War, which started as a resistance to white settlement, and occurred during the War of 1812. The Battle of Fort Jackson (choice A) was during the Civil War in 1862. Although white settlers did move into the Mississippi Territory (choice B), it is not the reason that the Creek Indians surrendered their land. The withdrawal of British soldiers during the Creek War in 1813 (choice D) did not occur until after the defeat of the British at Pensacola and New Orleans.

6. **B.** The APUSH exam will often insert "distractor" answer choices from different time periods. In this case, all of the presidents listed were popular, but only one held office during the Creek War, which was a part of the War of 1812, Andrew Jackson (choice B). Jackson led the Battle of Horseshoe Bend and the Battle of New Orleans, which made him highly popular; he served as president from 1829 to 1837. William Henry Harrison (choice A) also became a hero due to his military successes, but he fought in the Indiana Territory at the Battle of Tippecanoe, which was after the War of 1812. George Washington (choice C) fought in the American Revolution then became president in 1789. Theodore Roosevelt (choice D) was president during the Spanish-American War in 1898.

7. **C.** The perspective of the author, William Lloyd Garrison, clearly uses language that is unequivocal: "I will not retreat a single inch." The only correct answer is one associated with radical abolitionism, which would be linked to immediate emancipation, choice C. Remember to read the source information for "hints" about the author. Garrison's article about abolitionism points to the author's fight to end slavery—emancipation.

8. **D.** Garrison founded *The Liberator* (1831–1865), choice D. *The North Star* (choice A) was an anti-slavery newspaper published by a former slave, Frederick Douglass, in 1847. Choice B, *The Abolitionists,* sounds as if it would be a great name for a newspaper; however, it did not exist. Choice C, *The Missouri Gazette,* is not relevant to the time period; it was founded in 1808, inviting "liberties of the people."

9. **B.** The question asks you to correctly identify the "false" statement among the choices. The only answer choice that satisfies the criteria is the answer choice that uses the term "pro-slavery," instead of "anti-slavery," to describe the documents that were published, choice B (the abolitionists influenced domestic and foreign support by publishing pro-slavery documents).

10. **C.** The image depicts two post–Civil War "Redeemer" groups, the KKK and the White League, who resisted Reconstruction and terrorized African American freed slaves in the South; their attempts to regain political power were criticized by northern Republicans, choice C. The Redeemer groups served as the informal military arms of the southern Democratic Party. The image represents the violence used to control African Americans in the South and keep them from voting for or supporting Republicans. Choice A is incorrect because these groups were formed after the Civil War, not before the war. Choices B and D are not relevant to the question.

11. **B.** The Colfax Massacre of 1873, choice B, was organized by several paramilitary groups, including members of the KKK. The massacre represents the types of tactics used by the KKK. The massacre took place at the Louisiana city's courthouse after African American men surrendered. The men were shot down by white supremacists. It resulted in the deaths of approximately 100 African Americans, some of whom were Union veterans defending the courthouse. Choice A, the Enforcement Acts of 1870–1871, were enacted to "protect" African American voters and prohibited the KKK from interfering in elections. Grant's campaign called for peace, not violence, choice C. Choice D, Charles Sumner's caning in 1856, took place after his anti-slavery speech when he fiercely criticized slaveholders. Sumner was not attacked by the KKK and he was not African American.

12. **D.** The Supreme Court case *Plessy v. Ferguson* established the concept of "separate but equal" in 1896. This case upheld racial segregation in public facilities. The court decision was essentially the undoing of the Civil Rights Act of 1875. It represents the end of the Progressive rights that African Americans had gained during Reconstruction, choice D. Answer choices A (the pardoning of wealthy white southern planters by Andrew Johnson) and B (the enactment of the Black Codes restricting African American freedoms) occurred during the Presidential Reconstruction, when few Progressive acts were passed. Grant's use of the Enforcement Acts (choice C), otherwise known as the KKK Acts, was more likely to be viewed as an attempt to control violence in the South than as the end of African Americans' rights.

13. **A.** The excerpt reflects the tensions between Old and New Lights during the First Great Awakening, which occurred between 1730 and 1750, choice A. Led by George Whitfield, the religious revival polarized Christians. Notice the date referenced is 1743, a time of the First Great Awakening; therefore, choices B, C, and D are incorrect.

14. **C.** During the colonial period, the gentry's power was attacked through the religious revival of the Great Awakening (and tobacco agriculture), choice C. This created an evangelical culture that encouraged, not rejected (choice B), individual salvation, tolerance, and equality, and rejected the power of the Anglican Church, especially in the South. Choice A is incorrect because the Great Awakening later caused Americans to advocate for the separation of church and state in the future (not the joining of church and state).

15. **A.** Read the question carefully. This question asks students to look for a future development of the ideas expressed in the excerpt. Chauncy's words exemplify the division caused by religious tension. Therefore, the answer choice that best fits the question is the one that references the religious denominational division, choice A. Religion was used to spread Evangelicalism (choice B), defend pro-slavery arguments (choice C), and spark social reform movements (choice D) in the 19th century. Since Chauncy's words are described as "seasonable thoughts" in the title and seem to suggest negative developments that divide individuals rather than unite them, choices B, C, and D are incorrect.

16. **C.** After 1920, there was a significant decrease in U.S. immigration due to Nativist legislation that increased immigration restrictions and established quotas, choice C. Choice A can be eliminated because the Great Migration (1910–1940) was when African American southerners moved north in search of a better life; it did not involve immigration from outside of the U.S., but was focused more on internal migration. Choice B, the Chinese Exclusion Act, can also be eliminated because it occurred in the 1880s. Although white supremacist groups, choice D, were reestablished in the 1920s, the groups were not a cause of the decrease in immigrants.

17. **D.** Immigrants were drawn to cities, choice D, because of the Second Industrial Revolution (1870–1914) after the American Civil War. As a result of the large numbers of immigrant workers in urban centers like New York and Chicago, they were often devalued and poverty-stricken because of the exploitative practices of their employers. Choices A, B, and C are incorrect statements.

18. **B.** The bar graph shows that the lowest number of U.S. immigrants is from 1930 to 1939. Although the 1929 stock market crash, choice A, could be considered a factor in the decline, the *best* answer is choice B, a global economic depression. The "global" economic depression would have made it difficult for immigrants to obtain passage to the United States. The economic depression caused Americans to be less welcoming to immigrants than they had been in the 1920s. Choices C and D are from different time periods: World War I (1914 to 1918) and World War II (1939 to 1945).

19. **C.** Freehling makes reference to the enthusiastic nationalism of South Carolinians in 1816, which spread across the nation because of the War of 1812, choice C. Choice A (the nullification crisis had little effect on the people of South Carolina) can be excluded because Freehling references "extreme sectionalism" in South Carolina during the crisis. Neither of the topics in choice B (tensions over slavery developed in the North and South after 1816) or D (farmers and landowners resented high tariffs in the rural North and Deep South) are directly referenced in the excerpt.

20. **C.** In an effort to protect the Union and keep South Carolina from seceding, the Compromise of 1833 was enacted to prevent the escalation of the crisis, choice C. Jackson backed the Force Bill, which allowed the federal government to use military force to collect the tariffs (not lower the tariffs, choice A), which almost caused civil war. Choice B is incorrect because President Jackson reacted angrily to the crisis, not meekly. Most of the population supported secession, so choice D is incorrect.

21. **A.** Draw from your knowledge of U.S. history and the context of the time period to answer this question. The nullification crisis was generated because of economic tension between the North and South, choice A, over what the South deemed a biased tariff legislation. Lincoln was not president until 1861 to 1865, so the election of Lincoln, choice B, cannot be considered a development of the nullification crisis. The Era of Good Feelings, choice C, was from 1817 to 1825, so it too is not in the proper time frame to have developed from the nullification crisis. *Antipathy* means "opposed," but John Calhoun was well-liked in the South, eliminating choice D. Calhoun anonymously published "The South Carolina Exposition and Protest" opposing the tariffs, claiming that the tariffs were "unconstitutional."

22. **C.** Marshall's goal was to defend the U.S. decision to send economic aid to European governments in order to assist with global recovery programs, choice C. Choice A is incorrect because Marshall was not defending U.S. economic aid as a propaganda tool. Choice B (to reject economic assistance offered by Soviet interests) is not mentioned in the Marshall Plan. Although the U.S. continued to work toward global unity and peace, choice D, it was not the main goal of the Marshall Plan.

23. **A.** The Marshall Plan (1948 to 1952) was formally known as the "European Recovery Program." It was used as a tool to promote worldwide democracy and develop a marketplace for international trade, choice A. Choice B is incorrect because Germany, not the Soviets, led the aggression that began World War II. Choice C is the second-best answer, but capitalism was not the primary reason for the Marshall Plan; "privilege" in markets was a secondary goal (and a result of the plan), but it did not occur globally, only in the countries that received support, which excluded those that adopted Communist or Socialist governments. The U.S. intentions during the Cold War were to support nations that defended democratic principles, eliminating choice D. If European nations had a stable economy, they might be less likely to turn to Communism and Fascism in the future. No aid was given to countries that established Communist governments led by the Soviet Union.

24. **D.** The Marshall Plan encouraged production and dissemination of American goods in European countries like France and Germany, choice D. A rise in employment of African Americans and women (choice A), the enactment of the GI Bill (choice B), and an increase in German and Eastern European cultural exchange (choice C) were not domestic results of the Marshall Plan.

25. **B.** On the APUSH exam, you should be familiar with the causes of Bacon's Rebellion, but if you didn't remember the rebellion, the document provides hints to identify the colonial conflict. The royal governor, William Berkeley, directly references "Mr. [Nathaniel] Bacon," who was the leader of Bacon's Rebellion in 1676, an armed uprising of angry yeomen and frontiersmen who felt exploited by the royal government, choice B. The colonists wanted more support in their attacks on Native Americans. The Stono Rebellion of 1739, choice A, was an armed slave resistance. Choices C (battle between farmers and large landowners over tobacco inspections) and D (violent objection of indentured servants to extensions in service) are incorrect because farmers did not battle large landowners over tobacco and indentured servants did not rebel against extensions of service during this time period. Servants were more likely to run away than violently resist.

26. **A.** The yeomen farmers and frontiersmen who fought in Bacon's Rebellion were mostly composed of former indentured servants who purchased or rented inferior land after their terms of service were complete. As royal governors and wealthy planters became worried about the possibility of another uprising, they focused on African slaves as laborers to work their land, choice A. Wealthy landowners controlled slaves and used brutality and legal oppression to create racial divisions among poor whites and poor African Americans. White property owners, even those with small amounts of land, were further unified by economic interests. Although the abuse of power did exist during this time period, it was not the reason for a major turning point in history, choice B. Choices C (it drew attention to the unnecessary slaughter of peaceful Native Americans) and D (it suppressed the rights of black slaves through the Negro Act of 1740) represent developments from different time periods.

27. **D.** The cartoon depicts the presidential candidate divisions in the country during the 1860 election, choice D. As a result, Abraham Lincoln and Stephen Douglas did not even appear on the ballots of several southern states. The other candidates should be apparent from the date of the image and what you know about the presidential campaign of 1860. In the North, the candidates for election were Douglas and Lincoln; in the South, they were John Breckinridge and John Bell. The regions of the country engaged in national infighting, it was not just among the candidates themselves (choice A). Andrew Jackson (who is mentioned in choice B) is from a different time period and is not pictured here. Both northern and southern Democrats are included, not just southern Democrats, as choice C suggests.

28. **C.** The Republican victory in the 1860 election caused South Carolina to secede from the Union, choice C; other southern states soon followed, forming the Confederacy. The Battle of Fort Sumter, choice A, did not occur until 1861. Buchanan did nothing to divert war and kept a "low profile" during his period as a lame duck president, so since choice B implies a "strong objection" to the war, it is also incorrect. Booth was a sympathizer of the Confederate cause, but he did not assassinate President Lincoln, choice D, until after the Civil War in 1865.

29. **A.** During his debates with Stephen Douglas in 1858, Lincoln stated that he had no desire to ban slavery in states where slavery already existed, choice A. Lincoln simply believed that the expansion of slavery in additional states or territories should be prohibited. Choices B (Lincoln advocated a free-soil policy and promised to end slavery in the U.S.) and D (Lincoln was morally opposed to slavery, but believed it should not be banned anywhere in the U.S. due to the constitutional rights of slaveholders) are incorrect because they fail to recognize Lincoln's policy, which was not directed specifically at states that already possessed the right to own slaves. Choice C, the Emancipation Proclamation, was signed by Lincoln after the onset of the Civil War in 1862 and 1863, so it is not a reflection of Lincoln's attitude during the 1860 election.

30. **C.** The image depicts the Boston Massacre, a complex event that occurred when a mob of American colonists, angered by the Quartering Act, began to attack a group of British soldiers in Boston. To defend themselves, the British soldiers shot into the unarmed crowd, killing five colonists. Patriots, choice C, used this depiction as a portrayal of the British as aggressors, which rallied undecided colonists to their cause for independence. Choice A is incorrect, as colonists were neither innocent (they began the attack) nor were they slaughtered by British soldiers. The image is signed by Paul Revere (bottom right), so it is not a loyalist perception, eliminating choice B. Since it depicts the Boston Massacre which was used as Patriot propaganda before the war, it has nothing to do with the Continental Congress (choice D)—many delegates in the Congress were unsure about the rebellion. All of them would not have necessarily thought the Boston Massacre justified fighting.

31. **A.** The colonists' growing anger toward the Mother Country, Britain (and thus their attack on the British soldiers), was generated by Britain increasing taxes to pay for military expenses generated by the Seven Years' War and the French and Indian War, choice A. The Stamp Act (1766), the Townshend Acts (1767), and the Quartering Act (1765)—which taxed paper and goods and forced colonists to support British soldiers sent to "keep them in line"—were particularly reviled. Even though some of the legislation had been repealed, the animosity remained. While the colonists were angry about inaccessibility to Native American land (choice B), this was associated with the Proclamation of 1763, rather than the Boston Massacre, which occurred later. Choice C (General Gage's frustration during British occupation) and choice D (the British Crown's frustration with the treatment of its soldiers) place too much emphasis on the British to relay the actual circumstances of the act.

32. **B.** The Voting Rights Act of 1965, which ended literacy tests and prohibited racial or language discrimination in voting, was signed into law by Lyndon B. Johnson, choice B. Even if you are not familiar with this piece of legislation, you should be familiar with the time periods of U.S. presidential administrations. Kennedy (choice A) was president from 1961 to 1963; Eisenhower (choice C) was president from 1953 to 1961; and Nixon (choice D) was president from 1969 to 1974.

33. **D.** Martin Luther King Jr. led the infamous march from Selma to Montgomery on March 7, 1965. The peaceful march was designed to protest voter discrimination even after discrimination was outlawed by the Civil Rights Act of 1964. The march was first prevented by Alabama state troopers, who used tear gas and beat the peaceful protestors attempting to cross the Edmund Pettus Bridge. The troopers' cruelty and brutality was captured on television, which created widespread support for the protestors' cause, choice D. Even President Johnson was inspired to speak on national television to proclaim that he supported the marchers. With federal protection, the march continued on March 9, 1965.

34. **B.** Note the date on the portrait is 1789—which lets you know it was painted shortly after the end of the Revolutionary War in 1783. The mother in the portrait is also in a prominent position at the center of her children. The key words "early-American ideology" should lead you to the correct answer. The only early-American ideology among the choices listed is republican motherhood, choice B, which is connected to the ability of women to educate the next generation of republican children. Republican motherhood was seen as a key factor in the building of the new nation. While children's obedience (choice A), brave widowhood (choice C), and the elite family structure (choice D) might have also been viewed as important, none of these things were considered ideologies that would strengthen the fledgling country.

35. **C.** In the 18th century, many Americans thought that a woman's demand for equality was preposterous, but most men believed in the ideals of republican motherhood and respected their wives as the mothers of future citizens, choice C. This did not mean that men limited women (choice B), nor did it suggest that men granted women civil rights (choice A), and it certainly didn't mean they expected women to help support the family financially (choice D). More often than not, men simply believed a woman's rights were connected to the status of a male relative. Abigail Adams, wife of President John Adams and mother of President John Quincy Adams, was self-educated and a strong advocate of women's rights. She suggested that Congress "remember the ladies" when creating new legislation.

36. **D.** The Articles of Confederation were used during the American Revolution to unify the states and establish a weak central government (not a strong one, as choice A suggests) that could properly lead military battles, establish treaties, and settle disputes between the states, choice D. Since the document is identified as the Articles of Confederation and it is dated 1777–1781, choice B (the Albany Plan) can be automatically eliminated because it does not coincide with the time period. Although regional security (choice C) was a concern, the Articles of Confederation were not created to guarantee it.

37. **A.** A farmers' rebellion in rural Massachusetts led by Daniel Shays, choice A, revealed the limited power of the federal government as instituted by the Articles of Confederation. Shays' Rebellion demonstrated that a significant governmental weakness was the inability to gather an effective military force to quell an uprising, which could prove dangerous to the future of the new union. Neither infighting among colonies (choice B) nor the Continental Army's struggles at Valley Forge (choice D) are directly responsible for revealing the inadequacies of the document. The document is associated with the Second Continental Congress, not the First (choice C).

38. **B.** The Constitutional Convention (1787) was held in Philadelphia after Shays' Rebellion. American leaders—fearing the vulnerability of the new country—looked for ways to improve an ineffective central government and decided to replace the Articles of Confederation with a governing document that would prove to be more effective by giving the federal government more power while still protecting individual rights, choice B. The Articles of Confederation were not incorporated into state constitutions (choice A) but remained a separate document. Although the Articles could have been revised, the primary concern was not civil rights and liberties of individuals (choice C), but the power of the federal government. The idea that politicians might have been worried about losing support for their policies in state legislatures (choice D) is irrelevant; the question is asking about the document's ineffectiveness, not why it wasn't changed.

39. **A.** School desegregation did see a brief rise in the political beliefs and behaviors of the Dixiecrats (choice C); however, the more immediate cause of the Court's decision was associated with the South's blatant disregard for orders to desegregate in *Brown v. Board of Education,* choice A. Public school attendance (choice B) would not have been encouraged by this act because desegregation was unpopular in the South, and the Supreme Court's decision was not influenced by Nixon's "law and order" policies (choice D).

40. **D.** Busing protests were led by militant white citizens (choice D) who organized, demonstrated, and often attacked buses carrying African American children. Militant African Americans (choice A) and the NAACP and the ACLU (choice B) would have been fighting *for* the rights of black children to obtain desegregated education, not against it. Choice C is incorrect because the white citizens who participated in the busing protests were usually average middle- and working-class people, not business leaders.

41. **B.** The artist, Thomas Nast, aimed to depict the hope for the assimilation and political equality of diverse immigrants into the circle of an American national identity, choice B. This is evident in Nast's depiction of the ethnically diverse people from all over the world (German, Native American, French, British, African American, Chinese, Italian, Spanish, and Irish) as an extended family sharing a celebratory meal. This negates the idea that immigrants should be rejected and excluded (choice A) and works against attitudes associated with immigration quotas designed to turn away particular ethnicities (choice D). Since Nast's focus is inclusion, not education or "civilization," the White Man's Burden and imperialism (choice C) would be discouraged by the image, not encouraged.

42. **A.** The underlying political message is likely that Nast sought to support legislation that would expand citizenship (Fifteenth Amendment, which was up for ratification at the time); therefore, the image criticized nativist beliefs that sought to pass discriminatory legislation and limit citizenship, choice A. The Fifteenth Amendment ruled that all citizens had the right to vote no matter their race, color, or previous servitude. Uncle Sam is carving the turkey at the head of the table, which seems to indicate a welcoming atmosphere. Although Nast could have been hinting that immigrants contribute positively to the national economy (choice B), the image focuses on social interaction rather than interaction based on labor or finance. Since "endless immigrant assistance" was not given to immigrants by the government, choice C is also incorrect. Although one could interpret this as an ethnically diverse American heritage (choice D), nativist feelings were strong during Nast's lifetime. Therefore, that principle would have been rejected by many Americans, which may have prompted Nast to create such an image.

43. **C.** Discriminatory legislation and immigrant quotas began against immigrants in the late 19th century and continued through 1920, choice C. Immigrants were not subjected to the same amount of violence from white supremacist groups as African Americans, choice A. The Know Nothing Party, choice B, was from an earlier period. Labor organizations and political parties actually welcomed immigrant support, choice D.

44. **C.** The Knights of Labor was an early organized labor union that was formed to prevent employer abuses. The Second Industrial Revolution replaced human workers with machinery and tools of the industrial system. To protect workers' interests, the Knights of Labor was effective in working with employers and favored negotiations, rather than strikes, to demand better working conditions. It influenced employers, who paid low wages and offered no benefits to their workers, whom they considered replaceable with machinery or other laborers, choice C. Its concern was for workers, not employers who depended on cheap immigrant labor (choice A). It rejected the violence (choice B), and was more concerned with urban conditions than those of farmers or miners in rural or western regions (choice D).

45. **A.** The Knights of Labor was an early labor organization that inspired other coalitions of workers like the American Federation of Labor (AFL) and the Industrial Workers of the World (IWW), choice A. Populists did not unify with labor unions (choice B), an open class war (choice C) did not occur in the United States, and Gilded Age legislation did not encourage industrial regulation (choice D).

46. **B.** In the press, the Haymarket Square Riot (1886), choice B, was blamed on immigrant anarchists and militant labor activists. During a labor strike at the McCormick plant in Chicago, police shot two McCormick workers, and later a bomb went off, killing seven people. The riot destroyed the membership of the Knights of Labor, who had supported the strikers. While the Great Railroad Strike (choice A), Homestead Steelworkers Strike (choice C), and Pullman Strike (choice D) were also important events, they were not directly related to the destruction of the Knights of Labor.

47. **C.** Although you might be tempted to select choice A (the tensions in the New World associated with the Spanish monarchy's economic gain), the question specifically addresses the author's attitude, which distinctly focused on the treatment of Natives, choice C. The passage does not directly mention slavery (choice B), nor does it convey resentment (choice D), but instead expresses outrage surrounding how some of the "Indians" were being managed and treated.

48. **B.** The Spanish explorers were searching for a Western Hemisphere trade route that would allow the trade of spices and silk with India, choice B. When the Spaniards discovered land filled with gold and silver, they became motivated by the desire for economic gain, but it was unrelated to the stabilization of the European economy, choice A. Choice C can be eliminated because even though religious freedom was a desire of the later colonists like the Puritans, Catholic missionaries were established in Mexico and what would become the American Southwest. European agriculture was regulated, making choice D incorrect.

49. **D.** The Spanish settled in Florida and Texas, and U.S. conflicts arose to control these regions, choice D. In colonial America, tensions existed between slave owners and the Spanish in Florida, who offered slaves refuge. The Mexican-American War also began over conflicts associated with the Spanish (Mexican) settlement in Texas, but the U.S. acquired the territory in 1848. While the Spanish settled in what would become Louisiana, choice A, the territory was acquired by the French by the time Jefferson purchased the territory. The Patriots of the Revolutionary War received help from the French, not the Spanish (choice B). Dutch and British explorers did not battle with the Spanish in the Southwest (choice C).

50. **B.** World War I propaganda posters like the one shown had two goals: (1) to encourage Americans (expressed here as women) to support the war financially, and (2) to mobilize all citizens to do their part for the war effort. Hence, Americans would become emotionally attached to what began as an unpopular conflict. The correct answer is choice B. Since the poster encourages women to support a war that had already begun, the answer cannot be choice A (the end of isolationist foreign policies). The poster is also focused on all women, not just mothers (choice C), and although its intention is to inspire support for the war, it is not suggesting citizen groups should shame those who reject it (choice D).

51. **D.** The role of women during the war was important. The poster depicts a woman with consumer power, choice D, through the purchase of "war saving stamps." This is suggested as essential to "saving" the country, which is part of war mobilization. The poster is not an appeal to work in factories (choice A) or encourage women's suffrage or any other type of female political power (choice C). Although the draft was unpopular and needed support, the poster does not mention the draft or the need for women to support it (choice B).

52. **D.** The poster speaks directly to the power of women as consumers, which connects purchasing to patriotism, choice D. Although propaganda depicting Germans as barbarians was common during World War I (choice A), this poster does not include that sort of image, but rather portrays a woman as a warrior. Although it depicts a female military heroine, the poster does not encourage women to participate in the war by joining the military, choice B, or by working in factories (as many other posters did at the time). Since the poster suggests women are important "fighters" in the war, they are not shamed (choice C) but upheld as significant participants in the conflict.

53. **C.** Hammond's argument is about the Antebellum tensions between northern and southern legislatures, choice C. He is addressing tensions caused by his northern counterparts—powerful men whom he believed had self-righteous intentions that would end what he considered a successful economic and social system in the South. Although Hammond hints at the political power of the white masses, the power of labor coalitions and political legislation in the North (choice A) were not at issue until the Gilded Age and beyond. The idea that slaves were "happy" and "committed" to their masters (choice B) or that white southerners would grant slaves voting rights (choice D), as Hammond describes, is laughable.

54. **B.** Hammond explicitly states that he believes black slaves are both inferior and satisfied (content). He is echoing many of the pro-slavery arguments made by Antebellum white slaveholders, choice B. Since many northerners supported anti-slavery arguments, which are in opposition to his words, choice A (which mentions both northern and southern legislators) is incorrect. Hammond is neither promoting a class revolution (choice C) nor suggesting industrial managers should incorporate slavery into their factories (choice D), but rather attempting to legitimize the existence of slavery in the southern states.

55. **C.** Hammond's focus is the tensions created by the differing worldviews of those who promoted and those who rejected slavery. The American Civil War, choice C, was indeed influenced by sectional and political divisions over the expansion of slavery. While tensions regarding abolitionism and slavery played a role in the nullification crisis (choice A), there were other factors related to its occurrence. Also, the nullification crisis, like the American System (choice B) and Andrew Jackson's bank crisis (choice D) occurred *before* Hammond's speech, which eliminates every choice but choice C.

Part B—Short-Answer Questions

Question 1

Reasoning skill: *Continuity and change over time*

This question asks you to interpret documents on Progressivism. Keep in mind that the context of the documents suggests that you must analyze what these documents tell you about Progressive attitudes toward industries and corporations, which should help you narrow down your topic considerably. The first step is to link a historical event or development to the authors' points of view. The next step is to provide support for both Hofstadter's and Roosevelt's interpretations of Progressive intentions.

To receive full credit, you must address all three parts. The sample responses for parts (a), (b), and (c) in the table below are for instructional purposes only. On the actual exam, you must write ONE complete short-answer essay.

Part	Task	Explanation	Sample Response
(a)	Briefly explain ONE historical event or development that caused the frustration referenced in the passages.	Part (a) asks you to historically demonstrate why Progressives developed the attitudes suggested by Hofstadter and Roosevelt.	Like Hofstadter suggests, Progressives adopted many of their attitudes from the Populists, who became frustrated with the abuses of an unregulated economy and political corruption during the Gilded Age. Large corporations and industrial giants dominated financial, political, and marketing sectors, causing unprotected workers and farmers to object to unfair production and employment practices from 1870 to 1890.
(b)	Briefly explain how ONE specific historical event or development (not explicitly stated in the passages) could support Hofstadter's interpretation.	Part (b) can be answered by noting how Progressives began to organize, administer, and legislate industrial reform.	Many of the demands of the Populists, including calls to "clean up" political corruption and regulate the market, were absorbed by William Jennings Bryan's platform when he was running for president in 1896. Although Bryan did not win the election, other Progressives began to see their demands as legitimate and push for changes in legislation. Politicians, women, and volunteers were motivated by the poverty suffered by workers and the perpetual debt of farmers. For example, Jane Addams established settlement houses and pushed for legislation that would empower the poor, while Theodore Roosevelt promised to wipe out corruption.
(c)	Briefly explain how ONE specific historical event or development (not explicitly stated in the passages) could support Roosevelt's interpretation.	Part (c) can be answered by choosing specific evidence from Roosevelt's presidency.	Part of Roosevelt's Square Deal was to attach a sense of responsibility to legislation and to focus on destroying the power of large corporations. Roosevelt confronted the abuses of vertical and horizontal integration using the Sherman Antitrust Act as justification for destroying monopolies, like J. P. Morgan's National Securities Company. Unlike successive Progressive presidents (Taft or Wilson), Roosevelt supported the rights of large companies that he felt were serving the public interest, distinguishing "good" trusts from "bad" ones.

Question 2

Reasoning skill: *Continuity and change over time*

This question asks you to interpret an image that is associated with the Open Door Policy of 1899. You will need to closely examine and then analyze the actions of the figures in the political cartoon. Be sure to think of the image in the context of what you already know about global expansion and imperialism during this period. The question requires you to notice both supporting and opposing political or cultural perspectives and describe a historical event or development related to the U.S. that can be seen as causing a new way of thinking about the world.

To receive full credit, you must address all three parts. The sample responses for parts (a), (b), and (c) in the table below are for instructional purposes only. On the actual exam, you must write ONE complete short-answer essay.

Part	Task	Explanation	Sample Response
(a)	Briefly describe ONE perspective about America's role in global expansionism supported by the image.	Part (a) can be answered by considering the arguments that supported anti-imperialism.	The image references John Hay's Open Door Note, which called on France, Germany, Britain, and Japan to enforce an agreement that would allow equal access to China. This would allow global access to trade without having to sacrifice a nation's independence or become colonized as it had in the past. It was in response to anti-imperialists who were becoming disgusted with the growing demands for U.S. military power and occupation in the Western Hemisphere, including those who supported the Spanish-American War.
(b)	Briefly describe ONE specific historical event or development that led to the change in foreign policy depicted in the image.	Part (b) can be answered by focusing on the specific cause for a transformation in foreign policy from isolation to intervention.	U.S. foreign policy as a whole was beginning to move from isolationism to interventionism during the late 19th century. One possible reason was the Second Industrial Revolution, which created a surplus of goods through improvements in technology and better methods of industrial production. Anti-imperialists sought greater access to markets through nonviolent means—in this case economics—in order to ensure the sovereignty of other nations, a tenet of American democracy anti-imperialists claimed needed to be upheld.
(c)	Briefly explain ONE way in which the historical change depicted in the image was challenged between 1899 and 1917.	Part (c) can be answered by considering arguments that supported imperialism.	The opposing side of the Open Door Policy was the belief of imperialists. Imperialists were not averse to obtaining control of weaker nations through military force and political dominance. Many imperialists saw their views as an extension of Manifest Destiny and considered themselves beneficent individuals who were bringing "civilization" to people they considered underdeveloped, backward, or savage.

Question 3

Reasoning skill: *Comparison*

This question asks you to analyze the differences in the women's rights movement in the context of two particular time periods. You are being asked to compare and contrast the changes before 1865 and after 1865, which will require you to have some knowledge of both the early women's rights movement and the impact of the Fifteenth Amendment.

To receive full credit, you must address all three parts. The sample responses for parts (a), (b), and (c) in the table below are for instructional purposes only. On the actual exam, you must write ONE complete short-answer essay.

Part	Task	Explanation	Sample Response
(a)	Briefly describe ONE specific historical similarity between the women's rights movement in the period 1820–1864 and in the period 1865–1890.	Part (a) can be answered by analyzing one specific part of the women's rights movement from both periods that overlaps. Because the question is associated with the women's movement, gender norms and expectations might be considered to compose an effective response.	Both the Market Revolution (1815–1840) and the Second Industrial Revolution (1870–1910) sparked changes that enhanced women's roles in the public sphere. Both before and after 1865, many women advocated for their political rights and a greater role in social and reform organizations without jeopardizing the "cult of domesticity" or any other expected gender ideal or expectation. Although some women presented themselves as feminists who desired equality, most simply promoted their roles as mothers and moral authorities who deserved to comment and act on the problems they saw in the U.S. Women in both eras led campaigns for voting rights, temperance, prison reform, and social improvements.
(b)	Briefly describe ONE specific historical difference between the women's rights movement in the period 1820–1864 and in the period 1865–1890.	Part (b) can be answered by providing one specific difference in the women's rights movement from the two time periods. In this case, the break in the date comes before and after 1865, which should hint at the effect of the Fifteenth Amendment passed that year.	After the passage of the Fifteenth Amendment, which granted suffrage to black men, the women's movement became divided. Those who supported the amendment as a step toward universal suffrage for both genders were led by Lucy Stone and the American Woman Suffrage Association. Those who rejected the Fifteenth Amendment often became more militant in their pursuit of the right to vote. This group was led by Susan B. Anthony and the National American Woman's Suffrage Association. Divisions between women in the Antebellum Era, however, were often regional. Many women in the South, for example, rejected women who worked for the abolition of slavery and/or spoke publically about the issue.
(c)	Briefly explain ONE specific historical effect of the women's rights movement in either the period 1820–1864 or in the period 1865–1890.	Part (c) can be answered by providing a specific effect of the movement from either period. Since women became quite active in the public sphere after the Civil War, the second period might be easier to address.	Because women worked for greater rights alongside the Populists in many states in the West, they were granted suffrage long before the passage of the Nineteenth Amendment in several western states. Women also overcame their differences and established the powerful National American Woman's Suffrage Association, which recruited women for their cause through advertisements, legislative petitions, parades, and banners.

Question 4

Reasoning skill: *Comparison*

This question asks you to compare and contrast the differences and similarities of consumerism in the context of two different time periods: 1920s and 1940s.

To receive full credit, you must address all three parts. The sample responses for parts (a), (b), and (c) in the table below are for instructional purposes only. On the actual exam, you must write ONE complete short-answer essay.

Part	Task	Explanation	Sample Response
(a)	Briefly describe ONE specific historical similarity between the consumerism of the 1920s and the 1940s.	Part (a) can be answered by comparing the growth of advertisements and marketing in each period. Consumerism was a factor in the economic benefits and employment for average Americans that enabled them to have access to goods.	Both eras are characterized by employment that enabled Americans to purchase goods that increased the average consumer's living standard. After World War I, fiscal policies created mass industrial growth, which stimulated the economy and allowed individuals to obtain greater access to goods and credit lines. During World War II, the government provided large corporations with subsidies that encouraged the mass production of war necessities, which put people to work and ended the Great Depression. Both periods also saw the rise of merchandise advertisements in magazines, newspapers, radio broadcasts, and films that promoted particular products and lifestyles.
(b)	Briefly describe ONE specific historical difference between the consumerism of the 1920s and the 1940s.	Part (b) can be answered by providing a specific example from the time periods that noted the differences between the "uncontrolled" spending of the 1920s and the more "reserved" patterns of the 1940s, which was often limited by war rations.	People in the 1920s tended to spend more than they earned in order to attempt to make quick fortunes. Because investments and spending were not tempered with responsibility, the era is remembered for its wild speculation and greed. In the 1940s, however, the Office of Price Administration combated inflation by setting price limits and rationing items necessary for combat, so access to particular goods (like coffee, rubber, and nylon) was limited.
(c)	Briefly explain ONE specific historical effect of the consumerism of the 1920s or the 1940s.	Part (c) can be answered by providing examples from *either* time period. The sample response links consumerism to patriotism and support for the war. As a bonus, it extends the effect into a future era.	After funding was cut for the Office of War Information, propaganda to generate support for the war was turned over to advertisers. People began linking the purchase of particular products to the benefits of democracy (i.e., what soldiers were fighting for). Because Americans saw their ability to purchase items as a privilege of citizenship, a strong black market developed and the demand for new and better goods skyrocketed. Thus, consumerism that developed during World War II enabled the post-war economic growth of the 1950s.

Section II

Part A—Document-Based Question

DBQ Scoring Guide

To achieve the maximum score of 7, your response must address the scoring criteria components in the table that follows.

Scoring Criteria for a Good Essay	
Question 1: Evaluate the extent to which differing views about civil and social resistance affected the development of the African American struggle against institutional oppression during the 20th century.	
Scoring Criteria	**Examples**
A. THESIS/CLAIM	
(1 point) Presents a historically defensible thesis that establishes a line of reasoning. (Note: The thesis must make a claim that responds to *all* parts of the question and must *not* just restate the question. The thesis must consist of *at least* one sentence, either in the introduction or the conclusion.)	The thesis must answer all parts of the question while following a line of reasoning. This essay provides a coherent thesis and argument in each body paragraph. It also attempts to contextualize civil rights leaders' points of view without placing a judgment on their level of effectiveness or their beliefs.
B. CONTEXTUALIZATION	
(1 point) Explains the broader historical context of events, developments, or processes that occurred before, during, or after the time frame of the question. (Note: Must be more than a phrase or reference.)	A good response provides some historical context in each body paragraph. This essay discusses disenfranchisement, violence, institutional discrimination, and specific events to place the documents in the historical context of the 19th and 20th centuries.
C. EVIDENCE	
Evidence from the Documents **(2 points)** Uses at least *six* documents to support the argument in response to the prompt. OR **(1 point)** Uses the content of at least *three* documents to address the topic prompt. (Note: Examples must describe, rather than simply quote, the content of the documents.) **Evidence Beyond the Documents** **(1 point)** Uses at least one additional piece of specific historical evidence beyond those found in the documents relevant to the argument. (Note: Evidence must be different from the evidence used in contextualization.)	A DBQ response needs to address at least six of the documents to receive the highest possible points for this component. This essay uses all seven documents and provides perspectives from each author with historical evidence to support the documents. For example, Documents 1, 3, 5, and 6 provide examples of notable African Americans who led movements and/or protests to support social and political reform in black communities. Document 2 provides a historical perspective from an African American woman who organized reform efforts with white women. Document 4 provides evidence of a more radical reform movement, black empowerment. To provide outside evidence related to the topic question, this essay includes several pieces of evidence to explain the different legislation and racial advances that occurred during the Civil Rights Era and beyond, including the election of the first black president. For example, the Civil Rights Act of 1964 and the Voting Rights Act of 1965.

Continued

Scoring Criteria	Examples
D. ANALYSIS AND REASONING	
(1 point) Uses at least *three* documents to explain how each document's point of view, purpose, historical situation, and/or audience is relevant to the argument. (Note: References must explain how or why, rather than simply identifying.)	A good response should analyze at least three of the documents using point of view, purpose, historical context, or audience. This essay uses all of the documents. The essay notes the relevance of each speaker while comparing and contrasting different points of view. For example, Documents 1 and 3 focus on the goals of two late-19th-century African Americans who advocated for "cooperation" through education and training. In contrast, 20th-century African Americans Randolph and King (Documents 5 and 6) focused on pursuing change through marches and speeches in nonviolent movements.
(1 point) Uses historical reasoning and development that focuses on the question while using evidence to corroborate, qualify, or modify the argument. (Examples: Explain what is similar and different; explain the cause and effect; explain multiple causes; explain connections within and across periods of time; corroborate multiple perspectives across themes; or consider alternative views.)	A good thesis should both compare and contrast different attitudes and beliefs of various African Americans that affected their battles for civil and social rights. It should also note how these issues either stayed the same or changed over time. This response provides historical context to give the reader an overview of the topic. The sample essay argues that passive and aggressive approaches to resisting oppression existed throughout the 20th century and notes the impact of elitist and grassroots organizations.

DBQ Sample Response

In the late 19th century, at the end of the Reconstruction period, the disenfranchisement of blacks in southern states led African Americans into a distinctive struggle for equal rights. Although 20th-century black leaders agreed on the need for change, the leaders often disagreed about how to pursue social and civil rights. During the Progressive Era, tensions arose between those who placed hope in practical education and industrial cooperation and those who pursued legislative solutions, intellectualism, and reform. The Great Migration and the African American participation in both world wars led to reform movements that stimulated black pride and prompted more aggressive demands of white politicians, and aroused the African American community. Eventually, these early forms of resistance led to the intense civil rights struggles of the 1950s and 1960s. However, black leaders differed over the purpose of the movement, its challenges, and the forms of resistance.

Even before the 20th century began, African American educator Booker T. Washington started encouraging black men and women to pursue technical education and entrepreneurship. Made famous by the accommodation speech he gave in Atlanta in 1895 (Document 1), Washington saw black cooperation with white industrialists and hoped to quell the violence in the South by discouraging direct challenges to the Jim Crow laws and oppressive social practices. Washington was a prominent African American leader in the early 20th century who believed a strong black middle class could rise through efforts in labor to earn the respect of whites, and thus empower black Americans to achieve stronger economic, educational, and social positions in the U.S. W. E. B. Du Bois (Document 3) disagreed with Washington and advocated a classical education for the most intelligent 10 percent of African Americans in order to prepare them to lead the rest of the population to equality. Du Bois was not only an outspoken activist, but also one of the key founders of the NAACP, which fought to outlaw segregation and biased legislation through the U.S. Court system.

African American women have also played an important role in civil rights struggles. Middle-class Progressive black women like Gertrude Mossell (Document 2) participated in social reform like their white counterparts, hoping (as Washington had hoped) that blacks' behavior and social or political connections would stimulate a more positive view of African Americans in white communities. Black women worked with white women and politicians in projects that benefited their communities, and benefited the suffrage and temperance movements. Women saw their work as an implicit tool to uplift the black community that could step into the political vacuum left by the disfranchisement of their husbands and fathers. Unfortunately, like Du Bois, these women often occupied an elite social position that distanced them from the common African American woman's viewpoint. Washington's goals, although not ideal, occasionally appeared less dangerous and more accessible to people in black working-class communities, especially those who lived in the South.

The Great Migration and participation in World War I led to the rise of black pride through the Harlem Renaissance and movements like Marcus Garvey's Pan-Africanism (Document 4). An immigrant from Jamaica, Garvey argued that people of African descent should be proud of their heritage and globally unite to support black interests. Although his movement eventually fizzled out, it provided a basis for the black nationalism that arose in the 1960s, a more militant call for black pride and black rights that was supported by black leaders like Malcolm X, Stokely Carmichael, and Robert Williams. Unlike Martin Luther King Jr. (Document 6), who led nonviolent protests for black civil rights, Carmichael (Document 7) supported "black power," which included the use of violence for defense, the antagonistic takeover of white institutions that oppressed African Americans, and the rejection of interracial coalitions (when he took over the Student Nonviolent Coordinating Committee, SNCC, in 1966, he made it an "all-black" organization).

Carmichael and others in the black nationalist movement felt that King's nonviolent approach was not immediate or effective enough for the situation at hand. But King was influenced by Gandhi (the leader of the Indian Independence Movement, who employed nonviolent civil disobedience) and former civil rights workers like A. Philip Randolph (Document 5), who used the threat of marches and the rhetoric of democracy to pursue a "Double V" campaign during World War II (fight for African American democracy). Instead of pursuing militant policies, Randolph's work used Franklin Roosevelt's language of freedom and democracy to support both victory abroad and victory at home, which he hoped could help wipe out white supremacy, at least in employment and legislation. Randolph's threat to march on Washington inspired Roosevelt to compose Executive Order 8802, which banned employment discrimination in government defense industries and set up the FEPC to ensure that the law was followed. The freedom march did eventually come to pass in 1963, when Randolph helped King and his supporters organize a massive protest for "jobs and freedom." The highlight of the march was King's "I Have a Dream" speech, which envisioned a peaceful coexistence for people of all races. It is an example of the majority of his nonviolent work, which led to the passage of important legislation like the Civil Rights Act of 1964 and the Voting Rights Act of 1965.

A variety of approaches were used throughout the 20th century in the struggles for African American rights. All of them contributed to U.S. policies that have led to a greater degree of racial and gender equality. Although many black leaders would agree that the fight is not over, the African American community has made considerable progress since the time of Booker T. Washington and W. E. B. Du Bois. In 2008, for example, the first African American president, Barack Obama, was elected to office, something that would have been unheard of just four decades prior to its occurrence.

Part B—Long-Essay Question

Long-Essay Scoring Guide

Each point is earned independently (for example, you can earn a point for developing your argument and earn a point for providing evidence). To achieve the maximum score of 6, your response to ONE topic should use the scoring criteria that follows as a checklist to make sure that you have included all of the elements in your essay.

> Note: The directions asked you to choose ONE of the three LEQ topic options. The sample essay below is written for LEQ Question 4, but you can use some of the suggested ideas presented in the table below, "Scoring Criteria for a Good Essay," to formulate your written responses for Question 2 or Question 3.

Scoring Criteria for a Good Essay	
Question 4: Evaluate the extent to which internal U.S. migration fostered changes in American political alliances and citizen expectations from 1910 to 1990. _(Reasoning skill: Continuity and change over time.)_	
Scoring Criteria	**Examples**
A. THESIS/CLAIM	
(1 point) Presents a historically defensible thesis that establishes a line of reasoning. (Note: The thesis must make a claim that responds to *all* parts of the question and must *not* just restate the question. The thesis must consist of *at least* one sentence, either in the introduction or the conclusion.)	A good response to this question has a central thesis that must provide at least two changes related to political alliances and citizen expectations that resulted from internal migration in the U.S. It must also show at least two effects that are specific to these changes. This thesis addresses the changes in political alliances that were caused by these migrations as well as additional historical contexts that provide a basis for the shifts.
B. CONTEXTUALIZATION	
(1 point) Describes the broader historical context of events, developments, or processes that occurred before, during, or after the time frame of the question. (Note: Must be more than a phrase or reference.)	A good essay looks at the context of the big picture. This essay provides a context about the specific changes by starting with the New Deal period and then extends evidence for the thesis into the post–World War II era and a discussion about the Sunbelt, evangelicals, and the New Right.
C. EVIDENCE	
(2 points) Supports the argument in response to the prompt using specific and relevant examples of evidence. OR **(1 point)** Provides specific examples of evidence relevant to the topic of the question. (Note: To earn 2 points, the evidence must *support* your argument.)	The essay must provide multiple examples that will support the argument. This essay discusses the examples of African American voting shifts, the swing of conservatives in the Sunbelt, the political lobbying of evangelicals, and the patterns of migration that stimulated the changes. The writer also lists specific politicians and notes popular and unpopular policies and social factors that contributed to shifts in expectations and political loyalties.

Scoring Criteria	Examples
D. ANALYSIS AND REASONING	
(2 points) Demonstrates a complex understanding of historical development that addresses the question and uses evidence to corroborate, qualify, or modify the argument. (Examples: Explain what is similar and different; explain the cause and effect; explain multiple causes; explain connections within and across periods of time; corroborate multiple perspectives across themes; or consider alternative views.) OR **(1 point)** Uses historical reasoning (comparison, causation, or continuity and change over time) to frame and develop the argument while focusing on the question. (Note: Must be more than a phrase or reference.)	This essay demonstrates a complex understanding of the topic and also addresses the historical reasoning of changes and continuities. It addresses both changes and effects while noting the big picture. This essay connects shifts to the first and second waves of the Great Migration and the rise of conservatives in the Sunbelt. It also places the argument within a broader historical context of social, legislative, and economic developments during the New Deal, the Second World War, the post-war era, and the rise of the New Right, connecting them to policies supported by FDR, LBJ, Nixon, and Reagan.

Long-Essay Sample Response for Question 4

During the 20th century, several important shifts occurred as a result of internal U.S. migration. The most important changes are associated with transformations in political alliances and citizen expectations, which can be substantiated through African American Democratic allegiances during the New Deal, the rise of white conservativism in response to the Civil Rights Era, and militant political activism of the New Right of the 1970s and 1980s. Many of these changes are related to social and legislative policies of particular politicians, but others can be directly correlated with demographic shifts that resulted from the first and second waves of the Great Migration as well as movements associated with the rise of post–World War II industrialism in the South and West.

In 1936, black Americans in unprecedented numbers shifted their political loyalties from the Republican Party, which had fought for their civil rights during Reconstruction, to the Democratic Party, which promised to include them in the benefits of the New Deal. An important source of the change was the Great Migration of African Americans that occurred from the oppressive Jim Crow South to the North and West, first between 1910 and 1930 and later after the Second World War. An increased African American population in urban centers, like New York's Harlem, neighborhoods in Chicago, and Detroit, as well as the confidence obtained by black veterans who fought in World War I and World War II, led to a more confident black community, which became an impressive voting bloc. African Americans began to pressure Progressive Democratic politicians whose rhetoric encouraged democratic principles and equality to pass legislation that would discourage white favoritism and privilege while ensuring equal access to civil rights. Although it would be decades before ethnic and racial barriers were overcome, the expectations of black citizens grew as the federal government began to respond to their demands. The voting base established by the Great Migration served as a base for union membership during the New Deal Era, increased African American visibility in the political sphere, increased the demand for fair treatment in the workplace and the military, and applied legislative pressure against the South during the Civil Rights Era.

Unfortunately, because Democratic presidents of the 1960s like John F. Kennedy and Lyndon B. Johnson backed legislation that called for or increased African American civil rights, white conservatives also shifted their political support. Several causes for this shift existed, including LBJ's advocating of the Civil Rights Act of 1964, the Voting Rights Act of 1965, and programs pursued by various Democrats that increased welfare, Medicaid, and aid for the poor (Johnson's Great Society is just one of these programs). Although many scholars note the rise of conservatism as an increased call for states' rights and the Supreme Court's decision to enforce busing to desegregate schools, others attribute the change to the post-war need for industrial workers after World War II in the South and West, a region known as the Sunbelt. When white citizens migrated to these areas, they formed grassroots political movements that fought Democratic efforts to enforce civil rights or finance social reform. As a result of the efforts, white citizens developed a rhetoric that claimed to be neutral based on the "freedom to choose" their destinies, free from the interference of the government. Former Democrats, the citizens who supported these ideas became part of the Silent Majority of Republican president Richard Nixon, who responded to their demands by promising to reduce the programs they saw as "handouts."

The increased working-class white populations in the Sunbelt also influenced the spread of evangelical Christianity to these regions, which contributed to the formation of both the New Right and the rise of religious political lobbies that elected Republicans like Ronald Reagan and George H. W. Bush. The migration stimulated individual tendencies to ask for federal intervention to combat the counterculture movement that had developed in the 1960s. The rise in evangelical political participation transformed conservative coalitions during the late 20th century. Although New Right Republicans still heartily supported traditional policies—like a militant aggressive approach to the Cold War, or the deregulation of businesses—they also focused on "morality" and the culture wars. Evangelical groups like Jerry Falwell's Moral Majority and James Dobson's Focus on the Family demanded politicians reject laws that legalized abortion, upheld the separation of church and state, and granted rights to minority groups like African Americans, women, and homosexuals.

The composition of the New Right was not limited to evangelical Christians or disgruntled whites. In the 1970s, many Americans became disillusioned by government corruption and incompetence, which was visible during the Watergate scandal, the energy crisis, and the Iranian Hostage Crisis. Stagflation, the increase of both cost of living and unemployment, caused many people to lose their jobs and experience hardships. Defeated and disgusted with politicians, displaced union workers were forced to relocate within the U.S. to find jobs and frequently became "Reagan Democrats." Wooed by Reagan's optimism and positive, charismatic speeches in the 1980 presidential election, many people have voted Republican ever since, which—along with the factors previously mentioned—has contributed to the transformation of once solidly Democratic regions to areas that are now largely conservative (the South is a good example of this).

As a result of these migrations and the social and political shifts that occurred, U.S. citizens have begun to expect more from the federal government than ever before. During the New Deal, people responded to the need for Social Security and federal assistance. And while the Civil Rights Era caused many citizens to reject the intervention of the government into their private lives, American citizens in the 21st century continue to develop a relationship with politicians that promotes individual rights and basic needs.